D1432919

# THE LECTIONARY COMMENTARY

# THE LECTIONARY COMMENTARY

*Edited by*

Roger E. Van Harn

*Consulting Editors*

Richard Burridge
Thomas Gillespie
Colin Gunton
Robert Jenson
James F. Kay
Hughes Oliphant Old
Fleming Rutledge
Marguerite Shuster

# THE LECTIONARY COMMENTARY

*Theological Exegesis for Sunday's Texts*

THE SECOND READINGS

*Acts and the Epistles*

*Edited by*

Roger E. Van Harn

WILLIAM B. EERDMANS PUBLISHING COMPANY
GRAND RAPIDS, MICHIGAN / CAMBRIDGE, U.K.

CONTINUUM
LONDON · NEW YORK

Published 2001 in the United States of America by
Wm. B. Eerdmans Publishing Co.
255 Jefferson Ave. S.E., Grand Rapids, Michigan 49503 /
P.O. Box 163, Cambridge CB3 9PU U.K.
www.eerdmans.com
and in Great Britain by
Continuum
The Tower Building, 11 York Road,
London SE1 7NX
www.continuumbooks.com

Printed in the United States of America

06  05  04  03  02  01      7  6  5  4  3  2  1


**Library of Congress Cataloging-in-Publication Data**

The lectionary commentary: theological exegesis for Sunday's texts /
edited by Roger Van Harn.
p.      cm.
Contents: v. 1. The Old Testament and Acts (the first readings) —
v. 2. The Acts and the Epistles (the second readings) —
v. 3. The Gospels (the third readings).
ISBN  0-8028-4751-X (v. 1: cloth: alk. paper);
ISBN  0-8028-4752-8 (v. 2: cloth: alk. paper);
ISBN  0-8028-4753-6 (v. 3: cloth: alk. paper)
1. Bible — Homiletical use.  2. Bible — Criticism, interpretation, etc.
3. Common lectionary (1992)  4. Lectionary preaching.
I. Van Harn, Roger, 1932-  II. Common lectionary (1992)

BS534.5.L43   2001
251'.6 — dc21

2001040531


**British Library Cataloguing-in-Publication Data**

A catalogue for this book is available from the British Library.

ISBN  0-8264-5681-2 (Vol. 1)      ISBN  0-8264-5751-7 (Vol. 2)
ISBN  0-8264-5752-5 (Vol. 3)      ISBN  0-8264-5867-X (Set of 3)

# Contents

CONTENTS

CONTENTS

CONTENTS

## CONTENTS

CONTENTS

# *Preface*

Preaching pastors, ministers, and priests know how rapidly Sundays come and go in the pressures of parish life. Protecting time for study and theological reflection is an art not easily mastered once and for all. Flyby Sundays tend to collide with that steady resolve harbored since theological college and seminary to ground preaching in careful exegesis and extensive dialogue with biblical texts. The result is that sermon preparation suffers.

These volumes will not slow the pace of the weekly calendar, but they will provide tastes of theological exegesis for Sunday's texts that will stimulate reflection. These are not books of sermons. They leave homiletical work to the preachers, who are called to contextualize the gospel from biblical texts. Exegetes who have contributed to these volumes have come to name their work affectionately as exegetical "jump starts" for preaching. As such, they provide a place to stand in the text for starting a sermon.

The lections are all derived from the Revised Common Lectionary, Years A, B, and C. All the Sundays of the three-year cycle are included, as well as the texts for the Nativity of the Lord (Christmas Day), the Epiphany of the Lord, and the Ascension of the Lord. The pericope for each entry is identified in bold type in the heading and is accompanied by a listing of the other lections for the day. Although the responsorial psalm is not exegeted, it is listed following the first lesson and may be read or sung for liturgical purposes or used as a preaching resource. The applicable day(s) for each lection is indicated with each heading. Worded titles such as "Water into Wine," "Blind from Birth," or "The Prodigal Son" have been intentionally omitted. Such identifications may get ahead of the exegesis and may block the preacher's dialogue with and exploration of the text. When these happen, the preacher is prevented from seeing and hearing fresh possibilities for the sermon.

With seventy-eight exegetes representing a variety of traditions contributing to these volumes, the reader can expect a wide variety of styles and insights. No attempt has been made on the part of the editors to homogenize these styles. Exegetes have been asked to answer this question concerning their assignments: What does the preacher need to know about this lesson in order to preach a faithful sermon from it? The resulting literary and theological variety, therefore, is similar to the variety in the biblical genres themselves. The resulting unity derives from the story of what God has done for the salvation of the world in the history of Israel and in the person of Jesus Christ. Faithful preaching is not about Bible texts; rather, it proclaims the good news of God to which the texts witness.

Each exegetical essay includes some combination of three elements: engagement with the biblical text, theological reflection, and awareness of the context in which the sermon will be spoken and heard. While the reader will find these elements present in differing degrees, they suggest and stimulate the concerns the preacher brings to sermon preparation. The preacher will also bring the specific congregational context into dialogue with the text in order to discover and express the pastoral and evangelical purposes of the gospel. Wherever the exegesis illumines events of our history, features of our culture, or characteristics of the church that call for celebration or judgment, these may be indicated by the exegete or discovered by the preacher for possible inclusion in the sermon.

The three volumes are organized according to the first, second, and Gospel lections for each day. The lections are arranged in their canonical order in each volume. Each volume appends an essay for preaching: "Preaching as Worship," by Hughes Oliphant Old (vol. 1); "Preaching from the Letters," by Colin Gunton (vol. 2); and "Augustinian Preaching and the Nurture of Christians," by C. Clifton Black (vol. 3). Two indices provide a ready reference for the lections of the three-year cycle and the contributors to the three volumes.

Through the long months of preparation, the publishers are indebted to the consultants whose guidance gave shape and direction to the project: Richard Burridge, Thomas Gillespie, Colin Gunton, Robert Jenson, James F. Kay, Hughes Oliphant Old, Fleming Rutledge, and Marguerite Shuster. Their wisdom contributed to whatever value these volumes offer; lapses of good judgment and faithful insight are solely the responsibility of the editor.

Preachers who follow the Revised Common Lectionary will find these volumes useful. The organization and content will also serve other preaching patterns and possibilities such as a modified *lectio continua* or a thematically arranged series. However they are used, they are hereby offered as an aid to those commissioned to preach the gospel from biblical texts for the congregations they serve.

Roger E. Van Harn,
Editor

# First Sunday after the Epiphany (Baptism of the Lord), Year C

**First Lesson: Acts 8:14-17**
(Psalm 29)
Second Lesson: Isaiah 43:1-7
Gospel Lesson: Luke 3:15-17, 21-22

Give commentators who are to provide background for preachers, exegetes-for-a-day like me, a text like Acts 8:14-17, and you pose us precisely where we do not want to be — if our goal is to anticipate what hearers might want or need to hear and what of the good news might come through preaching on each text.

"We do not want to be" in the no-person's-land between factions of the Christian church. Being there is all right in the classrooms of seminaries, the killing fields called "denominational conventions," or in the company of the more genteel but stalemated ecumenical dialogue people. But a Christian congregation gathered on the day we observe the Baptism of the Lord does not come for the sake of debate. It is made up of people with hungry hearts, at least mildly curious minds, and souls in need of nurture. What good will come of turning their hearing occasion into a debate, with the preacher given the floor and respondents sitting in silence hearing argument, not good news.

The debate? It has to do with an element in this story. Precisely, whether baptism, water baptism, single baptism in the name of the Lord Jesus is sufficient, or must there be baptism, Spirit baptism, a second baptism, to complete the work?

How people answer such questions determines on which side of Pentecostal/non-Pentecostal, charismatic/noncharismatic lines congregations or halves of congregations are to fall. Woe to the preacher who walks in unmindful of the presence of these lines and factions on each side of them.

How to handle this in a Christian sermon? How to handle it, given the fact that barrels of ink, forests of trees, and plenty of sweat and blood have gone into the writing and publishing of books on one side or other of the debate? My advice would be: don't try to settle anything on this subject from the pulpit. Move on to other meanings in the text.

Warrant for that advice has to be more compelling than mere humanistic counsel. It is born, instead, from having listened to Paul the apostle when he dealt with the Corinthian church. It is very clear that he saw the Spirit working in special signs — speaking in tongues, healing, and inter-

1

preting tongues — but he also saw that claims for these could disrupt a congregation and lead to unintelligibility and chaos.

Most Christians have either fought to a draw on the issue, or agreed to disagree, or walked away with Spirit fatigue, or chosen other venues to probe and go deeper. Let's go to the story:

Philip has been a very successful spreader of the good news, even on the toughest terrain, namely, Samaria. This territory between Galilee and Judea was alien to dwellers in those two places. To make converts there was a significant breakthrough. Luke says "the apostles at Jerusalem heard that Samaria had accepted the word of God."

Samaria! One commentator, Ernst Haenchen, notes the obvious: that in the early days of the Christian mission there was a habit that led people to call a region or province Christian once a mission center had risen there. Only a few Samaritans were converted. Some seniors may remember maps prepared by denominational mission boards long ago. A nation would be colored black. Then a particular board sent two missionaries who converted four people. Suddenly a place like Japan would change colors from black to, say, green. Japan had been converted, or was poised to be so. (Even at its peak, Japan was only 1 percent Christian at most.)

Let Luke have his convention: enough was happening at Samaria to lead Jerusalem to send a checkup squad. Peter came, and with him the less frequently mentioned (in mission contexts) John. This is interesting: in Luke 9:54 John and James had called down fire from heaven on a Samaritan village that did not welcome Jesus. Now John and Peter are to help call down the fire of the Spirit, or to assess the credentials and results of those on the scene.

Here's the strange line: the Samaritans had been baptized only in the name of the Lord Jesus. So Peter and John laid their hands on them, "and they received the Holy Spirit." And here's another place to divert attention from the preaching of the good news to old though again not unimportant ecclesiastical argument.

Namely: What was going on here? Some see that this laying on of hands prefigures the rite of confirmation, and that there cannot be confirmation without laying on of hands and there cannot be fulfilled Christian development without confirmation. Over against that is the company who note that something like the coming of the Holy Spirit or like confirmation gets mentioned a number of times in the New Testament but never again with laying on of hands. If it is so important, why not stress it, command it, as there were commands about baptism itself and the Lord's Supper? (Tertullian, a couple centuries later, is the first to connect laying on of hands with confirmation.)

2

Let those two parties contend; we still have the issue of good news before us. And that good news announces that it is for everyone. That not only in headquarters or among "our people" can there be faith and fulfillment. That God works among "us" Samaritans, former outsiders, aliens, lesser people. That God, through disciples, messengers, and preachers, helps assure that all the gifts that come with the coming of the Holy Spirit are for everyone.

Whether or not that means that specific signs noted at Pentecost or at the time referred to in this text and sometimes spoken of as "the Samaritan Pentecost" are to be signs in the twenty-first century, and while texts like these induce valid debates, the coming and presence of the Holy Spirit upon the baptized whenever and wherever they gather "in the name of the Lord Jesus" is assured.

So modern Christians, across boundaries of time and space and race, identify with the Holy Spirit's working at the baptism of Jesus — though they bring to their own identification and baptism some needs that Jesus could not have had, namely, repentance. But repentance itself is also a gift of the Holy Spirit, and it is good news to rehear that.

*Martin E. Marty*

## First Sunday after the Epiphany (Baptism of the Lord), Year A

**First Lesson: Acts 10:34-43**
(Psalm 29)
Second Lesson: Isaiah 42:1-9
Gospel Lesson: Matthew 3:13-17

A cts is the great book of mission and the Spirit. To read it whole is to catch a glimpse of the biblical, missionary, evangelist God in action. It begins with a vibrant (re)entry of God into the pool of human history, among the first disciples of Jesus Christ, and to read on is like watching the ripples: from Jerusalem to Samaria to the ends of the earth.

The question Acts poses to each reader is the same question posed to

3

the main human characters in the book. They, like us, are led to ask, "Where is God the Holy Spirit leading?" with the clear invitation and challenge to join in and follow. The story of Peter and Cornelius, which this sermon deals with, follows this pattern and represents a big ripple in the unfolding story in that it marks the apostolic recognition that Gentiles — albeit God-fearers, but quite definitely non-Jews — are demonstrably included in God's plan of salvation. The days when followers of Jesus Christ are effectively a Jewish sectarian group are numbered.

This sermon arises out of two visions — one experienced by Cornelius (vv. 1-8), the other by Peter (vv. 9-16) — followed by two meetings/conversations — one between Peter and Cornelius's messengers (vv. 17-23a), the other at Cornelius's house (vv. 23b-33).

The sermons in Acts have been the focus of enormous scholarship over the last century or so. That they articulate the kerygma — a list of key Christian faith statements — has long been acknowledged, and several of those common themes are evident here. More interesting, though, are clear signs that here, as elsewhere in Acts, there is profound sensitivity to the congregation, an unequivocal attention to context. This is the first recorded sermon to a specifically Gentile audience, and it shows. So, unlike Peter's Pentecost sermon, this one contains no explicit quotations from the Old Testament. As is so often the case with Luke's writing, however, Old Testament imagery is never far away, and some commentators have made connections between (the difficult and convoluted) verse 38 and Psalm 107:20 and Isaiah 61:1. This implicit rather than explicit approach to employing Jewish Scripture intriguingly echoes the "halfway house" relationship of God-fearers to Judaism.

The sermon contains the most detailed account of Jesus' "earthly life" found in Acts. Unlike other kerygmatic sermons, especially Paul's, which limit information about Christ to his death and resurrection, here we are treated to a pretty full *curriculum vitae*. Indeed, the sermon is effectively a summary of Luke's Gospel, from the clear allusion to the angels' song at the birth of Jesus in verse 36 to the commissioning of the disciples in verses 41-42. Jesus' Galilean ministry, baptism, and the "Nazareth manifesto" in Luke 4 are also identified as significant points in the story that Peter comes to realize must be declared to the seekers in front of him. Speaking out of his own experiences as one of the Twelve, clearly for Peter this is not a gospel message that can begin with Jesus on the cross. Not that Jesus' death and resurrection are missing from this account. Far from it. These events are rightly evident and prominent. Here, however, in the context of non-Jewish hearers, Peter introduces the more general Old Testament theme that God's Messiah would hang on a tree rather than allotting blame to his own people for the crucifixion of Christ. In a number of ways, then, Christian preaching is here demonstrated to be more contextually sensitive than is suggested by those who see all such sermons as occasions for parroting a somewhat fabricated and wooden kerygma. Far from being a "show" sermon, as some suggest, words put in Peter's mouth, as it were, there is much to commend the view that this is genuine evangelistic preaching, an authentic, attuned presenting of the gospel of Jesus Christ to those who have asked to hear it. A homiletic lesson to us all, now as then.

Cornelius's level of ignorance about the gospel can be overexaggerated however. Twice Peter says, "you know . . . what took place . . . about Jesus of Nazareth." This may be simply an example of the preacher's trait of bringing the listeners "in," even if they actually "know" nothing. But given that Cornelius is an influential man, in a sizable social thoroughfare like Caesarea, with links in the synagogue and an interest in Jewish religious matters, it is highly possible he had picked up snippets of news about Jesus of Nazareth. Acts 8 suggests that Philip evangelized in this area, and it is not beyond the bounds of possibility that this gathering of Cornelius's family and close friends is an embryonic Christian congregation. As such they would have limited but real knowledge of the gospel, a fact that Peter both recognizes and supplements.

The similarities with Peter's Pentecost sermon in Acts 2 are marked. Luke leaves little doubt that this is a Gentile equivalent of what happened in Jerusalem, and on both occasions the proclamation of the Word precedes the anointing of the Spirit. The passage ends with Peter's sermon being interrupted by (or is it completed by?) the powerful arrival of the Holy Spirit. As at Pentecost, we are not privy to Peter's planned conclusion; he is cut short and the Spirit continues. As preachers, we know all too well that what we produce is never the final word!

At the heart of this sermon is the catching of a bigger vision of God's offer of salvation through Christ. Unquestionably the key theme, the theme that shapes the sermon, the theme made clear at both its outset (v. 36) and its ending (vv. 42-43), is the recognition and assertion that Gentiles are included in God's plan of salvation. This realization is the great leap in religious and spiritual understanding which Peter experiences throughout the whole story and expresses in this sermon: "I understand now that God is not one to show partiality" or "have favorites" (v. 34). Indeed, some suggest this is Peter's conversion (or *a* conversion), his Damascus road experience, the occasion when his perception of God, Christ, and salvation is turned upside down in order that it becomes the right way up! Peter, a member of the chosen race, declares in the house of a Gentile God-fearer his realization that God has no favorites. In the religious, historical, and cultural context of the day, the declaration that "everyone who believes in Jesus receives forgiveness of their sins" (v. 43) is simply wonderful. Christ is not a nationalistic messiah, not Lord of some, but Lord of all, and thus the perceived scope of God's salvation is expanded. Through Christ all can be saved. In this way Luke asserts a favorite and recurrent theme in both Gospel and Acts — that the gospel is for all, that it is universal in appeal. The use of "peace" in verse 36 makes this clear, the term, as is common in Luke's writings, becoming a metonym for salvation. "Peace by Jesus Christ" is not about the absence of war but reconciliation, and not simply reconciliation between Jews and God but between all people and God.

Significantly these assertions are made *prior* to the Spirit's coming upon Cornelius and the others, leading to the view that this "Gentile Pentecost" confirms what has already been recognized as the leading and will of God. We note also that Peter's profound change of mind arises out of God's revelation and initiative (the vision), encountering "godly" people (the meetings and conversations), and a little time on the road to mull it all over and pray — not a bad combination for Christian guidance!

The very magnificence of this appeal to a wider gospel "inclusiveness" — a very popular theme nowadays — is one easily capable of being wrongly understood and applied. It is important therefore that it is understood properly. There is no suggestion in the text that God is unconcerned with religious differences or considers all human beings automatically saved. Those who are "acceptable to God" are those "who fear him and do what is right" (v. 35). This "doing right" probably equates to hearing and receiving the message of salvation in Christ, as there is no suggestion that Cornelius is saved because of his piety, but because of his faith in Christ. The notion that general piety, of itself, makes everyone or anyone acceptable to God is therefore not supported here. Rather, God fairly judges all human beings and condemns wickedness wherever it is found. Salvation is not possible apart from Christ, but on the basis of his death for all, the gospel can be rightly offered to all and received by all those who are open and willing to accept it.

This Spirit-led and Spirit-revealed revelation about the place of Gentiles in God's plan of salvation represents a paradigm shift in terms of the Christian mission. Up to this point the idea of going "to the ends of the earth," promised in Acts 1:8, has been difficult to conceive given the limiting perceptions that Peter, as a Jew, wrestles with and overcomes. Now God's Spirit takes the lead, and such a global mission becomes not only possible but is the inevitable consequence of obedience and discipleship.

*Martyn D. Atkins*

# First Sunday after the Epiphany (Baptism of the Lord), Year B

**First Lesson: Acts 19:1-7**
(Psalm 29)
Second Lesson: Genesis 1:1-5
Gospel Lesson: Mark 1:4-11

In this section of Acts Paul moves from Corinth to Ephesus, where he meets some people Luke calls "disciples." The reader may immediately assume that these believers are disciples of Jesus, but subsequent events call this assumption into question. Paul must have made the same initial assumption, but something prompts him to investigate these "disciples" further. Are they really Christians, followers of Jesus, as they apparently say they are? Was it something they said that tipped Paul off? Perhaps it was something they weren't saying — not enough "praise the Lord's" in their conversations. Luke doesn't say what raised Paul's suspicions, but something about the Ephesian disciples prompts Paul to wonder what sort of Christians they were anyway.

So Paul gets out his stethoscope and blood pressure cuff and does a spiritual examination. He is going to get to the bottom of this. "I've got a couple questions for you," he says. "When you believed in Jesus, did you receive the Holy Spirit?" "Holy Spirit?" they respond. "We didn't even know there was a Holy Spirit." Well, that wasn't quite true. As Jews, they knew a Holy Spirit was mentioned in the Old Testament. And as those exposed to the teaching of John the Baptist, they had heard John talk about the coming one who would baptize with the Holy Spirit. But they didn't know that the Holy Spirit had been released and was now fully available. So the import of their reply to Paul was in effect that they didn't know that the Holy Spirit was now available. Their answer to his initial query does nothing to allay Paul's suspicions. Puzzled, Paul asks a follow-up question: "What baptism did you receive?" "We received John the Baptist's baptism," they reply.

How is one to regard these Ephesian "disciples"? Are they disciples of John the Baptist or Jesus? Those who regard them as disciples of the Baptist point out that they received his baptism of repentance. Those who regard them as disciples of Jesus point out that if they were simply followers of John the Baptist, Luke would have made this clear and Paul would not have exhibited the initial confusion that his questions belie. Perhaps the example of Apollos in the previous chapter of Acts offers some guidance.

Luke informs his readers that Apollos "had been instructed in the way

7

of the Lord, and he spoke with great fervor and taught about Jesus accurately, though he knew only the baptism of John" (18:25). As in the case of the Ephesian disciples, one wishes Luke would explain further, but readers are left to draw their own conclusions. The most one may be able to say is that while both Apollos and the Ephesian disciples were in some way followers of Jesus, their notion of baptism was incomplete. Christian baptism went beyond the baptism of John.

John the Baptist's baptism was one of repentance that anticipated a future baptism of the Holy Spirit. John preached thundering sermons about how God was about to do something big, and so after his listeners repented, he plunged them under the muddy waters of the Jordan River as a sign that God washed away their sin, a baptism of repentance. These Ephesians had approached God by repenting of their sins as John preached they should, and Paul in no way denies the authenticity or necessity of such repentance.

But however far these Ephesian disciples had moved toward becoming followers of Jesus — and perhaps they had moved less than Apollos — Paul suspects that they lack the presence and power of the Holy Spirit. After he detects this absence, he explains how Jesus is the coming one to whom John was pointing — no doubt in the process explaining the cross and resurrection — and he invites them to be baptized into the name of the Lord Jesus.

When Paul lays his hands on them — probably as part of the baptism rite — and prays, the Holy Spirit comes upon them in power. The Holy Spirit fills them, and they begin to speak in strange languages and convey messages from God under the influence of the Holy Spirit that remind one of the initial outpouring at Pentecost. What happens is fully in line with what Luke portrays as the normal order of things; the Holy Spirit and baptism into the name of Jesus always go together.

Now what if Paul were to subject Christians today to the sort of examination he performed that day in Ephesus? With us Paul might start by asking about repentance and the Holy Spirit. Repentance is absolutely crucial if someone is to experience the Holy Spirit as alive and active, whether that coming of the Spirit accompanies baptism or comes as a further filling thereafter. Conscious and obvious sin blocks the work of the Spirit. If believers flat out refuse to forgive, or hang on to anger, they block or inhibit the work of the Holy Spirit in their lives. If they refuse to turn away from particular sins to which God directs their attention, they grieve the Holy Spirit and make his work difficult. Repentance is the first step in preparation for the gift of the Spirit. One might call initial turning from sin to Christ repentance with a capital *R*, and those subsequent turnings as part of following Jesus as repentance with a small *r*.

8

But suppose that, like the Ephesians, we've repented and God has forgiven. Unlike those Ephesian disciples, we would at least have more solid answers for Paul's probing string of questions. Into whose name were you baptized? That's easy, we were baptized into the name of Jesus Christ — not only Jesus, but the Father, Jesus the Son, and the Holy Spirit. And orthodox Christians believe that anyone who believes in Jesus and is baptized receives the Holy Spirit. So, yes, Paul, we did receive the Holy Spirit when we believed.

And yet I wonder if Paul might not still have an additional question or two. He might say something like, "Are you sure you received the Holy Spirit when you believed?" Paul might observe that people in many contemporary churches often don't seem to be crackling with the power of the Holy Spirit. True, some Christians, these days still, prophesy and speak in tongues. There are churches today in which people cry, or fall down, or laugh with joy as the power of the Holy Spirit touches them. But we don't know, Paul, maybe something is wrong with us. Should we be speaking in tongues or something like that? Did we really receive the Holy Spirit when we believed in Jesus? We hope we did, but many Christians today are hardly flaming charismatics. How come so many Christians these days don't speak in tongues and prophesy like the disciples in Acts 19?

There may be several answers. I suppose some may speak in tongues or prophesy but keep what they do mostly secret. Many churches have not exactly emphasized or welcomed with open arms those sorts of expressions of the Holy Spirit: "We don't do that sort of stuff around here." Perhaps God has given some among us gifts that, for whatever reason, people have kept to themselves. So ask around.

Others have been given gifts by the Holy Spirit that could help us see evidence of the Spirit more clearly. But there is a problem. Maybe several problems. Some of us, I suspect, don't know that we have been given a particular gift by the Holy Spirit; we have somehow overlooked these gifts, not unpacked them. We may have left them under the tree or on a back shelf without realizing how wonderful they are and that they were meant especially for us. Paul says the Holy Spirit has given gifts to everyone who belongs to Jesus. So if people belong to Jesus, God the Holy Spirit has picked out and delivered a gift or perhaps several gifts for each one.

The Bible lists gifts of service, teaching, giving, mercy, leadership, healing, miracles, pastoring, wisdom, discerning spirits, intercession, and more. One of the most spiritually beneficial things persons could do for themselves as Christians is to discover what the Spirit has given and begin to use it in his power.

9

When people have discovered their gift (or gifts), they find that using it makes them feel alive to God. As followers of Jesus continue to use their gift, they have a growing sense that this is especially what God wants them to do. For instance, for people with gifts of mercy, God is never more alive than when they are bringing a casserole or delivering a floral arrangement in Jesus' name. And while the Holy Spirit comes into our lives only once, God can and does fill us with the power of the Holy Spirit time and time again. When Christians lay hands on each other and pray, God is often pleased to send his Spirit in power. God comes in power to empower his people.

*John M. Rottman*

## Fourth Sunday of Advent, Year A

First Lesson: Isaiah 7:10-16
(Psalm 80:1-7, 17-19)
**Second Lesson: Romans 1:1-7**
Gospel Lesson: Matthew 1:18-25

The opening verses of Romans establish Paul's authority and provide a framework for understanding what this letter seeks to advance, namely, the mission to Spain. Since the Roman Christians for the most part do not know Paul personally, he must lay his credentials on the table, so to speak. This pertains to the second word of the letter, usually translated "servant" rather than the more accurate word "slave," which seems puzzling because its degrading associations appear to contradict the claims about Paul as the one "called to be an apostle and set apart for the gospel of God" (1:1), the one who has "received grace and apostleship for the purpose of the obedience of faith among all the Gentiles" (1:5). However, this expression makes good sense in a city where influential slaves in imperial service proudly bore the title "slave of Caesar." More than four thousand slaves and freedmen associated with Caesar's household, his personal staff, and the imperial bureaucracy have been identified with this kind of title through grave inscriptions. Paul is therefore introducing himself with proper credentials as a representative of a great power, using the same title that members of the two churches within the imperial bureaucracy identified with Narcissus and Aristobulus (16:10-11) would have proudly carried. The proximity between "slave of Caesar" and "slave of Christ Jesus" suggests the agenda pursued throughout the letter concerning whose power is ultimate. To be a slave of Christ is to represent the most powerful force in the world, even in the face of Rome; this little word reflects an awesome responsibility for current preachers and evangelists who follow in Paul's steps.

Paul includes a confession in verses 3-4, which I translate and format as follows. The gospel that Paul brings as an apostle is one

3   concerning his son who was
     born from David's seed
     according to the flesh,
4   appointed Son of God
     in power
     according to a spirit of holiness,
     from out of a resurrection of the dead,
     Jesus Christ our Lord.

In *The Living Text* ([Lanham, Md.: University Press of America, 1985], pp. 99-122), I show that this was a composite confession that originated in a Jewish Christian group interested in the restoration of Davidic kingship. It was augmented by a Hellenistic Christian circle to show the distinction between the realm of the spirit and any realm of the flesh, such as a Davidic empire. Paul added the words "in power" and "of holiness" to give expression to his own viewpoint. Paul's emphasis on the power of the gospel is developed in the thesis of the letter, that the gospel about Christ is "the power of God for salvation" (1:16). Since the letter as a whole serves the task of world mission, the issue of power is central. Does the gospel of Christ really have the power to transform the world? This theme reappears in the benediction of 15:13; see also 15:19. The words "in power" stress that the power of God resides not in Davidic descent or the promise of a political empire, but in direct, divine appointment of Christ as Son of God. The words "spirit of holiness" make clear that the divine power celebrated in the confession entailed moral obligations. This theme is developed at length in Romans 5-8, which show that the new life involves a repudiation of fleshly passions and behaving "according to the Spirit." Paul makes plain that the Spirit given to Christian believers is the "Holy Spirit" (5:5), and that the law remains "holy" even for members of the new age (7:12). The key to the new ethic is giving oneself as a holy sacrifice for others (12:1). These themes are important in preaching, because the power of the gospel seeks to transform individuals and the world in the direction of holiness and justice. Although Paul and most of the Christians in Rome would be viewed today as "charismatics," filled with the power of God, Paul's concern is that the gospel should do more than turn people on; it seeks a total transformation of everyday life. In the context of the Roman house and tenement churches, holiness implied taking a welcoming attitude toward other Christian groups, a theme that is developed throughout the letter.

In contrast to other letters, this letter contains an address that avoids the word "church," which was apparently being used by only one of the groups in Rome (16:4). In 1:6-7 we find three expressions that constitute the address:

1. "the called of Jesus Christ"
2. "to those in Rome beloved of God"
3. "the called saints"

Paul's pastoral strategy is visible here: providing a model for later preaching to groups with diverse memberships. The expression "called saints" would have appealed especially to conservative, Jewish Christians, whose compatriots in Palestine are mentioned with this title in 15:25 and 31. In the Roman context, I think this address would include many of those Jewish Christian leaders banned under Claudius in A.D. 49 who have now returned to Rome, some of whom are being shunned by the Gentile Christian majorities in the house churches. One of the five groups that Paul mentions in chapter 16 also goes under this name (16:15), and the conservative group stereotyped as "weak" in chapters 14-15 probably overlapped with such "saints."

The expression "the called of Jesus Christ" seems to refer to liberal, Gentile converts who are using the term "Jesus Christ" as a kind of proper name rather than as a peculiar messianic title. The Gentiles reflected in 11:18 who boast that they had been elected to replace the Jewish branches in the divine olive tree of the chosen people would probably have felt themselves included with this expression. Insofar as the term "strong" in chapters 14-15 refers to Gentile Christians, it would roughly correlate with this expression "called of Jesus Christ." Most scholars currently feel that such Gentile Christians formed the majority of the membership of the house churches at the time Romans was written, which is perhaps why Paul uses this title first in his address.

The address, which does not match that of the social groupings in

Rome, is "the beloved of God." I think it is significant that Paul places this address between the two others so that it serves as a unification formula. The wording is explicitly inclusive: "*all* those in Rome beloved of God." This phrase suggests the theme of the letter, that God's love is impartial. No person on earth, whether Greek or Jewish, deserves such love, as 1:18–3:20 argues. But everyone receives such love in Christ, as 3:21–4:25 so eloquently shows. God is no respecter of persons, as 2:11 insists; all have made themselves into God's enemies (5:10), but all are included in the sweep of divine love. The offering of salvation "to *all* who believe" is virtually a litany of the argument of Romans (1:16; 3:22; 4:11; 10:4). In this sense the opening address of Romans sets the tone for the entire letter, offering the most inclusive program for global pacification found in the New Testament. If this gospel is understood and internalized, Paul suggests, the splintered house churches of Rome would become unified in cooperation while preserving their distinctiveness.

The history of early Christianity throws light on the validity of Paul's notion of the gospel as the power of God, capable of transforming the world by overcoming its hostile divisions. A recent book by Peter Lampe (*From Paul to Valentinus* [Minneapolis: Fortress, 2000]) shows that the majority of early Christian groups were situated in some of the worst slums of Rome. These small groups calling themselves brothers and sisters cooperated in creating arenas of relative safety and care, acting as the "beloved of God." The love feast system in early Christianity involved sharing food together on a regular basis in the context of a celebrative Lord's Supper. There is mounting evidence that these small groups of Christians in the crowded inner cities of the Roman Empire were coping with urban chaos, crime, unsanitary conditions, poverty, and plagues. In *The Rise of Christianity* (Princeton: Princeton University Press, 1996), sociologist Rodney Stark has described the revolutionary impact of Christian love and the social service systems developed by Christian groups. For example, he shows that when plagues struck these cities, the pagan doctors typically fled. They could not understand the cause of the disease but knew it was contagious. In the pagan worldview, plagues were indications that the gods did not care whether people lived or died. Christians, on the other hand, were convinced that God loved them, and that they were obligated to love one another. Thus only the Christians were willing to nurse the sick; their groups surmounted the plagues and took in surviving neighbors as converts. As it turned out, such factors help to explain why Christianity triumphed over the Roman Empire. If we take Paul's message seriously, the gospel still has the power to transform the world.

*Robert Jewett*

13

## Ninth Sunday after the Epiphany, Year A

First Lesson: Deuteronomy 11:18-21, 26-28
(Psalm 31:1-5, 19-24)
**Second Lesson: Romans 1:16-17; 3:22b-28, (29-31)**
Gospel Lesson: Matthew 7:21-29

There is general agreement that these verses provide the thesis of Paul's letter. When Paul states that he is "not ashamed of the gospel" because it "is the power of God," it seems natural to take this in the context of weighing whether the sovereign an ambassador represents is capable of achieving the purposes of the embassy. Shame is aroused when the power of the regent one represents is not commensurate with the countervailing forces. To put the question crudely, the language of 1:16 relates to the cynical query attributed to Joseph Stalin: "How many divisions does the pope have?" Paul in effect answers, "Plenty!" It is an extraordinary claim for the leader of a tiny minority group, writing to the center of power in the ancient world. Yet this claim sets the tone for the entire subsequent letter. As one can see from 1 Corinthians 1:20-31, the gospel was innately shameful as far as Mediterranean cultures were concerned. The message about a messianic redeemer being crucified was a "stumbling block to Jews and foolishness to Gentiles." A divine self-revelation on an obscene cross seemed to demean God and overlook the honor and propriety of established religious traditions, both Jewish and Greco-Roman. Rather than appealing to the honorable and righteous members of society, such a gospel seemed designed to appeal to the despised and the powerless. To use the words of 1 Corinthians once again, "God chose what is foolish in the world to shame the wise; God chose what is weak in the world to shame the strong; God chose what is low and despised in the world . . . so that no one might boast in the presence of God" (1 Cor. 1:27-29). There were powerful social reasons why Paul should have been ashamed of this gospel; his claim not to be ashamed signals that a social and ideological revolution has been inaugurated by the gospel.

At the center of the thesis of Romans in 1:16-17 is the paradox of power that in this shameful gospel that would seem to lack the capacity to prevail, the power of God is in fact revealed. The gospel *is* the "power of God," Paul contends, in that it shatters the unrighteous precedence given to the strong over the weak, the free and well educated over slaves and the ill educated, the Greeks and Romans over the barbarians. If what the world considers dishonorable has power, it will grant a new form of honor to those who have not earned it, an honor consistent with divine righteousness. All who place their faith in this gospel will be set right, that is, placed in the right relation to the most significant arena in which honor is dispensed, that is, divine judgment. Thus the triumph of divine righteousness through the gospel of Christ crucified and resurrected is achieved by transforming the system in which shame and honor are dispensed.

The means of transforming the world is the gospel itself, according to these verses. The gospel reveals the "righteousness of God," which means that it is God's means of restoring his righteous control over a disobedient creation. In effect, Paul presents himself in Romans as the ambassador of the "power of God," extending the divine Sovereign's cosmic foreign policy through the preaching of the gospel. When the gospel produces faith in the hearers, the distinctions of honor and shame are overcome and the inequalities of the human race are addressed. This is why Paul stresses that this message comes "to all who have faith, to the Jew first and then to the Greek." In a cultural situation where Jews were objects of discrimination even in the church, the message of Christ crucified reverses the honor system. The first are made last and the last first. And all who receive this liberating message are brought to participate in faith communities where justice is done and a new world is created in small house and tenement churches. It is essential at this point to recapture the social context of Paul's mission, rather than to allow our definition of salvation to be dominated by the later theological tradition.

An important purpose of preaching is to recapture the resonance these terms would have had for a Roman audience. Both in the missional program for the early church and in Roman imperial propaganda, salvation implies the restoration of wholeness on a corporate as well as an individual level; its primary scope in biblical theology and in Roman civil religion is the group, that is, the nation and the world, rather than the individual. The stunning feature of Paul's thesis, therefore, is its contention that preaching the gospel to establish faith communities, rather than force of arms or apocalyptic military miracle, is the means by which such righteousness is restored. In the establishment of faith communities as far as the end of the known world, in Spain, God will be restoring arenas where righteousness is accomplished, thus creating salvation. In place of the salvation of the Pax Romana, the propagandistic Roman peace based on force of armies, there is the salvation of small groups, cooperatively interacting with each other to extend their new forms of communality to the end of the world. The global offensive in behalf of divine righteousness envisioned by Romans is missional and persuasive rather than martial and coercive. It has to do with the restoration of holy and just communities rather than merely the conversion of individuals.

The much debated phrase "the righteousness of God" needs to be understood within this missional context. The long battle between orthodox Protestant interpreters stressing forensic dimensions of imputed righteousness and Catholic, Calvinist, and pietistic interpreters stressing ethical transformation shaped by righteousness failed to take account either of the background of Paul's language or the missional setting of Romans. These partisan controversies shared a mistaken premise that Paul's letter was a theological treatise aimed at refuting inadequate understandings of the doctrine of "justification by faith." Many scholars in recent years have pointed to the social context of the interaction between Jews and Gentiles as a decisive framework for Paul's doctrine. It is the inclusive gospel of Christ, which equalizes the status of Greeks and barbarians, wise and uneducated, Jews and Gentiles, that offers new relationships in communal settings to all on precisely the same terms. The early Christian mission is thus viewed as a decisive phase in the revelation of God's righteousness, restoring individuals, establishing new communities of faith, and ultimately restoring the whole creation. In *Romans 1–8* ([Dallas: Word, 1988], p. 48), James D. G. Dunn suggests that "Paul's experience of evangelizing the Gentiles gives Paul firm confidence that in the gospel as the power of God to salvation such early converts are being given to see the righteousness of God actually happening, taking effect in their own conversion." I would rephrase this in social terms, to avoid the individualism that often distorts interpretation. It is the conversion of houses, clans, and neighborhoods that is at stake here: the establishment of tenement churches and house churches that will provide the beachheads of the new creation. Paul's hope in writing Romans is that this inclusive and restorative righteousness will be allowed to heal the divisions between Christian groups and thus enable them to participate in the campaign to missionize to the end of the known world, as far as the pillar of Hercules in Spain, thus contributing to the unification of the world.

The citation from Habakkuk 2:4, that "He who through faith is righteous shall live," implies in this context that anyone, regardless of cultural background, can gain life and share in the restoration of righteousness by having faith in the gospel. This relates back to the theme of shame with which this short passage began. Traditional religion had taught that life is achieved by conforming to the rules of righteousness, but this fell into the trap of the ferocious competition for honor that marked the entire ancient world. If I and my group conform to the law better than you and your group, we have honor and you are shameful. The gospel of Christ crucified reveals that this approach is on the wrong track. The traditional approach to righteousness twists the law into a system of gaining honor, which produces lethal competition and hostility that thwart the justice the law was intended to ensure. Competition for honor produces discrimination and demoralization that erode the quality of life for winners as well as losers. To have faith in the gospel is to set this entire older system aside, to abandon the traditional quest for honor. The gospel of Christ crucified offers grace to all, regardless of their accomplishments or social status. It equalizes the relations between slave owner and slave, between males and females, between citizens and emigrants, between educated and uneducated, and in so doing provides a basis for a new kind of life together in the church. As small groups learned to live out the love of Christ, to treat each other as brother and sister, a new and more genuine form of "life" was created. These two verses sketch the contours of a tremendous revolution in human and divine relations whose full dimensions are yet to be realized.

*Robert Jewett*

## Second Sunday after Pentecost, Year A

First Lesson: Genesis 6:9-22; 7:24; 8:14-19
(Psalm 46)
**Second Lesson: Romans 1:16-17; 3:22b-28, (29-31)**
Gospel Lesson: Matthew 7:21-29

There is consensus among scholars that Romans 1:16-17 constitutes the theme statement (or *propositio*) for the letter as a whole, or at least for chapters 1–11. Romans 3:21-26 is the first and most important elaboration of the meaning of the saving righteousness of God alluded to in 1:16-17. The intervening material, 1:18–3:20, provides the prolegomena to 3:21-31, demonstrating that the whole world rightly stands under the power of sin, not only Gentile but also Jew, and that as such all are deserving of God's wrathful judgment. With every face flush to the ground, Paul in 3:21 picks up on the theme statement in 1:16-17 to explain more fully how it is that God makes a way — one and only one way — of escape.

Paul's declaration that he is "not ashamed of the gospel" (1:16) reacts against two objections that might be raised to the gospel: first and most importantly, that Paul's gospel is an ethical bust inasmuch as it makes the Mosaic law irrelevant and gives license for immoral behavior; second, that Paul's gospel, even if it could usher in salvation and transformed life for Gentiles, remains a disaster for unbelieving Israel, which, by gospel standards, is headed for destruction. The first concern is addressed in chapters 1-8; the second in 9-11.

1:16-17 points to six reasons why Paul is not ashamed of the gospel. *First,* the gospel "is the power of God to effect salvation" (v. 16); that is, it is the instrument that makes it possible for God to bring salvation. *Second,* this gospel has the capacity to save "everyone who *believes* [it]" (v. 16), a point repeated forcefully twice more in verse 17 with the phrases "from faith [in]to faith" (*ek pisteōs eis pistin,* meaning "on the basis of faith, from start to finish"; cf. 2 Cor. 2:16) and, in a quotation of Habakkuk 2:4, "from [or: on the basis of, by] faith *(ek pisteōs)."* *Third,* the gospel is capable of saving *everyone,* not just Jews but Jews and Gentiles. *Fourth,* despite the universal efficacy of the gospel, the gospel maintains a partial priority for the Jew: "to the Jew *first* and also to the Greek" (v. 16). Not only is Israel not left in the lurch by the gospel, it remains the top priority on God's list (Paul picks up this theme later in 3:1-2; 9:1-5; 11:11-32). *Fifth,* Paul is not ashamed of the gospel because in the gospel "the righteousness of God is being revealed" (1:17). The theme of God's righteousness dominates the argument in 3:3–4:25 and chapters 9-11 (esp. 3:5, 21-22, 25-26; 9:14; 10:3). The meaning of "the righteousness of God" *(dikaiosynē theou)* includes righteousness as an attribute of God, an activity of God, and a gift of God. *Finally,* Paul has no need to be ashamed of the gospel because its message is consistent with the message of (Old Testament) Scripture. Paul cites Habakkuk 2:4: "And the righteous [person] from faith will live," a text he also cites in Galatians 3:11.

Romans 3:21-26 cannot be adequately preached by beginning in verse 22b and ending in verse 28. One has to treat either 3:21-26 (note the *inclusio* established by the repetition of God's righteousness in combination with "now" in 3:21 and 26) or 3:21-31 in order to respect the integrity of the text.

Following an introductory "but now," the argument proceeds in two stages. First, in verses 21-24 Paul states the wondrous fact that God has now manifested his righteousness and then explains how it has been manifested. Second, in verses 25-26, redemption in Christ receives further elaboration, specifically as to how and why God mediated it.

Two elements come across clearly in this elaboration regarding Christ's death. First, *Christ's death as an "atoning" or "amends-making act" (hilastērion)*. Much ink has been spilled on whether the sense is *propitiatory* (if the object is God; i.e., serving to gain the favor of, conciliate, make amends *to*) or *expiatory* (if the object is sin; i.e., serving to atone or make amends *for*). The translation "atoning or amends-making act" (similarly, "a means of atonement or making amends") maintains the ambiguity between "propitiatory" and "expiatory": an act that makes amends *to* God or *for* sin. Both elements are likely to be included.

The concept of amends making, while here having cultic overtones, is not restricted to sacrificial imagery. Essentially the same concept, but in the guise of the commercial image of making compensation, arises in the language of "redemption" used at the end of verse 24. "Redemption" *(apolytrōsis)* means "buying back" or "ransoming" (e.g., slaves or captives) and by extension, "release, deliverance, liberation, setting free," with or without payment of a price or ransom. Here the thought of a "price paid" is evident (see "by his blood" in 3:25; "bought with a price" in 1 Cor. 6:20 and 7:23).

The second element is: *the vindication of God as righteous through the gospel*. The penultimate, anthropocentric purpose in God making amends for human sin is to achieve the remission of sins for Jew and Gentile alike. Yet even this purpose takes a backseat to a greater, theocentric purpose: the vindication of God's own righteousness. God and God alone effects salvation, and does so by exerting the ultimate cost: the death of his Son on behalf of sinners. "Precisely (*kai*; or: even) in justifying the one who lives by faith in Jesus," the one who has no personal merit, God demonstrates convincingly that he alone *is* in the right, *can* make right, and *chooses* to make right in gracious fulfillment of the promises of old. In so doing, God puts an end to all human self-boasting (3:27-28) and directs all boasting to himself (5:2-3, 11; 11:32-36; 15:6, 9-12).

Romans 3:27-31 focuses on faith in Christ as *the exclusion of boasting* by Jews for doing the works required by the law (3:27-28), *the inclusion of Gentiles* in God's salvation on the same terms as Jews (3:29-30), and *the confirmation of the law* rather than its complete disuse (3:31).

The exclusion-of-boasting theme in 3:27 is not unexpected given the negative references to boasting in 2:17, 23 and the emphasis in 3:3-26 on God's self-vindication/righteousness in both judgment and salvation. Humans can make no complaint when they are condemned and, given the surprising means by which God manifests salvation (apart from the law, by faith in Christ), no boast when they are saved. The phrase "law of faith," coined ad hoc by contrast to "law of works" (itself an inversion of the more typical "works of the law," deeds that the Mosaic law stipulates must be done), uses "law" generically to refer to a regulatory, governing, or operating principle, rule, norm, system, or demand (similarly, Rom. 7:23; 8:2). These are not two different ways of viewing the Mosaic law, but two different covenant jurisdictions: an old, provisional one that based salvation on the human impossibility of doing the law, and a new, permanent one that offers salvation based on God's doing through Christ's death and the giving of his Spirit, appropriated on the human side by mere faith.

This new regime or dispensation was necessitated not only by the goal of stifling human boasting, but also by the goal of asserting God's care and concern over the whole of his creation. The very "oneness" of God, as recited in the Shema every morning and evening ("Hear [O Israel . . .]," Deut. 6:4), is at stake. God is not "the God of Jews only."

The allusion to the Shema itself demonstrates that Paul is not repudiating every function of the law. Paul is emphatic that, despite the fact that God's righteousness is manifested "apart from the [works of the] law" (3:21, 28), God's now-revealed vindication is attested in the law itself (3:21), including (as Rom. 4 will show) the Genesis narrative of Abraham's faith in God's promise. In that sense "we do not leave the law unemployed *(katargoumen)*" but "cause the law to stand *(histanomen)*" (3:31) — not that the jurisdiction of the law, conceived as an entirety, remains in force.

If there is any one text in the New Testament the preacher should not try to overcrowd with illustrations, this is it. This text is a veritable gold mine of theology or (to switch metaphors) a feast for those hungry to be fed with solid food. Remarks could be focused on the following six main points:

1. The issue of theodicy and God's own self-vindication as revealed in the gospel, demonstrating God's faithfulness and truthfulness to the promises of old and, in the process, silencing every complaint ("But why can't I 'do it my way'?" as an old Frank Sinatra tune goes — only God can croon, "I did it my way").

2. The amends-making nature of the death of Christ, which, despite some contemporary theological trends to the contrary, must remain at the heart of the Christian faith. This theme is, after all, at the heart of our regular eucharistic celebrations. God did not all of a sudden decide to forget our sins. No, God paid the ultimate price for our release, making amends for those who should have made amends.

3. The demise of a system based on works and its replacement with one based on faith in the work that God has accomplished on our behalf. The Christ event has wrought a change in covenant dispensations and, with it, a change in the conditions for salvation.

4. The consequent end to salvation-historical barriers between Jews and Gentiles, offering salvation to both on one and the same terms. There is no "other way" for Israel or for anyone else on the planet. If there were, then Christ died for nothing (Gal. 2:21) and God would be in the wrong, not in the right, for allowing the unnecessary slaughter of his Son.

5. Respect both for the continuity between, on the one hand, the now-disclosed righteousness of God in Christ and, on the other, the ancient heritage of Israel. This respect calls for earnest prayer that gives priority to the salvation of Jews (Rom. 9:1-3; 10:1-2), and may lead to becoming a Jew to Jews (1 Cor. 9:20).

6. An unashamed proclamation of all the above (Rom. 1:16). What is there to be ashamed of in this wondrous salvation? (1) It's inclusive, extending to Gentile as well as Jew even while maintaining "the Jew first." (2) It's merciful, overcoming by divine action the problem of human sin, endemic to Jew as well as Gentile. (3) It's biblical, God keeping his promises to the patriarchs and matriarchs of old. (4) It's theocentric, putting an end to all self-bragging by stressing God's self-vindication as the only righteous one. And (5) it's ethical, stimulating the community of faith to boast joyously in God and thereby overcome internal disagreements over matters of indifference.

*Robert A. J. Gagnon*

## Second Sunday in Lent, Year A

First Lesson: Genesis 12:1-4a
(Psalm 121)
**Second Lesson: Romans 4:1-5, 13-17**
Gospel Lesson: John 3:1-17

One of the big surprises of Romans is that Paul gives his account of Abraham in chapter 4 without reference to Christ. This is quite in contrast to Galatians 3:6-18, where Paul declares Christ to be Abraham's offspring. On the other hand, the story of Abraham still is framed with Christology in Romans 3:21-26 and 4:24-25. Thus it is very significant that the revelation in the Christ event of the righteousness (or justice) of God is *for all who believe* (3:22). This has a forceful parallel in Paul's characterization of Abraham as the ancestor of all who believe in 4:11. The parallels between chapters 3 and 4 also indicate that the blessing promised to the descendants of Abraham (4:5-8) includes the forgiveness effected by God's act of redemption in Christ Jesus (3:24-25). Abraham's story is thus mediated through Paul's notion that God has acted in Jesus' death and resurrection. The absence of Jesus until 4:24 is astonishing. But he is hardly out of sight, because parallels between 3:21-31 and chapter 4 induce readers to view Abraham's story through messianist lenses. Interpreters should note, however, that the Christology has a theocentric focus. God is the one who acts in Christ for the blessing of all, and radical monotheism is essential to God's relationship to Jews and Gentiles (3:29-30). If we consider that chapter divisions are later and artificial, we could very well argue that this theocentric Christology is not absent from Paul's account of Abraham after all.

Paul presents the good news in Romans as both a promise of the past and a reality of the present. For the present, God has acted with power to raise Jesus from the dead. For the past, God made a promise to Abraham. Both the act of raising Jesus and the promise of the past are actions of God toward humanity with the purpose of creating a relationship with human beings, and Paul calls this relationship faith. Through faith God stands in a relationship with Jews and Gentiles as the God who acts for the blessing of all.

As important as faith is for Paul, nowhere does he define it. But Abraham is one of the most dramatic instances of faith for Paul. As a case in point, however, Abraham is filled with ambiguity. 4:1 can be translated at least three different ways. (1) What did Abraham our ancestor according to the flesh discover? (2) What did Abraham discover according to the flesh? (3) Do we discover that Abraham is our ancestor according to the flesh? In the first case, Paul would apparently be referring only to Jewish people when he speaks of "our ancestor" according to the flesh. It is highly unlikely that Romans is addressed only to Jewish people. The second case anticipates that Abraham discovers that God's promise to give Abraham and Sarah descendants is true in spite of the condition of his body (4:19). The third case implies that the answer is no, and the text then shows how Abraham is the ancestor of those who have faith like him. In any case, as the argument develops, Abraham as ancestor is clearly determined by the heirs of his faith and by the faith of his heirs.

Without a doubt, Abraham's justification by faith is played off against an alleged justification by works. But there is much discussion today about the meaning both of faith and works. Against a traditional Protestant understanding of works as "good works" to gain merit, a number of prominent scholars have suggested that the works Paul has in mind are Jewish practices of ethnic particularity, such as circumcision, food restrictions, and observance of the Sabbath. The context of 3:27-28 shows that Paul does have works of law in mind rather than good works in general. But three pieces of evidence still give some notion that Abraham is a countercase to attaining justification by deeds: (1) the analogy with earning wages as something owed to the one who works (4:4-5); (2) the explicit violations of law about which Paul speaks include stealing, adultery, coveting, and murder, and are not restricted to ethnic particularity (2:21-22; 7:7; 13:9); (3) the contrast between works and faith raises questions in Romans about how ethics is possible (3:8; 6:1, 15).

But the contrast between works and faith raises the question also of the meaning of faith. Traditionally we have understood the phrase "the faith of Christ" as "faith in Christ." It could just as well mean "the faith[fulness] of Christ." One can see this in the alternate translation the NRSV gives to 3:22. In Paul's interpretation of Genesis 15:6, it is clear that Abraham's act of faith is to believe God. But he also acts in accord with his belief. That is, an old, impotent man has intercourse with his wife, who is barren in the superlative degree — she was sterile in her childbearing years and is now aged, well beyond menopause.

The alternative between "faith in Christ" and "faith[fulness] of Christ" seems to me to split apart what is indivisible. As I suggested above, God acts in Christ to establish a relationship with human beings, and this relationship is what Paul calls faith. Paul thinks of this relationship with the God who has the power to raise Jesus from the dead as a dynamic relationship that bears fruit in those who stand in this relationship. From this perspective, faith is inevitably faithfulness.

The lectionary selection omits 4:6-12. But these verses contain two moves in Paul's line of argument that should not be neglected. One has to do with what constitutes the blessing promised to the heirs of Abraham (vv. 6-8). The second has to do with Abraham's relationship to Gentiles and Jews. I discuss these in reverse order. In the diatribe style, an imaginary interlocutor raises questions about Abraham's circumcision. Paul's version of the purpose of Abraham's circumcision is astounding, and it is part of a thematic development from 1:16. In 1:16 Paul implies that Jews have priority over Gentiles for salvation: "to the Jew first and also to the Greek." In Romans 2 Paul anticipates God's wrath for everyone who does evil, and his repetition of the same formula, "to the Jew first and also to the Greek," with

23

respect to wrath (2:9) clashes startlingly with the priority with respect to salvation in 1:16. Then in Romans 4 Paul gives an answer to the question of why Abraham was circumcised. Our general notion is likely that in Christ Gentiles are added on to Israel. Ordinarily, that is also the way Paul views things. But here Abraham is first of all the ancestor of Gentiles who believe without being circumcised. He is then circumcised so that he can be the ancestor also of Jews who are circumcised and believe.

The other matter in verses 6-8 is the nature of the blessing that comes in fulfillment of the Abrahamic covenant. Paul uses the testimony of Psalm 32:1-2 to indicate the content of the blessedness. It is clearly the forgiveness of sin. But it does not stop with forgiveness of sin, because the content of the blessedness links up with 4:13, which makes an outrageously astounding claim. It is so outrageous that it is virtually overlooked when it is read. Few take any notice when they hear that God's promise to Abraham and his descendants is that they should inherit the world — the whole thing. It has been possible to establish that there was a line of Jewish tradition that did not take God's promise of "land" to Abraham to have been fulfilled with the entrance of Israel into the land of Canaan. Rather, the promise was pushed into the future and universalized to include the whole earth as that promised land.

Law as a marker of Jewish ethnic particularity forecloses the universality of God's promise. If the promise is only for the Jewish people who have the law, then Abraham's descendants are members of one nation, whereas the promise to Abraham was that he would be the progenitor of many nations. If the promise is only for the people of the law, then Abraham and his descendants will not inherit the entire world. The promise to Abraham depends on a relationship of utter trust with God. When viewing things from a human perspective, Paul calls this relationship faith. It is in turn grounded in grace, which is nothing other than the same relationship from God's perspective.

*Robert L. Brawley*

## Third Sunday after Pentecost, Year A

First Lesson: Genesis 12:1-9
(Psalm 33:1-12)
**Second Lesson: Romans 4:13-25**
Gospel Lesson: Matthew 9:9-13, 18-26

Paul's characterization of Abraham as the father of us all is essentially about the character of God. Romans 3 raises the question of the justice of God (vv. 3-6). This is the problem of theodicy. How can God be just in the face of human disaster (e.g., envy, murder, strife, deceit [1:29])? But for Paul, when we engage in theodicy, we have our sock on the wrong ear. Theodicy is our attempt to justify God. But we discover that it is God who justifies us. God has acted in Christ by grace for the redemption of human beings through faith(fulness) (3:24). Thus God establishes God's place as the God of all by establishing all human beings as God's people. This universal perspective of Paul is grounded in monotheism, in the character of God (3:29-30). Abraham is for Paul a focal instance of how human beings can live in a right relationship with God on the basis of faith(fulness); namely, he is the ancestor of all who have faith.

Two very particular foci stand in relief against Paul's universal perspective. One is located in the distant past, the other in Paul's very recent present. The first is God's promise to Abraham. The second is God's act to raise Jesus from the dead. God made a promise to Abraham that he would be the ancestor of many descendants. Paul understands this in two ways. (1) Abraham and Sarah had a child of promise in their old age as a sheer act of God's grace and power. Through procreation God produced a child out of their bodies (4:19). This made Abraham and Sarah the progenitors of numerous descendants. But if this is understood only as the lineage through Isaac, the descendants, though numerous, do not fulfill God's promise to Abraham that he would be the ancestor of all nations. (2) Abraham believed God's promise, and so lived in relationship with the God who establishes God's place as the God of all people who have the same kind of belief.

Surprisingly, Paul gives his account of Abraham without any reference to God's act to raise Jesus from the dead. The context in 3:21-26 has a strong christological focus, particularly on the death of Jesus. 4:24-25 also appends Christology to the end of Abraham's story with a focus on both the death and resurrection of Jesus. Further, two conspicuous assertions characterize God by allusions to resurrection and creation. The God in whom Abraham believed is the God who gives life to the dead and calls into existence things that do not exist. Though Paul clearly alludes to the creation, he expresses it in the present tense so that the power of creation characterizes the God in whom Abraham believes. This power of the God of creation is also manifested in the birth of Isaac and anticipates resurrection in that the power of God brings forth a child from a body of a male and the womb of a female upon which death had already encroached — an outlandish case of impotence and barrenness.

But Paul believes in an outlandish God. For one thing, the God of Abraham in whom Paul believes makes an outlandish promise to Abraham and his descendants that they would inherit the world (4:13). For another, the fulfillment rests on the sheer promise of God so that it will remain nothing other than a promise. This stands quite in contrast to a scheme that makes only those whose identity depends on law heirs of the promise (4:14). In other words, the promise of the monotheistic God of creation and resurrection has sociological consequences. It establishes God as the God of all the nations of the earth so that no ethnic group can be God's favorite people. Romans 4 does not turn its back on consideration of salvation in individual terms. So everyone who is forgiven participates in blessedness, which is a part of God's promise to bless all the nations of the earth in Abraham (4:6-8). But the primary concern of Romans 4 is sociological — how Jews and Gentiles are equally parts of God's promise.

Almost as an aside, Paul comments that the law brings wrath. This has often been understood as the *purpose* of the law. Paul does not explain what he means here. Later he suggests that the law incites transgression by the forbidden fruit syndrome. But he also indicates that the law brings wrath because it shows sin to be sin. The law shows how sinful sin is. This happens first in a direct way. The law lets people know what transgression is. But the second way is much more subtle. The power of evil can usurp the law. It can make people think they are serving God when in fact they are serving the power of evil. One should note well that this is not inherent in the law. Rather, the problem is the power of evil. Sin is so sinful that it can deceive people to the degree that they take participation in evil as dedication to God (see Rom. 7). In 4:15, however, the function of the law to bring wrath appears to be more specifically for Israel, that is, the adherents of the law. I write the following words with extreme caution, because they should not be taken to degrade Israel or the law. But Paul has the notion that alongside Gentiles who rebel against God, Israel as a people failed to keep the law, and thereby incurred God's wrath (see Deut. 27:26). God's wrath to those who are under the law as well as to those outside the law also functions sociologically to place the people of Israel and the Gentiles in the same boat. In this way Paul argues that the law does not differentiate who the recipients of God's promise to Abraham are.

If Paul's God is outlandish, faith in such a God is derivatively outlandish. Thus the faith of Abraham is characterized by a bizarre hope. Paradoxically, when Abraham was beyond all hope, he hoped (4:18). In spite of my basically sociological emphasis in understanding Romans 4, I cannot help but say also that, pastorally, faith and hope go together. Enabling people to have faith has the function of enabling them to live in hope, and enabling people to have hope has the function of enabling them to live in faith.

It has often been noted that in denying Abraham the status of a hero for his works of law (see 4:2-5), Paul makes him a hero of faith and hope. Honoring heroes makes all of us liars, because we disregard everything that is not heroic about them. So also Paul suppresses parts of the story of Abraham. He claims that Abraham did not waver in unbelief concerning God's promise. People who know Genesis might wonder if Paul is reading the same story as the one in which Sarah almost ceases to be the mother of promise because Abraham passes her off as his sister or in which he participates in a scheme to have a child by Hagar. In a way, Paul is not reading the same story, because he is suppressing part of it in order to emphasize Genesis 15:6: "Abraham believed God, and it was reckoned to him as righteousness." Genesis 15:6 brackets the story of Abraham in Romans 4:3 and 4:22 and demonstrates how dominant that text is for Paul's story of Abraham.

Romans 4:23-24 adds an additional step in the interpretation of Genesis 15:6. Paul argues that "it was reckoned to him as righteousness" not on account of Abraham alone, but also on account of "us." The first-person plural is further defined as "those who believe in the one who raised Jesus our Lord from the dead" (4:24-25). The inclusion of all who believe, and even those who will believe, in the God who raised Jesus is a giant leap. God's word in Genesis 15:6 is directed to Abraham. Further, Genesis had its own historical audience, for whom Abraham was the primogenitor of Israel. So how does one verse in Genesis 15 become a universal word for "us"? There are two bases for an answer. (1) The word of God that reckons that Abraham is in a right relationship with God comes from the universal monotheistic God. (2) This universal monotheistic God made a promise to Abraham that he would be the ancestor of all the nations of the earth. For Paul, Abraham becomes a universal ancestor through those who believe after the fashion of Abraham. Believing in the God who raised Jesus is believing in the same God who brought forth a child from Abraham and Sarah and who brings forth new offspring to Abraham through belief. God's reckoning that Abraham is in a right relationship with God, the birth of Isaac, the resurrection of Jesus, and God's creation of new children of God from all nations as heirs of Abraham are all closely analogous and cohere in the character of one God.

*Robert L. Brawley*

## Second Sunday in Lent, Year B

First Lesson: Genesis 17:1-7, 15-16
(Psalm 22:23-31)
**Second Lesson: Romans 4:13-25**
Gospel Lesson: Mark 8:31-38

By citing the example of Abraham (4:1), Paul attempts to prove that God's new work ("but now," 3:21) of acquitting people on the basis of faith in Christ and "apart from the law" (Pentateuchal legislation) is really consistent with what the "law" itself (Pentateuchal narrative) says (3:21-31). He argues: "Are we then making the law useless through [a gospel predicated not on the deeds legislated by the law but on] faith? May it not be so; rather, we make the law stand [i.e., we establish or uphold it]" (3:31).

The real and enduring saving purposes of God, Paul contended, were first disclosed in the life of Abraham. In early Judaism Abraham was widely viewed as the first proselyte who forsook idols and circumcised himself. He kept the law even before it was given to Moses, and did so with perfect obedience. Arguably more important than his initial faith in God's promises was his repeated faith*fulness* amidst many tests (cf. Gen. 18:19; 22:16-18; 26:5), including endurance of persecution for his rejection of idols and idolaters, his departure to a foreign land, his circumcision of himself and his household, and his willingness to sacrifice his only son by Sarah, Isaac. (See esp. Sir. 44:19-21; Prayer of Manasseh 8; 1 Macc. 2:52; *Jub.* 19:1-19; 23:9-10; *T. Ab.* 10:13.)

Quite naturally, then, Paul moves directly to the example of Abraham in Romans 4:1: "What then shall we say that Abraham, our forefather accord-

28

ing to the flesh, has found [viz., in his dealings with God]?" The "our" refers to Paul and his imaginary Jewish dialogue partner; hence, "our forefather by race" (cf. 9:3, 5; 11:14).

Paul focuses on two sets of texts in the story of Abraham, Genesis 15:5-6 and 17:5, that delineate two crucial points: (1) the *content* of God's promise to Abraham (Gen. 15:5; 17:5) and (2) the *conditions* under which the promise became effective for Abraham and by which Abraham was regarded as righteous (Gen. 15:6). These texts (particularly Gen. 15:5-6) are important to Paul because they antedate Abraham's act of circumcising himself and his household in Genesis 17:23-27. They thus suggest a route to God for Gentiles that does not entail observance of the Mosaic law.

Regarding the content of the promise, in Genesis 15:2-5 God tells Abraham that he should try to count the stars in the sky, for "so shall your seed *(sperma)* be" (15:5; cf. Gen. 13:16; 22:17; 26:4; 28:14; 32:12). Paul cites this line in Romans 4:18 (see also the allusions to Abraham's "seed" in 4:13, 16). Yet Paul wants to understand this promise in light of a "clearer" formulation of the promise in Genesis 17:5 (cf. 17:4, 6, 16; 28:3; 35:11; 48:19), where God assures Abraham that "I have made you a father of many *nations*" (*ethnē*, a word that also means "gentiles"). Paul cites Genesis 17:5 explicitly in Romans 4:17, but its echo can also be heard whenever Paul refers to Abraham as a "father" (ancestor) of Gentiles (vv. 11-12, 16, 18). It is Genesis 17:5 that provides for Paul the best proof text that Abraham was destined to become the father not just of innumerable Jews but also of innumerable Gentiles.

Paul focused not only on the content of God's promise, but also — and even more importantly — on the conditions by which Abraham appropriated the promise and became righteous in God's sight. Paul's imaginary Jewish dialogue partner could have appealed to Genesis 17:9-14, 23-27 for establishing the means by which Gentile males became proselytes to Judaism, the rite of circumcision. Paul, however, latched onto Genesis 15:6: "Abraham believed God and it was reckoned (*elogisthē;* or: counted, credited, imputed) to him [or: to his account or advantage, in his favor] as righteousness." This passage serves as the leadoff text of Paul's discussion of Abraham both in Galatians 3:6 and in Romans 4:3. In the case of the latter, it functions as the primary proof text not only for 4:1-8 but also for the whole of chapter 4 (with the words "it was reckoned to him" requoted in 4:22). Paul's reason for choosing Genesis 15:6 is not hard to see. Nowhere else in the Genesis saga of Abraham (chaps. 12–25) are the terms "faith, believe" or "righteousness, righteous, justify, justification," either separately or in combination, applied to Abraham (cf. Gen. 18:19). Indeed, Genesis 15:6 is one of only two Old Testament texts (the other is Hab. 2:4, cited in Rom. 1:17) that combine the concepts of righteousness and faith.

In Romans 4 Paul comes at Genesis 15:6 from four angles to show that those who believe the law-free gospel about Jesus Christ "follow in the footsteps of the faith of our father Abraham while uncircumcised" (4:12). He shows *how* Abraham was justified, *when* Abraham was justified, *why* Abraham was justified, and *with what kind of faith* Abraham was justified.

First, in 4:1-8 Paul, through the citation of Genesis 15:6, establishes *how* or *on what basis* or *by what means* Abraham was justified: on the basis of faith, believing in God's promise, not on the basis of observing works of the law such as circumcision.

Second, in 4:9-12 Paul, through the citation of Genesis 15:6, establishes *when* Abraham was reckoned as righteous for his faith in the promise; namely, before he and his household were circumcised. In fact, if one considers the chronology of Genesis 12–17, Abraham received the promise in 15:6 at least fourteen years before the command to circumcise in 17:23-27. Under the circumstances, circumcision can hardly be regarded as a necessary prerequisite for receiving the promise or being accounted righteous.

Third, in 4:13-17 Paul, through the citation of Genesis 15:6, establishes *why* "the promise to Abraham and to his seed" came "through the righteousness of faith" (i.e., the righteousness that is attributed to faith) rather than "through the law" (4:13). One reason is that the law leads only to condemnation, not salvation. Had God made justification contingent upon observing the law, God would not have been able to keep his promise to Abraham because the law brings about only condemnation (4:14-15). Paul does not need to belabor the point here since it was already hinted at in 4:4-8 and extensively treated throughout Romans (3:3-20, 23; 5:20; 7:5–8:3; 9:30–10:13).

4:16-17 gives a second reason why the promise is "from [i.e., based on] faith" *(ek pisteōs)*: only faith-righteousness can be inclusive of both Jews and Gentiles, not just Jews, and only through faith-righteousness could God keep his promise to Abraham in Genesis 17:5. Romans 4:16 makes the transition from "the law only leads to condemnation" to "a faith-based promise includes Gentiles." The parallel with 4:12 makes clear that in 4:16 Paul means not that the promise is for *both* "the one who is from the law only" *and* "the one who is from the faith of Abraham," as though it were optional to replicate Abraham's faith, but rather that the promise is *only* fulfilled for those who, like Abraham, believe in the promise.

In 4:18-25 Paul reaches his fourth and final angle on Genesis 15:6: *what kind of faith* led God to justify Abraham. Already in 4:17b Paul has begun to transition to this point, in a clause that is syntactically tied to the preceding sentence: "before whom he believed, [namely,] God who makes the dead live and calls *into being* the things that are not [or: calls the things that are not *as though they were*]."

Even more important for Paul's discussion in 4:18-22 is that Abraham believed that God could exert a power very much like the power exerted in creation: making alive where there is no life and turning nothing into something *(creatio ex nihilo)*. For Abraham was already "about one hundred years old" (ninety-nine, to be precise) when he heard the promise again in Genesis 17:5 (cf. 17:1, 17). When Abraham "took a good look" *(katenoēsen)* at his body and at Sarah's womb, both of which for all procreative intents and purposes were "dead," he saw the situation as a prime opportunity for God, and God alone, to create out of nothing once more (4:19). Not only did Abraham not "weaken in faith" or "waver in disbelief," he actually "grew strong in faith, giving glory to God and being fully convinced that what has been promised God is also able to do" (4:19-21). In short, Abraham knew that no matter how impossible things looked, God the Creator could deliver the goods (cf. Heb. 11:8-12, 17-19).

Such a portrait of Abraham's faith might strike the reader as exaggerated in view of the Genesis narrative (see Abraham's missteps in 12:10-20; 16:1-4; 17:17-18; chap. 20). Whether Paul relied on Jewish apologetic traditions about Abraham to explain away the apparent wavering of faith, or whether he had a higher bar than ours for "weakening in faith" or "wavering in unbelief," is difficult to say. The modern reader, at least, can take some comfort in the fact that, despite Abraham's occasional setbacks over a twenty-five-year period, God graciously and patiently worked with him. Certainly by the time God tested his faith during the near sacrifice of Isaac (Gen. 22), Abraham had indeed "grown strong in faith" to a point where he believed that God, if necessary, was "able even to raise someone from the dead" (Heb. 11:19).

Quoting Genesis 15:6 once more, Paul provides at least a preliminary conclusion to this fourth and final section: "Therefore [it is written], 'and it was reckoned to him as righteousness'" (4:22). Such a faith, which was "against hope" (hope in what is humanly possible) and yet "based on hope" (hope in what God can do; 4:18), did not *earn* God's favor but was directed toward God's own saving words and deeds.

The concluding application in 4:23-25 belongs primarily with the section beginning in 4:18 (or 4:17b). Yet in a larger sense, 4:23-25 may do double duty as a conclusion to the chapter as a whole since only here does Paul make a direct christological link to the Abraham story: "us who believe in the God who raised *Jesus our Lord* from the dead." And here the hortatory device of diatribe with its use of imaginary interlocutors appears to give way to joint address to the audience at Rome. Paul shows that there is a typological correspondence to Abraham's faith and the faith of the believer in Christ. Both, of course, believe(d) in the *content* of the promise: that Abraham's faith would result in a harvest of blessing to the nations. Yet, Paul insists, both also believe(d) in the *divine means* of achieving this promise: God's power to raise from the dead. Abraham believed in a God who could raise a child from his own and his wife's figuratively dead (infertile) bodies; Christians believe that God raised Jesus literally from the dead. Or, put differently, when Jews and Gentiles "believe in the one who raised Jesus our Lord from the dead," they believe not only in the same promise but also in the same kind of God who, to fulfill the promise to Abraham, gives life where there is none and creates out of nothing.

How would this text have been heard by the Roman Christians? How was it an address to the particular circumstances of Christians in Rome? On a general note, the theme of Abraham believing "against hope [but] on the basis of hope" fits well with the next chapter where Paul exhorts the readers to "boast in the hope of the glory of God," even amidst such appearances to the contrary as the sufferings of the present time. This same theme is picked up at the end of the unit comprising chapters 5–8, in 8:18-39, underscoring its importance for the letter as a whole.

The preacher who respects the original purposes behind chapter 4 will focus on the how and when and, especially (since the focus of the sermon is on 4:13-25), the why and what of Abraham's justification. The aim of the preacher here is to inculcate in the congregation an appreciation for tying the gospel about Christ to its roots in the Old Testament. Some church members may have little interest in making such a connection, so the preacher may need to devote some time to talking about why that is important, namely, the sovereignty of God in history and Gentile indebtedness to Jewish heritage.

The preacher should also be prepared to treat the question of the church's contemporary relationship to Israel in light of the argument in Romans 4. Has the church, as some scholars claim, distorted New Testament texts about Abraham by arguing not only for Gentile inclusion in the Abrahamic tree but also for Jewish exclusion? Certainly the church has been guilty of anti-Semitic attitudes over the centuries. Romans 4 is not the last word on the relation of non-Christian Jews to Abrahamic paternity, nor is 9:6-9; for this, one has to read on in chapter 11, especially 11:28-29.

*Robert A. J. Gagnon*

## Trinity Sunday, Year C

First Lesson: Proverbs 8:1-4, 22-31
(Psalm 8)
**Second Lesson: Romans 5:1-5**
Gospel Lesson: John 16:12-15

The opening verses of Romans 5 are transitional. In chapters 1–4 Paul elaborates his understanding of the heart of the gospel — justification by faith. After announcing his theme in 1:16-17, he lays the necessary groundwork for appreciating the good news in Christ by rehearsing the sinful plight of all humanity (1:18–3:20). In a paragraph that rivals any other in the Bible for its theological density, he summarizes the source, means, and purpose of God's justifying work in Jesus Christ (3:21-26). 3:27–4:25 elaborates the key issue of faith and its universal availability, especially with respect to Abraham.

A respected tradition in Protestant Christianity views chapter 5 as the conclusion of Paul's discussion of justification. Advocates of this scheme often then see chapters 6–8 as an exposition of the doctrine of sanctification. But it is better to think that Paul moves into a new phase of his explanation of the gospel in chapter 5. Two features of the text in particular point in this direction. First, the opening words of the chapter, "Therefore, since we are justified by faith," suggest that Paul is now going to build on the reality of justification as he has explained it already. We should also note the shift here to the first-person plural — "we" — which has the effect of bringing the Christian reader into the argument for the first time. A second reason for thinking that chapter 5 begins a new argument is its relationship to chapter 8. In both 5:1-11 and 8:18-39, Paul argues that God's love and God's work in Christ and through his Spirit provide the believer with hope for the future. This theme of assurance frames chapters 5–8 and is the central idea of these chapters.

5:1-5 is therefore the bridge between two great doctrines in Romans: the doctrine of justification by faith and the doctrine of assurance. And this means that the preacher will have to establish some basis in the distinctively Pauline teaching of justification in order to bring home the message of these verses. But the focus of the verses is hope. Paul introduces this concept as the climax of his opening rehearsal of the blessings enjoyed by those who have been justified by faith (v. 2b); and he closes these verses with the same emphasis (v. 5). In between, quite significantly, Paul tackles head-on the matter of suffering.

After reminding us of our new status in Christ — "justified by faith" — Paul enumerates in quick succession three benefits believers enjoy: "peace with God," "access to this grace in which we stand," and "hope of sharing the glory of God." "Peace," reflecting the Hebrew *shalom*, refers to the overall well-being of the person in relationship to God. Paul uses the word "reconciliation" to refer back to this same concept in verse 11 (cf. v. 10). "Access into grace," the second of the blessings Paul lists, introduces a key theological idea in Romans. Nowhere exposited at length, grace runs through the letter to the Romans from beginning to end (cf. 1:5, 7; 3:24; 4:16; 5:2, 15, 17, 20, 21; 6:1, 14, 15; 11:5, 6; 12:3, 6; 15:15; 16:20). The concept of grace reflects the character of God. As "wholly other," God stands over all his creatures and is never constrained in his actions by them. What he gives to his creatures is therefore always a matter of his free choice. And the supreme manifestation of that grace comes in providing sinners with a new relationship to God in Christ. We can have a tendency to confine grace to God's act in conversion. But Paul's language here reminds us that grace is operative throughout our Christian experience: we "stand" in it and have constant "access" to it. The latter term was used in the ancient world to denote the privilege of entering into the presence of a king or other high dignitary. We who have been put in right relationship with God as an act of his grace have constant access to that grace for our continuing spiritual needs.

The three "blessings of justification" that Paul lists in verses 1-2 climax with the third. The hope of sharing the glory of God becomes the theme of verses 1-11 and, indeed, is the overarching theme of chapters 5–8 as a whole. The "glory of God" is that "God-likeness" that was marred at the fall (see 3:23) but will be restored in the last day to every Christian (cf. 8:17, 18, 21, 30). Believers may now "boast" in this hope. The word "boast" combines the ideas of "rejoice in" and "take confidence in." Being justified by faith means that we can have utter confidence that we will be transformed into the image of Christ himself (cf. 8:29) when he returns in glory.

But what about the present? Paul does not sweep under the carpet the difficulties that believers continue to face in this life. Indeed, quite the contrary, he insists that these "sufferings" are themselves a cause of boasting (v. 3) and that they will eventuate in a hope that is even more secure (v. 4). How can this be? Because, Paul argues, suffering is the catalyst for God's work in developing Christian virtue. The trials of this life are designed to produce "endurance," the ability to bear up under the pressures of difficult circumstances. And "endurance," in its turn, results in "character," a settled godly disposition that comes as the result of testing. Three issues relating to this teaching about trials in verses 3-4 are particularly significant for the application of the text. First, it is notable that Paul does not treat the evil of suffering as a "problem" to be overcome, but as an opportunity to be taken advantage of. God, Paul implies, brings difficulties into the lives of his people for a positive purpose. Only through the resistance provided by trials will the believer be able to develop his or her faith to the point where it is strong and unassailable. Second, the scope of the sufferings that Paul has in view here is not explicit. Many interpreters want to confine them to those difficulties that are the direct result of our Christian confession — persecution. But such a limitation has no good basis in the context and does not fit well with the breadth of tribulations that are mentioned in the related 8:31-39. It is better, accordingly, to identify these sufferings as any kind of difficulty faced by the believer, including, for instance, financial reverses, illness, and the death of loved ones. Third, we must not take Paul's point here too far. Paul is not teaching that "true" Christians will be joyful when trials come. This would be to deny the reality of evil. We are not called upon to rejoice, or "boast," because of the trial but in the midst of the trial. For we recognize that God has his purpose in that trial and that we can be joyfully confident in the spiritual benefit that will come from the trial when we approach it with a godly perspective.

The final verse brings us back to the key motif of these verses: hope. The hope that trials produce is no ephemeral thing: it will not "disappoint" us. The verb Paul uses here could also be translated "put to shame," and probably reflects the use of this same verb to refer to the judgment (see Pss. 22:6; 25:3, 20; Isa. 28:16). On the day of judgment, Paul is suggesting, our hope will be vindicated by the positive verdict that God will render over us. At the end of verse 5, Paul then begins to enumerate the reasons for our confidence on that day. And one of those reasons is the overwhelming experience of God's love. That love has been "poured into" our hearts through the Holy Spirit. The language alludes to the prophecy about the pouring out of God's Spirit on his people in the last days (Joel 2:28-32, quoted in Acts 2:17; cf. Titus 3:6). The Spirit convinces us deep within our beings that God loves us — and loves in such a way that he sent his only Son to die for us, unworthy though we were (vv. 6-8).

*Douglas Moo*

## Fourth Sunday after Pentecost, Year A

First Lesson: Genesis 18:1-15; (21:1-7)
(Psalm 116:1-2, 12-19)
**Second Lesson: Romans 5:1-8**
Gospel Lesson: Matthew 9:35–10:8, (9-23)

The first point to note with regard to the structure of the passage has to do with delimiting the text's boundaries. Preaching only from 5:1-8 will not do because the train of thought begun in 5:1 cannot be ended before 5:10 or 5:11. Moreover, the material in 5:12-21 was probably also conceived by Paul as part of the same argument; therefore, it should receive at least summary treatment.

The place of Romans 5 within the overall structure of the argument in Romans 1–11 is a subject of scholarly debate, with some putting it with the argument in 1:18–4:25, others with chapters 6–8, and still others as a transition between the two sections. In my view, the evidence decisively favors an understanding of chapter 5 as the beginning of a new section that concludes in 8:39. Chapter 5 and 8:18-39 constitute a "ring composition," bookends of grace sandwiching the moral exhortation and judgment language of 6:1–8:17.

Nearly all main translations of the Bible read for 5:1-3 a series of indicative verbs: "we have *(echomen)* peace . . . , and we boast *(kauchōmetha)*. . . . And not only [that], but also we boast *(kauchōmetha)*. . . ." Some indicate in the margins that a "let us . . ." is also possible for all three verbs. The key is whether to read the first main verb as the subjunctive *echōmen* ("let us have"; so the overwhelming preponderance of early manuscript evidence) or the indicative *echomen* (we have) — the difference between a Greek omega (long *o*) and omicron (short *o*). The subjunctive is strongly favored not only by the text-critical evidence but also by a proper understanding of the rhetorical purposes of the letter to the Romans as a whole. Note that *kauchōmetha* can also be interpreted either as an indicative mood or subjunctive mood. In context, the exhortation in 5:1 is to "have [i.e., possess, experience] peace toward God."

15:5-13 expresses the ultimate goal of the letter: to effect a joint "welcoming" among the Roman house churches through "glorifying" God "with one voice" "for his mercy" shown through Jesus Christ in joyous worship and praise (15:6-9). Only so can both "weak" and "strong" major in the majors (peace, joy, righteousness, love, and hope) and minor in the minors (in Stoic terms, *adiaphora* [matters of indifference] such as diet and calendar;

see chap. 14). This goal of utilizing joyous worship and praise of God as a means of unifying the isolated pockets of Christians at Rome requires their complete "renewal of the mind" (12:2). And this need for a thoroughly transformed vision of reality necessitates, in turn, a thorough exposition of the long-awaited but now-manifested "righteousness of God," God's salvific fidelity to "the promises to the patriarchs" (3:21-26; 15:8). Therefore, critical for the understanding of chapter 5 is the recognition that Paul is using the "indicative" explanation of the core gospel in 3:21–4:25 to develop a "theology of gratitude" or "debt theology" in chapter 5 and 8:18-39 (for "debtors," see 1:14; 8:12; 15:27).

Most translations render *kauchōmetha* in 5:2-3, 11 as "rejoice" or "exult," despite the fact that it means "boast" or "brag" everywhere else in Paul and in Greek literature generally (in Romans, see 2:17, 23; 3:27; 4:2; 15:17). The reason for this reluctance to give the verb its normal meaning is clear enough: boasting or bragging is usually thought of as a purely negative activity. However, translating with something other than "boast" or "brag" obscures an important contrast that Paul is making between two types of boasting: one in human attainments and one in God's accomplishments in Christ. Paul clearly derived this more positive sense from Jeremiah 9:23-24. Here Paul encourages three boasts in what God has accomplished in Christ: *first, bragging in the secure hope of sharing in God's glory (5:2b, 5-10); second, bragging amidst the pressures of life (5:3-4); third, bragging in God's reversal of Adam's sin through Christ (5:11-21).*

The first object of boasting is "the hope of the glory of God" (5:2b), which refers to the expectation of receiving a resurrected "glory-body," a material and heavenly existence described in the metaphor of being reclothed with garments of brilliant light. Paul mentions this boast only briefly before moving on to second boast regarding suffering (5:3-4), apparently in awareness of the experience of suffering as the key threat to this first boast. Once he establishes that suffering itself is no deterrent to boasting in future glory, he returns to the first boast in verses 5-10.

Verse 5 is a transition verse, wrapping up the previous point in verses 3-4 that "hope does not put us to shame *(kataischynei),*" that is, by offering no benefit in the present time to compensate for suffering. At the same time, it ties back to the first boast in verse 2b by demonstrating both the present solace (through God's interim presence) and the security derived from the future hope. The reason why hope does not "dishonor" or "shame" us in the present time is that, already, "the love of God [viz., God's love for us] has been poured out in our hearts through the Holy Spirit which was given to us." Normally, one would expect the language of "pouring out" to be applied to the Spirit. But Paul's point in his metonymic use of love is that every benefit of grace now experienced is a demonstration of the reliability of this one fact: the eternal inseparability of God's love from us who believe (5:8; 8:35-39). The gift of the Spirit is definitive proof of God's unfailing love, the "firstfruits" (*aparchē,* 8:23) or "down payment" (*arrabōn,* 2 Cor. 1:22; 5:5; Eph. 1:14) of the coming glory, a foretaste of God and a vehicle for God's interim presence during the time of "eager expectation" (Rom. 8:19). The theme is picked up again in 8:26-30, where Paul argues that the Spirit helps amidst our present weakness by translating for God what our real needs are behind our misguided prayers.

Not only is the gift of the Spirit a clear sign of God's love, and thus in turn of the security of the glory to come, but so too is the death of Christ. In one of the great formulations of the Christ event in Paul's letters, Paul in 5:6-10 underscores that if God could love us to such an extent that he allowed Christ to die for us even while we were weak, ungodly, sinners, and enemies of God (note the fourfold characterization of pre-Christian existence), then surely God's love will see us through to final glory.

In the first stage of the argument (vv. 6-8), Paul twice uses a "while . . . still *(eti)*" construction:

6: For, *still,* Christ, while we were weak *still* — at the right time — died for the ungodly

8: while we were *still* sinners, Christ died for us.

The point of the construction is self-evident: God must really love us if he *still* (= nevertheless) exerted the greatest possible sacrifice on our behalf while we were *still* (= continually) alienating ourselves utterly from God. The "for" or "on behalf of" us (*hyper,* 5:6-8), which frequently appears in Paul's letters among traditional creedal statements on the death of Christ as shorthand for "to make amends [atone] for," also emphasizes a point brought out more vividly in 8:31-34: "If God is for *(hyper)* us, who [can be] against us?" The parenthetical statement in verse 7 contrasts human behavior with God's: "*scarcely (molis)* on behalf of a *righteous* person *(dikaiou)* will someone die," whereas Christ died for the ungodly (v. 7a).

In the second stage of the argument in 5:6-10 (vv. 9-10), Paul employs what in Hebrew is known as a *qal wahomer* argument (lit. "a light and heavy matter," here a greater-to-the-lesser argument, *a fortiori*): "*if* that, *how much more* this." The how-much-more clause takes the discussion in 5:6-8 a step further, drawing the implications for the security of the future hope. Verse 9 and verse 10 are in synonymous parallelism:

9a:    How much more, then, having been justified now by his blood;
10a:    . . . how much more,    having been reconciled [to God through his son's death]
9b:    shall we be saved through him from the wrath [to come]?
10b:    shall we be saved by his life?

If we could be justified (a legal metaphor: acquitted) and reconciled (an interpersonal metaphor) by God "while we were enemies," then surely future salvation is secure now that we have been adopted as God's children (see 8:14-17) and cleared of the wrongdoing that once disrupted our relationship with God. A love that did not fail for enemies is not going to fail for children.

The second boast is bragging amidst the pressures of life (5:3-4). As mentioned above, the great threats to boasting in the coming glory are the discouraging hardships of the present life. Yet, Paul argues, we can boast even in such "pressures" (*thlipseis;* from *thlibein,* "to press"). How so? Using a chain of virtues common to moral exhortation in antiquity (see James 1:3-4; 1 Pet. 1:6-7), Paul argues that, far from dissolving hope, life's pressures can produce "endurance" *(hypomonē),* and endurance *dokimē* (usually translated "[tested, proven] character"), and *dokimē* hope. Probably a better translation of *dokimē* (a word not attested before Paul) is "proof" (as in 2 Cor. 9:13; 13:3). Endurance amidst hard times provides proof to believers that they are indeed serious about their faith, a proof that can only further verify the genuineness of their hope. Romans 5:3-4 suggests that believers can boast not only in their hope while undergoing pressures but also in the pressures themselves. Paul himself boasted in weaknesses and catalogued his hardships as proof of God's power operating in him and of the sincerity of his ministry; he also viewed hardships as a means of shifting trust and exaltation from himself to God (2 Cor. 1:3-11; 4:7-12; 6:4-10; 11:21–12:10). Romans 8:18-30 continues the discussion of the relationship between suffering and boasting, noting that the present sufferings are nothing in comparison to the coming glory (8:18-25); that the Spirit helps us in our weakness by interceding on our behalf (8:26-27); and that God can use sufferings to mold us more into the image of Christ (8:28-30).

The third boast is bragging about God's reversal of Adam's sin through Christ. Discussion of 5:11-21 takes us considerably beyond the parameters of the lesson. Nevertheless, it is important for the preacher to make clear that the boast continues on past verse 10. Although 5:12 is often regarded as the start of a new section or subsection, and the place of 5:12-21 within the larger framework of Romans 1–11 left in doubt, it is best to take 5:11

with 5:12-21 and see the whole as constituting the third of three boasts of chapter 5. The ultimate boast is not in the firm hope of being glorified, nor even in the pressures of life, but rather in God's own self. And boasting in that God becomes possible only "through" the work of Christ. The "if this, how much more that" construction, which carried forward the boasting in 5:9-10, is picked up again in 5:15 and 5:17, now with reference to the vastly superior effects of Christ's deed over Adam's.

Good preaching of this text will focus on three things: (1) the place of 5:1-8 (9-21) in the larger context of Romans; (2) the three different types of boasts propounded by Paul in Romans 5; (3) persuading the congregation that there is a valid place for boasting by Christians; indeed, boasting in God's work through Christ can become a means for overcoming disunity in the church.

In considering the last point, responsible preaching will point out both the pros and cons of a theology of boasting. Humans have a natural penchant for boasting. Indeed, boasting is often used as a motivating tool, most notably in sports and attempts to arouse patriotism. In Romans 5 Paul tries to channel boasting into something positive: God's work in Christ. Undoubtedly, some will interpret this as sheer triumphalism, to be eschewed at all costs. Such a reaction would be knee-jerk and naive. Stripping the church of all boasting in God does not result in a boast-free zone around the church; humans will find other ways of expressing their need to brag. Paul co-opts the worst in humans for God's use, gutting the concept of its typical manifestations (inflated self-estimate, egocentrism, arrogance, contempt for deficiencies in others, a winner/loser mentality) and replacing it with theocentric and christocentric elements. These elements are clear enough throughout chapter 5. Boasting in God's work in Christ stresses: (1) one's utter helplessness and undeservedness in the face of sin; (2) God's and Christ's *exclusive* rights to human adulation; and (3) the cruciform, self-denying character of Christ's atoning work. Boasting in God's work in Christ is at the same time an antidote to self-centered boasts.

*Robert A. J. Gagnon*

## Third Sunday in Lent, Year A

First Lesson: Exodus 17:1-7
(Psalm 95)
**Second Lesson: Romans 5:1-11**
Gospel Lesson: John 4:5-42

Verse 1: Paul often uses the word "therefore" with a comprehensive backward reference. Here he marks the beginning of a new section by drawing a conclusion from the entire line of argument from 1:18 to 4:25. Note that the first part of the conclusion is grounded in the perfect tense: *having been* (aorist in the Greek). Unfortunately, English translations often gloss over this important feature of Paul's syntax. Justification means that we *have been* made righteous, not as a legal fiction but as our reality in Christ, so that we are accepted without reservation by God. Justification is the stable basis, and not the uncertain goal, of the Christian life. The perfect tense indicates that God's acceptance of us is not partial but total, not conditional but unconditional, not imperfect but comprehensive and complete. The entire gospel may be said to rest on this use of the perfect tense.

Our reception of justification takes place *by faith*. It is not our faith that saves us, but Christ in whom we have faith. While faith is surely a human act, it is nonetheless entirely "passive," as Luther emphasized, in one notable respect. Faith does not contribute to the content of justification. Our actions do not in any sense constitute the righteousness by which we are justified. Our righteousness before God is a "passive righteousness." Faith is strictly the vehicle of reception, not an agency of production, by which lost sinners receive the unsurpassable gift of justification before God. (In the Greek the participle "having been" is not only aorist, but also in the passive voice.)

The gift that faith receives — justification — overcomes sin's terrible guilt and its fatal consequences. It ends our unacceptability to God and our painful estrangement from him. Justification means that we do not end in condemnation. It brings us *peace with God through our Lord Jesus Christ*. The perfect tense of justification, as received in the present by faith, has *peace with God* as its eternal consequence here and now. The preposition "through" suggests that the Lord Jesus Christ is at once both our legal advocate and our priestly intercessor. In Paul courtroom or forensic imagery (accusation, sentencing, judgment) is never far from priestly imagery (exchange, intercession, sacrifice). As our legal Advocate, the Lord Jesus Christ is the one through whom we receive acquittal or justification instead of condemnation. As our great High Priest, he is the one through whom we have peace with God by his cleansing us from all our sin and his clothing us with his perfect righteousness.

Verse 2: As our only Mediator and Advocate, the Lord Jesus Christ not only brings us to God in peace, but *also* brings *grace* to us from God. The prepositional phrase "through whom" continues to indicate, most especially, Christ's priestly work of mediation. That which we *have obtained* and that in which we *stand* are both stated, once again, in the theologically significant perfect tense. Through Christ's priestly mediation, *access to grace* is now so settled a condition that *in it* we may actually be said to stand. Apart from Christ's intercession this access would not exist, leaving us condemned only to fallenness. Moreover, the perfect tense of justification has consequences for the future that go far beyond the present. Having been justified gives us an unsurpassable *hope.* The object of this hope is *the glory of God,* and the subjective disposition toward it is one of "boasting" or *exultation* (cf. 2:17, 23; 3:27; 4:2). Because the lowly creature, and indeed the godless sinner, is exalted by Christ's righteousness into the glory of God, the subjective disposition naturally follows: exultation has exaltation in view. Those who have been justified by faith do not exult in themselves, but wholly in the gift of divine grace that promises to lift them beyond themselves into the glory of eternal life with God.

Verses 3-4: Paul knows both the *theologia gloria* and the *theologia crucis.* He will not do justice to the one without the other. Characteristically, he plunges directly from the vision of so glorious a hope to the sufferings of the present time. (See also, e.g., the transitions from 8:39 to 9:1 and from 11:36 to 12:1.) Just as exultant hope without reference to suffering reality would be irresponsible and frivolous, so present suffering without hope's prospect would lead only to resignation, cynicism, and despair. The genius and the realism of Paul's gospel is to hold hope and suffering together in full tension, remembering the Lord's death until he comes. Because in Christ crucified and risen we have so great a hope, we may *exult* even in our present *sufferings.* Indeed, in no small measure exulting in our present sufferings is what it means to *stand in grace.* Because Christ is present with us in suffering, having made our sufferings his own, we know that they are not meaningless. By grace they may be turned to serve that most biblical of all virtues — *endurance* or *hypomonē. Hypomonē* is an almost untranslatable term. It means waiting with patience upon the Lord, and with confidence in his faithfulness, despite all appearances to the contrary. Paradigmatic instances of this virtue may be found in the stories of Genesis (Abraham and Sarah, Joseph, etc.) and in Psalm 27. The objective hope in which we properly exult is a hope that sustains us through our sufferings and that, through our consequent perseverance or *hypomonē,* deepens hope as a disposition within us. Perseverance in suffering from hope to hope produces *character* in the people of God. It gives them integrity, compassion, and depth.

Verse 5: Resurrection hope is a hope that will not *put us to shame.* For it makes *God's love* present even now. The actual presence of divine love guarantees the final hope. In the midst of our sufferings, *the Holy Spirit* arrives as a *gift* from the future, *pouring out* divine love *into our hearts.* This pouring out is again an established reality that is spoken of in the perfect tense. This spiritual pouring out of divine love is the gift that, having once been given, continues to be given ever anew. It is hope's provisional sign and seal. As God's love enters our hearts profusely, it anticipates the life in which we enter God's glory eternally.

Verse 6: The subjective guarantee of final hope rests on a more objective ground. The love poured out into our hearts by the Holy Spirit is grounded in the reality of Christ's saving death on the cross. The love of God through Christ and in the Spirit is a love that turns everything upside down, because it has come and comes to lost sinners. God's love is directed, in other words, not to the religious but to the impious, not to the respectable but to the disreputable, not to the virtuous but to the *ungodly* — to those who merit the very opposite of the great love they are actually given. The ungodly are by definition culpably *helpless.* They are totally forfeit in themselves, totally lacking in any power of deliverance from the desperate plight into which they have plunged themselves. It is these for whom Christ came to die *at the appointed time,* according to the mysterious counsel and good pleasure of God.

Verse 7: The purpose of this verse is to underline our astonishment at the love of God. This love directs itself toward those — the unrighteous — whom anyone but God would have rejected without reprieve. It is precisely for such as these that God humiliates himself in Christ. It is for these that he takes their death away by dying it himself in Christ so that they might live.

Verse 8: It is not our repentance that leads us to grace, but God's grace that leads us to repentance. God does not love us because we are lovable, but we are lovable because God loves us. God's love is *shown* to sinners, odious and unrepentant, precisely while they are *still sinners.* It is these for whom *Christ died.* That is why God's love is called *agapē* rather than *erōs.* It is a love that loves not the lovely but the unlovable, even at the cost of death. It is a fathomless love that transforms sinners into those who are righteous, the ungodly into the godly, and enemies into friends. Paul knew this truth perhaps better than any other apostle. For while he was *still* a persecutor of

Christ and the church, with not one thought of repentance, grace had stopped him in his tracks.

Verse 9: Paul repeats the aorist passive of verse 1 — *having been justified* — but with a difference. Whereas he previously spoke of our having been *justified by faith* (v. 1), he speaks now of our having been *justified by his blood.* He shifts from justification's subjective appropriation to its objective ground. Whereas justification is appropriated by faith, it is grounded in Christ's blood, his sacrificial death for our sakes. The crucified Christ is the content, reality, and power of our justification; faith is the vehicle by which we acknowledge, receive, and partake of it. Only on this basis — Christ in his sacrificial death — are we assured of being spared from *God's wrath,* but on this basis the assurance of faith is secure. Divine wrath represents, for Paul, the just deserts of sin, as they will be manifest at the final judgment. The perfect tense of justification determines both the present and the future. In the present it pours out God's love into our hearts by the Holy Spirit, and then secures us by the blood of Christ (a term that always has eucharistic as well as direct priestly implications) on the last day.

Verse 10: The idea of reconciliation is stated twice in this sentence, each time in a verbal construction whose form is both perfect and passive. *Having been reconciled* is clearly a direct correlate for Paul of *having been justified.* Yet there are important differences. Since we cannot be reconciled to God without being made righteous, justification is the necessary subjective condition for being reconciled to God. No reconciliation without justification. But since reconciliation pertains more exclusively than does justification to the objective consequences of Christ's death, reconciliation is the external basis of our being justified by faith. No justification without reconciliation. (While the two ideas overlap in meaning, Paul never speaks of our being "reconciled by faith," but only "by Christ's death," whereas he does speak of our being "justified by his blood" as well as "by faith." Justification spans the objective and subjective aspects of salvation in Christ more fully than does reconciliation, whose connotations are more exclusively objective.) Paul's thinking here moves from the perfect tense to the future tense, and from Christ's death to his resurrection. In both cases we are spoken of in the passive voice, and therefore as the recipients of a free gift. Having *been reconciled,* we will *be saved.* Just as our reconciliation rests on Christ's death, so our deliverance from God's wrath at the last judgment, our being saved, rests on Christ's resurrection to new *life.* Being clothed in his righteousness, we are reconciled to God. Being invested with *his life,* we are saved from eternal death. The gift of sharing in Christ's righteousness grounds and guarantees the gift of sharing in his life.

Note again that this twofold gift (righteousness and life) comes not only to the undeserving, but to those who deserve the very opposite. The *ungodly* who as *sinners* have already been described as *helpless* are now described precisely as *enemies*. Sin is both a guilt and a power. The guilt of enmity underlies the bondage of the will that leads to ultimate death. Estrangement from God rests on hostility to God, sin as bondage rests on sin as guilt, leaving us without remedy in ourselves. The seriousness and the terror of the human plight, as well as the even greater magnitude of God's mercy, are revealed in one drastic resolution, *the death of his Son*.

Verse 11: Paul returns to the present tense, in which *we also exult in God*. This exuberant present, grace in the midst of suffering, is clearly placed between the times — between the perfect tense of reconciliation and the future tense of final deliverance into life, between the saving consequences of Christ's death and those of his glorious resurrection. The Lord Jesus Christ, *through whom* we have peace with God (v. 1) and access to the grace in which we stand (v. 2), is the very same Lord, Paul reiterates, through whom *we have received reconciliation* — again, purely as a free and perfect gift. God is the object not of terror but of joy, not of fear but of exultant hope, not of deadly estrangement but of fellowship in eternal life, for one and only one reason. He has bound himself precisely to lost sinners (cross), and lost sinners precisely to himself (resurrection), through the grace *of our Lord Jesus Christ*.

*George Hunsinger*

## First Sunday in Lent, Year A

First Lesson: Genesis 2:15-17; 3:1-7
(Psalm 32)
**Second Lesson: Romans 5:12-19**
Gospel Lesson: Matthew 4:1-11

Verses 12-14: Because the syntax of this statement is at least as difficult as its content, it must first be read in full. One thought tumbles after another, broken clause by broken clause, as though Paul's discourse were almost visionary or ecstatic. The reference at stake in *for this reason* is only the first of many difficulties. Clearly the argument has reached another turning point. Perhaps the best guess is that Paul is referring back to verses 9-11. If so, he would be setting out to explain the background of his directly previous point. The hope of deliverance on the last day (future tense) — as grounded in the cross of Christ (perfect tense) and received by justified sinners who exult in God (present tense) — arises within a larger, universal context. It is the context of hope that Paul intends to explain.

The general train of thought in this statement is clear: the world is prior to sin, sin is prior to death, and sin (with death) is prior to the law.

No real explanation is provided for the origin of *sin*. It has simply *entered into the world.* Sin is presented as a primeval event as contingent as it was catastrophic. Note that the whole catastrophe is introduced, almost offhandedly, by way of a relative clause. Sin's entry is the premise, not the focus, of Paul's interest. More important is the relation between the first human being and all others. It is a relation between the one and the many. Also important is the relation between sin and death. The one and the many are bound up with sin and death. This nexus is the first real focus of interest. It needs to be unpacked.

If sin is a kind of guilt, death is a kind of fate. Death as fate is a consequence of sin as guilt — *death entered the world through sin* — so that the guilt of sin stands behind the fate of death. The meaning of the word "death" seems to include but transcend mere biological death. The real point concerns how sin and death are related to God. Sin is enmity against God (v. 10), and death is exclusion from God's life. Death, like sin, is primarily spiritual in nature. It means being cut off from God and so from life in a way that is final and irrevocable. Presumably it involves what later tradition called both the pain of affliction *(poena sensus)* and the pain of loss *(poena damni).* It represents the supreme unhappiness and the worst of evils. If death is the fate that results from sin, sin is the guilt that justifies this fate. Immediately, however, the argument becomes obscure.

We can see how sin as guilt is a matter of free responsibility, and we can see how someone who is culpable deserves punishment. Insofar as the culpability of *one human being,* the very first, led to a deserved punishment (death for that human being), the sense is clear. The fate of the one, however, is also the fate of the many. *Death spread to all human beings,* says Paul, making its unlimited extension follow from the sheer contingency of what happened with the first human being. Death entered through sin, *and so* spread from the one to the many. The logic of this "and so," which is no logic at all, can only be descriptive rather than explanatory. We are not confronted with a followable connection, but with a non sequitur. The premise is, apparently, that sin and death are properly unintelligible. Any attempt to make them more intelligible (a temptation almost impossible to resist) would only gain in clarity by losing in descriptive adequacy. Sin and death are opaque actualities in a *world* created good by God. They can be acknowledged but not finally explained. Descriptive adequacy requires paradoxical formulations. Sin and death are, in Reinhold Niebuhr's memorable phrase, inevitable but not necessary — inevitable, because they describe a universal condition; not necessary, because grounded in the contingency of human choice. *Because all sinned,* Paul adds. Sin is as universal as death *(all sinned)*. It is somehow also the underlying reason for this universal human catastrophe *(because)*. Yet for the many who are not the one, sin itself seems to take on precisely the aspect of a fate, of an inherited condition — without ceasing to be a matter of guilt and so of free responsibility. How can the consequences of the first sin, we would like to know, *spread* to become the universal fate of the many? Moreover, if it does so spread, how can the many be held responsible? Ways in which the many in their sin and death are, and are not, like the one is a matter to be taken up later. A near pun in the Greek suggests, however, that for Paul the *spread* of sin *(diēlthen)* is as perplexing as its *entry (eisēlthen)*.

Paul breaks off this difficult line of thought, only to introduce another. He turns abruptly to a question that seems to weigh on his mind. Sin's relation to the law is a vexed matter. It calls forth some of Paul's deepest and most demanding deliberations. How sin and death are related to the one and the many cannot be separated in his mind from the question of sin and the law. As if answering the objection of some hidden interlocutor, Paul interrupts himself to remark on this question. He makes two points: sin is actual with or without the law *(sin was in the world before the law),* yet sin is not appreciated for what it is except by means of the law *(where there is no law, sin is not reckoned)*. The sense of the first point is clearer in the Greek than that of the second. If the interpretation suggested here is correct, Paul is saying that (a) sin's entry from the outset brought death to all (b) regardless of whether or not the law, which manifests wrath (4:15), was present to disclose sin's terrible significance. The law discloses sin, but sin precedes the law. With this brief digression, Paul returns, again abruptly, to his previous argument.

The reign of death is the point Paul now seems most eager to establish. It is at once primeval and universal, even before the law — *but death reigned from Adam to Moses* — precisely because sin is primeval and universal, even before the law. That death exerts a kind of spiritual reign implies that it stands

47

in direct conflict with God's lordship. How God deals with this alien, usurping power is a theme Paul intends to explore.

The statement (or string of broken clauses) ends unexpectedly on a tantalizing note. Adam is not just significant in himself, or only for his catastrophic role in the original position. He is *a type of the one to come*. There would seem to be another position foreshadowed by Adam, a position more original perhaps, or more ultimate. There is an encompassing eschatology that transcends sin and death. There is an Adam more fateful than Adam, a dominion more powerful than death. There is indeed sin, corruption, enmity, guilt, condemnation, and death's domain. Yet as Adam is merely a type, something greater is yet to come.

Verse 15: In the original position the *trespass* that occurred was also an *offense* (the latter being an equally good translation of *paraptōma*). It was an unspeakable affront and insult to God. However catastrophic, contingent, and inexplicable it may have been, it was nonetheless not the last word. The last word (therefore also the first) belongs to *the free gift*. Being a power for good and not for evil, a power that reverses the irreversible and retrieves the irretrievable, a power that wrests life from death, *the free gift is not like the trespass*. It brings life. It does so at the very point where the trespass brings death. Note that the one and the many in this scheme continue to form a kind of interpersonal system. What pertains to the one pertains to all. *Through the trespass of the one the many died.* The one is the center and the many are the periphery. What determines the center determines the whole. The offending trespass meant death for all. That is the penultimate word.

But an Adam more ultimate than Adam has come, *the one human being, Jesus Christ.* While the one and the many continue to form a system, Christ claims the center for himself. The old Adam is displaced by the new. The whole that was determined by death is determined by life. Something incalculable has arisen: *the grace of God and the free gift in the grace.* The old ground and consequence are superseded by the new: sin and death by grace and gift. Divine grace is the ground *much more* effectual than sin. Justification and life are the free gift *much more* ultimate than death. The free gift in the grace *has abounded for the many.* What exactly is the significance, we would now like to know, of free human choice in relation to the grace and the gift?

Verse 16: What verb tenses to choose in translating this verse is tricky. Fortunately, Paul's point seems more nearly logical than temporal. The new consequence, he wants to say, is not like the old. The free gift is not like the catastrophe. The catastrophic sequence was: one trespass–judgment–condemnation. The new sequence is: many trespasses–free gift–justification. The point is to bring out the difference between the middle terms. Even as it is not like the trespass (v. 15), so the free gift is *not like* what happened in the judgment.

The difference involves three factors: the result, the provocation, and the procedure. In the old sequence, the result of judgment was *condemnation*. In the new, the result of the free gift is *justification*. Courtroom imagery is evident in each sequence. *Judgment* results in either condemnation or acquittal (justification). The provocation is also different in each case. In the old sequence it was Adam's *one* catastrophic *trespass*. In the new it was the *many* ensuing *trespasses* of the entire human race. Finally, the procedure in each case is markedly different. In the first sequence, judgment upon *the one who sinned* meant condemnation also for the many. In the second, the freedom in the *free gift* is indeed decisive. Justification in the face of so great a provocation is intelligible only as a miracle of free grace. The perplexity in the old sequence is in the result: how the many can be condemned with the one. The perplexity in the new is in the procedure: how the provocation (many trespasses) can lead to the result (justification).

Verse 17: When the reign of death is replaced by the reign of life, the dominated become the sovereigns. No longer reigned over, they themselves *reign in life*. The change is not partial but systemic. The one at the center determines the periphery. In the old system, the one at the center was the one *through whom death reigned* by virtue of the original *trespass*. In the new system, the one at the center is the one *through whom* grace and the gift are *received*. The grace is *abundant,* the gift is *free,* and the new system surpasses the old beyond measure *(how much more)*. The accent falls on the incomparability of *the one human being, Jesus Christ*. It is through him — through his obedience unto death (Phil. 2:8) — that all blessing comes, so that as *righteousness* replaces sin, *life* overcomes death. Righteousness and life are clearly gifts to be received, not rewards to be earned. The free gift of righteousness trumps all deserving, most especially the deserts of sin. Righteousness brings life, and life means freedom. All are gifts of abundant grace. Finally, an urgent new question emerges: Who exactly are *those who receive?* Is the new system really coextensive with the old?

Verse 18: Although supplying the verbs is again tricky, Paul sums up his argument by bringing out two different systemic results for the one and the many. The latter are referred to (without the usual circumlocution) expressly as *all human beings*. (Here as elsewhere in the New Testament, *the many = all*.) In each case the one and the many form an interpersonal system determined by the one at the center. In the old system the sequence was: one trespass–all human beings–condemnation. In the new system the sequence is: one act of righteousness–all human beings–justification and life. In each system the middle term is again strikingly the same *(all human beings)*. In the old system the determining center was *one trespass*. In the new it is *one act of righteousness*. The entire life history of Jesus seems to be summed up as one righteous act. The whole, it seems, is in the part. Just as the whole of Adam's life was in the original catastrophic trespass, so the whole of Jesus' life was in the act of obedience by which he died for our sakes on the cross. It is this one seminal act of righteousness that brings to all what they have forfeit under the old system — *justification and life*. The consequences of the one trespass are reversed. Condemnation is not the last word. One act of righteousness avails for all. Again, Paul dares to speak as though the new system were coextensive with the old. Can universal hope be, as it seems, the last word?

Verse 19: In each system the one is spoken of, as it were, in the active voice, while the many are spoken of in the passive voice. In the old system the one was *disobedient,* whereas in the new the one was *obedient*. Sin and righteousness are to that extent clearly matters of free responsibility. In the old system, sin as a determining power is guilt before God *(disobedience)*. In the new, righteousness as a determining power is integrity before God *(obedience)*. For the many, however, sin and righteousness are spoken of in the passive voice. In the old system, the many *were made* sinners (aorist passive). In the new, they *will be made* righteous (future passive). Presumably in neither case are they made so without their full consent. The mystery of the respective processes by which they come to be what they are is suggested but not resolved. For the many, acting and being acted upon seem to form a unity-in-distinction in which being acted upon is predominant, yet without abolishing responsibility and consent. In each case, moreover, the system is not impersonal but interpersonal. In each, the center is occupied by a human being, even as the periphery is also occupied by human beings. The relation between the center and the periphery, in both cases, might be interpreted as one of participation or mutual indwelling. The one is in the many, even as the many are in the one. The relation of mutual indwelling holds whether the one is Adam or Christ. Because Christ is greater than Adam, and because grace is greater than sin, and because the center changes while the periphery does not, the verse ends on an exultantly positive note — *the many will be made righteous*. No more is said here about universal hope, but in Romans 8 and 11 it returns in a new light. If the previous suggestion has merit, however, we may conclude that, in the new system, with its new center, the many will be made righteous by way of participation, as Christ dwells in them and they in him.

*George Hunsinger*

## Fifth Sunday after Pentecost, Year A

First Lesson: Genesis 21:8-21
(Psalm 86:1-10, 16-17)
**Second Lesson: Romans 6:1b-11**
Gospel Lesson: Matthew 10:24-39

Verse 1b: May we continue in sin that grace may abound? We may assume that this question is not merely rhetorical. As with other such questions in Romans, especially those that receive the sharp rebuke "By no means!" we are confronted with an objection that would have been hurled against Paul by his opponents. We can easily see how the logic of Paul's argument could be misunderstood, above all by those hostile or unsympathetic. If grace is really as abundant as Paul has proclaimed, if it is so free in what it lavishes upon the ungodly, if it removes what they really deserve and bestows what they do not deserve, if indeed where sin increased, grace abounded all the more (5:20) — well, then, what does it matter if we go on sinning or not! Continuing in sin will only bring about more grace! With this debater's point, Paul is made to look absurd.

It is always a good sign when such objections arise — especially when people are offended — because it means that the gospel has really been proclaimed. The heart, as Luther observed, is naturally legalistic. It cannot tolerate the idea that grace is gratuitous. It cannot bear the thought that sinners might not get what they deserve. Nor can it bear the thought that sin cannot be overcome, and grace merited, by our earnest striving.

Verse 2: The stupidity of the question meets with Paul's impatience. The surface has not been penetrated. The gospel proclaimed has not been heard. Paul properly rebukes the question before he proceeds. *By no means!*

The explanation begins with an implicit question: Who are we anyway? The immediate answer is as provocative as it is astonishing: we are those *who died to sin*. One may well wonder when this dying happened — and how? What does Paul mean by putting this first-person-plural identity-description in the past tense — *we died* (aorist)? We died, says Paul, to the very sin that bound us to death. Death is no longer the false god that reigns over us, that we serve, that we placate, and to which we are in thrall. The service of this god is behind us. We *died* to it. We are set free from sin, and so from death — by our having died.

Verse 3: Those who are *ignorant* of this fact are ignorant of the gospel. How can any baptized believer actually fail to know what baptism involves?

51

The word "ignorant" takes a slight turn, apparently, toward sarcasm, perhaps because the objection arises from those who present themselves as champions of orthodoxy. Legalism often presents itself as orthodoxy — in the church. No better antidote can exist than the argument of Romans 6.

When baptized, we do not enter into union with Christ without entering into his death — without sharing in the power of the cross by which he destroyed the death that was ours, that we might be given the life that is his. It is *Christ* Jesus into whom we were baptized. Baptized into this royal man — into the death that conquered death — we ceased to be ruled by the reign of death. We can no longer live in sin (v. 2) by worshiping and serving death. No one who has entered the baptismal waters can be ignorant of the royal power of the cross.

Verse 4: When Christ was buried in the tomb, *we were buried with him.* His entombment was already ours in order that our burial might be enclosed within his. The event of his burial in the tomb did not signify the finality of what happened to him only, but also the finality of our being actually put to death — *with him.* When he died, we died. When he was buried in the tomb, we too were buried with him. Our death and burial are a thing of the past — in him. Something took place objectively with respect to us: *we* are spoken of in the past tense and the passive voice (aorist passive). Our *baptism* actualizes in us what has already happened to us in him. *Through baptism* we receive and take part in that which was done with us in him. Immersed in the waters of baptism, we were buried *with him* into sin's terrifying end before God, into final abandonment, affliction, loss — *into death.* The waters of baptism are the waters of death. No one who enters these waters will ever, upon emerging, be the same.

There is a finality beyond the finality of death. Beyond the terror of abandonment, affliction, and loss, beyond the just condemnation of the law, is *the glory of God the Father.* Hidden in the depths of the cross, this glory is disclosed in Christ's resurrection. The glory too pure to condone sin is the same glory too merciful to be satisfied by sin's mere destruction. The hidden glory in which Christ was sent to die is also that *by which* he was raised from the dead.

Those who belong to this royal man — those who were raised with him and through their baptism are joined to him — are freed from death's reign of terror. They are no longer servile and helpless. They are liberated from their bondage to sin. The old reign that held them in thrall is replaced by the new. They were not raised to live in anxiety serving death, but that they *might walk in newness of life.*

Verse 5: The emphasis in this grammatically difficult sentence seems to fall on "likeness" *(homoiōmati).* Union with Christ means participation in his death and resurrection, and participation in Christ means being conformed to the same. Those united to Christ through baptism are conformed to both aspects of his likeness. *Being united with him* has both objective and existential consequences. The objective consequences are eschatological. Participation in Christ's death and resurrection through baptism is something real, hidden and yet to come. The existential consequences, on the other hand, are a matter of spiritual formation and therefore of embodiment. Being conformed to Christ means being shaped by the community of worship and witness that, by word and deed, acknowledges him for who he is. The baptismal community that died and dies daily to sin is conformed to *the likeness of his death.* The baptismal community that was raised with Christ from the dead, and continues daily to be so raised, by Word and sacrament in the power of the Spirit, is also conformed to *the likeness of his resurrection.*

Verses 6-7: Paul states what those who are baptized must *know* that of which they cannot possibly be ignorant (v. 3). The royal man has taken over the center by putting Adam, the old human being, to death in himself on the cross. Since the royal man has embodied us in his death, and we were crucified with him (vv. 3-4), what happened was that the old Adam, *the old human being in us,* was *crucified with him.* Those at the periphery are now determined not by the old Adam but by the new humanity of the royal man.

Sin is a spiritual condition that is always embodied in community. The destruction of the old human being at the cross took place *so that the body of sin might be destroyed.* The old community determined by sin has been destroyed, and a new community determined by the royal man has come into being in its place. This community lives, for the time being, in tension between the cross and the resurrection, between the final death of the old and the final revelation of the new. The body of sin was indeed destroyed in order that it *might be destroyed* (subjunctive aorist passive) in the new community daily, by the royal man who reigns from the cross, until its accomplished destruction is made manifest, unambiguously, at the end of all things. The baptismal community lives from liberation to liberation in liberation.

This liberation, this baptismal transition to the new, is sure, because it is sealed by the death of the old. The three deaths that are one — that of the royal man, of the old human being in him, and of the old human being in us in him — are appointed to absolve us from sin. *For whoever has died is absolved from sin.* A fascinating wordplay in the Greek is impossible to reproduce in English. "Absolved" would more literally be translated by a word no less laden with meaning than "justified." Whoever has died can no longer be held responsible for sin. In that sense death means absolution. But when all have died in and with the royal man, sin's guilt has in fact been removed and its power is ended. In that sense death means being justified, and justification means being liberated from servitude.

In short, the finality of *our being crucified with Christ,* as acknowledged and received in baptism, assures three things: the crucifixion of the old human being in us, the destruction of the body of sin, and our finished and continuing liberation from a life of enslavement.

Verses 8-9: Again Paul insists on what the baptized must know (v. 3). Knowing in their baptism that Christ is *raised from the dead,* they know that he *will never die again.* The life that he lived on earth is now eternal in status and significance. Therefore, the question of the true Lord — Christ or death — is behind them. They know that the royal man is the Lord of death, not vice versa, that *death no longer lords it over him.* The baptized know that the reign of death has been vanquished by the royal man.

The baptismal community lives between past and future as determined by the obedience of the royal man, between his intercessory death and his triumphant life, between his cross and his final revelation. *But if we died with Christ, we believe that we shall also live with him.* That is the faith of the baptismal community. Its past is the cross in which it *died with Christ.* Its future is the resurrection in which it *shall also live with him.* Piece by piece Paul is building a christocentric definition of past and future in order to clarify the community's present.

Verse 10: Death is primarily a spiritual reality and power. It signifies God's fitting abandonment of us to our catastrophic abandonment of him. It includes and yet transcends death in the natural or biological sense. Therefore, all human death, by definition, is *death to sin* — death as determined by the reality and power of our collective human catastrophe before God. It is this death that the royal man, as one of us, died.

Life is also primarily a spiritual reality and power. God is the source of life, having life in and for himself. If anything else has life, it is necessarily on loan from God. Yet not all life is eternal life. Eternal life, without beginning or end, is the life proper only to God. The temporal life proper to the creature is obviously of a different kind, since it comes into being by nature and passes away. Yet human creatures with mere temporal life were created for fellowship with the eternal God. (It is this fellowship that was catastrophically forfeited by sin.) The life of the royal man has passed from cross to resurrection, from death as determined by sin to eternal life as determined by God. *The life that he lives, he lives to God.* Having vanquished death by death, he lives eternally to God. It is this life, perpetual and unending, that determines the baptismal community's future in God's sight.

Because of the royal man, sin and death have been made transitory and therefore past, to be remembered no more. They are the graveclothes left behind in Christ's tomb. Righteousness and life have, in turn, been made eternal and therefore future, to be bestowed ever anew. They are the heavenly robes received in baptism.

Verse 11: Members of the community — once dead in their sins, but having emerged from the baptismal waters — are to consider themselves in the present as already determined by the future. They are *alive to God*, not in themselves but *in the royal man*. His future is their future, because by his cross their past is null and void. Sin and death in them were crucified with him (v. 6), that his righteousness and life might clothe them eternally.

The members of the baptismal community are to *consider themselves* not as what they are in themselves but as what they are in the royal man, *Christ Jesus: alive to God*. Their fellowship with God is, and will be, eternally unbroken. In themselves, to be sure, the power of sin still tenaciously remains, even if only as that which is past. Though they live in union with the royal man, they are not yet risen with him from the dead. What baptism holds in prospect will come to pass. The baptismal community, and each one within it, must consider themselves to be what indeed they already are: *dead to sin and alive to God in the royal man*, despite what they so evidently still fail to be in themselves. Though they live in tension between the "already and the not yet," between what they are in Christ and are not yet in themselves, they *must* consider themselves not to be determined by sin and death, but rather by the royal man. He himself is their righteousness and life, and their eternal future. Because he is *alive to God* (v. 10), so will they also be *alive to God* in union with him. Everything depends on their grasping their true identity as received in baptism, and on their living by the true power that determines their future. Having emerged from the baptismal waters but not yet being raised from the dead, they have nonetheless died and risen in and with the royal man. Therefore they must consider themselves to be what they already are, but are not yet: *dead to sin and alive to God in Christ Jesus*. Any different or less complicated self-consideration would only falsify their baptismal reality.

*George Hunsinger*

## Sixth Sunday after Pentecost, Year A

First Lesson: Genesis 22:1-14
(Psalm 13)
**Second Lesson: Romans 6:12-23**
Gospel Lesson: Matthew 10:40-42

Verse 12: While living in the time before the end, the baptismal community must be exhorted to live according to the end of time. If it were already at the end, it would not need the exhortation. But if the end time had not already shattered the old aeon, the exhortation would have no force. Sin and death still remain, but only as fragments of the shattered aeon. They have been subdued by the royal man, who lords it over them (v. 9). His apocalyptic reign is exercised in the baptismal community. *The reign of sin* has been overthrown.

*The old lusts* are still present in the community: pride, greed, envy, bitterness, sensuality, gluttony, apathy. Their source is in the desires of the *flesh*. They promise life but deliver *death*. If baptism did not exist, their *fatal* deception would still triumph through *the reign of sin*. Sin reigns in deception by compelling *obedience* to these lusts. For the baptismal community this obedience has been broken and makes no sense. Having emerged from the baptismal waters, it knows a Lord greater than death, a reign greater than sin, and a truth greater than deception. It can therefore be exhorted to submit itself in obedience to the risen Lord.

Verse 13: The community of baptism — of the new aeon, of the royal man — is not to embody death but life, not injustice but justice, *not wickedness (adikia) but righteousness (dikaiosynē)*. *Sin* is the conjunction of behavior and lust, not just of lust alone. It concerns what we do, concretely, with the *members of our bodies*. Most particularly, it concerns *which lord we present them to*, which one we obey and serve, which one claims the desires of our hearts — the lord death or the Lord God.

The self for Paul is always the embodied and communal self. *Presenting yourselves* (second-person plural) is the same as *presenting your members*. When the community, and each one in it, *presents itself to sin* in the service of death, its members become *instruments of wickedness*. The poor are neglected, the vulnerable are oppressed, outsiders are humiliated, violence prospers, apathy prevails, and deception reigns. This is the pattern of the old aeon. Conversely, *when the self-presentation is to God* in the service of life, the community and its bodily members become *instruments of righteousness*. The hungry

56

are fed, injustice is exposed, brutality is renounced, the earth is honored, promises are kept, the lonely are visited, and the gospel is proclaimed to all creatures. This is the pattern of the new aeon.

Since the word for *instruments (hopla)* might equally well be translated as *weapons,* the implication seems to be one of combat. The royal man is in combat against sin and death. This combat is carried out, in some sense, within the baptismal community itself. That community has been transferred from the old aeon to the new. Its very *members* are at once instruments or weapons of righteousness and the site on which the conflict is waged.

Verse 14: In the old aeon it was impossible for the community, and each one within it, not to sin. *Non posse non peccare.* When the new aeon is at last manifested for what it is at the end, it will no longer be possible to sin. *Non posse peccare.* In the interim before the end, a decisive shift has occurred, and continues to occur — from the old and to the new. For the baptismal community, what was once impossible is now made possible: not to sin. *Posse non peccare.* Sin is essentially a spiritual rather than a moral reality. It is essentially a matter of which lord reigns in the community, which lord it worships, honors, serves, and obeys.

The power of the future — of the new aeon — is *grace.* It absolves the community of guilt and liberates it from bondage to sin. Grace is the reason why sin has no future. The reign of grace will triumph in the community — and despite it. The power of the past, on the other hand, is *the law.* The law belongs to the old aeon, not by what the law is in itself, but by what happened to it under the reign of sin. In the old aeon the law was capable of disclosing sin, but not of overcoming it. Having emerged from the baptismal waters, the community is *not under the law but under grace.* It belongs not to the law but to grace: not to condemnation but to righteousness, not to death but to resurrection, not to sin but to the royal man.

Verse 15: Paul returns explicitly to the question of verse 1. His argument has reached a plateau. Enough has been said to unmask the opponents' objection for what it is. Those *under grace* are under infinite obligation to the one who put them there. If they will not be condemned *under the law,* it is only because they belong to the royal man. Are they to *continue in sin* — as if he did not exist, as if he had not suffered for them on the cross, as if he had not bound them to himself in rising from the dead? Are they at liberty to contradict their baptism? To ask such questions is to answer them. *By no means!*

Verse 16: Paul continues with the running theme of *baptismal knowledge.* He insists on what the baptized must know precisely by virtue of their hav-

ing undergone baptism (vv. 3, 6, 9). This very knowledge should be sufficient to block the foolish question about the behavioral implications of gratuitous grace.

The question is not *whether one is to be a slave,* but *whose slave one is to be.*
Moreover, the question of whose slave one actually is can only be decided by
*who it is to whom one presents oneself for obedience.* If the community thought it
might just as well continue in sin (so that grace would abound), it would be
*presenting itself to sin.* It would therefore contradict its baptism *by becoming
sin's slaves.* The community cannot *obey sin* without becoming *enslaved to sin*
as an alien lord.

*How can the baptized community not know this?* How can they not know
that they belong to another Lord — the royal man? How can they not know
that they are liberated from the deceptions that *lead to death,* so that they
might continue *in obedience to him* on the path of baptismal righteousness
that *leads only to righteousness* and so to life?

Verses 17-18: Paul does not actually need to chastise the community for
presenting itself to the wrong lord. It is, after all, the baptismal community.
It is the community of those who presented themselves to Christ, bodily, as
having themselves died and been raised with him from the dead (v. 13). They
did this when they entered and emerged from the waters of baptism.

The act of baptism was preceded by a *form of teaching.* Their baptism was
not, as Paul reminds the community, undertaken in ignorance. It had been
prepared for by catechetical instruction. Paul gives *thanks to God* that this
teaching was not resisted (as it is by the spurious objection). It was in fact
obeyed gladly and *from the heart.* The teaching was obeyed when the catechu-
mens presented themselves, body and soul, to Christ in their baptism. This
teaching was undoubtedly the apostolic preaching of the cross. The power
of the cross is that which broke, and continues to break, the power of sin. As
conveyed in and through the teaching, it is the power that made baptism
possible.

The transition from sin to righteousness is not carried out by degrees. It
is an apocalyptic event. It moves drastically from death to resurrection. Sin
does not coexist with righteousness, as colored liquid might partially fill a
glass tube, nor righteousness with sin. A person cannot be bound in allegiance to both at the same time. To be bound to sin is to be a *slave to sin.* To
be bound to Christ is to be a *slave to righteousness.*

Verse 19: Paul knows the agony and the ecstasy of theological discourse.
He knows all too well that what urgently has to be said cannot be properly
spoken. He lives in the full tension between the urgency and the impropriety. Nothing could be more urgent than to refute the false conclusion about

the gratuity of grace. Yet in doing so Paul has had to stretch verb tenses and metaphors to the breaking point. He has had to speak of the real presence of realities like sin that are essentially past, and of those like the resurrection that are essentially future. He has had to speak of the obedience of a single royal man by which the entirety of the old aeon has been shattered once for all. He has had to explain a past and future apocalyptic event that is available for present participation. He has had to make manifest that which remains hidden while not hiding that which is still manifest. He has had to exhort the community to become what it is, because it is not yet that which it shall be. He has had to say that sin and death have been defeated because Christ is risen from the dead. He has been *speaking in human terms because of the weakness of your flesh.*

He again moves from the indicative to the imperative, and from the passive to the active voice. The baptized who were *made slaves of righteousness* (indicative/aorist passive) (v. 18) are exhorted *to present themselves as slaves to righteousness* (imperative/aorist active). As they once presented themselves (their members) to sin — to pride, greed, envy, bitterness, sensuality, gluttony, apathy — to the service of *uncleanness* before God through *an ever intensifying iniquity,* so now through a similar self-presentation, only this time to *righteousness,* they are to undergo the great reversal to *sanctification.*

Sanctification is the opposite of uncleanness, even as righteousness is the opposite of iniquity. The community knows what uncleanness and iniquity are. They have lived them. They must learn what righteousness and sanctification are. Again priestly metaphors coexist with courtroom metaphors and finally with governance metaphors. *Priestly metaphors:* Uncleanness is the defilement purged by the blood of Christ and washed away in baptism. Sanctification is the gift of participation in his holy purity. *Courtroom metaphors:* Iniquity is culpable self-seeking as manifest in the lies and violence that finally brought Christ to the cross. Righteousness is the utter destruction of that iniquity by wrathful divine condemnation for the sake of mercy. *Governance metaphors:* by turning from sin to Christ, the community is to live out the transfer of power from the old slavery and spiritual allegiance to the new.

Verse 20: *Slavery to sin* is false freedom, for it is freedom from all that brings life. *Freedom from righteousness* is no freedom at all, but bondage to that which brings death. Prior to baptism *(when you were slaves to sin),* the community and its members were separated from righteousness by an abyss of many waters. Moreover, slavery to sin was an objective condition to which they gave their full consent. They were slaves not by mere compulsion only, but by inward allegiance. Note again that righteousness and sin are not relative to one another, but complete contraries. That is why slavery and allegiance to the one excludes slavery and allegiance to the other.

Verse 21: Sin is a condition of bondage and allegiance with an inexorable outcome or *fruit (karpon)*. Often obscured in English translations, the word "fruit" is better retained, for Paul uses it regularly whenever he wants to indicate the result intrinsic to a spiritual condition. *Death* is intrinsic to sin. It is contained in sin as the fruit is contained in the seed. It is not an uncertain outcome that may or may not come to pass. Death is built into sin from the very outset. Death is the *end* or goal *(telos)* toward which sin essentially tends and in which it inevitably terminates. The harvest of sin, which promised life, has death as its bitter fruit.

The bitterness finds expression in *shame*. Although closely related, shame and guilt may be distinguished. Whereas guilt is the anxiety of being blameworthy for having violated a valid standard, shame is an acute sense of exposure for having been deficient in some fundamental aspect of being human. Whereas guilt pertains more to specific deeds, shame pertains more to one's essential being. One feels worthless as a person and unable to make oneself acceptable. Choosing a life of sin, Paul is saying, has subjective as well as objective consequences. It issues not only in death but in shame.

Verse 22: God will not coexist with sin, nor compromise with it, nor call it good. To be enslaved to sin means being "freed" from righteousness — and so from God (v. 20). Conversely, to be *enslaved instead to God* means being *freed from sin* (both verbs: indicative/aorist passive). Having emerged from the waters of baptism, the community has been brought from the old bondage to allegiance to the new. It has been freed from that to which it was in bondage (sin) and bonded to that from which it was free (God).

The new spiritual condition brings with it a new *fruit* and a new *telos*. *Sanctification* is contained in righteousness as the *fruit* is contained in the seed. Beyond that, *eternal life* is the *telos* of enslavement to God in righteousness. The new situation is notably more complex than the old. Whereas in the previous case of sin, fruit and telos could be indicated by one and the same term, "death" (v. 21), Paul now distinguishes the one from the other. When speaking of the new bondage and allegiance to God, he wants to distinguish the *fruit of sanctification* (as the opposite of *uncleanness,* v. 19) from the *telos of eternal life* (as the opposite of *death,* v. 21). The *uncleanness and death* of the old bondage to sin are thus replaced by *sanctification and eternal life* in the new bondage to God. Having been transferred from the one to the other through waters of baptism (which cleanse from shame and liberate from death), the community has *its fruit in sanctification and the end of eternal life.*

Verse 23: Paul concludes on a note that brings out the gratuitousness of grace — the point in question. By shifting from an organic metaphor (*fruit*) to a contractual metaphor (*wages*), he positions himself to validate the disputed gratuitousness that has been his underlying concern since verse 1. Whereas fruit and wages are both a kind of telos, wages differs from fruit in being a matter of earning or deserts. *Death* is not only the inevitable consequence of *sin*, it is what sin deserves (as well as the prize sin doles out as lord). *The wages of sin is death.* Eternal life, by contrast, is not what anyone deserves. Having emerged from the waters of baptism, no thanks to itself and its past shameful bondage to sin, the community has henceforth been transferred to a new Lord, to a new set of loyalties, obligations, and allegiances, to a new future, and therefore to a new form of life even now. It is to live in an ever new conformity to the likeness of the royal man. Having emerged from the baptismal waters, it has embarked upon a decisive and continuing exodus from the old and toward the new. *Shall we continue in sin that grace may abound? By no means! . . . For the wages of sin is death, but the free gift of God is eternal life in Christ Jesus our Lord.*

*George Hunsinger*

## Seventh Sunday after Pentecost, Year A

First Lesson: Genesis 24:34-38, 42-49, 58-67
(Psalm 45:10-17)
**Second Lesson: Romans 7:15-25a**
Gospel Lesson: Matthew 11:16-19, 25-30

In this passage Paul describes the divided ego. The passage falls into three main sections, each of which contains three parts. The sequence of the sections is the same each time: (1) the ego's knowledge of its sinfulness, (2) behavioral or experiential confirmation of this knowledge, (3) conclusion. The discussion intensifies as Paul moves through this sequence three times, from one section to the next.

This passage appears within a larger discussion in Romans about the law. Paul's view of the law is very complex. How to understand Paul on the

61

law is hotly contested in current scholarly discussion. The controversies cannot be resolved here. At least five themes can nonetheless be discerned: (1) The law is holy. (2) The law is the standard of God's will and so a yard-stick by which to measure our behavior. (3) The law does not liberate us from power of sin, but has been taken captive by it instead. (4) Under the dominion of sin, the law actually becomes an incitement to sin. (5) Under the dominion of sin, the law does not justify or acquit us, but condemns us; it brings us not life but death.

Whether or not the passage pertains to the Christian life is also hotly contested. I will assume here that it does. The interpretation suggested will thus be in line with classical expositors like Gregory of Nazianzus, Augustine, Aquinas, Luther, Calvin, and Barth. Among contemporary scholars, Kümmel, Betz, Cranfield, and Dahl would agree. Nonetheless, many scholars currently take a different view; among the most thoughtful are Käsemann, Beker, Moo, and Fee.

Paul situates the baptized community, and the baptized person within the community, in an apocalyptic context. The baptized exist in the turning from the old aeon to the new as determined by Christ's death and resurrection. They exist between past and future, between the old aeon determined by sin (now shattered by Christ) and the new determined by resurrection from the dead (now inaugurated). The power of the resurrection is really present to them — as that which is essentially future. Because of its presence, sin does not dominate them. They are freed, and continue to be freed, to live according to the future. Being free not to sin, they ought not to continue in sin. That is the theme of Romans 6:1-23. However, during the interim existence of the baptized, the power of sin is not absent. It too is really present — as that which is essentially past. Despite its having been vanquished, it maintains a tenacious grip. That is the theme of Romans 7:13-25: although the power of the future is predominant (Rom. 6), the power of the past remains (Rom. 7).

Verse 15a: "I do not understand my own actions." This statement gives us sequence element 1. Verse 14 has just indicated that the law is spiritual, but I am not. I am carnal, sold into slavery under sin. *This is the self-knowledge of the ego as disclosed by the law.* It creates a profound perplexity for the baptized person. Because, as Paul has previously established, that person, as a member of the baptized community, need not and ought not sin. Given the liberating power of resurrection, and the believer's new situation under grace (6:14), how can old bonds to sin still remain? And yet, as a matter of fact, in practice they do. *I do not understand my own actions.*

Verse 15b: "For I do not do what I want, but I do the very thing that I hate." This statement represents sequence element 2. It offers a behavioral confirmation of the ego's self-knowledge that the ego acts in conflict with the law. In some significant sense *the ego* of the baptized person actually agrees with the law. The ego actually *wants* what the law wants, so to speak, and actually *hates* what the law hates. While the desires of the heart are conformed to the real presence of that which is future, the deeds of the flesh are conformed to the real presence of that which is past. The behavior of the baptized ego shows it to be in conflict with its resurrection self (which agrees with the law), with the holiness of the law, and with the liberating power of baptism.

Verses 16-17: "Now if I do what I do not want, I agree that the law is good. But then it is no longer I that do it, but sin that dwells within me." These statements bring us to sequence element 3, and so to the end of round one. *They draw a conclusion that synthesizes the previous two elements.* The ego acknowledges (1) the truth of the practical conflict between the law and the ego as (2) confirmed by experience. The (1) goodness of the law is not invalidated by (2) the behavioral failures of the ego. The conflict between behavior and desire — *I do not do what I want* — indicates that the baptized person's desire is in agreement with the law — *I agree that the law is good*. The agreement between desire and the law coexists with the fact that the ego is still strangely captive to an alien power that grips it, not merely from without but within. This alien power is not identical with the baptized ego. *It is no longer I that do it but sin that dwells within me.*

The threefold sequence of section one has established: the baptized ego's agreement with the goodness and spirituality of the law, that same ego's lingering captivity to the power of sin, and so the ego's division between the law and sin.

Verse 18: *The flesh* is the real presence of that which is essentially past. It is the continuing presence of the old human being that was crucified with Christ (6:6). In this old humanity now relegated to the past, *the good does not dwell*. In some strange sense, I continue to be self-identical with this old human being. Two conflicting tendencies *are present in me* at one and the same time. *Wanting to do the good* is present, but *the ability to enact it* is not. The wanting represents *the presence* of that which is future; the inability, of that which is past. This is sequence element 1 as it appears at the beginning of round two.

Verse 19: The ego's self-knowledge is again confirmed in practice — sequence element 2. The baptized ego is strung out between what it wants and what it enacts, between the simultaneous real presences of the new aeon and the old. It does not do what it wants *(that which is good)*, and does what it does not want *(that which is evil)*. Practice again confirms the ego's perception and diagnosis of its plight. The power of the past, of the flesh, still *dwells in me* (v. 18). The ego has emerged from the baptismal waters, but is not yet risen from the dead. It is risen from the dead in Christ but not yet in itself. This apocalyptic eschatology of the already and the not yet represents the complex temporality of salvation. It is a christocentric eschatology of participation.

Verse 20: In sequence element 3, Paul *concludes* that the baptized ego is essentially identical with its future, not with its past. The ego belongs essentially to *what it wants* and so to the future, not to what it *still does in practice* under the power of sin. The persistent *indwelling of sin* no longer defines the ego, nor does it determine its future. The baptized ego belongs to Christ and his future.

The threefold sequence of section two has intensified what was established in section one: that the ego is and is not identical with the flesh, that the power of the past is confirmed by sinful practices in the present, and that the nonidentity of the baptized ego with the flesh means that, even in the apocalyptic interim, its true self is its resurrection self, as manifest in its dissatisfaction with what it does. Despite its behavioral failures, the baptized ego is essentially defined by a higher power, Christ the Lord, who determines its future.

Verse 21: Round three begins with a new statement about *the relation between the ego and the law* — sequence element 1. The statement is not easy to translate. Most English translations choose to speak of "a law," although the Greek undeniably speaks of "the law" *(ton nomon)*. Since Paul's larger purpose is to vindicate *the law* against possible (and existent) misinterpretations of how he actually views it, it would seem that he is not merely speaking here about some general principle of experience. The apocalyptic eschatology of the law shares in the general complexity of the turning of the aeons. Because the law is holy (7:12), it transcends the past and belongs to the future. When the baptized ego wants to do what is good, it is in conformity with this aspect of the law.

Because the law is co-opted by sin (7:7-12), on the other hand, it is a power that incites what it condemns. It is this aspect of *the law* that Paul has in mind here. Whenever the baptized ego *wants to do the good,* the power of the flesh reasserts itself as *the presence of the past (evil is present [parakeitai] to me).* In the old aeon, the law in the co-opted sense is enlisted to serve this carnal power. It is enmeshed in the power of the flesh. It *makes evil present* to the ego. Under the dominion of the flesh, the law cannot disclose evil without provoking the ego to commit it.

Verses 22-23: Paul does not really speak here of various different "laws." Everything depends on seeing that he speaks of the one law in two basic forms. In form one, the law transcends the past and belongs to the future. The law of God, the law in which the ego delights, and the law of its mind are not three separate laws, but three expressions for the one law in its transcendent or apocalyptic reinstatement. It is the law as essentially holy (7:12), freed from the past for the future. In form two, the law is co-opted by sin. Sin is really present only as that which has been made essentially past. *The law at war with the law of the baptized ego's mind, the law of sin to which that ego is made captive,* and *the law of sin that dwells in its members* are, again, not different laws, but three different expressions for how the one law functions in this, its persistent and still co-opted form.

*The inmost self* is not the Platonic soul, but the new *human being (esō anthrōpon)* of the future. It represents the real presence of the new aeon. It is the ego's apocalyptic reality that, in Christ, is at once real, hidden *(esō),* and yet to come. This apocalyptic human being, baptized into the reality of the future, delights in the promised future, in its real presence and the forms of its presence, and so *in the law of God.* Like delights in like, future reality in future reality. *For I delight in the law of God in my inmost* (apocalyptic) *self.*

The law of the flesh that the baptized ego *sees in its members* is *at war* with the law of its mind. When Paul previously spoke of *members,* in Romans 6, the idea of apocalyptic combat was also evident. In that context he described it from the standpoint of the future. The baptized community was summoned to present its members as "weapons" to be wielded against the powers of the old aeon. The baptized had been conscripted into the royal man's combat against sin and death. From the standpoint of the future, their members were "weapons of righteousness" (6:13). On the other hand, when described from the standpoint of the past, as still really operative in the present, that same combat looks very different. The "members" are at the same time still flesh. From the standpoint of the future, the baptized are already liberated. From the standpoint of the past, they find themselves *still being made captive.* These two countervailing identity descriptions are not harmonized. They are juxtaposed. Paul lets them stand in dialectical tension. These experiential matters represent the third round of sequence element 2.

Verses 24-25a: In and of themselves, even the baptized are still *wretched.* But they do not exist only as such, not even in the interim time, when they are buffeted between past and future, experiencing apocalyptic combat in their members from two antithetical directions. For their *Deliverer* is one and the same from either side. Prior to their actual resurrection from the dead, they still live *in the body of this death.* Although they are already joined to their Deliverer, the royal man, through baptism, they are more perfectly in him than he is in them. Throughout the interim time, they are summoned to persist each day in that once-for-all baptismal self-presentation of their members to him that they have already decisively made.

As they live in the turning of the aeons, they cannot live otherwise than *in thanksgiving to God through Jesus Christ,* for he himself has made them his own. And he will continue to do so. Despite the persistent power of sin that clings to them so closely, the baptized know that this malignant power does not determine their future. Despite the strange persistence of fleshly power, it is he who has transformed the catastrophe of sin and death into their past — so that it is really past. And despite the deferral of their actual resurrection until the final revelation of the end time, it is also he who has made his righteousness and life into their future — so that it is really future.

Bemoaning his wretchedness while yet exulting in Christ, Paul closes the last round with sequence element 3. The self-knowledge of the ego in relation to the co-opted law is not the last word. This self-knowledge, confirmed by experience, would not even be possible apart from the real presence of deliverance in Christ. By this deliverance, as entered by passing through the baptismal waters, the baptized may delight in God's law even now, see the apocalyptic combat in their members for no less but no more than what it is, and in all things live a life of thanksgiving.

*George Hunsinger*

## Eighth Sunday after Pentecost, Year A

First Lesson: Genesis 25:19-34
(Psalm 119:105-12)
**Second Lesson: Romans 8:1-11**
Gospel Lesson: Matthew 13:1-9, 18-23

In Romans 7:25b Paul, in terms of his own experience, depicts the dilemma in which he and all people have been caught. He says, "With my mind I am a slave to the law of God, but with my flesh I am a slave to the law of sin."

What is to be done? The answer comes in what *God* has done, and Paul declares it without equivocation: "There is therefore now no condemnation for those who are in Christ Jesus" (v. 1). "Now" refers not simply to Paul's, or our own, or anyone's present moment. "Now" instead refers to "the once-for-allness of the eschatological indicative, the opening of the new epoch effected by Christ" (James D. G. Dunn, *Romans 1–8,* Word Biblical Commentary 38 [Dallas: Word, 1988], p. 415). In Christ the age of the flesh, in which sin and death reign and conscript into their service even God's own holy law, that is, Torah, has been brought to an end, and the age of the Spirit has begun. Therefore those who are "in Christ Jesus," who have died with him and been raised with him and thus are incorporated into his body, the church, as attested in baptism (cf. Rom. 6:3ff.), are not condemned to a life of futility. They, and all whom Christ calls to be his own, have been freed by "the law of the Spirit of life in Christ Jesus . . . from the law of sin and of death" (v. 2).

This does not mean that those who are in Christ, whom Christ has called to be his own, no longer are capable of doing anything to displease God or to injure themselves or others or creation itself. They still can and do sin, and they most certainly die. But they do not now suffer condemnation. The "no condemnation" of verse 1 is emphatic; "condemnation is in every sense out of the question" (James Denny, "St. Paul's Epistle to the Romans," in *The Expositor's Greek Testament,* vol. 2, ed. W. Robertson Nicoll [Grand Rapids: Eerdmans, 1961], p. 644). That they do not suffer condemnation means that those who are in Christ do not have to live and die as if the law, sin, and death had the final say. "For God has done what the law, weakened by the flesh, could not do" (v. 3a). What the law thus weakened could not do — since, according to the flesh, the law is as much a temptation to sin as a warning to flee from it — is effect righteous judgment and secure among people that manner of life that God wills for people's benefit and for the flourishing of all creation under the will of God. In other words, the law could not effectively foster divine righteousness, the righteousness of God, which the gospel reveals and which Paul takes as the central theme of his letter to the Romans (Ernst Käsemann, *Commentary on Romans,* ed. and trans. Geoffrey W. Bromiley [Grand Rapids: Eerdmans, 1980], pp. 21-32).

But God effected righteous judgment, apart from the law, "by sending his own Son in the likeness of sinful flesh" (v. 3b), that is, precisely under the conditions of that form of existence Paul knew in his own personal and bitter experience to be prone to disobedience, injustice, and unrighteousness. God sent his Son as a sin offering, as expiation for sin (cf. Lev. 9:2; 14:31; Isa. 53:10; Ps. 40:6). God sent his Son to die a sinner's death, to bear the reprobation deserved by others, indeed all others, Gentiles and Jews alike. Thereby the Son atoned for human sin, "condemn[ing] sin in the flesh" (v. 3b) by enduring its consequence. God did this so the life of obedience required by the law "might be fulfilled in us, who walk not according to the flesh but according to the Spirit" (v. 4b). God, in his Son, the Second Adam, and in the power of the Holy Spirit not only condemned unrighteousness but accomplished — and continues to accomplish — for us human beings, and in us, and among us, and despite us, that obedience to himself from which the first Adam, and all human beings with him, turned and fell (cf. 5:12ff.). This is the confidence in which we "walk," in which we "live and move and have our being" (Acts 17:28): that no unrighteousness of any age or any life, including our own, can undo the righteousness that has been revealed in Christ Jesus our Lord. In that righteousness, which is not an indulgence or approval of sin but a forgiveness of it (John Calvin, "The Epistle of St. Paul to the Romans," *Commentaries*, vol. 19, ed. and trans. John Owen [Grand Rapids: Baker, 1989], p. 283), we stand; and from that righteousness we cannot fall.

In verses 5-11 of Romans 8, Paul further explicates his understanding of life according to the flesh and according to the Spirit. For Paul, "according to the flesh," as already has been suggested, is a technical term used to indicate the nature of life lived in rebellion against God and in disregard of God's righteousness. It does not imply a dualism at the heart of human beings. It has to do rather with one's habit of mind and the direction of one's "walk." To set one's mind on things of the flesh, then, is not simply to indulge on occasion a carnal appetite, though such indulgence certainly is included. More subtly, but as devastatingly, it is to give over one's thinking to such things as the good that is the enemy of the best. It is to surrender one's thoughts, often not self-consciously but inadvertently and out of habit, to the devious reign of sin and death through what is good (cf. Rom. 7:13). And its destiny, like its governance, is death. Life according to the flesh can be pious as well as self-indulgent. The elder brother in Jesus' most famous parable, for example, was as prone to it as the prodigal who, in a far country, "squandered his property in dissolute living" (Luke 15:13b). One can fast and offer prayer according to the flesh, as Jesus' teaching on fasting and prayer, recorded by Matthew, clearly indicates (Matt. 6:1-17).

This too should be noted: in Romans 8:5-11 Paul is speaking of capacities, tendencies, inclinations, and habits of thought common to humankind. To these any particular individual, Paul himself included, may be more or less conformed at any time (e.g., see 7:21-24). To set one's mind on things of the flesh consequently could involve the presumption that one's self-identity as a Christian woman or man is developed and sustained not by

God in Christ in the power of the Spirit, but by one's own efforts to be and to do what is well pleasing in God's sight (Pelagianism). One might even presume that laying claim to Christ as Lord and Savior obligates Christ; that is, that such an act of decision conditions Christ's own claim (Arminianism). According to the flesh, one could sing, "Blessed assurance, Jesus is mine," while failing to take account of the fact that such assurance, according to the gospel, is the outcome of that "blessed disturbance," as Paul E. Scherer referred to it, by which Christ has claimed, and still claims, people as his own, without seeking their prior concurrence in his claim. To put it starkly, would-be Christian righteousness can be pursued in disregard of the righteousness disclosed in Christ. It can take the form of self-righteousness and so epitomize life according to the flesh. As Paul said, however, "The mind that is set on the flesh is hostile to God; it does not submit to God's law [God's intention and manifest will] — indeed it cannot, and those who are in the flesh cannot please God" (vv. 7-8). So may piety run amok in pursuit of holiness while sensuality runs amok in pursuit of pleasure, and ambition in pursuit of vainglory.

Yet there is also a true piety, a piety of the Spirit, the yield of which is "life and peace" (v. 6b). It is marked by life lived not in pursuit of vainglory, intemperate sensual gratification, and self-righteousness, but in struggle against those lingering evidences of the reign of sin and death. And the peace that pertains to it is not merely peace of mind and peace and quiet, but that ultimate well-being God intends for his creation, namely, peace with God himself. Already the would-be enduring power of sin, death, and the law (weakened by the flesh) has been broken. And that brokenness cannot be mended. Therefore there is no need to dwell upon one's past "life according to the flesh," nor is there need to fear the future. Such dwelling, fretting, fearing would itself be to live life "according to the flesh." It is not that the evils and injustices of the past, the inadequacies of the present, or the likely failures of the future have no import. They in fact have considerable import, but that import is not decisive for the human prospect. If there is "now no condemnation" (v. 1), then there is now no evil or injustice that cannot at last be challenged successfully. There is now no inadequacy that cannot in the end be overcome. And there is now no future to appall. "Since we are justified by faith [i.e., by the free gift of trust in God], we have peace with God through our Lord Jesus Christ" (5:1). Jesus Christ has become our justification, our righteousness, our salvation. He is our peace. And what he is and is attested in Paul, and in the church at Rome, and in the church today, he is and will be attested in and among all human beings and throughout the whole of creation. God's reign in Christ, in the power of the Spirit in the church, and in and among its members is a prolepsis, a living anticipation of the universal manifestation of God's cruciform victory over sin and death in Christ Jesus. In consequence of that fact, it no doubt behooves those "in the Spirit" not to regard themselves as delivered from turmoil but into it and, through it, into God's presence, for "the power of the resurrection world breaks into the old aeon and brings about a worldwide conflict into which (cf. Gal. 5:16ff.) every believer is drawn both as the battleground and the instrument of his Lord" (Käsemann, p. 213).

"But you are not in the flesh; you are in the Spirit, since the Spirit of God dwells in you" (v. 9a). Here Paul shifts from a discussion of the contrasting conditions of life in the age of the first Adam, dominated by sin, death, and the law (weakened by the flesh), and the age of the Second Adam, inaugurated by Christ and given over exclusively to divine righteousness, and focuses specifically on the circumstance of the people of the church at Rome. By extension, of course, this word from Paul also is intended for people of the church today wherever they may be found. In effect, no questions asked, no reservations noted, Paul announces his readers' election, Jew and Gentile alike. They are elected not to a status, clearly, but to a vocation, a calling. That vocation or calling is to be the "battleground" and the "instrument" of the Lord in the conflict of the ages just mentioned. "Anyone who does not have the Spirit of Christ does not belong to him" (v. 9b) indicates that life is to be lived on the terms of the vocation to which one is elected, and that it is not to be lived on any other terms. "But if Christ is in you, though the body is dead because of sin, the Spirit is life because of righteousness" (v. 10). This verse means that the body, through the flesh, which is the means of access to the body for the reign of sin and death, suffers the divinely appointed fate of sin and death. It dies. But "the Spirit [not one's own human spirit but the Spirit of God, as Paul's use of the term throughout this entire pericope makes quite clear] is life because of righteousness" (v. 10b). The death of the body does not compromise the election and promise of God, for divine election and promise are vouchsafed to men and women in Christ through the indwelling of God's Spirit. This point is expanded upon in verse 11: "If the Spirit of him who raised Jesus from the dead dwells in you, he who raised Christ from the dead will give life to your mortal bodies also through his Spirit that dwells in you." Salvation is not disembodied, it is embodied. It is not accomplished "according to the flesh" but "according to the Spirit." And it is eschatological. It is yet to be realized fully. Nevertheless, the pledge of that full realization dwells within. The power by which Jesus was raised from the dead by the Father already is working righteousness in those who are in Christ. Those who are in Christ thus die as they live, not in despair, but in hope. The cruciform existence to which they are called and in which they are sustained by God in Christ in the power of the Spirit, while not giddy as in charismatic enthusiasm, nevertheless is marked by the charism, the Holy Spirit's gift, of "solemn joy" (Robert Browning, "Paracelsus V," in *Browning's Complete Poetical Works*, ed. Horace E. Scudder [Houghton Mifflin, 1895], p. 41).

*Charles L. Bartow*

## Fifth Sunday in Lent, Year A

First Lesson: Ezekiel 37:1-14
(Psalm 130)
**Second Lesson: Romans 8:6-11**
Gospel Lesson: John 11:1-45

Romans 8:6-11 is set within a context of the battle of the ages, the old age of the first Adam versus the new age of the Second Adam. The old age is the age in which sin and death reign, assisted by the letter of God's own law, weakened in application through human sin and rebellion (see 1:16-31 on human sin, rebellion, and failure to honor and glorify God; 5:1-21 on life in the age of the Second Adam as opposed to life in the age of the first Adam; 7:21-25 on the struggle of flesh and spirit in Paul himself). The old age, with its powers and the outcomes of the exercise of its powers, is what Paul has in mind whenever he speaks of "flesh" or of life "according to the flesh" (v. 5). In Christ the powers of the old age have been defeated. Sin and death have no power over Christ. Through death, resurrection, glorification, and the sending of the Spirit, Christ has inaugurated, even in the face of continuing unrighteousness and rebellion against God, the age of righteousness and obedience. To be "in him" is to be led by his Spirit. It is to die to the old Adam and to participate in the life of the new Adam. It is to die to sin (6:2) and to "walk in newness of life," as baptism attests (see 6:1-11). To "walk not according to the flesh but according to the Spirit" (v. 4) thus is to live in the light of Christ's victory over sin, death, and the law

71

(weakened by the flesh). Such is life under the aegis of God in Christ in the power of the Spirit as opposed to life under the aegis of the flesh. Ernst Käsemann speaks to the issue succinctly and memorably: "The Spirit unites the community [of saints or of believers] to the body of Christ, and thus creates for itself a field of earthly activity, a sphere of power which corresponds antithetically to the sphere of the rule of flesh or the 'letter' . . . the power of the resurrection world breaks into the old aeon and brings about a world-wide conflict into which (cf. Gal. 5:16ff.) every believer is drawn both as the battleground and as the instrument of his Lord" (*Commentary on Romans,* ed. and trans. Geoffrey W. Bromiley [Grand Rapids: Eerdmans, 1980], p. 213).

It is with this context in mind that Paul speaks of the importance of setting one's mind on the Spirit instead of on the flesh (vv. 6-8). To "set the mind" in either case is to focus attention deliberately and consistently on one or another way of being and acting. It is to develop a habitual and settled frame of reference for conducting one's affairs. Since it already is clear that sin and death reign in the flesh, to "set one's mind" on the flesh "is death." It is to think and act as if life, so to speak, swirled around and around to the hole in the sink. Paul does not here explore the attitudinal characteristics of such a life, but they can be imagined. To set one's mind on the flesh could mean to despair of finding meaning and purpose in life. It could be to nurse a gnawing melancholy born of the conviction that everything at last amounts to nothing and that everyone comes to nothing. Or, quite the opposite, setting one's mind on the flesh could lead one to nurture an exuberant mood: "Eat, drink, and be merry, for tomorrow we die." To set one's mind on the flesh could lead to a life filled with self-indulgence, or to a life filled with selfless service and rectitude. It could mean to set oneself to proving one's worth. It also could mean to fret over deeds of the past now regretted, to "stew in guilt." To set one's mind on the flesh could be to seek to abide by the letter of the law or to live in the law's despite. However understood or experienced, says the apostle Paul, to set one's mind on the flesh "is death." For it is to fail to set one's mind on the Spirit and on the gospel of God's righteousness (8:1-4).

On the other hand, "to set the mind on the Spirit is life and peace" (v. 6b). It is not to anticipate the possibility of life in denial of death (as is later made clear in vv. 10ff.). But it is to think and act in the assurance that sin and death (which reign in the flesh) do not have the last word. Thus "to set the mind on the Spirit" is to know peace, not just peace and quiet, peace of mind, or peace as an absence of conflict. For there can be no absence of conflict where the age of the flesh and the age of the Spirit contend with one another. "To set the mind on the Spirit" rather is to know "peace that passes understanding" (Phil. 4:7). It is to know "peace with God" (Rom. 5:1). The mind set on the flesh does not, cannot know peace with God, for it is set in opposition to God, even in its would-be goodness, even in its determination to pursue righteousness down to the last letter of the law. The mind set on the flesh, says Paul, is hostile to God even when the intention is to please God. This is so because the mind set on the flesh ignores the righteousness that has been provided in Christ "apart from the law" (vv. 3-4; and see Rom. 3:31). The mind set on the flesh thus does not, indeed "cannot please God" (v. 8). It still is in rebellion against God, no matter that the rebellion takes the "outward form of godliness" (2 Tim. 3:5) and, to the mind set on the flesh, seems motivated by a love for God. The love of God from a Pauline perspective, it must be remembered, is not an attitude, feeling, or determination generated from within the human heart. It is not a matter of doubling up one's fists, clenching one's teeth, and trying very hard to care for God deeply — against the odds of being able to do so. From a Pauline perspective, love for God is a relationship of affectional regard — and, from the human side, obedience — instanced and sustained by God himself, in the power of the Spirit. It is part and parcel of God's effectual calling of people, his enlisting them in and commissioning them for service to the divine righteousness and saving purpose already disclosed in Christ. If it is passionate, and it is, it is so because of being filled with Christ's own passion (see 8:28 and the exegesis for the second lesson, Tenth Sunday after Pentecost, Year A). One submits to the law — and so pleases God — not by seeking to obey the letter of the law, but by setting the mind on the Spirit of him who "has done what the law, weakened by the flesh, could not do" (8:3a).

It is not that the law itself is of the flesh and set against God. The law is of God and holy. It is in fact spiritual (see 7:4-14, esp. vv. 7 and 14). However, it is Christ who has fulfilled the law. Consequently, it is only in Christ that submission to God's law, that is, God's intent for human life, is possible (cf. 7:4). Some scholars contend that this means that the law as letter, as written code, cannot be used to provide guidance for the conduct of life according to the Spirit, for such a use of the law, it is argued, would indicate that human beings still had, and were seeking to exercise, a measure of autonomy in attempting to do that which pleases God (Käsemann, p. 218). Others see the "law" in verse 7b as *possibly* referring to Torah. But even Torah, in this view, would need to be interpreted in a new context, that is, "in Christ," and "in the Spirit," and thus in light of the fact of the justification of the ungodly (5:6-8). The law, in this view, could not justify and sanctify, but conceivably could serve to indicate what the Spirit was doing "so that the just

73

requirement of the law might be fulfilled in us, who walk not according to the flesh but according to the Spirit" (v. 4; see also John Ziesler, *Paul's Letter to the Romans* [London: SCM Press, 1989], p. 209). Still other scholars interpret submission to God's law in verse 7 as submission to God's will in the creation of human beings in God's image and for the praise and glorification of God. The parallel is 1:18ff., where to be subject to God's law is to be subject to God's will and to God himself in obedience, which is the only proper relationship of the creature to the Creator (James D. G. Dunn, *Romans 1–8,* Word Biblical Commenrary 38 [Dallas: Word, 1988], p. 443). Whatever the preacher might decide on this matter in the light of divergent scholarly opinion, it no doubt would be wise to stay focused on Paul's central point, namely, that the human mind is to be set on the Spirit, not on the flesh, not on the self and its possibilities for good or ill, and not on the law independent of and, according to the flesh, set over against the Spirit both as an accusation and a temptation, a letter that kills (2 Cor. 3:6). Pleasing God, that is to say, is not an achievement of the human being as an autonomous moral agent. It is, instead, an achievement of the Spirit, the "Spirit of God," "the Spirit of Christ" (v. 9) in those "who walk not according to the flesh but according to the Spirit" (v. 4b) and who, as a consequence, are led to set their minds on the Spirit.

"But you are not in the flesh; you are in the Spirit, since the Spirit of God dwells in you" (v. 9). At this point Paul cuts off his more general and somewhat impersonal mode of discourse and pointedly addresses his readers directly, using the second-person pronoun. He identifies them — apparently sans concern for the way they might have regarded themselves — as those who are "in the Spirit," by which he means that the Spirit of God dwells within them, inhabits them. And this is what it means to belong to Christ, for anyone who does not have "the Spirit of Christ" does not belong to him. But, to repeat, Paul says his readers *do* have the Spirit in Christ. He affirms that they therefore belong to Christ. The apostle does not leave the matter open to consideration and debate. He settles it in a peremptory fashion with an affirmation. The affirmation, that is to say, governs the explication that follows. The explication does not govern the affirmation and call it into question. Paul does not say here that "if you have the Spirit of Christ, you belong to him, but if you don't — and you may not — you do not belong to him." That would imply that his readers should start scratching around for evidence — superior to the apostle's affirmation — of the Spirit's residency. The residency is declared. Life then is to be pursued in light of the declared residency of the Spirit. In effect, Paul says, "If the Spirit is in you, Christ is in you, and, as your baptism attests, you are in Christ." This does not mean that believers own the Spirit as their individual or corporate possession, something they somehow have managed to obtain. Consequently, the presence of the Spirit in one's life, and in the life of the believing community, is not an occasion for boasting. It is rather an occasion for sober assessment of the fact that one's life, and the life of the communion of saints, is the dwelling place, the residency, of Christ in the Spirit. The Spirit is Christ's mode of being with and shepherding, governing, ruling in the affairs of those who have been baptized into his body. Their life now takes on the cruciform character of the crucified Lord. It is not so much a matter then of Christ belonging to believers as of believers belonging to Christ (v. 9b). "But if Christ is in you . . . the body is dead because of sin" (v. 10a) means there is no escaping the consequence of sin, namely, death. Nevertheless, the Spirit, that is, God's Spirit or Christ's Spirit (for Paul the terms are interchangeable), "is life because of righteousness" (v. 10b). The Spirit, in other words, in addition to being a witness among believers to the righteousness of God that has been revealed in the gospel (1:17), is an earnest of the resurrection they have not yet undergone but in the future are to undergo. This particularly is made clear in verse 11, which provides a thrilling conclusion to the pericope here under consideration: "If the Spirit of him who raised Jesus from the dead dwells in you" — and the Spirit does dwell in Paul's readers, so Paul has attested (v. 9) — "he who raised Christ from the dead will give life to your mortal bodies also through his Spirit that dwells in you."

Life is to be lived in the context of the promise of resurrection. The resurrection is an accomplished fact in Christ's own life. But for believers, the resurrection is a future to be anticipated. It is not a fact of believers' present existence. Believers yet remain both the "battleground" and the "instrument" of the Lord in the clash of powers of the old age and the new. Nevertheless, their cruciform life in the present, because it is governed by the promise of God, is joyful, whatever the ambiguities and sufferings inherent in it. The Spirit "will give life" to the mortal body of believers. The Spirit, that is, will not whisk away believers to some disembodied mode of existence that is quite unimaginable to Paul (and to anyone of Hebraic mentality). Rather, the Spirit will re-create bodily existence free from the temptations of the flesh and the reign of sin and death through the flesh. Bodily existence in the resurrection, in other words, is relational. It is a new being in community. It is personal life. But precisely because it is personal, it is life in relationship, which is what personal — as opposed to impersonal — life means. It is life in relationship to God, to other persons, and to the world, which is the sphere of persons in relationship to God and to each other (see Paul J. Achtemeier, *Romans*, Interpretation: A Bible Commentary for

Teaching and Preaching [John Knox Press, 1985], p. 133). Precisely in their cruciform — yet hopeful and joyful — life in the Spirit, under the reign of Christ as proclaimed in the gospel, that is, Christ crucified, believers together, which is to say in their ecclesial life, bear witness to, and so anticipate, the resurrection world where the cosmos and all its contents not only are restored but are made new (8:21b). The first lesson for the Fifth Sunday in Lent, Year A, particularly drives home the point of a corporate, as opposed to individualistic, reading of God's dealing with his people in the Spirit. What is to be restored there among the ancients, among the people of God in exile, is not a solo believer here and a solo believer there, but a full chorus of believers, "the whole house of Israel" (Ezek. 37:11). Much more then, to be in Christ, and to set the mind upon the Spirit, is not to withdraw into an intrapersonal reverie. It is to be caught up in a cosmic happening, an eventful life led by the Spirit of Christ "that dwells in you" (v. 11b).

*Charles L. Bartow*

## Trinity Sunday, Year B

First Lesson: Isaiah 6:1-8
(Psalm 29)
**Second Lesson: Romans 8:12-17**
Gospel Lesson: John 3:1-17

Romans 8:12-17 may at first seem an odd text for Trinity Sunday. What on earth has it to do with the doctrine of the Trinity as a way of identifying the God who is worshiped in the church and is to be obeyed there and in the world? On its surface, as is the case with the whole of sacred Scripture, it has little to do with a trinitarian understanding of the nature of God. But beneath the surface, and in its connections to the verses that precede and follow it, this pericope has a good deal to do with what has instanced trinitarian thought. Ecclesial biblical scholarship largely seems to be of one mind in seeing the immediately preceding verses, 8:1-11, as fertile ground for that kind of living and thinking in faith that in due course led to the formulation of the doctrine of the Holy Trinity (see, e.g., Ernst Käsemann, *Commentary on Romans,* ed. and trans. Geoffrey W. Bromiley [Grand Rapids: Eerdmans, 1980], p. 213). In addition, extensive scholarship attests the fact that verses 12-17 explicate further the issues of life according to the Spirit in contrast to life according to the flesh developed in verses 1-11, with particular reference to verse 9: "But you are not in the flesh; you are in the Spirit, since the Spirit of God dwells in you. Anyone who does not have the Spirit of Christ does not belong to him." In the second lesson for Trinity Sunday, Year B, then, the key to preaching the gospel of the triune God of Christian faith is the text's depiction of the person and work of the Holy Spirit.

In verse 9 alone one finds multiple ways in which the Holy Spirit is referenced: "Spirit," "Spirit of God," "Spirit of Christ." In earlier verses the Holy Spirit is named with these as well as other terms. For example, in verse 4 the single word "Spirit" is used, while in verse 2 reference is made to the "Spirit of life in Christ Jesus," and in verse 11 to "the Spirit of him who raised Jesus from the dead." Likewise, in verses 12-17 one finds the same variety of terms used to refer to the one known in the church catholic as the third person of the Trinity: "Spirit" (v. 13), "Spirit of God" (v. 14), and once again simply "Spirit" (v. 16). Beyond these observations, it has been pointed out that in verse 15 the phrases "spirit of slavery" and "spirit of adoption" may not necessarily refer to human attitudes and states of mind as is implied in the RSV and NRSV translations, in contrast to the KJV. To the contrary, as with the KJV, these phrases may refer to what those baptized into Christ on the one hand did *not* receive (a spirit of slavery) and, on the other hand, what they *did* receive (a Spirit of adoption), that is, the Holy Spirit (John Knox, "Epistle to the Romans," in *The Interpreter's Bible,* vol. 9, ed. George Arthur Buttrick [Abingdon, 1954], p. 516). What in any case is patent in all the variety of names used to identify the Spirit is that for Paul, and for the churches to whom he wrote, Christian experience of the preaching of the gospel and of the life to which it led could not be discussed and understood appropriately without reference to God, to Christ as God's Son, and to the Holy Spirit as the Spirit of God and of Christ dwelling with and among believers. And those terms, while combined in a variety of ways, finally could not be reduced to a single term.

What or who is the Holy Spirit? In the passage before us, Romans 8:12-17, it is conceivable that one could choose to make reference to the Holy Spirit with the neuter, impersonal pronoun "it." Yet the use of the personal pronoun may be even more readily conceivable. After all, in this pericope, as has been noted, the Spirit is identified as "of God" and "of Christ." Also it is through the Spirit that Christ dwells in those who have been baptized into him (vv. 10-11). Furthermore, the Spirit "leads" or, as it also may be translated, "drives" those who are called to be Christ's own (v. 14). Moreover, when the church, in the context of worship, cries out, "Abba! Father!" it is the Spirit who cries out to and with the church, inspiring that cry of acclamation and prayer. The Spirit cries out with or to the church's members that they are "children of God" (v. 16). What the Spirit does, God does, and what God does, Christ does in, for, and among those whom God in Christ in the power of the Spirit has called to be his own. So if the Spirit is not here depicted as a personality, to use contemporary terminology, neither is the Spirit depicted as a vaguely defined, impersonal force unrelated, so to speak, to the person of God, the person of Christ, or human persons. The Spirit, instead, is intimately related to God. And to those to whom the Spirit speaks, and in whom the Spirit dwells, God has become known intimately as the transcendent — yet also immanent — Father both of Christ Jesus, God's Son (v. 3), and of those who in Christ have been adopted as God's children and made heirs of that inheritance into which Christ himself already has come through death and resurrection and glorification (v. 17).

It is to the Spirit that people of faith are indebted instead of to the flesh (v. 12). It is by the Spirit that they are enabled to "put to death the deeds of the body" (v. 13). That is, by the Spirit people of faith are challenged to resist, indeed to seek to destroy, all that through the flesh tempts them to neglect or to oppose the righteousness of God revealed in the gospel of Jesus Christ (see exegesis for Rom. 8:1-11, Eighth Sunday after Pentecost, Year A). Through the leading of the Spirit, those who live according to the Spirit know themselves as children of God and not as slaves either to the law or to their own appetites. Beyond this they know themselves no longer as slaves of God but as freed men and women, duty-bound to God as to a loving parent (cf. 6:15-22). They know themselves, that is, as sons and daughters whose obedience to God is the joyful obedience of heirs destined to receive as an inheritance precisely what Christ Jesus, God's Son, has received already (vv. 15, 16, 17). Last but not least, it is by the Spirit that those who live according to the Spirit and not according to the flesh are sustained through the suffering which they must inevitably undergo because they belong to Christ. For to belong to Christ, to live under Christ's governance, is to participate in his passion (v. 17b) and only thus to have hope of sharing his glory. The Christ in whom those led by the Spirit live, the Christ whose glory the adopted children of God one day will share, is Christ crucified, the Christ of gospel proclamation. In light of all this, Paul can go on to say in verse 18, "I consider that the sufferings of this present time are not worth comparing with the glory about to be revealed to us."

Implicit in 8:12-17, then, is the articulation of an experiential basis for the development of an understanding of God as triune, that is, an understanding of God as Father, Son, and Holy Spirit. Insight into the experience of God that gave rise to trinitarian thought is provided in Paul's explication of the Spirit's presence and work in, with, and among those who have died with Christ, as attested in baptism, and have found their life in him. The experiential basis of the one God's triunity, that is to say, is not to be found in experience of God apart from the gospel in which the "righteousness of God is revealed from faith for faith" (1:17), but precisely in and through the proclamation of that gospel. For the Spirit which indwells the church and its members and all those Christ Jesus has called to be his own is the Spirit of God, the Spirit of Christ, the Spirit who testifies to and with the ecclesial spirit, "our spirit" (v. 16), that "we are children of God, and if children, then heirs, heirs of God and joint heirs with Christ — if [or perhaps since], in fact, we suffer with him so that we may also be glorified with him" (vv. 16, 17). What preachers therefore need to keep in mind in their Trinity Sunday sermons is that Romans 8:12-17 does not warrant a use of the gospel to preach the Trinity. Instead it warrants a use of the doctrine of the Holy Trinity to preach the gospel, the gospel of the cross, the gospel of the righteousness of God as opposed to any form of self-righteousness, the gospel of life according to the flesh come a cropper and life according to the Spirit made possible, the gospel of the power of sin and death done to death in the death of God's Son (vv. 3-4), and in the believer's life (v. 13). The text warrants, in a word, what it itself does. In 8:12-17 there is no vaunting of the text over the gospel. There is, to the contrary, the service of the text *to* the gospel. The gospel of the cross is what the text attests in and through all its varied nomenclature for identifying and explicating the Spirit's work. So it is the gospel, as attested in this text, that preachers themselves, with the assistance of trinitarian thought, are mandated to proclaim. The gospel in its apostolic attestation has led to the church's promulgation of the doctrine of the Holy Trinity. As a result, the usefulness and appropriateness of preachers' explication of that doctrine in their sermons must be assessed in terms of sermonic faithfulness in directing thought — and feeling and passion — to the apostolic attestation to the gospel given in the text.

Such an approach to the proclamation of the gospel on Trinity Sunday, in light of Paul's exposition of the work of the Holy Spirit in 8:12-17, will allow for challenges to various notions concerning the relevance of trinitarian thought for understanding the gospel and the claim of God upon human life. For one thing, it will allow one to challenge the idea that the doctrine of the Holy Trinity is an imposition upon the biblical witness, that it has little

79

to do with the gospel as we have come to know it through the biblical witness. Preachers also may challenge the idea that knowledge of God as Holy Trinity is purely speculative and not experiential, that is, that the doctrine of the Trinity does not issue forth from faithful response to the preaching of Christ crucified, risen, and regnant. It also will allow for a challenge to purely subjectivist understandings of experience and knowledge of God. For, claims the apostle Paul, the Spirit to whom we are indebted — instead of being indebted to the flesh (v. 12) — is not our possession by right nor something native to our interiority. In other words, the Spirit is not conjured from within. The Spirit, to the contrary, is "of God" and "of Christ," and the Spirit directs us, leads us, drives us to do those things which, more often than not, are opposed to our natural, "of the flesh" instincts and to our self-generated notions of well-being. The Spirit leads us — drives us, in fact — to put to death what the body, captive to the dictates of sin and death and the law (through the flesh), would have us do. We do not master the Spirit. The Spirit masters us. Through the Spirit Christ directs our life according to the righteousness of God revealed in the gospel (vv. 13-14) and forbids self-indulgence on the one hand, and self-righteousness on the other. In that much, then, the Spirit which, with the word of the gospel, brings us knowledge of God and of God's righteousness, far from ratifying our impulses, typically contradicts them and discomfits us.

At the same time, the Spirit's assurances also have an objective character. For instance, "Abba! Father!" — an echo of Christ's prayer in Gethsemane (Mark 14), which the church of Paul's time had incorporated into its liturgy as a cry of acclamation of the gathered, worshiping community (see the parallel use of the formula in Gal. 4:4-7) — as already noted, is a testimony of the Spirit to and with the church and its members. Through that testimony of the Spirit worshipers are assured that they are children of God by adoption, bound to come into that inheritance of glory — the glory of God — which Christ himself already possesses. Further, for the sake of that inheritance, even suffering may be endured. This is religion with a passion. But it is not a passion worked up from within. It is a passion infused from without. It is the passion of Christ crucified taking hold of people and making them what they otherwise could not, in fact would not be. It is not that human beings are divinized. But through the agency of the Spirit they are given, precisely in their humanity made new in Christ, a share in divinity's own triune glory. Says Ernst Käsemann: "Acclamation is inspired. It is thus an act of sacral law. When it takes place, the Spirit ruling in the congregation manifests objectively to the individual Christian what the Spirit given to him [or to her] personally says. Like the pagan in 1 Cor. 14:25, the congregation learns from the acclamation of ecstatics that God is present in their midst and that both to the whole and to the individual he gives assurance of sonship as participation in the *basileia*" (Käsemann, p. 228).

*Charles L. Bartow*

## Ninth Sunday after Pentecost, Year A

First Lesson: Genesis 28:10-19a
(Psalm 139:1-12, 23-24)
**Second Lesson: Romans 8:12-25**
Gospel Lesson: Matthew 13:24-30, 36-43

R omans 8:12-25 begins with the words "So then, brothers and sisters." This indicates that the exhortation given in verse 13 (in the second person and thus very directly, even pointedly, to Paul's readers as a warning and adjuration) erupts from the doctrinal affirmation of verse 11: "If the Spirit of him who raised Jesus from the dead dwells in you, he who raised Christ from the dead will give life to your mortal bodies also through his Spirit that dwells in you." By clear implication, Paul's readers are debtors to the Spirit, to live according to the Spirit. They are not debtors "to the flesh, to live according to the flesh — for if you live according to the flesh, you will die."

But, Paul continues (v. 13b), "if by the Spirit you put to death the deeds of the body, you will live." The implications to be drawn from this doctrinally governed exhortation are three in number. First, the adjuration, the moral imperative, as noted, erupts from the doctrinal indicative. So to speak, it is more a case of "you *are to be* doing something" than of "you *must do* something." The Spirit dwelling within believers impels them to do away with those deeds of the body which manifest the body's continuing susceptibility to the governance of sin, death, and the law — weakened by the flesh and enlisted in the service of sin and death (see exegesis of Rom. 8:1-11, Eighth Sunday after Pentecost, Year A, and Rom. 8:12-17, Trinity Sunday, Year B). Second, the line of demarcation between the first Adam and the

81

Second Adam, between the age of the flesh (marked by attempts at self-justification through the law on the one hand, and by self-indulgence or license masquerading as freedom on the other) and the age of the Spirit, runs right through the believer's own life as well as the life of the unbelieving world. Life in the Spirit, therefore, is not to be regarded as a status to be paraded, but as a calling to be pursued in fear and trembling and gratitude (gratitude not least of all for the inspiration and guidance of the Spirit provided by apostolic exhortation). Third, life in the Spirit leads not to quietude but to struggle. Already the victory of the Spirit over the flesh has been secured in Christ through death and resurrection. But sin, death, and the law (weakened by the flesh) still provoke a rearguard action in defiance of the Spirit. The temptation of believers is to live as if that rearguard action were a frontal assault, that is, that sin and death still had decisive power over them. So they might "faint and be weary" (Isa. 40:30). However, Paul's exhortation provides a reminder that believers not only are a site of struggle but are also, at the same time, instruments of the Spirit *in* struggle. Certitude of victory thus is given in the thick of struggle itself, not in attempted flight from it or disengagement in the midst of it. Through Paul's exhortation, then, the Spirit himself fixes the heart of the believer upon the righteousness of God revealed in the gospel, a salutary gift of the Spirit indeed; for, as Calvin observed in commenting upon Romans 8:13, "[T]here is no confidence in God, where there is no love of righteousness" ("The Epistle of St. Paul to the Romans," *Commentaries,* vol. 19, ed. and trans. John Owen [Grand Rapids: Baker, 1989], p. 283).

But where there is the love of righteousness, where there is engagement in a struggle to "put to death the deeds of the body," there is confidence in God. "For all who are led by the Spirit of God are children of God" (v. 14). Moreover, the children of God are not enslaved to an anxiety-ridden, fearful quest for self-righteousness according to the law. Neither are they held in thrall to "the elemental spirits of the world" (Gal. 4:3) or the importunings of their own flesh. Further, though they live in an appropriate awe of and respect for God, and are as much duty-bound to obey God as any slave would be, nevertheless they do not possess that dread and fear of God which is born of being out of sorts with God and having to anticipate God's enmity. For, justified by faith, they have "peace with God through our Lord Jesus Christ" (Rom. 5:1). What is more, having received the Spirit, they have received, with the Spirit, assurance of their "adoption" as children of God (8:15). Beyond this, when they cry out in acclamation or in prayer (as in the Lord's Prayer, though that prayer is unlikely to be specifically in view in this text) or even in desperation, upon being in desperate straits: "Abba! Father!"

(cf. Mark 14:36; Gal. 4:6), that cry itself, typical of the church at worship, is a testimony to the Spirit's prompting, leading, driving believers (Rom. 8:16), and affirming them as God's children. In that same cry the Spirit is witnessing to them that, as God's children, they are "heirs of God and joint heirs with Christ" (v. 17a), that is, heirs of that glory and kingdom and rule (see Rom. 5:17; see also Rev. 5:10; 22:5; cf. Matt. 19:28; Luke 22:30) inaugurated by Christ Jesus himself through crucifixion, resurrection, and glorification. And this rule, in the end, will be revealed to be none other than the very rule of God (see 1 Cor. 15:20-28). In all this breathtaking affirmation and commentary upon life in the Spirit, however, Paul, as consistently is the case throughout his epistolary discourses, never lapses into charismatic enthusiasm and triumphalism. As at the beginning of this portion of this pericope, Paul sustains an unflinching realism about life in the Spirit. The assaults of the flesh continue and need to be "put to death" (v. 13). Beyond that, an eschatological tension persists. Reigning with Christ, at last coming fully into the inheritance of the adopted children of God, lies in the future. Thus it entails participation in the sufferings of Christ in the present (v. 17b). The sign of Christ's reign in the present, in fact, is the sign of the cross. In all his doctrinal exposition, in his exhortation, in his affirmation and encouragement of believers, Paul consistently preaches Christ crucified (see 1 Cor. 1:18-25). The church is a Christocracy in precisely this sense: it lives not under a tyrant's sceptered sway, but under the word of the cross (see also the exegesis of Rom. 8:12-17 in the discussion of the second lesson for Trinity Sunday, Year B).

Beneath the cross, under the reign of God's Son, attested in the preaching of Christ crucified and sustained through the indwelling of the Spirit, life itself is cruciform. It involves suffering, and the suffering can be grievous. Nevertheless, Paul considers the sufferings of "this present time" — that is, the time between the would-be continuing reign of sin and death through the flesh, through the impulse to injustice, unrighteousness, idolatry, disobedience, and futility (see Rom. 1:18-32), and the time of Christ's victory over sin and death made manifest — as unworthy to be compared "with the glory about to be revealed to us" (v. 18). For Paul this consideration or reckoning is a matter of conviction. It is not a mere mental calculation (cf. 2 Cor. 4:17), for it is grounded not in Paul's powers to surmise but in the character of God disclosed in what God has done (see esp. Rom. 8:3-4). When the glory of God's Son at last is revealed openly, all those who belong to him, all those adopted as children of God through him, will themselves be transfigured. Believers' suffering in accordance with the preaching of Christ crucified is the contrary sign that attests the imminent "freedom

83

of the glory of the children of God" (v. 21b) for which creation itself "waits with eager longing" (v. 19). Such suffering, Paul reckons, is a trifling burden compared to the weight of glory that is to be revealed.

Paul's personification of creation, in addition to the content of his rhetoric, suggests an intimate relationship between humanity and the cosmic order into which human beings, made of the dust of the earth, yet in God's image, have been placed. What is called to mind particularly is the unique responsibility, that is, the dominion, human beings have been called upon by God to exercise in relation to the rest of creation (see Gen. 1:26-31). Paul presses the issue of human responsibility and accountability in the welfare of creation through a discussion of the fate of the earth — indeed, of the cosmos — in the light of humankind's fall (vv. 20-21). Specifically he alludes to God's curse upon human beings (Gen. 3:14ff., esp. vv. 17-19), which of necessity, since humanity was given stewardship of the created order, involved the subjection of the whole created order to the futility and to the "bondage to decay" (v. 21) to which human beings themselves were subjected or given up (see Rom. 1:24, 26, 28). The fall of humanity, in this view, is no "happy fall upward" into autonomy. It is, instead, a proud descent into condemnation through contradiction of God's purposes in creation. With human beings' abandoning of their vocation to govern the earth wisely as creatures made in God's image and for intimate communion and intercourse with God concerning the welfare of the cosmos, the cosmos itself was subjected to the Adamic curse. In other words, there can be no happy home for righteousness in the midst of unrighteousness. What a degraded humanity gets is a habitat subject to its own degradation. Is it all outmoded cosmological speculation and archaic mythology without enduring significance? Perhaps not. One thinks of rain forests despoiled, creaturely species for which autonomous humanity no longer feels responsible — in some cases even its own very young and elderly. One thinks of lakes and seas done to death through "deeds of the body" (v. 13b) not put to death. So perhaps John Calvin, speaking in the sixteenth century, has a word of comment on this pericope pertinent to people of the twenty-first century. With regard to the subjection to futility of the cosmos and its contents, Calvin observed: "[I]t is not happened through their own fault, that they are liable to corruption. Thus the condemnation of mankind is imprinted on the heavens, and on the earth, and on all creatures. It hence also appears to what excelling glory the sons of God shall be exalted; for all creatures shall be renewed in order to amplify it [i.e., the glory of the children of God], and render it illustrious" (Calvin, p. 283). Continuing the happier portion of Calvin's line of thought, divine righteousness, at last fulfilled in the glorification of the human being set free in Christ, will find for itself a happy home in a cosmos restored. This is the hope in which creation was subjected, and it belongs to humanity's own hope to see creation itself "set free from its bondage to decay" to "obtain the freedom of the glory of the children of God" (v. 21b).

Thus we have in Paul's theology, anthropology, and cosmology not a creation scrapped but a creation established, and set at liberty, with humanity, to enjoy and reflect the glory of the Creator. Just so are human beings as profoundly bound to the earth and to the heavens as to God. For its liberation, creation groans in exquisite anguish, as a woman laboring for the birth of her child. And in much the same way women and men in Christ, who have the "first fruits of the Spirit" (i.e., the secured promise of adoption fulfilled in an inheritance of emancipation and glory), groan, with a groaning made more vehement by the indwelling of the Spirit, for "the redemption of [their] bodies" (v. 23). "Bodies" refers to the redemption of the whole self, including but not limited to the physical self (Phil. 3:21; 1 Cor. 15:42-50). This is not resuscitation, for "flesh and blood cannot inherit the kingdom of God" (1 Cor. 15:50). Instead, it is a new embodiment (1 Cor. 15:35-50; 2 Cor. 5:1-5; Phil. 3:21), and a new creation as context for that embodied life (cf. Rom. 7:24; 8:11). None of this is seen. It is hoped for (vv. 24-25) as the future God brings. In fact, it is only in the context of hope as expressed in this passage (here and nowhere else in all Paul's uncontested writings — see Paul W. Meyer's article "Romans," in *Harper's Bible Commentary*) that Paul can speak of salvation in the past tense as something already accomplished. Hope is the form faith takes in response to the promise of glory vouchsafed to believers in the proclamation of Christ crucified. It is not self-induced "hope against hope." It is hope holding fast to what is hoped for, that is, to God, who has subjected creation (with and on account of humankind) to futility *in* hope (v. 20). Such hope is patient, not in the sense of being resigned to whatever happens, but in the sense of doggedly — and even cheerfully — suffering what it must, given what it means to live in Christ and to be led by his Spirit. In consideration of Paul's definition of hope, one might dare to suggest (if Paul's affirmation rightly may be rephrased as adjuration) that believers who in the twenty-first century want a sign of the end of the age and of the coming of the kingdom may well expect to be called upon to *be* one.

*Charles L. Bartow*

## Day of Pentecost, Year C

First Lesson: Acts 2:1-21
(Psalm 104:24-34, 35b)
**Second Lesson: Romans 8:14-17**
Gospel Lesson: John 14:8-17, (25-27)

In Romans 8:14-17 Paul, in short compass, declares his doctrine of liberation in Christ (cf. Gal. 3:23ff.; 4:1-11; and esp. 5:1). The use of "for" as a conjunction at the beginning of the pericope conceptually links the passage to verse 13, "for if you live according to the flesh, you will die; but if by the Spirit you put to death the deeds of the body, you will live." Verse 13, structured according to the pattern of Hebraic antithetical parallelism, sets before Paul's readers the claim of God's promise over against the absurdity of rejecting that promise in order to gratify the flesh (i.e., all that is experienced in the body as a rejection of the righteousness of God revealed in the gospel). The "deeds of the body" may take the form of carnal gratification or self-righteousness, licentiousness or the uptight pursuit of good apart from God. Paul's pressing of God's claim upon his readers is reminiscent of the articulation of the Deuteronomic covenant in Deuteronomy 30:15-19: "See, I have set before you today life and prosperity, death and adversity. . . . I call heaven and earth to witness against you today that I have set before you life and death, blessings and curses. Choose life . . ." (Paul W. Meyer, "Romans," in *Harper's Bible Commentary,* ed. James L. Mays [New York: Harper and Row, 1988], p. 1152). From Paul's point of view, for people to act as if they are claimed by the flesh, that is, held in debt to it (v. 12), and for people to fail to act as women and men claimed by God (and so in debt, so to speak, to the Spirit), is to choose death over life. But to act as people indebted to God and God alone, and in the power of the Spirit to put to death the deeds of the body, is to choose life. The challenge, and it is a challenge (issued in very direct, first-person language, "we," and then in second-person language, "you"), does not proffer options of equal merit. It is not a matter of "you pays your money and you takes your choice." Paul does not admonish his readers to exercise their moral autonomy and declare their preference. Too much is at stake — namely, the righteousness of God and the fate of humanity. To attempt to exercise one's powers of autonomous moral decision in the face of Paul's challenge is itself to choose death. Paul's adjuration is that his readers, and he himself, abide by the *Spirit's* preference, that they do what the Spirit, as opposed to the flesh, impels them to do.

The grounds for the challenge are given in verse 14; thus the use of the conjunction "for" as indicated above: "For all who are led by the Spirit of God are children of God." This verse too is packed with emotion. The word translated "led" could be translated "driven." The children of God are moved powerfully, from within, by the Spirit of God. They are moved to live according to the Spirit and not according to the law of sin and death, operating through the flesh and also through Torah weakened by the flesh (see Rom. 8:3-4). The children of God are not left desperately in search of a self-identity they must articulate for themselves. They have been given an identity by God through the eschatological judgment wrought by God in Christ in the power of the Spirit. They do not lead lives of autonomous self-interest, self-definition, and self-direction, for divine parental affection stirs within them and among them. In the Spirit, that is, the children of God are bound to God and to each other, not by their own choice or by duties prescribed under the law, but by God's free choice and determination to make them his own. In and through Christ Jesus they have been set free from the law as taskmaster or "disciplinarian" (Gal. 3:24). Also, they are no longer subject to "the elemental spirits of the world" (Gal. 4:3, 8-9). Both their identity and their conduct are determined by their stature as God's children. The children of God, then, are not constrained by *any* forces external to and not accountable to God in Christ, in the power of the Spirit, in the communion of saints. That Paul in 8:12 addresses his readers as "brothers and sisters" explicitly indicates what is implicit throughout his letter, namely, that he regards his readers as fellow saints in the household of God, that is, colleagues in an ecclesial communion. Not constrained by external forces unaccountable to God, believers are moved by "a deeply felt compulsion" (James D. G. Dunn, *Romans 1-8,* Word Biblical Commentary 38 [Dallas: Word, 1988], p. 459). However, that "deeply felt compulsion," that stirring of the Spirit within and among believers, is not at odds with the law, for it is the Spirit of God, moving powerfully in Christ, most particularly in Christ's death and resurrection, that has fulfilled the law. And it is that same Spirit that is at work in believers so that "the just requirement of the law might be fulfilled in [them], who walk not according to the flesh but according to the Spirit" (8:4). Pauline charismatic theology is not antinomian.

Just what or, perhaps better, who the Spirit is and what kind of impact the Spirit has had and continues to have on believers is spelled out in verse 15. Once again Paul uses direct, emotionally charged discourse and Hebraic antithetical parallelism to make his point clear and compelling. The RSV and the NRSV take the term "spirit" in verse 15 to refer to the believer's own spirit, his or her own internal attitude or state of mind. If this translation is

87

preferred, then the focus is on the subjective change in believers brought about by the impact of God's Spirit upon them. Believers, as women and men "led by the Spirit of God," have not received from God an attitude "of slavery to fall back into fear." To the contrary (the antithesis), they have received a "spirit of adoption." They have been endowed with the state of mind of men and women removed from a condition of forced servitude. Made legitimate members of the household of God, brought into kinship with God and Christ in the Spirit, they now enjoy the privileges of kinship, and so are moved to comport themselves in a manner suited to the dignity of kinship (James Denney, "St. Paul's Epistle to the Romans," in *The Expositor's Greek Testament*, ed. W. Robertson Nicoll [Grand Rapids: Eerdmans, 1961], p. 647). On the other hand, if the KJV translation is preferred (and it too is an option), then Paul's use of the term "Spirit" in verse 15, in keeping with his use of the term throughout chapter 8, refers to the Holy Spirit. According to this translation, the Spirit of God received by believers is not such a spirit as would keep them in a state of forced servitude under the law — and thus under the threat of divine wrath. To the contrary, the Spirit received by believers is the Spirit of Christ Jesus, crucified, risen, regnant. That Spirit, which has fulfilled the law and canceled its power to condemn through the flesh, governs believers' lives by drawing them close to God, through adoption making them kin of God and Christ. The aorist no doubt indicates that baptism, the public sign and seal ratifying persons' adoption by God into the divine family, is in view. Baptized into Christ, adopted as God's children, believers need not pursue the path of obedience to God out of fear. Such obedience as is required and rendered is prompted by the Spirit of kinship dwelling in and among them. In other words, God is at work in believers effecting the obedience that is demanded of them as children of God. Note that according to either translation (RSV/NRSV or KJV), the identity of believers is not possessed and secured by any deeds of their own. Identity as children of God is not thus earned. Grace, made known in the proclamation of Christ crucified, has secured believers' identities as God's children. Deliverance from anxiety and fear and servitude is through Christ, in Christ, in the power of the Spirit. That is what it means to be adopted as God's children.

Verses 15, 16, and 17 continue the emotional, even passionate speech that was found in the preceding verses. The cry "Abba! Father!" certainly is emotional and passionate, intimate and yet also public. It has the intensely personal, perhaps even desperate character of Christ's cry to God in Gethsemane: "Abba, Father, for you all things are possible; remove this cup from me; yet, not what I want, but what you want" (Mark 14:36). At the same time it is a cry, a shout, of the worshiping community similar to that other ecclesial, Aramaic acclamation cited by Paul in the context of the apostle's expectation of divine judgment upon those with no love for the Lord, "Maranatha!" meaning "Our Lord, come" (1 Cor. 16:22)! In this sense of communal, public cry, the Spirit-induced "Abba! Father!" shares something of the fervor, though not the conceptual content, of the gathered, worshiping people's "Amen" to the word of Christ. "Father," it is quite clear, is not used here simply to translate "Abba" from Aramaic into Greek. "Abba! Father!" is a single, two-word phrase, a prayer or a shout of the early church, and is plainly understood by Paul to be just that. It is a liturgical exclamation, whether uttered by individuals or the entire worshiping assembly. It is a liturgical exclamation inclusive of Jew and Gentile alike. It is not purely personal, exclusively intimate; and it certainly is not in the least sentimental. For the Father who in Christ and in the power of the Spirit adopts men and women as his children is transcendent, awesome, even as, in this cry, "Abba! Father!" he is affirmed to be an immanent, parental presence in the company of believers. The "Our Father in heaven" (Matt. 6:9b) of the Lord's Prayer thus shares in the spirit of the cry "Abba! Father!" even if, in the text before us, it is not specifically in view. Paul also makes it clear in these verses that the ecstatic, familial personal yet above all ecclesial cry "Abba! Father!" is prompted by God's Spirit. In fact, in the cry the Spirit bears witness to and with believers that they are children of God. How else would believers dare thus to call upon the One who has appointed Christ Jesus as eschatological judge other than under the influence of that "deeply felt compulsion" that is the moving of God's own Spirit within and among his adopted children?

In verse 17 Paul indicates what it means to be God's children: "if children, then heirs, heirs of God and joint heirs with Christ — if, in fact, we suffer with him so that we may also be glorified with him." Heirs are not those who have come into their inheritance. The inheritance remains to be possessed in the future. But *what* is to be inherited nevertheless can be anticipated, and what is to be inherited by God's children is the free, unfettered enjoyment of God's glory. One's inheritance, according to the Spirit, is to share in that glory. Already, through death and resurrection, Christ has received his inheritance, and so rules with the Father in glory. But the eternal kingdom, power, and glory that belong to God and to his Christ are manifest now under their contrary sign, that is, the sign of the cross, the gospel of Christ crucified, which is the word Paul preaches and under which he lives (see 1 Cor. 1:23; 2:2; Gal. 6:14). It is by means of this word, the word of the cross, that Christ, the eschatological judge, through the Spirit governs and makes himself known among God's adopted children who, with Christ, are to participate in the glory of God. This is the significance in the present of what it means to be "heirs of God and joint heirs with Christ." As the synoptics express it, there can be no hope of glory apart from the suffering implied in taking up one's cross daily and following Christ (see Matt. 10:38; 16:24; Mark 8:34; Luke 9:23; 14:27). Paul himself acknowledges that to people of the world, and even to religious people, such preaching is foolishness, a scandal, and something concerning which one might be tempted to be ashamed (see 1 Cor. 1:18-25; Rom. 1:16). But to live according to the Spirit and not according to the flesh is precisely to become a fool for Christ, to suffer the struggles and indignities that the Lordship of the crucified Messiah entails. The suffering Paul speaks of in this text does not have to do with suffering in silence in the face of injustice instead of combating it. In fact, combating injustice is part of what it means to "put to death the deeds of the body" (v. 13). It is not a matter of putting up with the immorality of imposed poverty, or the neglect or abuse of the earth and of those who inhabit it either. However, it does mean that in such struggles for justice, the claims of Christ take precedence over the claims of ideology. It also means that defeat in these struggles, on account of fidelity to Christ, is incumbent upon believers wherever victory would necessitate neglect of Christ's claims and neglect of the manner of his pressing his claims, that is, the cross. Ernst Käsemann has put it succinctly: "The Spirit points us back to the cross of Christ as the place of salvation. He thus continually actualizes justification, sets us unceasingly in the sphere of the power of the Crucified, and is . . . the earthly presence of the exalted Lord" (*Commentary on Romans,* ed. and trans. Geoffrey W. Bromiley [Grand Rapids: Eerdmans, 1980], p. 213).

*Charles L. Bartow*

## Day of Pentecost, Year B

First Lesson: Acts 2:1-21
(Psalm 104:24-34, 35b)
**Second Lesson: Romans 8:22-27**
Gospel Lesson: John 15:26-27; 16:4b-15

Romans has been likened to the cathedral of the Christian faith, and Romans 8 to the inner sanctuary of that cathedral. This lofty reputation arises from the way this chapter touches on so many of the benefits conferred on believers by the Holy Spirit. Paul uses the word "spirit" twenty-one times in the chapter, and all but two (cf. vv. 15a and 16b) probably refer to the Holy Spirit. Yet Romans 8 is not really about the Spirit. The Spirit is the constant motif, but the actual subject matter lies elsewhere. In this chapter Paul returns to the central focus of chapters 5–8 — Christian assurance — after the excursuses about sin and the law in chapters 6 and 7. So in 8:1 Paul summarizes the point he made in 5:12-21: the believer is no longer condemned because he or she is now "in" Christ and no longer "in" Adam. Paul switches to the positive counterpart of "no condemnation," "life," and elaborates the new life of the believer in verses 1-13. The Spirit confers life on believers now (vv. 1-4), sets us on the road to a new way of living (vv. 5-8), and guarantees future resurrection life as well (vv. 9-11). Believers are then to use the Spirit's power to claim that life for themselves as they turn away from sin (vv. 12-13). Another blessing conferred by the Spirit is adoption as God's children (vv. 14-17). Finally, dominating 8:18-30 is a focus on the Spirit's role in securing the believer's future glory. Verse 18 introduces this note — "the glory about to be revealed" — while verse 30 effectively frames the paragraph by returning to the same point — "he also glorified."

Within this exposition of the believer's secure hope for glory lie verses 22-27. The section falls into two parts. Verses 22-25 conclude a paragraph, begun in verse 19, that expands on "to be revealed" in verse 18. This paragraph emphasizes the tension inherent in Christian experience, as believers wait eagerly for the completion of God's work on the day his glory is revealed in us. Verses 26-27 then begin a paragraph (vv. 26-30) that encourages believers by reminding us of the support God gives us as we wait for that day of glory to come. Verses 22-27 thus bridge the two key points in this larger section of Scripture: the need for Christians to wait in patient endurance for the culmination of God's work in us, and the things God is doing to enable us to endure with patience till that end.

Verse 22 picks up the references to "creation" that begin in verse 19. Interpreters are divided over just what Paul intends this word to refer to. Some, noting that creation "waits" (v. 19) and "groans" (v. 22), insist that the reference must be to human beings or to angels. But Paul contrasts "creation" with believers in verse 23, and Paul would hardly teach that nonbelievers would "obtain the freedom of the glory of the children of God" (v. 21). Those interpreters, therefore, who think Paul refers to the subhuman creation are probably correct. Paul writes in the style of the psalmists, who pictured hills, meadows, and valleys "shout[ing] and sing[ing] together for joy" (Ps. 65:12-13), and the prophets, who attributed mourning to the earth itself (Isa. 24:4; Jer. 4:28; 12:4). We must read the text as a semipoetic personification of creation. Paul captures the "futility" (cf. v. 20) of the world of nature, deflected from its intended purpose and glory by the sin of Adam and God's resultant penalty on both humankind and the world itself. Yet the pain of this struggle has a positive outcome, just like the birth pains that women in labor suffer (v. 22).

But Paul's teaching about nature's travail, valuable though it is (see below), is not the point of these verses. The struggle and hope of nature is introduced to provide a foil for the similar struggle and hope that Christians experience. "We ourselves," like creation, "groan," Paul claims in the key verse 23. Though we possess the Spirit, we continue to struggle against sin, temptation, and the associated evils of this world. New Testament scholars like to use the somewhat inelegant "already/not yet" language to summarize the key theological concept that Paul touches on here. We who have believed in Jesus Christ are *already* justified, reconciled, adopted, etc. But we are *not yet* adopted in the final sense, we are not yet glorified. We live in two realms at once — the old realm of sin and death and the new realm of righteousness and life. And so we will continue to "groan" — a word that captures the burden of temptation and mortality from which we long to be delivered. But deliverance is sure. We wait for our final adoption with hope and patience (vv. 24-25). The content of that hope, "the redemption of our bodies," does not mean that we will be delivered *from* our bodies — a Greek notion of the afterlife that has little to do with the biblical hope for transformed bodies. It means, rather, the final rescue of our bodies, ourselves as embodied in this world, from both physical and spiritual decay.

How are we able to wait for this deliverance with "patience" (see the end of v. 25)? God does not leave us in the lurch. His gracious work in conversion (the "already") and his promised work in glorification (the "not yet") are bridged by the work of his Spirit (vv. 26-27), his providential care (v. 28), and the reliability of his promise (vv. 29-30). But just what is the work of the

Spirit to which Paul refers in verses 26-27? Two possibilities merit consideration. First, Paul could be referring to the Spirit's work in enabling our own incoherent prayer "groanings" to be turned into requests that meet God's will. The limitations of our current spiritual condition make it impossible for us ever to know God's will perfectly. Our prayers are often, then, hindered by our "weakness": we don't know just what to ask God for. And so sometimes we do not articulate requests in clear words; we simply mutter and stutter, depending on God's Spirit to interpret those requests. Second, Paul could be referring to the Spirit's own "groaning," an activity taking place completely "behind the scenes." In this case "groaning" would of course be a metaphor — but we are prepared for just such a use of the word by the reference to creation's "groaning" in verse 22. In either case, these verses encourage the believer who is struggling to pray intelligently and insightfully to remember that it is ultimately the Spirit who is praying the perfect prayer on our behalf. We do not need to bear the burden of perfectly discerning the will of God before our praying can be effective.

These verses therefore provide the preacher a marvelous opportunity to help Christians understand better who they are. Paul hints here at the balance needed if we are to have an accurate understanding of our spiritual condition. If we focus too much on what we already have, we will drift into the kind of triumphalism and unconcern about sin that marked the Corinthians. Too much focus on what God has yet to do will lead to despair and defeat. The preacher can help his or her congregation understand the need to live in the tension of the "already/not yet."

These verses are also important for a Christian perspective on the environment. The New Testament says little about the world of nature, and this is certainly not Paul's main point even here. But by reminding us that God intends to bring the world of nature into the glorious freedom of God's children, he makes clear that God still has concern for nature as such. It is not just to be considered a commodity for human beings to exploit for their own benefit. It has value in itself. Arising from this observation is the need for Christians to practice a careful stewardship of the earth, treasuring nature because God created it and is still concerned about its welfare.

*Douglas Moo*

93

## Tenth Sunday after Pentecost, Year A

First Lesson: Genesis 29:15-28
(Psalm 128)
**Second Lesson: Romans 8:26-39**
Gospel Lesson: Matthew 13:31-33, 44-52

Romans 8:26-39 is part exposition, part hymn, all ending in such exuberance and joy as words can barely express. It is not that the cross and the sufferings that carrying it entail have been left behind in the preceding verses. It is rather now that they are so taken up into — and transfigured by — the love of God in Christ made known through the indwelling of the Spirit, that Paul can hardly restrain himself. Verses 31-39, probably among the most read and best-loved lines of Scripture, feature Paul's rhetoric let loose in a celebration of the tenacity of God's jealous and holy love: Whom God calls, God keeps ever as his own, against the odds, however great, for who or what can withstand God? Ironically, the greatest assurance of this tenacious love is the sacrifice of Christ to which believers are joined through sufferings incurred because of fidelity to the Crucified. Through sufferings, that is, believers are drawn ever closer to God, and surety concerning God's love thus deepens even as the grip of adversity tightens. Auden, in celebrating the poetic achievements of Yeats, said: "In the prison of his days / Teach the free man how to praise" ("In Memory of W. B. Yeats," in *Selected Poetry of W. H. Auden* [New York: Random House, 1958], p. 54). This the apostle Paul has done. In nearly hymnic prose, in the Spirit, without artifice yet with an unguarded eloquence born of insight, he has taken the thoughts of the human heart as near to the heart of God as a word can lift them. But it would be a mistake to begin there in the heights of praise and wonder to which Paul would have his readers caught up with him in the Spirit. Better to start where Paul himself starts, in "the bottom of the night" (Auden) where believers do not even know how to pray (v. 26b), let alone sing.

"Likewise the Spirit helps us in our weakness . . ." (v. 26a). Use of the term "likewise" makes it clear that verses 26-27 are part of a discourse begun earlier at verse 19 and following. What Paul gives his readers in 19-27 is three testimonies to the glorious future vouchsafed to believers in the midst of ambiguity, disquiet, and every form of suffering: first the waiting, sighing, groaning of creation; next the yearnings and groanings of believers themselves, which are attested as "the first fruits of the Spirit" (v. 23); finally the sighing or groaning and interceding of the Spirit, an intercession not too ob-

94

scure but rather too deep for words. For the Spirit fathoms the depths of believers' predicaments and prays for what they need "according to the will of God" (v. 27b), this in keeping with the promise given of the Spirit's help to the beleaguered community of saints in times of persecution and trial (cf. Mark 13:11; Matt. 10:19-20; Luke 21:15. See Paul W. Meyer, "Romans," in *Harper's Bible Commentary*, ed. James L. Mays [New York: Harper and Row, 1988], p. 1153). Scholars debate exactly what is meant here by the Spirit's groaning. But the same Greek root is used to indicate the groaning of creation and the groaning of believers (see John Ziesler, *Paul's Letter to the Romans* [Valley Forge, Pa.: Trinity Press International, 1989], p. 224). Also the term "likewise," which may be translated "and similarly," clearly indicates that for Paul the groaning intercessions of the Spirit are similar to creation's groaning and the groaning of believers in that they all three attest God as the source of hope for "the redemption of our bodies," that is, the resurrection. The Spirit, of course, is the Spirit of God (v. 9), which is why God, rather obviously, "knows what is the mind of the Spirit" (v. 27a). The order of testimony seems ascendant: first creation groans, then believers groan, then the Spirit groans and intercedes for believers in accordance with the will of the one who is, in a typically Jewish description of God, the "Searcher of Hearts" (1 Sam. 16:7; 1 Kings 8:39; Pss. 44:21; 139:1-2, 23; Prov. 15:11; cf. Pss. 17:3; 26:2; Jer. 11:20; 12:3; 17:10. See James D. G. Dunn, *Romans 1–8*, Word Biblical Commentary 38 [Dallas: Word, 1988], p. 479). So Paul directs his readers' attention to the fact that God comes to the aid of believers through the intercession of the Spirit in the midst of circumstances where, even in believers themselves, flesh and Spirit still do battle (however certain the outcome in Christ). Therefore Paul, not infrequently and in a variety of ways and circumstances, provides testimony to divine provision for human weakness (see Rom. 5:6; 8:3; 14:1ff.; 2 Cor. 11:30; 12:9-10; 13:3-5, 9; and by implication, and with anguished precision, Rom. 7:24-25). James Denney, commenting on Romans 8:26-27, quotes R. W. Dale, who speaks movingly of the Spirit's descent to the "bottom of the night" of the believer's predicament: "The whole passage illustrates in even a startling manner the truth and reality of the 'coming' of the Holy Ghost — the extent to which, if I may venture to say it, He has separated Himself — as Christ did at his incarnation — from His eternal glory and blessedness, and entered the life of man. . . . His intercession for us — so intimately does He share all the evils of our condition — is a kind of agony" ("St. Paul's Epistle to the Romans," in *The Expositor's Greek Testament*, vol. 2, ed. W. Robertson Nicoll [Grand Rapids: Eerdmans, 1961], p. 651).

Next Paul says what only can be said "according to the Spirit" and "not according to the flesh" (see vv. 1-17), namely: "We know that all things work together for good for those who love God, who are called according to his purpose" (v. 28). Those "who are called," and who thus know that of which Paul speaks, does not refer to people who merely have been issued an invitation. Instead, "called" means summoned, enlisted, and commissioned to a task. Such people love God. Love here, quite plainly, is not to be understood as a feeling or sentiment. Instead, it is to be understood as a condition of relationship to God, instanced by and sustained by God's effectual calling. Such love is not without emotion. It is indeed passionate. But such passion as it has is infused, not worked up. Further, the passion is inseparable from the passion of him in whom believers have been and are being called and sustained in love, that is, the passion of Christ. Adopted brothers and sisters of Christ (vv. 14-17), who think and act according to the Spirit of Christ (v. 9b), know what simply cannot be known "according to the flesh." They know that "all things," including especially the sufferings earlier discussed in Romans 8 and soon to be graphically identified (vv. 35b-36), ultimately must serve God's good intention, that is, "the revealing of the children of God" (v. 19), for which the entire created order groans (v. 22). For the glorification of humanity thus set free holds promise (the promise of God and thus a promise made to be kept) "that the creation itself will be set free from its bondage to decay and will obtain the freedom of the glory of the children of God" (v. 21). Some ancient manuscripts, as the NRSV notes, render verse 28a thus: "God makes all things work together for good" or "in all things God works for good." In any case, the point is that suffering, never mind happier circumstances, not only cannot thwart but actually is co-opted to further the purpose manifest in God's calling people to be his own. Calvin expressed the matter this way: "All things which happen to the saints are so overruled by God, that what the world regards as evil, the issue shows to be good" ("The Epistle of St. Paul to the Romans," *Commentaries,* vol. 19, ed. and trans. John Owen [Grand Rapids: Baker, 1989], p. 315).

The point is developed further in verses 29-30, a part of which, according to Käsemann, probably is a hymn fragment or other liturgical piece used by the early church and quoted by Paul because of its aptness given his line of thought (*Commentary on Romans,* ed. and trans. Geoffrey W. Bromiley [Grand Rapids: Eerdmans, 1980], p. 244). The text speaks of those whom God foreknew and predestined in relation to his saving purpose for humanity and creation (v. 29). Calling to a purpose, foreknowledge, and predestination were integral to Jewish thinking and not at all novel with Paul. The point is that God does not act at random, but rather prosecutes a pretemporal divine purpose that moves history, and moves through history, toward an end God intends (cf. Ps. 33:11; Prov. 19:21; Isa. 5:19; 19:17; 46:10;

Jer. 49:20; 50:45 on divine calling, and Gen. 18:19; Jer. 1:5; Hos. 13:5; Amos 3:2 on foreknowledge and predestination). For Paul, those whom God foreknew and "predestined to be conformed to the image of his Son" (v. 29a) have in store for them not only the freedom and the glory that have come to Christ through resurrection but also, and more significantly in the context of history's unfolding, the obedience to the cross, to the point of death, to which Christ was subjected. It is thus that Christ is their Lord, that is, as he is proclaimed, Christ crucified. To be conformed to the image of the Son in time and history is to live in conformity to the word of the cross. The effectual calling of believers entails suffering on account of Christ, not as an accident of history (time, fate, circumstance) but as a result of God's prosecution of his purpose in and through history. Freedom, in light of predestination, is freedom for obedience, and through the path of that obedience it also is freedom to delight in the glory of God. *Neither* freedom is possible apart from God's effectual calling and preordination. And not least of all, Christ crucified, risen, regnant is the firstborn of a large family (v. 29b). This is, without a doubt, an allusion to Christ's role as the Second Adam: "For if the many died through the one man's [the first Adam's] trespass, much more surely have the grace of God and the free gift in the grace of the one man, Jesus Christ, abounded for the many" (Rom. 5:15b). Then on to the hymn, 8:30, which concludes with the glorification of believers spoken of in this text (and *only* in this text) in the past tense, as something already accomplished. It is not that the adopted children of God already have entered into their inheritance. It is rather that as they are conformed to Christ in his humiliation, so also they just as surely are to be conformed to him in his exaltation. The glory into which they will be resurrected — and so revealed (v. 19) — is, in Christ, an accomplished fact of which their sufferings are the contrary sign. "Those whom God now, consistently with his purpose, exercises under the cross, are called and justified, that they may have hope of salvation, so that nothing of their glory decays during their humiliation; for though their present miseries deform it before the world, yet before God and angels it always shines forth as perfect" (Calvin, p. 320).

Now at last the climax of it all: "What then are we to say about these things?" (v. 31). Verses 31-39 sum up not only "these things" just spoken of throughout chapter 8 — though they do that. Probably "these things" also refers to all that Paul has been speaking of since Romans 1:1: the righteousness of God revealed in the gospel, the justification of the ungodly, the putting to death of sin and death as powers that finally define human life, the fulfilling of the law in Christ (in whom all was accomplished among human beings that could not be accomplished because of the weakening of the law by the flesh), sanctification (as a continued working out of the implications of justification in the life of believers) through the action of the indwelling Spirit of Christ. Then comes Paul's depiction of salvation as the human being set free for the glory of God. The glory refused to God at the start (1:21) becomes a glory given by God to humanity (Dunn, p. 485). And with the freedom of "the glory of the children of God" (v. 21), there is the re-creation of the cosmos at the time of the revelation of the children of God, who now suffer with Christ so that they "may also be glorified with him" (v. 17b). In light of all this (and the amplification of it all through argument and evocative imagery), what is to be said? The scene is the last judgment: "For we will all stand before the judgment seat of God" (14:10b). Here the last judgment is prefigured as a vindication of God's righteousness in predestination, calling, justification, and glorification (v. 30). The rhetorical turn is to diatribe, Paul's favorite rhetorical device throughout Romans. Questions are pressed one upon another and answers are implied, stated, or expected. The response to it all is either "foolishness!" according to the flesh or "Amen!" according to the Spirit. Given Paul's readership, called to be saints, "brothers and sisters" (v. 12) in Christ, the expected response is "Amen!" And the church has been giving that response ever since this text has been read, preached, heard, and loved.

"If God is for us, then no testimony to the contrary can stand. He who spared not his own Son . . ." (vv. 31b-32). The reference is to the sacrifice of Christ as expiation for human sin (see esp. 8:3-4). The Old Testament allusion is to the Abraham/Isaac story of sacrifice, but now the story reflects not the faithfulness of the devout servant of Yahweh, but rather the faithfulness of God himself (though that too may be implicit in the original in the provision of a lamb). God's handing over his Son in grace answers his handing over of his creatures in wrath (Rom. 1:18-32; 8:20-21; see Dunn, pp. 500-502). "It is God who justifies. Who is to condemn?" (vv. 33b-34). The verb "justifies" is in the present tense. God not only justified the ungodly but does so even now through the once-for-all sacrifice of Christ. As for condemnation, since Christ, there is no one up to it, as the rest of verse 34 makes clear, echoing 8:1: "There is . . . now no condemnation." Paul goes on, his joy relentless as the surge of water through a massive, broken dam: "Who will separate us from the love of Christ?" (v. 35a). The answer is nobody and nothing, not even those terrors that Paul himself was led through for love's sake, because of his own effectual calling (cf. 2 Cor. 11:23-27). For, in the Spirit, suffering demonstrates the union of the believer with the Crucified, not the doubt of Christ's love (Dunn, p. 504). Paul then quotes Psalm 44:22, a lament concerning the suffering of God's people brought about because of their fidelity, not their infidelity. But in Christ lament is turned to praise, because sufferings themselves make clear to those in the midst of them how sure is the grip of divine love. The uncalculated eloquence of joy does not cease: "No, in all these things [the sufferings just mentioned] we are more than conquerors through him who loved us" (v. 37). The "more than conquerors" is a Pauline coinage. It means believers are "over-conquerors," a hyperbole that, for Paul, one may surmise, still falls short of expressing the victory (in suffering) that is to be celebrated. Then the list of existential and cosmic terrors that threaten to appall is cited. But since they all are creatures of God (Paul never separates the doctrine of creation from the doctrine of redemption as though one could choose between the two), they are subject to God's command, to God's purpose, and thus to the command and purpose of Christ crucified, the cosmocrator. Believers are not delivered from engagement with these powers, but are held fast in love, for glory, through engagement with them. The glad, thunderously joyful last thought is this, that the relentless, steadfast, tenacious love of Christ is nothing less than the very love of God (v. 39): "[T]he fountain of love is the Father, and . . . it flows to us in Christ" (Calvin, p. 332). The joy is unbounded because the preaching of Christ crucified transforms everything irrevocably. It is not that the love of God in Christ expects nothing of those it claims. That must be clear. Such love in fact expects, and works to effect, obedience to the redeeming purpose of God which includes in its compass all humanity: "For God has imprisoned all in disobedience so that he may be merciful to all" (Rom. 11:32). That nothing separates the beloved of God from the love of God in Christ Jesus is not a mantra for the vocationally indifferent. It is instead a word of comfort, that is, a word of encouragement and sustenance, for the vocationally challenged. "[A]s clouds, though they obscure the clear brightness of the sun, do not yet wholly deprive us of its light; so God, in adversities, sends forth through the darkness the rays of his favor, lest temptations should overwhelm us with despair" (Calvin, p. 326).

*Charles L. Bartow*

## Eleventh Sunday after Pentecost, Year A

First Lesson: Genesis 32:22-31
(Psalm 17:1-7, 15)
**Second Lesson: Romans 9:1-5**
Gospel Lesson: Matthew 14:13-21

Our text starts a new section of Paul's letter, but it picks up an issue that has been lingering in the background from the very beginning. Paul's special concern for Israel appears already in the thesis of the letter: the gospel effects "salvation for everyone who believes, both *to the Jew first* and to the Greek." In 3:1-2 the question of Jewish advantage comes up. The close structural similarities between 3:1-9 and 9:1-30 warrant the conclusion that the advantages listed in 9:4-5 are intended as a continuation of the single advantage listed in 3:2; and 9:6-29 develops further the qualification of those advantages, expanding on 3:3-8 by incorporating material similar to chapter 4. Israel's advantages, which are many, do not include an unconditional exemption from divine judgment for every single Israelite.

Against the backdrop of the triumphant language of 8:31-39, the lament in 9:1-5 is stark. Nothing, Paul boasts, can separate us from God's love. And yet, what of Israel? The abrupt transition in 9:1 signals the start of a new section, ending in 11:36, that deals with the question of Israel's failure: first absolving God of the charge of unfaithfulness (9:6-29); then putting the blame on Israel (9:30–10:21); and finally explaining how it is that God has not pushed aside his people (chap. 11).

A good exposition of 9:1-5 will hold in tension these two dimensions of Paul's thinking about Israel: (1) currently they are outside the sphere of salvation, and (2) the final chapter in God's dealings with Israel has not yet been written. A good exposition will also develop the reasons that motivate both Paul's anguish and his hope regarding Israel.

As for connection to the audience situation at Rome: First, Paul gives some indication in 11:18-25 of concern that most of the Roman believers might be tempted to brag about the turnabout of salvation-historical events. Paul warns that they should be mourning Israel's stumble, not gloating, and hoping for better. Second, Paul may be concerned to reassure other believers at Rome that, contrary to the slanderous rumors they may have already heard or might yet hear, Paul himself is not anti-Jewish or unmoved by Israel's plight (cf. 3:8). Third, for Gentile believers of all persuasions Paul seeks to show that God's record of fidelity in the case of Israel speaks to the reliability of God's assurances to the church (see chap. 5 and 8:18-39).

In 9:1-2 Paul strenuously insists that his grief over the current predicament of Israel is genuine. The doublet in v. 1, "I speak the truth in Christ, I do not lie," underscores Paul's sensitivity to the charge that his interpretation of the gospel played into the hands of anti-Jewish bigotry. The phrase "in Christ" is probably shorthand for "as one who takes seriously being joined to Christ and through whom Christ acts" (cf. Rom. 6:3-8; 1 Cor. 6:15-17; 2 Cor. 5:17; Gal. 2:20). Lest his readers think him self-deceived, he adds: "my conscience in [= fortified or renewed by] the Holy Spirit co-testifying to me" (cf. Rom. 2:15). The dual witness of Christ and conscience may echo the Deuteronomic requirement that admissible testimony be by "two or three witnesses" (Deut. 17:6; 19:15; quoted by Paul in 2 Cor. 13:1). The rhetorical effect of the doublet in verse 2, "I have great *lypē* and my heart has unrelenting *odynē*," both Greek words meaning "pain" or "grief" without any significant difference of meaning, is to emphasize again Paul's touchiness to the accusation of contributing to Gentile anti-Judaism. James Dunn sees an intertextual echo of Isaiah 35:10//51:11, the only place in the Septuagint where the words *lypē* and *odynē* appear together, intimating that Paul's pain and grief "shall flee away" only when "the ransomed of Yahweh shall return and come to Zion."

In verse 3 Paul illustrates the depth of his personal pain by means of an unattainable wish: "for I would pray [*scil.* if my fellow Israelites could be saved thereby] that I myself would be accursed *(anathema)* from the Messiah [Christ] on behalf of my brothers, my kin according to the flesh." If Paul could save his people through the destruction of his own life, he would do it. This statement, the one in 10:1, and the discussion in 11:17-24 make clear that Paul's anguish is over the possible damnation of most of his fellow Israelites because of unbelief concerning Jesus Christ. The extended discussion in 9:6–11:10 about why God is not at fault but Israel is confirms the seriousness with which Paul took Israel's precarious situation. However one gauges Paul's certainty that "all Israel" or "their fullness" would be saved, it was apparently not the kind of certitude that quieted in Paul's heart pain over the unredeemed status of the bulk of Israel; nor was it a "done deal" that precluded the need for earnest prayer and missionary strategy. In this readiness to die in their place, he patterns himself after both Christ and Moses. The intertextual echoes of Moses' intercession for Israel after the golden calf episode (Exod. 32:10-14, 30-32) suggest that even when Paul laments Israel's disastrous circumstances, he has reason to believe that God is not through with Israel — if for no one else's sake than God's alone.

The reference to his fellow Jews as "my brothers *(hoi adelphoi mou),* my kin *(hoi syngeneis mou)* according to the flesh *(kata sarka)*" underscores both Paul's ongoing ethnic and religious family tie to Israel (hence his anguish) and the limitations of this attachment. They are "my [Paul's] brothers" in a sense that precludes a reference to "your [Gentile believers'] brothers." Apart from two references to the Lord's (physical) brothers (1 Cor. 9:5; Gal. 1:19), Paul's remaining 130 uses of *adelphos* refer exclusively to fellow believers in Christ. The qualifying prepositional phrase "according to the flesh" is not entirely void of an implied contrast with "according to the Spirit" *(kata pneuma)*. Being an ethnic descendant of Abraham still counts for something in God's cosmic program, but in and of itself it cannot secure salvation.

The listing of eight tokens of divine favor toward Israel in verses 4-5 has as its purpose the further explaining of why Paul is in such great pain. It is not only a question of Paul's ethnic tie. It is also, more importantly, a matter of divine investment in, relationship with, and faithfulness to a particular people for more than a millennium. God's own reliability is at stake, as the immediate defense of God in 9:6-29 shows.

Scholars sometimes express greater certainty than context warrants regarding the meaning of the one-word individual tokens in verses 4-5 and their implications for Israel's current standing before God. The first six are arranged in parallel groups of three for stylistic reasons. There may be a further parallelism of content:

| 1. the sonship | and 2. the glory | and 3. the covenants |
|---|---|---|
| 1'. the lawgiving | and 2'. the (temple) service | and 3'. the promises |

"The glory" and "the [temple] service" in the second column belong together since God's glory was thought to reside in the temple. "The covenants" and "the promises" in the third column are closely related, as the phrase "strangers to the covenants of promise" in Ephesians 2:12 and the separation out of "the lawgiving" into the first column indicate. Even "the sonship" and "the lawgiving" in the first column form a natural pair since Israel's adoption *as a nation* is generally connected in the Old Testament with the events at the exodus, Sinai, and the plains of Moab.

Set off slightly from the list of six tokens of divine grace to Israel is that of "the fathers," which stands outside the symmetry of the first six and receives its own introductory "of whom (are)." This set-apartness suggests that for Paul this was the defining advantage of Israelites, the advantage from which flow all the aforementioned advantages. For all his insistence in chapter 4 and now in 9:6-13 that Abrahamic paternity is neither bound to nor limited by the literal "flesh" lineage, Paul cannot sit content with the thought that God would permit the permanent exclusion of the vast majority of the physical descendants of the "fathers" from the promises (hence 11:28-29). Nevertheless, this conclusion can be reached in Paul's thinking only after God's right to base salvation entirely on faith in Christ is firmly established. Like all the other advantages enumerated above, this one extends to Gentiles who so believe; they too can claim Abraham as their father (4:11-12, 16-25; cf. 1 Cor. 10:1).

Paul adds an eighth token of divine grace but prefaces it with "from whom" rather than "of whom": "from whom [comes] the Messiah [the Christ, the Anointed One], the [*scil.* 'from whom' being understood as] according to the flesh." The switch from "of whom, whose" to "from whom, out of whom" perhaps arises out of two circumstances: The Messiah as an exalted person cannot be said to belong to any human group, even less so to a group that has not embraced the Messiah as *its* Messiah. The phrase "according to the flesh," which forms an *inclusio* or brackets with "kin according to the flesh" just before the list in 9:3, places a strict limitation on the sense in which Jesus can be said to be "from" Israel (cf. Rom. 1:3-4). Still, the fact that the Messiah "has become a servant of the circumcised" is evidence of God's great regard for the Israelites, even if the ultimate aim of Jesus' Jewish ancestry was to make it possible for Gentiles to glorify God alongside of Jews (15:8-9).

How to interpret the concluding doxology has been a matter of vigorous debate among scholars. The two basic options are:

"Christ according to the flesh. The God [or: God] who is over all [be] blessed forever"
"Christ according to the flesh, who is over all. God [be] blessed forever."

In my view, the weight of evidence between the two main readings is closely balanced; no firm decision can be made one way or the other. The interpreter would benefit from a little humility in expounding the precise meaning of this verse.

Preaching this text faithfully requires that a heartfelt emphasis be placed on the unfortunate predicament that Jews find themselves in as a result of unbelief concerning Jesus. This means finding the high ground between supercessionist arrogance toward non-Christian Jews and an equally condescending and harmful false assurance of their salvation apart from Christ.

The enumeration of the divine tokens associated with the status of being an Israelite should temper any callous dismissal of Israel's prospects for salvation. God's concern for the salvation of the world is always "to the Jew first" (Rom. 1:16), and it will be easier for God to "regraft" Israel back into the Abrahamic tree "if they do not persist in their unbelief" than it was for God to graft the Gentile believers in (11:23-24). A sermon should point the congregation to 11:25-32 on the horizon as a means of generating hope beyond the current predicament.

It is often stated by scholars that it was necessary for Paul to establish God's ongoing faithfulness to Israel in 11:11-32 in order to assure those who believe in Christ of God's fidelity to them; and, to be sure, there is an element of this in Romans 9–11. Yet there is also another dimension to Paul's discussion. In 11:20-22 Paul uses the unfortunate circumstance of Israel to warn the Gentile believers in Rome that if some of the Israelite branches were broken off from the Abrahamic tree, they too could be broken off if they become arrogant and forgetful of God's unmerited kindness to them.

*Robert A. J. Gagnon*

## Twelfth Sunday after Pentecost, Year A

First Lesson: Genesis 37:1-4, 12-28
(Psalm 105:1-6, 16-22, 45b)
**Second Lesson: Romans 10:5-15**
Gospel Lesson: Matthew 14:22-33

Romans 10:5-15 is a subsection of the argument in 9:30–10:21 where Paul seeks to establish that Israel has only itself to blame for its present predicament of being accursed and outside salvation (9:3; 10:1). 9:30–10:21 is itself the second of a three-stage argument in Romans 9–11 which discusses the problem of the fate of Israel. As for the structure of 9:30–10:21, most scholars agree that a break in the argument occurs between 10:13 and 10:14, with 9:30–10:13 asking why Israel failed to attain salvation and 10:14-21 addressing the question of whether Israel had been given an opportunity to call upon the name of Jesus. Within 9:30–10:13, subsections are generally recognized for 9:30-33 (contrasting Gentile success with Israel's failure through law), 10:1-4 (Paul's remorse over and explanation for Israel's failure), and 10:5-13 (scriptural proofs for Paul's assertion in 10:4). Paul contrasts "the righteousness that is from [based on] the law," as exemplified in Leviticus 18:5 (Rom. 10:5), with "the righteousness that is from [based on] faith," as exemplified in Deuteronomy 30:12-14 (Rom. 10:6-10). Then additional proof texts from Isaiah 28:16 and Joel 2:32 are called on in Romans 10:11-13 to provide support for Paul's view that Deuteronomy 30:12-14 is referring to the doable nature of faith in Christ and its accessibility to all, Jew and Gentile alike.

A vocal minority of scholars contends that "the righteousness from the law" in 10:5 complements rather than contrasts with "the righteousness from faith" in 10:6. It is true that the *de* that introduces 10:6 could be rendered as a simple connective "and," though the more usual sense is a contrasting "but." The context of 10:5-6, however, leaves little doubt that a *contrast* between two different types of righteousness is being made. 10:3 develops a contrast between two very different forms of righteousness, "their own" and "God's," that appears to be carried through in 10:5 and 10:6. Romans 9:30-32, in phrasing virtually parallel to the two types of righteousness mentioned in 10:5-6, contrasts "a law of righteousness . . . from works [of the law]" and "a righteousness from faith." Within 10:5-13 itself there is an apparent contrast between *human doing* in 10:5 and *human believing* in God's doing through Christ (10:6-13). The quotation of Deuteronomy 9:4a in Romans 10:6 signals an intertextual echo from Deuteronomy 9:4b, denying that Israel's conquest of Canaan is due to "my righteousness," which in turn corroborates the view that 10:6b-7 criticizes the righteousness mentioned in 10:5.

Given that everywhere else in Romans and in Galatians insistence on righteousness from the law is presented as an obstacle to the evangelization of Gentiles, there seems to be no way to connect 10:5 (the necessity of doing the law's full range of commands) to 10:11-13 (righteousness by faith is Gentile-inclusive) other than by contrast. It is evident, then, that "the righteousness that is based on the law" is antithetical to "the righteousness that is based on faith."

What are we to do with Paul's unusual use of Deuteronomy 30:12-14? For that passage clearly identifies "the word" that "is very near you" (Deut. 30:14) as God's "commandments and statutes written in this book of the law" (30:10), speaking about the *law's* doable nature. Paul, however, equally clearly interprets this "near word" as "the word of faith that we proclaim" (Rom. 10:8), namely, the gospel about Jesus' Lordship and resurrection from the dead (10:9-10). Only this "word," Paul claims, is doable — precisely because it is based ultimately on *God's* doing through Christ. Humans appropriate this word not in the first instance by "doing" but by "believing" (10:9-11).

How can we explain Paul's radical transformation of the original meaning of the text? First, Paul's use of Scripture as a word that speaks *directly* to his own contemporary situation is standard procedure for Jews in antiquity. With respect to the use of Deuteronomy 30:11-14 by Jewish authors, there is some precedent for a free use of the text. (1) Philo was capable of vaguely identifying what is "near you" as "virtue" (*Quod omnis probus liber sit* 68) or as "the good" or "the good thing" (*De mutatione nominum* 236-37; *De posteritate Caini* 84-85). (2) Baruch 3:29-30 applies Deuteronomy 30:12-13 initially to the personified figure of wisdom. (3) The *Gospel of Thomas* 3 contains an alleged saying of Jesus that applies Deuteronomy 30:12-14 to the kingdom of God. Against the background of such interpretations, Paul's free application in Romans 10:6-10 is hardly unique, though it remains the most radical in terms of its antilaw use.

Second, it is likely that Paul viewed Moses in Deuteronomy 30:11-14 as prophesying a future time that would end the current jurisdiction of the law over the people of God, a law that Israel was incapable of doing. Already by introducing the citations of 30:12-14 with words from 9:4 ("do not say in your heart"), Paul appears to be signaling just such a move. For 9:4 resounds with echoes of Israel's inability to keep the commands of God in their present condition: "Do not say in your heart, 'It is because of my righteousness that the LORD has brought me in to occupy this land.'" Israel has proven to be a stubborn and rebellious people from the day God brought them out of the land of Egypt (9:5-24). The immediate context of 30:11-14 speaks of a future time when the curses of the covenant will fall on Israel for their disobedience (29:19–30:10). After a period of "exile," God "will circumcise your heart . . . in order that you may live" (30:6).

Third, Paul apparently found further confirmation for "word" = "gospel" in the specifics of Deuteronomy 30:12-13. Thus:

| Deuteronomy 30:12-13 | Paul's Interpretation |
|---|---|
| *Who will go up into the sky/heaven?* | That is, to bring Christ down. |
| *Who will go down into the abyss/underworld?* | That is, to bring Christ up from the dead. |

The spatial metaphors of bringing down from heaven and up from the abyss must have appeared to Paul as tailor-made for the message of the gospel. The stress here is entirely on the impossibility of attaining righteousness on the basis of human doing (the very basis demanded by the Mosaic law). Paul could see the fingerprints of the gospel all over Deuteronomy 30:14 as well. In his thinking, not only did the reference to "the word" suit his proclamation of the gospel (though here *rhēma* rather than the usual *logos*), but also the references to this word being "in your mouth" and "in your heart" connected up well with the reception of the gospel. Thus,

| Deuteronomy 30:14 | Paul's Interpretation |
|---|---|
| *the word* | the word of faith (= the gospel) which we proclaim |
| *in your mouth* | confessing with the mouth Jesus as Lord |
| *in your heart* | believing in your heart that God raised Jesus from the dead |

What makes the fit with Deuteronomy 30:14 especially good in Paul's estimate is that only in the dispensation of the new covenant does the faith emanating from the heart (and, by extension, the confession from the mouth), rather than doing what the Mosaic law commands, play the one most integral role in mediating God's salvation to the individual. So Paul stresses that "one believes for righteousness" and "one confesses for salvation."

In sum, Moses is not contradicting himself, in Paul's view. He himself defined two different periods of time: his own, in which Leviticus 18:5 would operate, and a future time, "the ends of the ages" that had now arrived with the coming of Christ (cf. 1 Cor. 10:11), in which Deuteronomy 30:11-14 would operate.

The subsection Romans 10:4-13 comes to a close in 10:11-13 with two additional Scripture citations: Isaiah 28:16: "Everyone who believes in him shall not be put to shame," and Joel 2:32: "Everyone who calls upon the name of the LORD shall be saved."

First, Paul confirms the link between believing and salvation/righteousness that he asserted in 10:9-10 (10:11: *"for* the scripture says . . ."). Only if Paul establishes this point can he seal his claim that Deuteronomy 30:14 refers not to the law but to faith. Neither Isaiah 28:16 nor Joel 2:32 explicitly links the words "believe" and "save," but they are linked when the quotes are combined.

Second, this faith of which Paul has been speaking is specifically faith *in Christ* (implied: not just any faith). Isaiah 28:16 speaks of believing "in him," which, in context, must refer to Jesus rather than God (cf. Rom. 9:33; 1 Pet. 2:6). The parallel reference to "calling upon the name of the LORD" in Joel

2:32 provides additional confirmation that Jesus is the object of the believing (cf. 1 Cor. 1:2; Acts 2:32; 9:14, 21; 22:16). Outside of some LXX citations, there is no unambiguous reference to God as Lord in Romans. In 10:9 Paul affirms that it is the central confession "Jesus is Lord" that leads to salvation. The expression "the same Lord" in 10:12 reappears in 1 Corinthians 12:5 of Christ. In 10:14 this one who is believed and called upon is also the one "proclaimed"; whenever Paul elsewhere follows the verb "proclaim" (*kēryssein*) with a personal object, it is always Christ, never God (e.g., 2 Cor. 4:5). In 10:17 Paul refers to "the word about Christ." There is no possibility, then, that Jesus is not being viewed as the object of faith in Romans 10:11-13 (14-17). The importance of this conclusion has monumental consequences for how one reads Israel's only hope for salvation in Romans 9–11. It is not enough for Israel to believe in God to avoid the judgment of the law, as if they could escape the law's curse by pursuing the law in a nonlegalistic fashion or by accepting a Gentile mission that did not mandate the observance of specifically "Jewish" requirements of the law. In Paul's view, the only way out from the law's curse for Israel is for Israel to believe in the Messiah Jesus, who alone makes escape from the law's legal jurisdiction possible.

The third and final point that Paul wants to communicate through the citation of Scripture in 10:11-13 is that this sole requirement of faith in Christ makes possible salvation for *all* who believe, "for there is *no distinction between Jew and Greek,* for the same Lord [is] over *all,* bestowing riches on *all* who call upon him" (10:12). The end of the law means not only an end to God's previous forbearance with respect to sins committed under the law's jurisdiction, but also an end to Israel's extraordinary "most favored nation" status (without obliterating Israel's priority, 1:16).

Starting in 10:14, Paul shifts the discussion from why Israel failed to obtain a righteousness that leads to salvation (9:30–10:13) to whether Israel had been given an adequate opportunity to call upon the name of the Lord (Jesus) and be saved (10:14-21). The four rhetorical questions in 10:14-15a and the comment in 10:17 establish a sequence of conditions that must be fulfilled before Israel can come to salvation (cf. 10:1), the very same conditions imposed on godless Gentiles: (1) sending emissaries to proclaim the gospel to Israel, (2) Israel's hearing of the gospel message, and (3) Israel's believing in and verbal confession of Jesus as Lord. Interestingly, Paul cites Scripture, read prophetically and christologically, to "prove" that the first and second conditions have already been met (for the first, Isa. 52:7, cited in Rom. 10:15; for the second, Ps. 19:4; Deut. 32:21; and Isa. 65:1 in Rom. 10:18-21). The citation of Isaiah 53:1 in Romans 10:16 "proves" that Israel has not believed the gospel proclaimed to them.

This text, especially 10:9-15, is wonderfully suited for instruction in the necessity and content of Christian evangelism and missions. In preaching from the text, however, a possible misunderstanding about the law should be dispelled. Doing away with the jurisdiction of the law was not intended by God as a license to do whatever we want. The message in Romans 6:1–8:17 is clear: God did away with the law precisely so that we would be able to keep its core requirements, especially that of loving one's neighbor (13:8-10; 8:4). Those who continue to live "according to the flesh" even after they receive the gift of the Spirit will still face the penalty of eternal death (8:13). Even so, the accent should remain squarely on the fact that salvation is something attained through what Christ has done, not through our own efforts.

*Robert A. J. Gagnon*

## First Sunday in Lent, Year C

First Lesson: Deuteronomy 26:1-11
(Psalm 91:1-2, 9-16)
**Second Lesson: Romans 10:8-13**
Gospel Lesson: Luke 4:1-13

This passage is a classic instance of Paul's interpretation of Scripture to make his point about the promise of the gospel. The quotation marks in my translation below indicate the scope of his citations.

8   But what does it say?
    "Near to you is the word,
    in your mouth and in your heart,"
    that is, the word of faith that we proclaim,
9   because if you confess "with your lips" the Lord Jesus
    and have faith "in your heart" that God raised him from the dead,
    you shall be saved.
10  For [a person] has faith in [the] heart toward righteousness,
    and confesses by mouth toward salvation.

109

11 For the scripture says,
   no one "who has faith in him will be put to shame."
12 For there is no distinction between Jews or Greeks.
   The same one is Lord of all,
   [bestowing] riches upon all who call upon him.
13 For, "all who call upon the name of the Lord will be saved."

In the context of his argument, Paul reinterprets these Old Testament passages in the light of his commitment to Christ's "triumph over shame." As I explain in *Saint Paul at the Movies: Triumph over Shame* (Grand Rapids: Eerdmans, 1999), in the ancient Mediterranean world the achievement of honor and the avoidance of shame were the supreme goals of life. Persons of low social status, who made up most of the early church, had been raised in the status of shame, treated by the rest of society as if they were worthless except to serve the honorable members of society. Now Paul claims that none of the groups that place their faith in Christ "will be put to shame" (Rom. 10:11). Their confession of Jesus as Lord in 10:9 and their "faith" in the gospel that leads to righteousness make them part of the new community that treats everyone with equal honor. Christ died a shameful death in behalf of shameful people everywhere, so everyone who accepts this message gains access to a new system of honor and shame, based on grace rather than achievement or prior status.

In contemporary preaching, the words of this passage echo an outmoded system of gaining honor by conformity to certain stereotypical formulas: "If you confess 'with your lips' the Lord Jesus, and have faith 'in your heart' that God raised him from the dead, you shall be saved." This verse has so frequently been cited by judgmental preachers, so often echoed on religious billboards, that its liberating link to triumph over shame has become opaque. In a profound subversion of the original message of redeeming grace, these words now tend to convey the message that making the right confession with the right words is the ultimate method of gaining honor. In the threatening rhetoric of some preachers, any failure to employ the proper formula of "confessing Christ as Savior and Lord" casts one in the situation of final shame. In the most extreme form of this subversion, religious extremists follow the pre-Christian Saul in persecuting nonconformists.

What this judgmental approach overlooks is that it was precisely the demand for religious and moral conformity that led to Jesus' death. In his crucifixion the entire realm of gaining honor through meeting the conditions of approved behavior and belief was overthrown. The salvation gained by confessing Jesus as Lord is not primarily in a guaranteed place in heaven, but a new life aimed "toward righteousness" (10:10). To confess Jesus as Lord was to join one of the new communities of faith that were springing up all over the Mediterranean world. Groups of between fifteen and thirty converts were forming house and tenement churches that met secretly in homes and shops with a new kind of social identity shaped by Christ crucified. They shared love feasts in which Jesus was thought to be present as host, honoring the shamed by his death for all and by his invitation to full membership in the family of God. To "confess" the "Lord Jesus" was not so much to make a dogmatic claim about his status as to reveal one's own identity as a convert. A "confession" in this biblical sense is a "slogan of identification" that marks someone "as belonging to Jesus," to use James D. G. Dunn's words in *Romans 9–16* ([Dallas: Word, 1988], p. 607). Since Jesus was the crucified one, the confession of 10:9 claims solidarity in shame. It binds the speaker to some-one else in final loyalty. To refer to Jesus as Lord "denotes an attitude of sub-serviency and sense of belongingness or devotion to the one so named" (Dunn, p. 68). This kind of confession designates to whom the speaker is committed but does not determine what attitude others should take. In con-trast to the later development of formulaic "confessions" in the Christian tradition, Paul had no intention of making this confession into a claim of honorable status that raises the speaker above others, using required lan-guage that others must employ to avoid peril. To "confess" in this context is also far removed from the traditional connotation in our culture, in which "confession of sins/guilt" is the dominant usage.

To "have faith 'in your heart' that God raised [Jesus] from the dead" (10:9) reflects the same distinctions found in the use of "confess." If the res-urrection of Christ really occurred, it confirms that the shamefully crucified one is the divinely authenticated Lord. The faith is "in your heart," therefore indicating that a "deeply motivating belief . . . is in view and not merely a recitation of creedal form" (Dunn, p. 609). To have such a belief is not to make any claim of superiority. It is rather evidence of having abandoned the traditional systems of earning honor and avoiding shame, because this Lord has the marks of the shameful cross on his resurrected body. The key ques-tion, therefore, is what is "in your heart."

The threefold reference to "heart" in 10:8-10 shows that for Paul faith is more than a head trip. It is more than a set of beliefs. It is related to the con-dition of the heart, that motivating center of mind, emotion, experience, and purpose. This is a realm ordinarily dominated by shameful secrets that faith in Christ crucified has the power to expose. As this text proclaims, the redeeming "'word is near you, on your lips and in your heart,' that is, the word of faith that we proclaim" (10:8). The apostle gives priority here to the message fastened deeply in the heart; it is already "near" them. In 10:12 Paul reiterates his conviction that this confession of Christ has already erased the boundaries of honor and shame: "For there is no distinction between Jews and Greeks. The same one is Lord of all, [bestowing] riches upon all who call upon him." The social distinctions that marked the Greco-Roman world have been eliminated by Christ, whose crucifixion and resurrection revealed that he is "Lord of all." His shameful death on the cross, which exposed the pretensions of those the world honors, was shown through the resurrection to have transforming social consequences. Social discrimination is now illegitimate. The "riches" of divine favor, which traditional religion has always believed would be bestowed only on the honorable, are now bestowed impartially "upon all who call upon him." It is not that such a "call," "confession," and "faith" qualify a particular individual or community for the blessings. It is rather that only those willing to accept solidarity with the shamed are in a position to receive such blessings. To "call upon" this particular Lord is to move beyond the wounds of ethnic, familial, and personal shame and take up a new identity as a member of a church that lives by faith in God's grace.

In 10:11 Paul quotes Isaiah 28:16 about believers not being put to shame, but adds the word "all" to the beginning: "All 'who have faith in him will not be put to shame.'" Although this is difficult to translate, its inclusivity is unmistakable. With this one word "all," the smear of shame is potentially removed from the entire human race. Whether Jew or Greek, barbarian or Roman, slave or free, male or female, no persons or groups "who have faith in him will be put to shame." But as we noted above, such faith is not self-honorific. The right confession and properly defined faith do not earn this triumph of not being "put to shame," despite centuries of twisted, self-serving theology. To "call on the name" of this Lord (Rom. 10:13) is to abandon any claim of already possessing honor and to take one's place alongside the dishonored shepherd and his disheveled flock. It is not the formulation of this faith that is decisive but a reliance on grace alone that makes all the difference.

*Robert Jewett*

## Thirteenth Sunday after Pentecost, Year A

First Lesson: Genesis 45:1-15
(Psalm 133)
**Second Lesson: Romans 11:1-2a, 29-32**
Gospel Lesson: Matthew 15:(10-20), 21-18

This reading comes as part of an extended exposition of Romans over sixteen weeks. On the two previous Sundays we hear, first, of Paul's "anguish" for his own people, the Israelites, who seem to have rejected the Christ and been "cut off" from the promises of God thereby (9:1-5). Yet these are the very people who have a special relation of "sonship" with God, who have received instruments of God's grace, like the covenants and the Law, and who have given birth, in the "flesh," to the Christ. Second (10:5-15), we hear of the gospel, the good news given in Christ, which proclaims justification by faith in Jesus for both Jew and Greek and oversteps the limited movement toward God given in Israel's earlier Mosaic covenant.

It should be noted that the parts of chapters 9–11 that are left out of these lections concern the more problematic historical realities that lie between these two affirmations — between the affirmation of Paul's love for Israel and its privileges, on the one hand, and of the gospel of justification in Christ for all, on the other. And this unread material deals specifically with the gap between Israel's call and the gospel's preaching to the nations that is constituted by Israel's disobedience and God's judgment upon it. Within this gap Paul does most of his reflective work in these chapters, following an argument that is driven less by neat premises and conclusions than by the serial trial of different possible understandings of how Israel's seemingly failed vocation can cohere with the grace of God's embrace of the Gentiles. It is the last of these attempts at making sense of this emotionally wrenching quandary that gives rise to the penultimate comments of chapter 11 which are appointed in this reading.

The entire question posed by these chapters — how can we explain Jewish disbelief in Jesus' messiahship? — leads Paul to address several seminal issues and finally propose a kind of resolution in this passage. First, there is the issue of Israel's vocation, experienced from the human side of things. If God has called Israel in a special way, it appears as if this call, for all its privileges (the covenants, Law, worship, etc.), has ended up being lived as a terrible burden whereby vocational responsibility creates the divine judgment that falls on disobedience. "They did not submit to God's righteousness"

113

(10:3), Paul says of his people as a whole, who seem almost willfully to have rejected the righteousness that comes by faith in Christ; Paul cites Isaiah 65:1-2 in this regard, who testifies that "all day long I have held out my hands to a disobedient and contrary people" (10:21).

The notion that divine vocation brings with it an awesome responsibility whose relation of intimacy with God makes God's judgment on disobedience all the more pressing, is one that Paul goes on to apply to all persons caught up in God's life, Jew and Greek together. "Do not boast," Paul tells the Gentiles brought close to God through faith in Christ (11:18). Launching into a metaphor of natural and grafted branches, he goes on to say that "they [Israel] were broken off because of their unbelief, but you stand fast only through faith. So do not become proud, but stand in awe. For if God did not spare the natural branches, neither will he spare you" (11:20-21). This reality of obedience and disobedience as a factor in the dynamic of relationship with God is the first element Paul then seeks to resolve at the end of the chapter. For how can one adequately respond to a divine call if its end is to crush us in our weaknesses?

The resolution is given from God's side, and it comes in an almost shocking form, at least in its final formulation here: God actually *furthers* the grace of vocation through making use of the disobedience of those called. This is the only way Paul can, in the end, maintain the value of Israel's election, as well as inject the character of hope into the newly called Gentiles. "I ask, then, has God rejected his people?" Paul asks at the opening of chapter 11. To answer in the affirmative would be both a denigration of divine vocation and a relativization of divine power to fulfill promises. After trying out an answer to this that makes use of the concept of the "remnant" faithful in Israel, always present while the majority of the people fall away (cf. 11:5), Paul leaves this possibility aside in favor of a far more sweeping vision: Israel's disobedience is *itself* an instrument in God's providence to open a door for the nations of the world by which they might come close to God. And the same grace that opens that door for the world must finally express itself in the comprehensive embrace of disbelieving Israel. "And so all Israel will be saved," Paul writes, once their falling away provides an opportunity for the gospel of salvation in Christ to be preached to the Gentiles (11:25-26).

This proves to be a powerful answer, upon which Paul ultimately rests his meditation: "Just as you were once disobedient to God but now have received mercy because of their disobedience, so they have now been disobedient in order that by the mercy shown to you they also may receive mercy" (11:30-31). Human disobedience is no barrier to God's mercy, and becomes *in fact* the temporal bearer of divine love. It is the sheer capacity of God to use even the rebellions of human hearts toward graceful ends that discloses the breadth of divine providence at work in reconciling human history. Paul ends the discursive portion of these three chapters with one of his most dramatically inclusive affirmations, which is designed to take in the whole of human experience within time: "For God has consigned all [people] to disobedience, that he may have mercy upon all" (11:32). And this kind of affirmation can only give rise to the cry of praise that ends the chapter (11:33-36).

Human disobedience as a divine instrument of grace is a shocking concept indeed, for it functions here as a kind of theodicy within the least expected of confines, that is, within the particularities of divine revelation and choice — Israel, the Law, Christ, and the gospel. Paul insists that these particularities of history are the very *means* of grace as it justifies the ungodly, even as the means themselves are rejected. And this insistence cuts against the grain of our modern sense that evil and brokenness derive from limitedness and its relatives, and can only be redeemed by something general that drives away the burdens of the particular. As Paul seems to imply, Israel's vocation of obedience, in its very attempt and failure, acted as a specific preparation for the world's exposure to God: the nations were to see, in Israel's life, the character of divine call — its holiness, its particular demands, and its integrity — and the consequences of human sin exhibited in Israel's own punishment.

Paul does not seek to elide or evade the historical realities of disobedience and judgment according to the particular demands of God given in the covenant and recounted in the Scriptures. Rather, a knowing confrontation with these articulated realities constitutes the "opening" by which, in the preaching of Christ, the nations could respond to God's call in a newly informed fashion. And this manner of response, read out of Israel's particularized historical experience of vocation, disobedience, and judgment, is etched in the forms of dependence, repentance, and redemption now figured in Christ. Human disobedience and divine grace, then, describe the proper relation, the "true" relation of God's love to human creation, given in Jesus. 11:32, shocking and sweeping as it is, thus represents a summary expression of the Christian gospel. And that expression is enunciated in the history of Israel as it is temporally tied to the larger human family.

What does it mean that one is "called" by God, and what does it mean that it is God who "calls"? Paul is clear on this matter: it means, respectively, the burden of demand and disobedience, and the transformation of punishment into new life for the world; it means, quite precisely and in an

115

unsubstitutable form, the life of Israel with God, as God offers Israel's life to the world in the figure of Christ.

At least two profound challenges to the church arise from this knotted Pauline reflection. The first is to look at oneself, as the Christian church, through the proper lens. That lens is the history of Israel. For the character of God's mercy is given — "revealed" — in the particular relation of God with Israel, in sin and redemption. And Paul's insistence that Gentiles, and the church made up of Gentiles mixed with Jews, be seen as a "grafted" branch upon Israel's root marks a rigorous limit upon Christian self-understanding: the character of our life as Christians is given only according to the chosen form of God's relation with Israel. "Salvation is from the Jews" (John 4:22) becomes, in this context and in the wake of Paul's wrestling in Romans 9-11, a comprehensive affirmation of a Christian historical and scriptural hermeneutic. Christian preaching, thinking, praying, and acting that is not somehow rooted in this affirmation is "proud," that is, drifting off the mark.

Second, it is imperative that the Christian church, in its relation of graftedness to the history of Israel, reinvigorate its self-understanding in terms of the history of our own experience within the realms of disobedience, judgment, dependence, and grace. Much of what the contemporary church encounters in struggle and dissent can only find its ultimate explanation within the form of Israel's life as it opens up to Christ. And in this regard, we are pressed to see the solutions to trials and uncertainties within our ecclesial bodies as lying less within the reach of our rational and strategic powers and more in the submission of our common life to the shape of God's providential usage of Israel's life for the sake of the world's salvation. We are to become *willingly* — not recalcitrantly — like Israel in her suffering at the hands of God. That, after all, is the form by which Christ turned the disobedience of all into an encompassing mercy.

*Ephraim Radner*

# Fourteenth Sunday after Pentecost, Year A

First Lesson: Exodus 1:8–2:10
(Psalm 124)
**Second Lesson: Romans 12:1-8**
Gospel Lesson: Matthew 16:13-20

This is one text in the New Testament that generates ideas for sermons with almost every word. It is a passage that stands as a timeless piece of instruction for our Christian sanctification. Personal sacrifice, nonconformity to the world, and the body life of the church are three themes that are woven into this passage from the seamless garment of grace. It might be important for the preacher to reflect on each of these three themes and perceive how they can fit together (or stand alone) before deciding which homiletical angle to take.

Paul had argued in the earlier chapters of Romans for justification by grace through faith. He then turned to the problem of his estranged Jewish nation, pondering the implications of grace for his people and their religion. In spite of his vexation and puzzlement over the fate of Israel, he ended chapter 11 on a triumphant doxological note praising God's mercy. Now comes chapter 12, with the need for corporate worship and proper conduct. Both personal and community ethics are seen as an important outgrowth of divine grace. Several key words spin the themes of the first two verses.

First, the reader is immediately struck by Paul's emphasis upon the body. After eleven chapters of pleading for the readers' hearts and minds, Paul makes an impassioned plea for Christians to worship by presenting their "bodies" *(sōmata)* to God. In contrast to modern Western culture, Paul does not argue that our bodies should be pampered in order to provide every opportunity to live a long and healthy life. They are, rather, to be laid upon the altar of sacrifice. What this means is not apparent until we read further, but clearly Paul is using familiar language about sacrifice in a new way. The traditional language of sacrifice is religious and cultic, and would have been well understood by both Jewish and Gentile audiences. Paul implies that the sacrifice of Christ is one that obligates his followers to imitate it — not to the same degree of course, because our sacrifice is one that, unlike his crucifixion, does not normally require our physical torture and death. Ours should be a "living *(zōsan)* sacrifice." Paul describes a seeming paradox in coining this phrase; for Christians to be presented as a "living

117

sacrifice" seems self-contradictory. Normal cultic sacrificial offerings died because they were cut to pieces and their blood drained. What then is required to make this sacrifice *live?* The living sacrifice is apparently an admonition to live sacrificially. The Gospels were not yet written when Paul penned these words, but he likely has in mind the teachings of Jesus to lay down one's life for a friend and practice charity much like the good Samaritan did. This entails a self-dying process, as opposed to a singular event, through which the follower of Christ attains a sober view of the self (see v. 3). Hence a life lived for God and in service to others becomes possible.

Sacrificial living, according to Paul, must merge with the traffic of everyday living. For the follower of Christ, the sacrificial has been transposed from a cultic sacrifice to an everyday ethic. In emphasizing the importance of the body, Paul is advocating that Christians make a daily ritual of self-giving.

C. S. Lewis also sprinkles his writings with an emphasis on the importance of being Christian in our everyday settings (see especially *Surprised by Joy,* and interestingly the Chronicles of Narnia). Everyday living is where our sanctification is worked out. It may not be dramatic or even look religious, but the ways in which we conduct ourselves in our bodies each day have vast spiritual implications. Much to the chagrin of a public, both ancient and modern, that loves spectacular cultic events and even the flow of blood, Christian faith is to be worked out in the twenty-four-hour segments of time that divide our days. No interactions with other persons in our workplace, school, or household are banal or unimportant — and neither are any members of the body of Christ (see vv. 3-8).

In spite of the fact that Paul wants us to sacrifice our bodies, the Bible rarely pictures our body as a cursed limitation. Our bodies are a blessing. As such they are the site of our sanctification. Not bodily existence in abstract or airbrushed to look like a model, but my own aching, aging, earthbound body is the arena of sanctification. Once again, the immensely practical and personal dimensions of the gospel come across loud and clear. In verse 1 Paul issues a summons to a concrete and personal commitment. There are few things we cherish as personally or intimately as our own bodies. Imbued with grace, we are challenged to sacrifice our bodies and break free from the entrapments of the surrounding culture which normally urges us away from such a costly way of living.

Second, coupled with a plea for self-sacrifice is an unequivocal summons to resist the influence exerted by the world (v. 2). The Greek word here for "world" *(aiōni)* is better translated "age." The spirit of the age *(zeitgeist)* should not set the believer's agenda. The Word of God should so shape our minds that we are transformed rather than conformed to our surrounding culture. Thus we prove what is the will of God not by our conformity to a strict set of laws, but by our willingness to die with Christ and also live in him (cf. 6:4).

The issue of nonconformity to the world presents a homiletical challenge. Nonconformity could be interpreted as a summons to wage cultural warfare. In present-day North America the so-called culture wars sell books and propel radio programs. While not being conformed to the world undoubtedly obliges the believer to follow certain moral guidelines, it serves as a poor witness for the church to reflect an embattled culture. The urge to humility which immediately follows (v. 3) is therefore well placed.

The specific conformities of each congregation and person most likely vary from place to place. In every culture and subculture loom certain stumbling blocks to sanctification to which the preacher must be alert. Each of us who proclaims the Word of nonconformity would do well to look deep within and honestly probe the areas in our own lives where an aggressively marketed secular culture has gained a foothold. If we begin by confession (not always from the pulpit), we may escape the dire straits of sounding either overly sanctimonious and rigid or so morally superior to our parish that we do not experience the same cultural temptations.

In the second paragraph the apostle develops his third point: he urges Roman Christians to celebrate their unity in Christ by exercising their diversity of gifts. Here the body is used as a metaphor for the functioning gifts of the church. While there is unity of body, there is commensurate diversity of members. Most agree that Paul is not attempting to be exhaustive here in his description of the particular gifts. A quick comparison with other passages that describe spiritual gifts (1 Cor. 12:12-31 and Eph. 4:11-13) helps round out the list, and it would not be out of order for the preacher to expand the list to include the personal offices, gifts, and needs of a particular congregation.

Today, even more than in the apostle's time, we can marvel at the simultaneous unity and diversity of the human body. A normal human body achieves a level of functioning that we should covet for the church. The uncovering of spiritual gifts within each congregation would be one step toward the realization of this smooth functioning. Another might be the appreciation we need to engender toward each and every gift represented by respective members and groups of members. Homiletical opportunities abound here: for example, just think of the ease with which we take one another for granted (document at your own risk), value public gifts over the private ones, and so on.

Two or three sermons could be spun from these eight verses. The theme of personal commitment and sacrifice, the following and connected theme of nonconformity to the world, and the third theme of the body of Christ and its members flow from Paul's pen in a logical progression. The grace-filled follower of Christ will normally wish to make sacrifices for Christ, should be vigilant to avoid being overly swayed by the allures and snares of the surrounding culture, and should eagerly seek out a niche in the local church body. The challenge of preaching this text is to make the believer feel compelled to follow Paul's timeless exhortation to make it so — and to do so with diligence, compassion, and, perhaps most of all, cheerfulness.

*Daniel J. Price*

## Fifteenth Sunday after Pentecost, Year A

First Lesson: Exodus 3:1-15
(Psalm 105:1-6, 23-26, 45c)
**Second Lesson: Romans 12:9-21**
Gospel Lesson: Matthew 16:21-28

This pericope opens with a maxim that serves as a thesis for the entire section: "[Let] the love be genuine." This wording shows that Paul assumes the presence of "the love" within the Roman audience. Such love rests on the prior gift of God's loving action to each believer. Since God's love for undeserving, shameful people was expressed in the life, death, and resurrection of Christ, the recipients of "the mercies of God" (Rom. 12:1) are called to pass it on to fellow humans. The use of the definite article in "the love" indicates that Paul refers not to love in general but to the specifically Christian form of love already manifest in the Roman churches. The social context of the early Christian "love feast" probably provided the primary resonance of this term for the Roman Christians. It is the nature of such love, poured into the heart (5:5) of each beloved member of the community (1:7), that it be both spontaneous and undiscriminatingly generous. Hence, Paul urges that their "love" be "genuine" in distinguishing between "evil" and "good" (12:21). As we all know, love is easy to fake and often surfaces in inappropriate forms. Congregational involvement in testing genuineness links this pericope very closely with 12:1-2, where the term "the good" was also used. The highly emotional verbs "abhorring" and "cleaving" in 12:9 imply a passionate commitment to the objective good for fellow members of one's congregation.

What contemporary readers might find puzzling is that some of the ways to abhor evil and cleave to the good are related to the seemingly minor arena of manners. The Norwegian scholar Halvor Moxnes makes some intriguing suggestions about 12:10, which I translate "having affection for one another with brotherly love, taking the lead in honoring one another." Moxnes has shown that by linking recognition with the egalitarian theme of brotherly love, Paul resists the cultural tendency to grant honor "on the basis of status or merits. There is to be no connection between service performed in leadership and honour and recognition above others. Honour is to be awarded solely on the basis of 'brotherly love'" ("Honour and Righteousness in Romans," *JSNT* 32 [1988]: 74). The congregational focus of the ethical admonition is expressed by the phrase "for one another" in this verse. That "brotherly love" would normally be perceived to include each other within a congregation would seem to be so self-evident as to make this admonition unnecessary, but the peculiar historical circumstances in Rome demanded the emphatic inclusion. The competing house and tenement churches were not in fact viewing each other as equals, as the evidence in Romans 14–15 reveals. The use of the term "affection" augments this appeal with a concept widely used in Hellenistic ethics: the solicitude typical for family and friendship is to be extended into the Christian community, particularly including persons in other house and tenement churches previously held in contempt. Family affection is to replace the harsh "judgment" (14:3-4, 10) and "contempt" (14:3, 10) that had poisoned relations between congregations.

An innovative feature in translation is to render 12:10 as "taking the lead." The translation of related verses that I developed in chapter 7 of *Saint Paul at the Movies: Triumph over Shame* (Grand Rapids: Eerdmans, 1999) is as follows:

> 12:9 [Let] the love be genuine,
>> abhorring the evil,
>>> cleaving to the good;
>>>> 12:10 [having] affection for one another with brotherly love,
>>>> taking the lead in honoring one another. . . .

> 12:13  sharing in the needs of the saints,
>      pursuing hospitality to strangers. . . .
> 12:16  being of the same mind toward one another,
>      not setting your minds on the heights,
> but being drawn toward lowly people,
>      "not being [wise] minded in yourselves" . . .
> 12:21  Do not be conquered by what is evil,
>      but conquer the evil with the good.

This translation takes account of the social context of honor that marked the Greco-Roman world, in which public recognition was the essential basis of personal identity. There is a similar Hebraic notion of the virtue of taking the lead in greeting others. Paul's wording fits the congregational situation in Rome, where members of competing groups were refusing to accept each other. If each group now "takes the lead" in showing honor to its competitors, the imbalance in honor due to social stratification and group competition would be transformed in a way that matched "genuine love."

Paul's interest in overcoming social discrimination based on Mediterranean systems of honor and shame is particularly visible in 12:16. As in 12:3, this verse combines three distinct sayings with the same component: "mind." The thematic progression is usually disguised by translators' preferences for graceful English expressions. In *Love without Pretense* ([Tübingen: Mohr [Siebeck], 1991], pp. 179-80), Walter T. Wilson has shown that the progression is marked by an opening maxim (16a) followed by a two-part explanation (16b-c), and concluded with a "direct application to the audience." There are close parallels in other Pauline letters, showing that the campaign against honorific discrimination is a major theme in Pauline thought. The expression "be of the same mind toward one another" is found with slight variations in 2 Corinthians 13:11; Philippians 2:2; 4:2; and Romans 15:5. To be "of the same mind toward one another" does not imply agreeing on particulars or achieving a consensus on general points that overcomes disagreements. It implies rather the admission of mental equality that enables people to work with each other. If love is to be genuine, it must abandon any claim of possessing superior insight or status. The admonition not to "set the mind on exalted things" and the exhortation not to be "wise minded in yourselves" carry forward the same impulse. Paul is demanding here that love (12:9) be allowed to draw one into association with the less enlightened. In the realm that Christ makes possible, superiority is replaced by equality, condescension by solidarity.

To be "wise minded in oneself" (12:16), which in the Hellenistic categories of the first century would have implied the self-sufficiency of a mind that believes itself superior, is essentially destructive to community. The wording of Paul's admonition in verse 16c is adapted from Proverbs 3:7 by changing the singular to plural and dropping the antithesis about fearing God:

> Do not be wise in yourself,
>     but fear God and refrain from all evil.

The effect of the minor alterations is to relate the citation more closely to the congregational situation in Rome so as to address the superiority claims of congregations and ethnic groups. The connection between conceit and community is specified by the antithesis between "exalted things" and associating with "lowly people" (Rom. 12:16b). The latter clearly refers to low social status. Only by repudiating the sense of superiority by those of higher social status is it possible to achieve genuine solidarity. If the overall argument of Romans is accepted by the recipients, they will see that all persons are in fact "lowly" because all have sinned and fallen short of the glory of God (3:9). Since all are honored equally by grace, the normal social distinctions are no longer relevant for the Christian community. Thus Paul advises converts with former social status and high intelligence not to be "wise minded in yourselves," which is also cited from Proverbs 3:7. It is significant that he omits the final line of this well-known proverb ("and the LORD will reward you"). The implication is that, by avoiding arrogance, the Roman Christians will overcome evil with good. The omission of a reward would clearly have been felt as a correction by an audience acquainted with the usual approach to ethics. In place of the promise of rewards from heaven, Romans offers an ethic motivated by a reward already received, namely, the grace of God conveyed by the gospel that restores right relationships everywhere.

The verb "conquer" that is used twice in 12:21 has a significant cultural resonance with honor. It was widely employed in the celebrations of the Greek goddess Nike and of the Roman goddess Victoria. The imperial authorities celebrated Victoria in monuments, coins, public inscriptions, triumphal parades, public games, and other propaganda as the key to world peace. The idea was that peace could only be achieved through Rome's victory over enemies. A subtle but profound interaction with the cultural context thus surfaces in the wording of 12:21, where Paul celebrates a new kind of triumph over evil: by civility and hospitality rather than by force. Even a drink of water given to a thirsty person or a civil word spoken to a slave becomes a means of expressing the love of Christ and thus extending the realm of divine righteousness. Given the beleaguered and marginalized circumstances of the Roman Christians, gathered in secret groups in tenement buildings, private dwellings, and workshops, this closing verse is a remarkable expression of courage and confidence.

*Robert Jewett*

## Sixteenth Sunday after Pentecost, Year A

First Lesson: Exodus 12:1-14
(Psalm 149)
**Second Lesson: Romans 13:8-14**
Gospel Lesson: Matthew 18:15-20

At first glance the opening sentence of this reading appears to contradict the theme of obligation developed in Romans 13:7. Whereas 13:7 urged "Render to all what is obligated," 13:8 insists that believers should "owe no one anything." Paradoxical antitheses like this are frequently found in classical Greek collections of proverbs and moral admonitions. In this instance the taxes, customs, respect, and honor owed in verse 7 are to be met, taken care of, paid off so that Christians are free to devote themselves to their new obligations. This implies that converts should avoid falling under the control of creditors or remaining entangled with patrons and thus erode the capacity of the members of house and tenement churches to shape their common life in Christ. Paul wants Christians to be slaves of no human, if they can avoid it, indebted only to mutual love. Their former social obligations are to be replaced by a single new obligation to meet the needs of fellow members in the church. That Paul has in mind the new obligation to love the members of one's house or tenement church as the new fictive family in which believers are embedded is strongly indicated by the wording of this verse and by close parallels elsewhere in the Pauline letters (1 Thess. 3:12; 4:9; 2 Thess. 1:3; Gal. 5:13). "One another" clearly refers to fellow believers, as elsewhere in Romans (1:12; 12:5, 10, 16; 14:13, 19; 15:5, 7,

14; 16:16). As I demonstrated in chapter 6 of *Paul the Apostle to America* (Louisville: Westminster/John Knox, 1994), these small congregations were regularly celebrating love feasts with shared resources. They were creating informal, urban communes that in some instances ate every evening meal together, during which the communion ritual was used as the frame around a potluck supper in which Christ was thought to play host.

There is a translation problem in the second half of verse 8, and as evident in my translation below, I feel the evidence supports the directing of one's love toward members of "other" Christian communities in addition to one's own.

8   Owe no one anything, except to love one another;
      for the one who loves the other has fulfilled the law.
9   For [there is] the [commandment],
      "You shall not commit adultery,
      You shall not murder,
      You shall not steal,
      You shall not covet,"
   and if [there is] any other commandment it is summed up
         in the [saying],
      "You shall love your neighbor as yourself."
10   The *agapē* does no evil to the neighbor;
      therefore the *agapē* is law's fulfillment.

The wording of verse 8 opens the door to consider the obligation to love Christians beyond one's small circle. This fits the historical context, because mutual acceptance of members and leaders from other Christian groups was a significant problem in Rome. This subtle widening of the love command to include the "other" Christian in 8b thus opens the door to the topic directly addressed in 14:1–16:23, the welcome of persons identified as the "weak." Love between Christians belonging to different groups is presented in 8b as the law's fulfillment, which addresses the question of whether one ought to have fellowship with persons who do not follow the laws of one's own group. The conservatives stereotyped as "weak" were evidently following kosher food regulations (14:2-14), while the majority who call themselves the "strong" feel free to "eat anything" (14:2). Sharing each other's love feasts thus raised the crucial issue of the status of the law, and Paul's claim is quite radical in that context. When love expresses itself in hospitality to "the other," the law of Christ is fulfilled.

Paul cites a series of commandments to illustrate his contention about mutual love as law's fulfillment. An interesting question is why these commandments were selected and the other commandments were not. I believe Paul selects issues of particular relevance for life in the urban environment of Rome, where interpersonal relations were tense, volatile, and full of temptations and provocations. The command "do not commit adultery" protects the sanctity of marriage, and the unconditional formulation is probably meant to include both men and women in the admonition. Neither the Jewish nor the Greco-Roman cultures shared this strict prohibition of sexual relations for both males and females outside of covenantal boundaries. It is likely that adultery was a significant problem in the ecstatic and closely knit communities of men and women from different families that made up early churches.

The command "you shall not murder" was also relevant for the urban environment of Rome, where life was cheap. The prominent place given to the prohibition of murder in the Old Testament, the reiteration of the prohibition of murder in Matthew 19:18, and the listing of murder in the catalogue of vices discussed above in Romans 1:29 confirm the high value accorded to the preservation of human life in the biblical tradition as a whole. Given the high incidence of crime and vigilantism in the slums of Rome, especially at night, and the violent conflicts that had already led to the banning of Christian and Jewish leaders under Claudius, this topic was a significant one for the audience of the letter. The prohibition "you shall not steal" refers to secretive theft rather than robbery, which has the connotation of violent assault. While some Jewish laws allowed theft from criminals or unbelievers like Samaritans, and the Roman moralist Horace satirized a pious citizen who would sacrifice "to Laverna, the goddess of theft, for the power to commit fraud and robbery while retaining his good reputation," the biblical prohibition against theft as quoted in this verse was formulated in an unconditional way. It had a direct bearing on church members living in close proximity, where the slum conditions made preservation of property difficult and the widespread poverty made theft appealing as well as damaging. The prohibition of coveting relates to the emerging solidarity of the communal systems of eating together in the house and tenement churches in Rome and elsewhere. The enemy of agapaic sharing is the desire for possessions under one's own control. This commandment is effectively recontextualized in this pericope to relate to the question of "loving one another," in a passage that climaxes with two explicit references in 13:10 to "the *agapē*," probably referring to the love feast.

The prohibitions from the Ten Commandments are followed by the open-ended formulation "and if [there is] any other commandment." This formulation may seem awkward to the current audience and is ordinarily smoothed out in contemporary translations, but it served the crucial purpose of including any commandment stressed by any group of Christians in Rome, even a law coming from outside Scripture.

A proper interpretation of 13:10 should continue the focus on local church relations throughout this pericope. But the persistent deletion by commentators and translators of the article "the" in connection with love in this verse serves to generalize the admonition and drive it in a theoretical direction not intended by Paul. The logical social corollary to "the love" in this verse is the *agapē* meal otherwise known as the love feast, the common meal shared by most sectors of the early church in connection with the Lord's Supper. As I suggest in *Common Life in the Early Church* ([Valley Forge, Pa.: Trinity Press International, 1998], pp. 265-78), the repeated use of the article in the expression "the love" in this verse would even justify the translation "the *agapē*." 13:10 contends that the love feast is inconsistent with doing any form of harm to a neighbor, understood here as a fellow Christian who may or may not be a member of one's small congregation. The social context of the *agapē* meal also fits the reiteration that such love is the "fulfillment therefore of law." It is not just any love that is in view here, but "the love" within the Christian congregation. The greatest barrier against such love in the Roman situation, according to Romans 14–15, was the insistence on conformity to various forms of law which divided the weak from the strong and prevented the celebration of love feasts together. It is essential therefore to translate "law" without the article, in conformity with the Greek text and in contrast to the usual translations in commentaries and modern versions. It is law as a principle, in its various forms, that is fulfilled in the *agapē* meal. The meaning of "fulfill" in this sentence is the entire completion of law, not the sum total of its individual demands. In effect, Paul is claiming that the final goal of law, in whatever culture it manifests itself, is achieved in the love feasts of early Christian communities. A challenge for contemporary ministry that arises from this close reading of the text is to find new ways to embody the love feast.

*Robert Jewett*

## First Sunday of Advent, Year A

First Lesson: Isaiah 2:1-5
(Psalm 122)
**Second Lesson: Romans 13:11-14**
Gospel Lesson: Matthew 24:36-44

Paul's words in this lectionary reading aim to retain a distinct identity over against a corrupt and violent world. He names some of the works of darkness that were particularly popular in the Rome to which this letter was addressed. In the translation I prepared for chapter 11 of *Saint Paul at the Movies* (Louisville: Westminster/John Knox, 1993), such works came clearly to the fore:

> 11   Besides this, knowing the time, that the hour [has]
>       already [come] for you to be awakened from sleep,
>          for the salvation is closer to us now than when we first
>             had faith.
> 12   The night has far gone,
>       the day has drawn near.
>       Let us therefore put off the works of darkness
>          but let us put on the armor of light.
> 13   Let us walk honorably as in [the] day,
>          not in carousings and drunkenness,
>             not in [sexual] affairs and indecencies,
>                not in strife and jealousy,
> 14   but put on the Lord Jesus Christ
>          and make no provision for the flesh [to gratify] its desires.

The first pair of works convey a life pattern of self-destruction. Both terms are in the plural, suggesting habitual repetition. The term translated here as "carousings" was used elsewhere for the lewd processions in honor of Dionysus, but in the New Testament it is always used in the negative sense of irresponsible carousing. A loss of self-control is typical for carousings and drunken bouts. One seeks to escape from responsibilities or troubles into a state of wild abandon and drugged insensibility. In the Rome of the first century, carousing and drunken stupors were typical of the rich as well as the poor. If you have seen the films *Claudius* or *Gladiator*, you gain some sense of the vicious scope of such debased behavior among the ruling elite, which was emulated on a less expensive scale by the urban poor. Paul disagreed with the idea that escapism is harmless. He was convinced that divine wrath was already visible in such self-destructive behavior. A society or an individual hooked on escapist patterns of behavior is likely to self-destruct. One day the roof falls in, the term is up, the grades are reported. People wake up after the last in a series of drunken parties to discover that they have lost out on life, that they have passed the point of no return, and that disaster is upon them.

The second pair of works of darkness that Paul names is "affairs and indecencies." The first term is literally "beddings," which implies sleeping with anyone who happens to be available. The second term, also in the plural, connotes behavior that experiments with sensations, lacking internal moral standards that might set any limits. Bedding on impulse and seeking sensual excitement fit in the category of exploitative behavior — using others for one's own pleasure, regardless of consequences. And again, in the Rome of the first century such sensual exploitation was generally viewed as harmless. A few moralists inveighed against the sexual depravities of a Claudius and a Nero and their associates; despised prophets from the Jewish or Christian traditions issued warnings about the wrath of God; but what Paul calls the "works of darkness" were among the most popular and widely discussed activities of the age.

The final pair of "works of darkness" that Paul lists is much more straightforward in translation: "strife and jealousy." These are the expression of what one might call the principle of domination. The desire to be number one results in endless quarreling; and the envy of those who are ahead is what Paul calls "jealousy." The one is typical of those who aspire to dominate, while the other is typical of those who have failed to dominate. The will to dominate thus lies at the root of both quarreling and jealousy. In the class-bound and highly competitive society of the Greco-Roman world, these traits were widely expressed and generally accepted. The personality type characteristic of the Mediterranean world of the first century was oriented to public recognition and status, as Bruce J. Malina demonstrated in *The New Testament World* ([Atlanta: John Knox, 1981], pp. 53-70). Self-identity was largely dependent on the admiration of others. To "be somebody" meant that you had to be ahead of someone, capable of evoking that person's jealousy. The social world in which the early church found itself was marked by chronic forms of squabbling and envy, which were thought to be the natural form of social relations. Social domination was simply assumed.

In this passage Paul was appealing for the members of the church in Rome to make sure that their pattern of life was consistent with the new age of Christ. "Besides this you know what hour it is, how it is full time now for you to wake from sleep. For salvation is nearer to us now than when we first believed; the night is far gone, the day is at hand." This verse could be used to correlate with the uncanny sense many people now have that darkness is upon us with full force. Escapism, exploitation, and domination seem to have won the day. The great temptation in such a time is to use the "works of darkness" to struggle against the darkness that surrounds us. The better alternative is to put on what Paul called "the armor of light." This metaphor is drawn from the apocalyptic depictions of the coming war between the forces of light and darkness, implying active struggle against evil. In our humane religious and intellectual heritage, there are sufficient resources to ward off the appeals of popular entertainments that can lure people into self-destruction. There remains a legacy of common sense and commitment to democratic processes that could be employed to make wiser choices about both the forms of entertainment we will support and the kinds of policies we will pay for. To wear the "armor of light" is to be realistic about the dangers of the "works of darkness," and to renounce them — over and over again. In Paul's view, to wear the "armor of light" is to wake up from escapism and mind-numbing addictions. It is to replace sexual and personal exploitation with righteous relationships in which the blessings of God can prosper and the young and the immature can be nurtured. To wear the "armor of light" means that there is no further need for domination; instead of quarreling and envy, there will be strength for cooperation and the mutual facing of the challenges that lie ahead.

Paul goes on to admonish the Roman Christians to "put on the Lord Jesus Christ" (13:14). The formula "Lord Jesus Christ" recurs here from 1:7, with the theme of Lordship in the place of emphasis. In the memorable words of commentator Ernst Käsemann, who struggled for these issues in gestapo cells, "Paul is concerned about the lordship of Christ which must be confirmed and passed on by every Christian and which stands in sharp opposition to the powers that rule the world" (*Commentary on Romans* [Grand Rapids: Eerdmans, 1980], p. 363). The One whose Lordship climaxed in shameful death in behalf of the shamed rules a new community in which the competition for pleasure and honor is no longer dominant. To stand under that Lordship is to put on Christ as a garment, to closely relate to him in every waking moment, to be guided by his love in every relationship. Whether in Rome or in the modern world, those who put on Christ march to a different drummer. Christian mysticism of the Pauline type places the transformed community under obedience to the Lord who rules the day and overcomes the shameful legacy of night.

Paul goes on in the last half of verse 14 to urge Christians to "make no provision for the flesh, to gratify its desires." The desires of the flesh are to gain dominance, pleasure, and prestige, to act in self-centered ways that demonstrate superior honor. These perverse expressions of twisted systems of honor and shame, whose successes and failures produce the "works of darkness," are countered by the shameful death of Christ in behalf of the shamed, and by the incorporation of the transformed community under the Lordship of Christ. The new ethos of light replaces the competition and exploitation of the darkling night with the mutuality of grace. But this ethos must be hallowed and preserved in the new community's constant battle against the "works of darkness" within and without. It is a battle in which the present church is regularly called to participate, and the ethical challenge is to make fresh distinctions between the works of darkness and the works of light as new challenges emerge. These are issues in which the entire Christian community is called to "ascertain the will of God" (12:2) through study, prayer, and public discussion.

*Robert Jewett*

## Seventeenth Sunday after Pentecost, Year A

First Lesson: Exodus 14:19-31
(Psalm 114)
**Second Lesson: Romans 14:1-12**
Gospel Lesson: Matthew 18:21-35

Paul intervenes in a hot conflict that threatens to split the Christian community in Rome (14:1–15:13). The situation is delicate, and Paul is never more brilliant. The surface issues have to do with the religious observance of dietary laws and holy days. The real issues, however, concern the identity of Jesus Christ and the community united to him. Only by reframing the communal conflict in christocentric terms can Paul keep the community from tearing itself apart.

Paul sides with "the strong" but repudiates their attitudes and prac-

131

tices; he opposes "the weak" but respects the integrity of their consciences. The weak do the wrong things, but in the right way. To go against conscience, Paul insists, even when it is mistaken, would be sinful. Paul will not force the weak to do this, and he admonishes the strong — who affirm the right things but in the wrong way — to abandon their scorn, self-righteousness, and sense of superiority. Paul understands that these attitudes are profoundly destructive of community, and repairing the community is the overriding consideration. For the sake of self-consistency and the beleaguered community, he must model the idea that the judgment of grace differs from graceless judgment. By penetrating to the deeper spiritual issues concerning union with Christ, and by openly upholding the truth of the matter while discriminating carefully among the vices and virtues of the disputants, Paul emerges as a masterful pastoral theologian.

The christocentric reframing of the dispute occurs in four sections. First, to counteract judgmentalism, Paul reminds the community that the Lord alone is the judge (14:1-12). Second, against the particular obtuseness of the strong, Paul reminds them that the Lord by his death showed a special solicitude for the weak (14:13-23). Third, to highlight that the strong have distinctive obligations, he shows how the Lord subordinated his own interests to those of others (15:1-6). Finally, he reminds them that while they were yet weak and impenitent, the Lord became their servant for the good of all (15:7-13). Only the first section will be discussed here.

Verse 1: There are members in the community whom Paul regards as *weak in faith*. In exactly what sense they are weak will emerge as the argument unfolds. By characterizing them in this way, however, Paul immediately signals his assessment of which party needs to be corrected in the disputes that endanger the community. Note that he does not describe them directly as the mistaken, however, but as *the weak*. The remedy that will need to be found requires their strengthening more nearly than their correction.

Since it is unlikely that the weak would need to be exhorted to welcome themselves, it seems that the personal address is directed to those who are not of this group. Those who are not weak need *to welcome the others,* implying that they have been less than welcoming. Paul aligns himself with their view of the disputed issues by calling the others weak in faith. But at the same time he uses his agreement with the strong to encourage attitudes and actions that are more generous. They are not to bar their opponents from the community; they are to be forbearing rather than forbidding; they are not to exclude but to welcome the weak in faith.

Verse 2: The disputed matter about which the quarreling has broken out concerns what it is permissible to eat. The weak feel they are permitted to *eat only vegetables*. Since they were initially described as *weak in faith* (v. 1), they presumably see themselves as bound by a sense of religious obligation, which is perceived to be at stake on both sides of the dispute. This threatens the very fabric of the community: the weak have a sense of religious obligation that the strong insist is simply false. The strong believe so strongly they may *eat all things* that they threaten to exclude the weak from the community, or at least do not welcome them. Paul has his work cut out for himself. He needs to expand the sense of religious obligation on both sides.

Verse 3: Although these statements would seem as evenhanded as one could wish, they contain certain nuances. Paul exhorts the one who eats *not to despise the other*. The attitude of scorn or contempt reflecting their sense of superiority seems to be a serious failing among those who are strong. Paul knows how corrosive scorn can be to the bonds of community, especially a community in conflict.

He exhorts the one who abstains, on the other hand, *not to pass judgment on the other*. The shade of difference would seem to be that whereas the strong despise the weak, the weak condemn the strong. The weak, being rigorists, would not perceive themselves as weak, or as rigid, but as upholding a high principle. They would perceive those who violated the principle as blameworthy, especially if they refused to mend their ways. Paul knows that judgmental attitudes will not enable the community to flourish.

Everything depends *on God — and on whom God has welcomed*. The members of the community have more in common than anything that sets them apart. The defining elements of their life together are not at stake: members on both sides of the dispute are baptized; they have all undergone catechesis, confessed the apostolic faith, and presented themselves in baptism to God. When they emerged from the waters of baptism, *God welcomed them —* all of them — as those who belong to Christ.

Verse 4: Although this critique of judging might seem to be directed primarily against the weak, the following sentence (v. 5) represents both groups as subjects of the verb "to judge." It seems advisable to continue taking these statements in an unrestricted sense as referring to both parties.

Neither the strong nor the weak has any jurisdiction or authority to pass judgment on the other. Neither is lord of the other. They are each *servants belonging to the household of another*, and judgment must be left to the lord to whom the servant belongs. Only by the judgment of the one who really counts will the servant stand or fall.

Paul is confident in the Lord, and he invites each party in the dispute to join him in this confidence. The servants who are correct will be strengthened in their stand. Those who have fallen into error, however, will be lifted up, so that they too will stand. Either way, it is the Lord, not they themselves, who is able to make them stand, and being a judge gracious to sinners, he has already done so. The two parties need to look away from each other to the Lord, and then back to each other again as those who belong to the Lord.

Paul has made his first move in separating the surface issues from the real issues. Dietary laws are a surface issue. They have led the community into a dangerous situation of mutual blaming and recrimination where members of the community stand in judgment over one another. The real issue has to do with *who holds the office of judge,* and that is the Lord to whom the servants belong.

Verse 5: Besides the observance of dietary requirements, the observance of holy days is also in dispute. Since these observances are perceived as matters of religious obligation, of devotion to God, *one must be fully convinced in one's own mind.* Ambivalence, lukewarmness, or insincerity would be out of place. Regardless of the substance of one's convictions (leading to observance or nonobservance), one's attitude must be appropriate to the case, even if one is mistaken.

But this is another surface issue; the real issue is honoring the Lord. Setting aside special days (over and above the Lord's day) for religious observance is not harmful, even if unnecessary or mistaken. Regarding every day as a special day is acceptable, even if no more virtuous than setting aside some days as holy. Everything depends on the quality of one's devotion to God, and there is no reason devotion cannot be properly maintained in either case.

Verse 6: The quality of devotion is not diminished on either side of the disputes. The Lord is acknowledged, thanked, and praised for who he is, regardless of the observance or nonobservance of days and food laws, and regardless of the propriety or impropriety of either course. The full weight of conviction is in evidence on either side. Paul highlights the subjective aspect of the practices as opposed to their objective content.

Verse 7: The argument takes an abrupt, unexpected turn. The floor is dropping out of the common structure assumed by both sides as Paul moves to a whole new level. Regardless of which side one may be on, not one of us is at the center. No one properly lives to himself, nor is he the ultimate reality and meaning of his life. No one properly takes himself as the object of ultimate devotion. Nor does anyone die to himself. No matter what illusions one may hold about oneself and one's religious rectitude, death unmasks them all. If in death we come *face-to-face with God,* the life we now lead takes on an aspect of seriousness and sobriety. Perhaps we ought not be too quick in scorning or blaming others.

Verse 8: All relativities of this life pale in relation to the Lord, even religious relativities, which are supposedly the highest. Such matters should not be made more important than they are. What matters in living and dying is the one to whom we ultimately live and die. It is a great thing to know that we live to the Lord because it de-centers us from being *homo incurvatus in se* (the human being turned in upon himself, Luther's famous definition of sin) and affords a proper sense of perspective.

If the ultimate reality of our lives is indeed the Lord, then we belong to him in life and in death: we were bought with a price. The community Paul addresses knows something of what that price was and who paid it, and knows that it is a fearful thing to fall into the hands of the living God. It knows that God is of purer eyes than to behold evil. Yet it also knows that God has turned his wrath to the service of mercy, his anger to the benefit of compassion. It knows that the Lord has lived and died as one of us, so that we might live and die to him. It knows in any case that he cannot be escaped.

Verse 9: Christ's death and resurrection are the enactment of his Lordship: through them he unites his eternal being to a temporal becoming. His life in our place, which we failed to live, was the one true life before God. Therefore he is *Lord of the living;* his death, in turn, was the death of death. By dying for us he conquered and abolished the death that was ours. Therefore he himself, not death, is Lord, and he is *Lord of the dead.* We have our future not in death but in him. He has triumphed in life and in death.

Because this Lord is able to make us stand (v. 4), and has proven his readiness to do so, we may approach him with confidence. But because he is also a righteous judge, we can only approach him at the same time with humble and contrite hearts, in fear and trembling.

Verse 10: *Meditatio* now becomes *applicatio.* Paul drives home his meditation on the real issue. Precisely who, he asks, is in a position to judge whom? The Lord who is able to make us *stand* (v. 4) will make us *stand* before the judgment seat of God, and not one of us will be excluded. It is not others who must give account to us, but we who must give account to God. We forget this destiny when members of the community turn upon others in judgment, as if the prerogative belonged to them.

Although each side to the dispute has sinned against the other, each has done so in its own way. The weak stand in judgment over the strong (v. 3), even as the strong despise the weak (v. 3). The weak condemn the strong for not being properly disciplined in devotion to God, and the strong scorn the weak for not robustly living out the freedom of the gospel. (The gospel, they believe, and Paul agrees, has liberated the community from superseded regulations about ritual purity [cf. v. 14].) But why do the weak — who remain

135

the *brothers and sisters* of the those on the other side — *judge* the strong? And why, in turn, do the strong despise the weak? How can each side fail to realize that their severe attitudes of blaming and scorn are all of a piece and threaten to destroy the community? How can each side fail to realize that the other side still belongs to Christ, and so cannot be shunned? How can each fail to see that in the name of God they are actually jeopardizing themselves — before God?

Verse 11: The word of the apostle stands in line with the word of the prophets. He reminds the community that he is not delivering his mere opinion, but serving the word of God. The Lord who spoke through the prophets is the same living Lord attested by the apostolic faith. Certainly, nobody other than God has life except on loan as God's gift. He is therefore worthy of thanks and praise and will be honored and confessed as the Lord, if not in this life, then before the throne of judgment on the last day; if not in the form of faithfulness, then in some other, less happy way. No one will be finally exempted from giving proper veneration to the Lord.

Verse 12: Paul closes the first section of his argument having met his two main goals: he has relocated the dispute into a new context, and he has spoken the judgment of grace.

When the disputants disregard the centrality of Christ, their perceptions of one another become twisted and broken. In the time between the turning of the ages, Christ does not guarantee that those who belong to him will never go astray. But he does establish bonds that determine how members of the community are to respond when they perceive brothers and sisters falling into error. Under no circumstances are members of the community to arrogate to themselves the authority that belongs to Christ alone. When errors emerge and conflicts break out, but essentials are not at stake, they are to do everything possible to preserve the bonds of community. Above all, they are to refrain from attitudes of blaming and scorn. Since the weak were probably mostly Jewish Christians and the strong mostly Gentile Christians, the fault lines appearing here were fraught with tragic implications for the future.

Because he keeps his focus on Christ, Paul is able to pronounce a judgment that is not graceless but gracious. He is able to discriminate as wisely among ideas as among attitudes and feelings. What the disputants have in common is a general and particular solidarity both in sin and in grace. Their general solidarity ought to remind them of the abyss from which they have all been delivered, and so to promote mutual humility and forbearance. Their particular solidarity, however, is that each has fallen into sinful attitudes that are sundering the very body to which they mutually belong, the body of Christ. Christ has made them and will make them stand, and will deliver them, as he has delivered them from the abyss, and so from their continuing failures and shortcomings. But he will nonetheless also make them stand before the judgment seat of God. That no one will escape the divine judgment is as much the Word of God as that Christ is Lord of both the dead and the living. That we live and die to the Lord does not preclude our living and dying to judgment. What we do to our brothers and sisters on earth has consequences for all eternity. The judgment of grace, though gracious, is nonetheless a judgment. Paul applies this judgment to the dire circumstances in the community with supreme objectivity — with proper passion but without spite or rancor — because he never loses sight of his vocation to attest the Word of God.

*George Hunsinger*

## Second Sunday of Advent, Year A

First Lesson: Isaiah 11:1-10
(Psalm 72:1-7, 18-19)
**Second Lesson: Romans 15:4-13**
Gospel Lesson: Matthew 3:1-12

This passage, Romans 15:4-13, encapsulates not only the practical outcome to which the whole of Paul's letter to the Romans points but also the practical outcome to which Christianity of every and any legitimate stripe points. It can expand the imaginations of believers beyond the confines of self-interest or even of provincial concerns. At the forefront is a vision that is at once theocentric, christocentric, and community centered. More specifically, it is a vision of church unity through worship effected by Jesus to the glory of God.

There is scholarly consensus that 14:1–15:13 constitutes a distinct literary unit, an exhortation to "welcome [*proslambanesthe;* or: take to oneself, receive, accept, i.e., as your partner, helper, or intimate friend] the person who is weak in faith, not for judgmental evaluations of positions" (14:1). The

137

same command is picked up at the start of the conclusion to this section: "Therefore welcome *(proslambanesthe)* one another" (15:7a). The same verb is twice employed in the indicative mood to justify the command: "for God welcomed him" (14:3; "him" being the one judged, whether for eating or abstaining); "just as also Christ welcomed you [pl.] to the glory of God" (15:7b).

Tensions among the Roman Christians had apparently arisen over dietary practices; specifically, over whether a vegetarian diet should be adopted (14:2-3, 6, 15, 17, 20-21, 23), and possibly over the drinking of wine (14:17, 21) and the observance of special holy days such as the Sabbath (14:5-6a). Although the Mosaic law nowhere required abstinence from all meat, the behavior of the "weak" can fit within the framework of Jewish thought. Jews sometimes avoided meat (and wine) altogether because of the difficulty of obtaining ritually pure supplies, the cultural association of meat and wine with idolatry and pagans generally, and the "unsavory" role of meat and wine in stimulating fleshly passions (for this last point see Dan. 1:8, 12, 16; Tob. 1:10-13; Jth. 10:5; 12:2; Additions to Esther 14:17). Paul accepted the label of "weak" for those who abstained from meat and wine and treated some days as more holy than others because, in Paul's view, such people maintained false scruples over matters of indifference (Stoic *adiaphora;* 14:5-6, 14, 17, 20, 22-23). Yet, since abstaining from foods could have no material effect on the salvation of the abstainer, Paul was more concerned to remove food from the arena of "hot-button" issues in the church than he was to have the "weak" corrected.

In the first subsection, 14:1-12, Paul gives equal attention to chastising the "weak" for "judging" the "strong" and the "strong" for "despising" the "weak" (14:3, 10; see also the retrospective summary in 14:13a, "let us stop judging one another," and the opening line of the conclusion in 15:7a, "be welcoming one another," both emphasizing reciprocity). Since the salvation of neither type of believer is at stake in their dietary or calendrical practices, they should mind their own business and leave it to the one who died for the express purpose that he might be Lord over both groups. In the second stage of the argument, Paul shifts from criticism of both groups to exclusive criticism of the "strong" or "able" *(hoi dynatoi,* 15:1), who apparently were the dominant group within Roman Christianity at this time. The "strong" or "able" (15:1) are urged to curtail voluntarily both their freedom to eat meat and their promotion of this right in order to avoid pressuring the "weak" into an activity that could, minimally, disrupt the unity of the church and, maximally, lead to the spiritual downfall of those who succumb to the pressure to engage in activity they regard as sinful.

Scholars generally see this second stage of the argument as ending in 14:23, with 15:1-6 constituting a distinct subsection. However, a better case can be made for concluding the second subsection with the "prayer-wish" in 15:5-6, since no shift in argument occurs with the onset of 15:1. Regardless, all recognize that the *dio* ("therefore," 15:7) signals the concluding summary for the argument begun in 14:1. Indeed, given that so many of the themes of Romans are repeated here and that the dispute in 14:1–15:13 factored significantly into Paul's reasons for writing Romans (the latter point is disputed by scholars but in my view warranted by the evidence), 15:7-13 functions as a summary conclusion for the letter as a whole. The lectionary reading of 15:4-13 thus cuts across two sections and does not represent a self-contained unit.

Although it is generally assumed that the "weak" and the "strong" divide along ethnic lines with few exceptions (the "weak" = Jewish Christians, the "strong" = Gentile Christians), both groups are likely to be predominantly Gentile, given Paul's exclusive address to a Gentile audience. This is essentially an intra-Gentile dispute over the interpretation and relevance of the Mosaic law for Gentile believers.

At the end of the second stage of the argument, Paul exhorts the "strong" to "please the neighbor for the good purpose of building up," just as "Christ did not please himself" (vv. 2-3a). In support of this christological assertion Paul cites Psalm 69:9b: "The insults of those who insult you have fallen on me." The fact that early Christian circles often heard the voice of Jesus in Psalm 69 (cf. Ps. 69:21, "they gave me vinegar to drink," with Mark 15:23, 36 par.; Ps. 69:9a, "zeal for your house has consumed me," with John 2:17) confirms that Paul understood the speaker as Jesus, probably in connection with his trial, scourging, and crucifixion. In effect, Paul is stating that what he is asking of the "strong" is nothing compared to the abuse Jesus suffered for the sake of others.

It is in this context that Paul in 15:4 refers to "whatever was previously written" as being "written for our instruction, in order that through endurance and through the encouragement [or: comfort] of the Scriptures we might have hope." The similar statement in 1 Corinthians 10:11 ("written for our admonition, on whom the ends of the ages have come") indicates that "our" has an eschatological connotation: "those for whom the Scriptures are now being fulfilled." How a text like Psalm 69:9b is intended to promote hope becomes clearer in the light of the prayer-wish of the next two verses: "Now may the God of endurance and of encouragement give to you the same mind-set [or: state of mind; NRSV's 'live in harmony' is too weak] among one another in accordance with [the same mind-set in] Jesus

Christ, in order that, with one passion and with one voice, you may glorify the God and Father of our Lord Jesus Christ" (15:5-6).

The summary conclusion in 15:7-13 also confirms this interpretation of 15:4-6. Skipping first to the parallel prayer-wish in 15:13, we can see the themes of hope, joy, peace, and faith brought together: "Now may the God of hope fill you with all joy and peace in the course of believing, so that you may abound in [viz., in a state of] hope in [viz., by means of] the power of the Holy Spirit." Here hope leads to joy and peace which, in turn, lead cyclically to abundant hope. Previously, in 14:17, Paul had made clear that "The kingdom of God is not a matter of food and drink but righteousness and peace and joy in the Holy Spirit." Earlier still in the parenetic section, Paul had urged his readers to "rejoice in hope" (12:12; i.e., hope brings joy) and had brought together "having the same mind-set" (the same phrase as in 15:5) and "rejoicing" (12:15). Similarly, with regard to peace, Paul exhorted his readers in 14:19 to "pursue the things of peace," had referred in 8:6 to the "mind-set of the Spirit" as "life and peace," and earlier still had introduced his bragging-in-God theme in chapter 5 with the appeal to "have peace toward God" (5:1, which should be translated as a hortatory "let us have," not as an indicative "we have"). Simply put, a community of believers at odds over issues that have no central bearing on the salvation of its members detracts from a united worship of God.

The same point comes across clearly in 15:7-9a. By "welcoming one another [as dearly beloved family members] just as Christ also welcomed you to the glory of God" (cf. the theme of pleasing others in imitation of Christ in 15:2-3), they can eradicate the divisions that threaten to undermine the main purpose of the church's existence: the glorification or praise of God. Again, Christ is the model: "For I say that Christ has become [viz., was and still is] a servant to the circumcised on behalf of [promoting] the truthfulness [viz., faithfulness] of God, so that he may confirm the promises to the fathers [or: ancestors, patriarchs], and that the gentiles may glorify God for his mercy." It would be the height of folly for Gentile believers, after Christ had already "welcomed" them "in the interests of God's glory" (15:7) alongside the remnant of believing Jews, now to turn around and behave toward one another in an unwelcoming fashion by judging and looking down on one another in matters as insignificant as dietary habit.

To confirm this objective of Christ's, namely, that of welcoming Gentiles to worship the God of Jesus Christ in a united voice alongside of Israel, Paul cites four Old Testament texts: two from the "writings" (specifically, the Psalms, in vv. 9b, 11), one from the "law" (v. 10), and one from the "prophets" (v. 12). This is another set of confirming witnesses to Paul's assertion in Romans 3:21 that the now-manifested righteousness of God through Christ is attested by "the law and the prophets" (cf. 1:2). All four quotes contain the catchword "Gentiles" and collectively refer to incorporating Gentiles into the worship of Israel's God or Messiah.

In the first citation, Psalm 18:49 in verse 9b, Paul probably understood Jesus to be the speaker (at least typologically) and God the addressee, along the same lines as his interpretation of Psalm 69:9 in 15:3: "For this I will acknowledge [or: confess] you among the gentiles and sing praise-hymns to your name." The "for this" in the context of Psalm 18:49 alludes to the triumph that God gives the Davidic king in "subduing" the nations (18:47-48). The image of captivity is elsewhere used by Paul for being brought under Christ's gracious Lordship (e.g., 2 Cor. 2:14; cf. Eph. 4:8).

In verse 10 Paul cites Deuteronomy 32:43c, in agreement with the LXX: "Rejoice, gentiles, with his people" (the Hebrew MT lacks this line and reads "O gentiles" for the first line of the verse where other versions read "O heavens"). Here the Gentiles are called on, along with the heavens and the gods, to join Israel in worshiping God.

In verse 11 Paul cites Psalm 117:1: "Praise, all you gentiles, the LORD and let all the peoples praise him." The reference to "praising" parallels the theme of glorifying God in Romans 15:6, 9. The following verse of the psalm (it is a psalm of only two verses) alludes to two themes important for the context here in Romans. The Gentiles are called on to praise God for "his mercy" *(eleos)* and for the "truth[fulness] *(alētheia)* of the LORD."

In verse 12 Paul cites Isaiah 11:10 in basic agreement with the LXX: "There shall be a root of Jesse [David's father] and one who rises to rule over the gentiles; in him shall the gentiles/nations hope." The MT differs in the second and third lines: ". . . which stands as a signal pole [i.e., a pole on which hangs a banner or flag or standard] to the peoples; of him nations will inquire." Although the two versions communicate essentially the same message, the version in the LXX is more suited to Paul's argument with its reference to "rising" (perhaps understood by Paul as a reference to Christ's resurrection) and to Gentiles "hoping" (Rom. 15:4, 13).

By means of these citations Paul attempts, in a manner consistent with his stated purpose of the Scriptures in 15:4, to reset the priorities of the Roman Gentile Christians. They have been saved not for the purpose of disputing about food and calendar but for the purpose of worshiping God, that is, ascribing glory and honor to God "with his people" Israel for the glorious hope accomplished by Christ's death and resurrection.

There is one basic message to 15:4-13: churches today are not going to be "filled with all joy and peace in believing" (15:13) if they are more focused on internal disagreements over relatively inconsequential matters than on the glorious hope that lies before them. Such differences need not cause division among believers. The ultimate purpose of Christ's redemptive work is to maximize God's praise among Jews and Gentiles for the manifestation of God's faithfulness through Christ. If Paul saw worship as a potential vehicle for bringing the church together, it is ironic that worship in our own time has become a source of division in the church. We need Paul's reminder that believers are obligated to "welcome" each other into their worship lest they alienate those whom God and Christ have welcomed.

*Robert A. J. Gagnon*

## Fourth Sunday of Advent, Year B

First Lesson: 2 Samuel 7:1-11, 16
(Psalm 89:1-4, 19-26)
**Second Lesson: Romans 16:25-27**
Gospel Lesson: Luke 1:26-38

The doxology that concludes the standard translations of Romans provides an opportunity to acquaint laypeople with a few basic issues of text criticism. It would hinder fundamentalism and encourage respect for the rich tradition of our faith through the ages if ministers would be frank about such matters. Believers should know that our biblical texts come down to us through a complex process of transmission by earlier church leaders, and that the history of their ideas and conflicts is visible at times in the variations of the New Testament texts themselves. A brief illustration of the issue would be suitable in a Bible class or even in a sermon on this passage, because Romans is a classic case in point.

Some of the early Greek manuscripts of Romans contain only the first fourteen chapters plus this doxology. Twelve other families of texts handle the doxology in various ways. In fact, one family lacks the doxology entirely, while others place it after 15:33, after 16:23, after 16:24, or even in some instances in two of these locations. What most modern translations provide is simply one of these thirteen options, and by no means the earliest. Standard translations reflect the late Greek edition of the New Testament that came to the West after the fall of Constantinople to the Turks in 1453, the text that provided the basis of the King James translation. Since that time thousands of earlier texts have been found. Scholars have applied scientific methods with increasing sophistication over the last four hundred years to explain the various versions of Romans.

The most plausible explanation is that this doxology was originally created to provide a conclusion to the fourteen-chapter version of Romans associated with Marcion, the radical second-century church leader who tried to erect an impassable barrier between Christianity and Judaism. He evidently disliked the final two chapters of Romans because of their greetings to Jewish leaders and their friendly attitude toward Jewish Christian groups. He would have been particularly offended by the idea of Christ serving the Jewish people in Romans 15:8. Marcion evidently found 14:23 a congenial place to close his version of Romans on a note friendly to his theology, that "whatever is not of faith is sin." This statement reiterated his contention that sin was no longer defined by the Jewish law but by faith in Christ. The resultant fourteen-chapter letter was published and distributed, but it lacked an ending that seemed appropriate for liturgical purposes. The widely accepted hypothesis is that some branch of the church that was using Marcion's fourteen-chapter version of Romans added the doxology, which probably had been used in that church's liturgy in some other context. The doxology shared some of Marcion's interest in eliminating the possibility of coexistence between Jewish Christians and Gentile Christians. The text of Romans thus reflects a phase in the long history of conflict between Judaism and Christianity.

If this hypothesis is correct, the doxology is what text scholars call an "interpolation," material written by a later hand. Those of us who believe in the authority of Scripture recognize that the doxology is part of God's word even though it was probably not written by Paul. Its vocabulary and sentence structure is non-Pauline, and it has what scholars have called a "supersessionist" perspective that Gentile Christians have displaced the Jews in the history of salvation. While many people today recognize that this perspective contributed to the later rise of anti-Semitism, and that in modern times such prejudice was a factor that encouraged horrendous crimes against the Jewish people, it is important to recognize that this doxology once played a positive role in ensuring the independence of Christianity. As the great Jewish historian Alan F. Segal has taught us in *Rebecca's Children: Judaism and Christianity in the Roman World* (Cambridge, Mass.: Har-

vard University Press, 1986), Judaism and Christianity were cousin movements, so to speak, in the first several centuries of the common era, and
both had to achieve independence in order to survive. They struggled
against each other for legitimacy, which both in fact enjoyed as children of
Rebekah and thus joint heirs to the divine promises. It is our task as interpreters to respect this rich tradition but at the same time to struggle against
its negative consequences.

I contend that we must read the doxology differently today than the believers in the early church were called to do. Since it is the Spirit of God that
leads to a proper understanding of the words of Scripture in each generation, current interpreters should be honest about the likelihood that what
one branch of the early church needed was quite different from what believers today should think about their Jewish conversation partners. This doxology is an ideal location to think these matters through with our congregations, and perhaps even to challenge some bright young person to learn the
languages and study the history of these problems, becoming a specialist
who seeks more adequate, scientific answers to the thousands of puzzles
concerning the transmission of our sacred Scriptures, of which this is only
one example.

The peculiar wording and rambling sentence structure of the doxology
are visible in my literal translation:

(25) Now to the one who is able to confirm you according to my gospel
and the preaching of Jesus Christ, according to the revelation of the mystery which has been kept silent for eternal periods (26) but now has been
disclosed, and through prophetic writings, according to the command of
the eternal God, made known for all the Gentiles for obedience of faith,
(27) to God only wise, through Jesus Christ, to whom [be] glory for aeons
of aeons. Amen.

The doxology to the "one who is able to confirm you" provides reassurance
to early Christians that God's power is sufficient to sustain their faith in the
face of public pressure from the Roman Empire and arguments from Jewish
conversation partners that Christ could not possibly have been the promised Messiah. The expressions "my gospel" and "preaching of Jesus Christ"
convey what to the period after Paul's death was considered the gist of his
theology, the standard of orthodoxy. Then as now, it was necessary for the
church to sum up its beliefs in a catechism that could be taught to the
young and serve as a litmus test in the struggle against heresy.

The phrase "according to the revelation of the mystery" reflects an interest in the disclosure of religious and mystical secrets, an interest also found in Judaism and some other arenas of Greco-Roman religion with whom early Christians were in conversation. While a number of New Testament passages have a similar revelation scheme, the most exact parallel in terminology is provided by Ephesians 3:3, "according to revelation the mystery was made known to me." The expression "kept silent for eternal periods" implies that the mystery in Paul's gospel had intentionally been kept silent since the beginning of time. While other late, New Testament writings (Col. 1:26-27 and Eph. 3:5-6, 9) speak of the hidden mystery that remained inaccessible because human finitude cannot grasp the transcendence of God, the doxology refers to silencing. In the context of the struggle against Jewish criticism, this doxology claims that God's truth was kept silent from Jewish interpreters but is now revealed, as the next verse claims, to the Gentiles. Both on the basis of the proper interpretation of the Old Testament as pointing to Christ as the Messiah and "according to the command of the eternal God," this mystery was "made known" to Gentile Christians. While the polemical situation requiring this claim is understandable today, its full implications need to be observed. The doxology claims that the prophetic message is accessible only through Gentile believers. Only they know the command of God. The Jews have turned away, and have been shattered in the great zealotic wars against which Jesus had warned, and which the Christian movement had tried to avert (in 66-70, 132-35 C.E.). So now the Gentiles alone inherit the promise of Israel and the key to its prophetic legacy. They are the new elite, who alone have access to the mystery hidden for ages. The doxology praises "God only wise," and by the phrase "through Jesus Christ" the Christian antithesis to Judaism was powerfully expressed in the claim that the revelation of God's wisdom came through Jesus of Nazareth. Paul's monotheistic theme in Romans 3:28-31 is modified by this wording; in place of God who is God both of Jews and Gentiles, now the "only God" sustains the Gentile supersession of Jewish prerogatives.

I believe it is important for interpreters to bring the full implications of this doxology to light, both to understand why it was important and useful for a small minority movement of early Christians under pressure by competitors who were better accepted by society, and to bring to awareness its risks for current believers.

*Robert Jewett*

## Second Sunday after the Epiphany, Year A

First Lesson: Isaiah 49:1-7
(Psalm 40:1-11)
**Second Lesson: 1 Corinthians 1:1-9**
Gospel Lesson: John 1:29-42

It is hard to imagine someone using this resource for preaching who does not have preconceptions about the Corinthians and Paul's letters to them. Already, before we approach the opening verses of the first letter, we have in mind those rascal Corinthian Christians and Paul's measured and cross-heavy corrections. That "noise" of what we already know makes it difficult to hear these opening nine verses with any sort of freshness. So, I say, bring it all to the exegesis-for-preaching table — all that you remember, all that you expect and anticipate, even all that you have forgotten. Put it all on these opening verses and listen to the dialogue between this text and your pre-text. Our question: How do we preach the gospel with 1 Corinthians 1:1-9 as a primary conversation partner?

We know that Paul is going to be dealing with problems in this letter — problems pertaining to sexual morality, lawsuits, marriage, food sacrificed to idols, apostolic rights, worship wars, women's role in the church, charismatic gifts, and resurrection. This letter, in fact, sets the paradigm for the Pauline apostolic ministry of the epistle: it allows Paul to be in two places at once, thus accomplishing what he would if he were present.

As Paul often does, he deploys clues in the salutation and thanksgiving for what comes later in the letter. So we see Paul mentioning "gifts," "call," "gnosis," and "speech" in the opening, all of which will be developed more fully later in specific response to the ways in which the Corinthians are misappropriating these gifts. Those called to preach the gospel from this text in specific contexts of problems and the misappropriations of gifts need to note the theological strategy that Paul takes to address the Corinthian situation. It is this strategy which will most inform preaching and carrying on the ministry of the gospel in faithful apostolic succession.

Paul is, indeed, setting up his later arguments through the salutation and thanksgiving by dropping certain key words into these nine verses. But even more, he is setting up his theological and christological strategy for dealing with the problems. For it is God and Jesus whom Paul asserts are behind, in, and throughout everything that he is, and everything that the Corinthian Christians are. It is for God's sake that the Corinthians'

146

ongoing sanctification requires of them certain changes of thought and behavior.

God is named six times and Jesus eight times in 1 Corinthians 1:1-9. God is the one who *calls* (Paul and the Corinthian Christians), who *wills* (Paul's apostleship), who *assembles* the community of faith, who *sanctifies,* who imparts grace and peace, who *receives* thanks, who *enriches* the Corinthians in Christ, in speech, in knowledge, *equipping* them with every spiritual gift and *strengthening* them for the end. Verse 9 is the exclamation point of Paul's assertions regarding God: "*God is faithful;* by him you were called into the fellowship of his Son, Jesus Christ our Lord."

By making such a claim, Paul changes the issue that lurks beneath all the other issues in Corinth. That issue is Paul's credibility as an authentic apostle. Many in Corinth, trained rhetorically in the classical tradition, were becoming outspokenly suspicious of Paul's credentials. Readers would have judged the persuasive efficacy of his letter, a form of deliberative rhetoric, primarily on their perception of the writer. Quintilian wrote: "What really carries greatest weight in deliberative speeches is the authority of the speaker. For he, who would have all men trust his judgement as to what is expedient and honorable, should both possess and be regarded as possessing genuine wisdom and excellence of character" (*Institutes of Oratory* 3.8.13; on 1 Corinthians as deliberative rhetoric, see Margaret Mitchell, *Paul and the Rhetoric of Reconciliation* [Louisville: Westminster/John Knox, 1991]). Rummaging through the entire Corinthian correspondence, we note the following criticisms of Paul:

- a Paul "group" (1 Cor. 1:12) implies opposition to Paul from the other groups;
- Paul's preaching lacked numerical success (1 Cor. 1:14-17);
- Paul's preaching lacked rhetorical polish and style (1 Cor. 1:17; 2:1-4);
- Paul is a "flatterer," one who says one thing but does another (1 Cor. 4:14-21; 2 Cor. 1:15–2:4);
- Paul is an incompetent and insincere orator (2 Cor. 1:12; 2:17; 3:5; 5:11; 6:3);
- Paul's demeanor was socially reprehensible (2 Cor. 4:7-15; 6:4-10);
- Paul offers an insufficient demonstration of charismatic gifts indicative of an apostle (2 Cor. 5:12-13a).

Stephen Kraftchick sums it up well: "The Corinthians failed to see in Paul enough evidence of the power of God" ("Death in Us, Life in You," in *Pauline Theology I,* ed. Jouette M. Bassler [Minneapolis: Fortress, 1991],

p. 165). Paul's affirmation that "God is faithful *(pistos)*" shifts the question from Paul's reliability to God's, the one on whom Paul depends and on whom he wants them to depend. The better question than "Can Paul be trusted?" is "Can God be trusted?"

The Greek backdrop to *pistos* connects it to meanings that have to do with "trusting," "trustworthy," "faithful," "reliable," and even a "means of proof" in the classical rhetorical sense of a proof in argumentation. The Old Testament backdrop pictures a God who is faithful in keeping covenant and showing steadfast love (Deut. 7:9; 1 Kings 8:23; Neh. 1:5; 9:32; Dan. 9:4). When God calls humans into covenant with himself, he is faithful to keep covenant even when they break it. For Paul, God's steadfast love is nowhere more evident than in the call to fellowship that God makes in Christ Jesus. Moreover, it is the faithfulness of God which guarantees Paul's own word (2 Cor. 1:18). Paul is convinced that in the relationship that God has created with humankind, God's faithfulness extends even to the point of God preventing unbearable situations of temptation (1 Cor. 10:13; 2 Thess. 3:3) while it works an ongoing sanctification of the believers within the faith community (1 Thess. 5:23-24). Paul wants them to know: this is not *Paul's* church and *Paul* is not their savior. Demote *Paul,* but then deal with him in relation to the *God* who did, in fact, send Paul to them.

In 1 Corinthians 1:1-9 Jesus is the Christ, the Lord, and the Son. He is the one who came and who will come again. Jesus is the one of whom Paul is an apostle, meaning that Paul's message has the authority of the one who sends him, Jesus Christ the Lord and Son of God. Christ Jesus is the location of being wherein the Corinthian Christians experience their sanctification. It is the name of the Lord Jesus Christ that is called on by Christians. Jesus, too, like God, is the source of grace and peace. God's grace comes to Christians in Christ Jesus. Their enrichment takes place in him. Their "testimony" or "witness" of or to Christ is "confirmed," "strengthened," or, perhaps better, "guaranteed" (a legal term). The Corinthian Christians' fellowship is not only "in" the Son, but "with" the Son as well.

It is likely that Paul emphasizes Jesus as the "Christ" as testimony to his true status as God's anticipated anointed one. Such would have been strong testimony to the Jews. His emphasis on Jesus as "Lord" would have struck a chord with Gentiles, especially in light of the Roman imperial cult that held Caesar to be Lord. Both assertions would be risky and polarizing to both ethnic segments of humanity, Jew and Gentile (cf. 1:22). But these risky and polarizing assertions are at the heart of Paul's stress in these opening verses. For Paul's emphasis on the grace-giving and strength-sustaining God and

God's Son, Jesus Christ the Lord, gives Paul a common confessional ground with the Corinthians which he will call on throughout the rest of the letter when addressing their problems. Gaining their nod regarding their God-given spiritual giftedness, their gifts of speech, and their knowledge, Paul then proceeds to explain to them the theological and ethical import of those gifts. Similarly, gaining their nod about Jesus the Messiah who is their Lord, he then proceeds to explain that this Messiah is the crucified Messiah whose Lordship consists of suffering ignominy. The implication of this christological orientation is profound for the way they understand Paul, other community orators in their midst, and themselves as a faith community, living in the world yet not of the world.

To preach the gospel is to name what God has done, is doing, and will do in the world to bring about new and redemptive situations that could not have been brought about by anyone other than God. As such, we see Paul asserting his own experience of the gospel as a preface to his correspondence to the Corinthians. Knowing that he is a target of criticism, he frames his own self-defense first in a sense of self before his God and his Lord, Jesus Christ. Paul's interest in this letter is not just that he be vindicated or "liked" and "affirmed" in his efforts, nor that the Corinthians bend their ways of being community and "doing" worship to Paul's preferences. Rather, Paul's burden for himself and the Corinthians is that they all find their sense of self, call, purpose, and source of relations in the life-giving, life-sustaining power and grace of God.

It could be, too, that we learn something important about overcoming difficulties with those with whom we are in conflict from Paul's use of first-century epistolary form. Paul frames what will become at times an emotionally charged correspondence with a blessing and a thanksgiving. Framing our difficulties with people this way — especially in view of who we are as blessed and prompted to thanks by God — gives us a new perspective for approaching them and releases us, too, to God's reshaping of our ways of responding to the slings and arrows of our critics.

One final matter haunted me as I wrestled with this text: What are we to do with the confessions "Jesus is Lord" and "Jesus is the Messiah"? Risky and polarizing in their day, they are functionally meaningless today, except as a kind of orthodox and sleepy church-speak. There are no Caesars among us requiring the title of "Lord" at the cost of our lives. The Constantinian cooling of confessional claims has become complete. Does proclamation accept this? Are we now in a noncompetitive time regarding Jesus' Lordship? Or are there ways of confessing Jesus as Lord today that legitimately reignite the flame of imperial powers which vie with the kingdom of God? What are those powers today? Where is the opposition — who is threatened by — our confession that "Jesus is Lord"?

The confession "Jesus is the Messiah" is a bit different. With the current surge of interfaith dialogue, especially between Christians and Jews, it is becoming less and less politically correct to make strong claims about Jesus' messiahship and Lordship. The goal of interfaith dialogue is understanding and fellowship, not polarization. The goal is communion and tolerance, not proselytization. Evangelism, as a form of "the testimony of/to Christ being strengthened among you," is not an activity which is sensitive to the hurt and shame that has been thrust upon Jews by Christians for centuries. Does Christian sensitivity to immoral actions by Christians mean, however, that we lose our confession that Jesus *is* the Messiah? In a post-Holocaust, pluralistic, postmodern world, is there a place for a Christian to say to a non-Christian (Hindu, Muslim, Buddhist, or Jew): "I believe Jesus is the Messiah, the Lord, the Son of God, and that God wills and calls you into the fellowship and the sanctification that is found 'in Christ'"? The kind of risk, polarization, and political incorrectness that attend such a profession of faith may "guarantee" that the gospel has not lost its potency to smell like death to some and life to others, to be wisdom to some and folly to others, to be received as the power of God to some while disdained as a scandal of moronic proportions to others.

*André Resner, Jr.*

## First Sunday of Advent, Year B

First Lesson: Isaiah 64:1-9
(Psalm 80:1-7, 17-19)
**Second Lesson: 1 Corinthians 1:3-9**
Gospel Lesson: Mark 13:24-37

As Thomas Long once noted, most people instinctively know how to sign a letter. The occasion and the receiver determine the matter. A letter to my mother will invariably end with "Love, Scott." However, were I a high school student requesting a letter of recommendation to a university, it is unlikely I would sign such a missive "Affectionately, Scott." No, such a formal letter will conclude with something along the lines of "Respectively Yours," followed by not just my name but any titles I can muster as well ("Reverend Scott E. Hoezee, Minister of Preaching . . ."). The signature alone can tell a person a lot about a letter. If you are romantically interested in someone and then receive a note from him or her which signs off, "Regards," your heart sinks. No love there!

The letter-writing tradition of the Greek world "signed" letters at the beginning. As Long notes, Paul was a master at finding just the right signature for various occasions. His opening signature in Philippians fairly radiates with warmth and love, setting up what may well be Paul's most affectionate letter. By stark contrast, Galatians opens with a ripping tirade which dispenses with the usual epistolary pleasantries (like "I thank my God always for you") in favor of an abrupt "I am astonished at you!" Right off the bat, discerning Galatian readers knew they were in for it!

Paul's signature in 1 Corinthians appears, at first blush, to be standard. But given what we know about the letter that follows, it becomes clear that in this particular signature Paul dripped with sarcasm and a cunning wit. The lectionary reading skirts the opening two verses, perhaps deeming them too routine. But to savor the ironic punch of verses 3-9 we need at least a quick glance at the opening two verses.

In verse 1 Paul introduces what will become the frame for this introductory signature, viz., the concept of being "called." Paul makes clear in verse 1 that he himself has been "*called* to be an apostle of Christ Jesus by the will of God." That is an important way to open this letter, given that in chapter 9 Paul will defend his apostolic credentials against some cynics.

Paul then says in verse 2 that the church of Corinth (the *ekklēsia,* or "*called*-out ones") is made up of holy people ("saints") who, along with everyone else who *calls* on the name of Jesus, are "*called* to be holy." The Corinthians are doubly called to be doubly holy even as they themselves call on the Name. Paul will return to this notion of calling in the final verse of this section when he makes clear that the Corinthians have been "*called* into fellowship with [God's] Son Jesus."

Why is this framework of holy calling vital to notice? Perhaps because the Corinthians were such an *un*holy mess at the time! They were divided on whether to follow Paul or Apollos or Jesus. They were hauling each other into court with lawsuits, arguing about marriage and food sacrifice to idols, turning the Lord's Supper into another example of classism, and some were denying the resurrection. God himself had *called* them to be different, to be distinct, to be holy. But holy-acting they were not. Paul's signature seems to be a subtle way of reminding the Corinthians just who it was who had called them and what the goal of that divine calling was.

The wider situation of the Corinthians makes some of Paul's other irony become likewise clear. In verse 5 Paul highlights the richness of their "speaking" and "knowledge." Might this have caused the people to squirm, given that the issue of speaking in tongues and delivering words of knowledge in worship services had nearly brought them to blows? In verse 7 Paul highlights the fact that they "do not lack any spiritual gift." True enough, but then squabbling over which gift was the best had plunged yet another dagger of division into the congregation. In verses 8 and 9 Paul mentions God's keeping them "strong" and "blameless," neither of which appeared to fit these folks very well. The last twist of Paul's sarcastic knife comes in verse 9 with the loaded word *koinōnia*, or "fellowship." They had been called into a godlike communion of hearts. Yet regarding their observance of the Lord's Supper (which was supposed to be a key sign of this heaven-sent fellowship), Paul writes in chapter 11, "I have no praise for you."

So in this lection is Paul being merely sarcastic? Or is he perhaps mixing in genuine admiration with a few wry allusions to the divisive issues still to come in the body of this epistle? Or does Paul's undeniable love for this troubled congregation lead him to sketch what he hopes may still be true somewhere below the surface of all these other unhappy things?

Perhaps it is difficult to choose exactly how to read this opening signature. But however Paul may have meant it, there is little denying that these verses are a summary preview for what is to come. Only one verse after Paul's soaring prose of verses 3-9 comes verse 10 and its blunt appeal for the Corinthians to "agree with one another" in the "quarrels among you" (v. 11).

But what does all of this have to do with the first Sunday of Advent? If we read this passage in the ways just suggested, it surely does not seem like a very good way to kick off the Christmas season. But perhaps it is precisely this passage's honesty, irony, and wit which can help congregations start their Advent reflections on a better note than the saccharine spirituality which too often floods this time of the year.

In the coming four weeks the Word of the gospel will come to congregations all over the world. Tidings of great joy regarding Jesus' first advent will be proclaimed. Anticipations for his second advent will be pondered. Children will stage Christmas pageants, and candlelight services will fill hearts with the warmth of the season. But in the midst of all this warmth and joy, 1 Corinthians reminds us that these gospel tidings *always* come to congregations which do not fully live up to the lofty callings of God — we are called to holiness, called to sainthood, called to godlike fellowship. But like the Corinthians, we always fall short at least a little (and sometimes a lot).

If Paul's purple prose of verses 3-9 caused some of the Corinthian Christians to blush the first time this letter was read, these words can function the same way in our lives. The details may be different, but choose almost any congregation and a similarly ironic paragraph could be written about it. Perhaps the perennially controversial issue of a building program has divided opinions in a congregation. You can almost see Paul writing, "I am thankful for the way you have *built yourselves up* in unity!" Maybe the worship wars of recent years have brought about mutual sneers among those with divergent musical tastes. "How wonderful it is that you sing your praises in the unity of the one Holy Spirit who moves the church to worship God!" And so on.

None of that is happy news, of course. Hence, most of it seems ill fitting in Advent. Traditionally, however, Advent was a penitential season, a time to recognize *why* God the Son had to become flesh as well as to see the ongoing stain of sin which should properly whet our appetites for the second coming of Jesus. The proof of how badly we and the whole world need the Christ of God is everywhere on display. The doctrine of depravity, it is said, is the one tenet of the faith which any given day's newspaper bears out clearly. Alas, sometimes the church bulletin functions the same way.

The message of Advent, in both of its poles of Jesus' first coming in Bethlehem and of Jesus' second coming at a day and hour we know not, is that the whole package came to us by grace alone "while we were yet sinners." God had to do it that way because sin is the one reality we cannot escape, not even in the church. If that does not seem a happy enough way to open Advent, perhaps that is because we've been co-opted into sentimentalizing Advent to the point where talk of sin is ruled out of order. But without some honest confession of sin, what we end up ruling out is the need for Jesus in the first place. In and through this passage Paul's aim was to bring home the message that comes at the very end of verse 9: the message that despite our sins, the God who has called us into fellowship with Jesus "is faithful." Just that divine faithfulness in and through our multiple failures is why we have an Advent message to proclaim in the first place.

*Scott Hoezee*

# Third Sunday after the Epiphany, Year A

First Lesson: Isaiah 9:1-4
(Psalm 27:1, 4-9)
**Second Lesson: 1 Corinthians 1:10-18**
Gospel Lesson: Matthew 4:12-23

Already in 1:10 Paul makes his appeal *(parakaleō)*. This is unusually quick for Paul. Normally his supplication comes after the laying of a deep theological substructure. But here he gets right to the problem at hand: "quarrels," "strife," "selfish fighting" (Gk. *erides*). His desire for them is that they "all be in agreement," that there "be no divisions," and that they be "united in the same mind with the same purpose."

"Chloe's people" have told on the Corinthians to Paul. We know nothing about Chloe or her people. We can conjecture that she and "her people" were considered reliable sources of this information since Paul takes it seriously. The nature of the quarreling is that they are dividing the church into subgroups based on preacher preference. Some say, "I belong to Paul," or "I belong to Apollos," or "I belong to Cephas," or "I belong to Christ." Nothing is known of Cephas's (= Peter's) relationship to the Corinthian church. This could be a group with loyalty to the mother church in Jerusalem. The "Christ" group is enigmatic, too, but in a fractured church they do not appear to be helping or healing matters by their desire to have allegiance only to Christ. Given Paul's direct references to eloquence, the other references to Apollos in the context, and Apollos's direct relationship with the Corinthian church, it seems that Paul's major difficulty is with the "Apollos" and "Paul" groups. Understanding the social-cultural backdrop of this problem enlightens the issues and the way Paul deals with them.

For reasons that only God knows, preaching is the perpetuation of Jesus' cross event, the crucifixion of the Messiah, for people's enlightenment, judgment, and salvation. This medium, though, caused some wires to cross for first-century consciousness. When Paul, or any preacher in the Greco-Roman world, stood up and began speaking in front of an assembled group, such a situation had a long precedent and would have been understood in very predictable ways. As George Kennedy asserts, "When early Christians spoke, wrote, or read religious discourse in Greek, even if relatively uneducated, they had expectations of the form the message would take and of what would be persuasive" (*A New History of Classical Rhetoric* [Princeton: Princeton University Press, 1994], p. 258). Duane Litfin underscores the way rhetoric shaped people's perception of a rhetorical situation and the way they treated the orators themselves: "The practice of eloquence was not something which merely existed during Paul's day; it was pervasive in Greece and had been for centuries. It was a prime ingredient in the cultural heritage which defined and gave the Greek mind its shape. . . . The reach of rhetoric was all but inescapable during the life of Paul, from city to town or village. The Greco-Roman people thrived on eloquence and lionized its practitioners in a way that is difficult for moderns even to conceive" (*St. Paul's Theology of Proclamation: 1 Corinthians 1-4 and Greco-Roman Rhetoric* [Cambridge: Cambridge University Press, 1994], pp. 13-14). This might make it easier to conceive: Rhetors were the first-century version of our rock stars. They were the celebrities in a society where one gained status, as one does now, by being seen with one of them or, better, by being perceived to be in the inner circle of the famous person. The system of patronage in the first century fed this and was one of the reasons why Paul refused to accept support from a church that he was currently serving.

Paul's problem with the Corinthian Christians' quarreling and party divisions is that they are acting just like the culture around them: they are "lionizing" the church's orators by dividing up in various "fan clubs." Though preaching the gospel can be seen from rhetoric's frame of reference as a situation identical to any other rhetorical situation, Paul insists that there are crucial differences in each key component — speaker, speech, and hearer. (For more on rhetoric as a powerful, nonneutral frame of rationality, see André Resner, Jr., *Preacher and Cross: Person and Message in Theology and Rhetoric* [Grand Rapids: Eerdmans, 1999].) The speaker is not a celebrity or rock star, but a slave and a steward (1 Cor. 4:1). The hearers are assembled together not so much to hear and judge a message based on its aesthetic characteristics and the speaker's powers of persuasion, but they are the community of faith assembled to worship and glorify God, and to edify and build one another up. The message of the day is not whatever the speaker decides, but the nonnegotiable word of the cross, the crucifixion and resurrection of the Messiah. Paul's task in 1 Corinthians 1-4 is to reorient the Corinthian church to the way they ought to think about their preachers, the message, and themselves, especially in distinction from the ways they had been trained to think about analogous situations of oration and assembly.

In 1:10-18 Paul differentiates baptism from preaching the gospel, and preaching the gospel from eloquent wisdom. He asks (in 1:13) a series of rhetorical questions, all of which assume a negative answer: "Has Christ been divided? Was Paul crucified for you? Or were you baptized in the name of Paul?" Stated in the affirmative, Paul is emphasizing that "Christ has not been divided, and neither should you be. Christ was crucified and is your sole allegiance. You were baptized into Christ, so disband the 'We Love Paul' party and let Christ be your chief identifying character." Paul's focus on baptism probably means that they were misusing it, perhaps by taking pride in the preacher who had baptized them. But just as he was willing to alienate the "Paul" group by his sarcastic questions of verse 13, he punctuates that alienation by thanking God that he hadn't baptized many of them so that they could use that as fodder for their schisms. "For Christ did not send me to baptize but to proclaim the gospel, and not with eloquent wisdom, so that the cross of Christ might not be emptied of its power." Though we know from the larger Pauline corpus of writing that Paul closely linked baptism to the gospel (cf. Rom. 6:1-11; Gal. 3:23-28), when baptism was being misused to cause division Paul drew a line in the sand and differentiated it from the gospel. Baptism thus becomes dependent on the preaching of the gospel, but — and this is important — preaching the gospel is not a tool for the human preacher to secure more baptisms for his or her record. Since preaching is the continuation of the cross event, the preacher is not permitted to manipulate it for the ends of personal self-promotion or the creation of personal fan clubs. Preaching is not a celebrity-making or celebrity-sustaining enterprise. And baptism is not a means by which people get in the inner circle of the famous person. Paul would rather baptize no one than have baptism misunderstood and misused, and the proclamation thus corrupted.

This brings us to Paul's second important differentiation. Paul says he deliberately refrained from using "eloquent wisdom" in preaching the gospel "so that the cross of Christ might not be emptied of its power." Some have interpreted this to mean that Paul used no rhetoric in his preaching, adhering rather to a wooden recitation of the cross event. If, however, Paul's letters give us a clue into his preaching, which most scholars believe is true, Paul was not averse to using rhetoric. In fact, his argument here "against rhetoric" is in the middle of a tightly and persuasively argued piece of deliberative rhetoric! (For more on this issue see Resner, chap. 3.) Paul's differentiation of "eloquent wisdom" from proclaiming the gospel must be seen not only as Pauline irony, but as part of the irony inherent to the gospel itself. It could be argued that there is no nonrhetorical way of preaching. The issue becomes: How does one use rhetoric in the preaching of the gospel in such a way that the gospel itself leads and guides rhetoric's use? Another way of getting at the issue is to ask which of the following carries the freight in preaching: the death of Jesus or the rhetorical forms employed by preachers who, by the mystery and power of God, continue that event into our present situations? Or what is the relationship between Christ's crucifixion and resurrection and our proclamation of that event in words and gestures? Though in the beginning the gospel was the event of Christ crucified itself, subsequent instantiations of that event have included the words we say and the lives we lead. Incarnation, revelation, and even salvation continue through the fragile means of personal witness and experience. How, though, do we use our words and our lives to bear witness in faithful ways to Christ without ourselves becoming the focus? This is the tension inherent to preaching, a tension which is sustained often by irony. The danger exists, however, for the misuse of the means and the subsequent contamination of the end.

Perhaps the most striking statement by Paul here is that the efficacy of the cross's power could somehow be affected by our (mis)use of eloquent wisdom. Any strong theology of the Word has a problem with the insinuation that the human component of preaching could hamstring what God desires to accomplish in the Word in any way. Yet that is how radical Paul's assertion here is. It is a word intended to give preachers and hearers pause, hopefully forcing a kind of personal introspection about the motives behind our preaching and our ministries. The message of our preaching, since it is more than a manipulable set of phrases but is in fact a locus point for the power of God, is inherently a cause for consternation or praise. "For the message about the cross is foolishness to those who are perishing, but to us who are being saved it is the power of God." Unlike other forms of oratory, like sales or the Toastmasters Club, the preacher's message is one that is known — maybe too well. Or, perhaps nowadays, it is one that has largely been forgotten, especially in its potency to alienate and attract. Paul states that the message of the cross was foolishness to the perishing but God-power to the one "being saved." Such comments assume something about the message that has been lost through time. Paul knows those for whom the gospel is absolutely moronic ("foolishness" = Gk. *mōria*). Here's why: it was a word which referred to an event that in that culture was indecent. The word was functionally an expletive. Moreover, to connect that event to any god and that god's chosen actions was illogical in the extreme. But for Paul, and for all those who had experienced the gospel's freeing action in their own lives, the word of the cross was ironically the power of God and even their new way of understanding the logic of existence. The cross was the new logic of the new community. Paul wants the Corinthians to use the logic of the cross in understanding the Christian assembly and Christian orators in that assembly.

These verses have important things to say to preachers and who they are, but also to the church and who it is. Preaching from such a text is humbling for preachers, especially as they call those assembled this Sunday to a rightful view of the preacher. All is in service to Christ and to the message of Christ crucified and risen. This is the church's center, its source for unity, and its hope and power for having the same mind and the same purpose. Paul does not mean that the church ought to be blandly uniform in its thinking or acting, but that its thinking operate from the same counter-cultural cross wiring of the cross event proclaimed.

Anyone who has had any experience with congregational "quarrels" or has pondered the divided state of Christianity today has to read Paul's words here with a mixture of amusement and sadness. But do we read them with hope, with the sense that genuine agreement and unity of mind and purpose in the centrality of the message of Christ crucified and raised is still a possibility? Was Paul merely naive in his first-century romantic notions of a church at one with itself? What would such a realization look like in the divided state of Christianity today, much less in the individual circumstances of one denomination or even one congregation? It's hard to say, but if it is to happen at all it is going to happen because God makes it happen. And where is the locus of God's power? That power persists in the ironic message of the cross of Christ. Let preachers focus there. Let Christians have their logical wires crossed there, and God can work miracles anew — even to reconciliation, salvation, unity (now?), and life everlasting.

*André Resner, Jr.*

## Third Sunday in Lent, Year B

First Lesson: Exodus 20:1-17
(Psalm 19)
**Second Lesson: 1 Corinthians 1:18-25**
Gospel Lesson: John 2:13-22

Assuming 1 Thessalonians is the only prior extant letter of Paul, we have here his first *theologia crucis*. In a sense it is not really a theology of the cross. There is nothing here about what God did in Jesus Christ on the cross (as in 2 Cor. 5:21 or Rom. 5:9). Paul is not working on the redemptive nature of the cross, but reflecting on how God works in history. The passage follows Paul's unhappiness with the situation in Corinth. There are divisions in the church. People are rallying around certain leaders. They named the various house churches after famous pioneers of the Christian faith: Peter, Paul, and Apollos. One church even had the gall to name itself after Christ. Presumably these house churches met in the homes of strong (wealthy?) leaders. Some of these leaders must have considered themselves pillars (1 Cor. 11:19), otherwise there would be no factions. But, claims Paul, God doesn't work through power, competition, and self-assurance. God doesn't work the same way the world works. The world seeks wisdom *(sophia)* while, in contrast, the effectiveness of God appears in foolishness *(mōria)*.

Wisdom is the key term in this passage. As we shall see, it has very broad implications. We can eliminate some meanings, however. It does not mean knowledge *(gnōsis)* or what we might call learned information. Or, while wisdom may imply intelligence, it is not necessarily a mark of education. Education *(paideia)* in the Greco-Roman world centered heavily on writing and communication (rhetoric). No, we suspect Paul here is using *sophia* in a rather narrow sense. It must be close to "verbal persuasion." This entire passage originates with Paul's reflection that he was sent to proclaim the good news, though not with skillful rhetoric: "For Christ did not send me to baptize but to proclaim the gospel, and not with eloquent wisdom, so that the cross of Christ might not be emptied of its power" (1:17). Paul did not want his listeners to be overcome by his speaking skills: "My speech and my proclamation were not with plausible words of wisdom, but with a demonstration of the Spirit and of power, so that your faith might rest not on human wisdom but on the power of God" (1 Cor. 2:4-5). Accepting the good news was not a matter of intellectual consent, but actualization in life of the redemptive nature of the cross. Instead of preaching wisdom, Paul preached foolishness ("through the foolishness of our proclamation" [1:21]). It may very well be that Paul was a great writer but not necessarily a good speaker. Later the Corinthians said of him, "His letters are weighty and strong, but his bodily presence is weak, and his speech contemptible" (2 Cor. 10:10). And Paul admitted that he was "untrained in speech, but not in knowledge [*gnōsis*]" (2 Cor. 11:6).

It is important to clarify Paul's use of wisdom in this passage. We need to note that, as a Jew, Paul certainly treasured wisdom. In Hebrew history the wise man (Job 29) and the wise woman (2 Sam. 14:1-14; 20:1-22; Jer. 9:17) played a very important role in the tribal structure. Wise people gave advice (Job 29:21), inspired confidence among the people, and made judgments that could protect the marginal (Job 29:10-17). Some readers suspect

159

this Wisdom at the gate was a feminine quality of God, perhaps even the fourth member of the Godhead:

> Does not wisdom call,
>     and does not understanding raise her voice?
> On the heights, beside the way,
>     at the crossroads she takes her stand;
> beside the gates in front of the town,
>     at the entrance of the portals she cries out:
> "To you, O people, I call,
>     and my cry is to all that live.
> O simple ones, learn prudence;
>     acquire intelligence, you who lack it."          (Prov. 8:1-5)

At least the female figure Wisdom was there from the beginning: "When he established the heavens, I was there" (Prov. 8:27). For the most part wisdom was expressed by elders in a local village (Ruth 4:2), but as the monarchy developed there arose also wise people who could discern signs and give political advice (2 Sam. 16:23). Joseph (Gen. 41:1-45) and Daniel (Dan. 2:47) would be good examples of the court type that had received the gift of wisdom. Both Joseph and Daniel were apocalyptic-type wise men who could discern dreams and mysteries *(razim)*. Paul himself identified with apocalyptic wise people. In something of a rhetorical tour de force, Paul claims he is a wise man and can interpret the mysteries of God ("But we speak God's wisdom, secret and hidden, which God decreed before the ages for our glory" [1 Cor. 2:7]).

So obviously, wisdom in itself is not the issue. It is smooth talk, persuasive speech. Indeed, Paul uses Isaiah 29:14 to compose a rhetorical question regarding the wise — not the wise people of the village, or even the court, but the scribe and the debater. Unfortunately for some of us, he is attacking the verbal methodology of professors, teachers, and preachers!

Paul's attacks on rhetoric were against the Greeks — Greek educators and philosophers. In contrast to the Greeks, the Jews seek a sign. The contrast is immediately apparent. Greeks (non-Jews) are moved to action by persuasion. Jews are moved to action by some event that indicates divine direction. Moses and Aaron gave signs to Pharaoh that he ignored. To the Jews Moses gave the sign of an outstretched hand (Exod. 3:12, 20). Their firstborn were saved by the sign of blood on the doorpost (Exod. 12:13). It didn't matter how persuasive Moses might have been, for the Jews required a divine sign.

Again Paul is treading on thin ice. First, non-Jews also sought a sign. Few major decisions and certainly few battles were fought without consulting an oracle (as at Delphi). Secondly, the cross itself was indeed a sign. The Jews had wanted Jesus to give them a sign: "The Pharisees came and began to argue with him, asking him for a sign from heaven, to test him. And he sighed deeply in his spirit and said, 'Why does this generation ask for a sign? Truly I tell you, no sign will be given to this generation'" (Mark 8:11-12; see also Matt. 16:1; Luke 11:16; John 6:30). Eventually Jesus did give them a sign — the cross. It was the wrong sign. It wasn't a sign of restored power or the coming of God's reign centered in Jerusalem. The sign rather was a symbol of failure, the Roman means of criminal execution. So while the cross was foolishness to the Greeks, it was a stumbling block to the Jews. The Greek word translated stumbling block is actually *skandalon,* an offense or cause for sin. Stumbling block is an appropriate translation. When a stone building was constructed, the cornerstone of the foundation extended out a few inches. As they rounded the corner, workers and others would sometimes trip over the extruding cornerstone. A cornerstone is necessary, but it can also impede progress for those who do not recognize it. Paul picked up this dual meaning, using both Isaiah 8:14-15 and 28:16, to say that Jesus is both the precious cornerstone of Zion and the rock of stumbling for those who seek a sign: "Why not? Because they did not strive for it on the basis of faith, but as if it were based on works. They have stumbled over the stumbling stone, as it is written, 'See, I am laying in Zion a stone that will make people stumble, a rock that will make them fall, / and whoever believes in him will not be put to shame'" (Rom. 9:32-33).

This is a painful passage for many of us. Like the Greeks, we have been trained to persuade. People in our communities often do believe that TV personality, that preacher, or that teacher who inspires the most. We know full well that persuasion only lasts as long as the persuader continues. Paul argues that self-giving action (the cross) creates a community that can exist without the rhetorician. At the same time, we can be excited about the Christian faith when we see growth in numbers, faith statements by prominent athletes, believers cured despite medical prognoses. They are signs! God is at work in the world! We, too, find the sign of failure, the cross, more than we can bear. Is God really speaking through the poor and are the wealthy doomed? Does the future of Christianity lie with the impoverished nations of Africa? Is the Christian civilization defunct? How can we read the sign?

*Graydon F. Snyder*

## Fourth Sunday after the Epiphany, Year A

First Lesson: Micah 6:1-8
(Psalm 15)
**Second Lesson: 1 Corinthians 1:18-31**
Gospel Lesson: Matthew 5:1-12

You need your glasses to find your glasses. If you wear spectacles, you know what I mean. You wake up in the morning, instinctively reach for your glasses on the bed stand next to you, and they're not there. You put them down somewhere different before getting into bed last night, somewhere "safe," and now you don't remember the safe place. So you start groping around, feeling the tops of tables and dressers, knocking things over. If you only had your glasses, it would make it a lot easier to find them.

That is a parable of what it is like to be "in Christ." "In Christ" you see things you don't, that you can't, when you're not "in Christ." You can be looking at the very same thing and see something different. That's what Paul says about preaching's message of the cross. "To us who are being saved it is the power of God," but "the message of the cross is foolishness to those who are perishing." To perceive this otherwise offensive, indecent, and illogical word as anything other than the functional expletive that it was in Paul's Greco-Roman setting, one had to have experienced, and be in the process of experiencing, the saving power of that Word of the cross. Insiders see what outsiders cannot. The experience of the cross becomes the lens for seeing the cross as lifeline rather than death nail, as glory rather than shame, as power and wisdom rather than futility and foolishness.

But why does Paul need to tell the Corinthians this? Since they are "in Christ," hasn't their vision been cruciformly corrected? Yes and no. They are not using their cruciform lenses in all the situations they ought to. They have found it more "natural" (*sarkinos*) to exchange their lenses of the cross for their cultural lenses on matters pertaining to the message, the preacher, and their community life. Paul stresses in these opening chapters of 1 Corinthians that it was the cross that got them into Christian community and it is the cross which continues to be their way of seeing rightly the nature of reality.

The wisdom (*sophia*) lens, the classical rhetorical tradition of philosophy, has failed to make God known clearly. Paul argues that God delights in confounding the world's so-called wisdom pursuit of the knowledge of the gods and the apprehension of meaning by choosing a means of revelation which conflicts with everything the world and its natural ways of perceiving would deem credible. "God decided, through the foolishness of our proclamation, to save those who believe" (1:21). The proclamation is foolish on two counts: (1) its content and (2) its form. Martin Hengel shows why Paul's message conflicted with both Jewish and Greek frameworks of rationality and decency:

> To believe that the one pre-existent Son of the one true God, the mediator at the creation and the redeemer of the world, had appeared in very recent times in out-of-the-way Galilee as a member of the obscure people of the Jews, and even worse, had died the death of a common criminal on the cross, could only be regarded as a sign of madness. The real gods of Greece and Rome could be distinguished from mortal men by the very fact that they were *immortal* — they had absolutely nothing in common with the cross as a sign of shame *(aischune)* (Hebrews 12:2), an infamous stake *(infamis stipes),* the "barren" *(infelix lignum)* or "criminal wood" *(panourgikon xulon),* the "terrible cross" *(maxima mala crux)* of the slaves of Plautus, and thus of the one who, in the words of Celsus, was "bound in the most ignominious fashion" and "executed in a shameful way." (*Crucifixion in the Ancient World and the Folly of the Message of the Cross* [Philadelphia: Fortress, 1977], p. 111)

Before this message Jewish hearers stumble *(skandalon)* and Greek hearers scoff in derision *(mōria)* (1:23). The message of the cross is incomprehensible from a worldly point of view, one which operates "according to the flesh" *(kata sarka)*. However, in the new community formed by the cross-event proclaimed, *kata sarka* has been dethroned. The cross requires a hermeneutics of suspicion regarding all humanly contrived ways of knowing. *Kata sarka* judgments, evaluations, and conclusions, such as those derived from rhetoric, no longer accord with "reality" as seen through the cruciform lens of Christian community and existence.

Why, then, do some believe this Word? Before one has one's glasses, how does find them? How does the unsightly word of the cross gain any adherents? Who can see well enough to find the means for one's sight?! For Paul, the answer to this question lies in the realm of God's mysteries. Those who believe are those "who are called" (1:24), "those who are being saved" (1:18), those who have come to believe through a servant of the word (like Paul or Apollos), but only "as the Lord assigned to each" (3:5). For just as belief unto salvation does not happen as the result of the powers of a persuasive preacher, neither does it happen due to the powers of a tenacious will on the part of any individual. Paul's frustrating evangelistic mantra is: "God gives the growth" (3:5-9). Those who discover that they see, therefore, see "Christ the power of God and the wisdom of God" (1:24).

Alexandra Brown helpfully summarizes Paul's argument to this point: "Thus far in Paul's discourse the cross has functioned in three central ways. First, it has dislocated its hearers by calling into question their ways of knowing (1:18). Second, it has revealed God's purpose to save, not through wisdom, but through the 'folly of the cross itself' (1:21-25); and third, it has demonstrated God's destruction of the old world (with its valued human assets of strength, wisdom, nobility) and creation of the new world (into which he calls the weak, ignoble, the nonexistent; 1:26-31)" (*The Cross and Human Transformation: Paul's Apocalyptic Word in 1 Corinthians* [Minneapolis: Fortress, 1995], p. 96).

This may explain why the "word of the cross" was heard well by those whose experience of the dominant culture was not the best (1:26-31). Since the dominant culture and social world tends to harm those who are not in power, those on the margins ("the weak, the ignoble, the nonexistent"), a word that stands outside of that dominating and oppressing realm can be seen as freeing. The apocalyptic word of the cross establishes in this world the community of the world to come, the eschatological *ekklēsia,* which functions as a subculture here and now that subverts the dominant and domineering patterns of worldly culture. In Paul's time this meant that those who had been societally controlled people, such as slaves, women, and Gentiles, were now set free to be full citizens in God's unusual kingdom.

The paradox which attends the message (1:18-25) is thus evident in the makeup of the church (1:26-31), as it is in the way Paul proclaims the message (2:1-5). Paul's "demonstration" *(apodeixis)* of its truth was not carried out *kata sarka,* nor in a way that the "natural person" (the *pyschikos* of 2:14) would necessarily understand. Rather, it was something that the Spirit of God undertook "so that your faith might not rest on human wisdom but on the power of God" (2:5).

Two results are driven home by Paul: (1) by God's ironic and paradoxical gospel, God shames the wise and the strong of the world, and (2) since God is the source of our life in Christ Jesus, there are no grounds for any human — preacher or believer — to boast other than "in the Lord."

"Shame" here is a strong word. It indicates that God is in no flirting contest with the world or its "powerful leaders" (cf. Sinclair Lewis's *Elmer Gantry* [New York: New American Library Classics, 1982] for a strident critique of American Christianity's inversion of Paul's vision). God doesn't need the world's "strong" and "wise" to do endorsements for the gospel, the church, or Jesus. In fact, God seems to delight in exactly the opposite. When the world's "strong" and "wise" sell the gospel, the possibility always exists that people believe simply because of the famous or beautiful person, or that they might be seen with the famous person and thus get in fifteen minutes of fame themselves. God's strange world of reversals subverts this way of thinking and operating. It resists such misuses. It is God who chooses (1:30), and God chooses the opposite of what the world would so that there is no confusion: this is the work of God, and it cannot be confused with the work of the world's brightest and best.

An ongoing question that this text raises is whether or not there is a material point of contact *(Anknüpfungspunkt)* in humankind for the gospel. Barth strongly said, "No!" Brunner said, "Yes, though in a fragmented, post-fall sense." (For a readable and evocative discussion of these crucial issues, see Garrett Green, *Imagining God: Theology and Religious Imagination* [Grand Rapids: Eerdmans, 1998].) Paul's words here could be construed to support either position. In this context Paul seems quite proto-Barthian in his insistence that those who are "in Christ" are there because of God's call, God's choice, and God's draw, without any reciprocal action on humankind's part. Even faith — unmentioned here — seems to be a gift given in God's miraculous move of salvation by fiat. But then Paul's proto-Brunnerian side shows in his calling of the Corinthians to consider their own experience. Is the fact that there are a majority of the world's weak and foolish in the church due to God's move by fiat or the attractiveness of such a countercultural community to the misfits and mistreated of the world? And how are preachers to preach if they are convinced that it's really nothing they do per se that causes people to believe? Where does the motivation for evangelism and sermon preparation come from if the power and efficacy of preaching are entirely the work of God? And how would anyone presume to judge preaching as "good" or "poor" knowing that it is God who empowers it?

Though much is unclear here, one thing is very clear for Paul: the message of the cross is more than a mere recitation of past events, ordered according to the rhetorical and aesthetic standards of the speaker or hearers currently present. Rather, Paul's gospel announces "Jesus Christ the Crucified and Risen One — to be God's eschatological act of salvation" (Rudolf Bultmann, *Theology of the New Testament,* trans. Kendrick Grobel [New York: Scribner, 1954], 1:3). This eschatological event broke into history once, but continues to break into every history in which it is proclaimed anew. When it does so, God works the miracle of salvation, reconciliation, and the creation of new community. By the grace and providence of God, preachers are

165

permitted to be involved in God's mysterious activities through means and toward ends that God controls.

*André Resner, Jr.*

## Fifth Sunday after the Epiphany, Year A

First Lesson: Isaiah 58:1-9a, (9b-12)
(Psalm 112:1-9, [10])
**Second Lesson: 1 Corinthians 2:1-12, (13-16)**
Gospel Lesson: Matthew 5:13-20

Does Paul here dismiss the whole of classical philosophy and rhetoric, as some have understood? Before we answer we must remember that his words of "dismissal" are themselves artfully eloquent in their persuasive power and intent. Paul's "radical Christian rhetoric" reminds me of David Jasper's words: "Orators, we know, are naughty in their art of persuasion, but to be no orator is to be truly naughty in mischievous subversion of art by art itself" ("The Christian Art of Missing the Joke," in *Rhetoric, Power, and Community* [Louisville: Westminster/John Knox, 1993], p. 136). Paul's potent irony reminds us that preaching the gospel is paradoxical in divine proportions. This is because although there is a speaker, message, and hearer in the situation of preaching — the classic components of the rhetorical situation — and though one can analyze the situation of preaching using all the sophisticated rhetorical and communication tools known to humanity, the essential of preaching the gospel — God — still eludes any human's hermeneutical and phenomenological grasp.

Good preachers are concerned that people believe their message. They care enough to prepare well, exegete the text and the context carefully, pair appropriate stories with Scripture's claims, and work hard with language so as to maximize the possibility of a hearing. They keep up on the latest and best in homiletical theory and read good literature so their service of the word in language and imagery is shaped in aesthetically faithful ways. They pray and attempt to live deeply, so that their preaching comes out of faith

166

even as it seeks to awaken and deepen faith. And yet, Paul tosses a lit stick of dynamite into the collective laps of not just grubby pulpit sophists but also of all the faithful proclaimers who do their best to do their homiletical duty to God and their churches. "When I came to you . . . I did not come proclaiming the mystery of God to you in lofty words or wisdom. For I decided to know nothing among you except Jesus Christ, and him crucified. And I came to you in weakness and in fear and in much trembling. My speech and my proclamation were not with plausible words of wisdom, but with a demonstration of the Spirit and of power, so that your faith might rest not on human wisdom but on the power of God."

Is this a call for bland, monotone, preacher-don't-get-in-the-way-of-the-message sermons? Or is it a refocusing of the preaching event as rhetorical event to that one aspect that humans and their wisdom cannot measure, manipulate, or touch, namely, God? The purpose clause in verse 5 drives it home: *"so that your faith might rest not on human wisdom but on the power of God."* The question remains, however: What do we do about the use of rhetoric or aesthetics in preaching? If Paul jettisons such for faithful preaching, then no matter how much they may nod their theological approval at Paul's admonitions, preachers and homileticians in America must confess to putting pragmatic hands over their ears and eyes. They know all too well that the reward system in churches and theological seminaries would have a hard time computing the antiaesthetic mandate of the apostle.

It is possible — we've probably all experienced it on one end or the other — to use language in such an outrageous, manipulated, or selfish way that even though our message is ostensibly the gospel, the preacher and his or her agenda or self is the focus. Is Paul arguing against this use of rhetoric? It is sure that he would oppose such misuse, but it is simply not clear what misuse of rhetoric Paul has in mind here.

One could argue that there is no purely nonrhetorical way of communicating. If that's the case, then we're really talking about a matter of degrees. Certainly Paul did not get up to preach and just say over and over, "CHRIST CRUCIFIED. CHRIST CRUCIFIED. CHRIST CRUCIFIED." What separates a parrot from a preacher? How much rhetoric is too much? How much did Paul use in his preaching? Where does one cross the line that separates the safe and good country of the gospel from the scary and dangerous country of rhetorical eloquence?

Everything we say about Paul's own oral proclamation is pure speculation. We have no sermons: no videos, no tapes, no sermon manuscripts or outlines. (Luke's account of Paul's preaching is generally considered inadmissible evidence, but if it were consulted we would see a keen aesthetic side to Paul's preaching.) All we have are his letters, which are themselves power-ful testimonies to Paul's rhetorical skill (for a discussion of this and perti-nent bibliography, see André Resner, Jr., *Preacher and Cross: Person and Mes-sage in Theology and Rhetoric* [Grand Rapids: Eerdmans, 1999], esp. chap. 3). Moreover, most Pauline scholars believe that Paul's letters give us a good window into his preaching. Therefore some speculation is better informed than others. The "aesthetics of rhetoric" question for preaching is not an "either/or" situation. It is, rather, a "how to" situation. For Paul's "every protest of ineloquence bows to the force of his masterful irony and para-dox" (Karl Plank, *Paul and the Irony of Affliction* [Atlanta: Scholars Press, 1987], p. 1). And there is one condition which lies underneath all of Paul's personal protestations of eloquence: God.

God is the condition of preaching. God is the source of preaching's effi-cacy. God is subject, verb, and object of preaching. Paul gives it all over to God. Paul cares that people believe, just as you and I do, but Paul knew — *he really knew* — that if and when someone believes, it is due purely to the work of God. This is why Paul insisted that his speech and proclamation were not "with persuasive words of wisdom" (2:5): because although the preaching situation looks just like a competitive situation like those one could see any day around Corinth, it was momentously different. For it was God who brought faith into and out of the preaching situation; Paul's preaching was "a demonstration of the Spirit and of power," not an argument of persua-sion in the classical sense. Even though Paul knew preaching entailed the person of the preacher, the logos of the message, and the people who stood and sat as hearers, all human components here must bow to the reality of God. For God is the source of preaching's power, even as God is the condi-tion of all true preaching.

"Power" must be understood in terms of the context's description of the ironic power of the gospel. Paul's preaching power would not have looked like power unless one were looking at it from the vantage point of the power of the crucified Christ. The paradox which attends the message (1:18-25) is evident in the makeup of the church (1:26-31) and in Paul's proclamation of the word (2:1-5). In this sense Paul's weak but strong preaching was "a demonstration of the Spirit." Paul's "demonstration" *(apodeixis)* of its truth was not carried out *kata sarka* ("according to the flesh") nor in a way that "the natural person" *(psychikos anthrōpos)* (2:14) would understand. Rather, it was something the Spirit of God undertook "so that your faith might rest not on human wisdom but on the power of God" (2:5).

Highlighting Paul's rhetorical astuteness, his "demonstration" *(apodeixis)* was a technical rhetorical proof which Quintilian called "a clear proof," or "a means of proving what is not certain by means of what is certain" (*Institutes* 5.10.7). The proof Paul demonstrates here is based in the Corinthians' own experience of hearing and believing the gospel, of receiving their salvation, and of being initiated into the "being saved" community — all impossible acts without God. Their current divisions indicate, however, that they were "immature," were following a "wisdom of this age," and were acting "naturally" and thus not as spiritually discerning Christians. Paul reminds them, "But we have the mind of Christ" (2:16). This assertion caps the discussion begun in 1:10 where Paul called them to "be united in the same mind." That "mind" of unity is the mind of the crucified Christ. It is a community mind-set that is shaped christologically. "What was begun in the dismantling of intellectual and social structures by the rhetoric of the cross now reaches its completion in the consciously cruciform mind" (Alexandra Brown, *The Cross and Human Transformation: Paul's Apocalyptic Word in 1 Corinthians* [Minneapolis: Fortress, 1995], p. 139). This "consciously cruciform mind" will result in a cruciform community of faith that lives out the gospel, that communicates the gospel, and that understands its community orators in ways that are consistent with the cruciform mind-set.

This is one of the most difficult and most debated sections of Paul's entire Corinthian correspondence. To preach on a text which is about preaching is meta-preaching at its height! This text again humbles preachers and church — all those in the household of faith — forcing all human ways of knowing to bow before the throne of God's own might and wisdom. It invites all into a world that is seen only through the window that the cross provides. It cajoles its hearers into a way of understanding and perceiving reality which is driven by the Holy Spirit of God, even — perhaps especially — a way of perceiving which will conflict with the world's ways of understanding. It reminds us that we are dependent — always — on God for what we know and experience in the new realm of the church. "We speak God's wisdom, secret and hidden, which God decreed before the ages for our glory" (2:7). We are reminded that our hope for unity is in "the mind of Christ" which we share, but that mind is defined perpetually in this world by the cross. Can the church live in the sustained irony that God gives through the cross? Can it encourage its preachers to shape their preaching ministries around the same paradoxical goal, even if at times that may mean a preaching ministry that is defined by criteria that the rhetorical aesthetes of our time disdain? Can preachers themselves put their lives and destinies in the hands of God, worrying more about the God who entrusted the ministry of the Word to them than about the temporal gains of the politically charged reward systems of this world?

*André Resner, Jr.*

# Sixth Sunday after the Epiphany, Year A

First Lesson: Deuteronomy 30:15-20
(Psalm 119:1-8)
**Second Lesson: 1 Corinthians 3:1-9**
Gospel Lesson: Matthew 5:21-37

Paul here describes the Corinthian Christians quite differently than he did in his thanksgiving (1:4-9). There he portrayed them as graced by God in Christ Jesus; as enriched in Christ in every way, in speech and knowledge of every kind; and as not lacking in any spiritual gift (1:5-7). Now they are people of the flesh, babies in Christ, breast-fed when he was with them and as yet unweaned. They are "fleshly" *(sarkinoi)* (3:1, 3 [twice]), "behaving according to human inclinations." One wonders how the rhetorical effect of Paul's argument would differ if the two sections were flip-flopped.

The evidence for their childishness (not to be confused with the positive quality of childlikeness) is just what he named back in 1:10-12: jealousy, quarrels, and party division over preacher preference largely because of a basic misunderstanding of the nature of orators in the church. To act like they are acting in their dividing up over preachers — only Paul and Apollos are named here — is to prove that they are failing to tap into the resources for discernment and community life that they have in Christ.

This, too, is ironical argument, since Paul attacks those who thought they were wise, mature, and strong and relabels them as fleshly. "Fleshly" does not imply any kind of sexual immorality in this context. Rather, it has to do with their manner of cognitive operation and spiritual discernment: they are thinking from a human point of view, specifically using the categories and standards of the classical rhetorical tradition in the way they view, value, and treat their community orators. Paul has to perform surgery on

170

their spiritual and cognitive organs using the cross as his scalpel. He must redefine for them who he and Apollos are, since from the classical rhetorical vantage point the community orators have been assumed to be celebrities from whom "groupies" could gain status by association. Paul reorders their universe by reidentifying himself: "What then is Apollos? What is Paul? Servants through whom you came to believe, as the Lord assigned to each. I planted, Apollos watered, but God gave the growth. So neither the one who plants nor the one who waters is anything, but only God who gives the growth. The one who plants and the one who waters have a common purpose, and each will receive wages according to the labor of each. For we are God's servants, working together; you are God's field, God's building."

Paul and Apollos, far from being celebrities from whom anyone can gain status by association, are "servants" *(diakonoi).* "Servant" is Paul's favorite term of self-designation. His biting questions, "What is Apollos? What is Paul?" are intended to express disdain. "So, you think you belong to Apollos or Paul? You think they're in competition for the greatest preaching, the greatest following, the most important, biggest budget, the most influential ministry? Do you not realize that they are nothing but servants?!" Paul pulls back the curtain on the Wizard and reveals to them that, though they may want to have such famous figures, every time this happens in the church — in Christ — it is a deception and a corruption. It is, in fact, a kind of idolatry. For the famous person is always the "idol" that the masses want to be around, get to know, have their picture taken with. Paul is clear that their idolization of preachers is the chief biblical sin since it is, like all other forms of idolatry, a placing of focus on something other than God. Anything that takes the place that only God should have is idolatry. Anything that occupies one's imagination more than God is an idol. The Corinthians are idolaters, and their preachers are their idols.

Paul knocks the idols off the cart and promptly puts them in their proper perspective and to their proper work, namely, serving God and the church. God has used them as agents of faith, but God assigned each. There is an ambiguity in the text just here: Does the Lord assign the faith of each who believes or the work of each servant who delivers the word? In this context, it is most likely a reference to the duties of each servant of the word. However, it is possible that double entendre is at work here, for both meanings are complementary to each other: (1) the Lord has assigned the service of each preacher, and because of this each servant of the word is nothing more than an agent of God's work; and (2) the Lord has assigned the faith of each believer, and because of this no preacher can boast that his or her skill brought about the faith of anyone who believes. Every link

171

in the chain of the proclamation of the gospel is owned by and dependent upon God.

Using farming or gardening imagery, Paul likens his and Apollos's work among the Corinthians to different necessary tasks in sowing and nurturing: "I planted, Apollos watered." Certainly such work needs to be done in order for things to grow, but these roles can be assigned by the field's owner to just about anyone. And though they are agents of the process, neither has ultimate power over the seed or the germination process. For "IT IS GOD WHO GIVES THE GROWTH." This is the Owen Meany–type mantra of the servant of the Word (cf. John Irving, *A Prayer for Owen Meany* [New York: William Morrow, 1990]). Paul is unafraid to trample on the self-esteem sensitivities of preachers. Though some go into ministry with unresolved self-worth-type issues, Paul would counsel pulpit abstinence for such until they could accept the servant role of the preaching assignment. For some, especially modern sermon-sophists who want to be entrepreneurial CEOs of their own ministry/corporation, Paul's cruciform reorientation of the preacher's role is a bitter pill to swallow: "So neither the one who plants nor the one who waters is anything, BUT ONLY GOD WHO GIVES THE GROWTH" (the "Owen Meany" emphasis is mine, though I think Paul would like it). Though different preachers may have different roles in the process of germination, they "have a common purpose." Literally, the Greek reads "They are one." There is no distinction. There is no competition. Those who are served, that is, the Corinthians, are not to equate the success of any servant's work to the power of that individual, no matter how impressively they turn the spade nor how accurately they slow-drip the water. Servants only plant seed that has been given to them. They water with water given to them. Any growth is due entirely to God. The servants are colaborers in territory that does not even belong to them. They receive their wages and work with, not against, each other. Neither gains any advantage on the other even as one builds on the other's work. "For we are God's servants, working together; you are God's field, God's building." Owned by God, given one's duty by God, empowered to one's service by God, and ultimately held accountable by God, the servant is a conscripted slave laborer by the ultimate of lords — the sole God of everything that is.

The rhetorical impact of Paul's argument here is to unhinge the Corinthian Christians' focus from their human leaders and reattach it to God. The disjunctive particle "but" *(alla)* in verses 6 and 7 is the strong form indicating a radical disjunction. "Paul planted and Apollos watered, BUT God gave the growth. The planter and waterer are nothing, BUT only God who gives the growth." This is Paul's goal here: to name their idolatry and cast it down, and then to have a renewed enthronement of the true and only God. If preachers are feeling marginalized by Paul's harsh words, he would say, "GET OVER IT AND GET FOCUSED ON GOD AGAIN." The almost over-used cliché is appropriate here for preachers and church alike: remember who you are and what you are, but even more importantly, remember whose you are. All is God's: preachers as God's servants; believers as God's fertile field and building under construction; the message as God's seed; the growth as God's mysterious yet ongoing creativity and recreativity.

*André Resner, Jr.*

## Seventh Sunday after the Epiphany, Year A

First Lesson: Leviticus 19:1-2, 9-18
(Psalm 119:33-40)
**Second Lesson: 1 Corinthians 3:10-11, 16-23**
Gospel Lesson: Matthew 5:38-48

In this reading Paul continues his discussion of the significance, or per-haps insignificance, of church leaders. Paul now changes images, however, moving from agriculture to the construction trade. The church in Corinth may be compared to a building. Paul as "founding pastor" laid the founda-tion; another now continues to build the edifice. In the previous verses Paul has reminded the Corinthians that the life of the church does not come from its leadership any more than growth comes from a gardener. Here, however, Paul calls himself a "skilled master builder." Quality of leadership is not irrel-evant after all. Skill and integrity make a difference both in construction and in church leadership. So each new builder must plan and build with care.

At this point Paul names the foundation. No foundation is possible for the church other than the one that has been laid, Jesus Christ. It is not en-tirely clear whether Paul is referring again to his own work, that is, to his own preaching in Corinth, or to the work of God, the one who has provided "the church's one foundation." The latter possibility is theologically more profound.

Earlier in the letter Paul told the Corinthians that the center of his role as an apostle was to preach the gospel (1:17). He is very specific about the content of that preaching: "We proclaim Christ crucified" (1:23). The foundation of the church was laid when the cross of Christ was preached and heard. In light of Paul's understanding of his role as an apostle and in light of his extensive discussion of rhetoric in chapter 2, we can be quite precise about what is at issue in chapter 3. It is not so much leadership, a vague and secular concept, that is at issue but the right preaching of the gospel.

It should be noted that Paul is not writing here of the church as a whole, but of its builders. In our day the clergy might be the equivalent of Paul and Apollos. If this is so, the difficult challenge within the text is directed not at our congregations but at us. It may be true that no other lasting foundation can be laid for the church than the Lord Jesus Christ. But that has not stopped the clergy from trying. Do we try to lay a foundation built from the popular spiritual notions of our day or from our own religious instincts and experiences? Do we substitute for the cross of Jesus Christ an ideology or a program, or ethnic or class identity, or one of a myriad other possibilities? The verse is a solemn warning not so much to the church as a whole, but to us who preach and lead.

This raises a question. If this material is really about leaders rather than the church as a whole, why raise it in a public letter to the whole church? And why raise it now in a sermon to a congregation rather than in an address to clergy or seminarians? In Corinth a "presenting problem" of the troubled church was that some Christians identified too strongly with particular leaders and formed too high an estimate of their significance. Hidden behind this text may also be Paul's awareness that some in Corinth had formed too low an estimate of Paul's own work. Analogous problems may face the church today. Anyone familiar with the situation of the contemporary church knows that the "building" can still be threatened by disputes over leadership. It was vital then, as also now, that the church as a whole form a right estimate of the role and significance of its leaders and preachers.

At this point the lectionary eliminates four verses, a peculiar and unfortunate decision. Preachers of traditions that allow freedom with respect to the lectionary ought to, if they plan to preach from the passage, restore the deleted verses. But even if we cannot do so, we preachers must "read, mark, learn, and inwardly digest." Let it be said again: this part of Paul's letter, both verses retained by the lectionary and those deleted, is directed not to the church but to the equivalent of the clergy. The preacher must hear these words even if the congregation does not. They are an invitation to self-examination by the preacher. We must ask, long before we mount the pulpit, what is the quality of our work, in preaching as in all other things? Will our preaching stand the test of fire?

The lectionary, however, jumps forward to verse 16. At this point we hear what kind of building Paul and the other laborers have been constructing. "Do you not know that you are God's temple and that God's Spirit dwells in you?" There may be a homiletical difficulty here. Some of our listeners may well interpret these words in light of the very similar words in 6:19: "Do you not know that your body is a temple of the Holy Spirit?" That verse is frequently used in moral exhortations, especially to young people, to avoid alcohol, tobacco, and sex. The echoes of juvenile moral instruction can be powerful and unpredictable in their effect. It is important therefore to emphasize that Paul is here speaking not of individuals but of the church as a whole. He is addressing "you" plural, the Christians in Corinth as a body.

The image of the church as temple, though not surprising to us, would have been a rich and powerful one for the Christians in Corinth. The purpose of a temple was to serve as the dwelling place of the divine and as a place of sacrifice. But for Paul the temple is no longer a physical edifice. Now the dwelling place of God's Spirit may be found in the life together of the Corinthians. The temple has become for Paul not primarily the name of a building but rather a metaphor for the shared spiritual life of the community. It is an image that Paul would develop at a number of points (cf. 6:19; 2 Cor. 6:16; also Eph. 2:21-22). The basic idea is also present wherever Paul uses the language of temple worship as a metaphor for Christian life, as, for example, in Romans 12:1: "Present your bodies as a living sacrifice."

There is both comfort and challenge in the image of the community as temple. A community that depends on a place or a building for its identity will not long survive, let alone thrive. In these days of declining churches, survival is again a matter of concern. Survival does not come from attachment to buildings. Our buildings are not the temple of God; we are. If the temple of God is found wherever there is a faithful people, God's presence can be found anywhere. It is that presence that alone gives life to the church.

There is also challenge in the image. This transfer of the idea of the temple from building to community raises the significance of the community's life together. The reverence which had once been attached to a temple must now be accorded to the community. To profane or destroy a temple would have been a horrible act of desecration worthy of death. But to destroy the fellowship of the church by any means — the preacher will have no difficulty thinking of church-destroying activities — is likewise sacrilege that will be punished (3:17). Christians often hold our church sanctuaries and even their furnishings in holy awe but can be remarkably casual about the people in the church. Paul reminds us to transfer that awe to those around us. Temples are holy, and a community that is understood as a temple requires holy living.

At this point Paul returns to material he discussed earlier in the letter. The preacher must read Paul's treatment of wisdom and foolishness in light of his discussion of the same terms in chapter 1. But now Paul becomes very specific indeed. Foolishness in the world's terms is a Christian duty. Paul strengthens his point with a combination of two loose quotations from the Old Testament. Human wisdom is futile, for God uses it only to deceive and entrap those who trust in it. If we place our trust in our own wisdom rather than in God, wisdom itself becomes the means of our destruction. (This may also be true of anything else in which we place our trust.) Perhaps the Corinthians had been placing trust not only in their own wisdom but in the wisdom of their leaders. But surely no one should boast in their leaders (cf. 1:29). Paul reverses the catchphrases of the Corinthians. They had said, "I belong to Paul, etc." But Paul says the revered leaders, Paul, Apollos, and Cephas, belong to the Corinthians. But not only that; all things belong to the Corinthians and all things are wrapped up in Christ, to whom they belong, who in turn belongs to God. This is reminiscent of Colossians 1:15-21 and is almost hymnlike in its spiritual intensity. When we truly understand with mind and spirit that we the church are the temple of the living God, we are mystically linked to the whole cosmos and to God's own self.

*Stephen Farris*

# Eighth Sunday after the Epiphany, Year A

First Lesson: Isaiah 49:8-16a
(Psalm 131)
**Second Lesson: 1 Corinthians 4:1-5**
Gospel Lesson: Matthew 6:24-34

1 Corinthians 4 is the conclusion and capstone to the argument that began in 1:10. Paul has had several tasks in this section: (1) to condemn the hero worship of preachers, which is a form of idolatry; (2) to reorient

and equip the Corinthian Christians with the discerning vision that comes via the cross event proclaimed; and (3) to shift the Corinthians' vision from preachers (and the temporal status they can gain from such associations) to God as the one on whom they, and their preachers, are both temporally and eternally dependent.

Though the kind of orator fixation in Corinth was common and could be expected in any other community of the time, for Paul this kind of activity was a serious breach of Christian community. Working from the vantage point of the cross, Paul reorients their natural Corinthian consciousness to reidentifying the objects of their adoration: preachers are nothing more than servants of God (3:5-15, *diakonoi*); the church is God's field and building.

In 4:1-5 the imagery shifts from agriculture to household: preachers are servants and stewards in charge of Someone Else's belongings: "Think of us in this way, as servants of Christ and stewards of God's mysteries." The word used for servant *(hypēretas)* occurs only here in Paul. It originally was used in reference to slaves who rowed in the lower tier of a sailing ship. Paul uses it as a synonym to *diakonos* and as a parallel to *oikonomos,* "steward." The steward was often a slave who had primary management responsibilities of the owner's household. The term implies a kind of delegated authority with which preachers of the gospel of Christ crucified have been entrusted. As stewards, preachers are accountable to God, who is the owner. Paul insists that he has applied *(metaschematizō)* all this to Apollos and himself for the Corinthians' benefit (4:6-7). In other words, the orators they are exalting are not operating with those criteria and are set to resist it. Benjamin Fiore's words here are helpful:

> Paul is intent on awakening his audience's attention to the fact that things are not what they seem to be. In fact, in using the term *metaschematizein* ("to transfer in a figure") . . . Paul expressly states the parenetic purpose behind his remarks. . . . At least the Christian patrons [wish] to resemble those of their groups around sophists and professional rhetoricians. If, then, it was these same highly placed Christians who were guilty of lionizing one teacher over another (1:10; 3:4), of vaunting their own knowledge (3:1; 6:12; 8:13), of making distinctions in the community rooted in pride (4:7; 5:2), or of slighting the poor at the assemblies (11:17-34), then Paul would have to proceed with caution. . . . Paul offers his own example . . . as a help for the community to see things for what they are and not take them as they seem to the world. ("'Cover Allusion' in 1 Corinthians 1-4," *Catholic Biblical Quarterly* 47 [1985]: 89-101)

Paul overturns the normal status indicators and invites the Corinthians to a different vision of the preacher, "Christ's slave *oikonomos.*" Moreover, he dismisses their judgment of him as inconsequential. Faithful, wise stewards recognize to whom they must give account: their owner. For preachers, this means God: "With me it is a very small thing that I should be judged by you or by any human court. I do not even judge myself. I am not aware of anything against myself, but I am not thereby acquitted. It is the Lord who judges me. Therefore do not pronounce judgment before the time, before the Lord comes, who will bring to light the things now hidden in darkness and will disclose the purposes of the heart. Then each one will receive commendation from God" (4:3-5). The normal "lord" of the classical rhetorical situation was the audience. The hearer would decide who was most persuasive, who won the rhetorical sparring match. Orators, knowing this and wanting to do all they could to win, would format their persons and message with the hearer foremost in mind. Aristotle's *On Rhetoric* is a masterful guide for helping rhetors do audience analysis with a view to projecting the kind of excellences *(aretai)* of character and speech that their audience prized. Astute speakers knew that their success depended on the hearer's judgment. Paul pulls the rug out from under this premise. Again he replaces the human court with the divine court. Using theological language to substitute humans instead of God as the ultimate judge of the preaching situation is a form of idolatry. Paul asserts God as the Lord and ultimate judge of the preaching situation, and the timetable of judgment as eschatological.

Although Paul's words here seem especially applicable for those who proclaim the gospel, 1 Corinthians 1-4 is not Paul's Lyman Beecher Lectures for preachers. They are words written to and for the church. Paul's problem is not with Apollos or Peter, but with a community of faith which is failing to operate out of the God-given spiritual resources for discernment that they have "in Christ." The cross shapes those resources and calls into question the idolization of preachers.

Preachers are at great risk in communities where they are accorded the wrong kind of identity and status, even if such imposition of status was well intentioned. For one thing, the elevation of preachers to celebrity or moral-giant status makes it hard for the preacher to be who he or she really is in the midst of the community. It can be fun and ego inflating to be worshiped. Those preachers at greatest risk are those whose egos, whose sense of self, whose identity is weakest. For they are more susceptible to the ecclesiastic neurosis of preacher worship than those whose identity has been and is continuing to be shaped most definitively by the cross event proclaimed.

A fascinating study by Ronald E. Osborn shows how certain models for ministers in America emerged out of the social and cultural matrix of each century. The eighteenth century sought the minister as saint, priest, master, and awakener; the nineteenth century desired the minister as pulpiteer, revivalist, builder, and missionary; the twentieth century required the minister to be manager, counselor, impresario, and teacher (cf. *Creative Disarray: Models of Ministry in a Changing America* [St. Louis: Chalice Press, 1991], p. 5). With "Jesus CEO" as a dominant christological image for the twenty-first century, what is to prevent the capitalistic, consumer-oriented, felt needs–driven church from desiring and selecting a minister to function partly as buoyant master of ceremonies and entertainer and partly as Wal-Mart-style manager and motivator, with the goal of happier, greater, bigger, and more?

The exclamation that is 1 Corinthians 4:1-5 is an ongoing word to preachers and congregations alike not to capitulate to the world's ways of thinking and operating. It is not easy to do, for faith is hard. It is easier for the church to slip into the praise, adoration, and comparison game of preachers than to stay focused on a God that cannot be seen as clearly. And sometimes, insidiously, churches slip into the game in the guise of and with the well-intentioned purpose of preacher encouragement. Congregations must remember that preachers of the gospel are most encouraged when they are called back to the cross, when they are called back to their God-given calling to be servants of Christ and stewards of God's mysteries. The temporal relief of misguided ego inflation of the preacher, even in the name of "encouragement" or "edification," is not worth the long-term cost of such idolatry-flirting, cross-skirting activity. Paul wants them to keep in mind two things: God and the end.

Murphy's Law may suggest that "what can happen, will happen." But Paul's eschatological perspective suggests something much more powerful and orienting for the Christian community: "What will happen, can happen." God will judge then, so let God judge now. All will serve and adore God then, so let all serve and adore God now. What does preacher loyalty look like from an eschatological perspective? What does a church divided up over favorite preachers, a church creating fan clubs and trying to grub for status look like from an eschatological perspective? Gaining an eschatological perspective is another aspect of grinding one's lenses for discernment in the here and now by the cross event proclaimed. It reorients preachers and hearers alike to the one from whom we hope to "receive commendation" in the end, namely, God. Such words of indictment and encouragement remind us of Jesus' parable of the talents in Matthew 25:14-30. Those whose focus has been kept pure, who know whose ministry this is, who remember their identity and role as stewards, who anticipate the re-

179

turn of the master, look forward to hearing the master's words of commendation: "Well done, good and trustworthy slave; you have been trustworthy in a few things, I will put you in charge of many things; enter into the joy of your master."

*André Resner, Jr.*

## Second Sunday after the Epiphany, Year B

First Lesson: 1 Samuel 3:1-10, (11-20)
(Psalm 139:1-6, 13-18)
**Second Lesson: 1 Corinthians 6:12-20**
Gospel Lesson: John 1:43-51

Of all the congregations Paul has established, the Christian church in Corinth seems to be dearest to his heart, yet it causes him more grief than any other. He wrote more to them than to any other group, and he deals with more concrete parish problems in those letters than in any others. He knows these people very well. They are united by their faith in Christ, but he knows that in other aspects of life they are a disparate group — Jews and Gentiles, rich and poor, illiterate and learned, etc. — and he knows how volatile these combinations can be as they deal with mundane affairs of everyday life, all in an environment hostile to their faith.

The larger context of this passage is the divisions in the Corinthian church (chaps. 1, 3) and the sexual impropriety in the Christian community, of which Paul has heard reports (5:1). There have also been instances of Christians suing each other in court (6:1-8), which would have discredited Christians among the Gentile society.

Today's text is a bridge between the chapters before and after this passage. The theme of this section is stated at the end of chapter 6: "glorify God in your body" (v. 20).

Paul's lead-in to this passage (not in the lectionary) reminds the Corinthian believers that "wrongdoers will not inherit the kingdom of God" (v. 9), after which he summarizes a whole list of immoral behaviors. Then he sets the stage by reminding them that they have been "washed . . . sanctified [and] . . . justified in the name of the Lord Jesus Christ and in the Spirit of our God."

With that Paul moves to the specific problem of this text. It is the issue which Paul confronts repeatedly: If we are saved by grace and freed from the law, what then are the "limits" to our freedom? It is only a slightly different version of the problem Paul addressed in the Letter to the Romans: "Should we continue in sin in order that grace may abound?" (Rom. 6:1). In his letter to the Galatians he ran into the same issue: "only do not use your freedom as an opportunity for self-indulgence" (Gal. 5:13).

This text addresses those who think Christianity is strictly a matter of the spirit. No doubt the Greek dualism of body and mind/spirit was a part of people's thinking in Corinth. Dualist thinking consigns religion to the soul and the spirit and can easily rationalize abuse and misuse of one's body, because the spirit is the locus of faith and religious life.

Paul's response to this thinking is the holistic Hebrew understanding of the whole person. The whole being is God's temple (1 Cor. 3:16-17), and abuse of the body is abuse of God's Spirit within us.

It is an appropriate text for us today, because there is a latent gnosticism in American society. Many people consider religion a matter of the spirit or heart, hardly affecting the body at all. If one starts from this kind of dualistic thinking so prevalent today, then adds the typical American misunderstanding of Christian freedom from the law — "Now I can do anything I want" — the result will be as twisted an idea of Christian freedom as anything Paul found in Corinth.

Yes, we are free from the law, Paul says repeatedly, but how do we use our freedom? Remove the law, and what are our guidelines?

Paul's answer, verses 12 and following, begins with a threefold pattern of "not this . . . but this," responding to the slogans he hears people mouth, then refuting them with arguments which would make sense even to Greek non-Christians.

1. "All things are lawful for me," one can say, but one also needs to ask what things are beneficial. Here Paul strikes Greek philosophy with one of its own maxims, namely, that self-indulgence is wrong when it is self-serving at the expense of others. His use of the term "beneficial" *(sympherei)* in 10:23 and 12:7 indicates that he has the good of the community in mind, not mere individual gratification. Even apart from Paul's biblical views, Greek thinkers would be persuaded by his appeal to what is beneficial.

2. "All things are lawful for me," but to succumb to a temptation may well mean one becomes dominated and enslaved by that particular activity.

What then becomes of freedom? Again Paul's argument appeals strongly to the Greek principle that an enlightened individual is one who is moderate in all things and does not allow himself to become enslaved to passion or desire of any kind.

3. Finally, "Food is meant for the stomach and the stomach for food," as if what one eats physically is totally unrelated to any spiritual issues. Exegetes question how far Paul continues quoting his opponents (since the Greek manuscripts don't include quotation marks), but Paul's point is clear: God's judgment falls as heavily upon physical sins as upon spiritual wrongdoing.

Paul leaves the issue of eating for a moment and moves straight to the heart of his thesis. The argument that physical actions are not important because God will destroy physical things overlooks the fact, Paul continues, that our physical bodies are members of Christ. To defile our bodies in any way defiles God within us. Paul bases his argument upon the resurrection of Christ's body (the argument which will be expanded upon in chap. 15): "God raised the Lord and will also raise us by his power" (v. 14). Therefore, as Christ's body was raised, so our bodies are members in him. The bodily resurrection of Jesus is Paul's refutation of the notion that the soul or spirit is the sole locus of God's presence among humans as well as Paul's affirmation that our physical bodies are also God's temple and therefore as much a part of our religious life as the things of the spirit.

Therefore immorality or abuse of any kind to one's physical body is a misuse of our being as God's temple. Paul illustrates this by citing union with a prostitute, which is giving one's body to fornication. The verb "united" is the same in verse 16, "united to a prostitute," and verse 17, "united to the Lord." Physical immorality is the same as any kind of spiritual sin, namely, taking what is the Lord's and giving it over to sinfulness. Paul understands sexual union as more than a physical act. Ever since creation the Old Testament considers sexual union as an intimate bond between man and woman, two people become as "one flesh" (Gen. 2:24). If we are "one flesh" as members with Christ's body, we are also one in spirit with Christ (v. 17). Therefore, to become "one flesh" with a prostitute is to be unfaithful to our union with Christ.

In verse 18 Paul returns to his method of argumentation from verses 12-14 by quoting what an opponent might say in rebuttal, "Every sin that a person commits is outside the body," as if what one does with one's body is not a sin in a spiritual sense. Paul refutes this argument by pointing out again that fornication is a sin *of* the body, that is, the temple of God. Paul's capstone argument follows: Our bodies are not our own to do with as we please. First, our bodies are part of God's creation. Second, and even more importantly, they were "bought with a price" (v. 20), a reference to Christ's sacrifice of his own body. His body was raised from the dead, prefiguring that our bodies will also be resurrected with his.

The passage is an affirmation of creation itself. On one hand Christianity has been plagued for centuries with a lingering gnosticism which perceives Christianity to be a matter of the spirit — exactly the same kind of misunderstanding Paul met among the Corinthians. If our bodies are creations and temples of God, then our concern for others should include not only the salvation of their souls but also the well-being and health of their bodies.

The other extreme we encounter today is a kind of narcissism of one's physical body, a notion rampant in our society. Healthy physical fitness is one thing, but an obsession with some artificial standard of beauty is quite another thing. Why is it that a high percentage of teenagers in our society suffer under the delusion that they're ugly? Why is it that millions of dollars are spent each year for cosmetic medical procedures which contribute nothing to health and well-being, but simply gratify one's desire to look younger and more attractive?

A Jewish Hasidic teacher once said, "Why do you worry about my soul and your body? Be concerned instead about your soul and my body." That advice is a corrective for many of us. The full truth, however, is that we should be concerned about body and soul, both our own and our neighbor's!

Take Paul's thinking one step further. If our physical body is to be revered as a temple of God, then is not the creation itself to be revered as God's work? Care of the world around us is care of God's temple, the creation. In 1967 Lynn White, Jr., a scholar of the Renaissance era, shocked readers when he argued that the Christian church is in large measure responsible for today's exploitation and pollution of the environment ("The Historical Roots of Our Ecological Crisis," *Science,* March 10, 1967). His point was that Christians interpreted Genesis 1:26, 28 ("let them have dominion over . . . subdue [the earth]") as if they could use creation however they pleased. Whether his accusation is true or not, Christians have come to realize that "dominion" means "stewardship" or "care of," because the earth is God's creation. This is not the central theme of this text, but it is related, since care for the physical world includes not only our physical bodies as God's temple but also the creation as God's world.

A sermon on this passage would affirm our physical bodies and the physical world as God's creation. Such a sermon would have as its center the resurrection of Jesus' body. The sermon would draw upon the broad concern Jesus had for the physical health of those around him. His healing work included both the forgiveness of sins as well as a healing of the body.

*Michael Rogness*

## Third Sunday after the Epiphany, Year B

First Lesson: Jonah 3:1-5, 10
(Psalm 62:5-12)
**Second Lesson: 1 Corinthians 7:29-31**
Gospel Lesson: Mark 1:14-20

The first twenty-eight verses of 1 Corinthians 7 are not in the Revised Common Lectionary, but the preacher needs to consider them to make sense of today's text. The chapter begins with admonitions about sexual morality and marriage. Paul's advice closely reflects his own experience. As a wandering missionary, often in trouble and jailed, and often moving quickly to avoid further difficulties, he was not suited to being married. Given the persecutions Christians face, he sees distinct advantage in being single.

Paul also opposes the legalistic Roman view of marriage. According to Roman law, the unmarried were taxed more heavily, and a person under the age of fifty who was divorced or widowed was required to remarry within a year. In a society where the Christian minority was surrounded by non-Christians, finding a suitable mate within a year may have been difficult, and Paul clearly sees the complications when a believer marries a nonbeliever (vv. 10-16). It is no wonder that what appears to us to be Paul's disparaging and pessimistic view of marriage is in part his reaction against laws which forced people into unsuitable marriages due to societal pressure.

Anyone who believes that Paul not only has a discouraging view of marriage but generally regards women as second-class citizens (and church members) should note that his description of marriage reveals a remarkable sense of reciprocal equality totally unknown in the first century: "The husband should give to his wife her conjugal rights, and likewise the wife to her husband. For the wife does not have authority over her own body, but the husband does; likewise the husband does not have authority over his own body, but the wife does" (7:3-4). First-century Greek men would scoff at such an outrageous idea. Such a notion comes straight from Paul's theology, that each of us is a redeemed child of God.

Paul's high view of marriage is also apparent in verses 12-16, where he addresses the situation of a Christian believer married to a nonbeliever, very likely a common situation in the early church. A person who considered marriage merely a convenient social institution might counsel believers to abandon their unbelieving spouses in order to preserve their own faith. Paul's advice is quite different: stay with the unbelieving spouse, first to protect the children from being considered illegitimate or orphaned, but more importantly, because the spouse might become a believer in time. One cannot prevent the unbelieving spouse from leaving the marriage, but the Christian spouse should not destroy the union.

This section can be read as Paul's positive view of marriage. There were probably those ascetics in the Corinthian church who believed that the Christian faith meant the disavowal of earthly life as an attempt to nurture one's spiritual life. Paul is telling these persons that their marriage is a commitment to which they should remain faithful.

As we read through this chapter, we gradually become aware that Paul's advice is predicated upon his assumption that the church is living near the end of time. Today's passage begins with Paul writing that "the appointed time has grown short" (v. 29). All of Paul's advice is given in the shadow of the eschaton. As long as the end is near, there is little sense in starting a family. If you have a family, nurture it, but don't launch out on any long-term new commitments. Follow God's will in your life as you are now (vv. 17-20).

Paul illustrates this principle with a two-verse discourse regarding one of his favorite admonitions: remain as you are with the time remaining. That is, if you are circumcised, let it be. If you aren't, don't seek to be.

The same is true of slavery. If Paul had foreseen Christians living twenty centuries into the future, his theology would surely have led him to crusade against the institution of slavery (see Gal. 3:28; Philem. 15-16). But with Christ soon returning to consummate world history, the wise course of action is to concentrate one's efforts on following God's will steadfastly in whatever circumstance one is living in. With time so short, one looks to eternity rather than earthly reform. Besides, Paul argues, for Christians the condition of slavery is altogether changed: "A slave is a freed person belonging to the Lord, just as whoever was free when called is a slave of Christ" (v. 22).

185

Next Paul addresses the unmarried. He begins with the interesting comment that in this topic "I have no command of the Lord, but I give my own opinion . . ." (v. 25). His principle is the same: "In view of the impending crisis, it is well for you to remain as you are" (v. 26). It is not sinful to marry, but with time so short it is better not to.

This brings us to the actual lectionary text, only three verses. Here Paul draws what sound like radical conclusions from his assumption that he is living near the eschaton. To advise husbands to live as if they had no wives does not mean to ignore their sexual relationship, which Paul already affirmed in verses 1-7, but simply that one's primary attention needs to be on the kingdom to come. Even such deep human emotions as mourning or rejoicing, or the possession of wealth, are less important than the overarching expectation of the world to come.

The remainder of the chapter, verses 32-40, continues with the same theme, that our consideration of marriage is always from the perspective that we are living in the end times. If one reads chapter 7 as a mere commentary on marriage, one might conclude that Paul did not value the institution. However, once we realize that Paul writes from the viewpoint of an eternity soon to come, it is clear that he not only has a high regard for marriage, but that his advice always takes into consideration the well-being of one's spouse.

Probably few sermons are preached on this text. Not only is the reading of these verses in themselves jarring to the modern listener, but a sermon requires extensive explanation of the text's full context. Since Paul's expectation of an imminent eschaton did not take place, we tend to disregard this text.

However, Paul's perspective here fits very well with the Gospel lesson for today, Mark 1:14-20. The three synoptic Gospels agree that Jesus' message as he began his public ministry was that, as Mark puts it, "The time is fulfilled, and the kingdom of God has come near . . ." (Mark 1:15; see also Matt. 4:17 and Luke 4:43).

We may or may not be living in the end times today, but the message of Jesus is that the kingdom of God has arrived among us. It is an eternal kingdom, but God's reign has already begun for God's people. We Christians might not arrange our lives as if the world is soon to end, but we do live knowing that we are already part of the kingdom of eternity.

From that perspective human life takes on a wholly different look. From the standpoint of God's eternal kingdom, the things that are important to people living only in this world don't seem so important.

Paul's conclusions in today's text are valuable for us today. Those who mourn need to remember that death and hardship are not the end of the story. Those who rejoice need to remember that joys on this earth, while real, may be short-lived. But the joy of eternity will last forever. The possession we buy now seldom adds to the happiness of life. "For the present form of this world is passing away" (v. 31).

The great irony of Christians living with the expectation of eternity is that they are more engaged with the present world than ever. Paul's advice to the married and unmarried was in the end an affirmation of their respective states. Some of the greatest movements for social reform in this world have come from those who have a confidence in the grandeur of a world to come, and who wish to work toward this vision even now.

*Michael Rogness*

## Fourth Sunday after the Epiphany, Year B

First Lesson: Deuteronomy 18:15-20
(Psalm 111)
**Second Lesson: 1 Corinthians 8:1-13**
Gospel Lesson: Mark 1:21-28

With this chapter Paul gives an example of the guidelines he has already laid down in chapter 6: "'All things are lawful for me,' but not all things are beneficial." As a bookend to this whole section, Paul repeats the verse once again in 10:23. How does one measure what is "beneficial"? In this chapter it is the good of the community. The issue at stake here is eating food which has been sacrificed to idols. This is not an issue for us now, but the principle Paul lays down is as valid today as it was in the first century.

Paul begins with an introductory contrast between knowledge and love, another of his favorite themes (vv. 1-3).

It was commonplace that after animals were sacrificed their meat was consigned to the local markets for sale. Any knowledgeable Christian would know that since idols don't exist, sacrificed meat carried no stigma, nor would eating such meat mean any tribute or concession to faith in idols or idol worship. People with that obvious knowledge might well feel rather superior to people who would worry about the implications of eating sacrificed meat. They might well look with a sense of smugness, even condescension, upon those who were apprehensive. After all, don't we all feel a bit superior to people who do things out of superstition or odd fixations? We *know* better!

How human it is to realize with pride that we know things others don't, when we can run machines while others stand by helplessly, or when we get a better grade than others, or when others have to ask us for advice because we know how to do something they don't. Who isn't guilty of that?

Such knowledge "puffs up," writes Paul. He knows what we're like.

What is the antidote to the superiority of knowledge? Love. Anything less than that is condescension or pity. So people who feel superior in knowledge are really ignorant of true knowledge, which begins with the assertion that God knows us and loves us — *all* of us, from the retarded child to the Ph.D. physicist. Once we acknowledge that, then we are all on the same level. Only love looks upon others as equal.

Another consideration is that the Corinthian church included both Jews and Gentiles. Jews considered eating meat sacrificed to idols idolatrous, to say nothing of unkosher. Gentiles, on the other hand, who still associated with friends and neighbors, would have difficulty avoiding such meat, both in private homes and on public occasions. For each group it was a problem, though in a different form.

What then should we do about eating meat sacrificed to idols, especially if served and eaten in a place which doubles as a pagan worship place (v. 10)?

Paul's answer is that since idols do not exist, we can of course eat such meat without blasphemy or sin. However, the problem is that "some [believers] have become so accustomed to idols until now, they still think of the food they eat as food offered to an idol; and their conscience, being weak, is defiled" (v. 7). This was clearly not a minor problem in the Corinthian church. Paul returns to this same theme again and again in this letter (9:4 and 10:23-33).

In verse 8 Paul quotes his opponents, a favorite rhetorical device in this letter: "Food will not bring us close to God," as if to say that what we eat doesn't make any difference to Christian living. Paul answers by taking his conclusion one step further: therefore "we are no worse off if we do not eat, and no better off if we do." That being true, then consideration for the faith of others becomes the guideline, and Paul states it thus: "But take care that this liberty of yours does not somehow become a stumbling block to the weak" (v. 9). Paul has brought the argument full circle, from our supposed freedom to the use of freedom *not* to eat such food.

The word for "liberty" (NRSV; "the exercise of your freedom") is *exousia,* normally translated "authority," translated "right" in 9:4. Paul concedes that believers have the right, or authority, to eat or not to eat such meat. But that is not the central issue.

Paul presses the point home in the following verses. What if those "who possess knowledge" eat meat and others who are not altogether free from adherence to idols compromise their faith by following their example, might not their faith be destroyed? One has acted out of knowledge but not out of love, and thus has caused a fellow member in Christ to be lost. The exercise of freedom has become a sin against a fellow believer.

The conclusion of the argument is clear: if by eating such meat I might cause another to fall from faith, I will not eat it. Love takes precedence over the exercise of freedom.

This is not the only place where Paul has confronted this problem. In Romans 14 he addresses the same situation with the same principle: "Those who eat must not despise those who abstain, and those who abstain must not pass judgment on those who eat" (v. 3). "[Let us] resolve instead never to put a stumbling block or hindrance in the way of another" (v. 13). "If your brother or sister is being injured by what you eat, you are no longer walking in love. Do not let what you eat cause the ruin of one for whom Christ died" (v. 15). "Let us then pursue what makes for peace and for mutual upbuilding" (v. 19). The key is always to ask what is beneficial (6:12; 10:23) for other brothers and sisters in Christ. What would be the loving thing to do (v. 1)?

After exegeting and understanding this text, how does one preach it? We don't have the problem of eating meat sacrificed to idols, but we confront exactly the same issue of one person or group wanting to do something which offends another person or group. Pastors live with that situation all the time. Can Paul instruct us?

At what point does one draw the line between exercising freedom in the gospel and offending or causing a faith crisis in another person? Back when faculty members smoked during faculty meetings, one seminary professor lit up a cigar next to a colleague who felt smoking was wrong. Was that an exercise of freedom, instructive to one who needed a lesson in evangelical freedom, or was it simply an offense to a brother?

A congregation once had an altarpiece where a translucent picture of Jesus was lit from behind with a neon light. Not only was it garish, but at the conclusion of parish events people would often call to somebody by the light switch, "Would you please turn Jesus off," which sounded disrespectful to many listeners. The church art committee removed the altarpiece, despite the objections of many who liked it. Was that an act of freedom or of love? Was it helpful or harmful to the community?

Every congregation contends with questions about worship. When some people propose more contemporary worship forms but longtime members resist, on what basis does one negotiate a resolution? Would such changes be a cause of offense, or even a crisis of faith, for some, or would these changes benefit the congregation as a whole?

Paul's response to these and similar situations would be the same: What is beneficial to brothers and sisters in the community? For Paul it is not an issue of which side wins. There are no winners in this kind of congregational struggle. Paul's advice would be to begin with the affirmation that we are one body in Christ, "believers for whom Christ died . . . members of your family" (vv. 11, 12). Rather than simply take a vote as in a government body, he would urge people to find a process to work the problem out together. Such a process does not always end in total harmony or avoid hurt feelings, but it is the correct way for brothers and sisters in Christ to resolve issues.

In real life the application of Paul's principle can be very complex. If a course of action is plainly the right one, it would be wrong to avoid it because some don't approve. There are also times when one cannot be held hostage from action by thinking opponents are weak and therefore shouldn't be offended.

Any time a person or group in a congregation proposes or does something which is opposed or resented by others, this text should be consulted. Paul's principle of love and benefit for the community is as valid today as in the first century, but it must be applied with wisdom and discernment.

*Michael Rogness*

## Fifth Sunday after the Epiphany, Year B

First Lesson: Isaiah 40:21-31
(Psalm 147:1-11, 20c)
**Second Lesson: 1 Corinthians 9:16-23**
Gospel Lesson: Mark 1:29-39

In this great passage we find Paul twisting and turning in very complicated explanations. Chapter 9 starts with a defense for apostolic salary.
Apparently there has been some complaint about support of the apostles,
perhaps even Paul himself. Paul argues vociferously for the right of support.
He even pulls out the old chestnut about not muzzling an ox while it grinds
grain (9:9). After reading verses 1-14, one would assume Paul is defending
his right to receive material support from the Corinthian house churches.
But not so. That is not the complaint about Paul. Quite the contrary, Paul is
not getting a stipend from the Corinthians. He makes tents to support himself while preaching the gospel (the original tent-making ministry). In verse
15 he says he writes simply to defend the other apostles — it doesn't apply to
him. It would appear that other apostles (and the brothers of the Lord, 9:5)
did receive some sort of support. The questions are very slippery. In 9:5 he
suggests the others had their wives with them. There is no reason to doubt
that (note Luke 8:1-3). If we translate *agamos* (1 Cor. 7:8) as "de-married" or a
"widower," then Paul had been married. Does he mean that when he was
married, he and his wife were refused support? Or that his wife was not with
him? Taking 7:8 seriously, we assume Paul's wife had passed away. Could
Paul support himself by tent-making because he had no wife — in contrast
to those who did and had to have support?

He would rather die than accept support from the Corinthians. Why? It
would take away his ground for boasting. Paul must be proud of the fact
that he does not need any of their resources, and they know it. Their real ire
hangs on his irritating independence, not his burdensome need for support.

The Corinthian issue is old and important. During the time of the classical prophets there was a constant question about the validity of prophecies made by professional prophets (Jer. 14:13-18; 23:9-40). In order to confirm the veracity of his prophecies, the herdsman Amos assured the priest
Amaziah that he was neither a prophet nor the son of a prophet (Amos
7:14). There is great power in the message of one who can speak without
fear of economic reprisal.

Paul's independence makes him free to be all things to all cultures.

Actually there is more involved than simply Paul's economic freedom. It is his attitude toward human culture. While the Jesus tradition, as seen in the synoptics, may have created a culture that altered Judaism, the Jesus tradition in Paul's thought made all cultural values relative. For Paul it was acceptable to participate in culture as long as you gave it no ultimate value. Paul stated this clearly in his *hōs mē* (as if not) passage: "I mean, brothers and sisters, the appointed time has grown short; from now on, let even those who have wives be as though they had none, and those who mourn as though they were not mourning, and those who rejoice as though they were not rejoicing, and those who buy as though they had no possessions, and those who deal with the world as though they had no dealings with it. For the present form of this world is passing away. I want you to be free from anxieties" (1 Cor. 7:29-32).

Paul's relationship to other people derives from these two foci: (1) he is free to preach the gospel without being beholden to any given group, and (2) no culture can claim ultimate authority. Paul then explains how he can be all things to other people in light of four cultures or subcultures: slaves, Jews, Gentiles, and the weak.

*Slaves.* Many of the first Christians must have been slaves or freed persons. One can see that in the large number of single names, like Fortunatus, based on virtues. It has puzzled many modern readers that Paul never opted for the abolition of slavery. He could encourage people to become free (7:21), but he never pressed for it. To the contrary, he urged people to remain as they were (7:21). He said this despite the fact that in Christ there is no slave or master (Gal. 3:28), and, having been bought with a price, no believer should be a slave to human masters (1 Cor. 7:23). But if culture is only relative, what difference does it make? Paul could speak of himself as a slave because he was a slave to Christ (Phil. 1:1), not because he had ever lived in the place of a slave. He did know what it was like to serve another with total obedience.

*Jews.* Paul, of course, was a blue-blooded Jew, born in Tarsus and educated in Jerusalem by a famous Jewish educator, Gamaliel (Phil. 3:4b-6; Acts 22:3). Culturally it would be difficult to be more Jewish. Yet the Jesus tradition released him from those elements of Judaism that separated Jews from other groups: circumcision (1 Cor. 7:19; Phil. 3:2-4a), kosher food or table fellowship (Gal. 2:11-14), and the Sabbath regulations (Gal. 4:10; 1 Cor. 16:2[?]). Despite his Jesus-based convictions, Paul was quite able to be a Jew. If we accept the witness of Acts, we know he frequently spoke in the synagogue on the Sabbath (Acts 13:14; 14:1). When he made his final trip to Jerusalem, he agreed to the wishes of Jerusalem believers by publicly going through the Jewish rites of purification (21:23-24). Paul simply would not let any particular rites or ceremonies stand in the way of his preaching the gospel.

*Gentiles.* Paul considered himself the apostle to the Gentiles (Gal. 2:7; Acts 22:21). As such he freely associated with Gentiles without asking them to change their cultural procedures or making exceptions for him because he was a Jew. According to the remarkable account in Galatians 2, Paul was eating with the Gentile Christians regardless of kashrut regulations. Even if, perchance, those who served Paul gave him kosher food and wine, still it was a break with his past simply to be sitting at the same table with them (Gal. 2:11-14). After Paul preached at the place of prayer in Philippi, he went to stay in the home of Lydia, a purveyor of purple (Acts 16:11-15). Even if Lydia had been a God-fearer, still Paul would have lived in a house that was not clean and would have eaten food that was not kosher. Few decisions were more important for early Christianity than Paul's willingness to "cross the line" and be all things to all people.

*The weak.* Undoubtedly the category "weak" will be the most difficult to define. One would like for Paul to say that, because of the Jesus tradition, he no longer identified with the powerful Sanhedrin or the leading Jewish party, the Pharisees. He no longer identified himself as a privileged Roman citizen. Instead he could identify with the poor and the powerless. As he made tents in the city market, he rubbed elbows with the homeless and gave food to the beggars. It will preach! I wish I thought it were true. Or better yet, it may indeed be true, but I don't imagine that is what Paul meant.

In 1 Corinthians 8 (see Rom. 14) the weak are those who have not assimilated their newly found freedom in the body of Christ. The weak cannot bring themselves to eat meat offered to idols (8:7). As readers we no longer know why they were so timid. Were they former Jews who had always refused to eat idol meat? Or former Gentiles who did eat idol meat but felt compelled to reject their former way of life? In any case, the weak here are those whose conscience will not allow them to ignore idolatry, to accept the nonexistence of idols (8:4). Paul would stop eating meat altogether rather than offend a sister or brother in Christ (8:13). Paul would become weak with the weak. He is all things to all people!

1 Corinthians 9:16-23 describes a critical point in Christian history. Not only was Paul willing to cross the Jew-Gentile boundary, but he was willing to identify with different social classes (slaves) and with those for whom acceptance of the good news resulted in a lifestyle different from his own. Community in Christ was more important than ideological correctness, or even revered tradition. Christianity grew so quickly in part because the faith community could include people of different races, classes, and

convictions. In the early centuries Christianity could include all kinds of people from the inner city. Perhaps in contrast to our time, Christianity did not do so well where the culture was unified.

*Graydon F. Snyder*

## Sixth Sunday after the Epiphany, Year B

First Lesson: 2 Kings 5:1-14
(Psalm 30)
**Second Lesson: 1 Corinthians 9:24-27**
Gospel Lesson: Mark 1:40-45

The theme of this chapter is the nature of Paul's life as an apostle. Verses 1-15 are not in the lectionary, but need to be considered to make sense of the remainder of the chapter. In the opening verses, 1-3, Paul defends his apostleship in terms of the freedom of the gospel in which he lives. Verses 4-13 follow with twelve rhetorical questions, the obvious answers of which make clear how Paul understands his work.

Lest anyone misunderstand his assertions, Paul then defends himself against any charge of boasting. In the familiar lesson for last Sunday, verses 16-23, Paul states that he is free in the gospel but "a slave to all, so that I might win more of them" (v. 19). How many people who use the phrase "all things to all people" (v. 22) even know it comes from this chapter, where Paul writes about his apostleship?

Why is Paul "all things to all people"? The next verse gives the reason: "for the sake of the gospel" (v. 23).

From there Paul concludes the chapter with today's text, where he returns to the analogy of athletics. Paul has used several analogies to describe Christian living, all of which imply struggle or contention — the good fight of 2 Timothy 4:7 or the armor of Ephesians 6:13-17. Here the analogy is a race where only one wins the prize (v. 24). Paul says the only way to win is to "exercise self-control," or in today's language, "work out," "get in shape," etc.

The analogy would strike home with the Corinthians, since the Isthmian Games, a biennial athletic spectacle surpassed in the ancient world

194

only by the Olympic Games, were held about ten miles outside Corinth. Very likely Paul attended the event himself during his sojourn in Corinth. Since it was necessary to construct a tent city to house the vast numbers of participants from around the empire, it is also possible that Paul, a tentmaker (Acts 18:3), was employed during preparation for the games.

Verse 25 is much stronger in Greek: "All those who strive with great effort [Vulgate: *in agone contendit*] exercise continence/temperance in all things." Paul's point would be quite clear to his readers, since self-control and temperance were virtues highly valued by the Greeks.

Paul wants to make clear that the stakes in life are vastly higher than a mere athletic contest. Hence verse 25b: "They do it to receive a perishable wreath, but we an imperishable one." Isthmian winners were considered heroes throughout the Roman Empire, but their immediate reward at the conclusion of the race was in fact a wreath of dried celery. The contrast in Greek is even stronger, since the word *stephanos,* "victory wreath," actually means "crown." Richard B. Hays suggests that a modern English translation of verse 25 might read: "If these athletes push themselves to the limit in training to win that pathetic crown of withered vegetables, how much more should we maintain self-discipline for the sake of an imperishable crown?" (*First Corinthians,* Interpretation: A Bible Commentary for Teaching and Preaching [Louisville: John Knox, 1997], p. 156). The word "crown" stresses the difference between a paltry wreath and the reward of eternal life in God's kingdom.

Paul's reasoning always points to purpose. *Why* do we do this? Staying with Paul's analogy, why do we stay physically fit — to look good, to stay healthy, to keep up with our jogging friends, to avoid heart attacks? In the concluding two verses Paul returns to purpose. Since he began the chapter defending his apostleship, these last verses bring his argument full circle, with himself as an example. He does not "run aimlessly, nor . . . box as though beating the air." He makes his point by shifting the metaphor to the point of absurdity. Spiritual discipline only for its own sake would be like a racer running about aimlessly or a boxer sparring against the air. Neither exercise accomplishes anything in actual competition — except for "shadowboxing" as a training technique. His efforts, on the other hand, always have purpose. They are always for the sake of the gospel. He is determined to be a creditable witness to that which he proclaims. In turn, his witness is for the sake of the gospel's outreach.

How do we preach today about the kind of discipline Paul urges? There is no hint of a monastic asceticism here. Nor does Paul prescribe a particular regimen of daily devotion or religious exercise. Still, one cannot avoid

Paul's plain argument that the Christian life is a life of discipline, and Christians need to deal with these questions.

What kind of discipline do we preach about? Usually we think of personal or individual discipline. We often speak as if whatever builds up or nurtures our own faith is beneficial in itself. Paul urges us to discipline, but its purpose is never limited to individualistic terms. The entire thrust of the Corinthian letter is that our efforts are always for the sake of the gospel, for the sake of reaching others.

Paul's use of the analogy of athletic competition to emphasize that the Christian life needs discipline and effort comes from his underlying assumption that evil is active in this world, and the Christian life is an ongoing struggle against the evil forces surrounding us. This is an altogether different view than the current New Age gnosticism that evil is really in one's mind, an ignorance of one's true person. No doubt the Christian church is paying the penalty of the "worm theology" so prevalent from pulpits of the past, where depravity and sinfulness were so heavily emphasized that people came away from worship burdened with residual and unresolved guilt. New Age thinking swings to the other extreme and sees only human goodness, attributing the evil rampant in the world to failure to reach one's potential. Paul sees both sides — the evil temptations surrounding us and the power of God's Spirit enabling us to live in Christ. The task of the preacher is also to present the depth of those two polarities. Depending on our theology, we call that the polarity of law and gospel, of sin and grace, of command and promise, or of judgment and assurance.

A possibility for preaching would be to focus on the word *stephanos,* since the English language does not do justice to Paul's contrast between the imperishable "crown" of a dried wreath and the imperishable crown of the Christian life, that is, eternal life. Paul sees human life from the cosmic perspective of God's eternal kingdom. Without that larger vision earthly rewards and successes are much like the Isthmian wreaths of dried leaves.

It is a mark of the secularism of our time that life has no reference beyond itself. If human life has no meaning outside the boundaries of birth and death, then how does one measure what is good and evil? Ivan, the cynical Karamazov brother in Dostoyevsky's novel *The Brothers Karamazov,* articulated this view: "If there is no God, all things are permissible." But if human life is measured by the will of a creator God, then our actions have cosmic and eternal significance. It is from that viewpoint that Paul's athletic analogies of running and boxing, plus the reward of an eternal crown, become meaningful for us today.

*Michael Rogness*

## Third Sunday in Lent, Year C

First Lesson: Isaiah 55:1-9
(Psalm 63:1-8)
**Second Lesson: 1 Corinthians 10:1-13**
Gospel Lesson: Luke 13:1-9

This reading is part of an extended treatment of the difficult issue of eating — likely in feasts within the pagan temples (cf. 10:21) — meat which had been sacrificed to idols. Paul had earlier conceded that idols have no genuine existence (8:4). Nevertheless, he has urged the Corinthians to use their undoubted Christian liberty to abstain from the meat offered to idols. They should make this choice out of love for the "weak," that is, those who might be tempted by this inappropriate use of Christian liberty into idol worship. In chapter 9 the apostle offers himself as an example of Christian liberty that does not insist on exercising all its rights. It appears from our reading, however, that idol worship is not just a threat to the "weak," but also to the "strong." Idols do not exist, but idol worship is very real indeed. Anything that smacks of idol worship offends the one true living God. So Paul says in a verse which lies just outside our reading but which is a summary of it: "Therefore, my dear friends, flee from the worship of idols" (10:14).

In a sense our reading is a health warning: "Idol worship is hazardous to your spiritual health." Health warnings often display pictures of the consequences of contracting disease. In this case the ancient Israelites are the sufferers and the consequence of the disease of idolatry is the wrath of God. And the results, Paul makes clear, are horrible indeed.

At the beginning of this health warning Paul calls the Israelites "our ancestors," two words with remarkable significance. Even the Gentiles among the Corinthians were in Paul's eyes spiritual descendants of Israel. Paul will explicitly make the same point with respect to Abraham in Romans 4 and Galatians 3. We may also call both the ancient Israelites and the turbulent Christians in Corinth "our ancestors." In the Christian faith "our ancestors" are always greater in number than our DNA would indicate.

In verses 1-4 Paul makes the stories of Israel contemporary to his hearers by his use of language. Thus the Israelites did not simply pass through the cloud or the sea; they were "baptized into Moses." They were not simply fed with manna and granted water in the wilderness. They "all ate the same spiritual food, and all drank the same spiritual drink." This is not, of course,

197

the language of the period of the exodus; it is the language of the early church. In our preaching we may apply to a text from Paul the technique that Paul long ago applied to texts from the Pentateuch. We may describe Paul and the Corinthians not only in first-century language but in the language of our own day.

This kind of thinking makes use of the technique of analogy, the recognition of a fundamental similarity despite differences between two realities. The experience of the Israelites is by no means the same as that of the Corinthians. They were desert wanderers while the Corinthians are citizens of a cosmopolitan city. There are, however, enough spiritual similarities that Paul can use the desert wanderers as an example for his readers. The fundamental similarity that makes the analogy between Israelites and Corinthians possible is the mixed blessing and danger of their spiritual situation. The Israelites had been rescued from Egypt and the Corinthians from spiritual darkness, a similarity that is implied in the exodus/baptism comparison. Both the Israelites and Corinthians had been fed by God's hand, with the manna and quails on one hand and the Lord's Supper on the other. (Paul will discuss the Lord's Supper both in this chapter and in chapter 11.) The Israelites had been given water from a "spiritual rock." Here Paul makes use of a Jewish tradition that Moses had not simply drawn water from different rocks at several points in the desert wanderings, but rather the same rock had followed the children of Israel on their journey. That spiritual rock, says Paul, was Christ. The equivalent to the miracle of water from the rock was the presence of Christ in the church. The Israelites are the ancient people of God, and the Corinthians are, for Paul, God's contemporary people. For the structure of Paul's argument, the most important point may be this: the God of the Israelites is the same God with whom the Corinthians must reckon.

"Nevertheless" — a key word — God was not pleased with most of them and struck them down in the desert. We can see now why Paul has worked so hard to establish an analogy between Israel and the Corinthian church. The Corinthians are indeed the people of God, but this does not mean they are "safe and secure from all alarms." The blessing of God ought never produce complacency. Just as the Israelites were punished, so might the Corinthians be punished. "These things occurred as examples for us, so that we might not desire evil as they did" (10:6; cf. 10:11). Behind the word "example" is the Greek word *typos,* from which we derive the English words "type" and "typology." A type is more than a moral example. It may well display something about the grace of God rather than convey a demand to the hearers. It is a pattern which can be perceived in the text which prefigures something in the life of the contemporary church. The process of reflection that leads to the recognition of types may begin with the text or the contemporary context. Always, however, the type in the Scripture enables the interpreter to see some reality in the present situation which might not have come to light without it. The task of the preacher is to use both the Israelites and the Corinthians as "types" through which we can see more clearly God working in our very different circumstances.

Paul does indeed use the Old Testament "types" as negative examples in the succeeding verses. We may observe a fascinating interplay between text and context in these verses. The first negative example concerns idolatry, which was, as we have seen, the presenting issue here. But Paul's words are also shaped by various accounts in the Pentateuch, and he explicitly quotes from Exodus 32:6 part of the story of the golden calf. The spiritual situation of the Corinthians is so precarious that they may rightly be compared to the children of Israel eating, drinking, and playing, unaware that they have provoked the anger of their God. This leads naturally to a warning against sexual immorality, a fault of both the Corinthians (1 Cor. 5:1) and the children of Israel (Num. 25:1-9). Nor must the Corinthians put Christ to the test, presumably by their participation in idol worship, as did their ancestors (Ps. 78:18). Neither must they complain and grumble, a habit that is not ascribed to the Corinthians by any particular verse but which seems to fill the background of both epistles to that church. Perhaps Paul has in mind here the constant sniping that he himself endures as an apostle. It is analogous to the complaints that Moses faced in his time (cf. Num. 21:4-9).

Behind all these verses is a very particular understanding of the nature of God. It is precisely this understanding that must have rendered these verses a stumbling block to the church in Corinth and may well do the same in the churches in which we preach. To the Corinthians God might have been "an abstract divine principle that sets us free from polytheistic superstition" (Richard B. Hays, First Corinthians, Interpretation: A Bible Commentary for Teaching and Preaching [Louisville: John Knox, 1997], p. 159). It would be anthropomorphic to think that such a God could become offended. It is hard to say what concept of God is held by most of our listeners, but it very likely does not make room for a wrathful God. A friend told me of entering a church in which a huge banner of Jesus was hanging. On the banner were the words "Jesus says, I'm Okay. You're Okay!" Such a Lord would never object to participation in whatever rituals our culture offers us. Paul's God is quite different. To Paul God is the jealous God who will not share the divine glory with another. Preaching that God in a society which often seems to view God as only infinitely accepting may be the greatest challenge this text poses to us.

199

Paul completes his warning to the Corinthians by repeating in almost identical words the substance of verse 6, a technique called *inclusio*. To the warning he adds an explanation of the urgency of his appeal. The present generation are those "on whom the ends of the ages have come." The children of Israel fell away from obedience; those who live in the last days should not do so. Paul then offers a clear word to those who might suffer from spiritual complacency: "So if you think you are standing, watch out that you do not fall."

Perhaps the mention of the end of the ages leads Paul to think of the troubles that would be, it was believed, precursors of the last days. These have not yet befallen the Corinthians; they have not yet experienced any unusual testing beyond that common to all people of faith. In the troubles they do experience, however, the Lord will always provide a way out. This verse is often quoted in connection with extreme and unusual circumstances. The context, however, makes it clear Paul is speaking of everyday life. If the Corinthians are faithful and flee idolatry, whatever troubles assail them because of that faithfulness will not, in the end, be able to destroy them.

*Stephen Farris*

# Second Sunday after the Epiphany, Year C

First Lesson: Isaiah 62:1-5
(Psalm 36:5-10)
**Second Lesson: 1 Corinthians 12:1-11**
Gospel Lesson: John 2:1-11

From the beginning of the letter Paul has displayed a pressing concern for the unity of the church in Corinth. That unity is threatened by disputes over the gifts of the Spirit, especially speaking in tongues. In our day when the unity of churches is still threatened by disputes over the charismatic gifts, the relevance of this discussion is obvious.

Paul begins his treatment of this subject, which will extend through chapter 14, with the simple words "Now concerning spiritual gifts . . ." The word "gifts" is supplied by the translators. But Paul could easily have written "gifts," *charismata,* if he had wanted to. In fact, judging by the variety of his vocabulary, he appears determined not to let the Corinthians think only of "gifts." The text could be translated either as "concerning spiritual persons" or, more likely, "spiritual matters." In fact, it would only be a slight paraphrase to offer the translation "Now, concerning spirituality. . . ."

Paul may be answering a question concerning this issue from the Corinthians themselves. Whether or not that is the case, it is not a good thing for them to remain ignorant concerning spiritual matters. The ignorance among the Corinthians stems from the fact that most of them had been Gentiles. As such, they had been led astray into the worship of useless idols. One can see here traces of the standard Jewish polemic against idolatry (cf. Isa. 44:9-20). Idols are useless in many different ways, but Paul focuses here on one particular disability: they are "dumb." By contrast, as we shall see, the Spirit of God enables all kinds of speech in the Corinthian church.

The question must arise for the preacher: Are we also ignorant about the things of the Spirit? One suspects that, despite our fascination with "spirituality," Paul would answer with a resounding "Yes!" In our day "spirituality" is a buzzword, but it is often very hard to discern what a speaker means by the rather elastic term. A useful exercise for the preacher would be to consider what in our present-day spirituality verges on, or actually is, idolatry. One thinks of the fascination with crystals, tarot cards, or other trappings of the so-called new age. A more respectable and very common form of paganism might be a near worship of nature. And how many church members read their horoscope daily? The pagan world surrounding the church in Corinth might not be so far away after all. It is still possible to be "led astray."

Even if we avoid the more obvious forms of idolatry, our spirituality may still be challenged by this text. Many in the church speak today of "Spirit" without the definite article and the identifying adjective "Holy." But for Paul the Spirit is very definite and works in very particular ways in the lives of Christians and that of the church. For those who would prefer a loose and ambiguous spirituality, Paul's specificity is awkward.

Paul begins with the negative: no one who lives in the power of the Holy Spirit can ever say "Jesus be [or is] cursed." It is unlikely anyone in Corinth actually ever said these words. It has been proposed, however, that they are a verbal summary of Paul's own life as a persecutor. He himself had lived as if Jesus were cursed. But that life, despite his apparently orthodox piety, had never truly been obedient to the Spirit. Such an interpretation, though inviting, is speculative. What can be said with confidence is that Paul uses the negative statement to introduce the positive "Jesus is Lord." These words were indeed said by the early Christians. This is perhaps the earliest Christian confession and stands in direct and conscious contradiction to another confession, "Caesar is Lord." The Spirit of God, says Paul, enables women and men to declare that "Jesus is Lord." Within the text Paul's concern may be to show the Corinthians that all members of the church who have made this confession are indeed shaped by the Spirit of God, whether or not they display spectacular manifestations of the Spirit. In our day the function of the text may be different. It reminds us that there can be no truly Christian spirituality that does not rest on the confession "Jesus is Lord."

Despite Paul's choice to abandon "lofty words or wisdom" (2:1), he himself is no rhetorical incompetent. In a carefully worded and beautifully structured argument, Paul asserts that despite the "varieties" of spiritual gifts and activities, there is an essential unity to life in the Spirit. The Greek word behind the English "varieties" is interesting. Though it is etymologically related to our word "heresy," it can be used either positively or negatively according to context, either to refer, as in this case, to a healthy diversity or to a "tearing apart" of the church. Differences in the church are by no means destructive in themselves. They enrich the church if an essential unity can be discerned behind the apparent variety of gifts and functions in the church. That essential unity lies in the reality that it is God who is at work in all the varied activities of the church.

The words that describe the work of God in the church ought to be particularly noted. First, there are various *charismata* but the same Spirit. This word is rightly rendered "gifts." The Corinthians were particularly interested in these *charismata*. These are not the only sign of the presence of God, however. There are also various forms of *diakonia,* or service, but the same Lord. Furthermore, there are varieties of *energēmata,* "activities." The English words that are derived from the Greek are obvious, and they give some sense of the breadth of the Spirit's work. The text invites the Corinthians to look beyond gifts, *charismata,* to other manifestations of the Spirit. A concentration on gifts can cause one to miss what services and activities God is doing in the church and the world. Some contemporary Christians prefer the spectacular manifestations that might be called *charismata.* Others might prefer the more sober and practical-sounding "service" or "activity." These preferences may be theological or merely a matter of temperament. But our preferences do not control the various workings of God's Spirit, none of which may properly be demeaned.

Note the three names for the divine: the Spirit, the Lord, and God. Paul is not anticipating the Council of Nicaea, nor is he attributing particular functions to divine "persons" in the technical sense, but such thinking is the raw material out of which the church will eventually shape the doctrine of the Trinity. One could call these words trinitarian without being Nicaean.

Paul himself recognized that some gifts were more valuable than others (12:31). Paul here gives a measure by which one may rightly judge the value of manifestations of the Spirit. It is interesting that Paul does not in fact use the word "gift" here. The more general word "manifestation" sums up all the "gifts," "services," and "activities" described in the previous verses. Each Christian is granted some manifestation of the Spirit for the common good. Paul clearly assumes that every member of the church in Corinth, not just a spiritual elite, is granted some such manifestation.

Paul then offers a list of possible manifestations of the Spirit. It may be that it represents roughly the variety of gifts claimed by various members of the church. For a detailed consideration of this list the reader must consult a technical commentary. Several more general observations may be made, however. The list does not pretend to be a systematic or exhaustive treatment of the various forms of the work of the Spirit. Elsewhere Paul will give slightly different lists (12:28-29; Rom. 12:6-8; also Eph. 4:11). Furthermore, the various manifestations seem to overlap. It is hard to differentiate, for example, between healing and the working of miracles. Nor is Paul here ranking the various manifestations according to their value. He appears to begin and end the list with manifestations that are of considerable value to the Corinthians, beginning with words of wisdom and knowledge and ending with kinds of tongues and the discernment of tongues. Hidden in the middle is the gift that he himself particularly values, prophecy, the gift of inspired speech.

Paul's list "is merely *representative* of the diversity of the Spirit's manifestations. Paul's concern here is to offer a considerable list so that they will stop being singular in their own emphasis" (Gordon D. Fee, *The First Epistle to the Corinthians* [Grand Rapids: Eerdmans, 1987], p. 585). The key thing about all these manifestations is that they are individually allotted by the Spirit of God. Two consequences must surely arise from this insight. Since they come from the same Spirit, they ought not be used to destroy what the Spirit has created. Secondly, no one ought to boast about something that is not an achievement but simply a gift.

*Stephen Farris*

## Day of Pentecost, Year A

First Lesson: Acts 2:1-21
(Psalm 104:24-34, 35b)
**Second Lesson: 1 Corinthians 12:3b-13**
Gospel Lesson: John 20:19-23

It would be inadvisable to suppose the term "Spirit" referred to the same experience among the early New Testament communities. One could say the understanding of Spirit seen in this important passage reflects only Paul's. In the synoptics the Spirit normally directs major events. For example, the birth of Jesus occurs by means of the Spirit: "Now the birth of Jesus the Messiah took place in this way. When his mother Mary had been engaged to Joseph, but before they lived together, she was found to be with child from the Holy Spirit" (Matt. 1:18). When John baptized Jesus, the Spirit descended like a dove (Mark 1:10). Jesus is a divine gift, and his ministry results from divine action. Luke speaks of the Spirit more than Matthew and Mark. For example, the revolutionary remarks of Jesus in the synagogue at Nazareth were inspired by the Spirit (Luke 4:18). Luke continues with the work of the Spirit in the book of Acts, where nearly every major move was caused by the action of the Holy Spirit (10:19; 13:4).

In the Gospel of John the Spirit performs quite another function. In John Jesus is the presence of divine reality. Jesus, who knows the will of the Father (6:38-40), could hardly be led by the Spirit. Rather, the Spirit continues the presence of God after Jesus is gone: "When the Spirit of truth comes, he will guide you into all the truth; for he will not speak on his own, but will speak whatever he hears, and he will declare to you the things that are to come" (16:13).

For Paul the Spirit develops the life of the faith community. Those qualities, skills, and personnel necessary for a viable community will be given by the Spirit. Put another way, the Spirit is the outer energy or dynamic that causes the communal organism to grow. We need not worry about the life of the group because the Spirit will eventually create what is needed.

In terms of the letter to the Corinthians, this passage comes as Paul's answer to their fourth question (concerning spiritual gifts [12:1]). It seems likely that one of the house churches (1:12) considered itself a "Spirit-led" church with no particular need for organization. In fact, their attitude toward tradition (the Jesus tradition) may be questionable. Paul then begins

204

his reply to them with the affirmation that a church led by the Spirit will also recognize the historical Jesus as Lord. Having attached the experience of the Spirit to the history of Jesus, Paul then proceeds to describe the life of the Spirit when it is realized in everyday life.

Paul begins with a rather amazing definition of the Trinity. There aren't many in the New Testament, so this becomes a treasure, so to speak. The Spirit gives the gifts necessary for the life of the community *(charisma);* the Lord leads the congregation in service and ministry *(diakonia);* God holds together everything, all the activities *(energēmatoi).* Let us state it again: God has overall supervision; the Spirit creates the community; and Jesus, as Lord, determines the nature of the congregation's ministry.

Paul then proceeds to list some of the Spirit's *charismata.* Some have the word (utterance) of wisdom *(sophia).* Paul doesn't refer to the rhetorical skill of persuasion mentioned negatively in 1:17, but to the gift of knowing the mystery of God's plan (2:7). This group understands what is happening. Another group has the word (utterance) of knowledge *(gnōsis).* They know tradition and procedures, so they can give direction to the congregation. Another group has the trust *(pistis)* of the congregation. They share leadership roles.

In addition to these congregational leadership roles, the Spirit also creates other roles that we often associate more with personal functions. So one group has the gift of healing *(iama).* Oddly enough, Paul seldom mentions healing and does not describe himself as a healer. Even Luke, who otherwise rather likes healing narratives, only once includes such a story about Paul. On the island of Malta he healed the father of the hospitable Publius, as well as some of the neighbors (Acts 28:8-9). On the other hand, Paul was well aware that illness could derive from a broken relationship with the faith community. In 1 Corinthians 11:27-33 he suggested there was illness, even death, in the congregation because they lacked consideration for each other at the Lord's Supper. Healing in the first decades surely was done out of compassion for the ill, but normally healing was also attached to some function of the congregation. Peter's mother-in-law became a deacon after she was healed (Mark 1:29-31). The Gerasene demoniac preached the gospel after he was healed (5:20). The gift of healing was a gift for the wholeness of the faith community.

The gift of working powers *(dynamis)* or miracles (NRSV) can be easily misunderstood. It doesn't refer to divine intervention, but to a manifestation of God's intention for the created world. For example, God doesn't will that babies be left exposed to die. When Christians cared for them, it was a *dynamis.* Some received the gift of prophecy. In the ancient Near East proph-

205

ecy usually referred to an ecstatic state brought on by wine, music, and/or self-flagellation (1 Sam. 10:5-6; Acts 8:9-24), but in the Hebrew Scriptures it normally referred to a person who spoke for God. In that case we should assume the gift of prophecy was that of preaching (see 1 Cor. 11:4-5).

The Mediterranean world was peopled with spirits. Of course, the nature of the spirits varied from culture to culture. The Romans were well aware of the spirits of the dead and, indeed, marked their tombstones with the acclamation *dis manibus* (to the spirits of the dead). Other cultures were closer to animism, believing that spirits lived in the trees, mountains, and rocks. One of the surprises of the Jesus tradition is the presence of more spirits there than are found in Judaism. Jesus dealt with good and evil spirits, clean and unclean spirits. Paul was well aware of the power of spirits to create a false teaching, a misleading direction, a false prophecy. So he warned that discernment of spirits will be necessary: "For you can all prophesy one by one, so that all may learn and all be encouraged. And the spirits of prophets are subject to the prophets" (14:31-32).

Of all the *charismata,* tongues may be the most difficult for us to understand. In our time it has been so identified with personal piety that we can hardly see its community function. Paul would hardly have listed it here unless it was given by the Spirit for the sake of community (14:1-12). In fact, Paul was aware that speaking in tongues could frustrate community development (14:13-19). Basically, speaking in tongues facilitated communication in the recently established congregations. Of course, there was the Pentecost experience of tongues in which each person present heard the message in his or her own language (Acts 2:6). But that is not meant here. Whatever was said needed an interpreter. In fact, one ought not speak in tongues unless there was someone with the gift of interpretation. Ideas, beliefs, convictions, no matter how personal, are all carried by language. When beliefs change they cannot, even dare not, be expressed by language that carries former convictions. For example, saying, "The Christ died on a cross," rips apart the old language about the Christ and marks the start of a new faith. One way for the language to shift is for the Spirit to send the gift of tongues (something not understood in the old context [14:2]). At the same time, someone interprets in a way that is new. Faith communication is an important gift of the Spirit; Paul was happy the Spirit had given it to him (14:18).

This extensive list of *charismata* comes in response to a question from the Spirit-led Christ house church. Gifts of the Spirit are not simply personal experiences but the action of the Holy Spirit to build up the faith community. Not everyone has every gift. Nor do those who do have the same gift band together to form a "miracles" group or a "healing" group. All these gifts are necessary for the body of Christ to exist. Spiritual gifts are not given for the sake of congregational harmony. It is true that the so-called "eye, ear, nose, and throat" passage (12:12-26) seems like Stoic harmony. Each person offers his or her skill for the upbuilding of the whole body. When all work together, functional harmony will exist. On the other hand, the gifts of the Spirit do not operate in the same way. First comes the life and direction of the body of Christ. The Spirit creates whatever roles are necessary to effect the direction of the body. This is good news for those of us who work with groups. It is not necessary to seek out skilled people. It is not necessary constantly to work for harmony among disparate persons. The Spirit will raise up in the congregation those functions that are necessary.

*Graydon F. Snyder*

## Third Sunday after the Epiphany, Year C

First Lesson: Nehemiah 8:1-3, 5-6, 8-10
(Psalm 19)
**Second Lesson: 1 Corinthians 12:12-31a**
Gospel Lesson: Luke 4:14-21

In this reading Paul introduces one of the most brilliant and memorable images of the entire Bible, the church as the body of Christ, a body in which the members, though many, are indeed one (v. 12). His language is vivid and concrete and at this point can serve as an example to the preacher. Would that Paul's style, and our own, were always so clear! But the very clarity of Paul's language might tempt us into too easy a reading of the text. We might see in this text only the well-worn catchphrase "unity in diversity." Such a summary of the reading would be true but not wholly adequate. The unity which may be found in the church springs from a very specific source. And a recognition of Christian diversity must issue not in independence but interdependence.

In the previous section of this chapter Paul discusses the work of the Spirit of God. A primary work of the Spirit is to incorporate individual per-

207

sons into one body (v. 13). Perhaps Paul is remembering here the work of the *ruaḥ,* the Spirit or the breath, in the creation story of Genesis 2. When the *ruaḥ* is given, the body of Adam comes to life. So it is with the body of Christ, the church. In the one spirit all were "baptized into one body — Jews or Greeks, slaves or free." This verse brings to mind Galatians 3:28. There are, however, certain differences. Here Paul notes that it is through the one Spirit that we are baptized. This emphasis on the Spirit links the image of the body to the discussion of the Spirit in the first part of the chapter. This is a rhetorically useful device, but it also makes a theologically profound point. The work of the Spirit is to link believers together into the one body of Christ that is the church. The one in whom the work of the Spirit is manifest will not necessarily speak in tongues but will have a tender care for the unity of the church.

As in Galatians, Paul rejects any differences between Jew and Greek and slave and free, but here neglects to mention the third pair, male and female. Possibly Paul was of the opinion that the Corinthians were already too careless of distinctions between the sexes (14:34-36). But Paul is not a systematic theologian, and it is more likely that he simply did not think of that pair here. In our time, however, we cannot be so forgetful.

The use of the image of the body as a symbol for a grouping of people is not unique to Paul. Scholars have noted that this was a reasonably common tactic in ancient rhetoric. But the use to which the image is put is remarkable on this occasion. In the examples from ancient rhetoric, the purpose of the comparison is to indicate that the "lower orders," whether the provinces of a state or individuals, should know their place and keep to it. To our ear, the opposite of such a hierarchical understanding of the body politic would be an egalitarian one, that everybody in the body is equal and ought to be treated in an equal manner. But Paul may not be egalitarian in the contemporary sense. His argument is more complex than that.

Both commenting on and preaching from texts dominated by an image are surprisingly difficult. An image is greater, more vivid, and more compelling than any assertions that may be drawn from it. The appropriate homiletical use of an image may not be explanation but rather multiplication. That is to say, the preacher may be well advised to lay beside this powerful image other complementary images that, like mirrors, will reflect and amplify its light.

We can consider, however, the use to which Paul puts the image. In the first place, he uses the image of the body to assert that no part of the church can cut itself off from the whole (vv. 14-17). No member can say anything resembling "Because I am not a hand, I do not belong to the body." At first sight this argument might seem beside the point. The problem in Corinth may not be that groups graced with particular gifts have cut themselves off from the body, but that they might try to cut others off. The strength of an image lies not in its complete logical consistency but in its ability to address us at several levels of our beings. Paul's intent here is to make his listeners feel themselves to be a part of an indivisible body. For this purpose his pictorial language works remarkably well. But considering this apparent failure in logic also might provoke us to ask ourselves a question. Might it not be in the very act of attempting to cut others off that we in fact cut ourselves off from this unique body?

Moreover, the diversity within the body is God-given. "God arranged the members in the body, each one of them, as he chose" (v. 18). Paul then asks the Corinthians to consider what the body would be like if it were all one member (v. 19). Let us step aside for a minute from this very solemn and respectable business of commenting on Scripture and do what Paul asks us. Picture a body as all one member. What a ridiculous and extravagant picture! This and other verses are meant to be funny. This part of 1 Corinthians ought not be read in a stained glass voice but in a "dribble glass" voice. Or to put it in a more scholarly manner: the passage contains elements of deliberate burlesque and ought not be read in a sacred monotone.

As a result of God's ordering, the body as a whole needs the unique contributions of its various members. Even the "weaker" parts (cf. chap. 8) are actually indispensable. Moreover, those parts which seem less respectable need to be treated with all the greater honor and concern. Paul is careful to use the word "seem" here. Neither he nor we can appropriately determine what is truly honorable in God's eyes. Nevertheless, there are indeed some members of the church whose functions are held in less esteem than those of others. It is to these that special honor must be paid.

Paul does not suggest that all Christians should be treated the same. Rather, he insists that those in special need should be treated with particular care. In the political economy of God there is always room for the special treatment of those with special needs. In a society that respects only the strong and the successful, there may be a surprising grace here. Equality is not the same as uniformity. The only "sameness" in the church is in the depth of mutual concern among the members. In such a church, both suffering and honor are shared among the members. We recognize that only the most wonderful of actual churches even begin to approach this magnificent reality. But in ecclesial as in individual ethics, Paul's fundamental command is "Be what you are." The church is the body of Christ. Now live up to that reality.

A perilously difficult balancing act is required of us in the church. On the one hand, a respect for diversity among members of the body ought never be interpreted in a laissez-faire manner. Paul's motto is not "different strokes for different folks." He is never indifferent to either doctrine or behavior. Some doctrine and some behavior are appropriately Christian; others are not. On the other hand, there can never be uniformity within the church. There have been many attempts in Christian history to impose uniformity in liturgy, church government, or doctrine. Such attempts are doubtless well meaning, springing as they do from a desire to express the unity that is ours in Christ. But uniformity is the enemy of true unity. Any attempt to impose uniformity leads only to a reaction which is very likely to destroy the unity that is sought by the advocates of uniformity. This balance between these two errors is easy enough to state. It is far harder to achieve.

Christians are members not just of the church but of Christ. And in God's ordering of Christ's body there are various gifts appointed by God. This list is not systematic or exhaustive. It is not identical to the list of manifestations of the Spirit earlier in this chapter or the list of gifts in Romans 12:5-7. But several observations can be made. The gifts are varied, just as the members of the body are varied. They are not, however, equal in value. Paul does not use the word "seem" here. Rather, in verse 31 he urges the Corinthians to strive for the "greater gifts." The various gifts are "appointed" by God, but they are also, it appears, realities toward which Christians can and indeed must strive. But any notion of hierarchy among gifts must be understood in light of Paul's teaching of mutual concern and support earlier in the chapter. And it also must be understood in light of the "still more excellent way" of which Paul will now speak.

*Stephen Farris*

## Fourth Sunday after the Epiphany, Year C

First Lesson: Jeremiah 1:4-10
(Psalm 71:1-6)
**Second Lesson: 1 Corinthians 13:1-13**
Gospel Lesson: Luke 4:21-30

This is surely one of the most difficult of all passages to preach. It is in the first place so beautiful that to add words of our own seems little more than a vain attempt to gild the lily. It is, moreover, so familiar, particularly from weddings, that listeners expect to hear nothing new in it. Finally, it speaks of love, a term so overused in our time that is in grave danger of becoming meaningless. It is almost as if these words belong on a greeting card rather than in a sermon. To surmount these difficulties the preacher is well advised not to treat the chapter as a freestanding hymn in praise of that popular but fuzzy concept love, but rather as a word directed forcefully to the troubles of the church in Corinth. Many Christians will then be able to recognize, by analogy, a word that comes to our troubled churches also. The preacher must get these words off the greeting card and into the life of a church.

The preacher ought, if at all possible, to depart from the lectionary slightly by beginning the reading with 1 Corinthians 12:31b. That this is the correct starting place for the reading is implicitly recognized by the lectionary authorities, who end the reading from the previous week at 12:31a. That this is the proper place to begin has also been known for centuries. Calvin, for example, called the present arrangement "a senseless division of chapters." Adding the extra half-verse helps to set the chapter in its proper context as a word to a church in conflict.

The "more excellent way" of love is the answer to the problems that bedevil the church in Corinth. It is sometimes argued that this chapter fits only loosely into its present context. That is an overstatement. The poem is indeed a self-contained unity which can be paralleled in Hellenistic and Hellenistic Jewish writings, most notably to a hymn to truth found in 3 Ezra 4:34-40. Nevertheless, the poem does accord well with Paul's pastoral and theological strategy. In the first place, it addresses the specific issue that is preoccupying the Corinthian church, the gifts of the Spirit, and, in particular, speaking in tongues: "If I speak in the tongues of mortals and of angels. . . ." Secondly, it picks up and amplifies a theme that Paul has touched on before when addressing the very specific troubles of the Corinthian

211

church: "Knowledge puffs up, but love builds up" (8:1). Thirdly, it accords with Paul's general strategy of linking the specific troubles of the Corinthians with a foundational Christian understanding.

At first sight it appears that Paul is altering his normal pattern of linking the present situation in Corinth to the work of Christ. It has even been claimed that there is no trace of Christology whatever in the poem. Christology is, however, omnipresent in the canonical context of the poem and in its use. The poem is an integral part of a letter written by "an apostle of Christ Jesus" (1:1) addressed to a Christian congregation that is "sanctified in Christ Jesus" (1:2). It follows a discussion of the Holy Spirit, whose presence may be known because through that Spirit believers can say "Jesus is Lord" (12:3). That Spirit makes the church the "body of Christ" and the Corinthian Christians "individually members of it." What is said about love in chapter 13 must be interpreted in this very christological context.

The mention of tongues, as we have seen, links this chapter to its immediate context. It is good rhetorical strategy to address a contentious issue using appeals to key values which the speaker knows he or she shares with the community, a "shared values" approach. This is not quite what Paul is doing here, however. Some Corinthians might well disagree with Paul with respect to the relative value of love and speaking in tongues. It is an appeal to core values indeed, but to core values derived from the work of God in Christ. This is a key point for contemporary preaching, because in our time the values shared by preacher and congregation may be those of the culture, not those of the Christian tradition.

In the first unit of this chapter, verses 1-3, Paul does not critique the world but the church. He contrasts love with specifically spiritual and religious activities. The first and most obvious, we have already mentioned, is speaking in ecstatic tongues. The person who speaks in tongues but without love is nothing more than a "noisy gong or a clanging cymbal." This may be more than a reference to musical instruments. The Greek word here rendered "gong" may actually refer to bronze acoustic devices used to amplify the voices of actors. The clanging cymbals may be associated with the ecstatic practices of the pagan cult of Cybele. Neither comparison is at all flattering to the Corinthians. It is as if Paul is telling them that their worship has become little more than "the empty echo of an actor's speech or the noise of frenzied pagan worship" (Richard B. Hays, *First Corinthians,* Interpretation [Louisville: John Knox, 1993], p. 223).

It should be noted, however, that these words are not an indirect attack on the practice of speaking in tongues, only on a concentration on tongues speaking in which love is forgotten. This is shown by the fact that Paul next

212

introduces another religious activity, prophesying, the gift of inspired and edifying speech. This is the gift that Paul himself particularly values (14:1-5). Nevertheless, even prophecy, if without love, is valueless. Similarly Paul will urge the Corinthians to give generously to the poor (2 Cor. 8:1-9), but such generosity, apart from love, gains the giver nothing. So it is also with a deep understanding of the mysteries of the faith, a gift held in particular esteem by the Corinthians, a faith powerful enough to move mountains. We think of self-sacrifice as a central tenet of the Christian faith. "If any want to become my followers, let them deny themselves and pick up their cross" (Mark 8:34), we quote. But it is not even enough to give up our very bodies to "be burned" or so that we might "boast." (The Greek is unclear in this detail, but Paul's point is not.) We must not miss the vigor of Paul's critique of religion. Without love, it's useless.

The second section of the chapter, verses 4-7, tells us what love is and what it is not. One of my mature students tells of finding a poster in the "summer of love," 1968, printed in the kaleidoscopic colors of the sixties. On it is printed a poem entitled "Love is. . . ." The words are familiar: "Love is patient. Love is kind; love bears all things, believes, hopes all things. Love endures all things," etc. And underneath is written, "Author Unknown." Our task is to introduce those who are aching for love to the author, not so much of the poem, as of the love. In a society in which the word "love" may have little meaning or too many meanings, the preacher is called to give love a content and even a name. For Paul there can be no doubt about the author of love. "God proves his love for us in that while we still were sinners Christ died for us" (Rom. 5:8). This is the love that bears all things and endures all things and will never pass away.

In the third and final section of the chapter, Paul reminds the Corinthians that their concerns are, compared to love, transitory. The section is dominated by a series of contrasts between "now" and "then." As elsewhere in his writings, Paul is sure that the "now" will unfold into the "then," and it is the reality of "then" that matters. Paul once again raises matters that are key to the Corinthians: knowledge, tongues, and prophecy. These are all "now" realities. This is a useful reminder to those of us who may become preoccupied with our own preaching. We preachers may appreciate the impact of the text more fully if we replace the word "prophecy" with "preaching": "As for preaching, it will come to an end . . . for we preach only in part." Knowledge, such as it is in the present world, will also pass away. But something is given to replace that which passes away. A new kind of knowledge will be given. "Now I know only in part; then I will know fully, even as I have been fully known." Strictly speaking, then, knowledge does not disappear; it is, however, changed utterly. Perhaps "then" it will no longer be a matter of what we know but of whom we know. For it is God whom we will know, just as it is God who knows us fully even now. And God, as we are reminded elsewhere in Scripture, is love.

As a final word to the present reality of Corinth and of our churches, Paul returns from "then" to "now." In the reality in which we presently live, three realities only endure: faith, hope, and love. "And the greatest of these is love."

*Stephen Farris*

## Resurrection of the Lord, Year B

First Lesson: Acts 10:34-43
(Psalm 118:1-2, 14-24)
**Second Lesson: 1 Corinthians 15:1-11**
Gospel Lesson: John 20:1-18

## Fifth Sunday after the Epiphany, Year C

First Lesson: Isaiah 6:1-8, (9-13)
(Psalm 138)
**Second Lesson: 1 Corinthians 15:1-11**
Gospel Lesson: Luke 5:1-11

In this fifteenth chapter of 1 Corinthians, Paul sets forth his theology of the resurrection. Paul demonstrates that the Corinthians' confusion about the resurrection is not just one problem among many that has undermined their ability to live together, not just another topic (along with such matters as sexuality, food offered to idols, and lawsuits) that requires his clarifying instruction. Rather, the resurrection goes to the very heart of the gospel. In this sense Paul's discussion of the crucifixion in chapters 1 and 2 and his discussion of the resurrection in chapter 15 represent bookends (or, as New Testament scholar Richard Hays has said, "sentinels"). Crucifixion and resurrection guard the gospel. They lay the theological foundations for the church's life and ministry. They protect the church from error and division.

In opening his letter to the Corinthians and pointing to the cross, Paul has declared that Christ crucified is greater than any human wisdom, stronger than any human strength. The cross eliminates any ground for human boasting. To live by the Spirit of Christ is to relinquish any claim to a self-centered, personal freedom, as though we could simply "eat and drink, for tomorrow we die" (see 15:32). When we know Christ crucified, his holiness claims us. We "have the mind of Christ" (2:16). We belong to the Lord, not to ourselves (6:15).

Paul's discussion of the resurrection in chapter 15 picks up and develops these themes. In chapter 1 Paul has argued that the crucifixion is central to the *gospel* (1:17); in chapter 15 Paul again "reminds [the Corinthians] of the *gospel*" (15:1), which is the good news of Christ's resurrection. Just as Paul in chapter 1 has *proclaimed* Christ crucified (1:23), Paul now *proclaims* what he knows about the resurrection (15:1, 2). The God who has chosen "what is low and despised in the world, things that are not, to reduce to nothing things that are" (1:28) is the God who, in the resurrection of Jesus, brings life out of death. Crucifixion and resurrection are two sides of the same coin. Each points to the other. Each makes sense only in light of the other. Christian faith and life rest on them both.

Paul uses a series of strong verbs to establish that belief in the resurrection, like belief in the crucifixion, is foundational to Christian faith and life. He reminds the Corinthians of the good news that they "received," in which they "stand," and through which they are being "saved," if only they will "hold firmly" to everything that Paul has told them (vv. 1-2). The fact that Paul has to make such a strong, urgent appeal to the Corinthians betrays the fact that they have gone astray. They are in danger of forgetting the faith to which they have been called. They are in danger of abandoning their theological foundations. Paul himself raises the possibility that they have "come to believe in vain" (v. 2).

But Paul is not about to give up on them. He appeals to the Corinthians to listen to the gospel again. He makes clear that this gospel did not originate with him. Nor is it an achievement of the human spirit, a distillation of human experience from every time and place into a timeless myth. Rather, the gospel is a testimony to what God has done at a particular time, in a particular place. The gospel is a witness to the life, death, and resurrection of Christ. The gospel is a confession of faith that seeks to awaken faith in others. Paul is handing on "as of first importance" what he has received (v. 3). He is making confession, in the hope that the Corinthians will confess again what they once believed.

This confession, probably a confessional formula of the early church, has the same movement from crucifixion to resurrection that characterizes 1 Corinthians as a whole. "Christ died for our sins . . . he was buried . . . he was raised on the third day . . . he appeared to Cephas, then to the twelve." Crucifixion and resurrection — both take place "in accordance with the scriptures" (vv. 3, 4). Crucifixion and resurrection are not the kind of facts that appear in the morning newspaper, only to be forgotten by evening. Crucifixion and resurrection fulfill God's purposes, to which the Scriptures of the people of Israel have witnessed. Crucifixion and resurrection reveal God's power and call us to a new way of life. They make us witnesses.

Paul does not mention an empty tomb. Nor does he speculate on the properties of the resurrection body. He suggests only that Jesus' followers had a visionary experience. But Paul makes clear that this visionary experience cannot be reduced to a psychological phenomenon. He carefully lists the witnesses. The one who died on a cross is the one who has shown himself to be alive. What is required of us is not a particular theory of the resurrection but an act of confession.

So Paul faithfully hands on what he has received. He aligns himself with a tradition. But he does more. Confession leads to confession. What God has done for us in Christ helps believers to see what God is doing for them in Christ. Paul repeats the church's inherited confession, then adds his own. The last phrase of the confession that Paul quotes, "He appeared to Cephas, then to the twelve," becomes but the first phrase of the confession that Paul now wishes to make. For Paul adds, "Then [Christ] appeared to more than five hundred. . . . Then he appeared to James, then to all the apostles. Last of all . . . he appeared also to me" (vv. 6-8). Christ is on the move, awakening faith. The circle of witnesses grows.

While the witness to Christ will continue from one generation to the next, Paul makes clear that he belongs to a select group. He is the last of the apostles, the last of those who have been granted a vision of the risen Christ. The witness of the apostles, Paul included, will become a new Scripture that confirms and continues the witness of the old. The risen Christ will now be known through Word and sacrament, not through special, visionary appearances.

For this reason, Paul knows that he must work hard. He must make the gospel known near and far. He acknowledges his unworthiness for the task. After all, he had not known Jesus personally. He had not belonged to the

Twelve. He had not experienced their confusion turned to joy on Easter. He had not received tongues of fire on Pentecost. On the contrary, he had persecuted the church (v. 9). Only by God's grace is he now what he is — an apostle — and only by God's grace has he "worked harder than any of them" (v. 10). He has given himself completely to the task of proclaiming the gospel.

This word "proclaim" frames our passage (even as it frames the letter as a whole). Paul begins his discussion of the resurrection by reminding the Corinthians of the gospel that he proclaimed (v. 1). He now reiterates that he and the apostles proclaim the gospel (v. 11). This proclamation sets forth the witness of the prophets ("the scriptures") and the apostles (those to whom Christ appeared), so that others might know Christ and believe in him. Paul will develop the implications of this witness to the crucified and risen Christ more fully in the rest of the chapter. He will show why his proclaiming and the Corinthians' believing cannot, must not, be in vain (compare vv. 1 and 13). In our passage, Paul is just warming up for what is yet to come. He is only preaching about why he is yet going to preach!

A passage that preaches about preaching might seem impossible to preach on today. A preacher is called to declare good news, not to get caught up in explaining where the practice of preaching comes from and why it matters. Nonetheless, this passage does preach if we remember that preaching for Paul is always preaching about the crucified and risen Christ. Paul insists that preaching is not a matter of unpacking abstract formulations such as love or justice, forgiveness or peace. Preaching is about setting forth Christ, so that people might encounter him as vividly and truly as Paul believed that he and the apostles had experienced him.

To preach, to set forth Christ, is to engage in confession. We are called to preach the church's inherited confession from Old and New Testament, and the church's confession as centuries of Christian tradition have given it voice. But we, like Paul, are also called to do something more. We are called to bear witness to Christ for ourselves today. The old confession must lead to a new confession — not a new confession that simply rejects or corrects the old, but a new confession that states as clearly for the present what the old confessed for its time and place. To preach 1 Corinthians 15:1-11 is to preach crucifixion and resurrection for today, so that people might believe.

*John P. Burgess*

## Sixth Sunday after the Epiphany, Year C

First Lesson: Jeremiah 17:5-10
(Psalm 1)
**Second Lesson: 1 Corinthians 15:12-20**
Gospel Lesson: Luke 6:17-26

The apostle Paul rarely speaks abstractly about philosophies or doctrines; rather, his epistles address real questions and problems addressed to him from living churches. This is why his epistles provide a timeless resource for preaching and church discipline. Word of a Corinthian church confused about the resurrection of deceased members reached Paul either by way of letter or report (1 Cor. 1:11). The apparent concern at Corinth was that believers who had recently died would not be able to participate in the resurrection Paul earlier proclaimed. Their doubts and fears about resurrection were practical, personal, and, to a degree, skeptical.

Paul had often faced intellectual opposition to his preaching on the resurrection; it came from several quarters. There were people in first-century Corinth for whom the resurrection of the dead required too much of an intellectual stretch. These were mostly Greeks and Romans who were swayed by their philosophers' teaching on the immortality of the soul. These philosophers exalted the rational faculty of the soul and often viewed the body as little more than an encumbrance. Thus the idea of retaining this fleshly encumbrance in the next life was likely to have troubled, if not repelled, many Corinthians (as it had a large portion of Athenians; see Acts 17:16ff.). But even in the Jewish temple and synagogues there were many who disbelieved in resurrection. Paul, as a zealous Pharisee, would have believed in the resurrection of the dead to final judgment on the Day of the Lord. His belief was opposed by the Sadducees — the same rulers who had tried to trap Jesus by showing the implausible implications of a resurrected husband faced with his seven wives in the next life (Matt. 22:23-28). Contrary to some modernist theologians, people in the first century were far from gullible regarding a person rising from the dead; the doctrine was in fact greeted with a good deal of incredulity from Gentile and Jewish audiences.

Upon his conversion Paul became more convinced than ever of a resurrection; however, his newfound resurrection belief was no longer predicated upon a doctrine taken from selected passages of the apocalyptic writers or the Mishnah, but on a specific historical event. Paul no longer needs to speculate about the resurrection because he has met the living One who conquered death. He encountered the risen Christ. What further proof is needed that the dead are raised? "Christ has been raised" is the linchpin of Paul's gospel.

Paul bases his belief in the resurrection on Christ's rising from the dead — nothing more, nothing less. In the verses that complete this chapter, he will try to explain how a resurrection can take place, drawing analogies from nature and employing a passage from Isaiah. Here, however, he lays the chief cornerstone: "In fact Christ has been raised from the dead."

Some would stumble over Paul's risen Lord, others would mock and jest. Nevertheless, resurrection is Paul's relentless message. One can only imagine Paul's deep disappointment when he heard that some of the Corinthian *believers* were beginning to have doubts and fears about the possibility of resurrection.

Paul employs a simple syllogism in order to guide the Corinthians back to this central belief. He begins the argument by supposing the skeptical Corinthians were right about the impossibility of resurrection. Supposing there could be no resurrection, what would be the logical implications?

If resurrection is impossible, then clearly Christ could not have been raised. If Christ has not been raised, then Paul's proclamation (*kērygma*, v. 14) must *not* be true. Paul would either be a liar or a dupe. A Christian proclamation stripped of the risen Christ would be vain, literally "empty" (*kenon,* v. 14), as would the faith of the Corinthian church. If there is no resurrection, there could be no faith (v. 17), no forgiveness (v. 17; he does not explain why).

Paul draws the conclusion that apart from a risen Lord, Christians would be "of all people most to be pitied" (v. 19). The syllogism is nearing completion. If the hypothetical possibility of no resurrection holds true, Christian faith would be a vacuous, pitiful illusion.

Paul's teachings about resurrection are remarkably unequivocal: resurrection is at the center of everything Christians are asked to believe. Ten times in this short passage he employs one form or another of the Greek verb "to raise" *(egeirō)*. Six times the verb occurs in the perfect tense, indicating the completed action with a present implication. Apart from Jesus' resurrection there is no resurrection of the dead and therefore no hope for the departed, no forgiveness of sins, and therefore only a pitiable shell of a religion.

"But in fact" (v. 20), which indicates a shift from the hypothetical discussion that precedes this to the first-person witness of Paul, "Christ has been raised." Here rings the note of triumph that is intended to push back the despair brought by the Corinthian skeptics. Here is the firsthand witness of a man who met a miracle.

219

This lesson illustrates that from ancient times to the present day, the Christian belief in the resurrection had to win its way forward at every turn. However, with the Enlightenment (eighteenth to early nineteenth century), belief in resurrection came under more scrutiny than ever. Some eventually relegated it to the category of myth, others more forthrightly proposed that Jesus' resurrection was a hoax executed by the disciples, or a serious misunderstanding, or a sentimental invention of the early church. Some far-fetched recent theories have promulgated the view that certain ossuaries in Jerusalem indicate the bones of Jesus and his family may have been found and possibly transported to western Europe. Another writer theorized that one of the thieves on the cross with Christ was Simon Magus, who was skilled at healing arts and revived Jesus within the tomb. These are but a few of many theories that recapitulate the doubts of many skeptics in the first-century Mediterranean world.

Add to the modern skepticism about miracles the influence of so-called multicultural and postmodern perspectives in the West, and we begin to see how relevant is this text for the twenty-first century. Paul proclaimed such a certainty of religious experience to the first-century Corinthians that he captured their attention and pulled together a church from a polyglot port city. Ancient Corinth parallels many cities in the Western world today. First-century Corinth was populated by an agglomeration of Romans, Greeks, and Orientals — some of the latter being Jews. Religious zeal could be found on every corner and hilltop. Immorality of every kind could be indulged in: some of it religious in form, other types merely the result of the city's location as a major port on the isthmus of the Peloponnesian Peninsula. Into the sometimes frenzied competition for religious devotion, Paul dared to put forth a message about a man, Jesus, who taught, lived, died, and then rose again to prove himself the chosen Jewish Messiah.

There is a decided otherworldliness about this text that may sometimes embarrass us, just as Paul's first-century proclamations could embarrass his hearers. Two things could be pointed out. First, the otherworldliness of the gospel is paradoxically the very thing that empowers its adherents to find staying power for this world. Heaven seeks to include earth within its moral borders (cf. Matt. 6:10); the resurrection demonstrates this great truth — serving as an echo of the incarnation. Second (this flows from the first point), the resurrection of Christ, and eventually all who belong to him, carries with it a paradoxical amount of social capital. People who believe this life is all there is seldom serve in soup kitchens and rescue missions. On the other hand, persons who have faith in the resurrection have no need to cling to this life. They are people who, the longer they follow Christ, the more

they become adept at spending their life in service. The preaching of the resurrection victory of Christ over death has spawned hospitals and clinics,
schools and better sewage systems, homes for the aged and ministries to
those infirm and dying. The final verse of this great chapter may warrant
mention each time a sermon is preached from any portion of it; it might be
paraphrased like this: "Keep working for the kingdom because nothing
done for such a cause will ever be in vain" (v. 58).

Finally, Paul's ultimate concern here is meant to be more than didactic
— it is pastoral. He presents his case forcefully so as to bring hope and light
to those who otherwise would have a short supply of both. His confidence
in the resurrection of Christ is still the best hope the Christian can find with
regard to the fear of death in all its various and sundry permutations.

*Daniel J. Price*

## Resurrection of the Lord, Year C

First Lesson: Acts 10:34-43
(Psalm 118:1-2, 14-24)
**Second Lesson: 1 Corinthians 15:19-26**
Gospel Lesson: John 20:1-18

S ome texts of the Bible deal with the daily affairs of life like not stealing,
what to eat and not eat, or how to care for domestic animals. Others
urge us to step back and open the eyes of our heart to a more vast pan-
orama. Big questions sometimes need to be asked, and Paul is not afraid to
tackle the big ones in this passage. Early in his letter to the Corinthians
practical issues are discussed at length. But in the latter chapters his interest
broadens to ponder matters on a larger scale. He thus probes for answers to
some of life's pressing questions: What is love? What does it mean to be
truly spiritual? Where, if anywhere, does a believer go after death? These
questions provide the main course in chapters 12 through 15.

Our passage begins with the apostle spinning an argument from a hypothetical possibility. Suppose the skeptics were right that bodies cannot be

raised from the dead. If this would hold true, then Christ has *not* been raised. If Christ has not been raised, there is a certain futility in placing our hope in him — let alone that he will impart immortality to his followers. The next verse begins our text, and follows with Paul drawing out the somber inference from the hypothetical situation: "If for this life only we have hoped in Christ, we are of all people most to be pitied" (v. 19). In fact, it would only increase the agony if Christ were not raised, because if Christ is not raised our belief would be futile and our hope to live beyond the grave seriously mistaken. With relentless logic Paul draws out the gloomy implications of skepticism toward resurrection.

The *de nyni* of verse 20 indicates a dramatic reversal to the preceding hypothetical situation. The "But *now*" of the KJV has the meaning of *"Now* hear this!"* (hence the RSV and NRSV "But in fact" is a better translation of the meaning, if not the literal wording). Paul shifts from gloomy "what if's" to historical certainties. He stakes his claim on his own firsthand experience on the Damascus road: "Christ *has* been raised from the dead." Paul is equally relentless in drawing out the implications of his own firsthand witness to the risen Christ: our hope of being raised is based in this man's being raised — nothing less. Just as Paul developed a hypothetical argument by drawing out the implications if Christ were *not* raised, he now develops the implications of Christ having *been raised.* Christ's resurrection is good news because it is a harbinger of many good things to come. Let us list them.

To begin with, Christ's resurrection is the first of many: the "first fruits" (v. 20) of an abundant harvest. Granted, Jesus was not the first to be revived from death (cf. Mark 5:35-43; Luke 7:11-17; and John 11:38-44), but his rising was the first to a new body that is endowed with immortality. In this sense Christ's rising presages our rising. The language here is taken from the sacrificial system, in which the firstfruits of the land are offered to God (Deut. 26:1-11). If Christ in his resurrection is taken to be the firstfruits offered to God, then there is much more of the harvest to come. The firstfruits may be sacred and celebrated, but the remaining fruits are what the people feed upon. His resurrection was unprecedented: it was the first, but it will not be the last. There is an abundance of resurrection life soon to be imparted to all Christ's followers.

Secondly, Christ's resurrection forecasts a reversal of the dismal condition of decay and death that has reigned since Adam. "Death came through a human being." Nevertheless, "the resurrection of the dead has also come through a human being" (v. 21). As surely as "all die in Adam," so "all will be made alive in Christ" (v. 22). The resurrection of Christ begins to reverse the sullen condition of the human race.

222

Among other things, the Adam-Christ typology in this passage reveals the social solidarity of sin and redemption. God may have created humans equal, but fallen human civilization does not often keep the playing field level. Many are born with two strikes against them. For example, the drug-addicted baby born with an absent father is unlikely to grow up and develop social skills that are considered normal. There is a web of sin into which some fall that is so powerful there is no escape apart from some intervening grace. We who have the advantage of understanding the psychological insights that have demonstrated the extreme importance of bonding to loving parents the first three years of life should have even more compassion upon the children of war, illegal drug use, and other sorts of abandonments that leave a child in a near hopeless condition. Fortunately the church has a good record of assisting vulnerable children. Unfortunately the apotheosis of the state has sometimes allowed us to show less concern for those born into abject poverty, hunger, disease, and abuse.

Nevertheless, the text brings us back to a sobering truth about our human condition. If we take Paul's Adam-Christ typology seriously, we are reminded that the truth is that we are all born into a stricken race. In an ultimate sense we are all Adam's offspring and thus "dead." Even the most powerful, intelligent, attractive among us are descendants of Adam, and thus the inheritors of death. We have struck out. That is the bad news. The good news comes in the form of the startling affirmation that due to the resurrection of Christ from the dead, "all will be made alive in Christ." We therefore will overcome every wicked ruler, power, and enemy — in the end, even death will be overcome (v. 26).

Some on the left wing of the church attribute *all* problems of the human race to sins of social hegemony: racism, sexism, and classism. The individual is almost forgotten in the shuffle of high-powered institutional concerns and hurling of social epithets. This is surely a truncated view of the human problem according to the Bible. On the other hand, those of the right wing of the spectrum tend to see the individual as the sole focus of the Bible; individual sin, individual repentance, and individual responsibility are the grid through which the biblical message is read and preached. Pronounced individualism is equally one-sided and inadequate.

The biblical message itself contains more balance than most of its readers. While there is here an undeniable social element to both sin and redemption, the individual is always made aware of his or her responsibility to the community. The preacher must keep the dynamic tension between these two truths always in view. We are individually responsible yet socially connected. Sin is a social web and also an individual choice. Likewise, salvation

223

is both socially liberating and personally demanding. The good news entails social justice and personal sanctification. Each apart from the other fails. Balanced preaching will include both, in order to convict of sins and provide a liberating word of grace. The Adam-Christ typology of this passage is not meant to make God so sovereign that human choice or responsibility is effaced. Rather, it informs us that while sin and brokenness are endemic to the human race, new life in Christ is a far greater force.

The universal scope of Paul's vision here is almost breathtaking. As death came through a human being, so resurrection came through a human being; as all die in Adam, all will be made alive in Christ. There is nothing more certain and universal than death. As certain as Paul is that all persons will one day die, Paul proclaims the sequel: he is equally certain that all will be made alive in Christ (v. 22). Is Paul talking about "all" within the church or "all" within the world? In this context the latter meaning seems more plausible because of the universality of the reality of sin. Adam's sin did not affect a few, or all those within a particular community, but, according to Paul's theology, "all" of the human race.

Finally, the fruit of the resurrection will become so far-reaching that it will actually bring about the end of history as we know it and allow Christ to consummate the Father's kingdom. It is a wonder how anyone could read this passage and still allow for a provincial gospel. Paul's scope here is absolutely sweeping; it is universal. Christ reigns until all enemies, including death, are put under his feet, and then he hands over the kingdom to God the Father. It is only with great restraint that the preacher can avoid slipping down to verse 28 and noticing that this final consummation of the kingdom results in God being "all in all."

*Daniel J. Price*

## Seventh Sunday after the Epiphany, Year C

First Lesson: Genesis 45:3-11, 15
(Psalm 37:1-11, 39-40)
**Second Lesson: 1 Corinthians 15:35-38, 42-45**
Gospel Lesson: Luke 6:27-38

F irst Corinthians reaches its climax in this fifteenth chapter. Throughout the letter Paul has been debating the Corinthians' claim that they have attained extraordinary spiritual powers. Life in Christ meant to them an ability to rise above the physical world and its constraints. Freedom meant an escape into the self rather than a deepened capacity to serve God's purposes in the world. Paul now links the Corinthians' failure to live responsibly in Christian community with their failure to believe in the resurrection. Only if the Corinthians recover a right understanding of what happened when Jesus rose from the dead can they recover a right sense of ethical responsibility.

Paul argues that belief in the resurrection is at the very heart of the gospel. He focuses first on the resurrection of Christ, then of believers. If Christ has truly conquered death, believers live within a new horizon of hope. Even though their experience of death has not been eliminated — even though death still seems to mock the gospel — they are now able to place the things of this world into the context of God's redemptive work. The God who created human flesh and called it good is also the God who redeems human flesh and calls it to do good.

In our passage (vv. 35-38 and 42-45), Paul turns to the nature of the resurrection body. The Corinthians were suspicious of embodied existence. They could not fathom that Christ would be raised in a body. Nor could they see any reason to hope for their own resurrection. They could not have imagined the resurrection body as anything more than a metaphor for pure, unrestrained, spiritual existence. They would have posed a series of mocking questions to Paul: "How are the dead raised? With what kind of body do they come?" (v. 35). It was as though they were saying, "Everyone can see that a dead body rots in the ground. It is spiritual, not physical existence, that really counts."

Paul refuses to play this game. As far as he is concerned, the fact that a body dies is evidence for the resurrection, not against it. Any "fool" can see that "what you sow does not come to life unless it dies" (v. 36). A seed of grain is transformed into a magnificent plant. The seed is no longer recognizable; it has "died." Yet the new thing is somehow in continuity with the

225

old. So it is with the resurrection body. "It is sown a physical body, it is raised a spiritual body" (v. 44).

Scholars have pointed out that the translation "physical" (NRSV) is misleading. Paul's point is not to contrast physical and spiritual, but the body that we now are with the body that, in and through the power of God, we will be. The Gospels' efforts to describe Jesus' resurrection body help to clarify this contrast. The resurrected Jesus has certain physical characteristics (he eats, he asks Thomas to place his hands in his wounds), yet it is unlike a physical body (he passes through closed doors). His body is recognizably the same (his disciples know that it is he), yet it is different — and people have to have their eyes opened before they are able to recognize him (Mary, the disciples on the road to Emmaus).

Paul, like the Gospels, refuses to allow a reading of the resurrection that would depreciate the flesh. It is not spiritual existence that truly defines us, as though we must escape mere physical existence. Rather, we are who we are, before God and in the world, as embodied creatures. There is no way to imagine any of us as truly *us* without a body. Redemption does not take place in opposition to our created nature but in fulfillment of it. The fact that Paul uses an oxymoron ("spiritual body") to describe the resurrection body ought to remind us that we have not the language to grasp what is an eschatological reality. Resurrection is a way of saying that God truly redeems us. If we are *redeemed,* we can no longer be subject to death and sin. We belong to a new creation. If *we* are redeemed, we somehow continue to be ourselves, even in the resurrection.

Christians have struggled throughout the centuries to unpack the meaning of embodied existence. (For a particularly illuminating treatment, see Caroline Walker Bynum, *The Resurrection of the Body in Western Christianity, 200-1336.*) The resurrection of the body also became a major point of contention between fundamentalists and modernists in North America in the early twentieth century. The fundamentalists argued that the resurrection of the body was basic to the Christian faith, and they classified it as one of the five fundamentals that every Christian should be able to affirm. For them Christ's resurrection was a historical event. It assured believers that their physical bodies too would be redeemed at the end of time. The modernists, by contrast, understood the resurrection of the body as a metaphor for a life no longer ruled by anxiety about death and sin but empowered to love God and others in the way of Christ. Resurrection was not a literal fact but a way of talking about discipleship.

The debate continues to this day in one or another version of these earlier debates. Yet the debate often bypasses what is most essential for Paul in the larger context of 1 Corinthians. Paul is never focused simply on what happens to us as individuals. Rather, he is always asking about our life in community. He cares about embodied existence not because he thinks that adherence to an abstract theological point is a good thing, but because the way we live in our bodies is closely related to the way we live in the body that is the church. It is interesting that so many of Paul's arguments with the Corinthians have to do with matters of the body, such as sexuality, food offered to idols, and worship in tongues. What we too often reduce to questions of personal morality is for Paul clearly a question of life together.

Just as God took human, bodily form in Christ, we are to set forth Christ to each other through our bodies (see Phil. 2). Just as God calls us to present our bodies "as a living sacrifice, holy and acceptable to God" (Rom. 12:1), we are to join ourselves to the body of Christ. 1 Corinthians 15 focuses on Christ and the individual believer, but its doctrine of the resurrection surely has implications as well for the body that is the church.

In this respect our passage offers particularly rich homiletical possibilities for churches in North America that are struggling with their own questions of life and death. Paul speaks of the body "sown in dishonor . . . raised in glory . . . sown in weakness . . . raised in power" (v. 43). Dishonor and weakness characterize not only mortal bodies but also the church. Just like the church in Corinth, many churches in North America today are rent by disagreement. The issues may be ones of personality ("I belong to Paul," "I belong to Apollos"), ethics (human sexuality seems to pose enduring concerns!), or theology. The church falls prey to envy, rivalry, and factionalism. One part of the church even files litigation against another (see 1 Cor. 6).

Paul extensively explores the image of the church as the body of Christ (see chap. 12). Like a human body, the church is composed of many different parts, and each part has its rightful part to play. But Paul suggests that the body, even when functioning well, has a tension built into it. The body has weaker and stronger members, and unless the stronger members care for the weaker, the body is threatened with dissension and ultimately death. "As long as there is jealousy and quarreling among you, are you not of the flesh, and behaving according to human inclinations?" (3:3). When strong and weak fight, the whole body becomes as weak as a baby's (see 3:1).

Dietrich Bonhoeffer once wrote, "God took humans upon himself, and they weighted him to the ground." The church is the body of Christ, but the body of Christ is not simply a whole, well-functioning body. It is also a wounded body, and its wounds are not always a result of external persecution. In our day, as in Corinth's, they are self-inflicted. A church in deep conflict crucifies Christ and therefore itself.

The body of Christ is the crucified body of Christ. Yet Paul knows that God has raised the crucified Christ to new life — is there not then hope for the church as well? "Sown in dishonor . . . raised in glory . . . sown in weakness . . . raised in power" — the God who promises every believer a spiritual body promises the church a spiritual body too, a body in which each member is fully present to the other. The resurrection is not merely a personal matter. It speaks to the very possibility of true communion with God and each other.

God calls us even now to embody this new way of life together — to bear each other's burdens, confident that God will redeem the church, even as God has raised Christ from the dead.

*John P. Burgess*

## Eighth Sunday after the Epiphany, Year C

First Lesson: Isaiah 55:10-13
(Psalm 92:1-4, 12-15)
**Second Lesson: 1 Corinthians 15:51-58**
Gospel Lesson: Luke 6:39-49

Almost every verse of this astonishing passage would provide the basis for at least one sermon, so rich are its possibilities. This introduction, therefore, will seek to identify and outline some of the central themes.

1. "I tell you a mystery." From the outset we must forget the popular connotation of the word "mystery." Here, as elsewhere in the Pauline literature, and especially in Ephesians, it speaks of revelation. Paul is informing the Corinthian Christians, some of whom appear either to have denied the resurrection or to have asserted that it has taken place for them already, that the resurrection is a fact made known to them in the gospel. It is a revealed teaching about human destiny, a destiny that can be known in no other way.

2. It follows that we are not concerned here with what is popularly known as "life after death" or the immortality of the soul. The whole of this letter is concerned in some way or other with embodiment, with what the

Christians to whom Paul was writing did in and with the body, in all the immense range of its sexual, social, political, and especially churchly relationships. Human destiny is not to end in some disembodied state, but with *this* life perfected in the age to come; not flight from the body but the perfection of what we have done in it. This is surely the point of the verse preceding our passage, that flesh and blood cannot inherit the kingdom of God. The reasons for this become apparent as Paul's argument continues, but for the moment the message is this: human destiny is a destiny for the whole person, body, soul, and spirit, and that destiny is not inbuilt into the person, as in many philosophical theories of the person, but has to be given by God in a transforming eschatological act.

3. The whole theology of the passage denies the philosophical teaching of the immortality of the soul. Apart from the resurrection, the miraculous resurrection brought about by the Holy Spirit, the only outcome of life and the world is death. A contrast of eschatologies will bring out the point. There are two alternatives which face us in the modern world: the eschatology of scientific prediction and that grounded in the resurrection of Jesus. The first sees the universe petering out into a hot or cold death; the second is perfection through that death and the death of all its living inhabitants by a transformative act of God. The revealed promise of the resurrection is of perfection not by escaping death, but by the transformation of that which is subject to death into a life beyond death. Verses 53 and 54 emphasize this strongly. The imperishable must be clothed with imperishability, the mortal with immortality. Paul here appeals, as the author of Revelation was to do later, to Isaiah 25:8: "He will swallow up death forever."

4. The reason for the need of such transformation is to be found in the manifest failure of things as they are to realize their true end. Paul writes elsewhere that the creation was subject to "vanity" and therefore must be liberated from it before it can attain its true perfection (Rom. 8:20-21), and such a theology of the fall must surely underlie what he says here. He is, however, here concerned primarily with human rather than universal destiny, for that is the meaning of the resurrection, despite the fact that it does indeed involve the human in the broader context of the created order — as is excluded in most immortality doctrines. Human beings are those made in the image of God, at the center of the universal reign of sin and death, and therefore the ones whose resurrection from the dead will signal the end of death's reign.

5. The enemies that will be overcome in the eschatological victory are sin, death, and the law. We know from verse 26 that the last and supreme enemy to be overcome is death, and that means two things. First, the gift and

promise of God is life, life in all its fullness, and in that regard death is that which prevents the promise from being realized. For Paul, almost certainly drawing on Genesis 3, death entered the world as the result of human sin (Rom. 5:12). Here death means more than merely the cessation of life, but includes the reduction of life to pointlessness or vanity. But second, the death of the body is also involved as that which represents the apparent failure to achieve that for which life was given. Whether or not Genesis 3 should be interpreted to teach that, had Adam and Eve not sinned, they would have lived forever cannot be decided here: suffice it to say that there has been a long history of dispute about the matter. For our purposes, the fact is that because of human sin the death that all human beings die is more than simply the cessation of life, for it also involves the failure of the life project with which God endows those who are made in his image. And that failure can be redeemed only by the act of transformation that is the resurrection. Redemption is begun and promised in baptism, which is the voluntary undergoing of death so that the life of Christ may take shape in those whose lives are misshaped by sin and evil; but that which it begins will be complete only at the end, when the promises of our passage are fulfilled.

6. The link between sin and death is on that basis easy to understand. Sin means a false relation to God, and therefore living a lie. Simply speaking in terms of the natural consequences of actions, those who live a lie — who worship the creature rather than the Creator — render themselves liable to death, for they walk out of the realm of life. A link between sin and the law, however, is less clear. We need to be very careful about what it should and should not be taken to mean. On the surface it is easy to understand, because, as Paul himself shows, perhaps especially in the argument of Galatians, the law prescribes the death penalty for those who break it. We need to bear in mind two aspects of the situation. (1) The link between the law and sin does not entail that the law, simply as law, is a bad thing. On the contrary, it is the good gift of God: a framework within which people and societies can structure their lives. More, as God's good provision for life in the world, the law is "holy and just and good" (Rom. 7:12). (2) Nevertheless, the law became necessary only because there was sin. The law is good because it enables life on earth and under God to be continued with minimal disruption, but it is, as Jesus said of the divorce law, given for the hardness of human hearts.

Why then does the law bring death? There are three reasons. The first is that the law must, being law, sentence those who break its requirements, and all do that. The second is that insofar as men and women believe that they can find their way back to God by its means, can claw their way back up to God by moral effort, they simply exacerbate the problem. In our refusal to accept our createdness, the fact that we are only what we are in dependence on God's grace, we replicate the very situation which caused the problem. In linking law and sin, Paul is making this point and this point alone. The law which is good is corrupted into a religious principle outside the relation to God which it is designed to realize. Many of Jesus' charges against his opponents also fit into this pattern. By their use of the law they harden their hearts, and so bring themselves and others into the realm of death. They use the law in such a way as to invalidate it.

Why does the law bring death? We come to our third answer, that not it but only a personal act of mercy by God himself in the person of his Son can bring back onto the path of life those who are on the way to death. Not the law itself, not the sacrificial system, not the rebirth of prophecy in John the Baptist — none of them can cleanse the conscience from dead works to serve the living God gladly and joyfully. That is why the Reformers were right — despite the fact that recent scholarship about Paul's thought makes it necessary to qualify some of their particular emphases — to argue that justification is the article by which the church stands or falls. The reason is that the wish to be God is the desire most entrenched in the human heart, and so the most difficult to eradicate, especially for those who are most deeply serious religiously, whether Pharisee or Christian. Only a heart-changing initiative from God can achieve that: only the redemption that is completed at the resurrection.

7. Our passage is rightly used at funerals, but is also essential to those who would proclaim life in Christ in the present. Because so much of what we do is far from perfect, what is needed is transformation; only so will the life that God gave be brought to its intended completion. The purpose of the resurrection is food for the Christian journey, not as an evasion of life in the body but to bring out its point. Our passage almost concludes with a call to action: stand firm, and get on with the Lord's work. But appropriately enough, the final words are again of promise. We can gladly pursue our godly calling, "because you know that your labor in the Lord is not in vain (lit. 'empty')." Perfection through transformation is the promise intrinsic in the message of the resurrection. Because Jesus was raised from the dead, the firstborn of many, those incorporated in him know that their lives are going somewhere.

*Colin E. Gunton*

## Seventh Sunday after the Epiphany, Year B

First Lesson: Isaiah 43:18-25
(Psalm 41)
**Second Lesson: 2 Corinthians 1:18-22**
Gospel Lesson: Mark 2:1-12

The fact that God exercises the "word of reconciliation," who is Jesus Christ, through the apostolic preaching office has always been diffi-cult for those who hear and those who preach. The preacher alternately feels too small or too big for the work, and the hearers swing between glorying in and killing the messenger. In this letter Paul is forced to address the fact that proclamation is the great finale of the eschatological work by which God ends the old flesh and commences the Lordship of the crucified Jesus Christ. Such a matter is rather tricky, as it is something like a sermon on ser-mons, a preaching about preaching, an exercise in the apostolic office about apostolicity. No wonder interpreters question whether Paul is just tooting his own horn or preserving his own turf. Since the connection of power and knowledge has been an especial concern of our times, Paul now appears doubly suspicious when he declares in verse 24, "Not that we lord it over your faith." Yet Paul knows the words of reconciliation are at stake: "All this is from God, who through Christ reconciled us to himself and gave us the ministry of reconciliation . . . God making his appeal through us" (5:18, 20). There is no other authority Paul can appeal to such as universal human rea-son, church institution, or tradition, since his authority comes from the cre-ative word he bears. So in times of trouble he can only resort to giving it again.

The difficult matter for Paul is that he had to spend a significant part of this letter speaking about himself ("boasting"). I suppose that for this reason Adolf Jülicher called 2 Corinthians the most personal of the letters of Paul. However, that is true only to the extent that his person had become an obstacle to his office. It is a *reluctantly* personal letter meant only to get his self out of the way so the gospel could be heard.

At the beginning of this letter Paul is reacting to earlier events. It ap-pears that in the time since the first letter false apostles had entered the Co-rinthian church preaching a glory newer than that of the cross. Subse-quently Paul's preaching of the gospel of the crucified Christ was doubted publicly. The doubt not only caused pain to Paul but threatened to cut the church off from the words of salvation like a parasite killing its host. His sharp reply in an earlier letter, the one of "tears" (not extent), caused a grief that Paul recognized as godly rather than worldly: "For godly grief produces a repentance that leads to salvation and brings no regret, but worldly grief produces death" (7:10). So when Paul writes the letter which begins our 2 Corinthians, the time had come for the Corinthian church to hear of "comfort" (with heavy dependence on Isaiah, "Comfort, comfort ye my people").

Much had happened to threaten the gospel for the church at Corinth, but since they had stood firm in their *faith* in the crucified Christ, not depending on signs of spiritual glory, it was time to exercise public forgiveness. Now the time had come to find the comfort that comes from sharing in Christ's sufferings: "For just as the sufferings of Christ are abundant for us, so also our consolation is abundant through Christ" (1:5).

If the general context of our lesson concerns what makes for a true and godly comfort, the precise context is Paul's defense of his faithfulness regarding promises. Attacks upon the gospel, which Paul recognized as ultimately the activity of Satan, may come as a rejection of the *message* or of the *messenger*. In the first case Paul took up the charge against his own personal trustworthiness. He did not return to Corinth a second time when he said he would (God willing). This led to a real problem, as he was perceived to be insincere, flighty, or perhaps uncommitted. Paul says: "I wanted to visit you on my way . . . back to you from Macedonia. . . . Was I vacillating when I wanted to do this? Do I make plans like a worldly person [this translation is important as a contrast with 'spiritual'], ready to say 'Yes, yes' and 'No, no' at the same time?" (1:16-17). One can easily imagine the gossip. A person who is not faithful in little matters may not be faithful in great ones. Ancient studies on rhetoric, like Aristotle's and Quintilian's, have long indicated what any preacher knows. The character of the speaker is closely scrutinized for trustworthiness, which in turn affects the trustworthiness of the message.

Thus, Paul lays out the story about how he came to be charged with making a promise about his travel plans that he didn't keep. Interestingly, Paul turns this around and addresses what is really at stake. It is *God* who led Paul from one place to another, and it was *God* who changed his mind, not Paul. God does what people do not always expect, but that only strengthens the surprising faithfulness of God in the gospel. After all, if God did what humans expected there would be no Christ, however hidden in suffering, no Spirit given as a "guarantee" while Christ's glory remains hidden, and certainly no making righteous of sinners under the law.

God's is a record of surprising faithfulness that simply continues what

233

was started with Abraham. Standing firm in faith depends utterly on these three: God's faithfulness in making the promise; the promise itself, who is Jesus Christ as the "yes"; and the Spirit, who guarantees the promise while we cannot see it. The comfort God gives is real and lasting, but it is not quite what people secretly wish. Connection to Christ means that faith happens when through suffering we are made to "rely not on ourselves but on God who raises the dead. . . . on him we have set our hope that he will rescue us again" (1:9-10).

In that light, the act of comforting is a matter of death and new life, not merely learning how to share sufferings and console others. God is the one who "raises the dead," but having such a God means death for us now and resurrection later: "We do not want you to be unaware . . . of the affliction we experienced in Asia." Paul says this not just as a plea for sympathy or as payment of a debt owed to the Corinthians, but as one who has undergone the work of the creator God who brings us to the point of death in order to raise us up to new life. Such comes with the office of the apostolic proclamation. Far from releasing him from suffering, faith in Christ makes Paul share Christ's prior death and resurrection, and in turn share suffering and comfort with all his churches: "for we know that as you share in our sufferings, you will also share in our comfort" (1:7).

Paul, apostle, is entirely at God's disposal now. He is not like those who, according the flesh, make their little plans and try to say yes and no at once to cover their behinds. Even if one despairs of life itself, receiving the death penalty at God's own hand, the promise is not withdrawn or forgotten. Christ stands as the one raised from the dead, and so we know that God is the one who raises the dead. This is what it means to have all promises find their "Yes" in Jesus Christ (1:19). We are right to say, even if experience is the opposite, that the Yes who is Jesus Christ remains "the crucified who was raised from the dead."

Paul uses a liturgical argument to make the connection between the cross and the Corinthians' charge against him: "For this reason it is through him that we say the 'Amen,' to the glory of God" (1:20). Why else are we saying the Amen through Jesus Christ, which otherwise would seem to be an abomination for breaking the first commandment — praying to another than God? Of course, this is the promise of the resurrection from death, accomplished in Jesus Christ though not a present glory for the faithful.

In what way does Paul make his plans, then, if not like an "earthly" person, vacillating and trying to please everyone? He does it with his desire: "I *wanted* to visit you." Yet he knows at the same time that his whereabouts are only *established* by God: "But it is God who establishes us with you in Christ and has anointed us, by putting his seal on us and giving us his Spirit in our hearts as a first installment" (1:21-22). Thus the charge against him is not only a misunderstanding of Christology, but of soteriology, of pneumatology, of the doctrine of the Trinity, and so we might also say of Christian anthropology and ecclesiology. What he preached is trustworthy, because he preached the Son of God, Jesus Christ, and in him God's faithfulness is accomplished. We are not waiting for election returns or hoping that God will pull a rabbit out of the hat. Even suffering unto death is only the presence of Christ crucified among us, who the whole while is there with his resurrection. So Paul says, "He who *rescued* us from so deadly a peril . . . on him we have set our hope that he will rescue us again." An apostle lives between these two, the remembrance of deliverance and the promise of deliverance. So too the community knit into Christ through the proclamation of the apostle lives between God's action in Christ and the hope of its completion. Though the cross delivers from sin, hope continues for deliverance from the last enemy, which is death itself.

In the meantime the Spirit is given "in our hearts as a first installment" (1:22). Paul isn't operating as an independent contractor. Neither is the congregation, though they are clearly tempted to consider Paul and thus themselves as "worldly," that is, without the Spirit of Christ. But this mistake is deadly to them and not just a personal affront to Paul. It is deadly because it requires not only separating themselves from their apostle, but thus from the Christ in whose name they say the Amen, and so from the one hope of deliverance at the sentence of death. The word of God which establishes "us with you in Christ" and "has commissioned us" (given us our authority to preach) is as certain as Christ crucified, raised, and established as Lord. The Spirit in our hearts is the guarantee, and this of course is experienced as the specific hope: "He who rescued us from so deadly a peril will continue to rescue us; on him we have set our hope that he will rescue us again" (1:10).

*Stephen D. Paulson*

235

## Eighth Sunday after the Epiphany, Year B

First Lesson: Hosea 2:14-20
(Psalm 103:1-13, 22)
**Second Lesson: 2 Corinthians 3:1-6**
Gospel Lesson: Mark 2:13-22

A t the beginning of the third chapter Paul returns to the question of his boasting: "Are we beginning to commend ourselves again?" Paul's boast of the conscience as his witness (1:12) whose guarantee is the Spirit (1:22) is the same thing as calling God to the witness stand. With God as his witness Paul defends his public confession: "It was to spare you that I did not come again to Corinth" (1:23). Paul was not frivolous in failing to return to Corinth as promised. He did it to "spare them," but spare them from what? He meant to spare them from pain (2:2). Pain *(lypē)* is the opposite of the comfort *(paraklēsis)* which is alone brought by the gospel.

If Paul's earlier letter "of tears" had caused pain, then it was not functioning as the Yes of Christ. It was experienced as Paul lording it over his Corinthian flock. However, Paul knew he could not in fact dominate people who were freed in Christ: "I do not mean to imply that we lord it over your faith" (1:24), as no one is Lord in faith except Jesus Christ alone. Paul believed visiting a second time in the midst of the church's turmoil would have worked as *pain,* not *comfort,* just as Paul's words in the letter of tears cut them: "For I wrote you out of much distress and anguish of heart and with many tears, not to cause you pain, but to let you know the abundant love that I have for you" (2:4). It meant at the same time that if Paul came, he himself would receive pain instead of comfort from his Corinthians.

What kind of body of Christ is it that causes not mutual comfort but mutual pain? How is it that the mutual comforting which they give each other, which they had received from Christ, had now turned to mutual "causing of pain"? Paul points to a specific offense. Someone from the church offended Paul in a way that was not merely a personal affront, but put the community in danger. It threatened to cut off the church from its apostle. Apparently someone saw Paul's boldness and preaching about the promises of Jesus Christ as lording it over others rather than giving the gospel. The majority apparently recognized this charge as a misapprehension of Paul's preaching and gave the offender an *epitimia* (reproach, reprimand, penalty), and Paul added, "This punishment by the majority is enough for such a person" (2:6).

236

The church's reproach of the offender was a matter of obedience, not to Paul but to the Lord whose affliction was for their comfort and salvation. A reproach is not comforting for either the receivers or the givers, but when it is necessary it should allow for the experience of patiently enduring sufferings as Paul had endured them for his community. In that situation, however, Paul's announcement of Christ's "Yes" could really only be heard as a "No," and so his change of plans was "in order to spare you." Again, spare them from what? Not from Paul's own anger, but from people who separate themselves from their apostle whom God has established and commissioned to bring the Word. The reproach spared the Corinthian church, in other words, from becoming angry at the word of comfort in their affliction. Their obedience to the Creator of new life was the all-important matter. It was not a personal matter for Paul.

Once Paul was assured that the Corinthians had not separated from their apostle, he then moved to exercise love for the original offender: "Reaffirm your love for him," Paul pleaded, lest he be overwhelmed with sorrow. This was what we might call an eschatological matter, not personal, and so the forgiveness and being forgiven is all "so that we may not be outwitted by Satan; for we are not ignorant of his designs" (2:11). All that matters is that the community be able to hear the Yes Jesus Christ speaks to them and not turn it into a No. Turning God's Yes into No is the advantage of the devil. Turning Yes into No is obviously quite possible to do and is not just a result of faulty thinking about God's words as "in general" being always gracious. Even the most gracious words of Christ preached to a community can be turned to their opposite. This is the meaning of "for we are the aroma of Christ to God among those who are being saved and among those who are perishing; to the one a fragrance from death to death, to the other a fragrance from life to life. . . . For we are not peddlers of God's word like so many; but in Christ we speak as persons of sincerity, as persons sent from God and standing in his presence" (2:15-17).

Paul is no peddler of goods that can only deal in death. Flannery O'Connor's Manly Pointer, the antagonist of *Good Country People,* is certainly taken as just such a peddler, and so she works an ironic tale around this passage. Paul was aware that such existed currently in the Corinthian church. This issue of authority and truth is especially important today in light of the significant criticism of rhetoric as mere ideology that asserts the power of one over another. The experts in suspicion that we have become will likely side with the poor, unnamed offender who may be speaking for us all as we hear Paul ply his trade. How dare he? What gives him the right? Isn't the whole book a self-justification? Is this not the rawest of power asserted over others and us? Is Paul merely being manipulative, or can he really be speaking the truth when he says, "Not that we lord it over your faith; we work with you for your joy, for you stand firm in your faith" (1:24)? Is Paul just one more peddler? Or does the difference lie here not in that he rises in his personality above others as greater, more remarkable, or to be praised, but that he really is sealed by the Spirit, really has been delivered, and waits to be delivered again? That is, is it not the case, Paul argues, that he has surprisingly become a servant of the Lord Jesus Christ? In short, the Yes in Christ is not because of Paul's person, but because it so happens that the true Lord has claimed him and given the Spirit as a guarantee. Paul is an apostle because of the *word* that he bears, and not as a result of *his* bearing it.

Of course, Paul famously turns this question back upon his hearers, saying, "You yourselves are our letter, written on our hearts, to be known and read by all; and you show that you are a letter of Christ, prepared by us, written not with ink but with the Spirit of the living God, not on tablets of stone but on tablets of human hearts" (3:2-3). Did not the promise of Jeremiah occur in your own hearing? "The days are surely coming, says the LORD, when I will make a new covenant with the house of Israel and the house of Judah. It will not be like the covenant that I made with their ancestors when I took them by the hand to bring them out of the land of Egypt — a covenant that they broke, though I was their husband, says the LORD" (Jer. 31:31-32). That is the surprising and powerful word that is Christ's Yes.

Paul's evidence is not his veracity or his authoritative personality, but the experience or effect of the preaching of the gospel. Did it do what it says it will do — free and deliver, bring comfort — or did it simply cause pain? Did it not fulfill all promises by writing on the heart rather than on tablets of stone? Did it not give certainty, even in the worst suffering or contrary evidence? The *diathēkēs* (3:6) referred to here, to which Paul is servant and so minister, is thus a new ministry of word, proclamation or preaching. It is not a service of or to a text or to an external law. Thus Paul's very preaching is the event of the fulfillment of Jeremiah's longing for a new heart. It is quite correct, then, to oppose some significant church teaching on this matter that identifies Christianity as a new law or a new interpretation of the Old Testament Scriptures via the method of spiritualizing or allegorizing. Letter and Spirit here do not refer to literal text and allegorical interpretations that are used to fit a new time or the coming of the perfect (as with Origen). It means quite simply that the passage from death to life (from letter to spirit) is the Spirit's own work. The tool for this passage is the preaching of a new word, gospel, as Paul himself was doing. The service of ministry is the delivering of this to the people who need it, the sinful ones.

There is no need for written recommendations, like those used by new preachers who have come in to Corinth, when hearts have in fact been changed! There is no need for anything more than the comfort in suffering and freedom from the letter that kills, the letter chiseled on stone tablets (3:6-7). Whatever letters the false apostles were spreading as recommendations mean nothing in comparison to what had already been written on the heart when Paul preached Jesus Christ's Yes to them. The distinction of letter *(gramma)* and spirit *(pneuma)* is between two preaching offices that Paul has just used and recited in the first part of 2 Corinthians. When Jesus Christ's Yes is taken as a No, and so does not comfort but gives pain, then a reproach is necessary. But this is not for the sake of lording it over someone; it is for the sake of getting the person in the place where he or she can again hear the promise of Christ, sealed in the Spirit, as the Yes of all promises. When that is possible, then the glorying in Christ can begin again: "For if there was glory in the ministry of condemnation, much more does the ministry of justification abound in glory!" (3:9). Freedom is wherever the Spirit is Lord, and that happens in preaching the gospel, however much the preachers are vessels of clay: "For we do not proclaim ourselves; we proclaim Jesus Christ as Lord and ourselves as your slaves for Jesus' sake" (4:5). Paul knew he was a vessel of clay, and yet he had been given the office of preaching which alone can give the comfort that overcomes the world, its sin, the devil, and his tools of death. The Spirit is his guarantee, and is the one who allows forgiveness to those who seek to attack the word (and its messenger) that alone gives life.

*Stephen D. Paulson*

## Last Sunday after the Epiphany (Transfiguration), Year C

First Lesson: Exodus 34:29-35
(Psalm 99)
**Second Lesson: 2 Corinthians 3:12–4:2**
Gospel Lesson: Luke 9:28-36, (37-43)

This passage is assigned in the lectionary as an explicit commentary on this Sunday's Gospel lesson describing the transfiguration of Jesus. It stands alone and not as part of an ongoing course of readings in 2 Corinthians, for the single purpose of elucidating the liturgical theme of the Epiphany season's scriptural culmination in the revelation of Jesus' divine being before the eyes of several chosen apostles. This liturgical context ought to guide our understanding of the passage, even as we remain aware that its original context is independent of such considerations. The common theme among all three appointed readings, of course, is the "glorious" nature of God's apprehended being before the face of the world, but the transfiguration of Jesus in particular is meant to set the parameters for our understanding of what such glory and apprehension amount to.

It is important, then, to allow the convergence of the Scriptures here to shape the meaning of the theme, and not the reverse. In particular, a hermeneutic key to the meaning of the transfiguration itself is given in Scripture in 2 Peter 1:16ff., and should therefore also inform the text from 2 Corinthians. In 2 Peter the author uses his eyewitnessing of Jesus' transfiguration as a proof for the claims he is making in his letter and preaching about Jesus: "For we did not follow cleverly devised myths when we made known to you the power and coming of our Lord Jesus Christ, but we were eyewitnesses of his majesty." He goes on to emphasize how his own "presence with [Jesus] on the holy mountain," hearing the very voice of the Father declare Jesus "beloved Son," attests to the truth of his teaching about the "Lord Jesus Christ."

The transfiguration is for Peter, therefore, a confirmation of the truthful authority of his affirmations concerning Jesus, Jesus' work, and the redemption he brings to the members of the Christian community. It is a confirmation much like the eyewitness testimony John recounts of the incarnate Word — "touched," "seen," and so on. And within the Gospel accounts themselves the story of the transfiguration clearly *does* function in this same confirmatory fashion. However, the episode is placed in such a way as to point the disciples (and readers) to an understanding of confirming authority that links it directly with the experience of sacrificial passion and death. Jesus, we are told, reveals his divine glory to those chosen disciples only after first revealing to them the secret of his arrest, rejection, death, and resurrection (cf. Luke 9:18ff.), a secret that Peter cannot at first receive (cf. esp. Mark 8:32ff.). It is a secret Jesus then applies to the very form of the disciple (Luke 9:23ff.), and reiterates a second time on his descent from the mountain (Luke 9:43ff.). Within this sequence of teaching, the transfiguration itself appears as a cipher by which apprehended "glory" is inextricably entwined with the cross. To "see" Jesus truly and to confirm the truth of that vision, that is, is to follow him in his sacrifice, a following that gains true "life" and is itself enveloped in the "glory" of the Father at the end of time (cf. Luke 9:26).

Paul's discussion of "glory" and "splendor" in relation to Christ, then, must be logically tied to this notion of confirmation through discipleship, glory through humiliation. In fact, the linkage proves not to be tendentious in the least, for aspects of just these themes inform the context of the actual passage. Much of 2 Corinthians deals with Paul's justification of his authority in the eyes of the Corinthian Christians, and in chapters 2–4 in particular Paul plays on the metaphors of shadow and light, veiling and unveiling, temporal limitedness and eternity in an attempt to frame the paradoxically confirmed claims for his qualifications as an apostle. The attempt itself follows a logic similar to the transfiguration Gospel's own reframing of confirmatory evidence for Jesus' divine Sonship.

Paul is apparently trying to answer the Corinthians' doubts as to his integrity, skills, and capacities as their leader, especially in comparison with other preachers the community has welcomed and perhaps found more effective. The end result of his argument is to confirm his authority on the basis of the humble and guileless character of his actions and relations with the Corinthian church: "We have renounced disgraceful, underhanded ways; we refuse to practice cunning or to tamper with God's word, but by the open statement of the truth we would commend ourselves to [everyone's] conscience in the sight of God" (4:2). But the paradox of this confirmation is that it arises out of a life that is otherwise *unspectacular*, indeed may even appear degraded. This is the burden of the grand admission that Paul accedes to just afterward in describing the "treasure" of God's inward glory that is borne in "earthen vessels," defined by "affliction," "persecution," and suffering (4:7ff.).

So, while Paul seeks to confirm his authority, and does so with the language of light and glory, he in fact does so in the course of explicating the almost *hidden* character of the power his ministry embodies. It is important to

241

grasp this point, for otherwise the contrasts he draws with the "old cove-nant" and with Moses, a contrast defined by "veiling" and "unveiling," will seem flagrantly chauvinist. The language — and reality — of light and glory, then, is properly expressive of the same humiliation to which Jesus' self-revelation on the mount points.

Thus Paul admits in the first place that his authority as an apostle among the Corinthians is "spiritual," and is, to this extent, not something that can be apprehended with the aid of external confirmations — its realm is that of the "heart," where the Spirit of God alone can touch, change, and bring "life" (cf. 3:3-4). It is the life with God, brought by the Spirit of God for which Paul is a "minister" (3:6), that stands as the criterion for true "glory"; but it is, as Paul says at the opening of the reading, a life that stands toward such glory as a "hope" (3:12) rather than as a reality already fulfilled.

The use of the image of Moses meeting God face-to-face on Sinai is per-haps somewhat confusing here. On the one hand, Paul wants to emphasize that the Spirit Christ gives the believer places him or her directly in commu-nion with the glory of God, with as palpable a sense of what that means as Moses' physical encounter with God. On the other hand, Paul wishes to un-dercut the ultimate value of that earlier encounter by emphasizing its im-permanence and transitory nature in comparison with the Christian's life in the Spirit, but in doing so he also subverts the palpable associations divine glory would normally have for his readers.

The "veil" (3:13), then, which he assigns to the vision of those still tied to the Law (after the image of Moses given him in Exod. 34:33ff.), is one that keeps them on the plane of physicality, of visibility, of common "splendor" — that is, much like the Corinthians' reactions to spectacular preachers and leaders. The "lifting" of the veil, however, displays the "hidden" light of the gospel (cf. 4:3), that is, the truth that the glory of Jesus is "seen" in the disci-pleship of the suffering servant (cf. 4:10).

To be "changed from one degree of glory to another" (3:18), which is the destiny of the disciple, is, quite literally, to be "changed into his — that is, Jesus' — likeness." We are meant to hear the transfigurative context of Je-sus' words here: "Whoever would come after me, let them deny themselves and take up their cross daily and follow me" (cf. Luke 9:23). For Paul this likeness, which the Corinthians ought to be able to apprehend in his own life and ministry among them, is exactly what confirms his authority, and nothing else. Like the life Jesus, his life displays "glory"; but like the glory of Jesus, that glory is the glory of the cross. (Cf. the image in John's Gospel [e.g., 13:31; 17:1-2], where the crucifixion clearly marks the moment of Je-sus' unveiling as the Son of God, which he describes as his "glorification."

242

Cf. also 1 John 3:2-3, where the "hope" of living with God is expressed in the present through the hard process of "purification," which itself renders the Christian "like" Jesus in appearance.)

The disciple, in passional terms, is the only one who "sees" the glory of Jesus, and indeed becomes one with it. Paul's own life and ministry represents this temporal and experiential outworking of the meaning of the transfiguration. Further, it helps to direct the doxological strain of the Christian faith toward its appropriate forum, that is, conformance with the life and passion of Jesus. While it is right to stress the "hopefulness" of the promise of ultimate communion the gift of the Spirit entails, it is always necessary to moor that hope in the practical patterns of discipleship that provide that hope its path of fulfillment. Questions of vocation, mission, Christian hope, and the character of the Christian claim to truth — all of which the preacher might appropriately raise in conjunction with this passage — must therefore consistently find their explication in the actual forms of Jesus' (and Paul's) life. In this sense the Scriptures here point directly to themselves, and not beyond themselves, and to the shapes of living they describe, just as Paul points his readers to his own way in the world.

*Ephraim Radner*

## Last Sunday after the Epiphany (Transfiguration), Year B

First Lesson: 2 Kings 2:1-12
(Psalm 50:1-6)
**Second Lesson: 2 Corinthians 4:3-6**
Gospel Lesson: Mark 9:2-9

The lectionary text begins abruptly in midstream: "And even if our gospel is veiled. . . ." Here in verse 3 Paul qualifies the claim he has just made in verse 2 that "we refuse to practice cunning or to falsify God's word; but by the open statement of the truth we commend ourselves to the conscience of everyone in the sight of God." Paul is confident in the power of the proclaimed word of God as the power of the truth itself (cf. 13:8). Because God's word works its sovereign will, Paul does not have to practice rhetorical tricks to make revelation "happen." Nevertheless, not everyone "gets it." Not everyone hears God's word in the words of the apostolic preacher, and not everyone sees God's glory manifested in the mundane event of apostolic preaching. How do we account for this?

Paul accounts for it by retrieving the metaphor of "veiling" that he employs in 3:12-18 in speaking of the "glory" manifested in the face of Moses at the giving of the Law. In Exodus 34:29-35 the glory of the Lord so "transfigured" Moses' face (cf. Mark 9:2-8) that its shining brilliance compelled him to don a veil when speaking to the Israelites following his conferences with God. In Paul's gloss on this narrative, what was really being "veiled" to the Israelites was the fact that the glory of Moses was already "passing away" (3:13). Only "in Christ" (3:14) is *this* veil, hiding the provisional character of the "old covenant" (3:14) and its "ministry of death" (3:7) or "condemnation" (3:9), removed.

But Paul's "gospel," too, proclaiming the "glory of Christ, who is the image of God" that accompanies the "new covenant" (3:6) and its "ministry of the Spirit" (3:8) or "righteousness" (3:9), can be "veiled" (4:3). In this latter instance, and the one with which our lection is concerned, the veiling of God's glory is not attributed to an anachronistic reading of the old covenant, but to "the god of this world," who "has blinded the minds of the unbelievers, to keep them from seeing the light of the gospel of the glory of Christ, who is the image [*eikōn*] of God" (4:4). The "unbelievers" here are the "perishing" (4:3; cf. 2:15). They are under the sway of "the god of this world" (*ho theos tou aiōnos toutou*, lit. "the god of this age"), a term Paul uses nowhere else, but as with the term "rulers of this age" (*archontoi tou aiōnos toutou*, 1 Cor. 2:6, 8), it aptly conveys the binding and blinding force of evil in its hostility to God and hatred for humanity. This malignant power, claiming to be "god," bends people to its will and blinds them to the glory of the true God.

But the gospel also knows a power greater than evil, and greater than ourselves, and so Paul declares: "For we do not proclaim ourselves; we proclaim Jesus Christ as Lord and ourselves as your slaves for Jesus' sake" (4:5). "Jesus is Lord!" *(Kyrios Iēsous)* was apparently a pre-Pauline liturgical acclamation and is found in Romans 10:9 conjoined with a confessional formula, and in the culminating stanza of the christological hymn in Philippians 2:6-11. Here the designation of God as *Kyrios,* used in the Septuagint translation of Isaiah 45:25, is transferred to Jesus. "Jesus is Lord" sums up the Christian message. This is what Paul proclaims. This is what faith acclaims and confesses, namely, that God has raised up the crucified Jesus above every power that sets itself in opposition to God. To preach "Jesus Christ as Lord" calls into question all authorities and powers of "this age" that tyrannically seek to dominate or determine human destiny. For this reason authentic preaching of the gospel always has political pertinence.

If Jesus Christ is our "Lord," then we are his "slaves" *(douloi),* to use the literal rendering of the NRSV. Since the division of human beings into "slave and free" is no longer operative "in Christ Jesus" or the community of the new creation (Gal. 3:28), the RSV translation "servants," with its connotation of service, better conveys Paul's intentionality than the translation "slaves." The latter rendering, with its negative connotations of enforced submission to arbitrary and dehumanizing authority, is certainly not how Paul understands his relationship to the Lord, for "where the Spirit of the Lord is, there is freedom" (2 Cor. 3:17).

Since he belongs to Christ, we might have expected Paul to say, "For we do not proclaim ourselves; we proclaim Jesus Christ as Lord and ourselves as *his* servants [*doulous autou*]," but instead Paul writes, "and ourselves as *your* servants for Jesus' sake [*doulous hymōn dia Iēsoun*]." Precisely as Jesus' servant *(dia Iēsoun),* then, Paul serves the Corinthians as theirs *(doulous hymōn).* This is Paul's reply to those who accuse him of working only to advance his own authority over the Corinthians (1:24). Paul does not flee from his apostolic authority, but he shows the Corinthians that it does not derive from an inflated self or from other patterns of domination typical of "this age," but rather from the pattern of Jesus Christ, who "loved us and gave himself for us" (cf. Gal. 2:20; Phil. 2:6-11). Thus Paul places his apostleship under the Lordship of Jesus Christ and in service to the church, thereby identifying and instructing true pastors.

The assertion "we do not proclaim ourselves" but "Jesus Christ as Lord and ourselves as your servants for Jesus' sake" (4:5) is inherently paradoxical. To proclaim only Jesus Christ as Lord excludes proclaiming ourselves as Lord, but to proclaim the Lordship of Jesus Christ is simultaneously to witness to who we are in relation to him. For this reason Paul can go on to speak of himself in terms of his hardships in serving the gospel (4:7-12), but these vicissitudes are understood as "carrying in the body the dying of Jesus" (4:10), that is, an embodied proclamation of Jesus' death for the sake of the Corinthians (4:12). Moreover, Paul writes metaphorically of the spreading gospel as "the fragrance" (2:14), while going on to state that he is himself "the aroma of Christ to God" (2:15). As Paul's double use of olfactory metaphors shows, proclaimers of the gospel are proclaimed as such, for they, too, belong to the life-and-death eschatological event of the gospel's manifestation (2:14-16). Because the identification between the Lord Jesus

Christ and his envoys (5:20), the proclaimers and the Proclaimed, is so strong, who are the authentic servants of the word and who are its counterfeiting "peddlers" (2:17) is not always easy for Christian communities to discern. As servants of Jesus Christ, we are called to resist substituting for his gospel one of our own making and to desist from subordinating his gospel to our own aggrandizing agendas. In so doing, "we do not proclaim ourselves; we proclaim Jesus Christ as *Lord*," and in this way are shown to be "servants" of those who hear the word.

This proper orientation of the proclaiming preacher toward the revelation manifested in the proclamation of the gospel, which serves as the basis for the claims made in verse 5, is summed up by Paul in verse 6: "For *(hoti)* it is the God who said, 'Let light shine *(lampsei)* out of darkness,' who has shone in our hearts to give the light of the knowledge of the glory of God in the face of Jesus Christ." Here Paul identifies the God of the gospel with the speaking God of the Scriptures. As Richard B. Hays notes, Paul does not directly cite but paraphrastically melds both Genesis 1:3a ("Let light *shine*," taking *lampsei* as a third-person imperative) and Isaiah 9:1b ("You who dwell in a land and shadow of death, light *will shine* upon you," taking *lampsei* as a third-person future indicative). It is the glorious God of Israel and of Israel's Scriptures, the God who creates and redeems through his word, that Paul proclaims "has shone in our hearts to give the light of the knowledge of the glory of God in the face [*en prosōpōi*] of Jesus Christ."

This glorious affirmation emerges out of conflict in Corinth over where God's glory is to be found. From Paul's references, we can follow J. Louis Martyn's contention that the pseudoapostles who invaded the Corinthian congregation (2 Cor. 11:13) were boasting "in outward appearance [*en prosōpōi*, lit. 'in the face'] and not in the heart" (5:12). Apparently these teachers proclaimed that those who see God, as they do "face to face" (cf. 1 Cor. 13:12), literally reflect on their own faces the "glory of God," as did Moses himself (Exod. 34:29-35). Paul does not compete with these teachers on their terms as to who has the more radiant image. Such contests belong to the "old age" and its accompanying judgments that have been put to death in the cross of Jesus Christ (2 Cor. 5:14-17). Given this turning point, Paul reframes the spirituality debate in Corinth by the christological criterion of the new creation: God's glory is now manifested only in the countenance of the Crucified! Christ, not Moses, is the true icon or image of God (2 Cor. 4:4), and the true knowledge of God's glory shines forth only from him (cf. Mark 9:2-8). To look at Jesus Christ "with unveiled faces" is indeed to be "transformed into the same image from one degree of glory to another" (2 Cor. 3:18), but this glorious transformation illumines not our "faces," but our "hearts" (2 Cor. 4:6; 5:12), whence our self-centered lives are remolded into the cruciform pattern of our Lord himself. In this Epistle lesson, then, no less than in the Gospel accounts, Paul proclaims the message said over Jesus at his transfiguration (Mark 9:7): "This is my Son, the Beloved; listen to him!"

*James F. Kay*

## Second Sunday after Pentecost, Year B

First Lesson: 1 Samuel 3:1-10, (11-20)
(Psalm 139:1-6, 13-18)
**Second Lesson: 2 Corinthians 4:5-12**
Gospel Lesson: Mark 2:23–3:6

## Ninth Sunday after the Epiphany, Year B

First Lesson: Deuteronomy 5:12-15
(Psalm 81:1-10)
**Second Lesson: 2 Corinthians 4:5-12**
Gospel Lesson: Mark 2:23–3:6

"But we have this treasure in clay jars," the NRSV translates verse 7, exchanging the more proletarian-sounding "earthen pots" for the "clay jars" of designer chic. In Paul's day people often hid their precious valuables in the cheap pots used for mundane household chores. A wastebasket, a garbage bag, or a throwaway cup might come closer in translating into our idioms the scandal Paul has in mind. In this self-deprecating metaphor, Paul is not just thinking of his human frailty but of his perceived expendability, the paradox that the glorious treasure of the gospel is embodied, and veiled to "perishing" "unbelievers" (vv. 3, 4), by an apparently unseemly, inglorious career (vv. 8-10).

This scandal is heightened when we pause to consider further what the apostle means by *thēsauros toutos*, "this treasure." The antecedent is probably found back in verse 6: "the light of the knowledge of the glory of God in the face of Jesus Christ." (For this reason the lectionary editors were arguably wise to include this verse with verses 7-12, even though it concludes the paragraph beginning at verse 1 and, along with verse 5, has already been commented on above.) This treasure does not shine forth unambiguously from Paul's face in the manner of a spiritual ecstatic (5:12); rather, it has shone in his heart (4:6) and only manifests itself in a cruciform life (4:8-12). Such a life has about as much prominence and prestige, in the minds of Paul's enemies, as a cracked pot has beside an elegant porcelain vase.

At verses 8-9 Paul employs a *peristasis* catalogue, that is, a listing of the hardships he has borne in service to the gospel (cf. 1 Cor. 4:9-13; 2 Cor. 6:4-10). It is composed of four couplets. Within each couplet the hardship is stated and then immediately qualified by *all' ou[k]*, "but not": "In every way, [1] we are afflicted, *but not* crushed; [2] perplexed, *but not* driven to despair; [3] persecuted, *but not* forsaken; [4] struck down, *but not* destroyed." While the outward vicissitudes of affliction, perplexity, persecution, and the "knockdown" or "takedown" are hardly "glorious," in no case do they push Paul to the breaking point. He is a "cracked" vessel to be sure, but he has not "cracked up"; a cracked pot but not a crackpot! Often put down, Paul has yet to be counted out. In every sense a survivor, Paul does not take credit for this amazing achievement. He gives all the credit to God. If his apostolic career can be likened to easily chipped pots, this makes clear that the treasure they hold and serve "belongs to God and does not come from us" (v. 7). The point here is not that adversity elicits admirable human "grace under pressure," a Stoic ideal still celebrated today, but rather that adversity elicits under its pressure the awareness of God's all-sufficient grace and power (12:9; cf. 1:4-7). Indeed, amid all the trials that reveal his weakness, Paul is continually preserved from crushing defeat, despair, abandonment, and total destruction by the treasure hidden within him, for such is God's own "extraordinary power" (v. 7). Thus Paul's hardships proclaim the power of God's gospel at work in human weakness (cf. 13:4), a paradox anticipated by the metaphor of treasure in earthen pots (v. 7) and elaborated further as the dying and life of Jesus borne by Paul in his own body (v. 10).

By means of the last term of the last couplet of verse 9, "but not destroyed," Paul makes the transition from the *peristasis* catalogue to the vocation and destiny of Jesus (v. 10). In this way Paul identifies his hardships as "always carrying in the body the dying [*nekrōsis*] of Jesus." The Greek word here can be translated "death," but *nekrōsis*, with its active ending, more readily suggests the process of dying or mortification. (Hence, in our contemporary medical usage necrosis refers to the localized death of otherwise living tissue, as when a portion of the retina dies due to a detachment from its blood supply.) So here, Paul is not recalling the death of Jesus as a punctiliar event of crucifixion, but rather the process of "the daily dying" of Jesus in the form of those sufferings that continually accompanied his vocation (Phil. 2:7-8) even as they "always" accompany Paul in his (cf. 1 Cor. 15:31). As Karl Barth, following John Calvin, declared, "The whole life of Jesus comes under the heading 'suffered,'" and the same could be said of Paul from the time of his conversion. But the point of such mortification is not masochism, but vivification or life. It is only through interpreting our sufferings as embodying the "dying of Jesus" that the "life of Jesus" also becomes visible "in our bodies."

Paul restates the paradox of verse 10 again in verse 11: "For while we live, we are always being given up to death [*eis thanaton*] for Jesus' sake [*dia Iēsoun*], so that the life of Jesus may be made visible in our mortal flesh" (cf. 6:9: "as dying, and see — we are alive"). From the standpoint of Jesus' death and resurrection, a reality and a hope into which we are incorporated at baptism (Rom. 6:3-11), no suffering or "wasting away" (2 Cor. 4:16), however unmerited, is simply pointless or tragic. But the apostle's "daily dying" is not for suffering's sake, but "for Jesus' sake," that is, "on account of Jesus," for the sake of knowing "the power of his resurrection" (Phil. 3:10), for the sake of proclaiming his "life" throughout the world (2 Cor. 2:14-16), and thus for the sake of the Corinthians themselves (2 Cor. 4:12).

"So," Paul and our lection conclude, "death is at work in us, but life in you." This does not deny, as verses 10-11 have stressed, that life too is at work in Paul, but verse 12 sharpens the paradox that the revelation of Jesus' risen life only comes through the death of Jesus embodied by its proclaimer. The life in question is not perceptible in Paul's body, as in the shining faces or radiant personalities of his opponents (5:12), but only becomes corporeally "visible" as the hearers of the gospel come to believe Paul's proclamation.

Thus verse 12 offers a concise restatement of a theme from verse 5, with which our lection begins: "For we do not proclaim ourselves; we proclaim Jesus Christ as Lord and ourselves as *your servants* for Jesus' sake [*doulous hymōn dia Iēsoun*]." Paul's apostolic ministry, in service to Jesus Christ with its ever accompanying hardships, is not exercised as an end in itself, but only in service to others (cf. 1:6). In this way "the word of the cross" (1 Cor. 1:18), which Paul embodies in his "daily dying" (1 Cor. 15:31), becomes for his hearers "the word of life" (Phil. 2:16).

*James F. Kay*

249

## Third Sunday after Pentecost, Year B

First Lesson: 1 Samuel 8:4-11, (12-15), 16-20; (11:14-15)
(Psalm 138)
**Second Lesson: 2 Corinthians 4:13–5:1**
Gospel Lesson: Mark 3:20-35

Our lectionary selection serves up a potpourri of themes and images: a scriptural citation on faith, a catechetical fragment on the resurrection, a discussion employing such contrasts as "outer" and "inner," "momentary" and "eternal," "seen" and "unseen," all concluded with a verse (5:1) introducing the contrasting metaphors of "tent" and "house," and which, in any case, belongs more appropriately to 5:2-10 than to 4:13-18. If we keep in mind that since 2:14 Paul has been defending the legitimacy and authenticity of his apostolic ministry in the face of rival apostles (11:13) who claim superior wisdom (1:12), possess "letters of recommendation" (3:1), and boast about their radiant faces (5:12) that reflect, like Moses', the glory of God (cf. 3:12-18; 4:6), then we begin to discover in our varied verses a common concern. Paul is saying that the glory of God or the risen life of Jesus reaches only us through the *dying* of Jesus (4:10) that the apostle proclaims; that our participation in this glorious life comes only through our participation in this ignominious death, that is, in our "daily dying" in service to the gospel; and that only in this way does the church confidently experience "daily renewal" or the anticipation of that final glorification which will verify the truth of Paul's apostolic gospel and ministry.

Since Paul lacked the sort of glamorous gifts and celebrity credentials much of the Corinthian (not to say, American) church prefers in its pastors and pulpits, usually in the name of "spirituality" told and sold with spellbinding eloquence, what compelled Paul to keep on preaching "the word of the cross" (1 Cor. 1:18) amid such opposition in the church? And what could keep us doing the same?

Well, Paul believes something, something not "seen" by everyone, but something that compels him to proclaim it. Here in verse 13 he quotes from Psalm 115:1a, as given in the Septuagint (= Ps. 116:10 in the Hebrew text on which our English translations of the Old Testament are based): "I believed, and so I spoke." To which Paul adds, probably embracing his coworkers: "we also believe, and so we speak [*laloumen*]," a term Paul employs with reference to preaching the gospel (2:17; 1 Thess. 2:2). That is to say, Paul does not preach on the basis of empirical "success" or "glory," but is rather impelled

250

by the "Spirit of faith" *(pneuma tēs pisteōs),* which can be taken in one of two ways: either as "the same" Spirit who prompted the psalmist's proclamation or (as suggested by the NRSV's lowercasing of "spirit") "the same" spirit or disposition of faith which Paul shares with the psalmist. Whether we take Paul's meaning as emphasizing the gift ("spirit of faith") or the Giver ("Spirit of faith"), in either case the faith given requires oral confession, requires proclamation (Rom. 10:8-17) — even if Paul does not proclaim the word of faith with the requisite oratorical displays (1 Cor. 2:1-5; 2 Cor. 10:10).

Moreover, Paul can preach because he and his coworkers "know" that the risen life of Jesus is not exhausted as a present possession, and its visibility "in our mortal flesh" (4:11) is seen only through faith (5:7), through hardship, suffering, and mortality (4:8-10); it is not an empirically demonstrable phenomenon evident in, say, a radiant personality, or a shining face, or the gift or craft of eloquence — as if such experiences rendered death irrelevant to human destiny. In contrast to this claim of Paul's opponents, the risen life of Jesus is outside ourselves, beyond ourselves, out on the horizon of the future where it promises to meet us. It is out of this hope that Paul and his coworkers speak the gospel. In the words of a catechetical formula adapted here by Paul, "We know that the one who raised the Lord Jesus *will raise* [egerei] us also with Jesus, and *will bring* [parastēsei] us with you into his presence" (4:14). What has happened to the crucified Jesus in his resurrection into glory now awaits not just the apostle, who carries in his body the dying of Jesus (4:10), but also the church, gathered now by the proclamation of faith, and which will also be gathered into glory by the power of God. Thus the glorious destiny of the church is none other than that of the Lord Jesus himself.

For this reason Paul declares to the Corinthians that "everything is for your sake" (v. 15); that is, his proclamation of Jesus Christ as Lord and all its attendant hardships are undertaken in service to the hearers of the gospel (v. 5), and therefore in service to their glorious destiny. Paul then elaborates, "so that grace, as it extends [pleonasasa] to more and more people, may increase [perisseusēi] thanksgiving, to the glory of God" (v. 15). Gratitude *(eucharistia)* is elicited by grace *(charis),* understood as God's saving power *(dynamis)* on our behalf (4:7; 12:8-9).

"So we do not lose heart" (v. 16) is the conclusion Paul draws for the present from the future. Paul is not overcome by cowardice but lives in the plenitude of gratitude; he does not base his proclamation or establish his commission to preach the gospel on the basis of "present trends" but on the coming future of God's glory. It is not that Paul is evading these trends in the church or in the culture; in fact, he is confronting them head-on in Corinth. But he is reframing them by a new reality not acknowledged by these assured developments, namely, by the radiance of the divine glory "shining in the face of Jesus Christ" that has also "shone in our hearts" (4:6).

In 4:16–5:1 Paul employs a series of metaphoric opposites to talk further about this divine glory or the risen life of Jesus in contrast to those deadly and otherwise disheartening "present trends" that he understands God's future to bracket and relativize. Here in verse 16 Paul speaks on the one hand of "our outer nature . . . wasting away," in contrast to our "inner nature" that "is being renewed day by day." The distinction between the "inner" (esō) and the "outer man" (exō anthrōpos) had a long philosophical lineage in Paul's world, but in this context "outer" refers to the "mortal flesh" of verse 11, the site of decay, hardships, and suffering. Here, life is "mortal life," existence lived continually under the shadow of death. To this "outer" man or woman of the old age that is passing away, there also corresponds the "inner" or authentic human self that is never our possession or achievement, but only a gift of grace to be received "day by day" (cf. 3:18; Gal. 2:20: "no longer I who live, but it is Christ who lives in me"). Our true life does not evade or annul our death; it does not grow organically out of our past, even by means of "spiritual formation"; but our risen life enters into our present "wasting away" only from the future, from God, just as it did for Jesus himself (v. 14).

In verse 17 Paul gives further grounds for why "we do not lose heart." Whereas verse 16 states the hope as the daily renewal of eschatological existence ("the inner man") amid the disintegration of this "mortal life" ("the outer man"), now Paul states the hope in terms of "this slight momentary affliction" that "is preparing us for an eternal weight of glory beyond all measure" (cf. Rom. 8:18). Notice here that the affliction, to which earlier reference was made in the peristasis catalogue (4:8-9), is characterized as but "momentary." In light of God's glorious future into which we will be raised (v. 14), our affliction, while not evadable, is nevertheless endurable because it is rightly understood as temporary. Because God's glory is an eschatological rather than an empirical phenomenon, language cannot fully comprehend it; it can only suggest a reality beyond all imagining: eternal, weighty, and "in never-ending abundance" (Bultmann). This is the framework of hope into which Paul places all his affliction. "Therefore, we do not lose heart"!

In verse 18 this framework of hope can be understood as a viewpoint that results from the turning point of the ages wrought in the cross and resurrection of Jesus Christ (5:14-17): "We look not at what can be seen but at what cannot be seen." This is not a fixated or hypnotic stare into a mystical abyss, but a keeping in view of the point that nothing in this world, including ourselves and our ministry, can be regarded apart from the destiny of Jesus Christ. This is not a "self-evident" truth this age can ever come to "see" with its own eyes or on its own terms (1 Cor. 2:7-8); it can be "seen" only in faith (2 Cor. 5:7); it can reach us only as a revelation from "the new creation" — and not as an extrapolation from the old (5:14-17).

Our text now concludes with 5:1, which the lectionary editors presumably included (despite its beginning a new paragraph) because it continues the pattern of antithetical metaphors stretching from 4:7. Recall that the career, or even body, of Paul is likened there to an "earthen pot," the antithesis of the gospel "treasure" it contains. But now in 5:1 Paul, the tentmaker (Acts 18:3), switches his metaphors. The "body" (5:8) is likened to a destructible "earthly tent" in contrast to a "house . . . eternal in the heavens." Our tattered flesh, in which the treasured gospel finds embodiment, strains forward to God's permanent provision for risen life. Treasured by God, eternal security awaits us in glory when we shall be "at home with the Lord" (5:8). "So we do not lose heart" (4:16, 1), and "we are always confident" (5:6) amid our present struggles on behalf of the gospel.

*James F. Kay*

## Fourth Sunday after Pentecost, Year B

First Lesson: 1 Samuel 15:34–16:13
(Psalm 20)
**Second Lesson: 2 Corinthians 5:6-10, (11-13), 14-17**
Gospel Lesson: Mark 4:26-34

The swath of chapter 5 that constitutes today's lectionary selection from 2 Corinthians falls into three parts: verses 6-10, which center on the present "walk" of the believer in light of the eschatological future; verses 11-13 (indicated as optional), which focus on the ethos or character of the apostolic proclaimer; and verses 14-17, which set forth the eschatological salvation event wrought in the cross-resurrection of Jesus Christ. These parts will be considered in sequence.

In contrast to the claims of Paul's opponents, the hope of glory is neither empirically evident to eyes accustomed to "this age" or so palpably present as to render hope superfluous as a promise already fulfilled. The enthusiasts (1 Cor. 4:8; 13:1) and the pseudoapostles (2 Cor. 5:12; 11:13; cf. 11:5; 12:11) in Corinth wanted no talk of dying, no talk of the cross, and no stammering forth of the gospel. They were into "spirituality" and "glory," basing their claim to apostolic authority on the brilliance of their radiant faces (5:12) and the razzle-dazzle of their pulpit oratory positively pulsating with power (1 Cor. 2:1-5; 2 Cor. 10:10). For them, seeing was believing.

By contrast, Paul's confidence is not grounded in the way things now appear (2 Cor. 5:7), on a world that is passing away (1 Cor. 7:31), in preserving his physique (2 Cor. 4:7-12), or in cultivating the power of human eloquence (1 Cor. 2:1-5). Paul looks the worst that can befall the world, our bodies, and our words straight in the eye, facing death itself. His gospel really is the gospel because it does not evade suffering but endures it all with Jesus. "So we are *always* [*pantote*] confident," declares the apostle (5:6), using the same adverb he used earlier in 4:10 in describing his ministry as "*always* [*pantote*] carrying in the body the dying of Jesus, so that the life of Jesus may also be made visible in our bodies." Amid the always constant pressure of death and dying, Paul is sustained in confidence by the always countervailing hope that death and dying do not hold the last word on our destiny but are themselves ultimately subject to the risen life of our crucified Lord. "We walk by faith, not by sight" (5:7).

Thus the Christian life is a journey, a pilgrimage, ever in transit, or bound for glory. In this context Paul uses the contrasting metaphors "to be at home" *(endēmein)* and "to be abroad" *(ekdēmein)*. From the standpoint of the end of our journey, "to be at home" is to be "with the Lord" (v. 8); from the standpoint of the pilgrimage now in progress, "to be at home" is to be "in the body" (v. 6). But whether we regard ourselves looking backward from the standpoint of where we are going or forward from the standpoint of where we are, in either case, "whether we are at home or away, we make it our aim to please him" (v. 9). That is to say, no hardship we undergo, and no concern for ourselves, sidetracks us from the goal of serving our Lord.

In this sense we are ultimately accountable in our ministry not to the voice (or applause) of the people, but to the Word of God enfleshed in Jesus Christ. In Pauline eschatology, sometimes it is Jesus Christ (1 Thess. 2:19; 1 Cor. 4:5) and sometimes it is God (1 Thess. 3:13; Rom. 14:10) who sits in the role of the final judge. In the context of 2 Corinthians 4 and 5, where

Paul has spoken of his own career and body as reiterating in the present the dying of Jesus, it is understandable that Jesus, who suffered before the judgment seat of Pontius Pilate, should now preside from the judgment seat of glory (2 Cor. 5:10). There is no higher court of appeal. But the one who is the Judge is the one God made "to be sin" for our sakes (5:21). The one who is the Judge is the one "who loved us and gave himself for us" (cf. Gal. 2:20). The one who was judged for our sakes unto death is the one who will be the Judge of all.

This means that no human judgments are final; all are penultimate at best. This is true whether they come down from the court bench, the stock exchange seat, the professorial chair, the bishop's throne, the "roundtable" pulpit, the "catbird seat" of a clever politician, the anchor desk, or the sofas of a focus group. All of us who sit on such seats of judgment and power, even the most "democratic" ones, will answer to Jesus Christ. Knowing this, we who are both issuing and receiving judgments, as we are and as we must "in this age," are freed "in Christ" from the withering tyranny of their finality and ultimacy. The arbiters of taste, public opinion, and political correctness do not have the last word. We can therefore commit our work and our lives to Jesus Christ. Only the one who loved us unto death can render the final verdict.

"Therefore, knowing the fear of the Lord, we try to persuade others" (v. 11a). That is to say, the confidence in which Paul and his coworkers undertake the ministry of the word is not the self-confidence of entrepreneurs (2:17), but the respectful obedience of those whose ambassadorial service is at the pleasure of Christ the Lord (cf. 5:9, 20). Commentators such as Bultmann have suggested that the word "persuade" be set in quotation marks because Paul has already made it clear to the Corinthians (1 Cor 2:4; 2 Cor. 4:2) and earlier to the Galatians (1:10) that he is not about persuasion, insofar as that term connotes reliance on clever rhetorical tricks to manipulate an audience. Rather, whether standing before God or before the Corinthians, Paul has nothing to hide (2 Cor. 5:11b). As he had already indicated to the Corinthians, "We refuse to practice cunning or to falsify God's word; but by the open statement of the truth we commend ourselves to the conscience of everyone in the sight of God" (4:2; cf. 6:3). Now Paul reiterates that "we ourselves are well known to God, and I hope that we are also well known to your consciences," not for the purposes of self-commendation, but in order that the Corinthians may refute the charges of duplicitous motives (11:7-11), financial fudging (12:16-17), cowardice (10:10), and ineffectual preaching (10:10; 11:6) that Paul's opponents were unleashing against him. The politics of destruction is well known in the history of the church!

Paul's opponents were bent on tearing him down and building up themselves. They were boasting "in outward appearance [*en prosōpōi*, lit. 'in the face'] and not in the heart" (v. 12). Moreover, their public displays of ecstasy seemed to confirm the Spirit-filled character of their proclamation. But unlike his opponents, Paul refuses to establish his apostolic authenticity on the basis of his ecstatic experiences. For Paul spiritual ecstasy is personal worship directed to God (cf. 1 Cor. 14:2, 28); it is not to be marketed to enhance ministerial reputations (cf. 2 Cor. 4:5; 5:15), as if true piety could be demonstrated by a radiant face or confirmed by an applause meter. What is directed to the Corinthians is a proclamation of the gospel that is sober, thoughtful, and frank: "For if we are beside ourselves, it is for God; if we are in our right mind, it is for you" (2 Cor. 5:13).

What, then, motivates Paul and his coworkers in the ministry of the gospel, if not money or success? It is nothing other than "the love of Christ" (v. 14). This is not to be taken as Paul's love for Christ, so that his motivation is ultimately a self-motivation, but rather as Christ's love, not only for Paul and the other preachers of the gospel, but "for all," emphatically indicated by the fact that twice in as many sentences Christ is said to have "died for all" (vv. 14, 15). It is this passion of Christ for all that becomes Paul's all-consuming passion for Christ. "For the love of Christ urges us on [*synechei hēmas*]," the NRSV translates, accenting the connotation of impulsion (cf. "impels," NAB) present in the Greek verb, but to the neglect of the connotations of control (RSV) or compulsion ("compels," NIV) highlighted in other translations.

Paul is "convinced that one has died for all [*hyper pantōn*]; therefore all [*pantes*] have died [v. 14b]. And he died for all [*hyper pantōn*], so that those who live might live no longer for themselves, but for him who died and was raised for them" (v. 15). These two verses are among the most succinct and important summaries of the gospel given in the New Testament, and they form the basis for Paul's subsequent and magnificent affirmations of the new creation (v. 17) and the reconciliation of the world (vv. 18-19). But before venturing to preach from this précis of the gospel, preachers need to consider matters that cannot be answered by exegesis alone but require dogmatic reflection. Two are tagged here: First, Christ died "for *all*." Does this "all" mean *all*, or only all *believers* (or all who are baptized)? Second, Christ died "*for* all." What is the force of this "for"? Does it mean "in place of" or "on behalf of"? In other words, in what sense do "all" participate in, or find themselves related to, the death of Christ?

What is clearer is that, since the death of Jesus Christ, a new way of living has entered into the world: "He died for us that we might die to ourselves" (Calvin). All boasting about externals is put to death; what comes to life is service to others, which is the service owed to Jesus Christ. Those who embrace the message of the cross "live no longer for themselves, but for him who died and was raised for them." The death and resurrection of Jesus Christ thus mark the decisive turning point in God's relationship to the world and humanity's relationship to God. This is richly developed in verses 16 and 17, which conclude today's lection. These verses will be commented upon below, where they begin our next lectionary selection.

*James F. Kay*

## Fourth Sunday in Lent, Year C

First Lesson: Joshua 5:9-12
(Psalm 32)
**Second Lesson: 2 Corinthians 5:16-21**
Gospel Lesson: Luke 15:1-3, 11b-32

Our lection is embedded in the broader context of 2:14–6:10, where Paul defends his apostolic ministry to a congregation beset by spiritual enthusiasts (1 Cor. 4:8; 13:1) and lately arrived pseudoapostles boasting of their superior credentials (2 Cor. 5:12; 11:13). In the face of these challenges to the founding gospel he proclaimed, Paul presents a point of view from which the Corinthians can discern authentic ministry of the word from its counterfeits. As in the first century, so today no Christian community can evade testing those claiming to speak "on behalf of Christ" (5:20), even if these preachers exhibit superior "spirituality" or perfect pedigrees of their "apostolic succession."

Regrettably, the Revised Common Lectionary severs 5:16 and its connective "therefore" from the antecedent grounds specified in verses 14-15: "For the love of Christ urges us on, because we are convinced that one has died for all; therefore all have died. And he died for all, so that those who live might live no longer for themselves, but for him who died and was raised for them." By rescuing these shorn verses from the editors' cutting floor, our text is restored to its kerygmatic context and content: "From now on, *therefore*, we regard no one from a human point of view [*kata sarka*]; even though we once knew Christ from a human point of view [*kata sarka*], we know him no longer in that way." Heard in context, "From now on, therefore" is not referring to some moment of conversion, whether Paul's or others', but to the more decisive and universal turning point that "one has died for all." From that axial moment there has come on the scene a new way of living ("no longer for themselves" [v. 15]) and a new way of knowing ("no longer according to the flesh" [v. 16]). Both are so radically opposite to the way "this age" (4:4) acts that Paul, perhaps echoing Isaiah (42:9; 43:18-19; 48:6; and 65:17-18), can exclaim, "So if anyone is in Christ, there is a new creation: everything old has passed away; see, everything has become new!" (v. 17; cf. Gal. 6:15). God's reconciling act in Christ entails not the rebuilding or repairing of the old creation, but its replacement by a new one.

Unfortunately, the NRSV follows the RSV in translating the prepositional phrase *kata sarka* (v. 16, lit. "according to the flesh") with the misleading phrase "from a human point of view." This translation makes no logical sense. From what vantage point could human beings ever see anything if not from a "human" one? Moreover, a "human point of view" could be heard as a "humane point of view," one consistent with love and reconciliation. But Paul is not asking the Corinthians to take leave of humane perspectives!

Exegetes have long debated whether *kata sarka* is to be taken adjectivally or adverbially. Scholarly consensus finds the adverbial reading more contextually appropriate and consistent with Paul's usage elsewhere. Paul is not forswearing people who are "according to the flesh" or a Christ who is "according to the flesh"; rather, he is heralding a new way of knowing that is no longer "according to the flesh."

What is this *kata sarka* way of knowing? It is a perceiving of others divorced from their destiny as beloved of God, that is, as those for whom Christ died and was raised. It is also a perceiving of Christ divorced from his destiny as the one who died and was raised for all. Hence the futility of all quests for the "historical Jesus," insofar as these *kata sarka* reconstructions proclaim as "saving" one known apart from his cross and resurrection. "So if anyone is in Christ" (v. 17), that is, under his Lordship and incorporated into his body, the church, there is a new way of perceiving and proceeding, namely, according to the Lord (2 Cor. 11:17), according to love (Rom. 14:15), or "according to the Spirit" (Rom. 8:4-5). In an earlier letter to the Corinthians, Paul characterized the contrast between these antithetical ways of knowing as "spiritual" and "unspiritual" (1 Cor. 2:6-16). But when the Corinthians attempt to demonstrate the power of their spirituality by manifestations of ecstasy (cf. 2 Cor. 5:12) while remaining in competitive patterns of communal life, their perceiving of the gospel is shown to be *kata sarka*, still bound to the dominant perspectives of the old age. This spirit, for all its exuberance, stands in opposition rather than orientation toward the love of Christ "who died for all." For this reason J. Louis Martyn has suggested that the opposite of knowing *kata sarka* is knowing *kata stauron*, "according to the cross" (cf. Gal. 6:14). At the juncture of the ages, the crucial test of all our God-talk and earthly ethics is not whether they demonstrate their power in ecstatic spirituality (cf. 2 Cor. 5:13), but whether they proclaim the cross of Christ as God's power to extinguish whatever prevents us from knowing and serving those in need (5:14-15). Such proclamation, in words and deeds, is a defining hallmark of authentic and apostolic ministry of the word.

Both this "ministry" (v. 18) and its "message [lit. *logos*, 'word'] of reconciliation" (v. 19) have been entrusted "to us" (*hēmin*, v. 18; *en hēmin*, v. 19), indicating here not only Paul but the church. In verse 18a Paul redescribes the message of the redemptive event (previously stated in v. 15) as an act of God, "who through Christ reconciled us to himself." Paul then explains this act in more detail as "not counting their trespasses against them" (v. 19a), which parallels his later discussion of reconciliation as the purging of sins wrought by God through the death of his Son (Rom. 5:1-11). If God's love discounts our trespasses, verse 21 immediately reminds us that this is only accomplished through divine judgment, an annihilating no, but one which God himself bears in Christ: "For our sake he [God] made him [Christ] to be sin who knew no sin, so that in him we might become the righteousness of God." Thus the "the word of reconciliation" is none other than "the word of the cross" (1 Cor. 1:18), which is "the word of life" (Phil. 2:16).

Several points can be made here, and all are worthy of sermonic development. First, whatever human actions led to the death of Jesus Christ, in this death God was at work to bring forth new life for all. Second, God did not need to be reconciled to the world; it is we who stood "helplessly" mired in hostility to God; and it is God who acted in love for us "while we still were sinners" (Rom. 5:8), "while we were enemies" (Rom. 5:10), and "reconciled us to himself" (2 Cor. 5:18). Third, God did not respond to our evil with evil, to our enmity with enmity, or to our violence with violence. God rejected all these old-world patterns and practices by overcoming them in a sovereign love that suffered unto death — and unto new life. Fourth, the "word of reconciliation" entrusted to the church is not the conciliatory imperative "Let's all get along!" Rather, it is the indispensable indicative proclaiming the reconciliation God has accomplished in Christ. The only basis of all pulpit pleas to "be reconciled to God" (v. 20) is that in Christ God has *already* "reconciled us to himself" (v. 18). Pleading the former without proclaiming the latter exchanges the enlivening gospel of God for the deadening moralism of a hectoring harangue.

Notice that 5:18-19 predicates two acts of God: (1) reconciling through Christ, restated as "not counting their trespasses," and (2) giving the "ministry of reconciliation," restated as the "message [*logos,* lit. 'word'] of reconciliation." The question arises whether these two acts are sequential or simultaneous, that is, two sides of one eschatological event. To say that God simultaneously instituted the deed and the word of reconciliation is to claim that Jesus Christ is savingly present whenever the word announcing his cross and resurrection as God's act on our behalf is proclaimed. For this reason, in Paul's letters faith in Jesus Christ and faith in the word (or kerygma or gospel) proclaiming him are one and the same (cf. 1 Cor. 1:21; 2:4-5; 15:2, 11, 14; Gal. 2:16; Phil. 1:27, 29; Rom. 10:14). While we cannot restrict God's contemporary saving work to the explicit proclamation of the gospel, we can claim that in this proclamation "God is making his appeal through us" (2 Cor. 5:20). This conviction is the basis of Paul's confidence in his apostolic ministry. Heard today as God's promise, it renews our own confidence that the "day of salvation," anticipated in Isaiah 49:8, now dawns in the ministry of the word (2 Cor. 6:2).

Thus, Paul likens his vocation not to "peddlers of God's word" (2:17), but to envoys with a message from God: "So we are ambassadors for Christ, since God is making his appeal through us; we entreat you on behalf of Christ, be reconciled to God" (5:20), and "we urge you also not to accept the grace of God in vain" (6:1). Here the apostolic preacher employs "we" and "you" language as he directly and authoritatively addresses the Corinthians *hyper Christou,* "in Christ's stead." Paul does not invent the gospel of God's reconciling act in Christ's cross and resurrection, and neither do we. As "ambassadors for Christ," we are entrusted with the gospel by God. The message is to be delivered not only to the world but also to the church entrusted with it. As Paul's entreaties to the Corinthians show (perhaps concluding our lection more fittingly at 6:2 than 5:21), the church never moves beyond its own need to hear the message of reconciliation it bears to others. Through the words of his ambassadors, God is now making his appeal, uttering his own creative word, thereby constituting and reconstituting cruciform communities impelled by the love of Christ.

*James F. Kay*

## Fifth Sunday after Pentecost, Year B

First Lesson: 1 Samuel 17:(1a, 4-11, 19-23), 32-49
(Psalm 9:9-20)
**Second Lesson: 2 Corinthians 6:1-13**
Gospel Lesson: Mark 4:35-41

The editors of the Revised Common Lectionary have followed the traditional chapter divisions by beginning our lection at 6:1-2, even though these verses continue the exhortation found in 5:20 and could therefore appropriately serve as the conclusion to a unit of thought stretching from at least 5:14. Since "one has died for all," and by means of this death God "reconciled us to himself through Christ, and has given us the ministry of reconciliation" (5:18), Paul proceeds to exercise this ministry by announcing to the Corinthians that "now is the day of salvation" (6:2; Isa. 49:8), urging them not "to accept the grace of God in vain" (6:1). If they reject Paul's apostleship in favor of newly arrived pseudoapostles (5:12; 11:13), they will reject God's ambassador (5:20) and, in rejecting this authorized messenger (2:17), will be rejecting the word he is entrusted to bring them. To be reconciled to Paul, therefore, is to welcome the divine "message of reconciliation" (5:19); conversely, to embrace this message is to welcome the apostolic ambassador who brings it.

At 6:3 Paul introduces a *peristasis* catalogue, that is, an enumeration of hardships (vv. 4-5) he has endured in his service to the word of reconciliation. Resumptive of those hardships listed in 4:7-12, Paul's catalogue enables him to commend himself (and perhaps coworkers such as Timothy [1:1]). He writes, "As servants of God [*theou diakonoi*] we have commended ourselves [*synistanontes heautous*] in every way" (v. 4). This claim seems to stand in tension, if not contradiction, to what Paul has said in 5:12: "We are not commending ourselves [*ou heautous synistanomen*] to you again, but giving you an opportunity to boast about us, so that you may be able to answer those who boast in outward appearance [*en prosōpōi*, lit. 'in the face'] and not in the heart." John T. Fitzgerald has observed that every time Paul speaks negatively of self-commendation he places the pronoun *before* the verb, as in 5:12 (and so also in 3:1; 10:12, 18; cf. 4:5). When he speaks positively of the same, he places the pronoun *after* the verb, as here in 6:4 (and so also in 4:2; cf. 7:11). The point is that there is a legitimate boasting "in the Lord" (1 Cor. 1:31; cf. Jer. 9:23-24). Such "boasting" is a way of blessing God. It does not arise out of egoistic motives or the cult of personality, typical of the self-

261

promotional strategies of the old age. Rather, this self-commendation is a way of praising God's faithfulness amid all the adversities that inevitably attend the ministry of reconciliation. To speak concretely of God's deliverance leads Paul to speak concretely of the vicissitudes he has undergone. In this way Paul does commend the blamelessness of his apostolic ministry (2 Cor. 6:3; cf. 1 Cor. 9:12) by witnessing to his own embodiment of the life-giving dying of Jesus that he proclaims (2 Cor. 4:10-12).

This paradox of "power . . . made perfect in weakness" (12:9), a manifestation of the new creation, is woven throughout 6:4-10 and serves to clinch Paul's argued defense of his apostleship (2:14–6:10). Paul begins by noting his "much endurance," listing nine hardships, in three groups of three items each, in which that endurance was demonstrated (vv. 4-5). The first group, "in afflictions, [in] hardships, [in] calamities," operates at the level of a general summary; the second group, "[in] beatings, [in] imprisonments, [in] riots," refers more directly to circumstances of punishment and persecution (cf. 11:23-25; Acts 16:19-23, 37; 18:12-17); and the third group, "[in] labors, [in] sleepless nights, [in] hunger," refers to the vocational hardships of a "tent-making" minister (11:27; 1 Thess. 2:9).

This catalogue of hardships is followed by one of "virtues" or powers. This second enumeration emphasizes not simply that Paul has endured adversity, but that he has endured it in "purity [of motive], knowledge, patience, kindness, holiness of spirit [*en pneumati hagioi*], genuine love, truthful speech," and fully armed "with the weapons of righteousness" (vv. 6-7). Even granting the NRSV translation, which takes here the arguable reference to the Holy Spirit as referring to the holiness of the human spirit, it is important to remember that for Paul all human "virtues" are fruits of the divine Spirit (Gal. 5:22) and not the cultivated habits of the human heart. Since his own endurance is the result of "the power of God" (2 Cor. 6:7; cf. 4:7-12), Paul's "virtues" are really charisms.

In verse 8a we find a brief catalogue of vicissitudes, followed in verses 8b-10 by seven antithetical clauses: "as impostors, and yet are true; as unknown, and yet are well known; as dying, and see — we are alive; as punished, and yet not killed; as sorrowful, yet always rejoicing; as poor, yet making many rich; as having nothing, and yet possessing everything." All of the initial theses, taken as exclusive characterizations of Paul apart from their antitheses, are caricatures because they are based on anachronistic *kata sarka* criteria (5:16). These old norms have now been relativized by those arising from the eschatological "new creation" wrought in the cross of Christ (5:14-15, 17), the salvation event that continues "today" in its very proclamation (5:18-20; 6:2). As an apostle, therefore, Paul embodies the gospel he preaches, living no longer for himself (cf. 5:15) but as a "new creation." But authentic apostolic existence cannot be seen or known by the norms of the old creation. Thus his opponents' perception of Paul as pitifully weak and without power (10:1, 10), and therefore an impostor (6:8), is decisively refuted only when reframed by criteria drawn from the cross and resurrection of Christ. Paul reiterates in the practice of his own ministry that "of our Lord Jesus Christ, [who] though he was rich, yet for your sakes he became poor, so that by his poverty you might become rich" (8:9; cf. 6:10). Paul exhibits the pattern of Christ himself, in whom weakness and power are joined (13:4). Thus Paul's weakness, like that of the crucified Christ, magnifies the power of God who gives life to the dead (1:8-9; 4:7), redounds to God's praise, and thereby shows Paul's apostleship to be authentic.

Today's Epistle lection closes with verses 11-13, Paul's personal and pastoral appeal to his beloved Corinthians: "Our mouths are open to you" *(To stoma hēmōn aneōigen pros hymas),* a locution meaning "We are speaking frankly to you" and probably not a reference to the "kiss of peace" (1 Cor. 16:20). Paul has spoken with candid openness to the Corinthians — and perhaps with more than his apostolic office required. He has made himself vulnerable to them in love ("our heart is wide open to you" [v. 11]). Now he entreats them to "open wide your hearts also" (v. 13).

Paul's Corinthian correspondence witnesses to the fact that fractious and contentious churches are not confined to the outset of our own century. If we place our congregational conflicts into the canonical perspective of the turn of the ages that has taken place in the cross and resurrection of Jesus Christ, we are compelled to reframe what "winning" and "losing" mean. Paul is a fighter, a warrior-apostle uninterested in pursuing appeasement with the forces of the old creation, even when the front line runs right through a community he has founded. Yet equipped with the gifts of the Spirit (6:6-7), Paul conducts himself on the battlefield in accordance with the message of reconciliation (cf. 10:3-6). That is to say, the means by which the gospel is advanced — and defended — must always be congruent with the claims of the gospel. For this reason, Paul speaks truthfully (6:7) and frankly (6:11), refusing to practice hucksterism (2:17), cunning, or deceit (4:2). If we relied on these anachronistic strategies to win the day, "our striving would be losing." But what does "victory" look like? Paul marches through the world in "triumph," but only as God's captive shouldering Jesus' cross. Paul's vocation becomes cruciform, "carrying in the body the dying of Jesus, so that the life of Jesus may also be made visible in our bodies" (4:10; cf. 2:14-16).

No doubt faithfulness to the Crucified, in battle against the illegitimate powers of the old creation, will occasion our own excruciations: suffering, hardships, or even martyrdom. Nevertheless, Paul never exhorts the Corinthians to seek suffering, or to embark on strenuous hardships like his own, or to court martyrdom. Where we take up our positions on the line of battle — and the sacrifices, or even casualties, those positions engender — belongs to our specific vocation. What is common to the calling of all Christians, armed with the gifts of the Spirit (2 Cor. 6:6-7; 1 Cor. 12:3), is that we embody the entrusted message of reconciliation not only for the world, but for each other; not only with our lips, but in our lives.

*James F. Kay*

## Sixth Sunday after Pentecost, Year B

First Lesson: 2 Samuel 1:1, 17-27
(Psalm 130)
**Second Lesson: 2 Corinthians 8:7-15**
Gospel Lesson: Mark 5:21-43

Second Corinthians 8, which concerns the collection for the saints in Jerusalem, is most often taken to be a separate business letter included in the book by later editors. Whatever its actual timing, it fits precisely with Paul's understanding of the life in the Spirit: "Since we have these promises, beloved, let us cleanse ourselves from every defilement of body and of spirit, making holiness perfect in the fear of God" (7:1). Goodness was a civic virtue far back in Hellenism. A benefactor who generously bestowed goods upon others was thought deserving of the highest praise among people and actually made cities run. Paul understood he was called by the Great Benefactor, the Savior, Jesus Christ the Lord, and so was very careful to point to Christ's grace and his own apostolic role as representative of the benefactor. He refuses to be paid for his public service, but works as a tentmaker. He emphasizes grace at every point. In that vein Paul uses a recent collection among the poor churches in Macedonia that "overflowed in a wealth of generosity on their part" (8:2) not only to goad Corinthians into giving, but to show the "the grace [benefaction] of God" (8:1).

264

Just as Paul had earlier recounted his own suffering in joy that came with bringing the gospel to the Corinthians, here he recounts the suffering and joy of the Macedonian churches and thus identifies the source of both as God's own grace. Macedonians became surprisingly liberal benefactors due to the liberality of this God. Not only did they freely give according to their own initiative, but in a surprising juxtaposition they *begged* from Paul the *grace* (favor) of being a *benefactor* (giver of favors) for the Jerusalem collection (8:4). What minister would not wish for such a situation! Here then is the fruit of the gospel, with the poorest churches begging to be benefactors, and their enthusiasm for the cause so great that Titus was to be sent to bring it off. All of this is bound up again with the concern of the entire second letter: the grace to give to others comes from giving themselves first to God, then to Paul and his fellow preachers (8:5). The pseudoapostles who troubled the congregation were bound to leave the Corinthian church dry and lifeless because they substituted a new law for the gospel. However, in the gospel — with this God and with these apostles (by God's own choice) — grace overflows in faith, word, knowledge, and zeal which comes with a new heart (8:7).

As true as it is that one cannot change his/her own will in relation to God, the will can *be* changed by God and thus made new. The Macedonians are evidence of that. It would be a significant misunderstanding of Paul's use of the Macedonian churches to take them as the new measure of cheerful and liberal giving. If competition among givers works to some extent to swell the coffers of the church, Paul cannot auction God's grace to the highest giver. What Paul is doing here is not what most commentators seem to think, that he is goading the Corinthians into giving or shaming them into it by craftily using the Macedonians. He is exhorting, and exhortation is not a new law. His words aim at people's hope and the faith in which Christ has created them anew, even with a new *desire*.

It is sometimes said that the purpose of a liberal education is to educate desire, but here Paul knows that desire is not educated so much as emboldened to emerge when God's grace has made a new will. Like a mare who nuzzles her foal into standing on its shaky new legs in order to walk and eventually run, Paul says it is time to stand on your own new legs. Freedom, not law, leads to generosity.

Paul is too often thought to be taking back all his earlier comments about becoming a new creature and always carrying in the body the death of Jesus (4:10, 5:16); here we also see how Paul reminds his enthusiastic Christians at Corinth that they are theologians of Jesus' cross. First, when he exhorts and even challenges them with the example of Macedonia, he is not giving an order or shaming them — that would be for an old time now past. He

265

is proving something to them, that is, that their new love is in fact genuine. Love is not otherworldly, nor so much of this old world's life that we simply fall back into manipulating people into being less stingy. The liberality that people fear is not really forthcoming in faith has shown itself "up north" as alive and well, Paul says, overflowing really, and is proof that the same love will show itself in Corinth because they have the same gracing God.

Exhortation like this often is perceived to fall back into using the Macedonians as a stick or as a gauge for determining how the Corinthians should now behave if they are going to live up to the proper Christian standard. Exhortation in Paul is always the gospel said in another verbal mode that encourages faith and even scorns that which is not. Your love is true (8:8), Paul assures them, it is not of the old type that has one thing going on inside a person and another outside. In Christ what is inside comes out and what is outside shows what is within. The basis for this is the gospel message: "For you know the generous act of our Lord Jesus Christ, that though he was rich, yet for your sakes he became poor, so that by his poverty you might become rich" (8:9). This echoes Paul's use of the Christ hymn in Philippians 2 and applies the theology of the cross to this situation of collecting money for the poor — even *from* the poor!

But how does one get from Christ's sacrifice on the cross to exhorting people in a collection for the Jerusalem churches? Is this not reducing the cross to a tit for tat, or merely making of Christ a new Moses who has come to provide an example of perfect selfless giving? For Paul giving freely is not a matter of asceticism that denies pleasure or worldly things for a spiritual purpose. Paul moves directly to the matter of "equality," which is the same thing in Philippians 2 that Christ did not consider a "thing" to be grasped. To understand what is going on, it is likely best to consider the old description of faith as a marriage of the sinner with Christ. In such a marriage an exchange takes place that takes what is the bridegroom's and gives it to the bride, that is, life, rightness with God, forgiveness, eternal life; in turn, what is the bride's becomes the groom's: death, sin, separation from God. Why would Christ do this? Not for gain, not for becoming more lovable in God's eyes, not for mere payment of a debt, but for love of the spouse. In that love there comes to be equality so that this new relationship forever determines who these two are, Christ and the sinner.

What Christ did on the cross he is now doing among his people in the churches. The bridal exchange, even between churches and peoples, results in the actual equality that otherwise is so elusive in this world. The "example" of Christ is not another law, but it is the gospel. The gospel is the self-giving of God in Jesus Christ, who gives us his desire for others even while they are sinners. This desire is not like our sinful desires that seek only our own selves and so eventuate in a master lording it over a slave. The desire of the new heart eventuates in actual, real, concrete equality. Paul is getting his Corinthians used to their new surroundings, as spouse of Christ, where there is true equality. In that place, "from each according to ability and to each according to need" is no longer a wishful dream but a reality. Paul saw it in himself and in the Macedonians, and now he exhorted the Corinthians to bring off what they themselves could hardly believe was possible: "so that their abundance may be for your need, in order that there may be a fair balance" (8:14). When the true gospel in Jesus Christ is proclaimed, giving comes from a certain hope. And hope gives even when we are in poverty on this earth, and not from selfish desire or fear: "I do not say this as a command, but to prove by the earnestness of others that your love also is genuine" (8:8, my translation, otherwise missed in the NRSV). There is no need to seek another gospel or establish a new law in order that liberal giving results. The proof is already out and about in the world, as the Macedonians showed.

Even giving money to the poor is a witness to the theology of the cross. It is worth remembering that Christians who are fixed in this old world at the cross, which is that juncture between old and new worlds, seem always to put the lie to the gospel that Jesus Christ has given all that is his to us and taken all that is ours for himself. No doubt this is the entrée for the pseudoapostles into Corinth. Why does the world seem so little redeemed, so little changed by the rather extravagant claims of faith, if the gospel is true? Faith seems small and unproductive, especially when it comes to the hard realities of running a church or giving to the poor. Why don't more putative Christians give freely like the Macedonians?

How often is it borne out that those who can afford it least give the most? Though there may be many reasons for it, in the case of the Macedonians it is simply trust by creatures of their Creator, and so gracing others out of grace received. The person fixed at the cross is thus the renewed person, who is not idle but participates in the ever widening works of God's grace: "Where the Spirit of the Lord is, there is freedom" (3:17), and in our text we may add, there is love, and where there is love there is actual, living redeemed equality. This is achieved through the cross of Jesus Christ, whose richness makes us rich and whose willingness to take on our poverty revolutionizes the structures of this world so that people like the Macedonians can become shockingly liberal in their witness to him. If it happened for them as a result of God's grace in Christ through faith, then it is proof that it can happen in Corinth and other corners of the world.

*Steven D. Paulson*

267

## Seventh Sunday after Pentecost, Year B

First Lesson: 2 Samuel 5:1-5, 9-10
(Psalm 48)
**Second Lesson: 2 Corinthians 12:2-10**
Gospel Lesson: Mark 6:1-13

The hearer of this passage will naturally be intrigued by the extraordinary religious experience tantalizingly described by Paul in the opening verses. Paul clearly wants our interest piqued in this way, but if he did only that he would disappoint us — and thereby capture our attention even more readily — by suddenly pushing the whole topic aside in favor of the far less spectacular religious experience of suffering with Christ and depending on God's singular grace in the midst of our "weakness" (v. 9).

Exegetical concern with the nature of the "visions and revelations" (12:1) that Paul subtly ascribes to himself, without naming himself (but cf. v. 7), is therefore a theological temptation to be avoided. The temptation to such experiential attractions is precisely what Paul wants his immediate hearers to resist, as they go more deeply into an apprehension of the truly "powerful" nature of God's work in Christ Jesus. In a manner consistent with his arguments in 1 Corinthians 12–14 over the exercise of the gifts of the Spirit, Paul here presses the church to measure the functional works of the Christian leader in terms of its imaging of the Christ's own embodiment of divine authority. Just as 1 Corinthians 13 would measure discrete activities like prophecy and tongue speaking and even sacrificial material giving by the range of embodied temporal habits given in suffering love — implicitly in the form of Jesus — so here Paul would frame the compelling character of the Christian leader in terms of the historically experienced "weakness" — both physical and relational — that Jesus both models and sustains in his followers.

As in much of 2 Corinthians, Paul's message seems determined by the context of his struggle to reassert and maintain his authority within the Corinthian church. Thus the question of "power" and "weakness" is here governed by the particular relation of leadership that Paul has with his listeners, a relationship that is both contested and misunderstood by the church's members. The text-critical issues surrounding the origin of the letter are much debated, in large measure because there seem to be several abrupt shifts in tone and perhaps even content in the course of the epistle, something which has led some commentators to wonder — and even assume —

that the current text is made up of an amalgam of diverse bits and pieces of different letters altogether. In its current form, however, there *is* a consistency of concerns between the opening and the final chapters, in the context of which this passage ought to be read; and that context is one defined by the dispute over the "apostolic" character that should demand assent and that Paul would claim for himself.

If the Corinthian Christians seem to Paul to be too easily swayed by visiting preachers (cf. 11:4), it is because these itinerant teachers cut a finer oratorical and perhaps ministerial figure than Paul himself (cf. 10:11). The result, in Paul's eyes, is that the Corinthian church has been tossed to and fro in its understanding of and practice of the gospel, listening and following whoever sounds and looks most impressive; and more seriously, the church has given in to the temptation of identifying that gospel itself with the allurements of human success and power. Paul sarcastically calls these visiting preachers "superlative apostles" (11:5; 12:11), or "super-apostles," with the same connotation as the phrase would have today. And the burden of much of his argument is therefore to defend himself as an embodiment of a true "apostle" of Christ.

The notions of "power," "authority," and "apostleship," then, are the key realities lying behind Paul's explication of his own experience in chapter 12. He has already begun this explication in 11:21 under the heading of a "boast," though in this case a boast given an ironic twist in comparison with that of his rivals in that what gives him cause for pride is precisely that of which the world (and too many Christians) are "ashamed." Paul's unique autobiographical sortie in chapters 11–12 is designed to paint a picture of the "true" apostle, who ought to exercise the true "authority" of the gospel. And that picture is one of a catalogued series of physical and emotional challenges and sufferings. (The unexplained "thorn in the flesh" of 12:7 falls within this general series, and therefore ought probably to be interpreted, not as a private ailment, but as a burden endured as a result of his ministry.)

In their initial description, this series seems calculated to leave one aghast at the deprivations and social failures of the apostle. Their true meaning, however, is given in the final verse of the passage under consideration (12:10), which acts as a summary of all that has gone before: "For the sake of Christ, then, I am content with weaknesses, insults, hardships, persecutions, and calamities; for when I am weak, then I am strong."

The true apostle with true power, then, is the one who lives and experiences the world "for the sake of Christ." The contrast is clearly made with 12:5, where Paul refuses to claim anything "for his own sake" (or "on his own behalf"). And so this "for the sake of" is critical to Paul's entire argument, though its meaning hangs on a simple preposition in the Greek *(hyper)*. For it seems to have, for Paul, a revelatory significance: in visibly — experientially — suffering "for the sake of Christ," Christ himself becomes visible to the world; his "power" in the world is "perfected" and "rests" upon Paul (12:9). This last description, often translated weakly as "rest," is in the Greek a wonderfully vivid image of setting up a tent or camp or even an actors' stage before the onlooking eyes of a viewing public — that is, Christ's power is there to be openly apprehended by the world right in the midst of and through the crushing weaknesses of Paul's own attempts at ministering the gospel.

Of course, this vision of Christ in the world, displayed through the apostle's suffering, is a "perfection" of divine power in the same way that Jesus on the cross "finishes" and perfects the purposes of God for creation. True apostles display, not their own weakness, but the very cross of Christ through the mirrored image of crucifixion inscribed upon their own life. This is a central conviction of Paul (cf. 1 Cor. 2:1ff.; 4:9ff.; 2 Cor. 4:10; Gal. 6:14ff.; etc.). And it is tied to Paul's understanding of what an "apostle" is in an almost technical way: persons whose calling has grown out of their personal "seeing" of the risen Lord (cf. 1 Cor. 15:3-11), and whose physical existences as they image Jesus' sacrificial body thereby become the vehicle for such "seeing" for others.

The experience of "vision," then, with which Paul begins this passage is not meant to be easily set aside. Paul's "visions and revelations" (12:1) of the "third heaven" are irrelevant to the gospel (though of precious value to Paul himself) precisely because they are private and interior, that is to say, visions without publicly accessible objects of sight. In terms of his argument about tongue speaking in 1 Corinthians 14:13-25, such visions do not "build up" because of their hermetic essence. But the "vision" — that is, the "spectacle" (cf. 1 Cor. 4:9) — of the apostles' suffering "for the sake of Christ" is that open declaration of the truth, faithfulness, and love of God (cf. 2 Cor. 1:19) by which the world is converted.

In the end, Paul would let his authority as an apostle rest on what the Corinthians simply see and hear in him (12:6), for these palpable forms of his life "for the sake of Christ," shorn of the veneer of social successes and gains, represent the form of Jesus — and the Son's life in him — openly and without guile. It is no less a challenging claim for the church in our day than in Paul's, our two eras being eerily similar in their characteristic temptations. To assert that Christ's self-revelation takes place historically in the truly "apostolic" life such as Paul outlines, is to encourage Christians and their churches to take the reimaging of the crucified Lord in their own corporate experience as a vocation that supersedes any strategies of alternative manifestation. What counts as "excellence" or "accomplishment" or "gain" for the Christian community must be resolutely and consistently reinterpreted in terms of the weaknesses of the passion.

It is probably one of the preacher's most demanding tasks to locate the objects of such reinterpretation and to facilitate their practical rearticulation. It is dismayingly relevant, as well, to realize that the character of "preaching" itself is explicitly relocated in the course of Paul's argument here: the "superlative apostles" are good speakers, while Paul himself is not (cf. 10:10). But what the Corinthians hear from Paul is inextricably tied to what they see in him (12:6), and these two aspects of authenticity and power demand nothing more for their efficacy than that each reflect the for-the-sake-of-ness embraced by the cross. This realization for the preacher is dismaying in that it undercuts the kinds of values often used to inform "good" preaching; it is also liberative, however, in that it turns the "communicator" into a disciple, first and foremost.

*Ephraim Radner*

## Trinity Sunday, Year A

First Lesson: Genesis 1:1–2:4a
(Psalm 8)
**Second Lesson: 2 Corinthians 13:11-13**
Gospel Lesson: Matthew 28:16-20

In the final verses of 2 Corinthians Paul bids farewell to his troubled but beloved congregation. Typically we have a string of imperatives (or passives) which are meant as exhortations aimed at the hope and faith of the church: mend your ways (or be restored), encourage others (or be encouraged), have a like mind, live in peace (13:11). Paul continues with two important concerns that we consider liturgical today: the holy kiss, and the apostolic blessing: "The grace of the Lord Jesus Christ and the love of God

271

and the fellowship of the Holy Spirit be with you all" (13:13). In these matters Paul recognized two truths for Christian churches. First, sin continues to oppose the communion of the Holy Spirit, refuses the grace of Christ, and does not recognize the love of God. For that reason forgiveness is needed, signaled by the holy kiss of fellowship and peace, especially in relation to others in the church.

The second is the abiding truth of communion in the churches as a gift from the triune God. It does not push Paul into the later mold of Nicaea to say that this communion is from the love of God, through the gift of Christ in whom God is reconciling the world through the cross (5:19), and with the Holy Spirit whom, we recall, gives life when the letter has done its killing work (3:6). This is why the church has taken this farewell of Paul's to be its closing benediction of a Christian worship service so as to identify the God who is worshiped there.

These verses are most helpful when understood in relation to the final section of 2 Corinthians, chapters 10-13. This section is sometimes considered a later letter, or fragments of several letters, and it concerns Paul's crucial explanation of the strength of Christians in weakness. The theological matter of weakness makes the salutation powerful: "For we rejoice when we are weak and you are strong" (13:9). Paul prays for the "mending" of the church that happens only with the Holy Spirit, through Christ, and by the Great Benefactor's loving grace. In this way the salutation becomes the conclusion to Paul's preaching about the cross.

In the final chapters Paul returns to the most ironic place for a preacher of the gospel of Jesus Christ. He says he "must boast" and become foolish (12:1). The gospel is not his own story, but his own story has been made an issue by the presence of "super-apostles" who boast literally "in the face" (5:12). Paul must respond to his critics without making himself the message. If doing so were only a power struggle for control of the church at Corinth, Paul's response would have been quite different than it is. As it stands, he once again uses his own story to preach the cross of Christ against the visible resurrection glory that was expounded by false preachers.

Who were these superapostles of whom Paul says: "And what I do I will also continue to do, in order to deny an opportunity to those who want an opportunity to be recognized as our equals in what they boast about. For such boasters are false apostles, deceitful workers, disguising themselves as apostles of Christ" (11:12-13)? The subject of false apostles was broached in the third chapter when Paul indicated he needed no letters of recommendation because the hearts of the Corinthians were his letters. It is the Spirit who gives life rather than the letters carved on stone and given to Moses.

Paul then distinguishes the glory of Moses' letters on stone from that which surpasses it: "Indeed, what once had glory has lost its glory because of the greater glory" (3:10). When Moses descended the mountain, he was asked to put a veil over his face, but Paul asserts that the veil was really to avoid seeing the fading glory (3:13).

Paul subsequently described the false apostles as preachers whose glorying is in the law of Moses, and so with a veil over their minds they are unable to turn to the Spirit in whom is freedom. Paul's own preaching is free and bold speech (4:2) about Jesus Christ, whose death works life in those who believe him and gives the knowledge "that he who raised the Lord Jesus will raise us also with Jesus and bring us with you into his presence" (4:14). Paul concludes, "We walk by faith, not by sight" (5:7). So we have two main themes regarding the superapostles (11:5). One regards their use of the law of Moses rather than the Spirit in whom is freedom; the other regards a false notion of glory which can be seen in signs, in wonders, and in "the face."

What is seen in this world, according to Paul, is the cross. One can't even see beyond this in Jesus Christ, as if the cross were merely a stepping-stone to get to the glory of the resurrection. When they looked at Paul, the Corinthians saw only suffering and human limitation. When they looked at the superapostles, they saw glory even in their faces, "those who pride themselves on a man's position and not on his heart." The translation must be more precise in order to identify the link in the argument between chapters 3, 5, and 13. Paul wanted his Corinthians to have an answer to "those who are boasting in the face (prosōpon)" (5:12). Their faces glowed just like Moses'! Yet their message "restricted" people; it did not free them. It presented a different Christ than the one who died on the cross and whose resurrection is our *hope*.

The mode of preaching for the superapostles fit precisely the mode of Corinthian enthusiasm seen in Paul's first letter, where the resurrected glory was already understood to be present in power and the cross was left behind. Paul runs through his list of reasons why he must boast in relation to the superapostles, though it is foolish: "Are they Hebrews? So am I. Are they Israelites? So am I. Are they descendants of Abraham? So am I. Are they ministers of Christ? I am talking like a madman — I am a better one" (11:22-23). The superapostles spoke eloquently, they spoke of obedience to the law, and they spoke, it appears, about revelations like those Moses himself was believed to have received. It is no wonder that in subsequent centuries speculation about the revelations to Moses on Sinai multiplies among Jews and Christians. In every case Paul turns his readers back to the cross and away from false glory. What they see and hear in Paul is a man with little elo-

273

quence; whose appearance is uninspiring; who has supported himself, was imprisoned, beaten, near death; and who bears daily the pressure of the churches he has begun (11:21-29).

Paul's final teaching for the Corinthians has to do with direct opposition to the glory of the superapostles. Glory appears in this world as weakness: "For the word of the cross is folly to those who are perishing, but to us who are being saved it is the power of God" (1 Cor. 1:18). Paul brings this home to his congregation in a most striking way. The connection between Christ and Christians is the cross which they are privileged to bear, and so he gives them the Lord's own words: "My grace is sufficient for you, for [my] power is made perfect in weakness" (2 Cor. 12:9). Between these two slogans, "the word of the cross" (which is folly to the perishing) and the promise that Christ's "power is made perfect in weakness," we have the whole of Paul's gospel to his Corinthians.

What kind of weakness is this? What kind of unexpected power is Paul speaking about? Getting and keeping power was and is a preoccupation, even with those who saw themselves as spiritual in Corinth. Paul used his own person to show how different this power looks and feels compared to that spiritual power propounded by the superapostles. Paul juxtaposes his third-person description of revelation to his intimate (and even pathetic) first-person account of his thorn: "Therefore, to keep me from being too elated, a thorn was given me in the flesh, a messenger of Satan to torment me, to keep me from being too elated" (12:7).

How much this rings of the experience of Jonah, for whom it is said God "appointed a worm"! How is God's power brought to its proper goal (perfected) through such a worm or thorn? One's relationship to the law of Moses and to the Holy Spirit hangs in the balance in this question. In fact, the understanding of the cross of Jesus Christ and its way of saving is determined here. Paul is not talking about mere humility that all should possess lest they be taken as fools. He is talking about the action of God himself, whose messenger is Satan in this case, as he was once for Job. God the Great Benefactor "gives" the thorn. What grace is given therein? It is the grace of weakness.

How does one who is spiritual, walking in the newness of life, resist flying from this world and the very cross of Christ within this world to the "third heaven" and beyond? How, in brief, does one not run from the cross as a past event, over and done with, to splendorous visions and a seeking after the glory of the face? Thank God for the thorn! It fixed Paul at the cross, where, after all, his Lord was in the world reconciling him to God. Paul had been given the working of the Spirit in a way very different from that seen in wonders, revelations, and glory like that of the superapostles. Certainly he did all those things as proof of his apostolicity. But he had been given the gift above all others that God in Christ seeks to bestow and only the Spirit can make possible. He had been given faith.

Faith is the perfecting (mending) of God's power in that it simply receives God's grace, receives Christ who is the Great Benefactor. Though this appears as weakness, as passivity, as being changed rather than changing, as suffering rather than success, it *is* nothing less than the power of God in Christ reconciling the world to himself. "He is not weak in dealing with you, but is powerful in you. For he was crucified in weakness, but lives by the power of God" (13:3-4). The Holy Spirit reveals Christ in his cross as the power of God reconciling the world to himself, and thereby saving the lost by giving them faith.

That is why Paul can actually "glory" in the words of Christ to him, which he now bestows on his Corinthians: "My grace is sufficient for you, for my power is made perfect in weakness." Paul's letter to the Corinthians, especially in this conclusion, is a sustained sermon on the suffering servant to whom the Spirit is sent. In him the glory of the Lord is revealed in the opposite of what appears glorious:

> Yet it was the will of the Lord to bruise him; . . .
> by his knowledge shall the righteous one, my servant,
>     make many to be accounted righteous;
>     and he shall bear their iniquities. (Isa. 53:10-11)

That is what makes God the Great Benefactor, and why Paul can boast in his weakness, where the power of God is carried out. Finally, he commends the same to the Corinthians for whom faith in Christ's cross is the power of being reconciled with God through the Holy Spirit. In that light, even though we are perishing and fighting, the resurrection remains our sure and certain hope of love, peace, and fellowship by Christ's grace.

*Steven D. Paulson*

## Second Sunday after Pentecost, Year C

First Lesson: 1 Kings 18:20-21, (22-29), 30-39
(Psalm 96)
**Second Lesson: Galatians 1:1-12**
Gospel Lesson: Luke 7:1-10

## Ninth Sunday after the Epiphany, Year C

First Lesson: 1 Kings 8:22-23, 41-43
(Psalm 96:1-9)
**Second Lesson: Galatians 1:1-12**
Gospel Lesson: Luke 7:1-10

The task of exegesis is to comprehend *what* the text says (its sense). Theological exegesis concerns what the text says *about* God (its reference). Authors make literary sense in two ways. One is by writing sentences, the basic building blocks of discourse. This is done by employing the lexical resources and grammatical conventions of their particular language (Koine Greek in Paul's case). Composing a literary work (even a formal letter), however, requires more than stringing sentences together one after another. They must be arranged into sensible parts, and the parts as a whole sensibly structured. Accordingly, an exegetical effort to *comprehend* the *sense* of the Letter to the Galatians must consider its structure and genre as well as the grammar and syntax of its individual sentences.

The easy part is the question of genre. The standard letter form in Paul's day included an opening prescript that identified the author, named the recipients, and expressed a greeting, followed by the body of the letter that bore the epistolary message, and concluded with a postscript that variously summarized the substance of the communication, sent greetings to others, and pronounced a blessing upon the addressed. Galatians clearly represents the apostle's appropriation of this basic form: prescript (1:1-5), body of the letter (1:6–6:10), and postscript (6:11-18).

Less clear, however, is the structure of the body of Galatians (1:6–6:10). The traditional division of the letter into history (chaps. 1 and 2), theology (chaps. 3 and 4), and ethics (chaps. 5 and 6) is both anachronistic and artificial. A much more satisfying and illuminating scholarly proposal is that Galatians is structured in accordance with the strategies commended in the ancient handbooks on Greco-Roman rhetoric for a deliberative (persuasive) address. In this case the body of the letter (1:6–6:10) may be structured broadly as follows: proem (1:6-10); first heading (ethos argument) (1:11–2:21); second heading (logos argument) (3:1–4:11); third heading (pathos argument) (4:12–5:12); and (without precedence in the rhetorical handbooks) parenesis (ethical exhortation) (5:13–6:10).

From this it is evident that the lectionary selection (1:1-12) includes the prescript (1:1-5), the proem (1:6-10), and the two introductory verses of the body of the letter (1:11-12). While this is artificial from a literary point of view, it has the advantage of focusing both the issue that occasions the letter (1:6-10) and the basic claim of Paul's response to it (1:11-12).

Later in the text the apostle will identify this issue thematically as "the truth of the gospel" (2:5, 14), but clues are already provided in the prescript (1:1-5). These are found by noting how Paul embellishes the conventional epistolary prescript: (a) author, (b) addressee, (c) greeting (cf. the canonical example of the simple standard form provided by the letter issued from the Jerusalem conference according to Acts 15:23-29). Observe how Paul expands on his name as the principal author of the letter. He writes as Paul, "an apostle." Moreover, he specifies that his apostolic commission is not "from a human source," nor was it mediated to him "through a human agent." On the contrary, his call came "through Jesus Christ and God the Father" (1:1). Later he will claim the same source and authority for his gospel (1:11-12). This may indicate that both his status and message were suspect in Galatia at the time of writing.

Observe also how Paul uses the prescript to point up the two events which he elsewhere identifies as matters of "first importance" in the gospel he proclaims: the death and resurrection of Jesus Christ (1 Cor. 15:1-5). Thus in the expansive greeting (Gal. 1:3-5), Jesus is identified as the one "who gave himself for our sins to set us free from the present evil age, according to the will of our God and Father" (1:4), and the latter is identified as the One "who raised [Jesus] from the dead" in the highly developed naming of the author (1:1-2a). The fact that this is the only mention of the resurrection in the letter underscores the importance of its inclusion here. With "the truth of the gospel" at stake, Paul uses the prescript to focus attention on the two primary events that constitute the core of his gospel, the death and resurrection of Jesus Messiah.

Moreover, this enactment of the will of God by Jesus and the consequent vindication of that act by God is also presented as the redemptive event that delivers us from the power of evil that grips the present time (1:4). The theme of this liberating act of God in Jesus Christ that is intro-

277

duced in the prescript will resurface at crucial points in the body of the letter (cf. 3:13; 4:4-5), but its prominent place in the opening greeting, where a simple "Grace and peace to you" would suffice, serves as an advance warning that this divinely ordained self-giving of Jesus is for some yet to be specified reason at the center of this struggle over "the truth of the gospel."

The purpose of the proem in deliberative rhetoric is to set forth the facts which occasion the speech (or letter). Here it should be noted that, apart from the Pastoral Epistles, the prescript in all the other canonical Pauline letters is followed by a proem in the form of either a prayer of thanksgiving (Rom. 1:8; 1 Cor. 1:4; Phil. 1:3; Col. 1:3; 1 Thess. 1:2; 2 Thess. 1:3; and Philem. 4) or a blessing from God (2 Cor. 1:3; Eph. 1:3). Galatians is the one exception (1:6-10). Evidently Paul is unable to thank or bless God for the ecclesial situation that compels him to write. Rather, he can only express his dismay ("I am amazed") at the "desertion" of some — perhaps many, possibly all — of his converts from the One who called them "in the grace of Christ" to embrace "a different (heteros) gospel," which is not merely "another (allos)" version of the one gospel. This other gospel, proclaimed by "some" who, as Paul views it, "willfully pervert the gospel of Christ" and thereby "confuse" the primarily Gentile congregations in Galatia, is so alien to the apostolic gospel that it is no gospel at all. No doubt these anonymous itinerant preachers would have found this assessment of their message and intentions a bit much, but the sharpness of Paul's accusation at least indicates the seriousness of the matter which divides them and occasions the letter.

If such a pointed accusation is offensive to postmodern ears attuned to theological inclusivity, what follows in the proem (vv. 8-9) is likely to be construed as intolerance born of fanaticism. For the apostle actually pronounces a curse (anathema) upon his opponents and anyone else, including "an angel from heaven," should they proclaim a gospel to the Galatians "contrary" to that which he and his colleagues proclaimed to them when they first believed (cf. 3:1-5; 4:12-20). Indeed, he then repeats the curse on "anyone" who proclaims to his churches a gospel "contrary" to the one they originally "received" (v. 9). How are we to take these curses? The answer is, seriously. Those who preach and those who receive the gospel are warned here that the apostolic message is vulnerable to distortion, misrepresentation, even falsification, with the result that it cannot mediate "the power of God for salvation" (Rom. 1:16) and set people free from the evil of the present age. The stakes are high when the issue is "the truth of the gospel."

Even by first-century standards, such an accusation and pronouncements were considered severe. Paul's readers then (as now) could be expected to inquire into what right or authority he presumes to exercise in privileging his gospel over that of his anonymous opponents in Galatia. His answer (1:11-12), which introduces the body of the letter, is that his gospel, like his apostolate, is "not of human origin," for he "did not receive it from a human source" nor was he "taught it." Rather, he insists, "I received it through a revelation *(apokalypsis)* of Jesus Christ" (1:11-12). Or, as he subsequently explains, there came that moment when God was pleased "to reveal *(apokalyptein)* his Son to me, so that I might proclaim him among the Gentiles" (1:16).

Most likely the reference here is to Paul's Damascus road encounter with the risen Jesus Christ. Luke reports this episode as a vision (Acts 9:1ff.; 22:6ff.; 26:12ff.), and the apostle himself speaks of it as both an objective ("Last of all . . . he appeared also to me" [1 Cor. 15:8]) and a subjective ("Have I not seen Jesus our Lord?" [1 Cor. 9:1]) visual experience. Yet the noun "revelation" and its verbal cognate are not synonymous with "vision" and "appear" in Paul's semantic field. The two sets of terms may refer to the same occurrence, but they denote different aspects of the event. To say that Jesus "appeared also to me" (1 Cor. 15:8) is to point up the *visual* aspect, while to say that God "reveal[ed] his Son to me" (Gal. 1:16) is to emphasize the *cognitive* aspect, in that "revelation" makes known to Paul the messianic identity of Jesus *as Son of God.* It is this *interpretative* or *hermeneutical* work of God that accompanies the redemptive work of God in Jesus which is intended by the apostle's appeal to divine "revelation" (Dieter Lührmann). What "revelation" provides is *a divinely given understanding* of what God has done in Jesus Christ to effect human redemption from the evil of this present age. It is an "invasive" event (J. Louis Martyn) in which the meaning of the cross and resurrection are made known (cf. 1 Cor. 2:6-16). It is this God-given understanding that Paul claims is normative for all gospel proclamation.

The crisis in the churches of Galatia that occasions this letter represents a full-blown hermeneutical conflict. Two different ways of construing the gospel have met head-on! Paul contends that the "different gospel" of his opponents "perverts" the gospel of Jesus Christ and thus renders it impotent to set people free. This connection between "the truth of the gospel" and its performative "power" is crucial. The gospel is ultimately authenticated by what it does.

*Thomas W. Gillespie*

## Third Sunday after Pentecost, Year C

First Lesson: 1 Kings 17:8-16, (17-24)
(Psalm 146)
**Second Lesson: Galatians 1:11-24**
Gospel Lesson: Luke 7:11-17

This reading represents the introductory verses of the body of the letter (1:11-12) and the first of three parts (1:13-24; 2:1-10; 2:11-21) which together compose its first heading, the argument from ethos (1:13–2:21). Because verses 11 and 12 overlap with the previous reading, we will build upon what is presented there (cf. also the exegesis of 1:1-12 for the overall structure of the letter as an example of ancient deliberative [persuasive] rhetoric).

In 1:11-12 Paul appeals to "a revelation" *(apokalypsis)* of Jesus Christ given to him by God at the time of his call to apostleship (1:16) as the source and ground of his gospel. The reference of this appeal is in all probability to his encounter with the risen Jesus on the road to Damascus that entailed a visionary experience ("Have I not seen Jesus our Lord?" [1 Cor. 9:1]; "Last of all . . . he appeared also to me" [1 Cor. 15:8]). Yet the term "revelation" (as well as its cognate verb "to reveal" [*apokalyptein*] in 1:16), as Paul uses it, denotes the *cognitive* rather than the *visual* character of that event. By means of "revelation" God grants *understanding* of his saving action in Jesus Christ. In a word, "revelation" is that divine activity which *interprets* Jesus as God's redemptive agent (cf. 1 Cor. 2:10-13, where the Spirit is said to "reveal" the "hidden wisdom" of God implicit in "Christ crucified").

The "revelation" of which Paul speaks, however, is not a unilateral event. The initiative lies with God, to be sure, and the apostle is clear about that: God "called me through his grace" (Gal. 1:15). But if the Jesus Paul met brought his identity as God's Son to that revelatory event, so also the Paul met by Jesus brought to it his own identity as one who lived "in Judaism," persecuted "the church of God," and was a zealot for "the traditions" of his ancestors (1:13-14). Among these traditions was the belief of the Pharisees in the resurrection of the dead, a tenet Paul no doubt shared as a member of this party (Phil. 3:5). The importance of this for understanding the theological content of the "revelation" that informed his gospel is difficult to exaggerate.

It may be recalled that the Pharisees believed in the resurrection of the dead, while the Sadducees did not (Acts 23:6-8; cf. Matt. 22:23). The basis of this difference was the absence of such a teaching in the Torah, the sole source of doctrine for the Sadducees. In point of fact, the resurrection hope came relatively late into Judaism, arising sometime following the Jews' return from Babylonian exile and becoming prominent in the period of Seleucid occupation and persecution. The determination of Antiochus IV Epiphanes to Hellenize the Jews by imposing Greek culture upon them and forbidding any observance of the Jewish Law under penalty of death created an understandable crisis of faith in Judaism. For the Law itself promised life and blessing to those who obeyed its commandments (Deut. 5:33; 6:24, 25; 7:12; 8:1; 30:6, 15-18), but now obedience brought suffering and death.

That the Pharisaic hope of the resurrection of the dead addressed this theological crisis is attested in 2 Maccabees 7, the story of the faithful Jewish mother who was compelled to watch her seven sons die horrible deaths under Greek auspices for their refusal to disobey the Law of God. Whatever the historical value of this highly stylized account may be, it demonstrates that the resurrection doctrine functioned theologically in intertestamental Judaism under conditions of unjust suffering as a *theodicy*. The implicit argument is that faithfulness to God's Law may bring pain and death *now*, but God will demonstrate faithfulness to his promises by raising the righteous to life *then*. Put simply, the resurrection event will vindicate (justify) both God and the righteous believer. Thus it was this understanding of the Pharisaic hope that informed the mind of Paul that day when he "received" his "revelation of Jesus Christ" from God.

This factor prompts the astute observation that Paul's gospel is "the exegesis of the appearance of the resurrected Jesus that he experienced" (Wolfhart Pannenberg, *Jesus — God and Man* [Philadelphia: Westminster, 1968], p. 73). Such an exegetical exercise leads to the following inferences. (1) The one who appeared to Paul was *Jesus* — Jesus of Nazareth, Jesus the *crucified*. That is to say, Paul met one whom he knew had been executed by the Romans on a cross, and thus one who had died under the curse of God's Law (Gal. 3:13, citing Deut. 21:23). (2) The crucified Jesus revealed to Paul was *alive*. The executed one, the one dead and buried, was encountered as *the living one*. Paul the Pharisee could only infer from this that God had raised Jesus from the dead, even as the Christians whom he persecuted claimed. (3) The Pharisaic view of the resurrection as an act of divine vindication of the righteous who die because of their fidelity to God compelled Paul to infer further that by raising Jesus from the dead God had *justified* the crucified Jesus as a *righteous* man, as a *faithful* Jew. (4) If God has so vindicated the crucified Jesus for his faithful obedience and obedient faith, then that includes the messianic claims made by Jesus during his earthly ministry. Accordingly, Paul speaks here of "a revelation of Jesus *Christ*" (1:12) and, in a messianic sense, of God's having revealed Jesus to him as "his Son" (1:16). (5) Be-

281

cause the messianic expectations of first-century Judaism were so varied and diverse, it was necessary now for Paul to give theological specificity to the claims of Jesus by addressing the paradox of a crucified Messiah. The question of why God would have justified a crucified and accursed man required of Paul a radical reinterpretation of the cross of Christ. Precisely such a hermeneutical exercise is represented by the Letter to the Galatians.

As noted, these two verses on the revelational source and authority of Paul's gospel introduce the first heading of the body of the letter, which in terms of the rhetorical strategies advocated for a deliberative speech (or letter) may be identified as an argument from ethos. According to Aristotle, there are three and only three modes of artistic proof: ethos, logos, and pathos. Paul employs all three modes in the Letter to the Galatians, and in that order. Ethos for Aristotle denotes "character," and this form of argumentation seeks to establish the credibility of the speaker or author with the audience or readership. Here the apostle seeks to give credence to his claim of apostolic authority and a revealed gospel by narrating (1) how God's call changed his life (1:13-24); (2) how he obtained public recognition of his gospel by the Jerusalem authorities, the "pillar apostles" Peter, James, and John, and thus preserved "the truth of the gospel" for his Gentile congregations (2:1-10); and (3) how he confronted Peter in Antioch when he and the other Jewish Christians, including Barnabas, did not "walk straightforwardly" (orthopodein) according to "the truth of the gospel" and withdrew from table fellowship with the Gentile believers under pressure from "certain ones" sent from James (2:11-21).

The first section of this narrative argument designed to enhance the author's reliability (1:13-24) covers a long period of Paul's life — indeed, from conception in his mother's womb, through his early life in Judaism, to his call to apostleship and his subsequent initial mission to the Gentiles, including his first postcalling visit to Jerusalem for the purpose of meeting Peter. What constitutes this passage as a literary unit is the stylistic device of *inclusio*. Notice how the verbs "to persecute" and "to destroy" are prominent in verse 13. Paul begins his narrative with an acknowledgment of his former intense persecution of "the churches of God," an activity aimed at destroying them. Note also how these same verbs reappear at the conclusion of this section in verse 23. Here Paul cites the report about him that was circulating among the churches of Judea to the effect that "he who once persecuted us now proclaims the faith which then he was trying to destroy." By thus beginning and concluding on the twin themes of persecution and destruction, Paul presents in this section what has been aptly called a "biography of reversal" (John Schütz).

282

Some scholars argue that this first narrative section of the ethos argument should be understood more as a "call" story than a "conversion" testimony. Actually it is both, attesting to a behavioral and theological "reversal" *in* Paul's life as well as a vocational redirection *of* his life. Like Jeremiah before him, Paul is given to understand that the God who now calls him to the apostolic mission has intended him for this task from his mother's womb (1:15; cf. Jer. 1:5). It is equally clear to the new apostle that God has called him "through his grace" (1:15), the latter term *(charis)* signifying God's unmerited, unearned, undeserved love. How could this turn of events be otherwise understood? The persecutor of the "churches of God" is summoned to the proclamation of "the faith" he once tried to destroy (1:23). In Paul's calling there is no place for any consideration of human merit or achievement. This insight carries over into the issue of how people become recipients of the redemption which God has effected in the death and resurrection of Jesus Christ. It is not fortuitous that the apostle addresses the Galatians as those God has called through the proclamation of the gospel "in the grace of Christ" (1:6). Everything Paul will subsequently say in this letter about how people receive the liberation from the evil of this present age which God has effected through the death and resurrection of Jesus is predicated upon the priority of grace (cf. 2:21; 5:4).

*Thomas W. Gillespie*

## Fourth Sunday after Pentecost, Year C

First Lesson: 1 Kings 21:1-10, (11-14), 15-21a
(Psalm 5:1-8)
**Second Lesson: Galatians 2:15-21**
Gospel Lesson: Luke 7:36–8:3

This lection falls within the last of the three parts (2:11-21) of the first heading, the argument from ethos (1:11–2:21), of this deliberative letter (cf. the discussion of its rhetorical structure in the exegesis of 1:1-12). Unfortunately, it excludes the incident in Antioch that occasioned it (vv. 11-

13) as well as the introduction (v. 14) to Paul's extended public rebuke of Cephas, which it continues. While the translations limit this direct address to verse 14, the lack in the Greek text of any typical Pauline linguistic *marker* that would signal a transition in subject matter at verse 15 warrants the view that the quotation extends through verse 21. Thus the lection is a continuation of Paul's speech (vv. 14-21). Further, the apostle's address takes the rhetorical form of "an *epicheireme,* or argument with the parts fully stated, which provides the conclusion to the first-heading" (George A. Kennedy, *New Testament Interpretation through Rhetorical Criticism* [Chapel Hill and London: University of North Carolina Press, 1984], p. 148). The correspondence between this conclusion of the first heading (2:14-21) and its introduction (1:11-12) should not be overlooked. For the argument from ethos, which has moved from personal testimony (1:13-21) to ecclesial decision (2:1-10), now appeals to the theological content of the "revelation of Jesus Christ" (1:11-12) that distinguishes Paul's gospel from that "different gospel" (1:6) of his opponents in Galatia.

Convinced that the Jewish withdrawal from the Gentiles at table in Antioch represented a failure to "walk straightforwardly" *(orthopodein)* toward "the truth of the gospel" (2:14), Paul confronts Cephas with this contradiction between belief and behavior by putting to him a question that places his apostolic colleague on the horns of a dilemma: "How can you, a [Christian] Jew who no longer lives under the [Jewish] Law, require Gentile [Christians] to live [under the Law] like Jews?" It is Paul's view that Peter the Christian "lives like a Gentile" and "not like a Jew" because he and Paul (the "we" of v. 15) "know" (theologically) as Christians that "a person is justified" *(dikaioutai)* not by *erga tou nomou* but through *pistis Iēsou Christou* (v. 16). This text requires three crucial exegetical decisions regarding: (1) the semantic value of the verb *dikaioun/dikaiousthai* ("to justify," "to be justified") in Paul's vocabulary; (2) the specific reference of the phrase *erga tou nomou* (works of the law); and (3) the grammatical identity of the genitive construction in *pistis Iēsou Christou,* whether it is to be understood objectively ("faith *in* Jesus Christ" = the faith that has Jesus as its object) or subjectively ("faith *of* Jesus Christ" = the faith of Jesus himself).

The semantic range of Paul's "justification" terminology includes *juridical, relational,* and *eschatological* nuances. The verb is juridical in that it connotes a divine judicial judgment (of righteousness upon the obedience of Christ and of forgiveness upon all for whom he died). It is relational in that it connotes the "rectified" (J. L. Martyn) relationship with God effected by the judicial forgiveness. And it is eschatological in that it anticipates the triumph of life over death in the resurrection (cf. Gal. 5:5). The Christian who is justified by God is thus one who is forgiven, related aright to God, and given the hope of victory over death. The question is on what basis and through what means this occurs.

The answer, Paul argues, is not "on the basis of" *(ek)* "works of the Law." The phrase *erga tou nomou* is traditionally understood in Protestant exegesis as referring to deeds required by the Law which justify the faithful in the eyes of God by achieving *dikaiosynē* (justification/righteousness) and thus meriting salvation. This traditional view of first-century Judaism as a legalistic religion that based salvation on good works is challenged by the seminal works of E. P. Sanders (*Paul and Palestinian Judaism* [Philadelphia: Fortress, 1977]; cf. also his later work *Paul, the Law, and the Jewish People* [Philadelphia: Fortress, 1983]). "Works of the law," he contends, refer simply to the rites and rituals of "covenantal nomism" (a proper name for early Judaism) — such as circumcision, dietary rules, and observance of religious days — that gave the Jewish people their ethnic identity. (It may be noted that when Paul specifies "works of the law" in Galatians, he mentions explicitly circumcision [2:3; 5:2-6; 6:11-16] and observances of a sacred calendar [4:10], and implicitly dietary regulations [2:11-13].) On this reading, Paul is merely warning his Gentile readers against adopting a Jewish way of life. Either way, however, his point is that neither good deeds nor a Jewish identity is a necessary condition of God's justifying action. For they entail in their respective ways what J. Louis Martyn calls *the circular exchange,* "this for that," the ever tempting quid pro quo in the relation of human beings to God ("The Apocalyptic Gospel in Galatians," *Interpretation* [July 2000]: 247). To Paul this religious strategy, however conceived, "nullifies" *(athetein)* the grace of God and renders the death of Christ "gratuitous" *(dōrean)* (v. 21).

Rather, God justifies *dia* (through) and *ek* (on the basis of) *pistis tou Christou* (v. 16). Traditionally, the genitive construction of this phrase has been read in an objective sense, meaning the Christian's faith in Jesus Christ. That this is important to Paul is clear from the immediately following statement that "even we believed in *(eis)* Christ Jesus" (v. 16b), but acknowledging the importance of the human faith factor is not the same as making it the ground and means of God's justifying action. For then it is difficult to explain how the human act of faith is not an alternative form of "the works of the Law." Accordingly, there is a growing agreement among exegetes, based on studies of Greek idiom in both the Old Testament (LXX) and the New Testament, that the subjective reading of the genitive in *pistis tou Iēsou Christou* is to be preferred (see esp. Richard B. Hays, *The Faith of Jesus Christ* [Chico, Calif.: Scholars Press, 1983], pp. 157-77). This accords well with Paul's revelational understanding of Jesus as the messianic claimant whom God "vindicated" by raising him from the dead. Jesus, the one who by faithful obedience and obedient faith "gave himself for our sins . . . according to the will of our God and Father" (1:3), is the "justified" Messiah. As such, he is both the ground and medium of God's justifying grace that liberates human beings from "the evil of this present age."

It is the *relational* aspect of God's justifying action that makes it possible for the apostle to shift from juridical terminology in verses 15-18 to the language of new life "in Christ" in verses 19-20. The phrase "seeking to be justified in Christ" in verse 17 bridges these texts by correlating Paul's two primary ways of speaking soteriologically — being "justified" and being "in Christ" *(en Christōi)*. The latter is variously explained as the apostle's "mysticism" (A. Schweitzer) or as his concept of "participatory union" (E. P. Sanders), but it is sufficient to think in terms of an intimate relationship between Christ and the believer — a relationship made possible by God's justifying act and established by faith. In this relationship the believer enters in the context of Christ's power and is subject to his Lordship. Put otherwise, God's justifying action as a resurrection event effects new life, given proleptically to believers "in Christ."

Verses 17 and 18 depict the way things in Antioch looked to the "certain ones" who came down from Jerusalem representing James. Finding Cephas, Barnabas, Paul, and "the rest of the Jews" eating with Gentile Christians without regard to the purity and dietary regulations of the Torah, they concluded that these Jewish Christians had joined the "sinners" *(harmartōloi)*, by Jewish definition those who lived outside the Law and thus beyond the pale of salvation. Paul considers this possibility in verse 17 and dismisses it on the ground that Christ, the agent of God's justifying action, cannot be thereby an agent of sin. In the concession of verse 18 that he would demonstrate himself as a transgressor only if he restored "these things *(tauta)*" that he has torn down, the reference of the demonstrative pronoun *tauta* is not the Law itself but the "works of the Law" as a condition of God's justifying activity. Thus Paul's argument is that if he reinstates the works of the Law which he has annulled as a basis of righteousness, he demonstrates that he is indeed a transgressor of the law because he is not faithful to its divine purpose, which is, after all, redemptive.

The notion of living or dying *to* something is difficult to express in English idiom. What is at issue in the statement of verse 19 seems to be something like a change in life "orientation." His life as a Pharisee was oriented to the Law in the conviction that he was thereby living to God. The "revelation of Jesus Christ," however, reoriented Paul to Christ as the means of living to God. That his consequent death to the Law in this sense occurred "through the Law" points to the confession "I have been crucified with Christ" (2:20). Paul reasons that the death of Jesus was a vicarious event that includes us. As he died "for us," even so we died "with him." Because Christ died under the curse of the Law (Deut. 21:23; cf. Gal. 3:10), becoming a curse for us (3:13), it may be inferred that he too died "through the law," and Paul therefore with him.

Having "died to the Law" in the death of Christ, Paul as the paradigmatic believer still lives. "I live, but no longer I [alone]" (v. 20). As one who "lives to God," he does so "in Christ" and thus "with Christ." The apostle's statement that Christ now "lives in me" is a personalized version of the early Christian confession "Jesus is Lord" (1 Cor. 12:3). Translated theologically, "Christ lives in me" means "I live under the Lordship of Christ and in his power." Put simply, our "justification" through "the faithfulness of Jesus Christ" effects a change of lordship (Käsemann).

*Thomas W. Gillespie*

## Fifth Sunday after Pentecost, Year C

First Lesson: 1 Kings 19:1-4, (5-7), 8-15a
(Psalms 42 and 43)
**Second Lesson: Galatians 3:23-29**
Gospel Lesson: Luke 8:26-39

The homiletical eye will focus on verse 28 as a text for a sermon on egalitarianism. What will be lost in the process most likely is the gospel basis for the apostle's remarkable claim: "There is no longer Jew or Greek, there is no longer slave or free, there is no longer male and female; for all of you are one in Christ Jesus." The lectionary itself encourages such a procedure by adumbrating an apostolic argument that begins in verse 15. It is necessary, therefore, to set this passage in its literary context.

The lection belongs to the second heading (3:1–4:11) of this rhetorically structured letter (cf. the exegesis of 1:1-12 for the broad outline). As an argument from logos (logic), it includes an introduction (3:1-5), an appeal to the

287

Scriptures (3:6-14), another appeal to the legal practices of testaments (3:15-29), an appeal to the juridical laws of inheritance (4:1-7), and a conclusion (4:8-11). The introduction attests to the evidential giving and receiving of the Spirit at the time the Galatians believed the message of Christ crucified (3:1-5), and the appeal to the Scriptures that follows interprets their experience of the Spirit as an instance of the fulfillment of God's promise to bless the Gentiles through Abraham (3:6-14).

The appeal to the legal practices of testaments (3:15-29), like the appeal to the Scriptures before it, falls into three parts that deal thematically with Abraham (vv. 15-18), the law (vv. 19-22), and Christ (vv. 23-29). With regard to the promise made to Abraham, Paul notes that "once a person's will has been ratified, no one adds to it or annuls it" (v. 15). Likewise with the covenant *(diathēkē)* of God (v. 17). The promises God made "to Abraham and his seed" are unconditional. Paul's point is that the law, which was given 430 years after the covenant was made, may not be viewed as a codicil that makes the fulfillment of that promise conditional upon law observance. To do so robs God's covenant of its promise character as an act of grace. For "God bestowed grace *(charizein)* upon Abraham through a promise" (v. 18). Moreover, appealing to the specificity of the fulfillment to clarify the ambiguity of the promise, the apostle identifies "the seed" of Abraham with Christ (v. 16).

In verses 19-22 Paul turns from the theme of Abraham to that of the law. Having denied to the law any redemptive function, he must now answer the inevitable question, "Why then the law?" His cryptic answer includes three points: (1) the *purpose* of the law ("It was added because of transgressions"); (2) the *provisionality* of the law ("until the seed should come to whom the promise was given"); and (3) the *provenance* of the law ("being ordained by angels through a mediator") (v. 19). Thus understood, the law is certainly not opposed to the promises of God. It simply is unable "to make alive" *(zōiopoiein)*. Otherwise, he explains, "righteousness" would come through the law (v. 21). This association of "righteousness" with the power "to make alive" alludes to Paul's conviction that God's justifying action entails the vindication of life over death through the resurrection. What the law cannot do, however, the Spirit does (cf. 2 Cor. 3:6). For the Spirit is the agent of the power that raised Jesus from the dead (Rom. 1:4). Thus the fulfillment of God's promise to bless the Gentiles through Abraham and his "seed" is "allowed to flow" (J. C. Beker) to "all who believe" on the basis of *(ek)* "the faithfulness of Jesus Christ" (Gal. 3:22; cf. the discussion of the latter phrase in the exegesis of 2:15-21). It is at this point that the lectionary selection picks up the unfolding argument.

The transition from the theme of the law to that of Christ is made at verses 23 and 24. Given the provisionality of the law established in verse 19 by the phrase "until the seed should come to whom the promise was made," and given the identification of "the seed" in verse 16 as "Christ," it is not surprising to read in verse 24 that "the law was our disciplinarian until the coming of Christ." What is surprising is Paul's identification of the subject of this advent in verse 23 as "the faith" and "the coming faith" (cf. v. 25, "But now that the faith has come . . ."). How is *pistis* to be understood here?

The possibility that "the faith" refers to the subjective act of human believing is ruled out by the fact that the apostle has attributed such faith to Abraham. Thus, temporally speaking, this kind of faith has already "come" (3:6). Other considerations reinforce this inference. The use of the definite article in each instance of the noun in the Greek text of verses 23 and 25 *(hē pistis),* for example, not only adds emphasis but functions grammatically as a demonstrative pronoun ("this faith"). Further, the faith that has now come is said "to be revealed" *(apokalyphthēnai)* in its advent. Also, by speaking of "the faith" interchangeably in terms of "coming on the scene" and "being revealed," Paul intimates the "invasive" nature of this event (J. L. Martyn) and points us in a theological direction. Finally, by speaking interchangeably of the coming of "the faith" and the coming of "Christ," the apostle clues the reader in on the fact that the former term functions either as a christological title in this context or, at a minimum, as a shorthand version of the fuller phrase "faith of Jesus Christ" in verse 22 (cf. 2:16).

Verse 25 marks the *terminus ad quem* of the law: literally, "The faith having come, we are no longer under a disciplinarian *(paidagōgos)*" = "no longer imprisoned" = "no longer under the law." The first argument of 3:6-14 concludes with the claim that Christ, by becoming a curse for us, has delivered us from the *curse* of the law. The conclusion of the second argument is that Christ has delivered us from the *jurisdiction* of the law. The point here is that those who are "in Christ Jesus" (v. 26) are so related to the one who is "the seed" of Abraham that for this reason they are themselves "seed of Abraham" and thus heirs of the promise (v. 29). The "inheritance," which is the fulfillment of the promise, is the "blessing of Abraham" which Paul has identified as "the promise of the Spirit" (3:14).

Notice that at verse 26, as at 2:17, there is a transition from juridical terminology having to do with "justification" issues to the language of personal relationship between the believer and Jesus Christ. Those who are "in Christ Jesus" are by faith "children of God." Although the term "Spirit" does not occur in verses 26-29, its reality is implicit in the reference to baptism in verse 27. Paul says the same thing differently in 1 Corinthians 12:13: "In the one Spirit we were all baptized into one body — Jews or Greeks, slaves or free — and we were all made to drink of one Spirit." Here the apostle affirms that "as many of you as were baptized into Christ have clothed yourselves with Christ." The clothing metaphor depicts personal intimacy, as in "as close as the clothes on your back." While the apostle is neither teaching Spirit baptism nor limiting the reception of the Spirit to the act of baptism, he is attesting that it is the work of the Spirit which leads to baptism, is confirmed by baptism, and is manifested in the resulting unity of believers in Christ. Baptism is thus oriented to Christology in this text rather than to ecclesiology as in the cited Corinthian text, but verse 28 makes clear that the community of "the children of God" formed by baptism is not out of view.

As sociological background for verse 28, it should be noted that the ancient world (even as our own) was fond of dividing humanity into two kinds of people, "us" and "them." The Jewish criterion of difference was religious, "us Jews" (who have the Law) and "them Gentiles" (who are outside the Law). For the Greeks the criterion was cultural: "us Greeks" and "them barbarians." The Romans, of course, trumped them all with the political card, "us freemen" and "them slaves." Common to all societies was the distinction between male and female, a distinction that had religious, cultural, and political implications that favored the male. The apostle was familiar with all these divisions, and each finds expression in his letters.

The apostle is not asserting here that "in Christ" *there is no longer any such thing as* Jews and Greeks, slaves and freemen, males and females. Scholars suspect that some members of the Corinthian church took Paul literally on this point, believing that in their baptism they had been released from the reality of all ethnic, social, and gender distinctions and thus causing all kinds of theological mischief in the congregation. Paul's point is more subtle but no less important. Among "the children of God," personal identity and status are given by God's justifying action. It is our uncommonly common relationship to God through Jesus Christ, based on divine grace rather than human merit, that makes us all "one in Christ Jesus" (v. 28). Not one and the same, to be sure, but one nonetheless. This is not to argue that unjust distinctions between people should be allowed to stand without challenge. The issue of slavery, for example, has been resolved politically if not socially and economically in favor of freedom for all. Similar progress is being made in regard to gender and age discrimination, among other forms. But who can doubt that our world will continue to be characterized by one type of divisive difference or another? This will continue so long as we locate our identity in and derive our sense of personal value from the things that make us different from other people. Paul's point is that where there is a deep and controlling sense of "belonging to Christ" (v. 29), there will be a concomitant sense of being "one in Christ Jesus" (v. 28).

*Thomas W. Gillespie*

## First Sunday after Christmas, Year B

First Lesson: Isaiah 61:10–62:3
(Psalm 148)
**Second Lesson: Galatians 4:4-7**
Gospel Lesson: Luke 2:22-40

Clearly liturgical interests have overridden literary considerations in the delimitation of this lesson. For it interrupts at midpoint an argument structured by two parts that represent distinct temporal periods, the former time (vv. 1-3) and the fullness of time (vv. 4-7). The redemption that occurs in the second period is like an answer without the question, apart from the enslavement that characterizes the first. Further, verse 3 (together with Paul's commentary on it in 4:8-10) provides an insight into how Paul's gospel of justification in Christ can be proclaimed and heard today. Thus the text should be read as a whole (4:1-7).

The argument is introduced by the transitional marker *legō de* (But I say) and concludes in verse 7 with a summary statement. It is predicated on the analogy the apostle sees between laws of inheritance and the human condition apart from Christ. Verse 1 depicts a boy in a wealthy home who is legally the heir *(ho klēronomos)* and so the "young master" *(kyrios)* of the family estate. Nonetheless, as a minor *(nēpios)*, he is under rules very much like a slave *(doulos)*. This period of minority, which is paternally determined, is the "former time" of which this part of the argument speaks. During this time the minor lives "under guardians and custodians" (v. 2), terms that have analogues in the "disciplinarian" *(paidagōgos)* and "the law" *(ho nomos)* in the immediately preceding argument (3:24). Thus the status of the minor child described in 4:1-3 is analogous to the situation of all who are under the law (3:23-25).

291

But it is also analogous to the situation of "Abraham and his seed" to whom God's promise has been given (3:16), for the future inheritance of the minor child, also assigned by the father, functions as a promise among the legalities that condition the period of minority status. Thus the laws of inheritance to which Paul appeals in 4:1-2 entail the themes of both promise and law which characterize the situation of Judaism prior to the coming of Christ (cf. the discrete arguments in 3:6-14 and 3:15-29).

In verse 3 Paul draws the analogy between the status of a minor and the human condition: "thus even we, when we were minors (nēpioi), were enslaved under the elements of the world" (ta stoicheia tou kosmou). The Greek term translated "elements" is a formal term denoting something that is basic to something else, something irreducible to anything else. Examples would be letters to words, numbers to arithmetic, and notes to music. As "elements of the world," they refer to the constituent parts of the universe that make it a cosmos rather than a chaos.

It is important to note three things about the "elements" in this text. (1) They have a nomistic character and function in the same manner as the "guardians and custodians" who exercise authority over the minor child, as well as the Law in its role as a "disciplinarian" (3:24). (2) Like the Law, they exercise religious dominion over human life (cf. Paul's comment in v. 8 that "formerly" the Galatians were "enslaved to beings that by nature are not gods," beings he identifies as "the weak and beggarly elements" in v. 9). (3) They are thus created realities ("of the world") rather than divine beings. His objection is not to their existence but to their idolatrous veneration.

Who is included in the first-person plural of the verb "we were enslaved" is ambiguous. Most commentators read it as a reference to all Christians, whether Jewish or Gentile. Alternative opinions refer it to Jewish Christians alone or to Gentiles alone with whom the apostle identifies himself here. The "we," however, has nothing to do with believers, Jewish or Gentile, but refers rather to the human situation in the world that includes both Jews and Gentiles.

That Gentiles are in view is evident from Paul's assertion that the submission of Gentile Christians to the Jewish law is tantamount to *returning* to their pagan servitude to "the weak and beggarly elements" (v. 9). That Jews are also included is equally clear from the fact that Paul repeats the phrase "under the elements of the world" (v. 3) twice by the equivalent rubric "under the law" (vv. 4, 5). The point is that Paul sees a parallel between the situation of all people under "the elements of the world" and that of the Jew "under the law."

Accordingly, the announcement in verses 4-5 that "when the fullness of time had come, God sent his Son, born of a woman, born under the law, in order to redeem those who were under the law" is good news for both Jew and Gentile. By "the fullness of time" Paul means simply "at the right time" or "in God's time." The sending of God's Son *(exapostellein)* picks up on the theme of the *advent* of "the seed" of Abraham (3:19), "the faith" (3:23, 25), and "Christ" (3:24), each signaling the coming of one and the same person who is identified in three ways. The notion of "being sent," in distinction from "coming," emphasizes the point that God's grace always enjoys the priority of initiative. The verb "redeem" *(exagorazein)* is repeated from 3:13, and both texts echo the identification of Jesus in the opening greeting of the letter as the one "who gave himself for our sins *to set us free (exairein)* from the evil of the present age" (1:4). Whenever Paul speaks of the human liberation effected by the coming of Jesus Christ, of course the cross is implicit even when not mentioned.

At the same time, the apostle makes clear in verse 5 that redemption is both *from* something and *for* something. In the immediate context it entails freedom *from* idolatrous servitude of the "elements of the world" (v. 3) as well as Jewish emancipation from a life "under the law" (v. 4). The purpose of God's redemptive act is to free us *for* the gift of "adoption as children" (v. 5b). Again the apostle restates a point already made (cf. 3:26), one he returns to in the summary of this argument (v. 7). One of the nuances of Paul's "justification" language is its relational character (see the exegesis of Gal. 2:15-21). The one "rectified" (J. L. Martyn) by God through "the faith of Jesus Christ" (2:16; 3:22) is thereby rightly related to God. This relational effect of justification accounts for Paul's ability to shift semantic gears into his "in Christ" terminology when speaking of the results of God's redemptive act in the death and resurrection of Jesus (cf. 2:16).

The reality of this new relationship is effected by the gift of the Spirit. Thus the apostle explains that "because you are children, God has sent the Spirit of his Son into our hearts, crying, 'Abba! Father!'" (v. 6). Here Paul takes up the subject with which he began this argument from logos (3:1 to 4:11), the work of the Spirit in human life (3:1-5). The Spirit is sent by God (again the verb *exapostellein*) into our "hearts," the term that designates in biblical understanding not the seat of our emotions and volitions but the center of our "multidimensional being" (Tillich), and is there pouring out God's love (Rom. 5:5). As Paul puts it elsewhere, "When we cry, 'Abba! Father!' it is the Spirit bearing witness with our spirit that we are children of God, and if children, then heirs, heirs of God and joint heirs with Christ" (Rom. 8:15-17). His argument here concludes in verse 7 on the same note: "if a child then also an heir, through God." Paul is clear throughout

Galatians that believers are "heirs according to the promise" (3:29), the promise being that made by grace to Abraham that through him God will bless the nations (3:18), the inheritance being the fulfillment of that promise in the giving of the Spirit (3:14).

Although Paul's "justification" language is not employed in this argument, its relevance to the discussion of "the elements of the world" is assured by the lawful character of these created realities and their requirement of something equivalent to the "works of the law." Theologically, Paul's "elements of the world" have been connected with what is called the "orders of creation" in Reformed theology by Hendrikus Berkhof (*Christ and the Powers* [Scottdale, Pa.: Herald, 1962]). As the basic structures of created reality, the "elements" represent the way the world is ordered. Because they exercise power over human life in this capacity, Berkhof translates Paul's phrase as the "world powers." They are our "guardians and trustees" in the sense that they hold together the world and preserve human life in it. Note that all of this is in keeping with the third characteristic of the "elements of the world" identified above, their created nature, and remember that Paul's polemic is directed not at these created realities as such but at their idolization.

Berkhof contends that the "world powers" are perceivable today in every realm of life, such as the state, politics, class, social struggle, national interest, public opinion, accepted morality, and the ideas of decency, humanity, and democracy. Clearly he is thinking here not merely of the order in the physical world but also of the ways in which God has located human beings in social, political, economic, sexual, and cultural orders of the created world. In these contexts, human life is considered "justified" by such "works of the law" as status, class, power, wealth, success, and recognition. Our modern society, including the churches, is full of people who look to the "world powers" for the meaning of their lives and whose piety consists in this subtle form of idolatry.

Such people are in a position to hear the gospel at Christmastide, that in the fullness of time "God sent his Son, born of a woman, born under the law, in order to redeem those who were under the law, so that we might receive adoption as children."

*Thomas W. Gillespie*

## Sixth Sunday after Pentecost, Year C

First Lesson: 2 Kings 2:1-2, 6-14
(Psalm 77:1-2, 11-20)
**Second Lesson: Galatians 5:1, 13-25**
Gospel Lesson: Luke 9:51-62


This reading combines the conclusion of the Sarah/Hagar typology (4:21–5:1) with the first two of three parts in the parenesis (exhortation) of the letter (5:13-15; 5:16-26; 6:1-10). It concludes the body of the letter because Paul's three major arguments in behalf of his law-free gospel (1:13–2:21; 3:1–4:11; 4:12–5:12) require him to address how such a gospel provides a basis for the moral life. The apostle was misunderstood in his own time as preaching "free grace means free sin" (Dunn). So the question of freedom as an ethical norm is taken up in the parenesis out of practical necessity, and is theologically integral to the argument of the letter as a whole.

Part one of the exhortation begins with a reminder to the Galatians that God has called them. The call of God is crucial for Paul's understanding of his apostleship (1:15-16), but it is equally central to his conception of the Christian life. The Galatians themselves heard God's call in the proclamation of the gospel (1:6; cf. 5:7-8). Now it is explicated as a call "to freedom" (the preposition *epi* with the dative indicating destination or purpose). Paul has prepared the way terminologically for this assertion by his conclusion of the Sarah-Hagar typology: "For freedom Christ has set us free; stand fast therefore, and do not submit again to a yoke of slavery" (5:1; cf. 2:4-5). But it is theologically grounded in the "deliverance" (1:4) and "redemption" (3:13; 4:5) God has effected in the death and resurrection of Jesus Christ. What these soteriological terms imply is now stated explicitly: "For you were called to freedom, brethren" (5:13).

The nature of this freedom is accordingly a crucial issue. From the Gnostics of old to the existentialists of today, freedom has been conceived in terms of life without limitations (cf. *Jonathan Livingstone Seagull* by Richard Bach). The fewer the restrictions, the greater the freedom. That Paul has no such concept of freedom is clear from the neuter adverb *monon* (only) that qualifies and thereby limits the opening declaration: "*only* do not use your freedom as an opportunity for the flesh" (5:13b). Freedom is indeed "opportunity" in the sense of the possibility of uncoerced action. It is what Jacques Ellul calls "the climate of all ethics" (*The Ethics of Freedom* [Grand

Rapids: Eerdmans, 1976], p. 108) in that freedom entails decision regarding how this possibility will be actuated.

Paul warns the Galatians that freedom should not be used "for the flesh" (*tē sarki:* a dative of advantage). Freedom used for this purpose effects what Paul calls and specifies as "the works of the flesh" (vv. 19-21). The term "flesh" in Paul's semantic world denotes primarily the material corporeality of human nature. But when life is reduced to the earthly, when it is merely "carnal" because of its separation from God's Spirit, the "flesh" becomes an isolated "sphere of existence" (Bultmann). Conduct oriented to the "flesh" has only the "flesh" for its norm, thereby becoming enslaved to "the desires of the flesh" (vv. 16-17). As the sphere of human life, the "flesh" pertains not merely to bodily instincts and sensual passions, but equally to human moral and religious efforts (as the "works of the flesh" catalogued in vv. 19-21 confirm). Used as "an opportunity for the flesh," freedom results in "self-indulgence" (NRSV).

Freedom, however, is also an "opportunity" to "serve one another through love" (v. 13c). In fact, freedom is the necessary condition of love. We can compel obedience and command respect, but love is given in freedom. By delivering and redeeming us, Christ sets us free to love. Paul understands love christologically, however, which means in terms of Christ's sacrificial service to others as attested in the key kerygmatic formulations of the letter (1:4; 2:20; 3:13; 4:4). In Christ the contradiction between freedom and its "ominous antonym" (Ebeling) — slavelike service *(douleuein)* — is resolved. More than a moral example is offered here, however. In the literal phrase "through the love serve," the preposition "through" *(dia)* identifies "love" *(agapē)* as that which makes possible the action of the verb. Further, the definite article before this noun is demonstrative ("that love"), namely, that of the Christ "who loved me and gave himself for me" (2:20). In sum, the liberating love of God in Jesus Christ creates "opportunity" for believers to serve one another on the ground of "that love" which calls them to do so.

Given the apostle's argument throughout the letter that Christians are no longer "under the law," it is surprising that he appeals to the law in verse 14 as the warrant for what has just been said: "For the whole law is fulfilled *(plēroun)* in one word, 'You shall love your neighbor as yourself'" (citing Lev. 19:18). Paul can say that the law (as Torah) is fulfilled in three senses: (1) the promises of God to Abraham have been kept in Christ (3:16, 19); (2) the divine purpose in later adding the commandments to the promises has been achieved in the coming of Christ (3:19, 24); and (3) the will of God that we should love our neighbor as ourselves has been accomplished in the sacrificial death of Jesus (1:4; 2:20; 3:13). In verse 14 it is the last sense that is in view.

Because Paul was accused of being antinomian (Rom. 3:8; 6:1-2), it may be asked what role if any the commands of God play in the moral life of those who are "in Christ"? Clearly none that *competes* with Christ as a redemptive agent and none that *completes* the redemption in Christ Jesus (cf. 5:4). Paul's appeal to the Levitical text in verse 14, however, does suggest a continuing pedagogical role for the law in the Christian moral life. This function is identified in the parallel text in Romans 13:8-10. There the apostle again cites Leviticus 19:18, but contends that this commandment both "fulfills" *(plēroun)* the law (vv. 8, 10) and "summarizes" *(anakephalaioun)* its particular requirements as well (v. 9). As examples of this latter function, Paul mentions commandments seven, six, eight, and ten from the second tablet of the Decalogue. While not synonymous, "fulfilling" and "summarizing" are complementary terms. If the love of neighbor fulfills the moral intent of the law as a whole and the command to love the neighbor summarizes its particular commandments, then the particular commandments serve to exposit what the love of neighbor requires. Thus, according to Paul, the love of neighbor precludes adultery, murder, stealing, and coveting. It is in this sense that the law functions pedagogically in the moral life of Christians.

Part two of the parenesis, marked by a typical Pauline transition formula ("But I say"), introduces the dichotomy that structures the entire passage: "Live by the Spirit . . . and do not gratify the desires of the flesh" (v. 16). While the "desires of the flesh" picks up on the "opportunity for the flesh" in verse 13, "the Spirit" is mentioned for the first time in this section of the letter. Yet the Spirit is implicit in the prior discussion of freedom and love. For Paul the Spirit is the necessary condition of freedom (2 Cor. 3:17) and the mediator of the love of God to the human heart (Rom. 5:5). And not to be overlooked is the role of the Spirit in our keeping the commands of God (Rom. 8:2-4). The reduction of the law to a singular requirement *(dikaiōma)* in this last text suggests the Levitical "summary" of the law (Rom. 13:9) and thus the role of the Spirit in its "fulfillment" (Rom. 13:8, 10; Gal. 3:14).

Because believers "live in the Spirit" (v. 25a), they are called to "walk in the Spirit" (v. 16), be "led by the Spirit" (v. 18), and "follow the Spirit" (v. 25b). This is no easy task in that "the flesh desires against the Spirit" and "the Spirit against the flesh," because they are "opposed to each other" (v. 17). As the law was given for the sake of boundaries that establish human accountability (3:19), so the Spirit is given "to prevent you from doing what you will" (v. 17).

Yet the apostle's parenesis is not based on "a charismatic ethic" (Dunn), with the Spirit providing instant and *de novo* guidance in each ethical situation. Walking in, being led by, and following the Spirit are simply other ways of speaking of fulfilling the summarized law by loving the neighbor as oneself (v. 14). That the moral pedagogy of the Spirit can be specified is clear from the vice and virtue catalogues in verses 19-23. Although not unique as a genre, these lists are nonetheless distinguished by their content. The "desires of the flesh" are "plain" to Paul, particularly those that deal with sexual immorality and idolatry, because they represent his Jewish moral sensitivities shaped by the law and the prophets. Those who are "led by the Spirit" are no longer "under the law" (v. 18) in the sense that they find their personal, social, and religious location before God in the law, but not in the sense that the commandments of God are devoid of moral imperative under the leading of the Spirit.

In contrast to "the works of the flesh" (v. 19), the apostle introduces his list of virtues as "fruit of the Spirit" (vv. 22-23). The difference is between behavior generated out of the self in its isolation from God and attitudes that grow out of a relationship with their source, the Spirit. It is the Spirit whose behavior is characterized by "love, joy, peace, patience, kindness, generosity, faithfulness, gentleness, and self-control." These virtues are learned by example from the ways in which the Spirit is experienced by those who "belong to Christ Jesus" and have for that reason "crucified the flesh with its passions and desires" (v. 24). For Paul the moral life of the believer in the gospel is informed by the sensitivities developed by attending to the commands of God and by the influence of the Spirit who, in relating to us in love, teaches us how we are to relate to our neighbor.

*Thomas W. Gillespie*

## Seventh Sunday after Pentecost, Year C

First Lesson: 2 Kings 5:1-14
(Psalm 30)
**Second Lesson: Galatians 6:(1-6), 7-16**
Gospel Lesson: Luke 10:1-11, 16-20

In terms of literary structure, chapter 6 of Galatians is composed of the third of three parts to the parenesis (exhortation) section (6:1-10) and the letter's concluding postscript (6:11-18). Of particular theological interest in this text are: (1) the concept of "the law of Christ" (v. 2); (2) the reality of moral accountability (vv. 7-10); (3) the notion of being "crucified" to "the world" (v. 14); and (4) the related idea of a "new creation" (v. 15).

The transition from the second to the third part of the parenesis section of the letter is marked by the vocative *adelphoi* (brethren). Here in 6:1-10 the apostle applies the general teaching of the previous two parts of his ethical argument to particular matters in the Galatian ecclesial context. The love of neighbor is spelled out in terms of dealing with one caught in a transgression (v. 1), bearing one another's (moral) burdens (v. 2), avoiding unwarranted pride (v. 3) and invidious comparisons (v. 4), accepting individual responsibility (v. 5), supporting those who teach (v. 6), and respecting the consequences of behavior (vv. 7-10).

It is in the context of the exhortation to "bear one another's burdens" that Paul speaks of fulfilling "the law of Christ" (v. 2). To what does this phrase refer? Is it (1) the law of love, or (2) the teaching of Jesus, or (3) the law which Christ himself is, or (4) the law which Christ has fulfilled and thereby made his own in the postresurrection situation? Paul himself provides a clue to the answer elsewhere in his discussion of his missionary strategy (1 Cor. 9:20-21). There he explains: "To those under the law I became as one under the law — though not being myself under the law — that I might win those under the law. To the lawless *(anomos)* I became as a lawless one — not being lawless *(anomos)* toward God but in the law *(ennomos)* of Christ — that I might win those outside the law *(anomos)*." Here Paul is engaging in a play on the words *anomos* (lawless) and *ennomos* (in law). While the latter term can denote "subject to law," its formulation by combining the preposition *en* (in) with the noun *nomos* (law) is suggestive of a locative sense in which one is "inside the law" as opposed to "outside the law" *(anomos)*. As one who is "in Christ" *(en Christōi)*, the apostle understands that relationship in legal as well as personal terms. The relationship between the believer and Jesus Christ is morally informed by "the law of Christ." "Bear one another's burdens, and so fulfill the law of Christ" in Galatians 6:2, therefore, is simply a reformulation of the statement in 5:14, "For the whole law is fulfilled in a single commandment, 'You shall love your neighbor as yourself.'" It is the law that Christ has made his own by fulfilling it through his faithful obedience and obedient faith, therefore, to which Paul refers here.

A note unheard in our contemporary culture of victimhood is sounded in verses 7-8: "Do not be deceived; God is not mocked, for you reap whatever you sow. If you sow to your own flesh, you will reap corruption from the flesh; but if you sow to the Spirit, you will reap eternal life from the Spirit." That believers "bear *(bastazein)* one another's burdens *(baros)*" (v. 2) does not eliminate personal responsibility, for ultimately "all will bear *(bastasei)* their own burdens *(phortion)*" (v. 5). Paul does not identify these burdens, but the context suggests temptations and moral failings (cf. Rom. 15:1, where the strong are encouraged "to bear *(bastazein)* with the failings *(ta asthenēmata)* of the weak"). Likewise the future tense of the verb in verse 5 suggests that the final judgment is in view, "burdens" thereby being viewed here as moral weaknesses and failures. It is in this context, therefore, that the warning against self-deception regarding moral accountability to God is stated. "God is not mocked," the apostle declares. The verb *myktērizein* occurs only here in the New Testament and denotes "to turn up one's nose at," "to treat with contempt," and thus the translation "to mock." His point is that those who "thumb their nose" at God do so at their own peril because they will reap what they sow. Human behavior, in other words, has inevitable and commensurable consequences. These are spelled out in verse 8 in terms of the "flesh"/"Spirit" dichotomy established in 5:16-26. Those who sow to their "own flesh" will "from the flesh" reap "corruption," while those who "sow to the Spirit" will reap from the Spirit "eternal life." Again the future tense of the verb "to reap" as well as the terms "corruption" and "eternal life" points in the direction of the final judgment before God. That Paul also recognizes the proleptic judgment of God upon human behavior in the present is evident from his repeated phrase "God gave them up" to the consequences of their idolatry in Romans 1:18-32 (esp. vv. 24, 26, 28).

The postscript to the letter is personally written by the author: "See what large letters I make when I am writing in my own hand!" (v. 11; cf. 1 Cor. 16:21). Large letters in Paul's day served to convey emphasis, much as bold type or italicized words function today. Postscripts provided a letter writer opportunity to summarize or highlight the main points of the epistle. With emphasis, then, Paul attacks the intruders into his churches in

Galatia who demand the circumcision of his Gentile converts, attributing to them motives of wanting "to make a good showing in the flesh" in order that "they may not be persecuted for the cross of Christ" (v. 12). This suggests that the Jewish Christians in Jerusalem and Judea were under pressure from non-Christian Jews for their religious association with uncircumcised Gentiles (cf. Gal. 2:11-14, where Paul reports Peter's defection from the Jewish/Gentile table fellowship in Antioch, together with Barnabas and all the Jews, "for fear of the circumcision faction"). For Paul this is tantamount to denying the efficacy of the death of Jesus on the cross, which alone is God's justifying act. "I do not nullify the grace of God," he has already declared, "for if justification comes through the law, then Christ died for nothing" (2:21). His opponents, who do not themselves keep the whole law, "boast" in the circumcised flesh of their Gentile followers (6:13). The apostle, however, expresses the desire never to boast of anything "except the cross of our Lord Jesus Christ, by which the world has been crucified to me, and I to the world" (v. 14).

This is the third time in this letter that Paul has spoken of crucifixion in such existential terms. With reference to his death "to the law" in 2:19, he confesses as a paradigmatic believer, "I have been crucified with Christ." With regard to the moral life of the believer in 5:24, he declares that "those who belong to Christ Jesus have crucified the flesh with its passions and desires." Now in the postscript he explains that by "the cross of our Lord Jesus Christ" he (again as the typical believer) has been crucified "to the world" and "the world" to him. Friedrich Gogarten observed that for the pre-Christian person the cosmos is the ultimate, all-embracing reality. The decisive issue on such a view is both that and how we may adapt ourselves and our actions to this order. The world thus becomes a religious reality and evokes a piety that consists in the worship of its order and powers (*The Reality of Faith* [Philadelphia: Westminster, 1959], pp. 40-41). It is Paul's view that Christ on the cross died to "the law," to "the flesh," and to "the world." Those who are "in Christ" have been "crucified with Christ," and thus participate in all the dimensions of that event.

Verse 15 requires comparison with two other Pauline texts that are formulated in a parallel fashion and inform each other materially:

For neither circumcision counts for anything, nor uncircumcision, but a new creation. (Gal. 6:15)

For in Christ Jesus neither circumcision nor uncircumcision is of any avail, but faith working through love. (Gal. 5:6)

For neither circumcision counts for anything nor uncircumcision, but keeping the commandments of God. (1 Cor. 7:19)

The cumulative point is that what matters decisively is the "new creation" in which "faith works through love" by "keeping the commandments of God." What distinguishes this obedience to "the commandments of God" from "the works of the law" — and thus preserves the integrity of Paul's gospel — is the context in which such acts occur. They are accomplished in the sphere of the "freedom" for which "Christ has set us free" (5:1). Gerhard Ebeling explains the difference as one between an ethics of law and the ethics of freedom. He writes:

> The former is based on unfulfillment, on the driving force of a demand. The latter is based on fulfillment, on the driving force of the Spirit. The former seeks to attain life and righteousness, the latter grows out of gratitude that life and righteousness have been granted by grace. The former must pay laborious heed to infinite detail, never attaining the whole. The latter knows the spontaneity of the Spirit through which the whole is grasped joyfully in the singular detail. The former necessarily concentrates on agents and their actions because they can never be sure of themselves. The latter counts on the self-forgetfulness of agents who enjoy freedom from themselves, concentrating entirely on who needs the agents and their actions. (*The Truth of the Gospel: An Exposition of Galatians* [Philadelphia: Fortress, 1985], p. 254)

For the apostle Paul, this is canonical. As he pronounced a conditional curse upon any and all who proclaim a "different gospel" in the proem of the letter (1:8), so he concludes his epistle with the conditional blessing upon "those who will follow this rule *(kanon)*" (v. 16).

*Thomas W. Gillespie*

## Second Sunday after Christmas, Years A, B, C

First Lesson: Jeremiah 31:7-14
(Psalm 147:12-20)
**Second Lesson: Ephesians 1:3-14**
Gospel Lesson: John 1:(1-9), 10-18

## Eighth Sunday after Pentecost, Year B

First Lesson: 2 Samuel 6:1-5, 12b-19
(Psalm 24)
**Second Lesson: Ephesians 1:3-14**
Gospel Lesson: Mark 6:14-29

After a two-verse salutation, the Letter to the Ephesians launches into an exuberant benediction, recounting God's multiple blessings mediated through Christ. The obvious theme of the sermon will be what God has done for us, and the list here is overwhelming. The challenge to the preacher will be to select the particular focus for the sermon, since the text covers virtually every topic of Christian theology!

The first thing to note exegetically is that God is the initiator throughout. Eight times "God/he" is the subject of a sentence. "We/you" is the subject of only four sentences, and in three of those we are recipients of God's blessings (v. 7, "we have redemption"; v. 11, "we have also obtained"; v. 13, "you . . . were marked"). Verse 12 refers to the consequences upon receiving this abundance of grace ("that we . . . might live").

The second thing to note in this passage is the sweep of its vision. It spans a limitless dimension of time, beginning even before creation (v. 4, "before the foundation of the world") and ending with the eschaton (v. 14, "our inheritance toward redemption as God's own people"). In between God planned in the "fullness of time," after making known his will in Christ, to "gather up all things in him" (v. 10).

Note the word "destined" in verses 5 and 11 and "inheritance" in verses 11 and 14. The use of these words, indeed the tone of the entire text, drives our vision constantly into the future. Nor is this an ephemeral or distant hope. The word "pledge" in verse 14 would be better translated "first installment." It was a legal term with much the same meaning as our "earnest money" in a real estate transaction. Hearing the gospel and believing marks us with the Holy Spirit (v. 13), which in itself is the first installment of our inheritance. It is not only a hope of the future; we have begun already to live in our inheritance. Look back at the verbs in this text. They are almost all past or perfect tense, that is, these actions and gifts of God have happened. This is what C. H. Dodd meant a half-century ago when he coined the phrase "realized eschatology." For Christians the future has already begun.

The broad sweep of the passage is also apparent in its portrayal of Christ's work. One of the problems of every preacher is a tendency to narrow our preaching to themes most important for us. This passage can be a corrective, since these verses are simply crammed with all God has done for us:

- "has blessed us in Christ"
- "chose us in Christ"
- "destined us for adoption as his children"
- "glorious grace that he freely bestowed on us"
- "we have redemption . . . forgiveness"
- "grace that he lavished on us"
- "has made known to us the mystery of his will"
- "good pleasure that he set forth in Christ"
- "gather up all things in him"
- "we have also obtained an inheritance"
- "we . . . might live for the praise"
- "were marked"

No other twelve-verse passage in all the Scriptures encompasses such a comprehensive list of God's actions, gifts, and blessing!

The third aspect to note in this text is the centrality of Christ in God's work of salvation. God's gifts come through Christ. The phrase "in Christ" occurs four times here, but we also read "through Christ," "in the Beloved," "through his blood," "riches of his grace," "on Christ," and "in him." The emphasis is set immediately in the first two verses: "who has blessed us *in Christ* . . . just as he chose us *in Christ*." God is the actor, but all God's actions, from the plan before creation to the consummation of all creation, are done in and through Christ.

The text may be divided into three parts, and Christ is at the center of each of them.

1. The basis of God's blessings in Christ (vv. 3-4). The impact of the opening verses is that God has chosen to bless us "with every spiritual blessing in the heavenly places," which means God's action in his own realm. Furthermore, God has chosen us before the creation of the world. There is

not simply an agreement between two parties, but a unilateral action with a cosmic dimension by the sovereign Creator of all things!

The opening phrase, "Blessed be the God and Father . . . ," follows the form of traditional Jewish prayers. These blessings are never a gesture of goodwill on our part toward God; they are always a response to the blessings we have received from God: "Blessed be God . . . who has blessed us . . . as he chose us. . . ."

2. The breadth of God's blessings in Christ (vv. 5-11). This compact section is full of descriptions of what Jesus Christ has given us. Preachers will recall from their seminary studies the variety of ways in which Jesus' work of redemption has been described throughout church history — prophet, priest, king, sacrifice, example, conqueror, etc. All this variety is included in these verses. The entire Christology of Christian theology is here!

We often wonder about God's activity in the world. Rather than giving up and thinking God unknowable or inscrutable, verse 9 uses the word "mystery" ironically: what was once a mystery has now been revealed in Christ.

After making the listener aware of the magnificent breadth of this vision, the preacher will need to make a decision on the specific focus of the sermon. One could preach a series of sermons on each of these rich phrases in verses 5-12.

3. The purpose of God's blessings in Christ (vv. 12-14). The "so that we" which begins verse 12 indicates a shift of intent. We move from the description of Christ's work to its purpose. All this has been done for us "so that we . . . might live for the praise of his glory." We "had believed . . . were marked" for this purpose.

This section gives the text an explicit trinitarian affirmation. The Christian life is life in the Holy Spirit, the breath and presence of God with us, the seal or guarantee of our life in Christ.

This text is appointed for the Second Sunday after Christmas in Years A, B, and C and the Eighth Sunday after Pentecost in Year B. Its placement with the prologue to John's Gospel as a Christmas text is a wonderful combination, with both texts focusing on the person and work of Christ. A sermon can easily incorporate both passages, as well as the glorious messianic vision of the Old Testament text for the day, Jeremiah 31:7-14.

In the Pentecost B series Ephesians is read as the second lesson for seven consecutive Sundays beginning with this Sunday. As is often the case with continual Epistle readings, it is not particularly connected with the other texts, but furnishes by itself a wealth for preaching.

In its own setting, the text spoke to both Jews and Gentiles. Jewish readers would note how Jesus Christ as God's Messiah is the center of God's redemptive work. Gentile readers would be accustomed to their panoply of divine beings who have a life of their own and scant interest in the lives of ordinary mortals. They would be struck how God's entire activity aims at the salvation of each human being.

Both aspects and meanings are equally apt today. For those who think of God in vague Deist or New Age notions, the crystal-clear message of this passage is that God has an intent for each human life, determined and destined before time, actively accomplished in Christ and already ushering us into a wonderful future.

Since many people think of the Christian faith as believing in a lot of propositions, a sermon on this text would be a corrective, because its theme is what God has done for us through Christ. The form of the sermon could be expository (marching one's way through the verses) or narrative (summarizing all God has done).

In a rootless society such as ours, or, as some would say, in this "now generation" or "me generation," people need to be connected to the past and to the future. This text grounds us in God's plan from the beginning, and pulls us toward the future as well, to an inheritance already begun.

A possibility for the next several Sundays is to preach a series of sermons on Ephesians. Its message is as powerful, rich, and appealing in our world as it was in its own time. The depth and breadth of its six chapters speak directly to any kind of congregation in any kind of community and circumstance. It is indeed a timely and precious letter to all Christians!

*Michael Rogness*

## Christ the King, Year A

First Lesson: Ezekiel 34:11-16, 20-24
(Psalm 100)
**Second Lesson: Ephesians 1:15-23**
Gospel Lesson: Matthew 25:31-46

## Ascension of the Lord, Years A, B, C

First Lesson: Acts 1:1-11
(Psalm 47)
**Second Lesson: Ephesians 1:15-23**
Gospel Lesson: Luke 24:44-53

This text is actually one long sentence, but English style calls for division. The four sentences in the NRSV translation can be divided into three distinct sections:

- Thanksgiving (vv. 15-16)
- Intercession (vv. 17-19)
- God's work through Christ (vv. 20-21, 22-23)

The text follows logically upon verses 3-14, where the author has listed all that God has done for us in Christ, an exuberant outpouring which encompasses virtually every aspect of Christology in Christian theology.

Verse 15 follows with an expression of thanksgiving, not only for the faith of the Ephesian Christians but also for their "love toward all the saints."

This first section ends with the author's assurance that the believers in Ephesus are remembered in his prayers. The focus of the prayer is thanksgiving, reminding us that our prayers too should be centered in thanksgiving. Intercession without prior thanksgiving becomes "gimme" prayers. If prayers shift to intercession without thanksgiving, the measure of prayer becomes its results rather than the goodness of God.

The opening two verses lead into the intercessions themselves, revealing the content of the author's constant prayers.

Note what is prayed for, which can be a model for our prayers as well. It is first a prayer for "a spirit of wisdom and revelation as you come to know

307

him" (v. 17). Many of the readers will be new to the Christian faith, and a wise grasp of God's revelation will be crucial. In our time faith and the sincerity of faith is valued more than its content, an utterly foreign notion in the Bible. These verses of intercession are in fact a prelude to the entire epistle, because the main body of Ephesians (2:1–3:16) is in fact an exposition of the content of the Christian faith.

Equally crucial is the "so that" which opens verse 18. The wisdom, revelation, enlightenment, and knowledge mentioned are never ends in themselves, but always lead to changed lives. They are given by God "so that" minds and hearts are opened and lives are indeed renewed. The tone of the prayer shifts to the consequences of God's revelation, asking that with the eyes of their enlightened hearts the Ephesians might know:

- the hope to which they have been called,
- the riches of the glorious inheritance,
- the immeasurable greatness of God's power for believers.

The concluding four verses describe the nature of this power. It is manifested specifically in the resurrection and ascension of Christ, the central miracles of the Christian faith. Christ's primacy is emphasized by listing four terms — "all rule and authority and power and dominion" (v. 21). This multiplicity of realms does not denote four separate or distinct entities, but rather intends to emphasize the all-encompassing sovereignty of Christ at God's right hand. No doubt the author used the four terms to include whatever powers Jewish or Gentile believers would see as oppressing them. Whatever any realm or power might claim, Christ is above it.

One might think of secular political powers; one might think of supernatural powers, dark forces of evil; a Gentile might think of the capricious meddling of Greek divinities in human life or the power claimed by other religions. The author wishes to make clear that whatever power or authority might threaten human life, nothing can supersede the power of the resurrected and ascended Christ at the Father's right hand.

To make this even more emphatic, the author states that Christ's name is above every name. Names were not simply verbal appellations. They carried within themselves the reality of that which carried the name. To name a name conveys the power of the person or thing so named. To name Christ claims the power of Christ over all other sovereignties. This passage reminds us of the Philippians hymn, where God designates the name of Jesus above every name,

so that at the name of Jesus
    every knee should bend,
    in heaven and on earth and under the earth.      (Phil. 2:9-10)

Beleaguered Christians in the Roman Empire of the first century may well respond to these verses with: "Who says all this is possible?" Sensing this, the author follows with a strong statement of the exaltation and power now given to the resurrected and ascended Lord Jesus Christ. This is not a power off in the distant future, but a power already exercised in Christ's resurrection and ascension.

This text is appointed for both the Ascension of the Lord in Years A, B, and C and Christ the King Sunday in Year A. (Having been read on those occasions, it is not repeated in the seven-Sunday sequence of readings from Ephesians during Pentecost series B.) In both cases its connection with the theme of the day and the accompanying texts is obvious, and the sermon will easily incorporate the other texts.

If one's Christology is oriented around Christ's work as prophet, priest, and king, this text focuses on Christ as king. If one's Christology is weighted toward Jesus the sacrifice for sin or Jesus the example of an ideal human life, the preacher will be broadened to proclaim Christ in his exaltation at the Father's right hand.

In a time when we often narrow our portrayal of Christ's work, the magnificent sweep of this passage blows open the horizons of our narrow thinking from Jesus the sacrifice or example to Jesus the incarnate Word of God now once again restored to his place "far above all rule and authority and power and dominion" (v. 21). Churches in Western Christendom traditionally feature the crucifix or empty cross as the centerpiece of their sanctuaries. For a complete portrayal of Christ, one needs also the iconography of the Eastern Church, where often Christ the supreme *pantocrator* looks majestically at his people from his exalted ascended state.

This is a forceful preaching text for our day. Whichever aspect of the text the preacher chooses to deal with, the theme of the sermon will be the centrality of Christ in all we say about God's redemptive activity.

On one hand we might speak to the widespread disillusion with the church as an institution. We live in a curious time when many people who are estranged from the church are still fascinated by Jesus. To them we need to make clear that the church is not the object of our faith. The gospel is, after all, the good news about Jesus Christ and what he means for our lives. Furthermore, at its heart the church is not an institution but a community, "God's own people" (v. 14), "among the saints" (v. 18), and, indeed, "his

309

[Christ's] body" (v. 23) on earth. To be a Christian is to accept what God has done for us in Christ, to be in Christ and thus united in a community with others in Christ.

On the other hand, the preacher might address the pervasive individualism of many Christians, who think the sum and substance of Christian identity is "Jesus and me" and who have no sense of their identity as members of a community at all.

Yet another possibility for preaching this passage is to consider the *content* of faith. We often speak of faith as if faith itself saves us, which makes faith a work. Faith does not save us; God saves us in Christ. We are saved *through* faith (2:8), by trusting in God's gifts. People need to hear that very clearly, and this text does make it clear. We speak so easily of Jesus as "Savior," but what does he save us from and for? This text, as well as the whole Letter to the Ephesians, speaks exactly to such questions. Such a sermon may well refer to passages in the following chapters which speak exactly to these questions.

Since Ascension brings the Easter season to a close and Christ the King Sunday completes the church year, it is appropriate to end each season on this strong note.

*Michael Rogness*


## Fourth Sunday in Lent, Year B

First Lesson: Numbers 21:4-9
(Psalm 107:1-3, 17-22)
**Second Lesson: Ephesians 2:1-10**
Gospel Lesson: John 3:14-21


G race is the dearest piece of good news the church has for the world. Grace is also, however, fiercely difficult to grasp. In the Bible, as throughout church history, grace has been a source of joy and celebration but also a source of consternation and even heresy. Jonah sneered at the grace of God which saved hapless Nineveh. "I just *knew* that if I preached to those folks you'd end up forgiving them, O God! I knew you were gracious, but I'd prefer you keep your grace at home in Israel where it belongs!"

Jesus embodied grace but was, for that very reason, an unpopular figure among the buttoned-down moralists of his day. "He eats with sinners," they cried in their shrillest tones of piety, and everyone understood where that left Jesus: on the outside of those who knew the ladder to heaven is built, rung by rung, by good deeds.

Meanwhile the apostle Paul was forever doing battle on two fronts. On the one side were the well-meaning folks who clung to the idea that circumcision and keeping kosher were the only ways to cinch one's place in the kingdom. On the other side were those who turned grace into an excuse to live however they wished, taking to heart what would later become the famous dictum of Heinrich Heine: "I like to sin, God likes to forgive. Really, the world is admirably arranged."

If there was one thing Paul, the former Christian baiter, persecutor, and fire-breathing Jesus hater, knew for certain, it was that getting saved has *nothing* to do with our deserving. But Paul made equally clear that once they were baptized, Christians were right to spend a good deal of time pondering how to cultivate Christlike deeds in their lives. Paul knew the riddle of grace: God's grace does not depend on how moral we are, and yet grace is simultaneously highly invested in the moral life!

This paradox is perhaps nowhere on better display than in Ephesians 2. Paul hammers home the assertion that human sin results in spiritually dead people, and dead people, by definition, cannot do anything for themselves. (There is a reason why morticians do not expect cadavers to lend a hand in the embalming process.) In sin, Paul says, we were dead, stuck, helpless. It was while we were in this condition of total inability that God scooped us up, redeemed us, and now loves us forever. It is by grace that we have been saved.

In this lection Paul mentions grace in verses 5, 7, and 8, bringing his soaring rhetoric of "grace alone" in for a landing at verse 9 where he wags a bony finger in his readers' faces to say, "It is not about your works. You don't have a leg to stand on or a single thing to be proud of in terms of your salvation." And that's the gospel. Period.

Or maybe we could better say not "Period" but "Semicolon." Because despite how neatly Paul has cut the legs out from underneath anyone who would want to trot out this or that good deed as contributing to salvation, Paul sees no contradiction in immediately moving on in verse 10 to say that we have been made over in Christ "to do *good works.*" It is the classic gospel paradox (the eschewing of which is what lies behind the age-old but finally misguided "Paul versus James" debate): we are not saved by good works, and yet we're not saved without them either. The same gracious Jesus who could not have cared less about the shape we were in before saving us ends up caring very much about the shape of our lives after saving us. ("If you love me, you will keep my commandments.")

This swift pivot from trashing works to promoting works can be seen throughout Paul's writings. Nowhere is Paul more visibly upset with people who had traded in grace for works than in the epistle to the Galatians. There Paul is in such a hurry to begin ripping into the "foolish" and "bewitched" Galatian Christians that he skips the usual epistolary niceties of giving thanks for them and proceeds immediately to bring them back to grace alone. Still, before that same letter is finished, Paul spends an entire chapter tracing out the fruit of the Spirit and, therefore, what it means to lead a good life!

Paul knew the power of grace. Grace is so powerful that it can (and does) forgive all sin. But anything this powerful does not merely wipe out a person's past but also opens up a new future. When the warhead of grace explodes at ground zero in a person's heart, the blast radius will affect everything in a person's life. Grace brings, as Paul says in Ephesians 2:10, nothing short of a new creation.

Fans of the *Star Trek* movie series may remember the fictional "Project Genesis" device. Genesis was essentially a torpedo whose ultimate goal was not destruction (though it would do this, too) but new creation. If launched onto a lifeless moon, the Genesis device would explode mightily, wiping out everything that was already there. But this was only the beginning, as Genesis would simultaneously take up into itself all the molecules and atoms from the destruction zone and then instantaneously reassemble them into preprogrammed new life-forms. As the Genesis wave would sweep over a lifeless moon, an advancing wall of fire would eat up whatever was there, but this firestorm would swiftly be followed by a wave of renewal as the atoms of this moon's surface would be assembled into lakes, grassy meadows, trees, mountains, and flowers. Within hours of the initial explosion of fire, the once-dead moon would be transformed into a verdant planet capable of supporting life.

Something like that seems to be Paul's view of grace: once it explodes in a person's heart, it changes what had been sinful into something that is now sacred. But it does not merely wipe away the detritus of the person's past life but also begins a transformation into preprogrammed patterns of love, graciousness, kindness, and joy (the "good works which God prepared in advance for us to do").

But the riddle of grace does not stop there. Because as Paul (and the

New Testament generally) knows, our struggle with sin is not completely finished in this life. Grace means new creation and new tendencies and new patterns, but it does not mean perfection. Each believer, with varying degrees of struggle, success, failure, and temptation, continues to sin. The abiding presence of grace means that we continue to be forgiven by grace as completely and freely as in the instant when faith first came into our hearts.

In Ephesians 2 Paul takes aim at what he calls "boasting." It is a mistake, however, to think that the only bragging Paul wishes to eradicate has to do with how we got saved in the first place. Paul equally wants to rid believers of any postconversion bragging over this or that good deed. Legalism, after all, is not just thinking that you can work your own way to heaven. Legalism rears its ugly, grace-wrecking head anytime we quietly think what attracted God to us in the first place was that we were just better candidates for the kingdom than the rest of those offensive "sinners" out there in the world. Legalism does a corporate takeover of the church anytime Christians take on the role of the world's morality police, demanding our brand of good living instead of preaching the grace of God (which alone can lead to such goodness).

Someone once said that if a preacher is never accused of being "soft on sin," he or she is probably not presenting the true punch of grace. An accurate portrayal of the free, free, free gift of grace always runs the risk of someone asking, "So what are you saying? It just doesn't matter how we live!?" And in one sense it doesn't, at least insofar as we never want to forget that those deeds have nothing to do with God's having come to love us in the first place (even as we do not want our deeds to eclipse the grace that enables those same acts). On the other hand, the tightrope preachers are forced to walk is evidenced by the fact that, like Paul, we are forced to speak much about bearing good fruit for God, thus running the risk of playing right into the hands of those who already quietly believe that somehow it is *only* our outward deeds of morality that get and keep folks in the kingdom. Preaching grace is no easy task.

But perhaps it is the cross which helps us keep our balance. The cross of Jesus which towers over Lent reminds us that whether we're contemplating the sins God forgave years ago or the sins he forgave earlier this morning; whether we are contemplating the good things we have already done in our Christian lives or the good things we hope to get around to doing next week, the one line from Ephesians 2 which perpetually inspires both gratitude and humility is, ". . . and this not from yourselves, it is the gift of God." Indeed it is. Lent is finally all about just that gift.

*Scott Hoezee*

313

# Ninth Sunday after Pentecost, Year B

First Lesson: 2 Samuel 7:1-14a
(Psalm 89:20-37)
**Second Lesson: Ephesians 2:11-22**
Gospel Lesson: Mark 6:30-34, 53-56

Peace flows from grace, and this peace-preaching paragraph in Ephesians flows irresistibly from the grace-filled preceding paragraph of 2:1-10. Combined with 2:1-10, 2:11-22 expresses the double theme of Paul's greeting: "Grace [2:1-10] to you and peace [2:11-22]" (1:2). While the peace Christ made and preached is creation wide, in this passage Paul focuses particularly on peace as meaning the inclusion of Gentiles in "the commonwealth of Israel" (2:12), "in Christ Jesus" (2:13), and in "the household of God" (2:19). This Christ-centered peace is embodied in a reconciled and holy people who serve as "a dwelling place for God" (2:22).

The peace theme in 2:11-22 serves as a subpoint for Paul's central proclamation in his letter to the Ephesians: God "has made known to us the mystery of his will, according to his good pleasure that he set forth in Christ, as a plan for the fullness of time, to gather up all things in him, things in heaven and things on earth" (1:9-10). Central to the plan of gathering up all things in Christ is the uniting of Jew and Gentile in Christ. As a new society, the church witnesses to the new creation. Bringing Jews and Gentiles together in Christ is not only a mystery "not made known to humankind" in former generations (3:5), it is also a mystery now "made known to the rulers and authorities in the heavenly places" (3:10). A reconciling church that embodies the peace of God as portrayed in 2:11-22 witnesses beyond itself to God's plan for all creation.

The centrality of reconciliation to the gospel of God's peace comes out as Paul turns to address explicitly "you Gentiles by birth" (2:11). While later in this letter Paul will contrast the Gentiles' former way of life with the new life they learn in Christ (4:17-24), here he contrasts the Gentiles' former status with the new status they have received "in Christ Jesus" (2:13). Gentiles "at one time" (2:11) — that is, before the death and exaltation of Christ (see 1:20 and 2:6) — were "without Christ, being aliens from the commonwealth of Israel, and strangers to the covenants of promise, having no hope and without God in the world" (2:12; cf. Rom. 9:4-5). That was then.

"But now" (2:13; cf. Rom. 3:21) their status has changed. Those far off have been "brought near" (2:13), and Gentiles are "no longer strangers and aliens, but . . . citizens with the saints and also members of the household of God" (2:19). The two major and related themes of 2:11-13 are, therefore, temporal and spatial: a "then versus now" change in status for Gentiles creates a new nearness to Christ, Israel, and God as members of God's covenant people. This good news for Gentiles flows from "the blood of Christ" (2:13), which leads to the next section in this passage.

Before proceeding to 2:14-18, however, a few more words on Jew-Gentile relations are in order. Pastors who preach this and other passages that speak of Jews and Gentiles will want at least some familiarity with the "new perspective on Paul" that is associated especially with the work of Jewish scholar E. P. Sanders. In *Paul and Palestinian Judaism,* Sanders provides massive evidence for his argument against "the view that Rabbinic religion was a religion of legalistic works-righteousness" ([Philadelphia: Fortress, 1977], p. 233). This view, according to Sanders, is "completely wrong," and yet it has informed much Protestant preaching of Paul and therefore needs to be corrected. To bring out the honor Gentiles have received by being grafted together with Jews into "the Israel of God" (Gal. 6:16), pastors will want to avoid equating Judaism with late medieval Roman Catholicism, and they will want to understand both the continuity and the discontinuity between Paul and Martin Luther. James D. G. Dunn helps pastors toward this goal in his survey *The Theology of Paul the Apostle* (Grand Rapids: Eerdmans, 1998). While Dunn and others who reflect "the new perspective" do not display much firsthand knowledge of Luther, they do offer a wealth of rich insights into the Jewish identity and mission of the "apostle to the Gentiles" (Rom. 11:13).

In Ephesians 2:14-18 Paul elaborates on the social expression of the gospel by emphasizing the basis for Gentile inclusion in God's covenant people. The basis is Christ: "For he is our peace" (2:14). Christ has made Jew and Gentile "into one" (2:14). He has made them into "one new humanity [*anthrōpon*]" (2:15) who form "one body" (2:16). Therefore, both Jews and Gentiles "have access in one Spirit to the Father" (2:18; cf. 4:4-6). Christ created this oneness by abolishing "the law with its commandments and ordinances" (2:15), which calls for a word of explanation.

Jesus said, "Do not think that I have come to abolish the law or the prophets; I have comes not to abolish but to fulfill" (Matt. 5:17), and Paul himself also claims to "uphold the law" (Rom. 3:31). Therefore, the abolition of the law he speaks of here has to do not with the holiness, justice, and goodness of the law (see Rom. 7:12), but with the law's involvement in the enmity that divided Jew and Gentile. The law's involvement in enmity expressed itself, for example, when "those who are called 'the circumcision'" would presume superiority over "Gentiles by birth, called 'the uncircumcision'" (2:11). It also expressed itself when the very structure of the temple included a "dividing wall" (Eph. 2:14; cf. Acts 21:28) that excluded Gentiles and prevented the temple from being "called a house of prayer for all the nations" (Mark 11:17).

Commentators disagree about whether the "dividing wall" of 2:14 refers explicitly to the wall of the temple in Jerusalem, but the point remains that Jewish observance of Mosaic law involved a separation between Jews and Gentiles that, because we are "flesh" (2:11), inevitably bred hostility. The coming of Christ in "the fullness of time" (1:10; cf. Gal. 4:4) ended the time for separation between Jew and Gentile. Therefore, even though commandments and ordinances such as circumcision, dietary restrictions, and Sabbaths are good in themselves and may be observed by some, they must not be allowed to divide believers (see Rom. 14–15). Christ has abolished the law in terms of abolishing the separatism and hostility that comes when observers of the law do not recognize the new era Christ has inaugurated. Christ's abolition of the law is for the sake of "one new humanity in place of the two" (Eph. 2:15). Christ does not force Jews to become Gentiles or Gentiles to become Jews. Instead, he allows for creative and historical diversity while endowing all believers with a new primary identity: the status of being "in Christ." In this way Christ is our peace and makes peace.

All this Jew-Gentile material may seem distant to believers today until pastors explain how Jew-Gentile unity offers a paradigm for all social relations in the church. Every congregation includes insider and outsider groups whose differences parallel the differences that divided Jews and Gentiles in the early church. Some believers feel very near to the traditions of the church; others feel far off. Some believers feel like strangers and aliens to the cultural convictions of others, and this can divide the church into warring camps. On top of this are denominational, national, racial, ethnic, class, gender, and other differences that compete with believers' primary identity of being "in Christ" (cf. Gal. 3:28). By dying on the cross, Christ revealed the need for members of all groups to be reconciled to God (see Eph. 2:16). By preaching peace to those far and near, Christ calls us all to be reconciled to each other (see 2:17). This can happen as Christ continues to preach in the church through the Spirit of Pentecost. Having announced the kingdom of peace in his earthly ministry, accomplished it on the cross, and proclaimed it after his resurrection, Christ continues to preach peace in and through the church, which includes Jews and Gentiles, "for through him both of us have access in one Spirit to the Father" (2:18).

In the third section (2:19-22) of the passage, Paul resumes his address to the Gentiles and reiterates their full inclusion in Israel and "the household of God" (2:19). Paul expresses this inclusion with the rich biblical image of "a holy temple in the Lord" (2:21). Holiness, which characterizes all the saints (cf. 1:1 and 2:19), has to do with being set apart for a particular relationship with God and purpose in God's plan. Believers grow into a holy temple as God relates to them in grace and works in them to display Christ as the destiny of the new creation. God's temple people will express this purpose insofar as they are "built upon the foundation of the apostles and prophets, with Christ Jesus himself as the cornerstone" (2:20).

This brings us back to the thematic passage of 1:9-10. Whether it is constructing an actual building or forming fellowship groups or carrying out any activity, churches can easily become subconsciously ingrown. The thematic verses of Ephesians remind believers that all church activities are for the sake of God's creation-wide purpose to gather up all things in Christ. The second half of Ephesians 2 alerts churches to how God's wide plan for a universal kingdom of peace can be expressed especially in relationships of reconciliation among groups. And the culminating image of the temple prods us to think how God's purposes and human reconciliation can shape everything believers do. Giving special attention to children at the Lord's Supper, working together to repair the church building or the neighborhood around the church, making our dinner tables into places where "people will come from east and west, from north and south, and will eat in the kingdom of God" (Luke 13:29) — these and countless other activities are all ways churches can be holy temples that witness to the day when there will be "no temple in the city, for its temple is the Lord God the Almighty and the Lamb" (Rev. 21:22). Faithful preaching of and listening to this passage can anticipate that day by allowing this passage to shape reconciled groups of believers into churches "built together spiritually into a dwelling place for God" (Eph. 2:22).

*Joel E. Kok*

# Epiphany of the Lord, Years A, B, C

First Lesson: Isaiah 60:1-6
(Psalm 72:1-7, 10-14)
**Second Lesson: Ephesians 3:1-12**
Gospel Lesson: Matthew 2:1-12

The Scriptures reveal God's concern for the world in personal, social, and cosmic terms. In this paragraph Paul combines personal, social, and cosmic implications of the gospel "in accordance with the eternal purpose that [God] has carried out in Christ Jesus our Lord" (3:11). Paul takes what has been "made known to me" (3:3) and passes it on to Gentiles (3:1-2 and 3:8), so that "through the church the wisdom of God in its rich variety might now be made known to the rulers and authorities in the heavenly places" (3:10). Paul calls the church to share his "understanding of the mystery of Christ" (3:4) in order "to make everyone see what is the plan of the mystery hidden for ages in God who created all things" (3:9). By listening obediently to this passage, churches can embody the gospel in a way that invites all people to "have access to God in boldness and confidence through faith in [Christ]" (3:12).

Ephesians 3:1-13 forms a unit that can be divided into two sections with overlapping themes. In 3:1-6 Paul expands on the theme of 2:11-22 by further explicating Gentile inclusion in "the commonwealth of Israel" (2:12). Under the heading of "mystery," Paul reiterates that, along with believing Jews, "the Gentiles have become fellow heirs, members of the same body, and sharers in the promise in Christ Jesus through the gospel" (3:6). In 3:7-13 Paul elaborates this theme yet further by tying it to his personal calling "to bring to the Gentiles the news of the boundless riches of Christ" (3:8). Paul's emphasis on the personal character of "the gift of God's grace that was given me" (3:7; cf. 3:2 and 3:8) does not hinder him from announcing the gospel to all creation. Rather, his personal involvement in the message stimulates him to expand the church's mission to include even beings who live "in the heavenly places" (3:10). This union of personal, social, and cosmic concerns makes the omission from the lectionary of the personal note in 3:13 puzzling. It also raises issues of authorship, to which we will return.

In this passage, however, as well as for the whole of Ephesians, questions of authorship are subordinate to matters of content. And one key word that unpacks the content of this passage is the word "mystery." In

318

common English usage a mystery is something beyond comprehension. Believers sometimes reflect this meaning of mystery when we speak of the mystery of the Trinity or the mystery of how divine sovereignty is compatible with human responsibility. This is a legitimate use of the English word, but it is not what Paul means by *mystērion*.

For Paul a mystery is something that was hidden but has now been revealed by God. (See 3:2; cf. 1:9; 3:5; 3:9; and also Rom. 11:25 and 16:25.) As noted above, the specific mystery made known in this paragraph is that Gentiles share "in the promise in Christ Jesus through the gospel" (3:6). God's gathering of Gentiles into Israel is one element in God's "plan for the fullness of time, to gather up all things in [Christ], things in heaven and things on earth" (1:10). God sends a message to all creatures "through the church" (3:10) by uniting Jews and Gentiles in Christ.

People familiar with Old Testament promises to the nations may well wonder how Paul can call the inclusion of Gentiles in Christ a "mystery hidden for ages in God who created all things" (3:9). Throughout the Old Testament the Creator reveals that "his compassion is over all that he has made" (Ps. 145:9; cf. Jon. 4:11). The very election of Abraham and his descendants serves as an occasion for God to promise that "in you all the families of the earth shall be blessed" (Gen. 12:3; cf. Gen. 18:18 and 22:18). And through Isaiah and other prophets, God repeatedly revealed his intention to gather all nations into his kingdom of peace (see Isa. 2:2-4; 11:1-10; 19:23-25; 42:7; 49:6; and 60:1-7).

The hidden aspect of these promises has to do with the radical equality of Gentile membership in God's messianic community. For example, one could read Isaiah 2:2-4 and easily conclude that Gentiles would share in the messianic peace by taking on the yoke of Torah (NRSV: "instruction") that God promised would go forth from "out of Zion" (Isa. 2:3). How else but by becoming observant Jews could Gentiles enter into the blessings of righteousness and peace revealed in the law and the prophets? Converting Gentiles into Jews could express the hope of Israel in a noble way. By teaching Gentiles to practice circumcision along with every jot and tittle of Mosaic law, God's people could signify that God's covenantal promises to Abraham had indeed been fulfilled in Jesus Christ (see Gen. 17:9-14 and Matt. 5:17-20).

For Paul, however, Gentiles may enter into Christ as Gentiles. They may "no longer live as the Gentiles live" (Eph. 4:17), but they do become "fellow heirs" (3:6) to God's promises as Gentiles. This happens not by obedience to the Torah but by "the obedience of faith" (Rom. 1:5 and 16:26), which God brings about among the Gentiles by grace through faith, which issues inevitably in good works (Eph. 2:8-10). God does not make Gentiles into Jews; instead God makes both Gentiles and Jews into new creatures in Christ (4:22-24). It took Peter and the early church repeated promptings of the Holy Spirit to begin to understand God's acceptance of people from "every nation" (see Acts 10–11), and the church is still learning "to perceive my [Paul's] understanding of the mystery of Christ" (Eph. 3:4) regarding this aspect of the gospel. Whether it grapples with societies characterized by polygamy or by serial divorce, the church continues to struggle with how the Spirit of Christ is embodied among diverse people who are renewed in diverse cultural contexts. The "rich variety" (3:10) of God's wisdom continues to call the church to recognize the manifold shapes of the one gospel as it becomes incarnate to all nations. (For a profound and fascinating exploration of these issues, see Andrew F. Walls, *The Missionary Movement in Christian History: Studies in the Transmission of Faith* [Maryknoll, N.Y.: Orbis Books, 1996].)

Besides "mystery," another key word in this passage is *oikonomia,* which the NRSV translates "commission" (3:2) and "plan" (3:9; cf. 1:10). God's plan to make the mystery of Christ known to all creatures included the specific act of God's revelation to and commissioning of Paul as apostle to the Gentiles. Amazingly, it was God's good pleasure to choose Saul the Pharisee to bring Christ's name "before Gentiles and kings and before the people of Israel" (Acts 9:15). As one who had violently persecuted the church and tried to destroy it (Gal. 1:13; cf. 1 Tim. 1:12-17), Paul saw himself as "the least of the apostles" (1 Cor. 15:9) and, in this passage, "the very least of all the saints" (Eph. 3:8). Some preachers may wonder how to reconcile the highly personal character of Paul's remarks in this passage with the fact that "about 80 percent of critical scholarship holds that Paul did not write Eph." (Raymond Brown, *An Introduction to the New Testament* [New York: Doubleday, 1997], p. 620).

While deciding what difference this critical consensus makes for preaching and teaching congregations, pastors can note at least three items. The first is that "even in the 20th century there have been major defenses of Paul as writer" (Brown, p. 620). The second is that the consensus of critical scholarship is often far more convincing to those inside the guild of biblical scholars than to those outside. Upon encountering the theory that a disciple of Paul wrote Ephesians, congregations may well share F. F. Bruce's "surprise that such a disciple has left no other trace, [along] with the observation that Paul's Roman imprisonment provides the most plausible *dramatic* life-setting for the letter" (*Paul: Apostle of the Heart Set Free* [Grand Rapids: Eerdmans, 1983], p. 424). The third and most important observation to be made in this regard is that a greater recognition of Paul's interest in Jew-

Gentile unity in his undisputed letters lessens the differences between them and the epistle to the Ephesians. As Markus Barth observes, "Certainly the apostle's teaching and preaching was much more politically, socially, ethically oriented than his individualizing and existentialist interpreters have been willing to acknowledge" (*Ephesians* [New York: Doubleday, 1974], p. 48).

These and other observations about the authorship of Ephesians can serve not so much to insist on one theory or another but, rather, to bring out the communal character of Paul's thought, especially as this theme emerges in Ephesians. In an age of individualism, it is crucial to see that, according to Paul's gospel, God's plan and wisdom become known "through the church" (3:10). Academic questions about authorship can lead to pastoral questions about how to produce disciples of Paul — and even more, disciples of Paul's Master, Jesus — who can display the gospel in not just personal but also social and cosmic terms. It is thrilling to consider that shaping individual members into a cohesive church body reveals God's otherwise hidden plan to gather all things — in heaven or on earth — under one head, Jesus Christ.

Finally, a few remarks on the "rulers and authorities in the heavenly places" are in order. Traditionally, these beings have been seen as angels and demons. In the modern era, some have demythologized them into social and political structures. Ministers will have to make up their own minds about this and will do well not to be overly dogmatic about the exact nature of these entities. It is worth noting, however, that Paul speaks of "the wiles of the devil" (6:11) and explicitly contrasts these cosmic powers and spiritual forces with "enemies of blood and flesh" (6:12). The traditional view, therefore, forbids demonizing human enemies while encouraging awareness of the spiritual world. Perhaps such awareness can stretch our imaginations as we bring to all people "the news of the boundless riches of Christ" (3:8). Certainly we will want to avoid all reductionism as we celebrate Epiphany and urge everyone to "have access to God in boldness and confidence through faith in [Christ]" (3:12).

*Joel E. Kok*

## Tenth Sunday after Pentecost, Year B

First Lesson: 2 Samuel 11:1-15
(Psalm 14)
**Second Lesson: Ephesians 3:14-21**
Gospel Lesson: John 6:1-21

In this paragraph Paul moves from explication of the mystery of Christ to intercession for its embodiment in the church. Those who have taken seriously Paul's exalted vision of the church in earlier passages in Ephesians will welcome Paul's prayer for the church in this passage. For the church to make known God's "plan for the fullness of time, to gather up all things in [Christ]" (1:10; cf. 3:9-10), it will need to be "filled with the fullness of God" (3:19). In fact, the church will need God "to accomplish abundantly far more than all we can ask or imagine" (3:20).

With the words "For this reason" (3:14) Paul returns to the introduction, to his prayer from which he digressed in 3:1. In 3:2-13 Paul had expanded on the theme of Gentile inclusion in Israel (see 2:19), which is his "understanding of the mystery of Christ" (3:4). Because of Christ, "both of us [believing Jews and Gentiles] have access in one Spirit to the Father" (2:18). This "access to God in boldness and confidence through faith in [Christ]" (3:12) expresses itself in prayer.

Some believers may hesitate to join in Paul's prayer because of the seemingly patriarchal character of the language he uses. In a play on words Paul announces that he bows his knees "before the Father [*patera*], from whom every family [*patria*, which, as the NRSV textual note indicates, can also be translated 'fatherhood'] in heaven and on earth takes its name" (3:14-15).

Rather than dismissing such prayer language as sexist idolatry, pastors can explain how it is rooted in a biblical tradition that sets believers free in Christ. When God commissioned Moses to "say to Pharaoh, 'Thus says the LORD: Israel is my firstborn son. I said to you, "Let my son go that he may worship me"'" (Exod. 4:22-23), God used the metaphor of father and son to set his people free. And this deliverance was not for Israel alone but was intended ultimately to make the Lord's "name resound through all the earth" (Exod. 9:16). It is this exodus tradition of liberation that Jesus called on when he taught his disciples to pray by saying, "Father, hallowed be your name" (Luke 11:2). Jesus did not reinforce structures of patriarchy when he said, "Call no one your father on earth, for you have one Father — the one in heaven" (Matt. 23:9). But Jesus did reveal the character of God when he said, "Whoever has

322

seen me has seen the Father" (John 14:9). It is God as revealed in Christ to whom Paul witnesses when he says, "You did not receive a spirit of slavery to fall back into fear, but you have received a spirit of adoption. When we cry, 'Abba! Father!' it is that very Spirit bearing witness with our spirit that we are children of God" (Rom. 8:15-16; cf. Gal. 4:6-7). And it is God the Father as revealed in Christ to whom Paul bows the knee in this prayer. (For a provocative defense of biblical language for the triune God, see "A Christian Women's Declaration," issued by the Ecumenical Coalition on Women and Society and available from the Institute on Religion and Democracy.)

Similar observations apply to the word *patria*. Paul's aim in his prayer is not to reinforce patriarchy but, rather, to emphasize God's universal concern for "every family in heaven and on earth" (Eph. 3:15). Appearing in the context of Ephesians, with its emphasis on the inclusion of Gentiles in the chosen people, the word "family" here echoes God's promise to Abraham that "in you all the families of the earth shall be blessed" (Gen. 12:3). Paul's reference to families "in heaven" expands our vision to include a glimpse into God's concern for "the rulers and authorities in the heavenly places" (Eph. 3:10). The phrases "bow my knees" (3:14) and "takes its name" (3:5) echo Isaiah 45:22-23 and Psalm 147:4 respectively, and they further support the universalistic scope of Paul's prayer. Those committed to biblical equality in the church may want to supplement Paul's prayer language, but they need not reject it. Indeed, developing Paul's theology as expressed in Ephesians as a whole and in his prayer in particular will serve the cause of biblical equality in the church with unparalleled power.

The content of Paul's prayer begins with a request for power. On behalf of the church, Paul prays that God "grant that you may be strengthened in your inner being with power through his Spirit" (Eph. 3:16). The "inner being" *(esō anthrōpon)* Paul speaks of here is the "inmost self" *(esō anthrōpon)* he agonizes over in Romans 7:22 and the "inner nature" (same terms in Greek) he says "is being renewed day by day" in 2 Corinthians 4:16. The difference between the beleaguered inner being in Romans 7 and the renewed inner being in 2 Corinthians 4 would seem to be the empowering "Spirit" for whom Paul prays in Ephesians 3:16. Paul's prayer for strength and power from the Spirit in this verse echoes his prayer for resurrection power and strength in 1:19-20. The connection between these two prayer passages carries the promise that when the inner self is empowered by the Spirit, "the new self, created according to the likeness of God in true righteousness and holiness" (4:24), can overcome "the old self, corrupt and deluded by its lusts" (4:22) in the life of believers. Beleaguered churches seeking renewal will find a strong ally in Paul in his prayers for the Spirit.

Having prayed to the Father for the Spirit, Paul goes on in a trinitarian way to pray "that Christ may dwell in your hearts through faith, as you are being rooted and grounded in love" (3:17). The Greek word for "dwell" here stands in contrast to a related word that means "to sojourn." The point to note is that believers who have already received Christ by faith will grow in their union with Christ as he dwells in them with ever increasing familiarity. To describe this growth, Paul happily mixes metaphors as he speaks of believers being rooted and grounded in love. The notion of rootedness echoes biblical imagery of plant life, such as the "trees planted by streams of water" in Psalm 1:3, the seed that is the word of God and needs to put down roots in good soil (see Luke 8:11-15), and the vine and branches in John 15:1-11. All these images share the characteristic of gradually growing strength. The same is true for the notion of groundedness. Here the image is of a building rather than a plant, but for Paul, believers are a living "structure [that] is joined together and grows into a holy temple in the Lord" (Eph. 2:21). The big idea in this petition is a stable but dynamic dwelling of Christ in believers. For Paul faith is not a onetime decision only but a union with Christ in which believers grow strong in obedience and are active in love (see Rom. 4:16-25 and Gal. 5:6).

Paul prays for this dwelling of Christ to take place in the "hearts" of believers. Before moving on to the next petition in this prayer, which is all one sentence in Greek, it is worth noting that for biblical writers the heart is the seat not only of feeling but also of willing and thinking (cf. Deut. 6:4ff. and Matt. 22:37, and see also Hans Walter Wolff's section on *leb* in *Anthropology of the Old Testament* [Mifflintown, Pa.: Sigler Press, 1996]). Paul reflects a biblically holistic view of heart and the human condition as he prays that believers "may have the power to comprehend, with all the saints, what is the breadth and length and height and depth, and to know the love of Christ that surpasses knowledge" (Eph. 3:18-19). Believers will need to stretch their emotions, thoughts, and motivations as they attempt to know what surpasses knowledge. To comprehend the love of Christ will take "all the saints" (3:18; cf. Heb. 11:40), and more. It will take God to fill us "with all the fullness of God" (3:19).

The word "fullness" appears earlier in Ephesians (1:23) and plays an important role conceptually in this epistle (see 4:13 and 5:18). Fullness and being filled are also key concepts in Colossians (Col. 1:9; 1:19; and 2:9-10). The term has generated much discussion with respect to its background, but Markus Barth reflects a consensus with respect to its meaning here when he translates 3:19b as: "May you become so perfect as to attain to the full perfection of God" (*Ephesians* [New York: Doubleday, 1974]). The idea is that, as believers mature "to the measure of the full stature of Christ" (4:13), and as they are "filled with the Spirit" (5:18), they will be filled with the fullness of God in terms of reflecting God's moral perfections with ever increasing brilliance. They will be perfectly inclusive in love as their "heavenly Father is perfect" (Matt. 5:48). They will be holy as God is holy (see 1 Pet. 1:15-16). They will "be imitators of God, as beloved children, and live in love, as Christ loved us" (Eph. 5:1-2). Paul's prayer for believers to be filled with the fullness of God echoes his Lord's prayer in John 17:26, where Jesus prays "that the love with which you have loved me may be in them, and I in them."

In his intercession for the church, Paul has led us to the heights of prayer, and yet he points us still higher by bursting into a concluding doxology. Whatever limits and sins may hinder our prayers, God, whose thoughts and ways are higher than ours (see Isa. 55:8-9), "is able to accomplish abundantly far more than all we can ask or imagine" (Eph. 3:20). Amazingly, according to Paul, the surpassing power of God is at work "within us" (3:20). And the surpassing glory of God is reflected "in the church" as well as "in Christ Jesus" (3:21). The good work that God is doing in the church will continue "to all generations, forever and ever" (3:21), and therefore carries a hope beyond what eye has seen or ear heard or "human heart conceived" (1 Cor. 2:9). To such a prayer the church can respond with a hearty "Amen" (Eph. 3:21), which means "This is sure to be! It is even more sure that God listens to my prayer than that I really desire what I pray for!" (Heidelberg Catechism, Lord's Day 52).

*Joel E. Kok*

## Eleventh Sunday after Pentecost, Year B

First Lesson: 2 Samuel 11:26–12:13a
(Psalm 51:1-12)
**Second Lesson: Ephesians 4:1-16**
Gospel Lesson: John 6:24-35

In this passage Paul makes a major transition from doctrinal to ethical instruction. The word "therefore" (4:1; cf. Rom. 12:1; Col. 3:5; and 1 Thess. 4:1) signals that Paul's imperatives — that is, his description of how believers ought to live — flow fittingly from his indicatives — that is, his description of what God is doing "in the church and in Christ Jesus" (Eph. 3:21). Since God's plan is "to gather up all things in [Christ]" (1:10), and since Christ came to "reconcile both groups [Jews and Gentiles] to God" (2:16), believers ought to make "every effort to maintain the unity of the Spirit in the bond of peace" (4:3). Because Paul's plea for unity does not entail uniformity but instead requires diversity, it is an apt application of his announcement of grace and peace to Jews, Gentiles, and all peoples.

The passage can be divided into two main paragraphs which emphasize unity and diversity respectively. 4:1-6 roots the unity of the church in the oneness of God, "who is above all and through all and in all" (4:6). 4:7-16 recognizes diversity among members of the one body by explicating how "each of us was given grace according to the measure of Christ's gift" (4:7). Tying the themes of unity and diversity together is the third theme of maturity. The one body composed of diverse members can build "itself up in love" (4:16) only if believers "grow up in every way into him who is the head, into Christ" (4:15).

Before focusing on the three main themes of unity, diversity, and maturity, it is worthwhile to notice a few details from the opening verses in which Paul makes his transition from doctrine to ethics. For example, Paul's exhortation that believers "lead a life worthy" in 4:1 may strike some readers as less than gracious. Believers rightly picture the gospel in terms of the father's acceptance of the prodigal confessing, "I am no longer worthy to be called your son" (Luke 15:21). How does the seemingly judgmental note of worthiness harmonize with the teaching that "by grace you have been saved through faith" (Eph. 2:8)?

The answer has to do with the transforming power of grace. For Paul, God not only accepts but also regenerates sinners by grace. Paul suggests this by means of his repeated use of the verb *peripatēsai*, "to walk," as a metaphor for the Christian life. (See 2:2; 2:10; 4:1; 4:17; 5:2; 5:8; and 5:15; the RSV brings out this walking metaphor for conduct more consistently than does the NRSV. For the Old Testament background of the metaphor, see Exod. 18:20; Deut. 13:4-5; 1 Kings 9:4; Ps. 86:11; etc. For important Pauline parallels, see esp. Rom. 6:4 and 8:4.) According to Paul, before receiving grace we "were dead through the trespasses and sins in which [we] once walked" (Eph. 2:1-2, RSV). Having been saved by grace through faith, however, we are "created in Christ Jesus for good works, which God prepared beforehand, that we should walk in them" (2:10, RSV). Therefore, when Paul exhorts believers to walk in a way "worthy of the calling to which you have been called" (4:1), he is simply describing the way in which God's grace manifests itself in daily conduct. Rather than walking "as the Gentiles do" (4:17 RSV), re-created believers will take on the righteous and holy character (see 4:24) of the God who saves them. By grace they will live "as beloved children[, who] walk in love, as Christ loved us" (5:1-2, RSV). They will not earn but will experience the blessings of light and wisdom (see 5:8 and 5:15) as they walk "not in the counsel of the wicked" (Ps. 1:1, RSV) but instead follow "the way of the righteous" (Ps. 1:6), which is the way "that leads to life" (Matt. 7:14). Believers who practice the Spirit-given virtues of humility, gentleness, patience, and love (Eph. 4:2) will discover in their own experience that this "walk" or way of life is indeed a blessing that flows from God's grace.

Believers will need all these virtues and more if we hope to speak with integrity with respect to Paul's plea to make "every effort to maintain the unity of the Spirit in the bond of peace" (4:3). Regarding the verb translated "making every effort," Markus Barth states, "It is hardly possible to render exactly the urgency contained in the underlying Greek verb" (*Ephesians* [New York: Doubleday, 1974], p. 428). Paul calls believers toward painstaking efforts on behalf of visible unity in the church. Given the divided state of the catholic church, this plea would be pathetic if it were rooted in human initiative alone. For Paul, however, "the unity of the Spirit" (4:3) has its primary basis in the unity of the triune God.

The God-centered, trinitarian character of the church's unity emerges overwhelmingly in 4:4-6. There can be "one body" only because there is "one Spirit" (4:4). There can be one church only because the "one Spirit . . . one Lord . . . [and] one God and Father" are three Persons who together are one God. This passage combined with parallel passages suggests that while Paul did not formulate a fully developed doctrine of the Trinity, he did conceive of God in a trinitarian way that is suggestive for the unity of the church.

Within Ephesians itself, Paul speaks in a trinitarian way when he states, "for through him [Christ] both of us have access in one Spirit to the Father" (2:18). It is no accident that this verse occurs in a paragraph devoted to Christ as "our peace" (2:14), who unites Jews and Gentiles as "one new humanity" (2:15) and "one body" (2:16). Elsewhere, Paul combines a binitarian description of God with an echo of the great Shema of Deuteronomy 6:4 when he states, "There is one God, the Father, from whom are all things and for whom we exist, and one Lord, Jesus Christ, through whom are all things and through whom we exist" (1 Cor. 8:6). Once again, Paul speaks of the one God in this multipersonal way for the purpose of uniting different groups in the church without insisting on uniformity. Later in Corinthians he does this again when he states, "There are varieties of gifts, but the same Spirit; and there are varieties of services, but the same Lord; and there are varieties of activities, but it is the same God who activates all of them in everyone" (1 Cor. 12:4-6). Bringing these passages from Corinthians into conversation with Ephesians 4:3-6 will help ministers to follow Paul in pleading for an inclusive unity in the church that reflects the oneness of the triune God. (Another important trinity-unity, ecclesial-ecumenical passage is John 13–17, especially Jesus' prayer that believers "may all be one. As you, Father, are in me and I am in you, may they also be in us, so that the world may believe that you have sent me" [17:21].)

The diversity section of this unity-with-diversity passage emerges in 4:7-16. This paragraph is reminiscent of Paul's body of Christ passages in Romans 12 and 1 Corinthians 12, though it reveals some development in his thought with respect to Christ as the head of the body. (For a brief but illuminating discussion of this development, see F. F. Bruce, *Paul: Apostle of the Heart Set Free* [Grand Rapids: Eerdmans, 1977], pp. 411-12 and 419-21.) The Ephesians version of this one body with diverse members metaphor is also slightly complicated by Paul's use of Psalm 68. Commentators arrive at different conclusions regarding both what version of Psalm 68 Paul quotes or paraphrases here and what he means by the phrase "lower parts of the earth" (4:9). However, the major points Paul makes by means of calling on Psalm 68 are clear enough. Christ's ascension signals his triumphal vindication of his people. Just as ancient conquerors received gifts from their captives and gave gifts to their people, so has Christ "made captivity itself a captive; / [and given] gifts to his people" (4:8; cf. the conquest imagery in Col. 2:15). That these gifts should be received and shared humbly is implied in Paul's assertion that the same Christ who ascended "also descended into the lower parts of the earth" (4:9). Whether this descent to the lower regions refers to the incarnation, the crucifixion, sheol, or something else, the Philippians 2 pattern of humility leading to exaltation is the big picture and pattern for believers who receive gifts not so that they may exalt themselves, but instead, so that they may serve and build up the body.

The building up of the one body through the humble sharing of gifts requires maturity on the part of diverse believers. After listing a few gifts explicitly, Paul explains that their purpose is "to equip the saints for the work of ministry, for building up the body of Christ" (4:12). Here is the theological basis for a priesthood of all believers that manifests itself as a ministry of all believers. For this vision of church life to become more than a slogan, believers must "come to the unity of the faith and of the knowledge of the Son of God, to maturity, to the measure of the full stature of Christ" (4:13).

The notion of believers attaining maturity as opposed to living as "children, tossed to and fro and blown about by every wind of doctrine" (4:14) could very well serve as a powerful image for those who want to express how Paul's vision for the church can be embodied in the lives of believers today. How do believers become mature? How do we grow in Christlikeness and live up to the manifold images for Christian conduct that Paul packs into this passage? How else except by walking humbly, gently, patiently, and lovingly with our fellow believers in the daily life of the church? Only by committing ourselves, for better and for worse, to the body of Christ will we "grow up in every way into him who is the head, into Christ" (4:15). Church life is the radically countercultural way of spirituality that Paul holds out to an individualistic, anti-institutional generation. Maturity in Christlikeness will come to each of us and to the church as a whole as each member humbles himself or herself in a way that "promotes the body's growth in building itself up in love" (4:16).

*Joel E. Kok*

## Twelfth Sunday after Pentecost, Year B

First Lesson: 2 Samuel 18:5-9, 15, 31-33
(Psalm 130)
**Second Lesson: Ephesians 4:25–5:2**
Gospel Lesson: John 6:35, 41-51

In this passage Paul issues the extraordinary command: "Therefore be imitators of God" (5:1). Apart from Paul's earlier theological and ethical instructions, the notion of imitating God would be either ludicrous or cruel. However, in the context of Paul's understanding of re-creation and conversion, this bold vision of the Christian life makes perfect sense. Believers who have been graciously forgiven by "God in Christ" (4:32) will find it graciously natural to imitate God by walking "in love, as Christ loved us" (5:2).

Scholars disagree about exactly how to outline the ethical section of Ephesians, which begins at 4:1. Some see 5:1-2 as offering a culmination to instructions that begin at 4:17. Others see 5:1-2 as introducing a related but new line of thought that ends at 5:20. And there are other possible outlines.

However one outlines Ephesians as a whole, the important point for dealing with the suggested lectionary reading is to see its organic relationship to the immediately preceding paragraph. As Peter T. O'Brien states in his introduction to this passage, "Paul now [at 4:25–5:2] proceeds to set forth specific, concrete exhortations which flow directly from the paraenesis of the preceding paragraph with its clear distinction between the old way of life and the new (4:17-24)" (*The Letter to the Ephesians* [Grand Rapids: Eerdmans, 1999], p. 334). One example of this close connection between 4:17-24 and 4:25–5:2 can be seen in Paul's choice of verbs in 4:22 and 4:25. Having described believers as those who "put away" (4:22) their former way of life, Paul goes on, by means of the same verb, to specify that this includes "putting away falsehood" (4:25).

The big idea in 4:17-24 is the notion of conversion from one way of life to another. Paul assumes all believers will experience conversion, and he describes the process with the metaphor of changing selves the way one changes clothes. As believers "put away" or take off the soiled old self, they will also "clothe [themselves] with the new self" (4:24). This conversion process involves intellectual effort on the part of believers as they are "renewed in the spirit of [their] minds" (4:23). But the human act of conversion is made possible by a divine initiative of saving grace, which Paul expresses in terms of new creation (cf. 2 Cor. 5:17). Renewed believers are "created according to the likeness of God" (4:24), and it is only because believers are re-created in the divine image that they can live the renewed life. For example, because the divine image includes "true righteousness and holiness" (4:24), believers can "speak the truth" (4:25). All the commandments for the converted life that Paul specifies in 4:25–5:2 are rooted in God's saving re-creation. This applies particularly to the otherwise impossible command: "Therefore be imitators of God" (5:1).

Working with a slightly different outline than that of the lectionary, John Stott succinctly summarizes the commands of 4:25–5:4 as teaching "the nitty-gritty of Christian behavior — telling the truth and controlling our anger, honesty at work and kindness of speech, forgiveness, love and sexual self control" (*The Message of Ephesians* [Downers Grove, Ill.: Inter-Varsity, 1979], p. 184). Stott observes further that, by guiding relationships among believers, each commandment supports the central theme of unity that pervades Ephesians. And he notes that Paul balances negative prohibitions with corresponding positive exhortations, while also providing a theological rationale for each command. "For in the teaching of Jesus and his apostles doctrine and ethics, belief and behaviour are always dovetailed into one another" (Stott, p. 184).

The theological reasons Paul provides for righteous and holy behavior encompass all reality, both visible and invisible. The first rationale he gives for godly living is that "we are members of one another" (4:25). The word "members" echoes the major theme in Ephesians of the church as Christ's body (see 1:23; 2:16; 3:6; 4:4; and 4:12-16). For Paul, believers as the body of Christ not only live in a way distinct from that of the pagan world (see 4:17) but also stand in opposition to "the devil" (4:27; cf. 6:10-20). The other invisible presence in this vision of the Christian life is "the Holy Spirit of God" (4:30). With the command "Do not grieve the Holy Spirit" (4:30), Paul attributes personal characteristics to the Spirit and thus continues to promote church unity in trinitarian terms (compare 4:30-32 with 2:18 and 4:4-6; compare also 1 Cor. 12:4-6). The ultimate theological rationale for all Paul's ethical instructions is his understanding of the character of God.

For Paul the character of God is revealed above all in Jesus Christ. This becomes overwhelmingly evident in 4:32–5:2. It is perhaps no accident that *chrēstos,* the Greek word for kindness with which Paul chooses to begin his short list of virtues in 4:32, echoes the sound of the word "Christ." The next virtue, the quality of being "tenderhearted" (4:32) or compassionate, is a quality that characterized Jesus' life and teachings on earth (see Luke 7:13; 10:33; and 15:20). And the practice of believers graciously "forgiving one another" follows directly from the example of how "God in Christ has forgiven [us]" (4:32). Any notion that Pauline teachings about salvation by grace and justification by faith compromise his teachings on the Christian life founders on Ephesians 4:32. Paul calls believers to live up to the highest ethical ideals imaginable. In describing Paul's moral vision, it is even possible to speak, along with E. P. Sanders, of "Paul's perfectionism" (*Paul* [Oxford: Oxford University Press, 1996], p. 101).

This brings us again to the command: "Be imitators of God" (5:1). Paul expects the "beloved children" (5:1) of God to reflect the character of the One who re-creates them in his own image (4:24). In this expectation Paul follows the example of his Master, who taught his disciples: "Be perfect, therefore, as your heavenly Father is perfect" (Matt. 5:48). Luke's version of this dominical teaching is also worth quoting: "Love your enemies, do good, and lend, expecting nothing in return. Your reward will be great, and you will be children of the Most High; for he is kind to the ungrateful and the wicked. Be merciful, just as your Father is merciful" (Luke 6:35-36). Other scriptural passages related to the theme of imitating God by reflecting God's character include Leviticus 19:2 and 1 Peter 1:15-16.

The notion of imitating God and all exhortations to moral perfection can be dangerous. Wrongly understood, they can provoke a variety of neurotic or despairing responses. Those seeking to present Paul's command to imitate God in a pastoral way will find illumination in the example of the apostle himself. Paul, who feels free to instruct believers to imitate him (see 1 Cor. 4:16 and 11:1; cf. also 1 Thess. 1:6), describes his own moral striving by confessing, "Not that I have already obtained this or have already reached the goal; but I press on to make it my own, because Christ Jesus has made me his own" (Phil. 3:12). Paul strove mightily not toward some abstract goal of perfection but rather "to know Christ and the power of his resurrection and the sharing of his sufferings by becoming like him in his death, if somehow I may attain the resurrection from the dead" (Phil. 3:10-11). Striving toward perfection in the context of this relationship to Christ did not exhaust but rather energized Paul to "press on toward the goal for the prize of the heavenly call of God in Christ Jesus" (Phil. 3:14). Paul says he "worked harder than any" of the other apostles, and yet exactly this effort led him to confess that "it was not I, but the grace of God that is with me" (1 Cor. 15:10; cf. also Gal. 2:20 and Phil. 2:12-13). The God Paul imitates is not some cruel tyrant but "the God and Father of our Lord Jesus Christ" (Eph. 1:3), whom we can approach "as beloved children" (5:1). Serious devotion "to lead a life worthy" (4:1) of such a God entails no denial of grace. Instead, it amounts simply to living in a way that "is proper among saints" (5:3). Imitating God comes naturally to those who, by grace, receive a new nature. Not effortlessly but willingly, believers will "clothe [themselves] with the new self, created according to the likeness of God in true righteousness and holiness" (4:24). If, like Paul, they know how "God in Christ has forgiven" (4:32) them, they will, like Paul, imitate this graciousness to those around them. (Those interested in a classic discussion of biblical conversion to Christlike perfection can find one in book IV of C. S. Lewis's *Mere Christianity*.)

As helpful as Paul's own example is for understanding what it means to imitate God, the supreme example that Paul holds up in this regard is Jesus Christ. To imitate God means, above all, "to live [more literally: 'to walk'] in love, as Christ loved us and gave himself up for us, a fragrant offering and sacrifice to God" (5:2). With Levitical sacrifices and Isaiah 53:10 serving as a background, Paul holds up Christ's sacrificial death for sinners as the ultimate incentive and model for imitating God. Those who survey the wondrous cross will inevitably share with Isaac Watts the desire to offer back to God "my soul, my life, my all." They can become living sacrifices (see Rom. 12:1) by giving themselves up for their fellow believers and fellow sinners. Such Christlike love, exercised in the ways Paul specifies in this passage, transforms bodies of believers into "a fragrant offering and sacrifice to God" (5:2).

*Joel E. Kok*

## Fourth Sunday in Lent, Year A

First Lesson: 1 Samuel 16:1-13
(Psalm 23)
**Second Lesson: Ephesians 5:8-14**
Gospel Lesson: John 9:1-41

The Letter to the Ephesians is selected for eight Sundays in a semicontinuous reading in Year B as well as the Second Sunday after Christmas, Epiphany, and Ascension. In Year A Ephesians shares these feasts as well as the Reign of Christ and the Fourth Sunday in Lent. When we look at the Lenten season of Year A, we notice that the Letter to the Romans appears for the first three Sundays and the fifth Sunday. Can one pericope from Ephesians that interrupts the readings from Romans provide a new possibility for preachers in the midst of Lent? Is its importance relegated only to a thematic connection with 1 Samuel 16 and John 9?

Some contemporary scholars suggest that Ephesians is a circular letter that was read among communities in Asia Minor. The letter is a treasure of numerous literary parallels to Colossians as well as Qumran communities and early Gnostics. One of its significant contributions to the church and early Christian literature is that it presents a baptismal sermon (for recently baptized persons) that is enclosed in a letter genre.

The verses of 5:8-14 constitute a small section within a literary unit of parenesis (4:17–5:20). In these few verses the author utilizes another type of rhetoric that is not found in the earlier Pauline letters where judicial and deliberative rhetoric predominates. The new type of rhetoric, that is, demonstrative *(epideictic)*, aims at persuading an audience of listeners (or readers) to choose some attitudes and disregard other, antithetical ones. In particular, the author wants the hearers to choose and be faithful to personal and social ethics that are fundamental values in Pauline churches.

In 5:8-14 the argument is carefully constructed and developed around the metaphors of darkness and light. The deutero-Pauline author addresses the community in the greeting as "saints who are . . . faithful" (1:1b). Later he exhorts them to reflect on their former, existential experience of being "darkness" (5:8a). The community is summoned to recall what they were like before they were baptized: "dead through the trespasses and sins in which you once lived" (2:1-2a); "following the desires of flesh and senses" (2:3b); "darkened in their understanding, alienated from the life of God be-

333

cause of their ignorance and hardness of heart" (4:18); "your old self, corrupt and deluded by its lusts" (4:22).

The metaphor of darkness *(skotos)*, which includes sin, ignorance, and lack of responsible relationships, has parallels in 1 Thessalonians 1:4, 5 (cf. 1QS 3.21-4.1; 1QM 1; 3-4). However, the author's understanding of "darkness" is much broader. It permeates creation. Listen to how it pervades the cosmos: "For our struggle is not against enemies of blood and flesh, but against the rulers, against the authorities, against the cosmic powers of this present darkness, against the spiritual forces of evil in the heavenly places" (6:12).

What enables the newly baptized to confront the darkness that is external and yet can seep into their souls? They are reminded: "but now in the Lord you are light" (5:8b). The phrase "in the Lord" *(en kyrioi)* designates a new way of being through baptism. Individuals remember their instruction to "put away your former way of life, your old self . . . and to be renewed in the spirit of your minds, and to clothe yourselves with the new self" (4:22-24a). However, "in the Lord" is not limited to an individual's change of body, mind, and spirit. It designates a new way of being in relationship to others. Baptism gives them membership as sisters and brothers in the household of God because each new self is created according to God's likeness (4:24b).

The baptismal catechesis, however, is more than persuasion to intellectualize an attitude. Their lives need to demonstrate its praxis: "Live as children of light" (5:8c), as adopted children of God through Jesus Christ (1:5). They belong to the household of God, individually and communally, because Jesus has redeemed them through his blood (1:7).

In the honor-shame society of the first century C.E., individuals received their honor and identity from being in relationship to others. Whatever the head of the household and the firstborn achieved in the public domain accrued to all in the private, domestic sphere. Each person had a responsibility to uphold the honor of the household lest a speech or action bring shame to everyone. Living as "children" of light refers to adult, responsible status and responsibilities on behalf of the household of God.

The metaphors of light and darkness continue the argument as the author contrasts the fruits of light with the unfruitful works of darkness. The "fruit of the light" is discovered "in all that is good and right and true" (5:9). There is no need for exhortations to virtue. The community has already listened to them (4:25-32). Rather, each member is encouraged "to find out what is pleasing to the Lord" (5:10). Earlier the author prayed "that the God of our Lord Jesus Christ, the Father of glory, may give you a spirit of wisdom and revelation as you come to know him, so that, with the eyes of your heart enlightened, you may know what is the hope to which he has called you" (1:17-18a).

Similarly, there is no need to develop exhortations against vices (5:3-7). Rather, the community is invited to expose the works of darkness: "For it is shameful even to mention what such people do secretly; but everything exposed by the light becomes visible, for everything that becomes visible is light" (5:12-14a).

It is life within the baptized community that needs attention. Members are to be responsible for one another by rooting out unfruitful works of darkness since each person is part of the household of God. The focus of the entire letter is the present life of the community. There is no sense of witness or mission to those who do not believe.

Finally, the author appeals to a fragment from an early baptismal hymn (v. 14b). It can be paraphrased to heighten the demonstrative rhetoric of verses 8-14. "Sleepers, you have been baptized into the household of God. Awake, now, to the glory of the new day and bathe in its light! Christ is the source of your light. Christ will illumine your living as children of the light."

Light/darkness and household are universal, religious symbols and central metaphors in Ephesians. What can they signify to us as preachers as we move and live and have our being in a world that is quite different from that of the first century c.e.? Are there ways to interpret the reading in front of the text where we and our congregations live in diverse North American cultures?

An immediate response is a contrast of worldviews and possibilities. Whereas early Christian communities were limited in their physical environment for providing light, we can have light twenty-four hours a day. While they had little control over darkness and seasonal changes, our scientific advances offer us many alternatives.

In addition, those who lived in an expectation of Christ's imminent second coming and/or changes in the Greco-Roman empire were focused on living a life of light to welcome the end times and change. Common household codes informed persons of virtues and vices (4:17–5:20) as well as a structure for accountability of women, men, children, and slaves (5:21–6:9). In contrast, we fear political, social, and economic situations as well as chronic and age-related illnesses that threaten to change our lives. Interpreting ethical issues and making decisions call for awareness of nuances that impact situations. Eschatological considerations are not often in the forefront of our consciousness.

In the Mediterranean world, belonging to a household with its minutely detailed roles gave each person the possibility of an honorable status. Today these specified roles are often reversed, blurred, or nonexistent. There is no guarantee of a responsible male and female to uphold honor, a division of labor, or recognition that each person needs to contribute to the household. However, neighborhood groups and centers often give identity and security to latchkey children and other vulnerable persons.

Early Christian communities became new households of "fictive kinship." Being baptized and gathering to celebrate the Lord's Supper offer a new identity with persons who are not necessarily related through bloodlines. Each time they gather, they are the household of God, the body of Christ (1 Cor. 12:14-26). Today many parishes and congregations invite and encourage "fictive kinship" through hospitality at the church, outreach to alienated persons in families and neighborhoods, and offering services to those in need. Individuals participate creatively in forming an inclusive community and other models of the household of God. Although centuries of cultural differences separate us from early house churches, there are possibilities today because of our common vocation (Eph. 4:1), gifts of grace (4:7), faith and hope in the "one God and Father of all, who is above all and through all and in all" (4:6).

*Mary Margaret Pazdan*

## Thirteenth Sunday after Pentecost, Year B

First Lesson: 1 Kings 2:10-12; 3:3-14
(Psalm 111)
**Second Lesson: Ephesians 5:15-20**
Gospel Lesson: John 6:51-58

In this brief passage Paul continues the ethical instructions he began at 4:1. He also builds on the theme of contrasting ways of life, which he introduced explicitly at 4:17. The notion of ultimately contrasting ways of life may seem foreign to many people — including believers — in our relativistic age. Especially those who are suspicious of "black and white" judgmentalism will perhaps find this and surrounding passages not only foreign but even uncongenial. However, by giving attention to the important biblical themes of wisdom (5:15-17) and the Spirit (5:18-20), preachers and teachers of this passage can present it in an attractive way that calls all people to find life by joining in the praise of God.

Before looking at specific items in the passage, a few more remarks about structure are in order. The passage has a topic sentence: "Be careful then how you live" (5:15), which is fleshed out by three "not/but" contrasts. Paul exhorts believers to live "not as unwise people but as wise" (5:15). He reiterates this by commanding "do not be foolish, but understand" (5:17). He then moves from a wisdom emphasis into a Spirit emphasis by saying, "Do not get drunk with wine . . . but be filled with the Spirit" (5:18). This last imperative regarding the Spirit is followed by a series of five participles ("speaking," "singing," "making melody," "giving thanks," and "subjecting") that leads several commentators to extend this passage to include 5:21. They then translate 5:21 not as an independent imperative but in its participial form: "subjecting yourselves to one another."

Emphasizing the participial form of 5:21 in this way serves to connect 5:15-20 very closely to the *Haustafeln,* or tables of household instructions, that Paul passes on in 5:22–6:9. The lectionary in this volume avoids this connection and excludes the New Testament *Haustafeln* (see also Col. 3:18–4:1; Titus 2:1-10; 1 Pet. 2:13–3:7; note particularly the exclusion of 1 Pet. 2:18) from its suggested readings. This offers further evidence that Paul's ethical instructions in this section of Ephesians may sometimes seem foreign and even uncongenial to contemporary believers. Once again this calls for wisdom and the ongoing guidance of the Holy Spirit on the part of pastors and teachers in the church. (For treatments of New Testament *Haustafeln* that find normative ethical guidance while avoiding patriarchalism, see John Howard Yoder's chapter "Revolutionary Subordination" in *The Politics of Jesus* [Grand Rapids: Eerdmans, 1972] and also Richard B. Hays, *The Moral Vision of the New Testament* [New York: Harper Collins; San Francisco: Harper San Francisco, 1996], pp. 62-66.)

Turning from the structure of the passage to its particulars, it is worth noting that, in the opening verse, the NRSV obscures an important verb. As the RSV indicates, Paul instructs believers to watch carefully how they "live" (5:15, NRSV) by watching how they "walk" (5:15, RSV). The verb "walk" *(peripateō)* appears several times in Ephesians (see 2:2; 2:10; 4:1; 4:17; 5:2; and 5:8; see also the essay on 4:1-16 in this volume) and is an important biblical metaphor for life-encompassing human conduct. The walking metaphor is important particularly in biblical wisdom literature, and Paul's reference to walking or living "not as unwise people but as wise" (5:15) makes this connection to the wisdom tradition explicit. (Note also that the suggested Old Testament reading for this Sunday is the story of Solomon's request for wisdom.)

In the biblical wisdom tradition, wise people recognize that there is a God-created "order within which the human race must learn to live" (Richard J. Clifford, "Introduction to Wisdom Literature," in *The New Interpreter's Bible*, vol. 5 [Nashville: Abingdon, 1997], p. 8). By actively seeking wisdom and by receiving it as a divine gift, human beings learn the best way to live. This Old Testament background matters to New Testament believers because "early Christians saw Jesus as a wisdom teacher and employed the tradition of personified wisdom to express his incarnation" (Clifford, p. 14). Therefore, when Paul calls believers to walk carefully and wisely, he is developing a wisdom theme that governs the whole of Ephesians 5: imitating God by walking "in love, as Christ loved us" (5:2). He is not locking them into one particular time- and culture-bound way of life. Instead, he is demanding that they think critically about how to live in the light of God's character as revealed in Christ.

The governing command of walking in love "as Christ loved us" (5:2) will help believers avoid misunderstanding and perhaps reject ethical instructions in Ephesians that may sound simplistic or separatistic when taken out of a wisdom context. At 4:17, for example, Paul commands believers no longer to walk "as the Gentiles live, in the futility of their minds." At 5:8 he contrasts darkness and light and commands believers to walk "as children of light." And at 5:15 he continues the stark dichotomy by distinguishing "unwise people" from the "wise." Does this mean that Paul wants believers to view unbelievers as nothing but fools? Does this mean Paul expects believers to separate from unbelievers to the point of going "out of the world" (1 Cor. 5:10)? By no means. Paul is wise enough to know that people cannot "be neatly separated into 'good guys' (us) and 'bad guys' (them) as in some simple 'cops and robbers' film. . . . Rather, we are all constantly placed before choices or steps ([Prov.] 4:12) that eventually shape paths, patterns, habits, a way of life, a form of culture that settles into character" (Raymond C. Van Leeuwen, "The Book of Proverbs," in *The New Interpreter's Bible*, vol. 5, p. 63). By presenting a distinctively Christian life in terms of walking and wisdom, pastors and teachers can clarify the important and even ultimate choices people actually do face without engendering self-righteousness or an un-Christlike separatism. This is God's way of wisdom for those who follow the way of Jesus.

Those who follow Jesus by walking as wise people will be characterized, according to Paul, by "making the most of the time, because the days are evil" (5:16). These references to "time" *(kairos)* and "days" raise the issue of eschatology in Ephesians. Speaking of 5:8-16, Richard Hays notes, "The language of this passage is reminiscent of the apocalyptic exhortations in other Pauline letters (cf. Rom. 13:11-14), but there is no explicit reference to the parousia or a future judgment." As Hays notes, this difference between Ephesians 5 and Romans 13 is part of a development in Pauline thought in which a "future-oriented apocalyptic hope" has been "supplanted by a belief in the progressive redemption of the world through the growth of the church" (Hays, p. 64). This development toward progressivism in Pauline eschatology offers rich resources for those seeking to combine urgency and stability in church life. Believers who want to witness to the future coming of Christ and his messianic kingdom in glory can call on the wisdom themes of Ephesians and the Scriptures as a whole in order to express this bold hope in everyday terms here and now. They can make the most of time in these evil days by gradually shaping congregational life in the light of the final day of judgment. By calling on Christlike wisdom to build up the body of Christ, the church can offer a cosmic witness to God's purpose "not only in this age but also in the age to come" (1:21). Ephesians balances wisdom and eschatology in an effective way, and congregations shaped by a discerning reading of Ephesians can achieve a similar balance. In this way they can fulfill Paul's exhortation: "Do not be foolish, but understand what the will of the Lord is" (5:17).

To attain the kind of wisdom and ongoing discernment Paul calls for in 5:15-17, believers will need the inspiration of the Holy Spirit, to whom Paul turns in 5:18-20. By means of his negative command: "Do not get drunk with wine" (5:18), Paul suggests the powerful influence that the Holy Spirit can have on believers. Those empowered by the Spirit will replace the passions of "debauchery" (5:18) with the passions of love. They will be mutually encouraging and edifying to one another, while "singing and making melody to the Lord in [their] hearts" (5:19). Even in difficult times they will be like Paul and Silas in prison, "praying and singing hymns to God" (Acts 16:25). As John Stott, following D. Martyn Lloyd-Jones, notes, while wine or alcohol is a depressant, the Holy Spirit is a stimulant (see *The Message of Ephesians* [Downers Grove, Ill.: InterVarsity, 1986], p. 205).

Not all believers will find Paul's exhortation about psalms, hymns, and spiritual songs stimulating, however, and preachers will want to avoid making Paul's vision of the Christian life depressing. To do this, they can call on the Old Testament theme that true life consists in the praise of God (see Pss. 6:5; 30:9; 88:10-12; and Isa. 38:18). They can encourage believers to heed the wisdom of Psalm 1 by walking "not in the counsel of the wicked" (1:1, RSV), but instead following "the way of the righteous" (1:6). In this way they can avoid the folly that leads to destruction and be a part of the new humanity God is creating in Jesus Christ (see Eph. 2:10; 2:15; and 4:24), which fulfills the command: "Let everything that breathes praise the LORD!" (Ps. 150:6). Groups of believers and whole congregations who seek wise and Spirit-inspired ways to teach and sing to each other while worshiping and thanking God will form bodies of Christ who pass on the life that comes with praising God. While distinguishing themselves from a God-denying world, they will bear glad witness to all creatures. They will urge everyone to discern with them God's "plan for the fullness of time, to gather up all things in [Christ], things in heaven and things on earth" (Eph. 1:10).

*Joel E. Kok*

## Fourteenth Sunday after Pentecost, Year B

First Lesson: 1 Kings 8:(1, 6, 10-11), 22-30, 41-43
(Psalm 84)
**Second Lesson: Ephesians 6:10-20**
Gospel Lesson: John 6:56-69

This lection concludes a lengthy section of exhortation that began at Ephesians 4:17. Many ethical concerns have been addressed, and now the writer turns to the church's life in the midst of a hostile world. While this concern over opposition to the church appears elsewhere in the Pauline corpus (e.g., 1 Cor. 5:5; 2 Cor. 11:14 and 12:7; Rom. 16:20; 1 Thess. 2:18), the concerns here are to make clear the nature of the forces arrayed against the church and to delineate the church's response in light of such supernatural opposition.

The writer of Ephesians envisions the battle in which the church finds itself as being not merely against human beings and their institutions, but against the cosmic powers that animate such antichurch forces. There is more than a whisper of the perspective of the book of Revelation in these verses. The implication is clearly that the community of believers cannot withstand the assaults of these opponents in its own strength and must therefore take care to defend itself in the strength of its Lord. It is often noted that the "whole armor of God" is almost all defensive in nature, and that therefore the battle against evil is God's, while the believers' task is to defend themselves (see, e.g., Walter Brueggemann, Charles B. Cousar, Beverly R. Gaventa, James D. Newsome, *Texts for Preaching: A Lectionary Commentary Based on the NRSV — Year B* [Louisville: Westminster/John Knox, 1993], p. 481).

As expected in such a hortatory text, the instructions are delivered in the imperative tense with a sense of urgency. This verb tense provides a sense of unity to the lection, even when it turns from the image of armor to instructions for various prayers in verses 18-20. The beginning imperative, "be strong" (v. 10), *endynamousthe* in Greek, is paired with "put on" (v. 11), *endysasthe,* the semihomonymic words again suggesting the theme of the whole lection: to be strong is to put on God's protection rather than relying on the power of the self (Brueggemann at al., p. 480).

The armor named would no doubt have been more than familiar to the Ephesians, who were accustomed to the sight of the battle-ready Roman soldier in their city. It is ironic that this image is chosen since the Roman Empire is among those agents of the cosmic powers that often proved hostile to the early Christian community. The enemy's all-too-familiar uniform provides the starting point for what constitutes "the whole armor of God," but the parts of that uniform are transmuted into distinctly Christian pieces of equipment. The Government Issue (GI) of the kingdom of God could scarcely be more different from the empire's GI. But both kinds of armor are intended to leave no part of the body unprotected (Ralph P. Martin, *Ephesians, Colossians, and Philemon* [Atlanta: John Knox, 1991], p. 76).

The armor begins with the belt of truth (v. 14). Truth is a most basic virtue, but in a world of spin, purposeful deception, and deceit, it becomes ever more precious and crucial. The dark powers are led, at least metaphorically, by the "father of lies" (John 8:44), and truth spoken in the name of the One who is "the way, and the truth, and the life" (John 14:6) is crucial defensive equipment. The temptation is ever to take up the methods of the enemy, to let noble ends justify ignoble means, to fight fire with fire. As the fire of evil is fought not with fire but with the waters of baptism, so the lies of the Evil One are resisted with God's truth with which the believer is to encircle himself or herself.

The "breastplate of righteousness" protects the vital organs, in particular the heart of the believer. Pursuing righteousness is not done by considering oneself as better than others, but by imitating Christ in word and deed. This imitation is undertaken regardless of whether or not such action and speech coheres with the practices of a world which has become the arena for combat with God's adversaries. Doing the right as led by reflection on the life of Christ and in submission to the Spirit's leading will indeed often place the faith community at odds with the world. But it is the pure of heart who are blessed (Matt. 5:8) with seeing God, and their heart is protected by righteous, not accommodationist, living.

Shoes not only protect the feet but also enable a much longer walk than do bare feet. And the task of proclaiming the gospel of peace is not accomplished on a short journey. Though the church may well be under attack, it still is entrusted with the task of proclaiming the gospel. It cannot retreat into such a defensive, preservationist posture that it loses its vocation (compare Rom. 10:14ff., citing Isa. 52:7, "How beautiful are the feet of those who bring good news!). The church "defeats" its human enemies by its long journey of faithfulness to its "ministry of reconciliation" (2 Cor. 5:18).

The Roman shield was large and rectangular, especially useful in protecting soldiers from arrows, flaming or not. Held side by side by many soldiers, the shield provided considerable protection. So it is with the believer's shield of faith: there is strength in numbers. Not only does the believer not attempt to face the forces of evil out of human strength alone, neither does he or she attempt to do so without the help of others. The community lives synergistically and is stronger than the mere sum of its believers. Its members need one another's encouragement in their efforts to live in trust of and obedience to that which has been revealed in Christ, that is, to live in faith.

The helmet of salvation protects the head, that part of a person which can reflect and learn. The community has been saved for a purpose: to enjoy and glorify God, as the *Westminster Catechism* puts it. It is able to grow in its ability to understand and to live out of that purpose by the renewal of its mind (Rom. 12:2). In the midst of conflict and assault, the temptation to retreat into old patterns may be particularly strong, and it takes considerable mindfulness to discern God's work in such times. Mindlessness, on the other hand, may lead to imitation of the world's ways or to forgetfulness regarding the path of salvation opened by Christ, and either can be fatal in the struggle to defend the faith community in fearful times.

At last, an offensive weapon is given — the sword of the Spirit. The craving for something with which to inflict some damage is finally satisfied! But the Roman sword was a two-edged sword, and so is the Christian's, for it is the word of God which judges both the believing community and its opponents. The (s)word of God is for the community's instruction and correction as well as that of the world.

The passage ends with requests, still in the imperative tense, for prayer. Though not so designated in the text, prayer is also part of the armor of God. It is a means by which one enters into communion with the God in whose strength the battle against cosmic powers must be waged. Prayer is the means by which even one imprisoned in chains by the enemy can continue to intercede in the fight.

These are the weapons God has chosen for the church. Their very nature and use will distinguish the church from its context. In times gone by, when the church was more closely aligned with the political powers of the world, when it did not find itself being pushed to the margins of culture in terms of influence and perceived relevance, the words of this passage may have sounded strange indeed (Brueggemann et al., p. 479). But in its present context, the church may be able to hear this text anew and find itself empowered for faithfulness by it. How the church is different from the culture is easier to see when the church is not so near the centers of power. The church's peculiar identity and vocation become clearer when it is ignored or confronted with disdain, and its message seen as unworthy of serious intellectual consideration.

When churches are vandalized or burned, when governments seek to curtail church-based ministries of compassion toward the poor, when religious leaders are not seriously consulted on public policy but only used for political advantage, when media regularly portray clergy as scoundrels or buffoons, then the church finds itself in a hostile time and arena where the assaults of evil are many, varied, and regular. When the church examines and critiques the values driving the culture — no-holds-barred capitalism, environmental destruction, materialism, hedonism, classism, excessive nationalism and ethnocentricity — then the church is afforded the opportunity to articulate clearly its gospel as distinct from that culture, both to itself and to those who have ears to hear in the culture (most likely its marginalized victims). This lection has been reopened for a church that badly needs its word in clarifying its identity apart from the world which no longer wants to hear it, and in saying no to all that which would seek to suppress its message.

*Lawrence W. Farris*

343

## Second Sunday of Advent, Year C

First Lesson: Malachi 3:1-4
(Luke 1:68-79)
**Second Lesson: Philippians 1:3-11**
Gospel Lesson: Luke 3:1-6

O
bserve closely this opening prayer of Paul. Themes will show up in the prayer that will continue throughout the letter. In typical fashion the prayer begins with thanksgiving. His reasons for giving thanks are both personal and theological. Deep friendship characterizes his relationship with the Philippian church here and throughout the letter. He is also thankful for God's dynamic work (*erg* is the root used — it means "work" as event) in the lives of the disciples in Philippi.

He then prays that three more results will become realities in their discipleship. First, that their love will grow in knowledge. Paul has united knowledge *(epiginōskō* means deep knowledge; the *epi* prefix, "into," has the effect of intensifying the word *ginōskō)* and love. He prays that his Philippian friends will experience and grow in a knowing, wise love. Love is decidedly not merely a sentimental feeling, but is an active agent that thinks and knows.

He also prays that the Philippians will have common sense (the word *aisthēsis* has this meaning in the first-century Greek). Paul does not want his friends to be unthinking or careless about ideas and interpretations of spiritual realities that they encounter.

His third prayer is that these Christians will be disciples who live out their lives with fruits of righteousness.

We are on a journey, and the concrete event that happened in us by faith will become more fully evident in our lives — until it is completed on the day when all of history converges into its final fulfillment in Christ: "the day of Jesus Christ." This term is used by Paul some twenty times in the New Testament. It also appears fifteen times in the Gospels (e.g., Matt. 7:2). It is part of the eschatological language of the New Testament and looks toward the vindication of our Lord on the day of his final triumph. This means that in Paul's view human history moves toward that convergence point. History for Paul is delimited by the acts of God in Jesus Christ, who as Lord stands at history's three most important points: as the Word at history's beginning; as the incarnate, crucified, risen one at its center; and as ultimate fulfillment at its end. He is the one who will sum up the whole of the story of life and history.

The Christian journey is dynamic and moves toward completions, toward the *telos,* the final completion at the day of Jesus Christ's ultimate triumph in history. Paul's use of the word *telos* is connected with the profoundly important Old Testament word *shalom* (peace). This Hebrew word with all its richly textured meanings of health and wholeness is translated in the Greek translation of the Old Testament, the Septuagint, by three Greek words: *sōtēria,* "salvation"; *eirēnē,* "peace"; and *telos,* "end, goal." *Telos* is the word that Paul uses here to say that God "will bring it to completion."

Paul's first concern for the Philippians is for their completeness and wholeness both as individuals and as a community. God is not only the true object of their faith; God is also the strong friend who has not abandoned these ordinary Christian believers on their life pilgrimage. God is at work in their hearts and minds and bodies to draw them step-by-step toward maturity and growth in grace.

The profound significance of Paul's prayer discloses that the Lord of life is the true constant in the experiences of life. To remember this constancy is to experience grace in a world where events can overwhelm and disorient us. Here is an encouragement toward a more trusting way of looking at life. Paul's prayer does not imply that every occasion or part of the journey will in itself be good, but that the God who began the good work in us will complete it. In spite of the negative experiences along the journey, God's goal is our shalom, our wholeness and peace, and God is at work to accomplish that goal in our lives.

Paul speaks warmly and personally to his friends: "I hold you in my heart," "I yearn for you." From these words they will realize how much he appreciates their loyalty to him throughout his imprisonments. Paul's next words show how he has integrated his theology and his life. He interprets these various imprisonments as a means by which the gospel has been *defended* and *confirmed.* This is not merely a rationalization or denial in order to put the best possible interpretation on bad circumstances, but a deeply felt understanding of God at the center of history and at the center of his own life. Paul also prays for the Christian character of the Philippians, that their love will grow more and more with the fruits of righteousness. In each of Paul's letters we find his strong concern for Christian piety and growth in grace. The prayer for the development of Christian character is essentially a prayer for integrity of faith and life, belief and behavior. The experience of the present generation of Christians indicates how contemporary is Paul's urgent prayer for the love that combines with righteousness.

Tom Wolfe's novel *The Bonfire of the Vanities* has created a patchwork quilt of the kind of people T. S. Eliot described in the opening lines of "The Hollow Men":

> We are the hollow men
> We are the stuffed men
> Leaning together
> Headpiece filled with straw. Alas!

One by one the characters in the story show themselves to be insubstantial and exploitative. No one can really help anyone else in the face of trouble because no one really cares that much during the long haul. Even parents, husbands, and wives are too distracted by tiny, self-serving motives to make a difference as the people around them collapse. Only one character seems real and substantial: the young daughter, Campbell. She asks her father the big questions, but he "solves" those questions with evasions and lies. The novel creates a deadening ache, or perhaps for some more cynical readers a yawn, but underneath his story of New York, Tom Wolfe has focused a very small and weak flashlight on the bankruptcy of human power. His story and a thousand like it in modern literature and films reach out to our own generation with a longing for substantial people who care and believe and hope.

We live with the bonfires of the vanities each day, but Paul's century was also inflamed with power, and he knows the emptiness that results from apparently limitless self-confidence. Human lives in his world were aflame with ambition and the desire for power in the apparently unlimited success of imperial Rome. Over against this ambition and power Paul puts a radically different power-love. It is what Martin Luther called "left-handed power." The "right-handed power" of the world is based on force and brute strength, whether military force or personal ambition. Right-handed power can always be defeated by a greater right-handed force. But left-handed power is the power of love, the power of forgiveness, the power of self-giving. There is no greater power in the universe. The cross of Christ is the greatest expression of God's left-handed power. The power of Rome that put Jesus to death turned out to be the instrument that ensured the victory of God's power of love and forgiveness.

Several years ago the distinguished pastor of the Young Nak Presbyterian Church in Seoul, Korea, Dr. Kyung Chik Han, was honored at a fifty-year class reunion of Princeton Theological Seminary. During an interview at the alumni banquet, he explained the theological examination process for elders in the Young Nak Church, which, with a membership of fifty thousand communicants, is the largest Presbyterian church in the world. He said that each prospective elder was examined in "Bible, Theology, Church History and Common Sense." The church in Seoul has borrowed its four criteria from Paul's prayer for the Christians at Philippi. Paul prays for a healthy dose of *aisthēsis,* that is, growth in common, practical sense, among the Christians so that they will choose the greater values over lesser values as they grow in the good fruit of righteousness.

*Earl F. Palmer*

## Eighteenth Sunday after Pentecost, Year A

First Lesson: Exodus 16:2-15
(Psalm 105:1-6, 37-45)
**Second Lesson: Philippians 1:21-30**
Gospel Lesson: Matthew 20:1-16

Paul writes Philippians to express his thanks for the gift the church has sent him while he is in jail (probably in Rome, possibly in Ephesus) and to encourage the church to stand united against the opposition of non-Christians and the doctrinal deviations of so-called Christians. 1:21-30 touches on both these basic concerns. The former part of the text (vv. 21-26) concludes Paul's opening sketch of his circumstances, while the latter part (vv. 27-30) inaugurates, and neatly summarizes, the exhortations of the letter.

After the salutation (vv. 1-2), Paul adds his typical section of thanksgiving for the Philippians (vv. 3-11). He hints at the gift the Philippians have sent him by thanking them for their "share in God's grace with me, both in my imprisonment and in the defense and confirmation of the gospel" (v. 7). In verses 12-18a Paul elaborates on these matters. He is especially concerned to help the Philippians discern the providence of God in his arrest and imprisonment. For these circumstances have given Paul himself the opportunity to make Christ known to his guards and has emboldened other believers to preach Christ more openly than before. In verse 18b he turns his

347

attention more directly to his personal prospects. He is confident that God will deliver him from his present confinement. But his greatest hope is that Christ will continue to be exalted through him, whether he lives or dies (v. 20).

It is just at this point that we find the well-known words, "For to me, living is Christ and dying is gain" (v. 21). As the "for" indicates, Paul here explains how it is that his living and his dying would equally exalt Christ. To continue to live "in the flesh" means further opportunity for ministry (v. 22). But dying would mean being "with Christ," which, for him, is a "far better" thing — "gain," as he calls it in verse 21. Since, then, people like the Philippians will benefit from Paul's continuing ministry, Paul is convinced that it is God's will for him to be freed from his current imprisonment (vv. 24-26).

This first paragraph requires two further notes. First, on background. If, as is likely, Paul is writing from Rome, the letter probably comes toward the end of the two-year stay in the city that Luke informs us about at the end of Acts. Evidence from the first century suggests that Roman judicial procedure would have imposed a two-year statute of limitations in a case such as Paul's. He would therefore know that the outcome of this imprisonment, one way or the other, was imminent. It is for this reason that Paul can express his hope to come and see the Philippians again in the near future (v. 26; cf. also 2:24). Second, on theology. Paul's discussion of his own prospects gives us a window into his understanding of life after death. Paul makes clear that he thinks of dying as a transition into the presence of Christ. As he puts it in 2 Corinthians 5:8, to be "away from the body" is to be "at home with the Lord." As Christians, we can be confident that death ends our earthly life but inaugurates our heavenly life. And while harboring natural fear of the "last enemy," we should also emulate Paul's deep confidence about the true "gain" that death brings in terms of the spiritual life.

Philippians contains few specific rebukes — as we might expect in a letter of thanks. But one issue does seem to be a problem in the church: unity. Paul urges the Philippians to have "the same mind" (2:2) by imitating the humility exemplified by Jesus himself (2:5-11). They are to leave off "murmuring and arguing" (2:14), and specifically, Euodia and Syntyche are to come to terms with one another (4:2). The focus on unity in 1:27-30 is therefore no passing allusion but reflects one of the letter's key concerns. In preaching these verses one penetrates to the heart of Philippians.

Paul opens with a general exhortation: "Live your life in a manner worthy of the gospel of Christ." "Live your life" translates a verb (politeuomai) that has particular application to the Philippians. Philippi was one of the few cities in the east with the special distinction of being a Roman "colony." As such, her inhabitants, though far from Rome geographically, could nevertheless pride themselves on being citizens of Rome. As such, they would seek to emulate the values and lifestyles of their true "homeland." The verb Paul uses here, along with the related noun in 3:20 *(politeuma)*, refers to being citizens. "Live as citizens" we could translate this verb — citizens of your true homeland, "heaven" (cf. 3:20). The Christians in Philippi should be much more concerned to live out the values called for by the gospel than those called for by the emperor.

After this general, but quite striking, opening, Paul moves quickly to his chief concern: that the Philippians exhibit a united front in their resistance to opponents. Paul does not identify these opponents here. They may be the same as the false teachers he alludes to in 3:2-4, 17-18. Or Paul may not have any definite group in mind. Contemporary social theory helps us understand that groups with very specific identities are always defining themselves over against hostile elements in the culture around them. Paul may therefore be deliberately vague here, as he simply acknowledges the opposition that those called to a distinctive set of values will always experience. Indeed, a key point that emerges from verses 27-30 is the expectation of opposition in the Christian life. Paul writes from personal experience. As he notes in verse 30, the Philippians know how Paul himself has had to struggle with opposition. They "saw" his imprisonment when he first brought the gospel to them (Acts 16:11-40), and they have "heard" about his fresh arrest and imprisonment.

The message is sorely needed in some parts of the world, where Christianity is still generally accepted and many believers find themselves at very comfortable points on the socioeconomic scale. The tendency can be to compromise with the standards of the culture around us in order to maintain and consolidate that comfortable position and, at the same time, to find the notion of suffering for Christ quite foreign. But Paul quite boldly claims that suffering, just like believing, is a gracious gift of God to us (v. 29). The strength of this assertion needs to be stressed from the pulpit so it is fully felt in the pew. Suffering — a gracious gift from God! Such a notion conflicts violently with the assumption of "health and wealth" that so many Christians seem to think God has promised them. God, Paul here implies, has his purpose in bringing his people through difficult experiences. As other texts suggest (see Rom. 5:3-4; James 1:2-4; 1 Pet. 1:6-7), God knows that our tendency to settle down into this world, gradually but steadily taking on un- or even anti-Christian values in the process, can only be halted by reminding us sharply, if unpleasantly, that this world is not as comfortable as we might think. Suffering is, then, a gracious gift, because it forces us to reconsider and recommit to the values of heaven that are so easily suppressed when things are going well for us.

While several preaching points emerge from Philippians 1:21-30, the overarching idea perhaps is the notion of the right "thinking" that is incumbent on those who consider heaven their true home. Such people will put petty issues aside as they recognize the overwhelming need for unity in fighting for the truth of the gospel. They will see suffering as a means by which God draws us further from the contaminating values of the world around us and closer to himself. And they will rejoice that death itself means "gain": to be with Christ is "far better."

*Douglas Moo*

# Nineteenth Sunday after Pentecost, Year A

First Lesson: Exodus 17:1-7
(Psalm 78:1-4, 12-16)
**Second Lesson: Philippians 2:1-13**
Gospel Lesson: Matthew 21:23-32

The word translated "mind" means *perspective, frame of mind, outlook*. Paul is continuing a theme he introduced in his opening prayer. He wants his friends to think things through under the authoritative guidance of Jesus Christ. This perspective will bring the kind of unity he is seeking in these Christians. It will also enable them to put each other ahead in line (this is the meaning of the phrase in v. 3). At this point Paul illustrates his encouragement theme over against its opposite, the selfish ambition, conceit theme.

The integrity of faith demands that we give up the illusion of perfection and face the truth about the world, ourselves, and the church. And this is what Paul does. There is one problem in the church at Philippi that now surfaces in Paul's letter. There are tensions in the congregation that cause certain members to oppose each other instead of teaming together in the unity of soul and spirit. Later Paul will name three people in the fellowship who are involved in the arguments that now endanger the unity of the church.

Controversies in churches are not new. They occurred in the New Testament churches, as each of the letters of the New Testament makes clear. We can understand this as both an encouraging and a discouraging fact.

On the one hand, it is unfortunate that very early in the life of the Christian fellowship there should have been the sort of conflict that threatened the effective witness of the Christian church in the world. Here in Philippi, for example, we have evidence of "in-house" struggles that use up the energy and time of the Christians. What a waste!

On the other hand, struggles show that God uses that which is imperfect. This less-than-perfect fellowship at Philippi that must face up to some serious internal problems is the same fellowship used by God to send help to those suffering in Jerusalem, to be the witnessing church in Philippi, and to send concrete help to Paul. In spite of the flaws of disunity and controversy, God makes use of such a fellowship, and he works with a church like the one at Philippi through the letter Paul wrote to them. As Karl Barth said, "There are no letters in the New Testament apart from the problems of the church." And even this letter, so warm and heartwarming, is a letter that must deal with a very real problem in the church.

One positive result is that the New Testament letters make it impossible for us as twenty-first-century readers to idealize the early Christian church. The realism of the letters prevents us from creating in our minds a fantasy portrait of the first-century church as a fellowship of faultless saints who, because of perfection, had such a tremendous impact on their generation. When idealized portraits of the church of the New Testament era replace the accurate record of what really existed, the result will be dangerous both theologically and historically, because it will make it impossible for us to build healthy discipleship models for Christian fellowships today. The church then becomes a divine ideal instead of a divine reality. Dietrich Bonhoeffer warned in his book about the church, *Life Together,* of the dangers of this kind of wish-dream idealism in defining and understanding the Christian church. These idealizations do not help us to really understand either the true situation among the first-century believers or their mandate and enablement, which is the mandate and enablement that are also ours today. "The Christian Church is not a divine ideal but a divine reality" (*Life Together* [New York: Harper, 1954], p. 27).

Our task at the beginning of the twenty-first century is not to try to be like an imaginary and totally inspired first-century church or to try to learn special spiritual secrets which they know but have somehow been misplaced through the centuries. We have a better hope. The same Lord Jesus Christ who was Lord of the Philippian fellowship is Lord today, and we need his real presence and grace today even as they needed his grace and presence in the middle of their century. Another aspect of this first-century letter becomes clear when we recognize that the problems that proved to be troublesome for the Philippians in their time have their analogies and parallels in each generation. The people who make up our churches are real people who have convictions about almost every subject. This is not a weakness of the church — it is part of what makes the church actual and visible. But conviction produces colors that clash with each other as well as those that harmonize.

It is this shared humanity and the same living presence of Christ that make all the letters of the New Testament contemporary documents of the Christian church in every age. For example, we know from letters written to the church in Philippi by Polycarp and by Ignatius sometime early in the second century that the Philippian Christians still struggled with problems of "factionalism" (as Ignatius called it) many decades after Paul wrote his letter. Divisions in a community of believers had a way of persisting then as they do now.

Notice how Paul grapples with the factions at Philippi. Paul begins by stressing the need for unity: "Stand firm in one spirit, striving side by side for the faith of the gospel." But Paul does not stop there. He knows that the Philippians are well aware of the problem and that they realize that disunity is wrong. He does not scold. Rather, he tries to move the Philippians away from focusing on their disagreements toward an appreciation of the grace they have experienced as a community. He uses words of encouragement and asks the Philippians to think about the meaning of those words.

He makes four statements beginning with "if." If these four things are true, if the Philippians have experienced them, then the church in Philippi has a solid foundation for unity, and this foundation is what they must now focus on. The first of the four statements is the most important: "If there is any encouragement in Christ." The word translated "encouragement" is *paraklēsis*. It comes from a root that means "to call alongside" or "to come alongside." This is the same root from which is derived the word used for the Holy Spirit in the Gospel of John when Jesus promises the "Comforter" *(paraklētos)*, the one who will come alongside to teach us all that we need to know concerning Christ. The "if" implies a question: Has there been any concrete coming alongside, any concrete companionship, any encouragement in Christ? Before disunity reared its head, was there an experience of mutual encouragement in Christ, who is the only basis for unity?

Second, have they experienced any motivation and personal strengthening that had its source in mutual love? Third, have they experienced fellowship *(koinōnia)* in the Holy Spirit? And finally, have they experienced that warm affection that comes from their very deepest being, and have they experienced any acts of mercy in the past? Paul knows that the church in Philippi has experienced all of these, and he asks the Philippians to remember the positive experiences of God's love at work in their own lives, experiences in which they have all shared. This positive exercise in remembering becomes the harmonious background against which he will draw the stark contrast with the controversy and negative anxieties that have made many members of the church highly critical of each other.

Here the apostle Paul becomes the originator of the theological and historical basis for the "power of positive thinking." Paul asks the Philippians to make a choice, much like the psalmist who calls upon Israel to remember the goodness and faithfulness of God (Ps. 103). Will they build on the concrete experiences of encouragement that they have received and experienced in Christ and among themselves, or will they ignore that foundation of encouragement in favor of the anger and destructive divisions in the church and the culture around them?

It seems ironic that the anger-producing memories that many people have of the church stem from interpersonal disappointment more often than from doctrinal disagreement. Someone had his or her feelings hurt, and that experience of harm done to that person becomes the major source of most church conflicts. Paul challenges the Philippians — and us as well — to focus on the encouragements that we have found in Christ, so that we can be less terrorized by the discouragements and grievances we have so carefully catalogued against the people we know. He warns us as Christians against isolating ourselves because of real or imagined grievances and self-righteousness. In this context he warns the Philippians against the way of conceit *(kenodoxia,* "empty glory").

Paul advocates the oneness of love, and now from prison he urges his friends to choose that way. He is realistic in that advocacy, however, and recognizes that such a decision on the part of Christians will be costly: they will lose the right to feel superior in relation to other Christians.

The decision in favor of the way of encouragement is, in Paul's view, the better way, but it is also the way that requires humility and a profoundly and deeply rooted concern for the sisters and brothers. The sentence "count others better than yourselves" (Phil. 2:3) has been an awkward sentence to interpret because, taken by itself, it sounds very much like the sort of self-depreciation that few self-respecting modern men or women would ever take seriously. He has made use of a first-century expression that is best translated "put others in line in front of yourself." When we understand this sense of Paul's statement, we realize that he is not advocating the loss of self-esteem or self-respect, but on the contrary, is offering this behavior as evidence of the dignity they have in Christ.

The result is a powerful poem, which has become the great hymn of Philippians 2:5-11.

Following the dramatic hymn, Saint Paul calls to the Philippians to make an event of the salvation that God has granted them in Jesus Christ. This response on the believer's part is so awesome that Paul uses two strong fear words, "phobia" and "trauma," to accompany the challenge. *Phobos* is a common word for fear, from which we derive our word "phobia," and *tromos* means "shaking, quivering," especially from fear. We must be very careful to note that Paul is not telling his friends to earn their salvation by fearful and wakeful work and worry. There is no hidden theology of "salvation by works" now enveloped into the letter to the Philippians. Paul makes it quite clear that the miraculous gift of God's forgiveness originates from his grace and is prior to our response.

Paul combines his exhortation that we must work out *(katergazesthe)* our own salvation "with fear and trembling" with the promise that "God is at work *(energeō)* in (us), both to will and to work for his good pleasure." This is what makes the mandate both possible and joyful. But it is, on the other hand, the very thing that makes it a matter of great consequence.

In Paul's Greek sentence there is an emphasis that is somewhat obscured in the English translations. In New Testament Greek the verb often is put in the first part of the sentence, but here Paul puts the verb last, which gives it special force. We could render his statement something like this: "Therefore, with fear and trembling, your own salvation, work it out — for God is at work in you."

Only I can make my salvation concrete in my everyday life; at the same time, it is only God who can accomplish this salvation in me. Paul combines the freedom of our faith and the sovereignty of God in these two verses in what seems to be a paradox. I am not on my own! But I do have the option to make this event of grace an event in my own life.

God is at work to carry out his gracious will, to make real in our lives the reality of Jesus' life. But we must equally be at work each day of our lives to spell out the implications. This means that we rest in the great fact that our salvation is a gift that all of our work and working could never achieve. Nevertheless, we work because that salvation is so total and so complete that it demands a practical, everyday response from us.

*Earl F. Palmer*

# Palm/Passion Sunday, Years A, B, C

First Lesson: Isaiah 50:4-9a
(Psalm 118:1-2, 19-29)
**Second Lesson: Philippians 2:5-11**
Gospel Lesson (Year A): Matthew 26:14–27:66
Gospel Lesson (Year B): Mark 14:1–15:47
Gospel Lesson (Year C): Luke 22:14–23:56

Notice the play on words by Paul. The word "conceit" in Greek is *kenodoxia,* and it literally means "empty glory" (v. 3). Paul then tells of Jesus Christ, who shares in the very essence *(morphē)* of God and then empties himself of his rightful prerogative *(kenoō,* "empty" [v. 7]).

He became a real man *(morphē,* "essence," is used again, v. 7). Jesus identified with human beings, *homoiōma,* and even looked like man *(schēma* means outward form, v. 7). This profound identification extends to his death on the cross. From that lowest point God has highly *(hyper)* exalted him, declaring that his name is above all names. Jesus deserves universal worship to the glory *(doxa)* of God.

This is the greatest single christological paragraph in all of Paul's writings. Paul wanted to show how Christ modeled mutual care for one another by his own way of humiliation on our behalf. But Paul's illustration, his Christ model for encouraging the Philippians, expanded into a song of majestic praise to celebrate Christ's profound humility. The result is that the apostle has given the world the greatest hymn to the humiliation and exaltation of Jesus Christ that can be found anywhere in the New Testament. What began as an illustration became a profound and astounding song of wonder at the personal and costly love of God.

Paul begins with a portrayal of the person of Jesus Christ in his eternal nature and true divinity, and then sketches his historical acts on our behalf in his true humanity. Paul describes Jesus as being in the "form of God." The word for form is *morphē,* which means the essence of a reality, what J. B. Lightfoot calls "its specific character" (*St. Paul's Epistle to the Philippians* [New York: Macmillan, 1896], p. 38). Jesus was equal with God. But he did not count equality with God "a thing to be grasped" *(harpagmos).* This word is used only here in the New Testament. Its exact meaning in this verse has been much disputed, but the most likely meaning is something like "prize" or "booty." It can refer to either a prize that has already been obtained or a prize that is sought after. Either way the point is clear: Jesus is willing to surrender his claim to equality with God.

At this point in the great hymn of the apostle we hear the powerful and costly word *kenosis:* Jesus *emptied* himself, "not of his divine nature, for that was impossible, but of the glories" (Lightfoot, p. 38). He took upon himself the essential form (again the word *morphē* is used) of a servant/slave. And he was born in the likeness of a man (*homoiōma,* "likeness," indicates that Jesus was fully human). Paul now adds one more word of Christ's identification with us. He took on human form (*schēma,* "outward shape"). This Jesus, who has the essence of a slave, is really like us as a human being, and even looks like us, is the same Jesus Christ who from the beginning is of the original essence of God.

Paul has given us a portrayal of the uncompromised, total humanity and total deity of Jesus Christ. This Jesus is the one who has humbled himself and has identified with us by living as a human being. But he went beyond that. He identified with us to the point of voluntarily experiencing death. It is difficult for us to grasp the full impact of this because the death that Jesus faced was the death of total rejection and curse: death by crucifixion.

But now we discover the greatest surprise of all: this humiliation becomes a victory. The low point of Jesus' human life turns out to be the high point of human history. In his voluntary humiliation on the cross, Jesus Christ has won the victory over sin and death and the dreadful power of evil. Christ has broken the apparently permanent grasp of all three of these foes in the ultimate display of the surprising openhanded power of God. As Augustine sums it up in his *Confessions,* "Proud man would have died had not a lowly God found him."

But God has "highly exalted" him (Paul uses a luxuriously compounded word by adding the prefix *hyper* to the already powerful word "exalt"). And God has given Jesus the Name that is above every other name. In the first century a man's or woman's name often signified his or her dignity or character. This was to some extent also true later, when people were often identified by their parentage (Johnson, "John's son") or by their occupation (Baker) or by the location of the family home (Green). But Jesus has the character and the dignity above all others in the story of names: Jesus is Lord not only on earth, which is understandable to us, but also in heaven, which is beyond our understanding, and even in the shadowy realism of the places of death. In this great hymn we see the exaltation of Jesus Christ as the Last Word, as the Lord over life and death, over heaven and hell. He reigns, and every tongue shall one day agree (the literal meaning of "confess") as to who he is. All this is to the glory of God. Now we see, as wrote

Karl Barth in his *Dogmatics in Outline,* that "the omnipotence of God and the love of God are the same thing."

There is a profound poetic play on words within the structure of this hymn. In verse 3 Paul cautioned against conceit, *kenodoxia,* which literally means "empty glory." In verses 5-11 he shows the contrast between our empty glory and the greatness of Jesus Christ. Jesus Christ "emptied himself" *(kenoō)* and by doing so was exalted, to the glory *(doxa)* of God the Father. If we try to establish and prove our own glory, our own superiority, it will turn out to be empty and worthless. It is in the emptying of ourselves of any false claim to glory and praise from people that God's power can work in and through us. In the seeking of God's glory it is Jesus Christ who will be exalted.

Notice the word progression in this poem from *kenodoxia* to *kenoō* to *doxa.*

Jesus did not have conceit (empty glory), but he emptied himself in his humiliation on our behalf, and it is God the Father who has given to Jesus honor and glory.

The poem is a profound christological hymn that flows from Paul's exhortation to the Philippians. As he begins his illustration, he breaks into poetry. The NRSV is correct in presenting this text in poetic form. The poem belongs in this context and therefore should be interpreted in the light of its place in the letter.

As in his other letters, Paul cannot speak of any theme without seeing that theme within its larger context of meaning. In this case his encouragement exhortation needs a center from which to receive its full sense. That living center is Jesus Christ.

Perhaps more than any other passage in Paul's writings, this marvelous hymn shows that Paul cannot talk about any major theme without relating it to Christ. For Paul, Jesus Christ is the foundation, the center, the focus that gives meaning to and integrates all of life. When he talks about ethics, about how we should live and act, he always goes back to the only motivation we have as Christians: the living Jesus Christ, who makes it possible for one human being to have the resources to love another human being. Paul realizes that we cannot live by the requirements of the law or by trying to make up for previous failures. The effort to be good or to do better when it is motivated by fear or the threat of possible punishment does not succeed.

Paul's motivation for ethical behavior is not fear. It is grace, and the source of grace is the person Jesus Christ. The problem of our guilt has been resolved. Christ is therefore the fundamental starting point of Paul's total perspective. Karl Barth explained this in his comments on the great second

357

article of Christian theology in *Dogmatics in Outline:* "'I believe in Jesus Christ the Son.' That is why Article II (of the creed), why Christology, is the touchstone of all knowledge of God in the Christian sense, the touchstone of all theology. 'Tell me how it stands with your Christology, and I shall tell you who you are.'"

*Earl F. Palmer*

## Twentieth Sunday after Pentecost, Year A

First Lesson: Exodus 20:1-4, 7-9, 12-20
(Psalm 19)
**Second Lesson: Philippians 3:4b-14**
Gospel Lesson: Matthew 21:33-46

## Fifth Sunday in Lent, Year C

First Lesson: Isaiah 43:16-21
(Psalm 126)
**Second Lesson: Philippians 3:4b-14**
Gospel Lesson: John 12:1-8

Paul tells us that from the perspective of the first-century Pharisees, his impeccable credentials should have won him first place. If anyone had reason to place his confidence in his moral excellence, his ancestry, and his religious devotion, it was Paul. His life conformed to the law from his eighth day, when he was circumcised. He was from the high-ranking tribe of Benjamin. Both of his parents were Hebrews. Add to this privileged ancestry his religious achievements: faithful Pharisee, zealous persecutor of the church, above reproach as a keeper of the law of Moses.

Pharisaism was a lay movement that began after the Jews returned from the Babylonian exile under Ezra and Nehemiah. As a separatist movement, it developed during the time of the Maccabees. Paul compares his life as a

Pharisee with his new life in Jesus Christ through a series of contrasts, including one that contains what even by first-century social standards would be understood as a crude literary expletive. By these contrasts Paul shows the surpassing worth of Jesus Christ compared to his former life. None of his former credentials can compare with what Paul has found in the gospel of Jesus Christ, in whom this former legalist has found a righteousness "not based on law, but that which is through faith in Christ." By comparison, all his former achievements he considers *skybalon,* "dung, excrement, leavings, refuse." What he thought was the feast of God's approval was nothing but the garbage left over after the feast. Note that Paul does not reject God's law, but he rejects the confidence that he had in himself because he kept the law. Justification before God has come through *God's* fulfillment of the law in Christ. For Paul there can never again be "righteousness of my own based on law." Such hope is empty pretense; it is "refuse."

Paul's contrast between his former life under the law and his new life of faith in Jesus Christ discloses a deep issue in the New Testament. We know from the letter of Paul to the Galatians and from the record of the first ecumenical church council in Jerusalem (Acts 15) that a major question that troubled the early church was this: Is it necessary for a non-Jewish believer in Christ to be circumcised as a vital part of the journey of faith? That is, should a Gentile believer first become Jewish, become part of God's covenant with Abraham, before that person can fully partake of the gospel of Christ?

Paul himself treasured his Jewish ancestry and legacy, and if anyone could claim to have the correct credentials for being a true Jew, it was Paul. At one point Paul himself circumcised his Greek friend Timothy (Acts 16:3), but when Paul saw that this symbolic entry into the tradition of the law and the prophets had become theologically distorted, so that some Jewish Christians in Jerusalem saw circumcision as an essential part of a person's experience of the promises of the gospel of Jesus Christ, Paul stood firm and refused to allow the circumcision of another Greek friend, Titus (Gal. 2:1-5). He explains in Galatians that he rejected the need of circumcision in this case because such an act would have distorted the integrity of the gospel.

Therefore Paul and Barnabas and the church at Antioch requested a meeting of the church leaders in Jerusalem. At that meeting the question was settled by the early Christian church. The non-Jewish believer does not need to become a Jew in order to know Christ's grace. Peter spoke movingly at the close of that historical meeting: "We believe that we shall be saved through the grace of the Lord Jesus, just as they [the Gentiles] will. . . . Therefore my judgment is that we should not trouble those of the Gentiles who turn to God" (Acts 15:11, 19).

But bad theory and bad practice have a long and persistent staying power — even when the church has decided in favor of the greater truth. This is why the church in every generation needs the purifying, reforming, and correcting ministry of sound teaching and sound doctrine. We are always in danger of going astray, and usually our going astray is motivated by attraction to a half-truth or by a theory that appears more reverent and more devout than what others in the church are teaching. False teaching is often very difficult to sort out because it has an aura of sincerity and truth about it.

The false teachers in Philippi exhorted the male Christians to prove their real devotion to the Lord by an act of discipleship that is more demanding and more "spiritual" than the apparently "easy" gospel they had heard from Paul. These teachers may well have accused Paul of compromising with the culture, and done so by quoting Scripture. They would be able to quote Old Testament texts that tell of the sign of circumcision and its importance as the true sign of the covenant God made with Abraham.

Paul has been very specific and definite in his insistence that righteousness comes only from Christ and cannot be a "righteousness of our own." Since he has argued strongly against works righteousness, we might expect a peaceful doctrine of restful complacency. But Paul has nothing like that in mind. His experience of grace has produced more positive motivational energy than he had ever known in the self-righteous motivation of legalism.

In the next few verses Paul uses an image from the experience of the athlete committed to a race. There are two kinds of incentives that motivate team athletes. The one is the pressure of an athlete who is trying to win a place on the team. The other is the pressure to excel that comes to a player because he or she is already on the team. Paul is describing that second motivation. We run the race, not in an attempt to somehow make the team, but because we are already on the team. The secret of Paul's motivation lies in his deep awareness of Jesus' unconditional acceptance. Paul presses on to make full identification with Christ his own because "Christ Jesus has made me his own." Paul's is not the motivation of fear, nor of guilt or of pride. It is the motivation of grateful belonging. "I belong in this race. I was made for this event. This is my moment."

This awareness of being accepted gives Paul the freedom to focus on what is most important. He says he does one thing: forgetting what lies behind and straining forward to what lies ahead, he presses toward the goal, the "final tape at the end of the runner's race." Every track-and-field competitor knows what Paul is talking about! In a race there is a forgetfulness of everything but the race itself. It is this forgetfulness and intensity of focus that Paul combines in these unforgettable sentences. Jesus' gracious acceptance enables Paul to focus his life purpose on Christ in ways he has already described: to know Christ (v. 8), to gain Christ (v. 8), to be found in Christ (v. 9), to have righteousness in Christ (v. 9), to know the power of Christ's resurrection (v. 10), and to share Christ's sufferings (v. 10). Truly Paul could say, "For to me to live is Christ" (1:21).

Paul is able in this passage to be open and forthright about his own lack of perfection. He states twice in verse 12 that he has not yet "arrived": "Not that I have already obtained this or am already perfect." Paul's realism and his self-awareness do not immobilize or demoralize this runner because Paul has experienced the powerful grace of the Lord. This is both a comfort and a warning. It is a comfort to those of us who feel inadequate as Christians. Paul had not yet arrived. We have not yet arrived. God does not expect us to have won the race, he expects us to run the race.

But it is also a warning for those of us who think we have arrived spiritually. People who are spiritually self-satisfied are in danger of dropping out of the race and not reaching the goal at all. Later, in verse 15, Paul says, "Let those of us who are mature be thus minded." The word for mature, *teleois,* is from the same root as the word "perfect" in verse 12: "Not that I . . . am already perfect." This may be an intentional play on words on Paul's part: if you are mature, you know that you are not perfect; if you think you are perfect, you are not mature.

"Forgetting what lies behind and straining forward to what lies ahead." What is Paul advocating in these words? We often are unable to enjoy the present and to focus on what is truly important today because of guilt about our past and anxiety about our future. Guilt is the sense that we have done something wrong, whether it be a specific, all-too-well-remembered act or a vague sense of being guilty without being able to put our finger on exactly what we did wrong. We can feel guilty only about the past; we cannot feel guilty about the future. Anxiety, on the other hand, is what we feel about the future: uncertainty about what may happen. Just as we cannot feel guilty about the future, we cannot be anxious about the past, although guilt and anxiety may be related. In his forgetting what lies behind and straining forward to what lies ahead, Paul faces up to the past, present, and future.

There can be no whole perspective on life or the development of a philosophy of life that does not resolve our relationship with each of the three tenses of our life: past, present, and future. Paul covers all three in one sentence: "Forgetting what lies behind [past] and straining forward to what lies ahead [future], I press on [present]." He can make this statement with full conviction because the grace of God has resolved the guilt of his past and removed the anxiety about his future.

But we must read his statement in the light of what he has just said: "I am not yet perfect." The truth of God's grace is certain, but our understanding and appropriation of that grace are not yet perfect. Growing in grace means learning more and more to live in the awareness that our guilt has been forgiven, that our future is secure in Christ, and that as a result we are truly free to live in the present. God will continue to do the work that he began in us when we came to Christ until we see him face-to-face.

*Earl F. Palmer*

## Second Sunday in Lent, Year C

First Lesson: Genesis 15:1-12, 17-18
(Psalm 27)
**Second Lesson: Philippians 3:17–4:1**
Gospel Lesson: Luke 13:31-35

Paul now advises his readers to imitate the pattern of life they have observed in him. This advice does not contradict his earlier words of caution about blind and unthinking obedience to false teachers. Paul has made it clear that each believer is to think things through carefully, but now it is appropriate to remind them also that one of the proper ways we learn is by watching more experienced companions who are alongside us on our common journey. We learn by watching others.

Johann Sebastian Bach watched and listened carefully to the great organist-composer Dietrich Buxtehude. Bach's many trips to Buxtehude's church had a very definite influence upon the style and vitality of Bach's music and helped to shape the young Bach, who would then go on to become an even greater genius than his mentor. Nevertheless, Bach needed the example and inspiration of this lesser genius. Similarly, we cannot grow in grace by ourselves.

Paul then goes on to warn against those who are "enemies of the cross of Christ." He has already warned against the legalism of the Judaizers who taught that Gentiles must submit to the law of Moses as a condition for belonging to Christ. Here another shadow crosses the page. Paul warns the Philippians against the opposite danger of allowing their freedom in Christ to justify whatever behaviors they chose to indulge in. Paul may have in mind here not only the legalists he challenged earlier, but also another movement which had its beginnings around the time he wrote this letter and posed a serious threat to the integrity of the gospel — gnosticism. The gnostics taught that the body has no importance since we have a mystically spiritual relationship with Christ assured by secret knowledge. This would mean that the fully initiated believer is so totally spiritual that his or her personal actions are indifferent in the sight of God. This view would lead to ethical and moral chaos.

If Paul is indeed on the attack against rigid legalism on the one side and antinomian chaos on the other side, it is interesting that both attacks could be mounted in the same sentences. This is because both legalism and gnosticism are opposed to the all-sufficiency and total Lordship of Jesus Christ over all of life — body, soul, spirit. In different ways we know that they each troubled the Christian churches of the first century.

Paul had warned against the Judaizers (legalists) with anger; now he warns against the gnostics (antinomians) with tears. He describes them in terms that contrast with what he had testified about his life in Christ. Their end is destruction (v. 19), not the resurrection life. Their purpose is to satisfy their desires, not share in Christ's sufferings. Their glory is not in God's work in Christ, but in their own "shame." They are not minded to be identified with Christ, but to possess earthly things.

The argument Paul gives against both legalism and gnosticism is that "our commonwealth is in heaven." Paul here uses the word *politeuma*, "commonwealth" (literally "citizenship"), which is the noun form of the verb he used earlier in 1:27: "Let your *manner of life* be worthy of the gospel of Christ." Heaven is here portrayed as a city-state that holds our citizenship. Our rights and responsibilities and the resulting lifestyle are ordered by the authority seated in that city. In chapter 1 Paul encouraged the Christians at Philippi to be real people in the real place where they live, so that their citizenship, that is, their total community involvement and life, will show in concrete ways the gospel of Christ. Citizenship brings with it both privileges and responsibilities, and Paul had urged the Philippians to take their social and political responsibilities as citizens seriously.

But Christians have a second set of privileges and responsibilities as citizens of heaven. The two citizenships are intertwined. If we fulfill our responsibilities as citizens of heaven (whose royal law is, "You shall love your neighbor as yourself" [James 2:8]), we will also be able to fulfill our responsibilities as citizens on this earth. On the other hand, if we are irresponsible citizens here and now, we cannot be responsible citizens of heaven. We live Christian lives in the real present with its concrete street addresses and political and social realities because we belong to a permanent citizenship that is God's gift to us here and now.

Some citizens of the United States live and work for a period of time in a foreign country where they are required to live responsibly under the laws of that foreign country, just like its citizens. But at the same time they are subject to the laws of the United States. Therefore, no matter how wonderful the foreign country is for American citizens, the United States is still home, the place where they ultimately belong and where they will go once their work in the foreign country is done.

But there is a difference. When we will finally fully claim our heavenly citizenship, Jesus Christ "will change our lowly body to be like his glorious body." The requirement for heavenly citizenship does not involve either the legalistic requirement of circumcision or the special gnostic secrets of spiritual superiority. Our bodies will be transformed, and this solid expectation is the best protection against religious leaders who insist upon either a religious rite like circumcision or on mystical religious secrets to make our bodies somehow acceptable to God. Such cosmetic religious acts are unnecessary since Christ will change our bodies as he chooses in accord with his grand design.

At the same time, this expectation is the strongest argument against those who reject the body as of no importance. The whole point of our hope of resurrection is that it is our whole being — body, soul, and spirit — that is loved and redeemed by God in Christ. Real human beings really matter, and that means our concrete self, our personality, our emotions, our distinctive characteristics — the total mixture of who we are — is beloved by Jesus Christ, and it is the particular "who we are" that has a destiny in the fulfilled commonwealth.

Integrity involves both these citizenships. We cannot have integrity in our everyday affairs if we are not willing to take seriously our responsibilities as citizens of heaven. And we cannot possibly have integrity as citizens of heaven if we neglect our interpersonal, social, and political responsibilities as citizens here on earth.

The image of the track event, the race, emphasizes the strenuous activities of forgetting the things behind, straining forward to what lies ahead, and pressing on to the goal until we reach the finish line. The image of our heavenly citizenship makes of us a *waiting* people. No one image can exhaust the fullness of our life in Christ. Pressing on to the future prize, we also await the future deliverer (v. 20). When he comes, he will complete in us the good work he has begun (1:6), and will remake us in his own likeness (3:21).

Paul concludes this section with an appeal to "stand firm in the Lord." And he makes that appeal a very personal one. He asks the Philippians to stand firm, because he personally cares very deeply for them: "My brethren, whom I love and long for, my joy and crown . . . my beloved." The word *stephanos,* "crown," is the Greek word for an athletic crown of victory, such as the wreath that would be worn by an athlete. It should not be confused with the word *diadem,* which is the Greek word for the crown worn by a king. Paul does not have notions of kingly reign for himself, but he does have the vision of the wreath of acknowledgment for the race run, and he tells the Philippians that they have been for him already that good wreath. In effect he tells them, "You're my celebration wreath, my gold medal."

*Earl F. Palmer*

## Twenty-first Sunday after Pentecost, Year A

First Lesson: Exodus 32:1-14
(Psalm 106:1-6, 19-23)
**Second Lesson: Philippians 4:1-9**
Gospel Lesson: Matthew 22:1-14

Who are Euodia, Syntyche, and Clement? The first two are common first-century names, and we know nothing more about them than what we have in this narrative. Clement is also a common first-century name, but the early church fathers Origen and Eusebius were convinced that this Clement is the man who later became a bishop in Rome and wrote the letter of Clement to the Corinthians (A.D. 110-20). Some interpreters of Philippians have constructed an elaborate interpretive scheme to explain these names, proposing that the two female names symbolize two parties or factions within the church, "the Jewish Christians and the Gentile Chris-

365

tians." Such an interpretive model is totally artificial and in the end much less helpful than the simpler, literary approach. The most valuable interpretive model to follow in all Old and New Testament studies is the hermeneutical rule "lean is better than luxurious." The simplest and most obvious meanings of words and names should be the primary method of interpretation. We must assume that what we have here is a direct reference by Paul to three actual people who are members of the fellowship at Philippi. It is not clear from the paragraph whether the argument only involves Euodia and Syntyche while Clement is one of the yokefellows who is to assist in their reconciliation, or whether Clement himself is also in some way a party to the dispute and for that reason is named by Paul.

A point of great importance is that Paul has not become so involved in the gossip and stories of conflict that he is willing to make the connections clear to us. The members of the church at Philippi who received this letter knew the answers to the questions we have about the dispute. But from Paul we will learn no gossip about particulars. Instead, what we have in these few simple sentences of the apostle is the example of a remarkably sensitive pastor-counselor who manages to become involved in a way that preserves the integrity of all parties and the high reputation of each person, while at the same time realistically facing up to the fact of an interpersonal crisis in the church community. He asks these friends to agree in their deepest loyalty, in Christ. He does not presume to take sides in the issues at debate. The wise mixture of pastoral elements in these few lines from Paul is very helpful for those of us who must face similar conflict situations in a fellowship. Notice what Paul says and what he does not say. He does not take sides in the dispute. He does not from a distance try to produce a narrative of the causes of the crisis. He does not give the church detailed disciplinary instructions. He does not threaten or scold the persons involved, nor does he scold the church. Yet at the same time he does not gloss over the crisis in a vague or indirect way.

Notice what he does say. He names the persons in a forthright way. He admits to a crisis of disagreement in the church. He calls on the parties involved to agree in the Lord. While acknowledging that there are points of view or convictions or behavior patterns in which they do not stand together, he encourages them to meet where they do stand together — their common bond in the Lordship of Christ. The advice is profoundly theological. Paul points to the fact that because of Jesus Christ we as Christians are not left alone to figure out and solve our interpersonal relationships as if our direct relationship with other fallible and imperfect human beings were all we have. Dietrich Bonhoeffer made the profound observation in *The Cost of Discipleship* that, because Christ is the Savior Lord and because of his radical intervention, we now have *mediated* relationships with each other in the family of faith as well as *mediated* relationships toward those outside faith and indeed toward the whole created order. "Christ stands between us and God, and for that very reason he stands between us and all other men and things."

Paul calls out to his friends to rejoice, then to become moderate (*epieikas,* literally "gentle"). He is describing an unflappability that has its source in one great fact: the Lord is nearby. Because of Christ's closeness to us a series of results follow: the privilege of prayer and the gift of peace that is in itself our guard (*phroureō,* "to garrison").

He then offers a list of virtues that follow and calls upon the Christians to compute these into our lives. (*Logizomai* means to think carefully.) He calls out to his friends to make up their mind about their discipleship response in order to learn from Paul their mentor and then to put into practice what they have learned.

This paragraph is reminiscent of the Old Testament book of Proverbs. Paul adopts the wisdom approach of the Old Testament proverbs in order to alert his readers to virtues which are all directly related to the gospel. The Hebrew word that is translated "wisdom" in the Old Testament means "skill." As we read the wisdom texts of the Old Testament, such as the book of Proverbs and the Psalms, we discover in that literature the rich Jewish tradition of the teaching of ethical, moral, and spiritual skills to young men and women so that they will know how to live as God intended them to live. Paul decides to play that ancient role with the Philippian Christians, not to reintroduce legalism, but instead to help them grow in the gospel. Paul's point is that we as growing Christians need to examine values that make up the whole range of possible behavior patterns so that we will choose the substantial patterns that we have observed in the lives of people like Paul himself and then put into practice what we know to be true and healthy.

Paul has put his finger on a very important truth about spiritual-ethical maturity. Growing as a Christian in a healthy way requires thousands of day-by-day decisions about values. Each of these options we must evaluate for ourselves, and we must then follow up our choices by putting them into practice. We, and only we, are able to choose what behaviors will become our own. But inevitably those day-to-day choices make up the portrait of who I really am. The large, grand goals, such as peace and justice, are easy to embrace and admire with the rhetoric of abstract beauty and perfection. But all too often we are like the *Peanuts* character Linus, who said, "I love mankind, it's people I can't stand." The large, grand goals become reality in a human life on the basis of the day-to-day, small-scale choices that we make in supermarkets, on the freeway, in crowded workstations, at home, and in a thousand other forks in the road where we make the real choices that either express or diminish the grand goals that have won our respect.

For this reason Paul calls the Christians at Philippi to choose the ways that honor the substantial values. Paul is encouraging us to make a habit of the virtues we treasure so that they become a regular part of each day. He wants us to practice these virtues just as we practice an athletic skill in order to make it a regular and natural part of our daily lives.

Paul is giving the right advice to his friends. Honesty needs to be the practical everyday pattern in our lives. There are countless opportunities to practice honesty in the many small details of ordinary interpersonal encounters. Great moments for great acts of sacrificial love rarely announce themselves to us with adequate lead time. Instead, we stumble into the most important moments in odd places and seemingly insignificant situations, so that it is only later that we understand what really happened.

Courage is like that. Brave people whom we honor with awards for public courage are usually ordinary people who stayed close to danger just a few seconds longer than everyone else, and while they stayed they thought up something concrete to do that turned out to be a courageous act at a time of intense stress. They were just as frightened as everyone else, but something made those added seconds possible. In most instances it was their pattern of living and their habits that played the big part. We gradually become brave just as we gradually learn how to really communicate with our children or our parents. Paul wants to develop the kind of Christians at Philippi who, like a weight lifter working out every day, will be people who daily practice their virtues. It means putting them into practice when no one is watching.

Whatever the conflict or dispute in Philippi that lies behind these words, Paul counsels the people to find peace. Prayer can bring this result: "The peace of God . . . will keep your hearts and your minds in Christ Jesus" (v. 7). Practicing the virtues Paul modeled can bring this result: "The God of peace will be with you" (v. 9). The "peace of God" is a gift of "the God of peace" through faithful prayer and practice.

*Earl F. Palmer*

## Third Sunday of Advent, Year C

First Lesson: Zephaniah 3:14-20
(Isaiah 12:2-6)
**Second Lesson: Philippians 4:4-7**
Gospel Lesson: Luke 3:7-18

This is a good place to notice Paul's emphasis on *joy* throughout this letter. "Joy" or "rejoice" appears in 1:4, 18, 25; 2:2, 17, 18, 28, 29; 3:1; 4:1, 4, and 10. Here in verse 4 the call to rejoice is repeated. It is too much to say that *joy* is the *theme* of the letter because nowhere does Paul describe it or treat it as a subject. But because it permeates his message, we can say that *joy* is the *spirit* of the letter. The apostle who once sang hymns with his partner Silas in a prison in Philippi (Acts 16:25), now writes a letter of thanks to Philippi from another prison. With his life in danger, Paul calls the Philippians to rejoice with him in the Lord.

First Paul says, "Let all men know your forbearance." The word for forbearance, *epieikes,* means "yielding, gentle, kind." The word carries the connotations of openness, relaxation, moderation, and gentleness. It is the same word used in James 3:17: "But the wisdom from above is first pure, then peaceable, *gentle,* open to reason, full of mercy and good fruits."

"Have no anxiety about anything." The word translated "anxiety" (*merimnaō*) literally means "a divided mind," and it carries the sense of being "harassed by care." Earlier, however, Paul did not criticize Timothy for being anxious for the welfare of the Philippians (2:20). Apparently there is a wholesome anxiety (care) born of concern for others and a destructive anxiety born of lack of trust. It is the destructive kind that he calls them to put aside here. It is the word Peter uses in his famous sentence in 1 Peter 5:7: "Cast all your anxieties on him, for he cares about you." It is also the word used by Jesus in the Sermon on the Mount: "Therefore do not be anxious about tomorrow" (Matt. 6:34).

Paul now encourages the Christians at Philippi to challenge the real harassment of anxiety by bringing the requests they have in their hearts and minds directly to the Lord. Paul draws two words together to explain the act of prayer by which we bring our requests to the Lord. *Proseuchomai* is the word translated by the English word "pray" in the New Testament. Because of the prefix *pros,* it should more precisely be translated "pray toward." The *pros* gives a vital clue to the reader that biblical prayer is focused primarily

369

on or toward the one to whom we pray, rather than on the act of prayer or the practice of prayer as a religious act of the believer.

The word *deēsis* is translated "petition," and it means the specific request made to God. Prayer in the Bible is specific and tied to real-life concerns. Prayer is what we bring to God when we lay our life and thoughts before God. Paul encourages exactly this kind of thoughtful prayer by his use of this word. We are invited by Jesus Christ, who showed us how to pray in the Lord's Prayer, to bring the requests and real concerns of our daily lives, including our need for bread, to our Father in heaven. Now Paul reminds the Philippians of that generous invitation.

The third key word in Paul's invitation to prayer is "thanksgiving." We must focus not only on what we need, but also on who the Father is and on what the Father has given us. Thanksgiving is a response to the gracious generosity of God. Paul urges that prayer be offered *in* everything, *with* thanksgiving. Just as he called them to rejoice at all times (v. 4), he also urges them to pray with thanksgiving in all circumstances. This is possible only through trusting that God's greatest gift is already ours: in life and death we are not our own, but belong to God through Jesus Christ (1:19-24).

Paul has accompanied his exhortation to rejoice with three specifics, each dealing with a different relationship: gentleness toward others, setting aside anxiety toward the world and the future, and a prayerful relationship with God. Now he adds a fourth, which is the result of the first three and concerns us individually and collectively as the church: "And the peace of God, which passes all understanding, will keep your heart and your minds in Christ Jesus." This is the peace that belongs to God and is his alone to grant.

As we have seen earlier, "peace" in the Old Testament Hebrew is the word *shalom*, which is a very rich word that contains the sense of wholeness and health. Paul here writes in Greek, but the rich and ancient Hebrew word certainly stands behind this first-century expression. This peace is not merely the absence of conflict, but the presence of harmony that comes from having everything in the world and life back in its proper place and function. Chaos is disorder; shalom is restored order. The kind of prayer Paul urges here restores us to our place as God's people in God's world for God's purpose. That is the beginning of shalom.

This peace far exceeds, is far above, every thought and will guard our lives. "Guard" is a better word than the RSV "keep." The word *phrourēsei* means to "guard" or "garrison," and its noun form is the word for "fort" or "fortress." One can imagine Paul writing this letter from prison while being attended by an armed guard. He sees the guard standing over him and makes him into a parable. Paul declares that God's peace is able to guard our hearts and our minds from the pressures that bring harassment and fear.

For many centuries these words of Paul were treasured for their poetic beauty but hardly for their realism. But look again. The massive fortresses of ancient and medieval history have been replaced in Western history by weapons and strategies of war. Because of the technological achievements in weapon invention, we who live in the nuclear generation are now able to really understand the profound relevance and realism of Paul's affirmation that peace is indeed a fortress.

If two people are standing across the room from each other and the floor is covered with gasoline, the best protection for each person is to talk with the other and to keep away from matches. The extensive firepower of modern weaponry has produced just this sort of mutual restraint between highly armed nations, who now realize that the world's surest fortress for each country on the globe is peaceful arms-reduction negotiations between nations that will hopefully lead to peace in this nuclear, gasoline-on-the-floor world.

But Paul has in mind the even more profound peace that comes from the love of Jesus Christ at work in the hearts and minds of people. This sentence directs our eyes toward the mystery of the gospel of Jesus Christ that is able to create new beginnings and heal brokenness. When warfare is raging in a human life, the result of this inner conflict is that we cause harm to the neighbor unfortunate enough to be nearby. There can be no realistic peace in human life, nor between human beings, unless this most basic of all warfare is slowed down and finally resolved.

But our own experiences with the harsh realities of human sin and our own skill at doing harm have made us pessimistic about real solutions. Paul fully understands our difficulty in expecting any lasting resolutions of this long-term crisis, and that is why he announces the power of the peace that comes from Jesus Christ as the peace that surpasses our best estimates or expectations.

*Earl F. Palmer*

## Eighth Sunday after Pentecost, Year C

First Lesson: Amos 7:7-17
(Psalm 82)
**Second Lesson: Colossians 1:1-14**
Gospel Lesson: Luke 10:25-37

Preaching the opening verses of a letter always poses the challenge of covering the necessary "background" material touched on in those verses. Identifying the author and his circumstances, pinning down the date, recognizing the location and status of the addressees, etc., can indeed provide insight into the letter. But rather than treated as topics in themselves, such material is better brought into messages on the letter where it can serve to illuminate or illustrate a point from the text. We will thereby save our hearers from the boredom of a "history lesson" even as we illustrate just how valuable such data might be for understanding and applying the text.

In the case of Colossians 1:1-14, therefore, the preacher would be well advised to move over verses 1-2 quickly or, indeed, not treat them directly at all. To be sure, the situation of Colossae as a cosmopolitan trade center plays a role in the false teaching that Paul opposes in the letter. And that false teaching itself, as the context out of which Paul's own teaching arises, is significant for our understanding of many passages in the letter (esp. 2:16-23). But Paul says nothing about false teaching in these verses, so these points can perhaps be profitably left to other sermons. Nevertheless, we should at least contextualize what Paul says in verses 3-14 by recognizing that he already has at least one eye on this false teaching. His thanksgiving for the Colossians (vv. 3-8) and his prayer for them (vv. 9-14) take the offensive, as it were, by setting out positively some crucial teaching that will serve to counteract the negative thrust of the false teaching. We may therefore justly apply the words of Paul's prayer for the Colossians to all Christians, and especially those facing similar kinds of false teaching.

Paul's thanksgiving falls into two major sections. Verses 3-5a begin with a focus on the traditional triad of "faith," "love," and "hope." Paul thanks God that the Colossian Christians, in faithfulness to their calling as "saints" (v. 2), exhibit each of these three standard Christian virtues. But the careful reader of these verses will be struck by an unusual way of introducing hope in verse 5. Rather than paralleling this virtue with faith and love, Paul introduces it as the basis for the other two — "*because of* the hope laid up for you in heaven." As the language "laid up in heaven" makes clear, hope here is not the subjective attitude but the objective reality, not our hoping but what we hope for. Faith and love are strengthened when we keep our eyes fixed on the blessing of heavenly deliverance and reward that awaits us. The certainty that this blessing awaits us in the life to come provides the foundation for a faith that takes risks and a love that reaches beyond our comfort zones.

In the second part of his thanksgiving, Paul's gaze turns to "the word of truth, the gospel" (v. 5b). It was this message of good news in Jesus that proclaimed the hope the Colossian believers now have. Standing out as particularly important in these verses is Paul's emphasis on the power of the gospel. This gospel has been "bearing fruit and growing" all over the world. And it has been having the same effect on the Colossian Christians ever since they were converted (v. 6). The inherent ability of God's own word in the gospel to transform human beings is a basic theological conviction of the New Testament writers. Luke, in the book of Acts, is particularly fond of emphasizing this point. At critical points in his narrative he attributes the spread of the early church to the activity of the word itself. "The word of God continued to spread; the number of the disciples increased greatly in Jerusalem, and a great many of the priests became obedient to the faith" (Acts 6:7). "But the word of God continued to advance and gain adherents" (12:24). "Thus the word of the Lord spread throughout the region" (13:49). "So the word of the Lord grew mightily and prevailed" (19:20). Conversion and growth in Christ, suggest both Paul and Luke, are to be attributed not (ultimately) to the teacher or preacher but to the word the teacher or preacher proclaims. Ministers and laypeople alike need to recommit to this vision of the active, powerful word of God. Our job will be to facilitate its growth and to seek to be faithful conduits of its power. And it is at this point that we might bring in briefly the circumstances of the letter. Paul writes, at Epaphras's request (vv. 7-8), to counter false teaching that has come into the Colossian church. Scholars continue to debate the precise origin and thrust of this false teaching. But it is at least clear that it urged believers to supplement their spiritual resources with additional practices and beliefs. Paul's reminder to the Colossians here of the power of the word as it has been manifest in their lives ever since their conversion is a not-so-subtle jab at this false teaching. To contextualize Paul's point, then, we will have to ask whether any similar kind of false teaching might be affecting our own churches, a false teaching that, however subtly, questions the efficacy of God's word in and of itself to bring believers to spiritual "fullness."

Similar preemptive strikes against the false teaching can also be observed in Paul's prayer for the Colossians (vv. 9-14). Two themes in particular emerge from these verses. First is a focus on the importance of spiritual "knowledge." Paul uses several terms to get at this idea: "knowledge [of God's will]," "spiritual wisdom," "[spiritual] understanding" (v. 9), and "knowledge [of God]" (v. 10). The knowledge Paul prays that we might have is clearly more than intellectual. True biblical knowledge is known by its fruits. As Paul says, the result of such knowledge is that "you may lead lives worthy of the Lord, fully pleasing to him, as you bear fruit in every good work." One must press beyond the simple understanding of Scripture to the implications of Scripture for the way we think and live. But we should be careful not to indulge the postmodern tendency to depreciate "head" knowledge. Knowledge of God and his word must go beyond the head — but it must begin with the head. Patient study and careful reflection on what Scripture teaches are indispensable to the knowledge that will enable us to honor and do the will of God in practice. And again, as we recognize the context of false teaching, we can apply Paul's insistence on knowledge especially to situations in which someone might be trying to encourage the church to look beyond knowledge of God's will for spiritual growth.

A second key theme, also of particular relevance to the false teachers, is the status of the believer. Verse 11 shifts the focus, as Paul moves from his prayer for knowledge to his prayer for spiritual strength. Only by tapping constantly into God's own power, through prayer and meditation, will we be able to endure the various trials that come our way in the Christian life. When we use God's own power to stand fast in the face of the threats to our faith and, positively, turn to God in thanks, we will confirm and rejoice in the benefits God has given us. The "inheritance" is Old Testament language for all that God promises his people (v. 12). That inheritance now belongs to the saints. In verse 13 Paul switches images, making one of his few references to the kingdom. In conversion we are rescued from the realm of sin and death — "the power of darkness" — and brought into the realm of God's own Son. And in that Son we enjoy "redemption." As used in the first century, the Greek equivalent of this word *(apolytrōsis)* suggests the freedom gained by a slave in exchange for a sum of money. So God brings the forgiveness of sins to his people by paying the supreme price of his own Son. Contemplating the blessings that God has already conferred on us should make any false teaching that promises greater spiritual experiences rather unimportant to us. It is when we fail to appreciate what we have that we are tempted to search for more.

*Douglas Moo*

## Christ the King, Year C

First Lesson: Jeremiah 23:1-6
(Luke 1:68-79)
**Second Lesson: Colossians 1:11-20**
Gospel Lesson: Luke 23:33-43

T his text is fitting for the Sunday of Christ the King for several reasons. It speaks of Christ's "kingdom" (1:13), contains royal imagery ("thrones," 1:16), affirms his preeminence over all things (1:18), and confesses him as head of the church (1:18).

Although the letter to the Colossians is attributed to Paul on the basis of statements within it (1:1; 4:18), it is often considered deutero-Pauline (pseudonymous). In any case, the author addresses a community that is plagued by certain false teachers who claim that people are governed by so-called "elemental spirits of the universe," which are cosmic powers hostile to God (2:8, 20) and stand as roadblocks interrupting communion between God and humanity. These false teachers also promote the worship of certain angels (2:18a), mysticism (2:18b), and aspects of Jewish law, including dietary regulations (2:16a), Sabbath and festival observances (2:16b), and laws of purity (2:20-21). The "philosophy" (2:8) they promote seems to be a syncretistic blend of Jewish traditions and current cosmological speculation. The passage assigned for this Sunday alludes to, and presupposes, that worldview.

Just prior to the assigned passage, the author mentions that he continues to pray for his readers. Specifically he prays that the Christians at Colossae may be filled with knowledge, wisdom, and understanding, which culminates in good works (1:9-10). Our reading begins with his wish for the congregation (1:11), which coincides with the petitions of his prayer: that the church at Colossae be strengthened "with all the strength" (NRSV) or, better, "with all power" (RSV, NIV; *dynamis* in Greek) that comes from God's own "might" (*kratos* in Greek). The author thereby discounts the idea that Christians are ruled by "powers" of an alien kind. The power that comes from God is able to provide strength to endure in times of trouble.

In the verses that follow (1:12-14) the author exhorts his readers to give thanks to God, and the reason for thanksgiving is God's redemptive work in Christ, by which Christians have an "inheritance," eternal salvation as a gift. Using the indicative, the author speaks of Christians as being delivered and transferred — that is, they have had an exchange of lordships — from the powers of darkness to Christ. It is probable that in the author's view this exchange took place at the time of his readers' baptisms. In any case, believers belong to Christ and his destiny. Belonging to him, they have "redemption," which is consequent to the forgiveness of sins.

At 1:15 we begin reading a hymn, the so-called Colossian Hymn. But while it certainly begins at 1:15, it is not clear where it ends. The twenty-seventh edition of the Nestle-Aland *Greek New Testament* (1993) has the entirety of 1:15 through 1:20 indented and printed in a poetic format, as though all of 1:15-20 is a unit. That judgment may well be correct. The other view is that the actual hymn that has been put to use is contained within 1:15-18a (ending with "head of the body").

In either case the author makes use of a hymn concerning Christ and creation. By using this hymn — which may well have been familiar to his readers as well — he refutes the views of his opponents that the "elemental spirits of the universe" reign over the lives and destinies of people. Instead, he declares, it is Christ in whom and for whom all things were created, and in whom all things "hold together." By saying that everything, "visible and invisible," has been created through Christ, the hymn has a background in the wisdom tradition of Israel. In Proverbs 8:22-31 "wisdom" is personified as God's assistant or agent in the creation of the universe. That concept is also found in apocryphal/deuterocanonical literature, such as Wisdom of Solomon 9:1-4. In various literary expressions of early Christianity, the preexistent Christ was identified with wisdom, taking on the role of being involved in the creation of the universe. In addition to Colossians 1:15-18a, the best-known texts on the role of Christ in the creation of all things are John 1:1-3 and Hebrews 1:1-3.

Beginning with the words "the church," the remainder of 1:18 and the material of 1:19-20 could be the author's own composition. Even those who think all of 1:15-20 is a single hymn claim the author of Colossians made additions to this material, including "the church" (1:18), "through the blood of his cross" (1:20), and perhaps other items. In any case, this portion of the text marks a shift away from Christ and creation to Christ and redemption.

As the "firstborn from the dead," the now-reigning Christ heads up the new humanity, the church, and in fact is preeminent over all things. One of the most striking and memorable expressions concerning the incarnation is set forth in 1:19: all that can be known of God was manifested in his Son. The next verse (1:20) sets forth one of the most striking and memorable expressions concerning the work of Christ, his reconciling of "all things" to himself. As explained more fully in the verses that follow (1:21-22), which are not included in the assigned reading, Christ has reconciled to himself (and thus to God) all who were estranged from God by their evil deeds. He has reconciled them (translating literally) "by means of the body of his flesh through death" (1:22, NRSV: "in his fleshly body through death") in order to present them "holy and blameless and irreproachable." Christ took upon himself the sins of humanity and bore in himself the penalty to its ultimate conclusion, death. As a consequence, those formerly estranged are blameless. Their sins have been forgiven (1:14; 3:13). The result of his reconciling work is universal peace — both in heaven and on earth.

The theme of the day is kingship. In the first lesson the promise of God is set forth, in which it is said that God will raise up a descendant of David who will "reign as king and deal wisely, and shall execute justice and righteousness" (Jer. 23:5). And in the day's Gospel reading the inscription on the cross at Jesus' crucifixion reads: "This is the King of the Jews" (Luke 23:38). Moreover, one of the criminals crucified with him cries out, "Jesus, remember me when you come into your kingdom" (23:42).

Christ is portrayed as king also in this second lesson. It is this reading, in fact, that speaks of Christ as king between the times of his being exalted as king through his death/resurrection, on the one hand, and his manifestation to all as king at his parousia. In short, this lesson portrays him as king in the present of our Christian existence. God the Father has "transferred us into the kingdom of his beloved Son" (Col. 1:13).

A sermon on this passage might well center on the twin themes of Christ's being "firstborn of all creation" (1:15) and "firstborn from the dead" (1:18). These two phrases can be used to gather up the main thoughts that are there.

Although modern Christians (or people in general) do not share the stark features of the cosmology presupposed by those at Colossae in ancient times, many share their sense of helplessness and fear. The cosmos can be perceived and experienced as a threat to both one's well-being and security. All manner of forces, both visible and invisible, can make life perilous. These include meteorological, economic, social, political, and even religious forces and systems.

But the message of the reading is that Christ is the "firstborn of all creation." That does not mean that he is a creature created, but that he is supreme over all. When God created the universe, it was not "out of control" but integrated by being placed under his beloved Son, in whom there is full integration and peace. Since the creation is integrated under him, we should know that above, around, and underneath all that seems hostile or out of control, Christ reigns, holding all together in his care. We can live in hope, anticipating that God's will for cosmic wholeness will be fulfilled in God's own time.

In the meantime, God has inaugurated a new era and a new humanity through Christ, "the firstborn from the dead." Christ heads up this new humanity, the church, within the present era. By means of Christ's resurrection, the "already" of the new age has invaded the "not yet" of the old one. We who belong to that new humanity — and belonging is a matter of faith, not sight — have a share in the destiny of Christ. Through him "all things" (1:20, a marvelous thought!) have been reconciled to God. What God has in store for the creation is realized "already" in the community of believers, the community of Christ the King.

*Arland J. Hultgren*

## Ninth Sunday after Pentecost, Year C

First Lesson: Amos 8:1-12
(Psalm 52)
**Second Lesson: Colossians 1:15-28**
Gospel Lesson: Luke 10:38-42

In many churches the reading of Scripture is followed by "This is the Word of the Lord," to which the congregation responds, "Thanks be to God." This lection from Colossians 1, however, is so stunning that the line "This is the Word of the Lord" could best be met with a dropped-jaw gasp! A congregation's collective sharp intake of breath would be a poignant indication that the theological and cosmic wallop of these words had properly struck people right between the eyes.

There is much in Colossians 1:15-28 that amazes, but as striking as anything is how the passage concludes. Verses 15-20 are perhaps better known than other portions of this lection. Paul's soaring rhetoric on what has been called "the cosmic Christ" is a beautiful statement on the nature and identity of Christ Jesus as both the sovereign Creator of all and now the glorious Redeemer of all. The depiction of Christ as the Ruler of all things, whether visible or invisible, and the theological assertion that the entire universe comes together in Christ are as grand a set of beliefs as one is likely to find in such a short compass. The claim that a Jewish carpenter's son who had lived his whole life within the relatively small geographical confines of Palestine is now the Lord of lords who rules the galaxies in a supremacy unlike any other, is a claim which properly scandalized first-century Jews and Romans alike.

However, Paul does not leave it at that. Instead, in verses 21-26 he moves to the proclamation of this news. But then comes verse 27, which is the gasp-inducing climax to all this: when anyone hears and believes this mysterious message which Paul proclaims, the result is "Christ in you."

*Christ in you.* In just three short words Paul has clamped together the lofty cosmic picture of verses 15-20 with our very concrete lives right now. The *same* Christ who created and redeemed all that we know (and all that we can neither see nor know), the *same* Christ who rules with a supremacy we cannot begin to fathom, can also be localized in the heart of any and every believer on the planet! The "glorious riches of the mystery" is every believer's connection to the wider scope of God's creative and redemptive work.

The homiletical directions in which a preacher could justifiably take the sweep of Colossians 1 are many and varied. But in this article I will suggest just two possibilities. One ties in with people's perennial desire for a touch of divine mystery in their lives (a human tendency which flared brightly in the late twentieth century as various forms of "spirituality" — especially experiential, mystical forms of spirituality — became very much in vogue). The second possibility has to do with the need, in an increasingly pluralistic and fragmented world, to find some kind of overarching unity and coherence to reality.

First, the mystical element of Colossians 1. Richard Mouw relates an anecdote about a friend who, once upon a time, had been the quintessential 1960s radical, eschewing *all* religion (and especially the Christian faith) as just so much nonsense mumbo jumbo. Thirty years later, however, in the heady days of the 1990s and that decade's spirituality fads (with all those mystical books about angel visitants, conversations with God, and New Age channeling sessions to get in touch with past lives), Mouw's friend had changed. Upon meeting up with him again for the first time in many years, Mouw told him that he was still a Christian. His friend could not believe it. "How can you go in for a religion that is so *tame?!*"

In many ways Christianity is distinct from the more mystical elements of various Eastern religions as well as from New Age amalgamations of those faiths. The Christian faith is a world-affirming religion, not a world-shunning one, which is perhaps why there are no words from Jesus in the canonical Gospels which suggest (or even hint at) the need for mind-emptying meditation techniques or mantras by which to transcend the plane of this existence in order to commune with higher (and presumably better) spiritual realms. Colossians 1, for all its mystical poetry about invisible realms, likewise affirms the integrity of the physical creation as well as pointing to the fact that it is precisely *this* world and all its creatures which Jesus both made and saved.

Still, there are some profoundly mysterious teachings in this passage as well. There are, to paraphrase Shakespeare, more things in heaven and on earth than can be imagined in our typical apprehension of religion and philosophy. There are realms we know little, if anything, about. God, however, knows about every real thing. What's more, Christ has united all those realities in his very self by redeeming them through his blood shed on the cross. The sublime mystery of Golgotha is that in Jesus' horrific death things got set back to right in the entire cosmos.

Faith is the conduit through which Christ and all the riches of his gospel are accessed by each and every believer. Faith is the electrical lead through which the power of Christ, via the Spirit, gets wired into our hearts. But far from a personalized "Me and Jesus" perspective, Colossians 1 reminds us that what we tie into through faith is the whole of reality. There can be no union with Christ without also sharing a communion with all the other things and people Christ redeemed. That is a profoundly mystical teaching. It is also a theological assertion redolent of hope: the entire creation does have a future.

A second line of thought dovetails with this mystery in pointing to reality's larger sense of purpose, order, and coherence in Christ. Biographer William Manchester relates the story of the time young Winston Churchill, at the tender age of eight, was shipped off to a boarding school in England. The headmaster met the future prime minister and immediately handed him a Latin grammar, ordering Winston to memorize the declension for the Latin word *mensa* and stating that he would return shortly to see how Churchill had done. The headmaster returned a few minutes later, and Winston reeled off a perfect recitation. But then Churchill asked, "What does it mean, sir?" and was told that *mensa* is the Latin word for "table." Ever the quick study, young Churchill quickly grasped that the vocative form he had just recited would mean "O Table!" Churchill asked why this was necessary and was told by the headmaster, "That is the form you would employ when addressing a table." "But I never do!" Winston blurted out, only to be chastised mightily for his insolence.

It did not make sense or add up to Churchill. Mere memorizing of data ought never be the goal of education, yet increasingly it seems that merely being able to access facts quickly has become a substitute for true intelligence. In recent decades the world has entered the information age. High-speed Internet connections, e-mail, and an ever burgeoning set of worldwide websites now make it possible for people everywhere to access almost any kind of information instantaneously. Indeed, the highly interconnected nature of this planet is revealed each time some computer hacker launches a virus via e-mail. The "Love Bug" virus in early 2000 circled the globe in less than two hours, moving from Hong Kong to everywhere in record speed.

But for all that interconnectedness, a larger sense of life's meaning seems to be still lacking. The so-called information superhighway is a road that leads to everywhere in general but to nowhere in particular. Bits and pieces of data are more readily available now than ever before, but do students (or adults) today have the mental and spiritual equipment necessary to assemble all of that into a larger, meaningful picture of existence? Is it merely a coincidence that in recent years the very high school and college students who know more information than any previous generation are the same young people who routinely express despair (sometimes leading to suicides, if not mass shootings)?

Colossians 1 holds out the hope that in Christ it all comes together. It is possible to understand reality through faith in the God from whom all things came, by whom all things have been saved, and in whom the entire universe is now held together in hope. This is not a simple message or a simple formula, but it is the gospel recognition that reality is not a booming, buzzing confusion and history is not (contra Henry Ford) a random string of "one damned thing after another." Reality does hang together. Exploring that in Christ is the abiding task of Christian teachers and preachers because this belief is nothing short of the "mystery, which is Christ in you, the hope of glory."

*Scott Hoezee*

## Tenth Sunday after Pentecost, Year C

First Lesson: Hosea 1:2-10
(Psalm 85)
**Second Lesson: Colossians 2:6-15, (16-19)**
Gospel Lesson: Luke 11:1-13

D ealing with an incursion of false teaching that questioned the sufficiency of Christ, Paul insists throughout Colossians that a vital relationship to Christ is all anyone needs to attain spiritual perfection. But nowhere does this central theme of the letter surface so clearly as in 2:6-15.
This passage may rightly be considered the linchpin of the argument of the
letter. Its essential message is simply stated, using a play on words that Paul
himself utilizes: because "the whole fullness of deity" is found in Christ
(v. 9), people who are in Christ have come to "fullness" (v. 10). The positive
and negative exhortations of verses 6-8 are built on the theology of verse 9,
and verses 11-15 elaborate verse 10 by showing how believers have become
"full" in Christ.

As he has elsewhere in the letter (cf. 1:6), Paul begins by reminding us of
our initial Christian experience: we received "Christ Jesus the Lord." But a
preferable translation is "Christ Jesus *as* Lord" (NIV). This rendering puts
the emphasis where Paul's grammar probably intends it to be, on the fact
that our faith is directed, from the beginning, to one who is Lord. If, Paul
suggests, our initial Christian experience had to do with nothing but Jesus
himself, Lord of the universe, there is no reason why our progress in the
faith should require any other focus. We should, he says, "continue to live
[our] lives in him." The precise intent of Paul's "in Christ" language, so
characteristic of his theology and very prominent in these opening verses
(see also vv. 7, 10, 11), is not easy to pin down. But it probably arises from
his conception of Christ as "second Adam," a corporate figure who includes
within himself all those who, by faith, have come to belong to him. Without
lapsing into an unbiblical mysticism, we can compare Christ to the atmo-
sphere in which believers live. Our connection with Christ is to be, then, the
source of all future spiritual development, as the varied metaphors of verse
7 bring out.

Verse 8 presents the negative counterpart to verses 6-7. If the complete
sufficiency of Christ means that we must continue to live in him for spiritual sustenance, it also means that we must resolutely resist all temptation
to search for spiritual meaning anywhere else. Certain teachers, apparently

offering the Colossian Christians the "next step" in their spiritual pilgrimage, were presenting just such a temptation. But Paul condemns their teaching, claiming it is human in origin and operates according to "the elemental spirits of the universe." This phrase is very perplexing, scholars arguing at great length whether it refers to "worldly" teachings or to spiritual beings. Since reverence for spiritual beings plays a prominent role in the "Colossian heresy" (2:18; cf. 1:15, 20; 2:10, 15), we may prefer the spiritual beings interpretation. But whatever our final interpretation, the crucial point surfaces in the last, negative, characterization of the teaching: it is "not according to Christ."

Paul's use of "fullness" language in Colossians and the closely related Ephesians might suggest that he was deliberately picking up terminology popular among the false teachers. They were, perhaps, promising their adherents "spiritual fullness." Paul responds by pointing to the true source of all spiritual fullness: Christ, himself God (v. 9). All that can be known of God, Paul implies, is found in Jesus; one need look nowhere else. Paul is not, of course, denying the deity of Father or Spirit. Jesus does not exhaust deity; he simply exhaustively mediates deity to those who seek it.

The fullness found in Jesus is experienced by all who are "in" Christ, the "head of every ruler and authority" (v. 10). "Head" here, as elsewhere in Paul, is a metaphor for functional superiority (see also 1 Cor. 11:3; Eph. 1:21; 5:23; Col. 1:18). Practically, in this context the point is that one cannot find any spiritual benefit by associating with those spiritual beings who have been placed under Christ. How did we become "full" in Christ? Verses 11-15 explain. Paul turns to another metaphor in verse 11, drawn from the Old Testament/Jewish world: circumcision. Paul likens our conversion to the cutting away of "flesh" that takes place in circumcision. Unlike children in the Old Testament, Christians do not have physical flesh stripped from them, but they do have the spiritual power of sin that Paul calls "flesh" stripped from them. "Circumcision of Christ" at the end of the verse, then, probably refers to "the circumcision done to us by Christ" rather than (as a few scholars suggest) "the circumcision done to Christ." The point of the verse, then, is that our relationship to Christ puts us in a totally new relationship to sin, in which sin no longer has dictatorial power over us (see also Rom. 6).

Paul continues to use imagery found in Romans 6 in verse 12 by associating believers, in their conversion, with Christ's burial and resurrection. And all this is linked as well to baptism. The precise relationship of this identification with Christ's burial and resurrection, baptism, and our own faith (see the end of v. 12) is difficult to unravel. This much, however, is clear: Paul views baptism as closely aligned with faith and sees it as a part of the larger "conversion experience." And we should also note that he does not, in this text at least, compare baptism to circumcision but to spiritual circumcision.

Identification with Christ in his resurrection means new life (see again Rom. 6:4-5), so it is natural for Paul in verse 13 to claim, in the next of his descriptions of our entrance into Christ's fullness, that we were made alive with him. In our pre-Christian state we were "dead" — insensitive to God's will and doomed to die because of our sins. But God in Christ has forgiven us our sins and so paved the way for a new life. Verse 14 uses yet another metaphor to elaborate on this forgiveness. Paul now turns to the legal realm, suggesting that our sins have been recorded in a "record" that stood against us. The word translated "record" (cheirographon) could be paraphrased "IOU." Paul pictures every human being as having a document that pledged unconditional obedience to God. Since our sins have broken that pledge, we owe to God debt that we can never repay. But God took that record of our sins, nailed it to the cross, and so frustrated the spiritual powers that held us in their sway (v. 15). This last verse introduces yet another metaphor, drawn from the "triumphs" that honored victorious generals when they returned to Rome. They would enter the city in a long and elaborate procession, leading in their train the captives they had taken in the victorious campaign. So God, Paul suggests, leads the spiritual powers in triumphal procession, broadcasting his victory over them on the cross of his Son.

This incredibly rich passage poses two serious and related challenges to the interpreter: how to bring alive the evocative metaphors that Paul uses in verses 11-15, and how to do justice to the text in a single message. Metaphors that created an immediate picture to Paul's first-century readers do not always have the same effect on a contemporary audience. And so the preacher must do his or her research and patiently unfold the metaphors one by one. Yet this takes time. And so the preacher may choose to elaborate one of the metaphors only, or to summarize verses 11-15 while focusing on verses 6-10.

And there might be good reason to focus on these earlier verses. For they elaborate a theme that should be a focal point of faithful preaching of the Scriptures in our present cultural climate. Postmodernism has brought in its wake a pervasive relativism. People in our culture hear, in various guises, explicitly and implicitly, the message that all religions are the same and that the search for God need not be confined to one particular tradition or faith. That message leads many Christians to think they might be able to find deeper spiritual fulfillment by adding to their Christianity elements of

other religions, whether it be New Age, Buddhism, transcendental meditation, or whatever. Colossians 2:6-10 stands as a clear warning against any
such dalliance with other religious traditions. Only in Christ is the true God
to be found, and only in him can spiritual progress be made.

*Douglas Moo*

## Resurrection of the Lord, Year A

First Lesson: Acts 10:34-43
(Psalm 118:1-2, 14-24)
**Second Lesson: Colossians 3:1-4**
Gospel Lesson: John 20:1-18

Much of Colossians appears to be a kind of baptismal catechesis, instructing Christians in the kind of life appropriate to those who
through faith and baptism have "been raised with Christ" and "whose life is
hidden with Christ in God." The language here echoes that of Paul's instruction on baptism in Romans 6, with one important exception. There
those who have been buried with Christ by baptism into his death are called
to walk in newness of life. Here they are described as "raised with Christ."
We should, however, not make too much of this, inasmuch as Colossians
goes on to urge the same kind of conduct as Romans. In Romans Christians
are said to have died to sin. In verse 5 here, immediately after this pericope,
the Colossians are called on to "put to death, therefore, whatever in you is
earthly." The new life in Christ is central in each, and that is plainly the focus here.

This argument is not intended to put to rest the issue of whether or not
Colossians is authentically Pauline, but it is intended to render the question
moot. There are good arguments either way, but even if Colossians is not
from Paul's hand, it is so close conceptually as to be very much Paul's even if
from the hand of a disciple. Moreover, the comparison between Romans 6
and Colossians 3 shows, contrary to some arguments, more similarity than
difference. The argument that Colossians has a more spatial conception of

salvation and a more realized eschatology is a fairly minor observation that may not prove much at all. In any case, its canonical position and "orthodoxy" remain beyond question.

The baptismal imagery is part of the reason for its assignment to Easter Sunday. The lectionary was created by the Roman Church, in which the Vigil of Easter is the preeminent time for baptism, especially of adults. We do well to picture this text being read to people who have been baptized for less than a day, as we reflect on it for preaching and before we apply it to the whole congregation. We should also put ourselves in the position of "newborn babes" being instructed afresh as to the implications of baptism and faith.

The other reason for its assignment to Easter Sunday is even more obvious. Verse 1 says, "So if you have been raised with Christ, seek the things that are above, where Christ is, seated at the right hand of God." It is the language of resurrection, and it is the language of baptism into the death and resurrection of Jesus, such that Paul can say to them and to us, "You have died, and your life is hidden with Christ in God." Baptism is not something over and done with at once. It is to be lived out; hence he says to seek the things that are above and set our minds there.

It is sacramental language, language of the mystery of our union with the Lord. In Colossians the language of life in Christ and in the Spirit in the church simply rolls over us. We are, to reiterate, buried and raised with him in baptism. We are also "filled with knowledge" to "bear fruit" and "grow." God has "transferred us into the kingdom of his beloved Son." We are joined to him in whom "all the fullness of God was pleased to dwell" as the body is to the head. Paul completes in his own body the afflictions of Christ. In him we "were circumcised with a spiritual circumcision." Ethnic distinctions fall away. We get rid of vice and "Christ is all in all." Some years ago I used this text on Easter Sunday, and the following paragraphs are an adaptation of some of what I said.

None of this is so unearthly as it might sound. Paul is not calling for some New Age ascent to a higher mental state. Indeed, he is resisting such notions, as is apparent in chapter 2 and in other warnings that seem aimed at a kind of mild, Judaized gnosticism which seems to be the primary problem in this otherwise healthy congregation.

So Paul talks about orienting and structuring our lives here in terms of the resurrection of Jesus. Think about *him*. Remember: your life is all wrapped up in his. "Your life is hidden with Christ in God" does not mean that it is gone, extinguished, but that the fullness of the life of God belongs to you. Your life is hidden in God's, and God through baptism and faith is in you. You are not obliterated; you have been given the Holy Spirit, the Lord and Giver of life. You are as real and alive as God himself.

The impact of the resurrection is that we get our life back, the freedom to live as we ought in full dignity and responsibility as children of God. We can tune our actions to the commandments and to the model of Jesus because we have died and risen with Christ. We have not just a promise ahead of us when we die; we have God and life and Jesus now. Change, growth, and a closer walk with God are real and attractive possibilities for us now.

For an example I used a scene in the movie *Dead Man Walking*. As the execution of Matthew Poncelet approaches, we see a fine portrayal of what such renewal and regaining of life can mean. Poncelet is a bitter, cynical, hardened, and justly convicted murderer. Through an odd set of circumstances Sister Helen Prejean becomes his spiritual adviser as his time is running out. Out of deep Christian conviction she seeks to discover his buried humanity, to show him the face of love, and also to bring him to genuine repentance.

At one point he tells her that he has been reading his Bible and is now confident that Jesus will be waiting for him when he is executed. His theology is correct as far as it goes, but Sister Helen reacts almost in shock. She says, "That's not how it is, Matthew. It's not like a ticket you hand in. You have to participate in your own redemption."

Those with strong Protestant upbringings will recoil at what seems to be works righteousness of the worst sort. "Isn't that just like a Catholic, telling somebody who has come to believe that he still has to work his way into heaven?" But something is utterly correct in Sister Helen's counsel. Poncelet, the condemned killer, is not really "seeking the things that are above." He only wants to save what's left of his miserable hide. She wants him to know, to possess, and to enjoy the fullness of his redemption. (By the way, this episode takes place right after Easter in the movie.) What she wants him to do is finally admit his full responsibility for his sin and to repent not only to God but to the parents of the young people he killed.

At the end he does. He finally admits that he did rape the young woman and that he indeed pulled the trigger and killed the young man. Strapped cruciform to the gurney with the IV needle in his arm, awaiting his execution by lethal injection, he at last admits his role to the victims' parents witnessing his death and expresses his profound sorrow for his deeds.

He has participated in his own redemption. He has claimed his baptism. He has refused to offer excuses or alibis for his sin. He has stopped treating God as miraculous helper at the moment of crisis or death, and he has set his mind on the things that are above. He is thinking like God, and in the moment of his death he finally lives with dignity. His weak, self-serving faith has come to real life. His life is hidden with God on this side of the grave, so that there can be no question with whom he will be on that side of the grave.

By the grace of God things don't become that extreme for most of our hearers. Their struggles to seek the things that are above will be worked out in less drastic ways. That can be harder! It's not a matter of final confession before execution but of dealing with the really hard stuff: money, family, friendship, work, sex, attitudes, politics, neighborliness. It is a matter of using the gifts of the Spirit — love, kindness, faith, self-control.

Participating in our own redemption will mean reordering our desires. What ruins us is that we desire the wrong things — security, autonomy, wealth, happiness of our own choosing and making, control of others. On Easter we are reminded again, in the words of Colossians, of "Christ who is [our] life." He is risen. We are his. We are to set our minds, that is, our desires, where he is.

We are freed by the resurrection to desire what we truly need, God and his mercy and a life oriented to him and to the love and service of all. It is disordered desire that kills faith and vitality, beauty and goodness. But God in giving life calls us to be fully alive. And we can desire what is truly good for us as we struggle to die to sin and to set our minds and hearts on Christ who is our life.

Such is the way faith apprehends and puts to work the baptismal mystery that our "life is hidden with Christ in God." When he is fully revealed, we will share with him in glory.

*Leonard R. Klein*

## Eleventh Sunday after Pentecost, Year C

First Lesson: Hosea 11:1-11
(Psalm 107:1-9, 43)
**Second Lesson: Colossians 3:1-11**
Gospel Lesson: Luke 12:13-21

Mixing specific injunctions with theological principles, Colossians 3:1-11 provides the preacher with a golden opportunity to set out some of the basics of New Testament moral teaching. In this passage Paul moves continually back and forth between the "indicative" and the "imperative"; that is, he alternates between telling us what God has done for us and what we are to do as a result. While, therefore, we may be tempted to focus on some of the specific concerns that surface in the passage — sexual morality, greed, truth telling — we will give more respect to the essence of this text by helping our people understand how their status in Christ leads to a new way of living. "Being precedes act" is a cardinal principle of New Testament ethics, and no text illustrates the truth of this principle better than Colossians 3:1-11.

Paul writes to the Colossians to counter some false teaching that has infected the church. The false teachers are questioning the sufficiency of Christ for spiritual perfection, urging that believers add to their faith in Christ reverence for other spiritual beings, the observance of certain Jewish customs, and an ascetic regimen. The paragraph previous to this one, 2:16-23, tackles this program of the false teachers head-on. Paul urges the Colossians to resist the pressure to follow this route to spiritual maturity, claiming that it is a human and ultimately futile program. In 3:1-11 Paul sets forth the Christian route to holiness, in three stages. He begins, in verses 1-4, with basic commands and general principles. Verses 5-8 become more specific, as Paul details some of the forms of behavior that Christians are to discard. He finishes with a prohibition of lying, grounding it in a final general assertion about the change in status that Christians have undergone (vv. 9-11).

In what might be the key paragraph of the letter (2:6-15), Paul has argued that Christians have been "raised with him through faith in the power of God" (v. 12). This is his starting point in 3:1-11. The idea of a present, "spiritual" resurrection with Christ is a distinctive idea in Ephesians and Colossians (see also Eph. 2:6 and possibly Rom. 6:5, 8). It is not that Paul replaces the future eschatology of bodily resurrection with a present eschatology of spiritual resurrection. Rather, he uses the language of resurrection to convey the entrance into a new state of affairs created by the resurrection of Christ. With Jesus' death, resurrection, and the coming of the Spirit, the new age of salvation and transformative power has been inaugurated. By faith Christians identify with Christ and therefore enter with him into that new age. What Paul, then, calls on us to do in verses 1-2 is to live out the implications of that change of status. We are continually to be seeking (present tense in Greek) "the things that are above" — that is, to pursue actively and daily the values and lifestyle of heaven itself. The command in verse 2 is parallel, focusing, however, more narrowly on the mind-set of the believer. Verse 3 returns to the theme of the beginning of verse 1 by reminding us, this time negatively, of the change in status that we experience in coming to Christ. In 2:20 Paul reminds us that believers have "died to the elemental spirits of the universe." Scholars continue to debate the exact referent of these "elemental spirits." But suffice to say that the phrase ultimately connotes any religious system that is not derived from Christ. When a person comes to Christ, Paul implies, the person undergoes a fundamental change of state, equivalent to going from death to life. It is this idea that Paul briefly alludes to in verse 3. The end of verse 3 and verse 4 add a further perspective on this change in status. To be "hidden with Christ in God" suggests protective care. But it also implies that our true status as "new age" people is not evident. Using the traditional language of Jewish apocalyptic, Paul proclaims that what is now hidden will one day be revealed: when Christ appears in glory at the end of history, his people will be glorified with him (see also Rom. 8:18-22).

In verse 3 Paul reminds us that we have "died." Now, reflecting a tension between "indicative" and "imperative" that is typical of the New Testament, Paul urges us to "put to death . . . whatever . . . is earthly." God's decisive act on our behalf does not exclude but in fact makes possible our own response to him. In verses 1-2 Paul used the Greek present tense to urge a constant "seeking" and "setting the mind on" the things of heaven. Now he uses the aorist tense to exhort us to "put to death" the things of this earth. Some interpreters have been guilty of overinterpreting the aorist imperative, as if it generally connoted a once-for-all action. This is not true. The aorist simply states the need for the action, without regard for its frequency or duration. Paul probably shifts to the aorist because he wants us to take clear and decisive action with respect to these "things that are on earth." Paul deliberately uses a vague phrase, encompassing any way of thinking or behaving that is typical of this world in its opposition to God. The interpreter needs to be careful of overinterpretation here again. We must not give the impression that everything relating to this life on earth is evil and to be avoided. Many of the activities and pleasures of this world continue to reflect the "goodness" of God's creation and are given to us to enjoy and praise God for. Only those forms of behavior contrary to our new heavenly identity and typical of our life outside of Christ (cf. v. 7) are to be shunned. Paul provides some examples of these forms of behavior in verses 5 and 8. These two short lists are similar to lists of vices that are found throughout Greco-Roman literature. What is important to recognize is that these lists are usually not carefully thought out or exhaustive. Writers seemed rather to provide off-the-cuff examples of the kind of behavior they had in mind. We should therefore note the specific sins that Paul lists in these texts but not assume that these exhaust the kinds of behavior that he has in mind.

In verse 9 Paul adds a final prohibition, against lying. And he grounds it in a final reminder of the change of status that Christians have experienced. This reminder, while directly tied to the prohibition of verse 9, grounds, by extension, all the commands and prohibitions in the passage. Paul uses the language of taking off and putting on clothes to depict the believer's removal of the "old self" (v. 9) and his or her acquisition of the "new self" (v. 10). Paul uses the contrast between old and new self twice elsewhere in his letters to depict the radical transformation of the believer (Eph. 4:22-25; Rom. 6:6). Just what Paul intends by the metaphor is debated, some insisting that we are to think of the "new self" as added to the "old self" at conversion, others conceiving of the "new self" as replacing the "old self." However, what Paul says here in verse 11 hints at another direction entirely. While this is obscured by the NRSV rendering, Paul pretty plainly indicates that the erasure of ethnic, religious, and social barriers takes place "in" the new self. The "new self" appears, then, to be not a part of each human being, but a corporate entity. "Self" translates the Greek *anthrōpos,* which can also be rendered "man." And Jesus, Paul suggests elsewhere, is himself the "new man," while those who belong to him, who are "in Christ," take on that identity (Eph. 2:15). What Paul therefore suggests in these verses is that coming to Christ means severing our tie to Adam, with its consequences of slavery to sin and death, and establishing a definitive and vital tie to Christ, providing for a new life of righteousness and life. And while it is not a major emphasis in this text, the preacher might well want to dwell on the way all kinds of people, tied to Christ, make up the variegated "new self" that is the church.

*Douglas Moo*

## First Sunday after Christmas, Year C

First Lesson: 1 Samuel 2:18-20, 26
(Psalm 148)
**Second Lesson: Colossians 3:12-17**
Gospel Lesson: Luke 2:41-52

The immediate context for this parenesis is in the first portion of Colossians 3. There, responding to the pressures from strains of ritualism and gnosticism in the church at Colossae, Paul reminds the Colossians of their baptism into the death and resurrection of Jesus. They have been raised with him, and their lives are hidden with him. They await, and we await, the fulfillment of his revelation, which will be his glory and ours. This strong paschal emphasis on the Sunday after Christmas is not a problem theologically or liturgically. After all, we only celebrate Christmas because of Easter. Were the baby Jesus not the crucified and risen One, his birth would be of no importance at all.

So this reading from Colossians provides the preacher with a good opportunity to link Christmas to Good Friday and Easter, the incarnation to the crucifixion and resurrection. And that is exactly as it should be.

Verses 1-4 lay out the theology of baptism and resurrection. Verses 5-11 warn of things to be avoided by those who have been joined to Christ and are called to set their "minds on things that are above" (v. 2). At the end of that section Paul moves toward the positive image of stripping off the old and clothing "yourselves with the new self." In this selection for the Sunday after Christmas, he will spin out that imagery further. This is still basically baptismal catechesis flowing from the beginning of chapter 3, but this section gives a more positive description of what the faithful life looks like, just as the previous section illustrated what needs to be avoided.

One might wish that verses 5-11 had been chosen instead. The contemporary church tends to flee the lists of vices. The church is too often co-opted by the culture of self-esteem and easy tolerance, and it is weakened by a tendency to gain the world, or at least a market niche of it, by not giving offense. The desire to accentuate the positive has a pastoral place and the sermon as jeremiad is not a very effective way to communicate either the law or the gospel, but accentuating the positive can tempt modern Christians toward the denial of sin and of the need for repentance and change.

Biblically, however, the need for repentance and change is communicated as powerfully in "positive" instruction as in words of judgment. We should not miss that, and so we can utilize the pericope assigned for this day to talk about themes that have long been understood to be important in the Christmas feast. The second lesson for Christmas Eve for centuries has been Titus 2:11-14 with its reminder that the Savior came to redeem and purify for himself "a people of his own who are zealous for good deeds." Christmas is very much about renewal. Even the vulgar secularization of the feast is full of language of peace and goodwill, and this is a good thing, even if it is most of the time hopelessly disconnected from the birth of the Messiah.

In the church, however, we know that all this is about the birth of the Messiah, and the forgiveness of sins attained by the coming of the Christ is for the purpose of the redemption and purification of a people who are zealous for good deeds, repentance, and renewal. Or in the image of the pericope under question, those who celebrate the birth of Christ are to put on the right clothes. Note the echo of Galatians 3:27: "As many of you as were baptized into Christ have clothed yourselves with Christ," another baptismal catechesis closely related to today's text. Note also the resurrection imagery of being "clothed with our heavenly dwelling" in 2 Corinthians 5 and the way 1 Corinthians 15:53 speaks of putting on the incorruptible and immortality. Being rightly clothed is an important New Testament picture for the new life of those who have come to faith and baptism. It would certainly be appropriate to refer to the swaddling cloths in which Jesus was wrapped or, less biblically, to the new clothes people tend to get for Christmas. Those churches that employ baptismal garments in their baptismal celebrations offer another opportunity to drive the image home.

Still, the most important thing to remember is that what we have here is another of the many occasions in which the New Testament letters follow up glorious theological assertions with the most down-to-earth advice about morality, life in the community of the church, and the behavior appropriate to the righteous. The following section of Colossians is a *Haustafel,* a table of duties for those in various states of life. We have been raised with Christ, therefore we should show patience and be good husbands, wives, and children. This is not a collapse from the sublime to the ridiculous. It is the gospel getting real.

Because the secular Yuletide is so profusely, albeit superficially, moralistic, this text gives the preacher an opportunity to flesh out the moral implications of the incarnation. It is not just a matter of thinking warm thoughts about others and throwing some coins in the kettle. It is about reclaiming the new identity that is ours in Christ. The baptized (v. 12) are "God's chosen ones, holy and beloved." Therefore they should clothe themselves in "compassion, kindness, humility, meekness, and patience."

393

In keeping with Christ's instruction and example in the Lord's Prayer (could that be in the background here?), we are to forgive as we have been forgiven (v. 13). Here the preacher can find occasion to talk about the seriousness of sin and the need to deal with it honestly and directly in ourselves and in our churches. In a culture that thinks reasons are excuses, the preacher can talk about what forgiveness really is and how our excuses are part of our sin.

Peace and love are not just empty slogans. In verses 14 and 15 they are part of the new identity, the new clothing, that is ours *in Christ*. Peace that does not get its meaning from the Prince of Peace is deficient. Love that is not the clothing of the new identity he gives can easily degenerate into ephemeral sentiment, and in our culture it surely does. There is an opening here to talk about how poorly love is understood in our culture, torn as it is between cynicism and romanticism. Love is exemplified by the self-giving of God, apparent in the birth of Christ as well as in his death. When peace and love are properly understood, we can be thankful, as the last short sentence urges us to be.

Verse 16 again addresses life in the church. We are to teach and admonish each other and sing psalms and hymns and spiritual songs. Jesus did not come to give a ticket to heaven to a host of rugged individuals. He came to create a body who in peace and love would reveal the truth of God to the world and live as his representative people. Christmas and the incarnation are about the church and its worship, and since it is one time of the year when everybody likes the hymns, some words about the place of worship and praise would be in order. We are called to love God and our neighbor, and that implies real acts. The love of God is no mere sentiment any more than love of neighbor. It is worship, adoration, contemplation — singing.

The last verse puts all of the new life in the context of the "name" of Christ and "giving thanks to God the Father through him." Sacramental churches will find this last reference at least partially eucharistic. Preachers in all traditions will welcome the way the last line "puts Christ back in Christmas." This selection for the First Sunday after Christmas is no afterthought. It helps place Christmas in its proper relation to the death and resurrection of the newborn babe and to the new life, the new garment, that is ours because of his coming. Just where the preacher needs ammunition for countercultural witness, this text provides it.

*Leonard R. Klein*

## Twenty-second Sunday after Pentecost, Year A

First Lesson: Exodus 33:12-23
(Psalm 99)
**Second Lesson: 1 Thessalonians 1:1-10**
Gospel Lesson: Matthew 22:15-22

*Introduction.* Even in these high-tech days of Internet technology, e-mails, chat lines, and video conferencing, people still write letters. Not surprisingly, the letters we write also reflect the context and the audience to which they are addressed. There are fundamental differences of style and content between letters to colleagues, parents, and friends and an intimate love letter to a spouse or partner. Exactly the same is true of Paul's letters or epistles to the flourishing church communities over which he exercised some authority and control. They all reflect the intimate pastoral and personal relationship Paul had with these fledgling Christian communities. 1 Thessalonians is a good example of one such epistle, and because it is one of his earlier letters, it exhibits certain tendencies and emphases which throw into stark relief the underlying theological, missionary, and pastoral concerns and practice of the apostle and his colleagues, Silas (Silvanus) and Timothy (1:1; see also 2 Cor. 1:19; Acts 15:22; and Acts 16:1).

*Epistolary context.* Recent archaeological evidence supports the consensus that Thessalonica was a thriving, cosmopolitan, and highly successful commercial port city of the Roman province of Macedonia beneficially situated at the head of the Thermaic Gulf. The city enjoyed Roman patronage and yet retained its Greek inheritance particularly in terms of its institutions of internal governance. The city was controlled by several politarchs (Acts 17:6, 8), and the close religious and political ties fostered by the imperial cults of Rome guaranteed economic prosperity and other social privileges to those citizens who did not stray too far into the more exotic religious milieu of the mystery cults and the new religious movements such as that represented by the apostle Paul and his missionary colleagues. Scholars generally concur that the actual circumstances of the mission to Thessalonica should not now be deduced from the Lukan account (Acts 17:1-9) which demonstrates certain conventional Lukan themes and editorial concerns, but from Paul's own account of his missionary activity, particularly that described in Galatians 1–2. Consequently, it is possible to place the Thessalonian mission within the period between the two Jerusalem visits mentioned in Galatians 1:18 and 2:1, that is, the fourteen-year period be-

395

tween his first missionary sortie into the areas of Syria and Cilicia and his return for the important apostolic conference in Jerusalem. From Paul's own correspondence we know that his itinerary led him from Philippi along the Egnatian Way to Thessalonica (1 Thess. 2:2; Phil. 4:16) and eventually to Athens (1 Thess. 3:1). Luke adds an intermediary stop in the more favorable environs of Berea (Acts 17:10-11). However, if we work with the assumption that the senders of the Thessalonian missive are the same as those who were involved with Paul in the Corinthian mission (2 Cor. 1:19; see also 2 Cor. 11:9 and Phil. 4:15-16), then a subsequent stopover in Corinth before reaching Athens is likely. The Corinthian mission can be dated with some accuracy to the midforties, and Corinth probably became the base for Paul's Achaean mission, in which case we can date the mission to Thessalonica in the early forties and the correspondence to the midforties, probably from Corinth and Athens.

*Epistolary style.* While there is a certain scholarly consensus that 1 Thessalonians is probably comprised of two letters given that we have two thanksgiving sections (1:2-10 [compare with Phil. 1:3-8] and 2:13 [compare with Rom. 1:8-9 and 1 Cor. 1:4-7]) and the presence of other puzzling textual anomalies, the most significant factor is that all Paul's letters demonstrate a certain distinctive epistolary style. All except Romans mention at least one cosender, and in 1 Thessalonians his repeated use of the first-person plural ("we") and the lack of any term of self-description (i.e., as an apostle or a prisoner for Christ Jesus) perfectly illustrate his intimate relationship to this community as a missionary cofounder who is reluctant to impose apostolic authority. Secondly, his deployment of parental imagery (2:7, 11) and the frequent use of the familial term "brother(s)" (which occurs twenty-one times in 1 and 2 Thessalonians) reveal a pastor/leader who is frequently concerned and at times deeply anxious about the spiritual nurture and development of these recent converts. Finally, the ethical, ecclesial, and eschatological concerns represented respectively by 4:3-8, 9-12, 13-18, and 5:1-11 exemplify Paul's apostolic credentials as an important theological adviser on all pertinent matters of faith and doctrine.

*Epistolary greeting.* The community or gathering *(ecclesia)* of the Thessalonians to which Paul refers in his opening greeting is one that is defined over and against the pluralistic religious environment of the city by its monotheistic focus, and therefore the rejection of all other gods and idols, (1:9) and its christological grounding in the death and resurrection of Jesus (1:10). It is God the loving Father who chooses (1:4), calls (2:12), gives the Spirit (4:8), wills the believer's sanctification (4:3), and will eventually make us all perfectly holy (5:23). All these benefits are made present reality through the believers' incorporation into Jesus Christ, who has died and been raised for their sakes (1:10; 4:14; 5:10); who is the source of their salvation of grace, peace, and hope (1:1, 3, 10); and who is consequently the Lord who exercises sole authority and power over creation, humanity, and history (5:9-10). Paul's shortened greeting ends with an echo of the Aaronic blessing of Numbers 6:24-26.

*Epistolary thanksgiving.* While Paul's thanksgiving prayer plays a crucial role in opening up some of the important themes of his letter, which is generally the case for all his thanksgivings (Phil. 1:3-6 and Philem. 4-6), nevertheless it reminds us that those who are called to be missionaries, leaders, and pastors of Christian communities are also called to a ministry of continual prayer and thanksgiving in support of such communities. There is a universality, concreteness, and mutuality to such continual prayer that expresses the bonds of love and attachment that unite believers in a common allegiance to Christ (5:17, 25).

None of the three essential Christian virtues Paul mentions (1:3) can be separated from the dynamic of their corporate life as the people of God that defines their ecclesial existence. Their faith grounded in the saving reality of the death and resurrection of Christ is a dynamic, active force that eventuates in a true labor of love both for one another and for those as yet outside their community. It is, as Paul says elsewhere, a "faith working through love" (Gal. 5:6) that resolutely reorientates them toward an active future hope in Christ's return.

*Epistolary certainties.* Overruling Paul's natural fears and anxieties for this new Christian community is his certainty of divine election. Just as God chose Abraham and his descendants, the people of Israel (Deut. 4:37; 1 Kings 3:8; Isa. 41:8, 9; 43:10; 44:1; 45:4; 49:7), in order to reveal himself to the nations, so Paul is convinced that Christians are similarly called, chosen, and justified instruments of God's saving purposes for the whole of humankind (Rom. 5:1-2). God chooses some in order to save all. Believers are a remnant of Israel "according to election of grace" (Rom. 11:5), but that same election now includes people from every nation. Believers were chosen "before the world's foundation" (Eph. 1:4), yet called in their own time and place (2 Thess. 2:13, 14) to be "conformed to the image of his Son" (Rom. 8:29) to receive the gospel which is manifest among them as a message of salvation redolent with spiritual power and conviction (1 Thess. 1:5) so that they can become imitators of the apostles (1:6), enduring the suffering of the cross and scorning the shame and derision of their contemporaries (1:6; 2 Thess. 1:4; Heb. 12:2; Rom. 5:3-5). Election is a missionary prerogative that results in the apparent paradox of joy in the midst of persecution (1 Thess. 1:6; Rom.

5:3, 5; see also Acts 14:22). It is a lasting joy which is both a grace and fruit of the Holy Spirit's presence (Gal. 5:22), and so permits the Thessalonians to become an example to other believers throughout the respective provinces of Macedonia and Achaia. A missionary prerogative founds a missionary community whose resolute faith, welcome embrace of the gospel and the apostles, coupled with their rejection of the economic and political patronage of Rome, like the seismic shocks radiating outward from the center of an earthquake, literally shakes the whole region to the core of their social and political life. Now all have to attend, quite literally, to the reality of the resurrected Jesus who is enthroned as Lord and king of the nations (1 Thess. 1:8-10; Rev. 11:15). Now the eschatological hope of future judgment and salvation becomes both a moral imperative and a gracious invitation to those who wish to turn away from the vain glories of this world (Acts 14:15).

1 Thessalonians sets before us the distinctiveness of a vibrant Christian community in the midst of a pluralistic religious environment. For any pastor, minister, or church leader, it would be worth asking if the missionary context we share with our fellow believers, the homiletic style we use in addressing our congregations, the greeting and thanksgiving we exhibit in our pastoral work radiate with the same confidence and certainty in God's electing grace, Christ's inclusive salvation, and the Holy Spirit's joyful presence as that exhibited by Paul in his opening remarks to this Christian community.

*Colin J. D. Greene*

## Twenty-third Sunday after Pentecost, Year A

First Lesson: Deuteronomy 34:1-12
(Psalm 90:1-6, 13-17)
**Second Lesson: 1 Thessalonians 2:1-8**
Gospel Lesson: Matthew 22:34-46

*Introduction.* It is often the case after a particularly hard and demanding period of work, public ministry or shared common endeavor, that we can look back and see just when the personal battle was won or lost. The benefit of hindsight is that it allows us to examine our motives and appraise whether we were successful or not in realizing our aims and objectives. Indeed, many successful business executives, corporate companies, and now of course Christian ministers and senior pastors expect their staff to regularly undergo personal appraisals so that they can learn from their successes and failures and so increase their effectiveness in whatever sphere of work is their particular responsibility. The importance of this passage from 1 Thessalonians and the tremendous insights we gain from it is that it takes us to the heart of the life-and-death struggle the apostle Paul and his missionary associates endured for the sake of the gospel and the credibility of their public and pastoral ministries. We are introduced to some striking rhetoric, pertinent autobiographical appraisals, and extraordinarily honest and candid accounts of personal motivation and missionary strategy. Elsewhere in his correspondence to the Christian churches Paul can point to difficult contexts where both his life and the effectiveness of his public ministry were on the line, so to speak (2 Cor. 4:7-12; Phil. 1:12-26; Col. 1:24-29). In these verses, however, we are granted a rare glimpse into the soul of an apostle who knows only too well both the fragility of the human earthen vessels and the significance of the divine treasure they contain.

*The morality of public preaching.* More recent investigations of this passage have focused less on Paul's presumed apologia, or defense of his ministry in the face of specific accusations, and more on what we could call his justification of the morality of public preaching. It would appear that Paul employs the language and rhetoric of contemporary preachers of public morality to distance himself from the fame-and-gain activities of charlatan preachers and the sophistry of Cynic philosophers. There are striking similarities between how Paul describes his foundational visit to the Thessalonians and the language used by Dio Chrysostom to denounce the activities of a diverse array of public speakers. What Paul claims he did not do is precisely the kind of deplorable public rhetoric Dio accuses contemporary moral preachers of orchestrating.

On the other hand, no one could accuse Paul of not being interested in success or effectiveness, and that is why he begins by reminding the church at Thessalonica that what he shared with them was not empty rhetoric and so, correspondingly, his visit did not result in failure or rejection. He directs the Thessalonians to their shared experience of a rhetorical contest and struggle similar to the hostility and opposition he endured at Philippi (Acts 16:19-24). The lot of Christian preachers in the public arena was not always a happy or enjoyable experience; rather, they were frequently subject to verbal and physical abuse. The book of Acts is after all a succession of riots and revivals!

The verb in verse 2 often translated "to suffer" and taken to refer to a

399

context of persecution has a more active sense synonymous with the idea of an athletic contest or a vigorous personal struggle (see, e.g., its use in Phil. 1:27-30). So, Paul and his associates struggled valiantly for the sake of the gospel in the face of public opposition and the scoffing of hostile crowds. Again Dio Chrysostom sets the scene for us: "was I not to fear your noise, laughter, fury, hissing, mocking jokes, means by which you scare everyone and always take advantage of everyone everywhere?" (*Oration* 32.22). In contrast Paul, using the rhetoric of Greek political philosophy, points again to the morality of public preaching. He and his associates engaged in "open or free speech" not as a form of harsh moral rebuke, but as public speakers accountable to God, in the context of a strenuous rhetorical contest for public truth, that is, the gospel. Similarly their qualification to engage in such debate was not based on their readiness to endure public scorn and abuse as did the Cynic philosophers, but as God's appointed emissaries or ambassadors (2 Cor. 5:20) with no other motive or credentials than that.

*The morality of apostolic motivation.* Paul introduces the important theme of personal motivation in the context of making a public appeal on behalf of the gospel to the often boisterous and agitated crowds who gathered frequently to listen to the sophistry and persuasive rhetoric of contemporary moralists. He dramatically contrasts the missionaries' motives to those of the charlatan itinerant preachers. Their public appeal did not spring from error or delusion (v. 4) that consists in seeking the praise and adulation of mere mortals (v. 6). They were not tricksters using vain flattery or loquacious, pedantic sophistry in order to achieve short-lived fame and financial reward. Neither did their motives spring from impurity, usually thought to refer to sexual immorality as it obviously does in 4:1-8, but much more likely in this context to refer to the deliberate distortion of the truth for the sake of personal popularity. Finally, they refused to use deception to gain a following, again a common practice of the charlatan moralists, who, Dio Chrysostom informs us, "play upon the credulity of lads and sailors and crowds of that sort, stringing together rough jokes and much tittle-tattle and that low badinage that smacks of the market place" (*Oration* 33.9). By contrast, the morality of public preaching encompasses three crucial areas of deep-seated personal motivation. It is either a question of pleasing God or a public appeal that deliberately distorts the truth out of self-interest. Similarly it leads to either self-promotion or respect and concern for the integrity of others, and it results in either blatant deception and manipulation of public opinion or proclamation with a demonstration of the Spirit's power (1 Cor. 2:4-5; 1 Thess. 1:5-6) on behalf of those entrusted with the guardianship of the gospel (see Rom. 3:2; 1 Cor. 9:17; Gal. 2:7).

If verses 3 to 4a concentrate on the morality of personal motivation, verses 4b to 5 concentrate our attention on the reality of divine examination. Pleasing God rather than pandering to human expectations is a common Old Testament theme particularly when linked with the daily practice of prayer and righteous living (Gen. 5:22; Ps. 69:31; Wis. 4:10), but here it is again applied to the trustworthiness of the missionaries' public proclamation of the gospel. Now Paul is clear that he equally refused the temptation to entertain and pander to the whims and fancies of his audience, either through ribald entertainment, cheapening the gospel message, or resorting to elevated philosophical discourse. Instead, using political and judicial terminology, Paul argues that in much the same way as political candidates are scrutinized and approved by their benefactors, so he and his colleagues were "examined, tested and approved" by God as ministers of the gospel. It is always God, who calls, elects, and justifies, who also scrutinizes the deep recesses of our personal motivations. Paul insists that he did not resort to flattery, which is the opposite of genuine friendship because it involves manipulating others for our own ends. Aristotle concurs with this judgment: "the man who joins in gratifying people . . . for the sake of getting something for himself in the way of money or money's worth is a flatterer" (*Nicomachean Ethics* 4.6.9). Again, Paul insists that he did not act out of avarice to earn a fast buck all in the name of popularity and profitability. He was not looking for "human renown" (v. 6) from either the Thessalonians or the other churches in Macedonia, because the work of God among the Thessalonians established different criteria of success, namely, "you are already our renown and joy" (2:20). Paul clearly wished to establish the independence of his missionary work from any unhealthy reliance on human support or human criteria of success, whether that be establishing a popular public profile, achieving a personal following, founding his own school of thought, or advancing his own reputation. In that sense, as he emphatically declares elsewhere, he and his colleagues "have renounced disgraceful and underhanded ways" (2 Cor. 4:2).

*The morality of missionary strategy.* While Paul is clear that he was prepared to be bold, frank, and robust in his spirited public proclamation of the gospel, he is equally clear that he was not prepared to resort to authoritarian and coercive missionary strategies in seeking the allegiance of the Thessalonians to their newfound faith in Christ (v. 7). He refused to rely on status or to appeal to his apostolic authority; instead he invokes the metaphor of a nurse gently caring for and attending to the needs of her own children. The preferred methods of the missionaries were not unlike those of the Cynic philosophers, that is, gentle persuasion, admonition, and leading by example. Human beings cannot be coerced into the kingdom, and it is only the constant love and affection of spiritual leaders and pastors that encourages new converts to "lead lives worthy of the God who calls them" (2:12). Paul frequently uses the parental model as the only appropriate way to be an effective missionary and leader. Whether as father (1 Cor. 4:14-15), parent (2 Cor. 12:14; also 6:13), or mother (Gal. 4:19; 1 Thess. 2:7) — and to individual converts always as father: Timothy (Phil. 2:22; 1 Cor. 4:17) and Onesimus (Philem. 10) — he heightens the affective and philanthropic dimensions of missionary activity. The missionaries set high standards of fellowship and intimate friendship that went well beyond the call of duty, reflecting instead the close connection between the gospel they preached and the lives of self-sacrifice they lived (1 Thess. 2:8).

The pertinence and probing relevance of all that Paul is saying in these eight verses to every form of Christian ministry should be abundantly clear. For those entrusted with the proclamation of the gospel, there is a morality of public testimony, personal motivation, and effective missionary strategizing that invokes the highest standards of personal and public integrity. When we attend carefully to such criteria of success, then, like Paul, we may be opposed and ridiculed as we seek with others to advance the cause of the gospel, but we will never be ashamed of its inherent power to bring salvation to everyone who believes (Rom. 1:16-17).

*Colin J. D. Greene*

## Twenty-fourth Sunday after Pentecost, Year A

First Lesson: Joshua 3:7-17
(Psalm 107:1-7, 33-37)
**Second Lesson: 1 Thessalonians 2:9-13**
Gospel Lesson: Matthew 23:1-12

*Introduction.* There is clearly an integral relationship between the discussion and themes of these few verses and everything we have been seeking to understand and interpret in the first eight verses of chapter 2. In fact, we are very obviously deep in the same territory of Paul's pastoral and missionary concerns. We have been, and still are, listening in on a very frank and revealing discussion between the apostle Paul and the leaders of the Christian community at Thessalonica. As in many important and significant conversations to which we may be privy, the interpretive key to the whole discourse often lies in some apparently throwaway remark the speaker articulates toward the end of what he or she is describing or recounting.

Such is the case with these four significant verses. If we are truly to understand the apostle Paul's concerns and the passion of his argument, we must look to verses 17 to 20, which describe for us a broader context of interpretation that throws into stark relief the whole tenor and intent of his remarks.

*Moral imperatives that derive from eschatological convictions.* In verses 17 to 20 of chapter 2, we locate the theological foundation to the apostle Paul's concept of Christian ministry, which, more than anything else, fundamentally disassociates him from the urbane sophistry and moralizing of the Cynic philosopher. All of Paul's moral imperatives and injunctions derive from the belief that his pastoral and practical ministry and that of his associates are set in the context of the great eschatological struggle that will herald in the end times (see Mark 13:10; Matt. 24:14).

Paul believes he is part of a wider cosmic drama where his real adversary is not just the inevitability of misplaced plans or limited human resources, but satanic powers and forces. He views his ministry as one of constant vigilance because Satan, the supernatural adversary (1 Thess. 2:18), the crafty deceiver (2 Cor. 11:14), is out to destroy believers by undermining their allegiance to Christ (1 Cor. 5:5; 2 Cor. 2:11), and so thwarting the divine plan and harassing God's ministers (1 Cor. 7:5; 2 Cor. 12:7). In the end his power will be removed (Rom. 16:20), but it is because Paul sets his own concerns and expectations within this wider eschatological context that he feels so intensely the pain of separation, like parents deprived of their children (1 Thess. 2:17).

Similarly, the reason he and his colleagues exhausted themselves in constant effort and sheer hard work was that Paul believed they would be judged before the throne of God on the basis of the integrity of the communities they had founded. Strong Christian believers were the evidence of their missionary stewardship, the culminating achievement of a lifetime of missionary endeavor (Phil. 2:16; 2 Cor. 1:14; 5:10; 1 Thess. 2:19-20). With this wider eschatological context in mind, we can better understand his formidable defense of the morality of public ministry and pastoral care.

*The morality of public ministry.* Verses 9 to 13 make a clear link with 2 Corinthians 11:27. In both instances Paul is referring to the toil and hardship associated with working to support himself so that he and his associates were not a financial burden to the new converts. Here was further proof that he did not preach the gospel for avaricious reasons, but, rather, sharing himself (v. 8) entailed sharing the responsibility and putting in the long hours associated with hard work (v. 9). If indeed 1 Corinthians 4:11-12 and 2 Corinthians 11:27 suggest that Paul and his associates, like the Stoic and Cynic philosophers of the time, were of the artisan class, then the workshop provided both a means of financial support and a further opportunity to share the gospel.

We know that the early Christian missionaries preached and shared the gospel in a variety of contexts. So, whether it was preaching in the city forum, or accepting invitations to share the gospel in households, or evangelizing from the artisan's workshop, in all instances Paul was concerned to allow the morality of public ministry to speak for itself. His basic principle was to put no impediment or "obstacle in the way of the gospel" (1 Cor. 9:12).

While elsewhere he could maintain the inherent right of the missionaries to receive financial assistance or support (1 Cor. 9:3-7; Phil. 4:15-16) from the Christian communities who chose to act as benefactors of the apostles' cause, he was in all circumstances diligent not to compromise the free gift of the gospel, which in turn was the basis of his own freedom of ministry (1 Cor. 9:19-23).

As if to underline his resolve in this regard, he has recourse to three rarely used adverbs (v. 10): "devoutly," "uprightly," and "blamelessly." The first describes Paul's fidelity to the principle just described, the second his loyalty and determination to act properly and justly toward the Christian community in Thessalonica, and the last to divine approbation or evaluation of their conduct. The third phrase therefore acts as a summary statement because, as the eschatological context of Paul's remarks suggests, it is God who opens up the opportunity for future ministry among the Thessalonians (1 Thess. 3:12), and so it is God who will complete the good work begun in them so that in turn they are rendered blameless in the final judgment (3:13).

*The morality of pastoral care.* If Paul has been at pains to lay out the basic moral principles of his public ministry, verses 11-13 take us into the equally important and sensitive realm of the morality of pastoral care. Having argued for the blameless conduct of the missionaries in the former regard, he wants now to establish some important principles of Christian nurture and spiritual development.

Again Paul uses the metaphor of parenting. If the former image of the nursing mother (v. 7) refers to the preaching and sharing of the gospel as the means toward the birthing or conversion of the Thessalonian Christians, here he adopts the model of the disciplining father who is responsible for the moral and spiritual instruction and nurturing of the new converts. Both mother and father should retain an essentially affective relationship with their children. Indeed, as both are responsible for attending to the individual needs of their children, so Paul recognizes the individual nature of long-term pastoral care and nurture.

Christian nurture, again, unlike the moral banditry of the charlatan preachers, does not resort to bullying or endless cajoling of reluctant conscripts. Rather, the fundamental moral principles or virtues of pastoral care are encouraging, comforting, and urging or imploring (v. 12).

Encouragement to greater effort and higher resolve is a frequent Pauline term (2:12; 3:2, 7; 4:1, 10, 18; 5:11, 14); "consoling" is a rarer term and seems in this instance to refer to a context of personal loss or grief, or indeed bereavement, suggested by the content of 4:13–5:11, dominated as it is by the theme of death and eschatological uncertainty (see also 1 Cor. 14:3; Phil. 2:1 for the use of the term in other contexts). Imploring or urging the new Christians to live a life worthy of their calling in Christ takes us into the ethical injunctions and instructions listed in 4:3-12 and 5:12-24. In verse 12 it is clear that the ethical injunctions are initiated by God's call and determined by the nature of his kingdom. In other words, the reality of the kingdom is both a present down payment and first installment (2 Cor. 1:22) of a future destiny where we share in God's glory (Rom. 8:23). That glory we are called to share is reflected in the risen Christ and mediated through the Spirit (2 Cor. 3:18), which in turn is experienced as salvation through Jesus (1 Thess. 5:9).

The inclusion of verse 13 in this lectionary Epistle may seem something of an anomaly given that some commentators believe it is the introduction to another thanksgiving section which was the start of Paul's original letter. In some sense we could argue, however, that the theological concerns of the verse override the apparent literary hiatus. Here Paul directs us again to the powerful sustaining reality of the word of God which, because of its human mediation, establishes the importance of the apostolic office (1 Thess. 2:19-20), and because of its divine significance, manifests itself in living faith and spiritual vitality, both of which are the sustaining center of pastoral care and nurture.

For those who teach or are involved in pastoral practice and spiritual direction, these verses are an important reminder of the biblical virtues and practices that underlie such endeavor. So often we resort to a therapeutic model of pastoral practice borrowed from the human sciences, or to a form of evangelical moralizing which has little or no relation to the morality of public ministry and pastoral care Paul outlines for us here. There is a fundamental integrity to all that Paul outlines for us in both respects, which is based on distinctive eschatological convictions. These, in turn, derive from a theological appraisal of the nature of the gospel as the freedom we enjoy when we live out of the resources of the nurturing and sustaining word of God.

*Colin J. D. Greene*

## First Sunday of Advent, Year C

First Lesson: Jeremiah 33:14-16
(Psalm 25:1-10)
**Second Lesson: 1 Thessalonians 3:9-13**
Gospel Lesson: Luke 21:25-36

*Introduction.* The season of Advent is traditionally regarded as a time of both waiting for and anticipating Christ's imminent return. Paul's epistles, and particularly 1 and 2 Thessalonians, reflect the white heat of radical eschatological expectation. In today's consumer society such an expectation seems to barely apply, and so our churches often lose touch with the pressing urgency of Christ's imminent return that animated New Testament faith and witness.

Perhaps we can rediscover something of the value of this advent theme by reflecting on the sense of waiting and eager anticipation that permeates the whole third chapter of 1 Thessalonians.

In one sense this chapter is a summary of previous concerns and themes outlined in chapters 1 and 2. Hence we find certain recognizable epistolary formulas linked to previous topics of concern such as a clear disclosure formula: "you yourselves know" (v. 3); statements of reassurance: "we often warned you that we would certainly . . ." (v. 4); and statements of responsibility: "such is our appointed lot" (v. 3). These literary devices actually reflect the anxiety and anticipation of an apostle caught in an agony of waiting. Paul was waiting both for Timothy's imminent return from his second visit to the Thessalonians and in keen anticipation for Christ's return so that no longer would both the missionaries and the new converts have to endure the present difficulties that threatened to overwhelm them (v. 3). We need to inquire further into the nature of these difficulties and trials to find the key that unlocks the meaning of verses 9 to 13.

*Shared difficulties and trials.* The usual way of explaining the nature of the trials and tribulations Paul appears to be alluding to in verses 3-4 is to interpret them in terms of Luke's account of the mission to Thessalonica in Acts 17. Here the clear inference appears to be that the new converts, like the missionaries themselves, suffered overt persecution and hostile opposition at the hands of zealous Jews.

The term *thlipsis,* however, occurs forty-five times in the New Testament, and particularly in the Pauline corpus it covers a range of meanings. It can mean oppression, suffering, affliction, or trials and troubles, all of which require careful interpretation in terms of the context in which they are used. So, for instance, suffering can be viewed as instrumental in character building (Rom. 5:3), or it can refer to the difficulties and hardships endured by the missionaries themselves (2 Cor. 1:8), or indeed the anguish experienced by Paul in writing to his fellow Christians (2 Cor. 2:4), or again, not surprisingly, the sufferings associated with the end time (Rom. 2:9).

In terms of the Pauline use of *thlipsis,* it has three dominant strands of meaning. It can refer to the trials and difficulties that are simply an integral part of Christian existence in the world. It can mean the continued suffering of Christ, who shares in the afflictions of his servants and disciples. Or it can denote a context of eschatological tribulation. In 1 Thessalonians 3:3-4 it would appear to refer mainly to the reception of the gospel in a context of great difficulty that Paul alludes to in 1:6. In other words, it highlights the social and cultural ostracization that the new converts experienced through their adoption of a radically new value system associated with their conversion to Christian faith.

So, what Paul and his associates often warned the new Christians about was not the inevitability of brutal persecution by hostile Jews, although this did sometimes occur, but much more likely the more insidious alienation and hardship that occur when a group of people adopt the standards and values of the crucified Savior. The lot of the committed minority who subvert the value system of the dominant ideology is never an easy one, and this experience Paul and his fellow missionaries knew only too well (v. 7). The allusion to the influence of the tempter or Satan, in verse 5, supports this interpretation, because the efforts of the Christian missionaries in sharing the gospel would only have been rendered null and void if the new converts had been seduced back into the old allegiances and commitments associated with life in a pagan environment.

So the splendid news Paul received from Timothy (v. 6), which occasioned the outburst of joy and thanksgiving that permeates verses 9 to 13, was the assurance that the Christian community in Thessalonica had stood firm and remained faithful to Christ. They had done so as well in the face of the inevitable difficulties and hardships associated with Christian discipleship and witness in a context of religious pluralism where the Christian value system was inimical to that of the dominant state religion. The civil religion of Rome that absolutized the power of the emperor was a means toward social and political advancement. In contrast the gospel of the crucified and risen Jesus, as Paul makes absolutely clear elsewhere, was both a stumbling block to the Jews and foolishness to the Greeks and Romans (1 Cor. 1:23), and unfortunately, therefore, often a means toward social, economic, and political oblivion. In verses 9-13 Paul reflects on the necessary ingredients of the Christian value system that both sustain the Christian community living in such a difficult context and paradoxically anticipate the coming of Christ that will put an end to all such disadvantageous social and political relationships.

*Persevering faith.* Chapter 3 begins with an extraordinary, strong statement of Paul's deep anxiety and concern for the well-being and health of the faith of the Christian congregation at Thessalonica. It was for this reason that Paul, against his best interests, sent Timothy on a second visit to the church at Thessalonica (v. 1). Timothy came to test the mettle of their faith (v. 5), to encourage and instruct them in the art of persevering faith (v. 2) that can withstand the trials and difficulties that accompany those who, forgetting what lies behind, press on to obtain the prize of heavenly citizenship (Phil. 3:13-20).

Timothy returned with encouraging news about the quality of their faith (vv. 6-7). Here perseverance is couched in the idiom of steadfastness or standing firm in the Lord (v. 8b). Again the term covers a range of meaning: from resisting unbelief (Rom. 11:20), to maintaining the unity of fellowship (Phil. 1:27), to experiencing and withstanding the difficulties and trials that accompany subversive Christian witness (Phil. 4:1 and 1 Thess. 3:8).

Why, then, if these Christians are standing firm in their faith, which correspondingly helps and encourages the missionaries in the midst of their own difficult circumstances (v. 8) and is the occasion for Paul's deep, abiding, prayerful joy in the presence of God (v. 9), does he crave another opportunity to visit them to supply what appears to be still lacking in their faith (v. 10)? Some commentators assume that the faith of the new converts was consequently still deficient in some crucial respects and that the ethical and eschatological teaching that follows in chapters 4 and 5 was designed to meet this lack. Such an interpretation would appear to nullify the veracity of that steadfastness of faith that both Paul and Timothy found so encouraging.

Perhaps it is as well to keep in mind at this juncture the wise words of Walter Elliot, that perseverance is not one long race but many short races, one after another. It was for this reason that Paul prayed that God would "direct our path to you" (v. 11) so that the very presence of the missionaries among the Thessalonian Christians would be an example of persevering faith which they could emulate (1:6), and an encouragement to continue standing firm in the faith (2 Cor. 1:24).

*Expansive love.* Timothy has reassured the missionaries not just about the strength and vitality of the Thessalonians' faith but also about their expansive love which manifests itself in a radical concern for others (v. 6). It would not be surprising given the intimidating environment of overt and covert ostracization that we have already referred to that a Christian community would develop strong bonds of mutual love and support. Indeed, "love for one another" (v. 12; see also 5:11) becomes a major concern in all of Paul's subsequent epistles precisely because he regards such love, unity, and fellowship as constitutive of ecclesial existence. In verse 12, however, Paul prays for a superabundance of love that reaches beyond the fellowship of Christians to embrace outsiders. He calls upon the one who defined kingdom living in terms of love of God and one's neighbor and who was installed as Lord because he became the servant of all (Phil. 2:9-11), to bring about an overflowing increase in what he would later describe as "the most excellent way" (1 Cor. 12:31b). In other words, even in the face of the difficulties the Thessalonians were experiencing from those committed to other value systems, a ghetto existence was not an option. Instead, Christian existence in the world must be defined by an extravagant expansiveness of love that reaches far beyond the confines of committed believers (1 Thess. 4:9-12; 5:15; Rom. 12:16-18; 13:8-10; Gal. 6:10).

It is the combination of these virtues, persevering faith, and expansive love that would render the Thessalonian Christians blameless in holiness in the presence of God when Christ returns (v. 13). Paul ends his prayer of thanksgiving with a direct reference to Zechariah 14:5, imagining the returning Lord accompanied by his "holy ones" or angels. Clearly then, for those of us surrounded by the dominant value system of consumerism, it will not be easy to adopt an alternative stance. The trials and difficulties we may experience can, however, be offset by the knowledge that steadfast faith active in love anticipates a much richer future and reward.

*Colin J. D. Greene*

## Twenty-fifth Sunday after Pentecost, Year A

First Lesson: Joshua 24:1-3a, 14-25
(Psalm 78:1-7)
**Second Lesson: 1 Thessalonians 4:13-18**
Gospel Lesson: Matthew 25:1-13

In 1 Thessalonians 1:3 the apostle Paul speaks of three virtues, "faith," "love," and "hope," which in various ways he treats in his first letter to the Christian church in Thessalonica. In 4:13-18 he treats the third virtue, "hope."

Paul desires that the believers of Thessalonica not be ignorant concerning those "who are asleep," that is, those who have died, lest they "grieve as others do who have no hope" (4:13). A tomb inscription from Thessalonica well illustrates how few of the pagan population of this city had any hope beyond the grave: "Because of her special disposition and good sense, her devoted husband Eutropos created this tomb for her and also for himself, in order that later he would have a place to rest together with his dear wife, when he looks upon the end of life that has been spun out for him by the indissoluble threads of the Fates" (*CIG*, 1973). After death, Eutropos's only hope of rejoining his late beloved wife is in his burial next to her in the family tomb. A sad letter from Egypt expresses similar hopelessness: "I am sorry and weep over the departed one as I wept for Didymas. And all things, whatsoever were fitting, I have done, and all mine, Epaphroditus and Thermuthion and Philion and Apollonius and Plantas (have departed). But, nevertheless, against such things one can do nothing. Therefore, comfort one another. Fare well" (P.Oxy. 115).

410

Christians may well grieve the loss of loved ones, but they need not grieve as those who have no hope. This is so because we believe that as Jesus died and rose again, "even so, through Jesus, God will bring with him those who have fallen asleep" (4:14). Because of the resurrection of Jesus and the promise of his return, we may have hope in life beyond the grave. But Paul goes beyond assurance of future life; he clarifies the fate of those who have died before the time in which the Lord returns in glory. "We who are alive, who are left until the coming of the Lord, shall not precede those who have fallen asleep" (4:15). The question is pertinent, for it was raised in Jewish as well as pagan circles. The seer in 4 Ezra 5:41-42 (late first century) asks God: "'Yet, O Lord, you have charge of those who are alive at the end, but what will those do who lived before me (and have died), or those who come after us?' He said to me, 'I shall liken my judgment to a circle, just as for those who are last there is no slowness, so for those who are first there is no haste.'" 4 Ezra's understanding is quite similar to Paul's: the living will not precede the deceased, for "the dead in Christ will rise first; then we who are alive, who are left, shall be caught up together with them" (4:16-17). Indeed, some pagan epitaphs spoke of loved ones being "snatched" away, but Paul affirms that those in Christ will be "snatched" up to join the Lord in life everlasting.

The assumption that those who have died are somehow at a disadvantage when the Messianic Day arrives is easy to understand. There are many intertestamental Jewish texts that speak of the special blessedness of those who are alive when the Messiah and/or the kingdom of God arrives. The sage Jesus ben Sira (second century B.C.) declares: "Happy are those who will live in those days and who will be permitted to see the salvation of the Lord" (Sir. 48:11; cf. Isa. 40:5). Similarly, we read in the mysterious *Sibylline Oracles*: "But as many as are pious, they will live on the earth again when God gives spirit and life and favor to these pious ones. Then they will see themselves beholding the delightful and pleasant light of the sun. Oh most blessed, whatever man will live to that time" (4:187-92). The author of the *Psalms of Solomon* (first century B.C.) declares: "Blessed are those born in those days to see the good fortune of Israel which God will bring to pass in the assembly of the tribes" and "May God cleanse Israel for the day of mercy in blessing, for the appointed day when His Messiah will reign. Blessed are those born in those days, to see the good things of the Lord which he will do for the coming generation" (17:44; 18:5-6). Finally, the author of 4 Ezra asserts, in the words of the Almighty, "Understand therefore that those who are left are more blessed than those who have died" (13:24).

Paul states that the dead in Christ will be raised first and then the living will be caught up (or "snatched up") "to meet the Lord in the air." This meeting of the Lord midway (i.e., midway between earth and heaven) probably conjures up the image of celebrants who leave their city and joyfully intercept the approaching king or victorious general, escorting the dignitary to their city. Likewise, the risen, exalted Jesus "will descend from heaven with a cry of command, with the archangel's call, and with the sound of the trumpet of God." In response to this heavenly summons and fanfare, the saints will immediately spring from the very earth to meet and then escort their triumphant Lord.

Paul's descriptive language of Jesus' parousia is parallel to various New Testament expressions (e.g., Matt. 24:31; 1 Cor. 15:51-52; Rev. 11:12, 15) and echoes various eschatological passages in the Old Testament, for example, Isaiah 27:13 ("in that day a great trumpet will be blown"), Zechariah 9:14 ("the Lord God will sound the trumpet"), Joel 2:1 ("Blow the trumpet in Zion . . . for the Day of the Lord is coming"), Zephaniah 1:14-16 ("the great day of the Lord is near . . . a day of trumpet blast"), and 4 Ezra 6:23 ("and the trumpet shall sound with a din, and when all hear it, they shall suddenly be terrified"). But his descent/ascent language may very well allude to Psalm 47:5 (LXX 46:6; MT 47:6):

> God has gone up with a shout,
>     the Lord with the sound of a trumpet.

Paul seems to have utilized this language. This possibility becomes probability when we take into account the evidence that the early church understood Psalm 47:5 in reference to the ascension of Jesus (cf. Luke 24:51; Acts 1:9-11). Because Jesus would return in the same manner as he departed, the language of Psalm 47:5 was also applied to the return of the Lord (cf. Justin Martyr, *Dialogue with Trypho* 37-38; John Chrysostom, *Expositions in the Psalms* on Ps. 47:5; Eusebius, *Demonstratio Evangelica* [Griechischen christlichen Schriftsteller der ersten drei Jahrhunderte 23.2]). God has gone up with a shout, with the sound of a trumpet; in like manner God will return.

In view of Christ's resurrection and scriptural assurances of his return, the faithful may "comfort one another" (1 Thess. 4:18), knowing that the grave is not the end and there is indeed hope in Christ.

*Craig A. Evans*

# Twenty-sixth Sunday after Pentecost, Year A

First Lesson: Judges 4:1-7
(Psalm 123)
**Second Lesson: 1 Thessalonians 5:1-11**
Gospel Lesson: Matthew 25:14-30

"Now about times and dates we do not need to write to you." If only that could have been true throughout church history! Perhaps the Thessalonian Christians didn't need reminders to avoid fretting over the date and time of Jesus' return in glory, but the same cannot be said for a great many Christian groups ever since. In the last thirty years of the twentieth century, precisely such an obsession with times and dates became a cottage industry. A few authors and their publishers even reissued the same books several times, having changed nothing in the text except the predicted date of Jesus' return and just which geopolitical conflict would be the decisive one (the previous date and scenario having come and gone without incident)! Strikingly, these volumes sold almost as well when they were republished with the adjusted information as when they were first released with predictions that had proven patently erroneous.

People want to know what's next. Although obsession with chronological time is nothing new, it seems this tendency has spiked in recent centuries. Desk and wall calendars, day-timers, daily planners, PalmPilots that can hold years' worth of a person's schedule, and the ubiquitous clock all force us to think continually about pegging the future to a certain set of dates. In a global society, doing this well has become something of an art and a skill. Businesspeople and others face challenges that were unknown a few generations ago: we now need routinely to take into account time zones, international date lines, airline schedules, and Greenwich Mean Time. Many people's lives are scheduled out to nearly the hour and the minute to the point that they can barely do anything that is *not* scheduled. In a recent film about the president of the United States, staff workers for the world's most powerful office are seen scurrying furiously day and night to keep up with the demands of their work. At one point one presidential aide says to another, "Well, why don't we knock off to celebrate a little Christmas." The other aide responds, "It's Christmas?" to which his friend replies, "Didn't you get the memo?"

1 Thessalonians is the earliest letter we have from the apostle Paul — indeed, many commentators regard it as the oldest part of the entire New Tes-

tament. It is estimated that Paul may have written this letter around A.D. 48-51. The epistle itself is among Paul's warmest and most affectionate, as he tries to guide this group of fledgling Christians into greater understandings as to the nature of discipleship. We now know that Thessalonica was awash in cults and idol worship, and thus Paul focuses a lot on what could be called "the basics."

Especially in chapter 4 Paul reminds the Thessalonians that they should control their sexuality, control their speech, love each other and their neighbors from the heart. In 4:11 Paul gives remarkably simple advice on what it means to be a Christian in the midst of a non-Christian city: "Make it your ambition to lead a quiet life, minding your own business, doing honest work with your hands." At the end of chapter 5 Paul returns to these basic ideas, urging the Thessalonians to be patient, to smile a lot, to be kind. Being a Christian may mean more than just being nice, but apparently it does not mean less!

Sandwiched into the middle of all that is this lection, which makes it clear that the Thessalonians, like all Christians, eventually had to make sense of their faith also in the cemeteries of life. If anyone thought the message of Easter meant there would be no more funerals, they were quickly proven wrong. So in 4:13 Paul says, "Listen: Jesus lived, died, and rose again. That means death is not the end. Our dear departed brothers and sisters in the faith are with Jesus now. When Jesus comes again, they'll be with Jesus. We will see them again."

This reference to Jesus' coming back leads very naturally to the question, "When will that be?" So, starting in chapter 5 Paul says, "Now, now: I don't have to talk to you about times and seasons, right? We covered that when I was with you. In short, nobody knows." Paul then goes on to say that while Jesus' return will scare some people in the world half to death, it won't be that way for Christians. To those who do not believe, Jesus' return will be like a thief in the night. But Jesus can never seem that way to believers! Jesus cannot appear like a thief to you if he's already been a guest in the house of your heart for years! The only thing that will be different on the great Day of the Lord is that we will at long last be able to *see* Jesus with our own eyes. That may startle believers for the same reason you can jump half out of your skin when you are lost in thought in your den only to have your four-year-old suddenly burst through the door saying, "Hi, Daddy!"

That can scare you so badly you spill your coffee all over your shirt! It's not that you didn't know the child was in the house, you just didn't expect her to bomb in at precisely that moment. But once you overcome the initial fright, you're not terrified to see your child. So also for Christians: we may practically faint with surprise the same as everyone else when the last trumpet sounds. But once that wears off, life will make more sense than it ever did before.

The point of chapters 4 and 5 is to encourage. In 4:18 and again in 5:11 Paul says to remember these basic elements of the gospel, to remind one another of them often, and so to encourage one another mightily. God's got everything under control. And so we live always with the suspenseful awareness that the reality we can see with our eyes is not all there is. God's got more in store for the cosmos, and it's only a matter of time before Jesus returns to make it so.

Yet what's truly remarkable in this chapter is that Paul nestles this advice in the middle of all that other material about leading a quiet and holy life. Paul says that even with the outrageous knowledge that at any moment Jesus could return, we are to lead quiet lives of honest simplicity, kindness, hope, prayer, and joy. In history, when people have so much as suspected that something apocalyptic may be in the offing, they have mostly started to act crazy and changed everything in their lives. Paul says believers *know* how the world will end and that it could be anytime now, but even so, they are to lead quiet, normal, holy lives, not panic-driven, eye-on-the-sky ones.

Raymond Brown has asserted that precisely because 1 Thessalonians may well be the oldest extant document of the New Testament era, its words and theology are arresting. Just imagine, Brown writes, that you were alive about A.D. 50 in the city of Thessalonica. And just imagine you wandered into that little congregation's worship service the day Paul's letter was read for the first time. Already in what we now call the first ten verses of chapter 1, you would hear about the Fatherhood of God, about God's Son who is now a Lord named Jesus, about a Holy Spirit who works in people's hearts by faith, about the resurrection of Jesus from the dead, and about the hope of this same Jesus' return (see *An Introduction to the New Testament* [New York: Doubleday, 1997], pp. 464-65).

Most of Christianity's salient beliefs were already available by the time Paul wrote this very early letter. Compared to the Thessalonians, we know so much about the world, the physical universe, the human body, and so much else that it's not funny. But when it comes to knowing the truth of history and the cosmos, when it comes to what you need in order to live and die in hope, the Thessalonians knew everything we know (or need to know). And it's enough — enough to face the future with confidence that in all things we are the Lord's. The one thing we don't know, according to Paul, is also the one thing we need least to know, namely, the exact date and timing of Jesus' return. Although knowing that would be interesting, according to

Paul it would not change much. Our task would still be the same as it is now: to lead quiet lives of holy simplicity that themselves bear witness to the daylight of God's kingdom presence in which believers already live every day.

*Scott Hoezee*

## Third Sunday of Advent, Year B

First Lesson: Isaiah 61:1-4, 8-11
(Psalm 126)
**Second Lesson: 1 Thessalonians 5:16-24**
Gospel Lesson: John 1:6-8, 19-28

*Introduction.* As we indicated in our study of 1 Thessalonians 3:9-13, Advent inevitably redirects our attention to the context of radical eschatological hope that dominated the faith horizons of the early Christian churches. Indeed, as 1 Thessalonians demonstrates, the apostle Paul casts all his pastoral concerns, his ethical injunctions, and his practical theology of ecclesial life into the searchlight of the imminent return of the Lord of life and death (4:14). There is no sense that the eschatological passages in 1 Thessalonians (1:9-10; 2:19-20; 3:13; 4:13-18; 5:1-11) are in anyway unrelated to the everyday business, joys, and tribulations of Christian life and witness. In fact, the reverse is the case.

So, for instance, Paul's eschatological prayer in 3:13 provides the necessary reason for making sure that the love the Thessalonians enjoyed between themselves also reached beyond their fellowship to embrace outsiders (v. 12). Similarly, the advice he offers in 4:13-18 is directed toward those who have been devastated by the loss of loved ones and are in danger of losing hope. The final section of eschatological reflection, which functions as the introduction to chapter 5, is equally a challenge to those who are speculating about dates and times to be more concerned about the state of vigilance and readiness that should typify those who are children of light and children of the day (v. 5).

416

So in all the sweeping up of various ecclesiological concerns that we find in 5:12-24, the same applies. It is because Paul is convinced that God did not destine his fellow believers to suffer wrath but to attain full salvation through the Lord Jesus Christ (5:9), that he takes the time in these verses to advise the Thessalonians to inculcate certain attitudes and patterns of conduct that will ensure that they remain blameless at the coming of our Lord Jesus Christ (v. 23).

While the lectionary reading begins at verse 16, to adequately put verses 16 to 24 in context we should actually commence at verse 12. We can then discern the striking similarities between 1 Thessalonians 5:12-22 and Romans 12:9-18. The parallels are of a thematic and linguistic nature.

| 1 Thessalonians 5 | Romans 12 |
|---|---|
| 13b *peace* among yourselves | 18 *peace* with all |
| 15 *do not repay evil for evil* | 17a *do not repay evil for evil* |
| 16 *rejoice* always | 12a *rejoice* in hope |
| 17 *pray* continually | 12c persevere in *prayer* |
| 19 don't quench the *Spirit* | 11b be fervent in *spirit* |
| 21b hold fast what is *noble* | 9b hold to *good* |
| 22 abstain from *evil* | 9b hate *evil* |

While the similarities are indeed striking, the differences are also important, reflecting by and large differences of context. The exhortation to reject evil and choose the good in Romans 12 is directed toward the maintenance of community life, while in 1 Thessalonians 5 it is concerned with the discernment of prophetic activity (v. 20). Verses 12-14 offer no parallels with the other passage, while the more general advice of 15-17 corresponds most closely with the text of Romans. Similarly, while there are linguistic parallels between verses 19-22 and the corresponding passage in Romans, the context of the former concerns the presence and activity of the Spirit and in the latter it has to do with the resources that sustain community love. Nevertheless, both passages reveal that combination of general ethical injunctions and more specific pastoral advice that was typical of Paul's theology of pastoral care and leadership.

*Attitude toward fellow laborers and benefactors.* The first group of people we are introduced to in verses 12-13 are the *kopiaō*, a general term Paul uses to designate those who are to be highly regarded because they either render assistance to the community or counsel and guide them in Christian discipleship. The terms could include people like Phoebe, Priscilla and Aquila, and many of the others listed in Romans 16 who minister as missionaries or teachers, or in a more general sense those who are deacons or generous benefactors. In that sense the most obvious parallel is Romans 12:6-7, where Paul is referring to the gifts, functions, and ministries individuals exercise within the community under the Spirit's provision and directed toward the edification of the whole community in love, unity, and spiritual maturity (Eph. 4:12-13). So Paul does not appear to be referring to leaders who exercise pastoral oversight but to those who exercise charismatic gifts and ministries and whose ministry, like those of the founding missionaries, should be held in high esteem.

*Attitude toward fellow believers.* The theme of peace introduced in verse 14 is designed to allow Paul to focus on three other groups within the community who are causing some concern. The first group, described as the *ataktoi*, probably does not refer to the idle (see 2 Thess. 3:6-12), but to the disorderly who are violating what Paul regards as acceptable norms of Christian behavior. So Paul would appear to be briefly reiterating the ethical and pastoral advice given in 4:3-8 and 9-12, asking those within the community to challenge the disorderly to "conduct themselves properly" (4:12) and so live "in a holy and honorable manner" (4:4). Peace is not simply the absence of conflict; it is a state of spiritual harmony and concord that is an anticipation of life in the full presence of Christ (5:23).

The second group is referred to as the fainthearted or discouraged, which, as we have already indicated, most likely encompasses those who have been recently bereaved. As Paul offered eschatological advice in order to increase their reserve of hope (4:13) and comfort them in their suffering, so he asks the rest of the community to act likewise (5:14). Mutual encouragement enables those who are fractured and despairing through the loss of loved ones to face the future with renewed hope and confidence (5:10).

The third group is designated as the weak, which probably does not refer to the physically infirm or the morally lax but simply to those who find the Christian life a socially and individually hard road to travel. The temptation to return to a more socially acceptable and less personally demanding form of religious belief was always present, and with this in mind Paul advocates putting on the armor of faith, hope, and love (5:8) so as to avoid just such a deviation and instead remain steadfast in the faith (3:8).

While verse 15 could be perceived as an example of general moral advice, there is a sense in which it functions as a summary statement in regard to how the community should treat the three groups of people to which Paul has just referred. Here Jesus' teaching concerning nonretaliation, love of God and neighbor, including our enemies, comes readily to mind (Matt. 5:38-48; Luke 6:27-36). Paul advocates a similar response to the disorderly, the fainthearted and discouraged, and the weaker members of the Christian community.

*Attitude toward the Father, Son, and Holy Spirit.* With all this in mind, that is, Paul's careful injunctions in regard to proper Christian attitudes and conduct toward fellow ministers and benefactors as well as those within the community who are more difficult to support and encourage, we can more readily understand Paul's advice in verses 16 to 24. Essentially, what Paul is suggesting is that the believers' attitude and conduct toward others stems from their own spirituality of joyful response to the Christ event. There are clear similarities between verse 16 and Philippians 4:4-6 and Romans 12:11-13. In all three contexts continual prayer and a life of joy and thanksgiving stem from gratitude toward Christ's saving death and resurrection and the recognition that not only is this God's will for our personal spiritual life, but it also provides the resources out of which we can practice hospitality, encouragement, and support toward others.

The importance of both acknowledging and respecting the activity of the Holy Spirit within the Christian community is something Paul has alluded to already in 1 Thessalonians (1:5-6; 4:8). At this juncture he is concerned to remind the Thessalonians of the value and importance of the charismatic gift of prophecy in terms of the building up, encouragement, and consolation of the whole community (1 Cor. 14:3; 1 Thess. 2:12; 5:11). Presumably Paul also has in mind the fruits of the Spirit (Gal. 5:22-23), which he has rejoiced to see in abundance in their community life and which he hopes will enable them to both discern and hold on to what is good in the prophecy delivered and reject that which is inimical to community life (see 1 Cor. 14:29-31).

In verses 23-24 Paul directs the attention of the community toward the eschatological goal of their corporate existence. The God of peace is the one who is in control of the eschatological future and so "will soon crush Satan under your feet" (Rom. 16:20). He is also the one who can guarantee lives of social concord (Phil. 4:9; 2 Cor. 13:11; 1 Cor. 14:33). But here, as in Romans 15:33, he is the God of peace whose sanctifying power will render the believer holy and blameless at the return of the messianic Son. The gift of eschatological holiness is also the reality of personal wholeness, the integration of the human personality in such a way that every dimension of our existence — spirit, soul, and body — mirrors the faithfulness of the God who calls us, the love of the Son who claims us, and the joy of the Spirit who empowers us.

The question remains how we are to appropriate and embrace the eschatological and ethical injunctions that Paul offers to the church at

419

Thessalonica by way of his closing remarks. In that sense verses 23-24 are the key that will unlock the rich texture and meaning of all Paul's advice.

The church in the twenty-first century must similarly learn to live within the tension of the already and the not yet in such a way that the search for holiness is not an extravagant exercise in personal fulfillment but an authentic expression of human wholeness grounded in the vicarious humanity of Jesus Christ.

*Colin J. D. Greene*

# Twenty-fourth Sunday after Pentecost, Year C

First Lesson: Habakkuk 1:1-4; 2:1-4
(Psalm 119:137-44)
**Second Lesson: 2 Thessalonians 1:1-4, 11-12**
Gospel Lesson: Luke 19:1-10

This reading, assigned to the twenty-fourth Sunday in the long season of Pentecost, will be preached on infrequently because the church year rarely makes it through twenty-four Sundays in Pentecost. It will appear only when Easter is very early and thus the Pentecost season is very long. When the Twenty-fourth Sunday after Pentecost does make it into the church year, it's at the tail end of Pentecost, with one eye on Advent. Combined with the story of Zacchaeus and the passages from Habakkuk, which already echo the Advent themes of watching and waiting, this passage can seem benign, almost a throwaway introductory salutation to this letter.

But a close read (a recommended way to approach it, expository style, line by line) invites preaching on how Paul's thanksgivings (vv. 1-4) and the content of his prayer for the church in Thessalonica (vv. 11-12) spell out essential aspects of the Christian life. Without a close read, this passage will seem no more than typical salutatory material.

Paul wrote 1 and 2 Thessalonians to a newly formed church, and these letters are intended to aid the Christians there in the ongoing formation of their life together in Christ amid persecution. We do not know the nature of that persecution (it is referred to in Acts 17:1-10 and 1 Thess. 1:6), and it is not transferable to the lives of most modern Western Christians. But the object of Paul's thanksgivings and the content of his prayer for the Christians in Thessalonica are transferable, and are invitations to reflect on our own faith as we continue to be formed by Christ in his body.

The usual greeting in 1:2, "Grace to you and peace from God our Father and the Lord Jesus Christ," is no throwaway. It can be seen as a summary of all of Scripture, describing what God is up to. God's grace given to us leads to peace: peace within ourselves and peace among us, which Paul talks about in many places as unity. As the church heads into Advent, preparing for the coming of the Prince of Peace, this salutation is an opportunity to proclaim God's peace in contrast to lesser worldly versions. Is this what the watchman waits for on the tower in the reading from Habakkuk?

Paul makes the unusual statement in 1:3 that "We *must* always give thanks to God for you." Here the obligatory nature of thanksgiving arises not out of a sense of imposed duty or in response to a command, but from the quality of Paul's relationship with the Christians in Thessalonica. Gratitude is foundational for life in Jesus Christ. It is the foundation of our life in him, culminating in the Eucharist. The deep sense Paul has of how he must give thanks for God's people invites preaching on gratitude and may stimulate the preacher's own thanks for the people she or he serves.

Paul tells the Thessalonians that he must give thanks first for their growing faith, and second for their increasing love for one another. Faith identifies their relationship to Christ, and love for one another is the fruit of their faith. One is not complete without the other, and Paul sees both at work in them. The connection between faith in God's love in Christ and our love for one another deserves a sermon — perhaps every week! One of the mystics, Theresa of Ávila, wrote that she could not learn anything of the love of God for over twenty years because she could not love the sister who sat next to her in choir! In the Gospel lesson for today, Zacchaeus exemplified both: his response of faith to Jesus transformed his relationship to others.

Paul writes here not about the relationship of church members to the wider society, but about relationships of church members toward one another. Growing faith and increasing love provide a vision of the church as a fellowship where these are learned, practiced, nurtured, and developed. While Christian love extends to our neighbor and even to our enemy, Paul's language about "the love of every one of you for one another" within the church suggests that the church provides the basic training for responsible loving in our wider neighborhoods.

Giving thanks to God for their growing faith and increasing love is closely related to Paul's boasting *(enkauchaomai)* of them among the churches (v. 4). Because we give thanks to God for you, *therefore* we boast of you. In Paul's teaching and usage, boasting of human accomplishments according to the law is forbidden (Rom. 3:27). However, boasting of what God has given us by grace in Jesus Christ is freely expressed and practiced (Rom. 5:11). In his first letter Paul wrote about boasting of them "before our Lord Jesus at his coming" (1 Thess. 2:19, 20); here he boasts of them as a witness to other churches.

The contrast between boasting "in Jesus Christ" and boasting "in the flesh" is clearly made in Philippians 3:3: "For it is we who are the circumcision, who worship in the Spirit of God and boast in Christ Jesus and have no confidence in the flesh — even though I, too, have reason for confidence in the flesh."

Following Paul's thanksgiving for them (1 Thess. 1:1-4), the lection for the day skips forward to describing his intercession for them (1:11-12). Paul's prayer for them, "asking that our God will make you worthy of his call" (1:11), is reminiscent of Ephesians 4:1 where Paul begs the Ephesian Christians "to lead a life worthy of the calling to which you have been called." There Paul identifies the qualities appropriate to the pursuit of God's calling: "with all humility and gentleness, with patience, bearing with one another in love, making every effort to maintain the unity of the Spirit in the bond of peace" (Eph. 4:2-3). These qualities belong in the church in Ephesus, in Thessalonica, and wherever God's calling is heard. Since these qualities are appropriate to the pursuit of God's call, they belong to the "worthiness" that Paul encourages and pleads for in 1 Thessalonians 2:12 and prays for in 2 Thessalonians 1:11.

Paul prays for God's action in them and spells out this prayer so they remember that it is God who gives the growth. Likewise, this prayer expresses the confidence that God will fulfill what he has started in them, will fulfill by his power (not theirs or Paul's) every good resolve and work of faith. The purpose? So that one day what is new for them and hard for them, challenged as they are in persecution, what is only partially seen and known by them, may be fully revealed: the Lordship of Jesus Christ, his glory.

This is the goal of their faith, growing within them and becoming more evident in their love for one another. But the Lordship of Jesus Christ is also the source of their faith. He has planted the seed, watered it, and given the growth. The continuity of the thanksgiving for growth and the fruit of growth and the prayer here that the growth may continue until fulfillment invite the preacher to lay out the full Christian life as a long, God-led process. We can continue to deepen our faith with confidence, even in difficult situations, with thanks and hope and longing for the day when we will see and reflect the full Lordship of Jesus Christ.

As the church prepares to enter Advent and the Christmas season, the focus of many people's energy is directed to family and family celebrations. This passage at the tail end of Pentecost reminds us that we are, in effect, united with one another in the church, the new family of God. With love, thanksgiving, and prayer, this is who God has made us in and through his Son. It is through loving one another in the church that we learn and reflect God's love for the world.

*Annette G. Brownlee*

## Twenty-fifth Sunday after Pentecost, Year C

First Lesson: Haggai 1:15b–2:9
(Psalm 145:1-5, 17-21)
**Second Lesson: 2 Thessalonians 2:1-5, 13-17**
Gospel Lesson: Luke 20:27-38

In the parish, one of many pastoral and theological challenges is responding to people who are caught up in writing about the parousia. Whether it is biblical or current Christian literature on the end times that parishioners are reading, the challenge is to take their concerns (of whatever nature) about Christ's second coming seriously while focusing them on the ongoing Christian life of sanctification and love of neighbor. Strangely enough, it seems that such concerns about the end times are rarely elicited by Advent, the season the church devotes to Christ's first and second comings. This reading, at the tail end of the long season of Pentecost, already has its sights set on Advent and Christ's second coming.

The selection of the particular verses for this Sunday's reading, with much of Paul's response to the Thessalonians' alarm of talk about the parousia omitted (2:6-12), underscores Paul's own pastoral and theological response to the Thessalonian Christians' concern about the end times. This

423

reading is not so much about what will happen at the end. Paul wants to set the record straight, as he does in 2:1-5 (and continuing in vv. 6-12). His real interest is in focusing the Thessalonians on the assurance of their salvation because of what Jesus Christ has done for them. The future he wants them to keep in the front of their minds is not the alarming descriptions of the end times, but their full participation in Christ's glory, as he says in 2:14b. That future, full participation in Christ's glory, that promised future, because of God's love and actions in Jesus Christ, is what is to shape our minds (Rom. 12:1) and give us the strength to stand "firm" (see Eph. 6:10ff. as well as 2 Thess. 2:15).

The "but" at the beginning of 2:13 has enormous significance and shapes the theological emphasis of this reading. It shapes our preaching as well, laying the weight of this passage on God's actions and not predicting the time of Christ's return. Whether Paul or the preacher is speaking of the end times or election and sanctification or, in the midst of alarm and deception, the need for strength to stand firm, Paul's deepest assurance is that God's actions are before and behind us and this world's evil. In other words, God is in charge. Such conviction, such confidence, which leads to thanks (2:13), underlies preaching on this text.

Paul begins this passage by begging his readers not to be "quickly shaken in mind or alarmed" by what some are telling them about the end times. He doesn't believe that what they're being told is simply misunderstanding, but deception (2:3). We don't know what they were being told specifically, but here Paul argues that the Day of the Lord cannot be here yet because certain events, both public and cosmic, haven't taken place. He is writing to Christians relatively young in their faith, and most likely was concerned that their faith would come unhinged, given their alarm, or at the least that they would be sidetracked from Christ's gifts in love. Paul's concerns about how quickly their minds have been shaken invite the preacher to step out of this passage to look at what can shake the minds of parishioners today, new or mature Christians, beyond deception about Christ's second coming. The state of our minds — their ability to be shaken contrasted to our call to live by the renewing of our minds (Rom. 12:1) — is one theme elicited by this Scripture passage.

This passage then jumps, skipping a good chunk of Paul's explanation about the end time, to the recounting of what God has done for them, beginning with choosing them as firstfruits (vv. 13-17). In effect, the "but" is not only a transition but also an answer to the question of how we keep our minds from being shaken or easily alarmed. How do we avoid getting sidetracked by the deceptions and issues of the day that have the capacity to stir us up and divide us? How do we do it? We remember, recount, believe, and give thanks for God's choosing us as his beloved.

Terms such as "firstfruits," "salvation," and "sanctification" need unpacking so that they are living language to the ears of Christians today, so that they ring not only with assurance but with meaning also. Some translations read "from the beginning" in 13b and others "first fruits" to describe when God chose them. It can be read either way. The *when* seems less important than God's choice out of love ("beloved by the Lord") and the connection between being chosen in love and being given a purpose. God's love and election always comes with a call (John 15:16). God's love cannot be separated from God's purpose. God is never "just" Immanuel, that is, just with us, but rather with us in love and calling us. Too often people want comfort but not strength. Paul prays for both for his friends in Thessalonica, both God's comfort and God's strength (2 Thess. 2:17).

The explanation of what God has done leads us to action (v. 15), standing firm, holding fast. If we believe and stay focused on what Christ has done in his death and resurrection, that Christ has conquered evil; that the cross rises above any tragedy, conflict, or violence; and that he has chosen and prepared us to participate in the glory rising from his resurrection, perhaps the call to stand firm and hold fast will make sense. The image of standing firm is rich, especially when our instinct is to do battle, to take on whatever forces assault the gospel. Paul's call to stand firm is a test of our confidence both in Christ's victory and that we do and will participate in his glory. To stand firm calls us not to take things into our own hands, but to rest on our confidence that they are in Christ's pierced hands and Christ has taken care of them for us. Given the combative nature of many issues in our times, both in and outside the church, his call is a challenge, to say the least.

This call here is mentioned specifically in terms of the teaching on the end times in contrast to the deceptive teaching that has alarmed them. At the end of Ephesians, however, Paul uses this same wonderful imagery in a larger context. Put on all the armor of God and do what? Battle? Go after the enemy? Drive out those teaching something other than the tradition? No, stand firm (Eph. 6:10ff.).

The purpose for which God has loved, called, and sanctified us is, of course, to participate in his glory of Jesus Christ (v. 14), which brings us full circle to the questions about the end times and God's call to stand firm because of Christ's victory. Can we somehow in our preaching give Christians a sense of where they're going, into Christ's glory, and that this end, this promised end for which God has done so much to make possible, shapes our living now? Our minds should be fixed on this and renewed by this and not unraveled or sidetracked by worries about when or how the end times might come. Such speculation, with their apocalyptic special effects, can be seductive. But our eyes need to be set on Christ's glory because this is the purpose for which he has loved us, called us, and chosen us. It is this same glory, revealed on the cross, that allows us with confidence to stand firm now in the face of all those opposed to Christ and his reign. We can stand firm because the glory we will fully obtain at his second coming, we now participate in by faith.

The preacher has the great privilege of directing the ears and eyes of his or her listeners toward Christ's glory so that they and we may claim it as our own future. At the same time, we must draw our listeners back to today and tomorrow, when we are called to stand firm in whatever seeks to alarm and unravel us. Christ's glory shines there are well, and even more, it is the "armor" we need for such a stance.

*Annette G. Brownlee*

## Twenty-sixth Sunday after Pentecost, Year C

First Lesson: Isaiah 65:17-25
(Isaiah 12)
**Second Lesson: 2 Thessalonians 3:6-13**
Gospel Lesson: Luke 21:5-19

This passage will not come up in the lectionary often, since the church year rarely makes its way through a full twenty-six weeks of Pentecost. Some preachers will be glad of that because this passage, with its stern command from Paul about not eating if you do not willingly work, seems tone-deaf to the gospel — at first glance. Some universalize it and read it as a statement against government welfare programs. Others react negatively to Paul's use of authority, that is, "we command you." But if we read it in light of Paul's exalted ecclesiology, mindful that this addresses and pertains only to situations within Christian community, we have an example of how Paul addresses a pastoral situation that has the potential to fracture the body of

Christ. It is that community, its unity and right relations, that Paul cares about deeply. He knows what is at stake.

To preach on this passage is an invitation to raise the bar, so to speak, in the local parish. How we treat one another matters. What we assume of others or unconsciously place on their shoulders matters. We are not, after all, a self-selected special interest group, a sect, or a social club. We are Christ's very flesh, God's chosen vehicle of light and grace to the world.

Paul's ecclesiology is perhaps best laid out in his letter to the Ephesians. Here in 2 Thessalonians the implications of that ecclesiology get lived out. In the third chapter of Ephesians Paul speaks of the function of the church as "to make all people see what is the plan of the mystery hidden for ages in God, who created all things; that through the church the manifold wisdom of God might now be known to the principalities and powers in the heavenly places" (Eph. 3:9-10). This cosmic function happens as "the saints and members of the household of God" are built into a holy temple "as a dwelling place of God in the Spirit" (Eph. 2:20-22). And thus Paul calls the body to lead a life worthy of this calling, "*eager* to maintain the unity of the Spirit in the bond of peace" (Eph. 4:3). By living in unity and peace, we are built up into a dwelling place for God, with Christ as the cornerstone, so that through us no less than the principalities and powers in the heavenly places may know God's wisdom.

Thus to fracture Christian community is to fail at our calling and to fail to understand what a high calling God has given us in the church. It is to fail to see that how we treat one another in the church casts a light that is visible even in the heavenly places. Paul's stern command to the Thessalonians invites the preacher to explore the passions and convictions that are at the root of his admonitions. What light do our parishes cast beyond their doors?

Paul's admonition to the idle brothers and sisters here repeats and expands his admonition in his first letter (1 Thess. 4:9-11 and 5:11), there put in the context of love for one another. Apparently some did not work because they were certain that the end was near. Paul does not address this belief here, only their relationships to one another in Christian community. Nowhere does Scripture suggest that the nearness of Christ's return alters his command to love one another and to be eager to maintain the bonds of unity and peace. No Christian belief, passion, longing, or theological position is license for disregarding, diminishing, or dismissing our sisters or brothers in Christ. We are bound to each other in and through Christ.

The economic implications of some in the community not working,

427

and thus asking others to carry their load, cannot be replicated today, since members of parishes are not so financially interdependent as they were in Thessalonica, especially in a time of economic scarcity. But this same dynamic still exists. To give a concrete example, by my unwillingness to give generously to the church, I am implicitly asking my neighbor in the pew to take on her shoulders part of my financial burden. If financial giving were spread evenly over all the shoulders in a parish, the burden would be light (and the stewardship great). How a preacher addresses concrete situations in his or her parish in light of this passage calls for pastoral discretion. But helping parishioners see the unconscious burdens we place on the shoulders of others in the body, by our own unwillingness to give, is to cast light on our call as Christians in Christ's body. As Paul says in Ephesians, when *each* part of the body is working properly, it grows and builds itself up in love and into Christ, who is its head (Eph. 4:16).

Rather than let the situation sort itself out, Paul directs the Christians in Thessalonica to take action. (One can speculate on what might have happened to this community if the situation was left to work itself out.) He instructs them "to keep away from believers living in idleness," to imitate his example (not the example of the idle), not to regard the idle as the enemy but to warn them as unbelievers, and finally to remember the command he gave them while with them, that those unwilling to work should not eat. Likewise he directly addresses the idle to "do their work quietly and to earn their own living" (2 Thess. 3:6ff.).

The challenge of Paul's plan of action is how to continue to see the idlers as part of the church and yet to keep away from them. They are not to eject them, certainly not to admire or copy them. It would be easier to kick them out and see them as the enemy, as Paul tells them not to in 3:15. But Paul continues to know them as a part of the body. It is not for the members here to decide who is and who is not a part of Christ's body. It is, however, for them to decide whom to imitate and whom not to imitate. Ultimately Christ has decided that for the body.

The role of imitation of another Christian, as a part of our formation in the body of Christ, is at the center of Paul's command to them and his recommended action. Imitation includes whom to imitate and whom not to imitate. While with the Thessalonians, Paul went to great lengths so as not to be a burden to them. Though he had the right to receive food without working (other than preaching the gospel), he intentionally surrendered this right to the higher good of not burdening the community and establishing an example to imitate. This is the pattern we are to imitate, having in mind our relationship to our sister or brother rather than our own rights. It is Christ's own pattern of giving up equality with God and taking the form of a slave for our sakes (Phil. 4:5-9).

Where in Philippians Paul says they are to have this mind of Christ among them, to the Thessalonians he gives himself as an example of this Christlike mind and commands them to imitate it. Paul is an example of the Christian life shaped by life in the body of Jesus Christ, with Christ's own example at its head. That body, born and sustained by Christ's willingness to give up his rights, is the place we also learn to imitate such Christian love.

The powerful role of the body of Christ, both in its God-given role to reveal God's love in the heavenly places and to shape our understanding of what it means to follow Jesus, is a powerful message in a culture of private, individualized Christianity that thrives on individual rights. It is by learning to live with such people as the idlers, in that difficult situation — not letting their behavior fracture community, neither excommunicating them from it — that they learn about their place in God's great plan for the cosmos.

*Annette G. Brownlee*

## Seventeenth Sunday after Pentecost, Year C

First Lesson: Jeremiah 4:11-12, 22-28
(Psalm 14)
**Second Lesson: 1 Timothy 1:12-17**
Gospel Lesson: Luke 15:1-10

1 Timothy is occasioned by Paul's fear that false teachers may subvert the ministry of the gospel in Ephesus (1:3-11) and by his firm commitment to Timothy, his young colleague and "child in the faith" (1:2), who is assigned the difficult task of organizing Christian congregations there. The community's "rule of faith" is Paul's own interpretation of God's "glorious gospel" entrusted to him (1:11). The present Epistle reading is autobiographical and reminisces on Paul's conversion to Jesus — an experience of divine calling but also of divine mercy that evidently funds the content of what he proclaims as gospel.

429

Whatever one's position on whether Paul actually wrote these words, and scholars remain divided on this matter, their rhetorical intent is perfectly clear: God's gospel, entrusted to Paul (1:11), is centered on "Christ Jesus, [who] came into the world to save sinners" (1:15); and that he might be put on public display in the transformed lives of those sinners who "come to believe in him for eternal life" (1:16). The implication of this evangelical calculus in light of Paul's warning about false teachers is that their preoccupation with myths, genealogies, and endless speculations rather than with the faithful management of God's household (1:4) stands in radical contrast with the content and practical results of his gospel ministry.

Noting that Paul begins this passage with a note of gratitude, some scholars suppose that its overarching role in 1 Timothy is similar to Paul's use of epistolary thanksgivings to introduce and ground his letters in particular claims about God. Similar in form if not also in function, the passage begins with thanksgiving and concludes with a formal doxology (1:17). In this case, however, his referent is "Christ Jesus our Lord" rather than God, and the subject is himself rather than his audience, since it is the living Jesus who encounters him on the Damascus road both to convert and to commission him as a Christian missionary. It nevertheless seems clear that Paul uses his reminiscence of that life-changing experience to clarify the core theological terms of his gospel and its transforming results in sinners. I doubt that he is doing so to defend himself or his gospel; rather, he is interested in supplying his young colleague with an example to follow as he contends against false teaching.

Paul begins his personal testimony with the grateful admission that Jesus has "strengthened . . . and appointed me to his service" (1:12). The verb "to give strength" refers more to Paul's self-confidence or personal authority than to his individual talent, his powerful rhetoric, or his substantial theological education; it derives from his "appointment" to preach the gospel. Significantly, while the critical Greek text prefers action in the aorist tense, positing Paul's authority in his prior encounter of Jesus and probably on the Damascus road, an alternative reading of this verse, attested very early, prefers the present tense, which suggests that Paul's authority and appointment to preach the gospel are predicated on his ongoing and dynamic relationship with the living Jesus and are not tied to some past encounter with him (Luke T. Johnson, *Letters to Paul's Delegates*, New Testament in Context [Valley Forge, Pa.: Trinity Press International, 1996], p. 118). If the portrait of Paul in Acts shapes our reading of Pauline autobiography, both meanings are possible and even likely. Without question, Paul's authority according to Acts is not tied to an apostolic office but to his Damascus road commission; however, it is also clear from Acts that Paul is authorized and led by his ongoing encounters with Jesus, whether mediated through his Spirit or via visionary episodes.

The crucial catchphrase of Paul's testimony is "But I received mercy" (1:13, 16). The idea of "receiving mercy" is central to Paul's own conversion experience and funds his understanding of God's salvation. On the one hand, Paul carries over from the Old Testament the substantial weight of a theology of God's "mercy" — God's covenant faithfulness to a promise made to Israel that obliges God to maintain good relations with Israel even though Israel does not deserve them. God's mercy offends all notions of fair play: God routinely shows kindness toward the unfaithful. On the other hand, Paul's idea of God's mercy is active: *mercy is a verb of God's activity that is conjugated in Paul's own experience.* The experience of being "mercy-ed" by God is in contrast ("But . . .") to Paul's prior human and religious experiences. This contrast frames for Paul the concrete, real results of God's mercy and the persuasive power of his gospel: once a sinner, but now saved. It must be this transforming effect of God's mercy in the sinner's life that Paul has in mind when he says Christ assesses him to be "faithful" when appointing him, an ignorant sinner, to preach the gospel (1:12). Paul's spiritual capacity to complete the missionary tasks given him are evidently related not to what he was but to what he would become by God's mercy.

The transforming effect of God's mercy in Paul's life cuts two ways. Before he encountered God's mercy in the living Jesus on the Damascus road, Paul was "a blasphemer, a persecutor, a violent man" (1:13). The referent of this catalogue of vices within a Pauline autobiography is, of course, Paul's preconversion life. Rarely does Paul refer to himself as a sinner, as here; however, when he does, the purpose is paradigmatic of Christian conversion and so of the gospel he is called to proclaim.

We are certainly familiar with Paul the persecutor (1 Cor. 15:9; Gal. 1:13; Phil. 3:6), perhaps even with his violence against the church (cf. Acts 8:1-3), but not with Paul the blasphemer, which strikes us as odd (cf. Phil. 3:6; Acts 22:3-5). Paul's intent here is probably rhetorical — to draw even more sharply the contrast between his pre- and postconversion personas. As recipient of God's transforming mercy, his violent (i.e., insolent, contemptuous) treatment of others is turned into "love," and his blasphemy (i.e., disrespect, "unbelief") of God is turned into "faith" (1:14).

Some have noted an implied contrast between the source of Paul's sin, which is "ignorance" (1:13), and the false teachers, who are "blasphemers" (cf. 1:20), even though they have heard the gospel and are no longer ignorant of its claims. If so, Paul is not likely optimistic that these opposing teachers will share in a similar conversion experience; rather, his purpose is to issue a sharp rebuke of their practices that should justifiably result in their removal from Christian fellowship (cf. 1:20).

Paul's experience of God's transforming grace is formulated into a memorable saying of faithful people: "Christ Jesus came into the world to save sinners, among whom I am foremost" (1:15; cf. Luke 19:10). The text remains unclear whether Paul appeals to this saying to provide support for his personal experience of God's mercy or whether this saying interprets that experience. The choice the expositor makes is critical. If the former, then church tradition stands prior to and tests human experience, whether Christian or not; but if the latter, then church tradition is the theological precipitate of and follows from our experience of God's grace. The logic of Paul's argument to this point of his letter would seem to require the latter reading. Paul was hardly ignorant about God or of the Scripture's witness to God, yet he remained ignorant of God's mercy, which he came to know through his experience of conversion and transformation. His condemnation of the false teachers, who "desire to be teachers of the law" (1:7), is not a condemnation of Jewish tradition, which has its legitimate uses (cf. 1:8). Rather, his condemnation of them is that they lead sinners to the wrong fount to confirm the gospel — to the law rather than to a robust experience of mercy, which comes by trusting in Jesus Christ for eternal life (1:16).

Finally, Paul's testimony of his conversion evokes a doxology (1:17) that gives thanks to God, the only God, for this gift of eternal life, reminding Timothy that God is the sole source of Paul's transforming experience and the hope of the salvation they share.

The expositor will note several connections between this passage and the Gospel lesson from Luke 15:1-10. First, Jesus identifies with sinners who draw near to him, ever aware of their need for a Savior (15:1). The religious conflict this provokes among the Pharisees (15:2) may be reread by the testimony of the Pharisee, Paul, whose initial hostile response to Jesus was the result of his ignorance; that is, the Pharisees "murmured" in response to Jesus' table fellowship with sinners because they were ignorant of his true identity as Son of God Messiah and the announcement of God's salvation he brings near to them. Second, both parables Jesus tells (15:3-6, 8-9) and their common lesson of heaven's delight in a single sinner's conversion (15:7, 10) may well be the Lord's testimony of Paul's own conversion: Paul is that sinner wandering on the Damascus road, who is found by a merciful Lord seeking to rescue the lost (cf. 19:10). Finally, the climax of both parables is the joyful celebration of the heavenly community when even one sinner is saved (15:6, 9). The incomparable value God places on the church's mission to the lost is the subtext of Paul's testimony to Timothy and should encourage us to bear witness to the "glorious gospel of the blessed God" in the world.

*Robert W. Wall*

## Eighteenth Sunday after Pentecost, Year C

First Lesson: Jeremiah 8:18–9:1
(Psalm 79:1-9)
**Second Lesson: 1 Timothy 2:1-7**
Gospel Lesson: Luke 16:1-13

Timothy's difficult vocation is to organize Christian congregations in pagan Ephesus. Cued by the exhortation "I urge you," the present lesson begins an extended catalogue of Paul's practical instructions covering a range of issues (cf. 1 Tim. 2–3), addressing several challenges his young colleague must face in living out his vocation as a minister of the gospel (cf. 2 Tim. 1:6-7). Various proposals have been put forward as to whether Paul's advice to Timothy evinces an organizing theme. Probably so: most commentators suppose that Paul aims to form Christian congregations after the pattern of a household — as a "household of God" (so 1 Tim. 3:15). Properly functioning households were considered the cornerstone of an orderly, stable society in Paul's world. Issues of authority, proper manners, and responsible relationships were of central concern to the moral philosophers of the day, and the New Testament routinely adapts these same concerns to the social life of the church.

In the present passage, two different — often competing — human families are in view, the one constituting a secular household, with "kings and those in high positions" (2:2) as head, and the other a sacred household, with God, the only God (2:5), as head. Paul's instructions are given in part to resolve the tension created by the competing loyalties and values between the sacred and secular households in which believers are citizens. In the case of 1 Timothy, however, the social stability of congregational life serves a missiological (rather than sociological) end. If God desires everyone saved (2:4) and initiated into eternal life (1:16), then the practices of God's "household" should aim its common life in the same direction: at the salvation of all people.

This passage forms a compact unit which commands the congregation to pray for all people. Paul's instruction regarding prayer is noteworthy, not only by placing it "first of all" (2:1) but by its sheer length: it is the longest discussion of prayer in the New Testament. Some suppose this emphasis is due to the presence of false teachers in Ephesus, whose work threatens to subvert Timothy's ministry. This emphasis on prayer is a tacit rebuke of those "teachers of the law" more interested in religious sophistry than piety (cf. 1:4-5). The "therefore" that begins Paul's instructions (2:1) assumes that Timothy has heard the relevant contrast made in chapter 1 between the false teachers and their miserable destiny (1:18-20), and Paul, the exemplar of Christian ministry (1:12-17). Others think there are divisions within the congregation that make corporate prayer impossible. Paul's emphasis on praying together is another way of encouraging an increased unity of life and Christian witness.

In either case, two brief observations about the importance of congregational prayer should frame any exposition of this text. First, God's household must be ordered to serve God's purposes. The prayers of the household are an essential exercise by which its members grow in their spiritual understanding of God's purpose for them in all of life. One should not make too fine a distinction between the four general terms used to describe the congregation's prayers — "petitions, prayers, intercessions, and thanksgivings" (2:1). Paul's intent is rather to emphasize that the congregation's communication with God should cover all aspects of life.

Second, if that purpose is to advance the gospel in the wider community, then prayer must support the congregation's outreach program. In Paul's mind evangelism is the church's primary social ministry, and prayer serves that ministry when the congregation prays "for everyone" (2:1) so that "everyone [is] saved and comes to the knowledge of the truth" (2:4). The universal scope of the church's evangelistic concern is reflected by the next phrase, which repeats the preposition "for" (*hyper*) to underscore those the congregation might be inclined to omit in their prayers: "rulers and those in high positions." Paul knew well the practice of praying for pagan authority from the Diaspora synagogue — wisdom learned from Daniel's example to ensure peaceful relations with hostile powers. In other writings Paul extends this wisdom to a theological principle, so that civil authority is ordained by God to maintain a public morality that accords with God's de-

434

sire for good works (cf. Rom. 13:1-4; 12:2). Luke Johnson points out that Jews and Christians of the first century felt a deep solidarity with their social world as a faithful response to the Creator's provident care for all things (*Letters to Paul's Delegates* [Valley Forge, Pa.: Trinity Press International, 1996], pp. 129-31).

Paul's intent is quite different here: the congregation should pray for the conversion of their pagan leaders as the means of social reform. The terms of the purpose clause describe prayer's result as a "quiet, peaceful, godly, and respectful life" — all terms used in the Pastoral Letters to describe a genuinely Christian life. The public prayers of the Christian community hardly reflect a program of social domestication as some suggest, then, but a Christian mission that boldly evangelizes the surrounding pagan culture from top to bottom.

At this point Paul begins to articulate the theological (and more subversive) foundations for prayer. The prayers of believers are not duties performed by "good citizens" to favor the Caesar, for Christianity is not a civil religion. Christian prayers are offered to God according to God's standard (2:3) and intend to mark out this household as belonging to God. The subtext of Paul's instruction to pray to the "one God" (2:5) for the Caesar's salvation is clearly political, however, since such prayers refuse to admit that the Caesar is sovereign or has ultimate control over the church's destiny. Paul's use of "acceptable" *(apodektos)* may allude to the Old Testament liturgy of offering acceptable sacrifices in worship of God (cf. Lev. 1:3-4; 17:4; et al.). Again, the issue at stake is not so much that prayers have replaced sacrifice as the normative mode of Christian devotion, but rather that what pleases "God the Savior" are prayers that seek the salvation of all people (2:4), including pagan rulers.

The inclusiveness of God's redemptive plans probably intends to overturn an element in the doctrine of salvation pressed for by Timothy's opponents. Paul's concluding emphasis on his call to carry the gospel to the Gentiles (2:7) may well reflect the principal controversy provoked by his Gentile mission, namely, the demand by some Jewish believers that Gentile converts to the faith must become Jewish proselytes (cf. Acts 15:1-5). Paul of course rejects this Jewish convention, arguing that God's desire is that everyone be saved (2:4), whether Jewish or Gentile and whether or not they ultimately accept the truth of the gospel. Indeed, the central truth of the gospel is that God, the only God, is "our Savior" (2:3), who alone establishes the pattern by which everyone is saved. All competing notions of what is true about God's salvation, including those held by those who oppose Paul's mission, are exposed by the congregation's prayers as fraudulent.

435

The opening "for" *(gar)* that frames verses 5-6 introduces a "footnote" to the final phrase of verse 4, "the knowledge of the truth," and serves to define in formal theological terms the universal scope of God's plan of salvation. In fact, Paul's concluding though awkward phrase, "this [saying] was attested at the appropriate time" (2:6b), probably qualifies what has been written here as an official summary of the "knowledge of the truth."

1. "There is one God." This apt summary of Jewish monotheism serves not only to locate "kings and all who are in high positions" in their proper place but also to challenge any notion that supposes God has multiple plans of salvation, one for Jews and another for Gentiles. One God has one plan.

2. "There is one mediator between God and humankind." Although this is a christologically laden phrase with inferences of the crucified Christ's mediation of God's new covenant (see esp. Heb. 8–10), Paul's primary meaning here is more diplomatic: God's offer of universal salvation is tendered by a single ambassador; to receive it from any other source on any other grounds is bogus. In this context, Paul's subsequent reference to himself as herald and apostle (2:7), appointed by command of God (1:1), is suggestive of an ambassadorial role: he is "undersecretary" of God's kingdom, who mediates the gospel of God in Christ's absence.

3. "Christ Jesus, himself human." The reference to Jesus' humanity seems awkward at first. Some suggest that it goes best with the next phrase, which speaks of Jesus' death; certainly Paul's Adam Christology requires the connection of the Lord's humanity with his atoning death (cf. Phil. 2:6-8). Yet I doubt this connection is intended here. Rather, Paul extends his reference to Jesus' role as an effective broker of God's salvation to all people on the basis of shared humanity. My sense of this phrase, then, is more incarnational: God discloses God's desire to save everyone by becoming one of us.

4. "[Christ Jesus] gave himself a ransom for all." Again, Paul employs a theologically rich idiom. In Paul's social world, payment of a "ransom" freed slaves from indenture; and perhaps the most important theological symbol of Paul's Jewish world is of a God who liberated an enslaved Israel from their captivity to a foreign power to live in a land all their own. Yet the reader may well have expected him to conclude this saying with a more traditional Pauline doctrine of redemption: "who gave himself a ransom *for sin*" (cf. Titus 2:14). Instead Paul repeats "for all" *(hyper pantōn;* cf. 2:1) because under the present circumstances he is pressing for the universal scope of God's salvation as the principal theological reason why the congregation should pray for everyone, even for their pagan rulers. Sharply put, Chris-

tians pray for pagans because Christ died for them according to God's plan of salvation.

Paul has already mentioned to Timothy that this gospel that seeks the salvation of all has been entrusted to him (1:11), and under spectacular circumstances (1:12-16). The concluding verse of this unit (2:7), however, focuses on two new elements of Paul's autobiography. First, according to his apostolic vocation, his primary tasks are to *preach* (or "herald") and *teach* this gospel to the Gentiles. The book of Acts, which supplies the biblical reader with a narrative context for reading Paul's letters, underscores the universal scope of Paul's mission: if the plan of God's salvation according to Scripture includes Jews and Gentiles, then so must Paul's mission. In Acts Paul, challenged by Diaspora Judaism, understands himself as a teacher of Israel (even though his primary success as a missionary is in establishing a Gentile church). In 1 Timothy Paul, challenged by Jewish Christians, understands himself as a teacher of Gentiles.

His instruction, as with the community's prayers, aims at bringing Gentiles to a knowledge of the truth about God's salvation (cf. 2:4). The addition of "faith" here is interesting, in part because of how faith words are used in the Pastoral Letters. Rather than referring to the act of saving faith, "faith" is here used to refer to the beliefs and practices of Christian faith, which any Christian teacher would seek to clarify — especially in a setting where false teaching influences, as here, the direction of Christian formation.

This New Testament lesson helps illumine the Gospel lesson, Luke 16:1-13. The lesson learned from the clever but unscrupulous manager of Jesus' controversial parable is this: use worldly wealth in service of your heavenly Master, since "no slave can serve two masters." The purpose and content of the congregation's prayers, Paul asserts, must serve absolutely the purposes of God the Savior, who desires to save everyone and not just a few. Our prayers, as with all of life, must reflect such single-minded devotion to God's redemptive plans rather than the spiritual schizophrenia that elevates other commitments, whether acquiring wealth, a successful career, or some other worldly devotion, to the same level as our obedience to God's will.

*Robert W. Wall*

## Nineteenth Sunday after Pentecost, Year C

First Lesson: Jeremiah 32:1-3a, 6-15
(Psalm 91:1-6, 14-16)
**Second Lesson: 1 Timothy 6:6-19**
Gospel Lesson: Luke 16:19-31

Typical of Paul's letters when he turns them toward the end, this passage at first glance consists only of miscellaneous exhortations and instructions, and lacks coherence. Closer analysis, however, discovers a sharp focus that contrasts Paul's ideal pastor with the profile of his opponents in Ephesus — a contrast that is the subtext of the entire composition. In this sense, then, the present lesson is a summing up of Paul's letter to Timothy.

In the first half of the present lesson (6:6-10), Paul's famous concern for "the love of money" (6:10) actually concentrates what for Paul is the primary motive for the misconduct of his opponents and their teaching, which "does not agree with the sound words of our Lord Jesus Christ" (6:3): greed. Such an assessment continues the familiar verdict of Jewish wisdom (as well as the currents of popular secular philosophy in Paul's day), expressed well in the Old Testament wisdom book of Ecclesiastes: material and transitory pursuits should be considered "vanity" in contrast to a life with God that lasts forever (cf. Eccles. 5:15). This same sentiment is found in the New Testament book of James, which is deeply indebted to the Jewish "piety of poverty" tradition and its core value of a richness of one's faith in God over the trappings of material well-being.

The believer's primary disposition toward wealth is rather "godliness combined with contentment" — a memorable phrase that brings together two important words in a Pauline glossary of the Christian life. Paul claims there is "great gain" in a life so characterized. "Godliness" *(eusebeia)* is a catchword used frequently and importantly in the Pastoral Epistles of a life that is truly and distinctively Christian. Recent critics suppose that it reflects the later Pauline tradition's accommodation with the secular order, since it is a favorite word of secular philosophers. Nothing could be farther from its Pauline usage, however, which routinely refers to the courageous practice of God's will according to Christ's example (1 Tim. 3:16; 2 Tim. 3:12) and teaching (1 Tim. 6:3).

The moral gravity of this catchphrase, however, lies on "contentment," which here characterizes the minister's godliness. According to secular philosophy, the noble person lived with such "contentment," which meant self-sufficiency in two ways. First, the contented person is sustained by his own internal resources — soul food — rather than by material possessions. Second, the contented person is not acquisitive, constantly longing for a new and better "toy." This connotation is drawn out in 6:7-8, where Paul combines proverbs about the long view of life ("from dust to dust") and the basic material necessities of life. The subtext may well be from the "sound words of our Lord Jesus Christ" found in the Gospel lesson, where Jesus contrasts the destiny of the rich man, who received good things in this life, with Lazarus, whose creaturely comforts awaited him in the age to come (Luke 16:19-31). Paul's solidarity with the poor in his own ministry makes him profoundly suspicious of both wealth (cf. 1 Tim. 6:9-10) and the wealthy (cf. 6:17-19). The tensions provoked by a memory of Jesus' teaching, carried forward by Paul in these concluding exhortations, are more likely more severe and serious in an urban church, where public pretensions of wealth and status were more prominent.

Although Paul's wisdom serves the rank and file of the community, his particular focus here is upon its leaders who, like Timothy, "teach and urge these duties" (6:2). Thus the contrasting vices of those who are ambitious for wealth and fame, described in 6:9-10, frame the character of those who seek to lead with a false gospel in hand and subvert the practices and faith of Christian witness as a result. In Paul's mind they do so simply because they are greedy people, and he leaves no doubt in Timothy's mind what their destiny is as a result: they are "plunged into ruin . . . and are pierced with many pains." The collection of vivid and familiar images of destruction found in 6:9-10, stated in hyperbole, underscores the great peril of wealth. Paul's intent seems both to remind Timothy that at "the root" of lasting contentment is "godliness," but also to encourage an honest appraisal of the true costs of pursuing a career for a paycheck — an ambition that is at "the root" of those entanglements and activities that destroy a person's life.

The second half of this lesson (6:11-19), which concludes with a positive exhortation to the congregation's wealthy (6:17-19), concerns the lifestyle of its leaders. The precise meaning of Paul's charge to "keep the commandment" (6:14) is unclear; however, it is probably best to understand it in reference to the various moral qualities Paul has made clear to Timothy throughout this letter. Paul charges Timothy to be a certain sort of person, whose moral purity exemplifies the God he serves and heralds the coming triumph of God at Christ's epiphany (6:14). Indeed, the remarkable theological claim on the "man of God" (i.e., Timothy) found in this passage is of paramount importance for Paul. Timothy's life is modeled after a generous God (6:18), the only God (6:15), who alone "gives life to everything" (6:13), richly providing for our present enjoyment (6:17) even into the coming age that will never end (6:15-16). This is, Paul asserts, "the life that really is life" (6:19).

This positive, hopeful orientation toward life, deeply rooted in who God is, forms a very different outlook toward wealth than that which threatens Paul's opponents, who "love money." Rather than the preoccupation of one's life, wealth funds "good works" and the purchase of future dividends that will be cashed out in the age to come. The catchphrase "good works" is frequently used in the Pastoral Epistles of activities that please God and accord with God's will. If God is generous with life, then the wealthy "man of God" must embody that same generosity toward others. This particular duty of the wealthy to care for the poor is well attested both in biblical wisdom and in secular philosophy. In Paul's hands, however, a radical criticism of wealth takes place, based not only on practical principle (do not bank on "the uncertainly of riches" [6:17]) but also on theological conviction (bank rather on a future with God, "who alone has immortality" [6:16]).

Paul's economic policy is framed by his profound confidence in the future of God: the believer spends money on projects of mercy that build spiritual revenues for the coming age. This same forward thinking is what earlier prompts the prophet Jeremiah to purchase land near his home in obedience to God's word, even though he was imprisoned and the Babylonian armies were destroying the very land he purchased! According to the Old Testament lesson, the prophet's spending habits, while perhaps foolish in the eyes of the local bankers, are symbolic of his hope for Israel's future restoration.

*Robert W. Wall*

# Twentieth Sunday after Pentecost, Year C

First Lesson: Lamentations 1:1-6
(Psalm 137)
**Second Lesson: 2 Timothy 1:1-14**
Gospel Lesson: Luke 17:5-10

Paul's opening salutation (1:1-2) to his "beloved child" and young colleague Timothy supplies the reader with much useful information, which helps to frame the rest of this letter. At first glance Paul opens his letters the same way: he introduces himself as an apostle, identifies his recipient(s), and greets him/them with similar salutations. Upon closer inspection, however, there are important differences that define more carefully the nature of his relationship (and thus that of his letter) to a particular audience. For example, the reference to Timothy as "beloved child" (rather than "faithful child," as in 1 Tim. 1:2) indicates that this correspondence presumes a more intimate relationship between sender and recipient and anticipates advice that explores in personal ways the nature of Timothy's vocation and service to God.

Paul's apostleship, and the authority this status presumes, is always linked to Christ Jesus, who called him into the gospel ministry in accordance with God's will — like the prophets of old. In this case, however, Paul adds the phrase "the promise of life" to his assertion of apostolic authority. While several reasons for this addition have been suggested, it no doubt is given here as a reminder to Timothy that even as his apostleship serves the redemptive interests of God, so must any form of ministry patterned after Paul's (cf. 2:2). The real prospect of entering into this promised life is not only on Paul's mind as he nears death (4:6-8) and his ministry draws to a close; it also is the central exhortation of Timothy's future ministry and present experience (cf. 1:10-11; 2:8-11).

Typical of his other letters (cf. Rom. 1:8-15; 1 Cor. 1:4-9), Paul's greeting turns into thanksgiving for Timothy's faithfulness (1:3-5). The real purpose of Paul's thanksgiving is to report the content of his prayers for Timothy in anticipation of concerns he will develop in the main body of the letter. Intercessory prayer becomes the occasion for Paul to "remember" certain things about Timothy (1:3) that serve to encourage his ministry. With extraordinary poignancy, Paul "remembers" Timothy's "tears" and "longs" to see him (1:4), images of a close friendship; and he recalls Timothy's faithfulness cultivated from youth by his mother and grandmother (1:5), images of a Christian household (1:5). That Paul intercedes for his friend "continually" and longs for him "day and night" suggests more than a deeply felt friendship; it suggests that Paul is committed to Timothy's future success in ministry. In fact, some commentators (e.g., Luke T. Johnson) have found here a subtext of doubt: Paul is worried that Timothy has yet to bring to full maturity that "sincere faith" necessary to continue his mission in Ephesus, which prompts Paul's exhortations in 1:6-14.

The combination of these various themes — friendship, household, faithfulness — brings to light what is for Paul his most profound worry: the importance of transmitting his gospel intact to the next generation of Christians. 2 Timothy is both a profoundly felt "last will and testament" from Paul to his dear friend and also something of a "great commission" that charges Timothy, Paul's successor, to continue to be the sort of person Paul is and to do those kinds of things that characterize the apostle's mission. Even as Paul continues with "clear conscience" in the faith of his Jewish parents (1:3), as does Timothy (1:5; cf. Acts 16:1), so must Timothy remain loyal to and continue in the faith tradition he has established (thus 1:13-14). Many think this sentiment betrays the author's post-Pauline perspective: the historical Paul highlighted the discontinuity between his Jewish past (and Judaism) and his Christian present (so Phil. 3:4-9). But this is certainly not true of the Paul of Acts, who repeatedly defended his Jewish background and practices (Acts 22:3-7; 23:6; 24:10-23; 26:4-8). Nor is it true that Paul's theological commitments envisage a sharp break from their Jewish moorings. While dramatic changes in Paul's religious outlook necessarily resulted from his Damascus road encounter with the living Jesus, it seems clear from his letters that his reading of Jewish Scriptures maintained continuity between his Jewish faith and his devotion to Jesus as Lord and Savior. Such now is what he wants for Timothy.

Toward this end, Paul gives the first (1:6-7) of three related exhortations, linked to the previous prayer-report by similar verbs for "remind": even as Paul remembers "sincere faith" (1:5), so now he reminds Timothy to continue to cultivate that faith by "rekindling the gift of God within you." The gravity of Paul's friendly recollection lies on Timothy's gift for ministry (cf. 1 Tim. 4:14). The verb "rekindle" envisages someone fanning a fiery flame — an image Paul draws from the Old Testament (cf. Num. 11:26-29) and associates with the Spirit in 1 Thessalonians 5:19. In this context, however, where images of friendship evoke Timothy's loyalty to continue Paul's gospel ministry, the Spirit's gift is confirmed by (*dia*) apostolic authority. The act of "laying on of my hands" is personal ("my hands") rather than congregational (cf. 1 Tim. 4:14), and suggests that Paul has anointed Timothy as his successor after the Old Testament (Moses/Joshua; Deut. 34:9) pattern. Paul's reminder, then, underscores two integral points: Timothy is gifted for ministry by the Spirit and is authorized to use this spiritual gift by the apostle as his chosen successor.

Significantly, the Spirit's gift is "within" Timothy — the Spirit's role has to do first of all with the formation of Timothy's character, not with empowerment for ministry per se (cf. 1 Cor. 12). According to Paul, ministry is the public demonstration of the believer's spiritual transformation that results when the Spirit brokers God's salvation-creating grace in those belonging to Christ (Rom. 8:1-17; Gal. 5:16-24). No doubt due to his worries about Timothy's flagging fortitude, Paul reminds him that the personal yield of living in the Spirit's realm is not "timidity." The public quality that the Spirit produces in the genuine believer is not a cowardly response to difficult situations, which is the opposite of "sincere faith." God's powerful grace works in opposite directions to produce a public persona whose characteristics are "power and love and prudence" (which Johnson broadly defines as "moral right thinking"). While these are qualities the Spirit cultivates in all believers, they seem especially relevant for church leaders like Timothy, whose spiritual gift is pastoral ministry and whose personal vocation is to succeed Paul, who exemplifies such a persona brought to maturity by the Spirit (see 3:10-14).

The second exhortation, "do not be ashamed," has important currency in Paul's social world, as in our own. Feeling inward shame or being publicly shamed is often a means of maintaining social order. Typically, only those with influence over us, or those important to us, can say or do something that evokes feelings of shame. Elsewhere (Rom. 1:16; 1 Cor. 1:18–2:5), as here, Paul speaks of shame in connection with the proclamation of the Christian gospel of the suffering Messiah, which both Jews and Greeks think shameful even though for different reasons (see 1 Cor. 1:22-23). Evidently various opponents of Paul's Gentile mission contend that his message is bogus, and the costs of advancing it — imprisonment and suffering according to 1:8 — seem complete lunacy to outsiders. Of course, the irony of Paul's exhortation is that Timothy's cowardice (1:7) may well be due to a "prudence" that supposes the costliness of Paul's witness to Christ is simply not worth the price. What Paul makes clear by this exhortation is that if Timothy is to succeed him in the mission, it is not only a continuity of theology and ministry that he envisions but also of self-sacrifice.

Paul first appeals to God's power, as he does in Romans 1:16, and only then to his autobiography (1:11-12) to warrant his exhortation to shameless courage. Again, the kind of personal transformation that is consistent with

443

Timothy's calling, set forth in the triad of "power-love-prudence," is deeply rooted in a "sincere faith" in God. I. Howard Marshall notes that Paul's intricate definition of this power from God, which follows in 1:9-10, has the form of a traditional Pauline confession of faith (*The Pastoral Epistles*, International Critical Commentary [Edinburgh: T. & T. Clark, 1999], pp. 700-702). That is, this statement reminds Timothy of the nonnegotiable content of the gospel learned in his household at a young age (1:5) and then from Paul (3:10-15). The very terms of Paul's gospel supply the theological warrant for Timothy's courage (cf. 1:10): (1) God, the only God, has saved "us" (Paul and Timothy) because of God's grace and not "our" works; (2) God's salvation, promised "ages ago," is now realized ("appeared") in Jesus, the only Messiah; (3) because of him, death is replaced by life.

The meaning of the famous biographical sketch that follows in 1:11-12 is famously disputed, reflected in the disagreements of various translations (esp. 1:12b). The initial emphasis in the index of Paul's authority as "preacher, apostle, teacher" falls on the middle term, "apostle," since the other offices are shared with others, including Timothy; and no doubt Paul understands his vocation as the primary reason he suffers so (cf. Acts 9:15-16). What is not as clear is the final element of this sketch, whether Paul has shamelessly entrusted his life of costly service to God (NRSV, NIV, JB) or whether God has entrusted God's gospel to Paul (RSV, NEB, NAB). The decision we make turns on two prior decisions: (1) Should we think 1:11-12 concludes the second exhortation that begins with 1:8, or does it introduce the third exhortation found in 1:13-14? If concluding the second exhortation, then likely it is Paul entrusting his life to God; however, if we take it as introducing the third exhortation (1:13-14), then the likely meaning of this phrase is that God has entrusted the gospel to Paul and his successors. The grammar and natural sense of the text prefers the first meaning. (2) Should we think, then, that Paul entrusts some deposit he makes to God, who then guards it? Probably, and if so, then it is Paul who entrusts his gospel ministry to God, who stands guard of him until the "Day" — that is, the return of Christ.

The third exhortation (1:13-14) follows naturally from the first two: confident of God's powerful help (1:8-12) in rekindling and safeguarding Timothy's witness to the gospel (1:6-7), Paul finally encourages him to combine a godly life ("faith and love that are in Christ Jesus") with a commitment to preserve and pass on the "sound (or 'healthy') words" learned from Paul. Aware that his death is imminent, Paul's "last will and testament" to his "dear son" is his gospel ministry, which Timothy continues "by the Holy Spirit who dwells within us."

Paul's concerns about Timothy's "sincere faith" are reflected in the Lord's response to his apostles' presumptuous demand, "Increase our faith!" (Luke 17:5). In Luke's Gospel "faith" manifests itself in faithful living. Jesus' initial response to their request (17:6) is to correct their implied assumption that the resources for faithful living are somehow found outside of themselves: the source of extraordinary practices is an inward trust in Jesus as Lord. Yet, the faithful disciple should not suppose that a practiced piety is the means to gain great honor or receive an award from God (17:7-9). Rather, the inward decision to follow the Lord Jesus obligates such faithfulness as a matter of course (17:10). And so it is with Timothy, whose "sincere faith," cultivated from youth within his home and by Paul, obligates faithful, even suffering service in the ministry of the gospel.

*Robert W. Wall*

## Twenty-first Sunday after Pentecost, Year C

First Lesson: Jeremiah 29:1, 4-7
(Psalm 66:1-12)
**Second Lesson: 2 Timothy 2:8-15**
Gospel Lesson: Luke 17:11-19

In this passage the main theme of 2 Timothy comes to clear focus: Christian ministry serves the redemptive interests of the Lord, for whom one should expect to suffer. In continuing this theme, today's New Testament lesson (2:8-15) continues to explore ideas introduced earlier in Paul's exhortation for Timothy to share in his suffering (cf. 1:8-12): Paul "remembers" the risen and living Jesus (2:8a; cf. 1:3, 9-10), who supplies the theological core of his gospel ministry (2:8b; cf. 1:8, 11); and his own suffering and imprisonment (2:9; cf. 1:11-12), which illustrates devotion to his calling. He claims that the purpose of his gospel ministry is the eternal salvation of those who are in Christ Jesus (2:10; cf. 1:9-10), and lists yet another "faithful saying" (or, "a saying of the faithful"; 2:11-13; cf. 1 Tim. 1:15; 3:1; 4:9) that promises future reward for faithful believers. Once again, the act of remembering these things "reminds" Timothy why he should not waste energy on "disputed teachings" (2:14; cf. 1:13-14) or feel "ashamed" of his own spiritual gifts and calling for Christian ministry (2:15; cf. 1:12).

The meaning of Paul's exhortation to "remember" Jesus (2:8a) is as unclear as its formulation is odd. One would expect Paul to recite the christological confession as it must have been first drawn — in chronological order — reciting first Jesus' Davidic descent, then his resurrection (cf. Rom. 1:3-4). If we explain this odd sequence by pointing out that Paul merely wanted to lay stress upon the Lord's resurrection, perhaps because some Christian teachers in Ephesus were arguing against it (2:18; cf. 1 Cor. 15), or more simply to illustrate the ultimate purchase (i.e., exaltation) of suffering, we still are left to explain why he should include a reference to David and to Jesus' royal messiahship. Perhaps Paul's intent is to claim a second, traditional messianic proof that his gospel asserts, especially important if Paul's gospel ("my gospel") is also challenged by Jewish teachers who seek to subvert his claims that Jesus is Israel's Messiah.

The powerful contrast between a "fettered" Paul and the "unfettered" word of God (2:9) conveys meaning on several different levels. Paul recognizes that he (and Timothy by implication) is but a mortal agent who serves an eternal purpose. Such an honest perspective on Christian ministry, similar to what we find in the book of Acts, is the subtext of the succession theme in this letter: because of their shared mortality, Paul charges Timothy to continue his mission and message after his death (cf. 4:6), which he is to pass on to others who will teach still others as their successors (2:2). Paul's capacity to respond to his suffering with patient endurance (*kakopatheia*, 2:9; cf. 2:3; 4:5) does not derive from stoic self-will but from his confidence that God will call out still others to advance the gospel without him. Perhaps Paul is here also challenging a reason for Timothy's timidity (cf. 1:7). Timothy may not only be worried that he will end up imprisoned like Paul; his reluctance to embrace his gift and vocation for gospel ministry may also have to do with the real purchase of a gospel that claims God's salvation from suffering and death when those who proclaim it are suffering and dying, seemingly without God's protection. If so, then, Timothy's confidence in the trustworthiness of God's "unfettered" word that proclaims the prospect of "eternal glory" (2:10), as well as his own participation in the coming age, is encouraged by remembering that "Jesus Christ [is] risen from the dead."

The relationship between Paul's suffering and his saving gospel is made even clearer in 2:10. In fact, Paul clearly thinks that those ushered into God's salvation during his evangelistic crusades are the fruit of his suffering! In my opinion the subtext of this causal connection between Paul's suffering and the salvation of "the elect" is not supplied by Jewish mysticism (as in Col. 1:24); nor does Paul suppose that Timothy must suffer in order to be successful as a Christian evangelist. Paul is no masochist! His comment is simply a deeply felt personal reflection on his present situation in light of his commission to carry the word of God and so share in Christ's suffering (cf. Acts 9:15-16) — the very sort of comment we would expect to find in a literary "last will and testament." The larger principle expressed is this: a believer's life is empowered by God's grace, even to endure great suffering, in order to bear witness to the truth of the gospel.

But what are we to make of Paul's reference to "the elect" (cf. Titus 1:1)? I take it that he is not referring to a group of nonbelievers who are predestined by God to believe in Christ, since the term is used in Scripture only of those who have already believed (see I. Howard Marshall, *The Pastoral Epistles* [Edinburgh: T. & T. Clark, 1999], p. 737). Paul's point is rather that he endures the costs of his demanding ministry in order to ensure the *future* salvation of those Christians who came to faith during his evangelistic crusades. The importance of this point extends to the succession theme mentioned above: Paul exhorts Timothy to succeed him in ministry, not only for the sake of the nonbelievers who will be initiated into God's people as a result, but also to encourage those already saved to endure to the end in order to "obtain salvation in Christ Jesus with its eternal glory."

The "faithful saying" added in 2:11-13 expresses four conditions that, when met, "obtain salvation in Christ Jesus." Several similar sayings are found elsewhere in the Pastoral Epistles (1 Tim. 1:15; 3:1; 4:9; Titus 3:8), all confessional in tone and all tidy summaries of Pauline thought. The grammar of these conditions alternates between present faith and future blessing: if we remain faithful to the Lord in our present suffering, then he will bless us in the age to come. The first two lines of this confessional (2:11// 12a) form a forceful parallelism and stipulate the positive condition: "if we die/endure, then we will live/reign with him." This parallelism captures the sense of Paul's important baptismal formula, given famous expression in Romans 6:1-11, that by faith in Christ we participate in and truly experience the redemptive results of his death and resurrection. The third line (2:12b), however, restates this theological truth as a negative condition — as a warning, followed by the first half of the fourth conditional statement (2:13a): "if we deny him/are faithless, then he will deny us." No doubt Paul has his opponents in mind (cf. 2:16-18); he considers them apostates, and their eternal destiny is imperiled. However, Paul breaks this negative pattern in the second half of the fourth line (2:13b) in a striking way to conclude on a positive note: "[Christ Jesus] remains faithful since he cannot deny himself."

447

The rhetorical effect of ending the "faithful saying" in this way is to underscore the immutability of divine promise, which, while dependent upon human agency for its fulfillment, is nonetheless independent of any human influence since God, being God, is ever faithful to promises made. Sharply put, whether or not Timothy finally agrees to succeed Paul in the gospel ministry, which evidently remains an open question, his decision will not affect God's decision to grant eternal life to those who trust in Christ Jesus. The presumption, of course, is that if Timothy fails Christ, God will raise up and gift another person to succeed Paul. Our faithlessness grieves the Lord but does not subvert or reverse his love for us and the real prospect of future blessings for those who remain faithful to him.

To underscore this present contrast between enduring for Christ and denying him, Paul supplies Timothy another contrast between God-approved workers "who rightly handle the word of truth" (2:15) and Paul's opponents, who "subvert the faith of some" (2:14, 16-18). It is proffered in the form of a personal exhortation, which brings the preceding saying more directly to Timothy: "Remind [the faithless] of this and charge them before the Lord. . . ." What are the contrasting characteristics of these two kinds of teachers? The most prominent difference Paul notes is contrasting teaching styles. Paul's opponents are prone to "word games" (2:14) and "profane chatter" (2:16) because their teaching does not aim at a redemptive or evangelistic purpose. God's "worker," on the other hand, feels no "shame" because s/he is confident in God's power to make clear the gospel's truths (see 1:8) for the salvation of the lost.

In this regard, Paul also notes contrasting content between what these two groups teach. Rarely does Paul indicate to Timothy or Titus what their opponents teach, but in 2:17b-18a he divulges that two teachers in particular, Hymenaeus and Philetus, have departed from a Pauline understanding of the resurrection (cf. 1 Cor. 15:12), presumably denying the first article of the community's confession of faith mentioned earlier (2:8, par. 2:11). A few important ancient manuscripts of 2 Timothy omit the article of "the resurrection" and simply refer to an unspecified resurrection. If we retain the article, as most do, "the resurrection" can only refer to the future resurrection of the body (see 1 Cor. 15). Evidently, some of Paul's opponents had rejected this teaching as gospel truth and replaced it with doctrine that asserted believers are already resurrected with Christ — in a spiritual or mystical rather than a bodily or physical sense — thereby gutting the "word of truth" of its "blessed hope" in the coming, cosmic triumph of God at Christ's parousia.

Finally, such false teaching "subverts the faith of some" (2:18b); their talk "eats away" at Christian faith "like gangrene." These are bad results that clearly indict the content of the competing gospel as false. Luke T. Johnson notes that medical metaphors were often used in the Greek world to distinguish between truth and falsehood. Truthful instruction produces moral and spiritual health, whereas falsehood produces spiritually sick people. To characterize false teaching as "gangrene" is to contrast its unhealthy result in Christian formation with that of the "word of truth" (cf. *Letters to Paul's Delegates* [Valley Forge, Pa.: Trinity Press International, 1996], p. 76). Elsewhere in the Pastoral Epistles, Paul speaks of the importance of "sound [lit. 'healthy'] doctrine" (cf. 1 Tim. 1:10; 6:3; 2 Tim. 1:13; 4:3; Titus 1:9, 13; 2:1-2) to underscore his didactic calculus that the content of what one teaches, whether true or false, is tested in the community's life by whether it reproduces sacred or profane actions.

This connection between the content of what one accepts as true and the health of one's lifestyle is aptly illustrated by the Gospel lesson, Luke 17:11-19. Jesus, who is now traveling to Jerusalem to carry out his messianic mission on the cross, happens upon a leper colony. There Jews and Samaritans mingle together since all were equally cursed by their sickness. Ten lepers appeal to Jesus as merciful "Master." As an observant Jew, Jesus follows Torah's teaching (Lev. 13:49; 14:2-4) and tells them to seek out priests through whom God's purifying mercy would be found. They obeyed and were cleansed. But only one worshiped the Son — strangely the Samaritan, who would likely have sought out the priests of the temple cult in Gerizim, not those in Jerusalem. Observant Jews despised Samaritan priests as false teachers, and Samaritans as renegade Jews. In fact, Jesus names the Samaritan leper by the derisive term "this foreigner." Despite this, he got Jesus right, and his faith in Jesus made him well.

*Robert W. Wall*

## Twenty-second Sunday after Pentecost, Year C

First Lesson: Jeremiah 31:27-34
(Psalm 119:97-104)
**Second Lesson: 2 Timothy 3:14–4:5**
Gospel Lesson: Luke 18:1-8


S aint Paul urges Timothy to continue to grow in his journey of faith. That journey is seen by Paul as having its roots in the sacred Scriptures which are the authoritative source of his understanding. This understanding leads to the salvation we find with Jesus Christ. For Paul the person Jesus Christ is the fulfillment of the Old Testament story which anticipates the salvation won by Jesus Christ. Paul is describing the sources of biblical authority to his young friend.

The early church, by its agreement upon the canon of Holy Scripture, interpreted Paul's testing principle as follows: all doctrine must be tested by its submission to the historical witness that surrounds Jesus Christ, the texts of the Bible, consisting of the Old Testament and the New Testament. As we trust in Jesus Christ, we trust the witness to him. We have been convinced by the Holy Spirit of the Jesus Christ we meet in the biblical witness to him. The church's doctrine of the inspiration of the Scriptures rests on the belief that the Holy Spirit has preserved the faithfulness and trustworthiness of the documents and that the Holy Scriptures are the books God wants us to have. They point us faithfully to the center. The Bible derives its authority from its witness to Jesus Christ. Since the historic Jesus of Nazareth is the only Redeemer and the good news is complete in him, therefore there are no hidden new gospels to be found or revealed.

This conviction of the total sufficiency of Jesus Christ underlies the meaning of the doctrine of the infallibility of the Bible. By that doctrine we agree that only the one word which has been spoken in word and work — Jesus Christ himself — shall have final binding authority over our lives and our doctrines.

Every new doctrinal statement, therefore, must be tested by that biblical witness. Every Christian doctrine, therefore, should itself begin with its own willingness to be tested. The Barmen Declaration of the German Confessing Church of 1934 began in just such a way: "Try the spirits, whether they are of God! Prove also the words of the Confessional Synod of the German Evangelical Church to see whether they agree with Holy Scripture and with the Confessions of the Fathers. If you find that we are speaking contrary to

450

Scripture, then do not listen to us! But if you find that we are taking our stand upon Scripture, then let no fear or temptation keep you from treading with us the path of faith and obedience to the Word of God, in order that God's people be of one mind upon earth and that we in faith experience what he himself has said: 'I will never leave you, nor forsake you.' Therefore, 'Fear not, little flock, for it is your Father's good pleasure to give you the kingdom.'" The word "inspired" (*pneuma* is the word for wind or breath in Greek; *theopneustos* means God-breathed) is Paul's alert to Timothy that he should trust the sacred Scripture (Old Testament) as the faithful witness that reveals and teaches the character of God. Since the word "righteousness" always has to do with the true character of God, "training in righteousness" is training to live and act in keeping with who God is and what God is like.

The basic principle involved here is that the biblical Christian is prepared to order faith and life on the basis of the gospel. Biblical Christianity has Jesus Christ as center. What matters here is the daily walk of the Christian man and woman with Christ by faith. Prayer, simple obedience, confession of our sins, and acceptance of God's gracious acceptance of us are the ingredients of the Christian life that the Bible invites us to enter into and enjoy. As a result of the personal relationship with the living Christ and the empowerment of the Holy Spirit in the life of the people of God, the biblical witness draws us into the mandates of the way of discipleship in the world. When it comes to forming the content of faith, the biblical Christian asks this question: "What does the Bible teach?" If the Bible teaches a doctrine, it becomes part of what we confess. Discipleship does not depend on the ability to describe the Bible in exalted language, but rather on how we answer this question: Are we prepared to order how we live and what we believe by what the Scriptures teach? The purpose of the Scriptures is to equip God's people for every good work (2 Tim. 3:17).

Biblical Christians do not worship the Bible; we worship Jesus Christ. The Bible, taken seriously, never stimulates false worship, but by its texts and themes, its history and poetry, its yearnings and prayers, its real people from Moses to John, points us to its Lord. Therefore, when the Bible is truly authoritative for our faith, there is little danger of that faith becoming sidetracked with insignificant themes and cultic curiosities.

Because of the timelessness of Jesus Christ himself, the Bible's witness to his ministry is also timeless. The biblical Christian is not in bondage to the tyranny of the current, to the oppressive pressure of the latest cause. The James party at Galatia troubled many Greek Christians with the "new word" that true Christians should not only believe in Christ but also keep the law of Moses and submit to circumcision. But Paul had the deeper truth of the gospel to apply to their claims, and out of that controversy the book of Galatians became a declaration of independence for all Christians who have ever been tempted by the latest fad or movement. The biblical Christian is free from false gods because the Bible has bound us to the true God whom we know in Jesus Christ.

Biblical faith does not blunt one's ability to be a perceptive observer of the contemporary scene. Paul surely had gospel-sharpened insights into the context in which both he and Timothy were called to minister. He saw it coming because it was already present: "For the time is coming when people will not put up with sound doctrine, but having itching ears, they will accumulate for themselves teachers to suit their own desires, and will turn away from listening to the truth and wander away to myths." The gospel has the power to instill in us a sharpened sensitivity and inquisitiveness toward what is happening in our world. Changes and trends provide the context in which we are called to witness to the truth of the gospel. Researching both the riches of the gospel and the characteristics of our times is essential in raising a faithful witness to the gospel of Jesus Christ.

There is a doctrinal wanderlust that often takes hold of a person. It tends to create its own momentum, and within it an insatiable appetite for the new and different for their own sake. This wanderlust should not be confused with the research instinct that we have been describing, or the hard work of theological inquiry. The restlessness in research is founded upon the whole principle of testing followed by meaningful response to truth discovered, whereas the restlessness of doctrinal wanderlust is dominated by inner moods, by the current immediate impression. Wanderlust is not freedom, though it disguises itself as freedom. In the classic river scene in *Huckleberry Finn*, it is the slave, Jim, who is truly free because Jim knows who he is. Huck at that point in the story is not free because he is simply a young boy adrift on the Mississippi. Freedom to explore comes from knowing who and why we are.

Paul writes to remind Timothy of who and why he is. In a world of change where trends seem unfavorable to the preaching of the gospel, Paul urges Timothy to "proclaim the message; be persistent whether the time is favorable or unfavorable; convince, rebuke, and encourage, with the utmost patience in teaching. . . . always be sober, endure suffering, do the work of an evangelist, carry out your ministry fully" (4:2-5).

Paul's description of Timothy's world sounds much like the world we have come to call "postmodern." The "modern" world with its confidence in science and reason to solve human problems has been dismantled by its dis-

452

mal consequences. Postmodernism puts its faith in absolute relativism and encourages "itching ears" that attend to "teachers [who] suit their own desires" (v. 3). Paul's words to Timothy are no less urgent for our time: "Do the work of an evangelist, carry out your ministry fully" (v. 5).

*Earl F. Palmer*

## Twenty-third Sunday after Pentecost, Year C

First Lesson: Joel 2:23-32
(Psalm 65)
**Second Lesson: 2 Timothy 4:6-8, 16-18**
Gospel Lesson: Luke 18:9-14

The synopsis of Paul's life reads like an epitaph: "I have fought the good fight, I have finished the race, I have kept the faith." These final words to his friend Timothy were written from a setting of extreme trial and surprising grace from prison. Paul does not say, "I won the race," but "I finished the race." The crown that awaits him (v. 8) is not the kingly crown, *diadem,* but the athlete's award, *stephanos.* The reader can sense the nonchalance of trust as he reviews his life and anticipates his death.

Paul was in prison at Rome during the horrific days of Nero's severe persecution of Christians following the fire in Rome. Tacitus tells of the circus events where Christians were punished in the games and sent before the lions as scapegoats for Nero, whom many in Rome suspected as the one who started the fire that swept out of control and burned a vast part of the city. Paul had carried on his ministry throughout the time of his imprisonment to the extent that he could inform the Philippians that members of the Praetorian Guard in Rome had heard about Christ because of his imprisonment (Phil. 1:13). Indeed, his imprisonment in Rome had contributed to the progress of the gospel (Phil. 1:12).

Paul wrote the letter to Timothy from Rome under circumstances that were intense and dangerous. Rome was a cruel and angry city at the time Paul wrote to his young friend. Nero had become emperor in A.D. 54

through murder and intrigue that had been actually sponsored by his ambitious mother, Agrippina. Britannicus the son of Claudius should have become emperor by right of birth as eldest son of the emperor, but he and his father were no match for Claudius's latest wife, Julia Agrippina.

Agrippina's son, Nero, was a teenager when he began his rule as emperor. The opening years of his reign were essentially peaceful and moderate because of the regency authority of Afranius Burrus and Lucius Annaeus Seneca, who together skillfully governed the Roman Empire in Nero's behalf until the young emperor at age nineteen decided to take full power into his own hands. From that point until Nero's death in 68, the Roman Empire descended into a period of terrifying cruelty and sadism sponsored by the depraved Nero himself.

Nothing could stand in Nero's way or interfere with his personal desires or his lavish plans for Rome. He instituted daily gladiatorial contests in the arena; these became progressively bloodthirsty and decadent. Seneca wrote with dismay in his memoirs about these daily events at the Colosseum. After one such gladiatorial contest he wrote, "I felt as if I had been in a sewer." Nero became impatient with the moderation of Burrus and Seneca, dismissed them from their posts, and finally arranged for their deaths. He murdered his own wife and finally arranged for the assassination of his mother, Agrippina. Her last words tell something of the horrifying story of Nero. "The one good thing about my death," she said to her executioners, "is that the womb that bore Nero is now dead."

Tacitus the historian accused Nero himself of starting the infamous fire in Rome in 64 in order to clear the way for his own grand plans for new buildings in the city. But what was to have been a small fire grew into a great conflagration that destroyed much of the city. Following this fire Nero, in the cynical style that marked his reign, blamed the small but growing band of Christian believers in Rome for the arson and meted out to them some of the most horrible punishments that have ever been chronicled in a civilized society. Tacitus describes the terror of that persecution:

And so, to get rid of this rumor, Nero set up as the culprits and punished with the utmost refinement of cruelty a class hated for their abominations, who are commonly called Christians. Christus, from whom their name is derived, was executed at the hands of the procurator Pontius Pilate in the reign of Tiberius. Checked for the moment, this pernicious superstition again broke out, not only in Judea, the source of that evil, but even in Rome, that receptacle for everything that is sordid and degrading from every quarter of the globe, which there finds a following. Accordingly, arrest was first made of those who confessed (i.e., to being Christians); then, on their evidence, an immense multitude was convicted, not so much on the charge of arson as because of hatred of the human race.

Besides being put to death, they were made to serve as objects of amusement; they were clad in the hides of beasts and torn to death by dogs; others were crucified, others set on fire to illuminate the night when daylight failed. Nero had thrown open his grounds for the display and was putting on a show in the circus, where he mingled with the people in the dress of a charioteer or drove about in his chariot.

All this gave rise to a feeling of pity, even toward men whose guilt merited the most exemplary punishment; for it was felt that they were being destroyed not for the public good but to gratify the cruelty of an individual. (*Annals* 90.44)

This is the city where Paul the Christian was imprisoned. At first his situation was tolerable. At the close of the book of Acts Luke tells us that upon Paul's arrival in Rome as a prisoner in about 63, he was probably under house arrest for at least two years and was during that time able to receive visitors "quite openly and unhindered" (Acts 28:31).

But by the time Paul wrote his final letters from Rome (Philippians and 2 Timothy), his safety was very precarious and the conditions of his imprisonment had become harsher as the situation in Rome itself had become more chaotic and ominous. He gave at least two clues in the Philippian letter that it was written from Rome and that he was being held prisoner in one of the several prisons in that city, perhaps located near or actually in the vast villa at the southwest border of the Forum where the emperor himself lived.

First, there is Paul's reference to the Praetorian Guard (Phil. 1:13). This is almost always a reference to the troops that were attached to the emperor and served as his personal guard. They were stationed in Rome and traveled with him when he left the city.

The second clue is even more intriguing. Paul sent greetings from the Christians in Rome to the friends at Philippi and added the surprising statement, "especially [from] those of Caesar's household" (Phil. 4:22). Did Paul want to give his readers a clue as to which of the five principal prisons in Nero's Rome he was being held? Was the apostle at that time being held in the prison at Nero's Villa Vale? We cannot be sure. What is clear, however, is that this letter and the letter to the Philippians were not sent from the comfortable safety and stability of Caesarea on the Palestinian coast, but from Rome itself, from the very heart of the decadent empire of Nero, and

455

that it was written at the most unstable and, especially for Christians, dangerous period in that city's history.

Perhaps guards from the Roman cohort, the Praetorian Guard, had become acquainted with Epaphroditus as he served the prisoner Paul. There were speculations in the early church that Paul, during his final imprisonment, had been visited by Roman officials who were themselves troubled on the one side by this remarkable new message about Jesus Christ the Lord and on the other by the increasing decadence and inhumanity of the reign of the emperor Nero. There are accounts in early church writings that Seneca, the brother of Gallio whom Paul had met at Corinth (Acts 18), visited Paul in private, as well as reports of visits by the historian Suetonius.

We cannot conclude such visits from this text, but we do know that there were persons in the Roman Praetorian Guard who had become Christians during this time. This handful of people in Caesar's household would expand over the years, while the Roman Empire continued on its course toward disintegration.

In danger of death, Paul also suffered desertion. But the protecting presence of the Lord sustained him and empowered him with the grace to forgive (2 Tim. 4:16). The persecutor-turned-apostle had received forgiveness from the dying Stephen (Acts 7:60; 8:1), and now extends that forgiveness to his deserters. Paul's message and mission remained intact (2 Tim. 4:17), and God received the glory (v. 18).

*Earl F. Palmer*

## Nativity of the Lord (Christmas Day), Years A, B, C

First Lesson: Isaiah 9:2-7
(Psalm 96)
**Second Lesson: Titus 2:11-14**
Gospel Lesson: Luke 2:1-14, (15-20)

The challenge of preaching on Christmas Day is to supply a theological co-text for the wonderful tradition of exchanging gifts with friends and family, which will surely be the preoccupation of most parishioners!

The present New Testament lesson, which seeks to clarify God's gift of salvation, supplies an excellent resource to meet this challenge. At least one important commentator (Spicq) calls this passage "the very heart of this letter." I agree.

Much like 1 Timothy, Titus is a practical letter, filled with useful instructions regarding how best to organize Christian congregations in non-Christian places. As in 1 Timothy, the structure of this letter combines life-centered instructions with theological summaries that provide both the foundation and explanation for Paul's pastoral advice to his young associate Titus. In this particular passage Paul has just encouraged Titus to instruct his congregation about the character of exemplary relations within the household of believers (2:2-10a) — relations that befit "sound doctrine" (2:1), so that in every relationship the community "may adorn the doctrine of God our Savior" (2:10b). Paul's grand pretext in providing these moral instructions to Titus is that the Christian life embodies the truth claims of the Christian gospel for all to see — a sight that is hardly repulsive but rather highly attractive to those who look on (2:5, 8, 10).

The theological summary that Paul attaches to his ethical exhortation is carefully crafted. In fact, our lesson begins with "for" *(gar)* to cue the reader that what follows explains what precedes it. Closer scrutiny shows that Paul has just concluded his instructions with a purpose statement: the positive aim of the community's life together is to "adorn the doctrine of God our Savior" (2:10b). The verb "adorn" *(kosmeō)* comes from the "cosmos/-ic" word family, and its most popular connotation is of the "cosmetic" that one applies to make one's public appearance more appealing. According to Paul, healthy relationships between believers provide the external "cosmetic" that makes the inward beliefs and values of our faith — "sound [or 'healthy'] doctrine" — more presentable to the world: believers should be the very picture of theological and spiritual health! This crucial claim is made even clearer by repetition of key words that link together this purpose clause (2:10b) with the opening line of the theological summary (2:11): "in *all* things" is picked up again by "*all* people," and the very character of "God our *Savior*" is envisaged by the action phrase "for the *salvation* of all people." Pauline theology is missionary theology; it is never preoccupied with declining the nouns of God's existence but rather with conjugating the verbs of God's saving activity in the world. Sharply put, then, if the household code given in 2:2-10a is the moral "cosmetic" the church applies for the world to see, then 2:11-14 is the doctrinal statement of God's salvation that provides its theological explanation. The preacher must never moralize without first theologizing!

The uncommon language of this passage, both in beauty and in vocabulary, suggests that Paul uses a Christian confession of faith already known to Titus. Further, it forms a single sentence in the Greek text, suggesting that its various parts form a complete and coherent whole. Here, then, Paul reminds Titus of the two core beliefs that constitute the "doctrine of God our Savior." The first belief is that "the grace of God has already appeared [lit. 'epiphany'], bringing salvation of all people" (2:11). The unusual personification of grace is a poetic way of recalling the person of Jesus, whose appearance in human history is the subtext of this entire passage, as made clear by 2:14. Even so, Paul clearly wants Titus to reflect upon the community's actual experience of God's grace — grace alone, its meaning and singular importance for advancing the gospel.

This passage mentions two elements of this experience of God's saving grace, both with implicit reference to the prior instructions for the household of faith (2:2-10a). (1) The sphere of God's grace extends to all people. Although the reason to press for the inclusiveness of salvation here is not clear, Paul probably has the household code (rather than his opponents) in mind. That is, the grace of God is for everyone in the community and excludes no one by gender, age, or social class. For this reason, every member and every relationship of the household of God must exemplify the results of God's grace in their life together. (2) The grace of our divine Benefactor saves us not only *from* sin and death but also *to* live in new ways that accord with God's high standards. Grace not only forgives sin but transforms lives. It is a power from God already at work "in the present age," since God's grace has already appeared for us on the cross and its power demonstrated to us in the empty tomb. The sharp contrast between vice ("impiety and worldly passions") and virtue ("self-controlled, upright, and godly") in 2:12 expresses Christian conversion in practical terms: their real experience of God's grace "trains" or shapes believers into a moral people of the kind described in 2:2-10a. Again the personification of grace presumes a subtext: the effect of divine grace in Christian formation is mediated by the Spirit through word and sacrament. In particular, the use of the verb "train" invokes images of education, when new converts learn the gospel under the instruction of teachers such as the older women who mentor the young women of the community (see 2:3-5).

The second core belief about God our Savior concerns the future appearance of the "glory of our great God," for which the community must await the coming "of our Savior, Jesus Christ" (2:13). The confusing syntax of this passage is reflected in its different modern translations. Does the phrase "the glory of our great God" refer to the first or second person of the Holy Trinity? Any response to this question is complex and remains contested (for an expert's discussion of this question, see I. Howard Marshall, *The Pastoral Epistles,* International Critical Commentary [Edinburgh: T. & T. Clark, 1999], pp. 272-82). In my opinion, Paul understands that the Old Testament promise of God's glorious presence in a restored Israel is ultimately realized at Messiah's return to earth to complete his mission to deliver all things from sin and death. Although the text's grammar suggests (but does not demand) that both "God" and "Savior" refer to Jesus Christ, the theological claim it enshrines suggests that the statement refers to both persons, even though Paul does not conceive of the Father's present grace or future glory as somehow independent of the Son's death and parousia: "God our Savior" and "our Savior, Jesus Christ" make up the divine team of world saviors.

To what does the "glory of our great God" refer that has its epiphany at our Lord's return? For what exactly is the faith community waiting? To understand this is to explain what prompts the community's "blessed hope," which surely is the principal motivation to live in transformed ways during the present age. The "glory of God" is a prophetic idiom (esp. Isaiah and Ezekiel) and refers to the power and splendor of God's character that finally "will fill the whole earth." Certainly Paul's primary concern lies with the concrete demonstration of God's glory at the end of human history. As with God's grace, this consummation is linked with the (re)appearance of Christ on earth. God's grace has already made its appearance in the messianic mission of the Suffering Servant "for the salvation of all people." Yet this salvation and its transforming results (2:11-12) are harbingers of God's restored *creation* in which the redeemed community will live forever (cf. Isa. 66:18-23).

The subtext of this striking personification of God's grace (2:11-12) and glory (2:13) to fulfill God's promised salvation is of course christological and is now stated with profound clarity in 2:14. The past arrival of the Savior's grace and the blessed hope of the future arrival of the Creator's glory are both predicated upon the Lord's atoning death. Christ volunteers himself, a sacrifice for sin, both to "redeem us from sin" — the sinner's "new exodus" out of his "Egyptian" captivity to sin and death — and "to purify a people for himself" — a liberated Israel's Passover in preparation for their long journey to their future promised land.

With the final phrase of 2:14, "zealous for good deeds," we come to the key to the interplay between moral teaching and theological confession we find in Titus. Why must the congregation of believers live according to the standard Paul establishes in 2:2-10a? Because the grace of God, which has already appeared with the death of Jesus "for us," is the power of a transformed life, purified from sin to live a life of "good deeds" — a life that heralds the coming triumph of God over sin and death once for all. Indeed,

Moses establishes the logic of covenant keeping when he bids Israel to behave as a "holy nation" by being "zealous for good works" in response to God's liberating grace (Exod. 19:3-6).

Under the light of this Pauline confession of faith, hear again the wonderful claim of the angelic canticle: "Give glory to God in heaven, for on earth the real experience of God's promised shalom is now possible among those graced by God."

*Robert W. Wall*

## Nativity of the Lord (Christmas Day), Years A, B, C

First Lesson: Isaiah 62:6-12
(Psalm 97)
**Second Lesson: Titus 3:4-7**
Gospel Lesson: Luke 2:(1-7), 8-20

This second Christmas lesson from Titus extends the teaching of 2:11-14 in supplying the theological foundations for Paul's exhortations regarding the Christian life (see my study of Titus 2:11-14). Both passages use common themes and language to summarize Paul's account of God's purpose and plan of salvation. The dynamic interplay between Christian beliefs and Christian behavior, characteristic of Titus, envisages the deep logic of Paul's gospel: God's grace, which saves the sinner from a death sentence, also transforms the believer to live in new ways. This transformation of "convict into convert" is well illustrated by the sharp contrast Paul makes between his exhortation to be "good citizens" in 3:1-2 and the catalogue of human vices found in 3:3. The imperial cast of Paul's exhortation in 3:1-2 is not without controversy, since his appeal to do the bidding of those in charge seems to some to subvert the countercultural dimension of Christian community. Yet this contrast between virtue and vice illustrates well the theological point expressed in the confession of faith that God is our Savior (cf. 2:10), whose grace saves sinners (so 3:3) for eternal life and regenerates them in their present lives to live for God (so 3:1-2).

This Pauline confession of faith, articulated in 3:4-7 in a single sentence (or as a "faithful saying," so 3:8a), begins with a summary of the history of God's salvation (3:4). The temporal phrase "but when" not only introduces a soft contrast with the vice list of 3:3 but recognizes that a decisive change of direction has already taken place in human history because God's grace has already made its appearance "through Jesus Christ our Savior" (3:6) and, at Pentecost, "in the Holy Spirit" (3:5; cf. 2 Tim. 1:8-10). As a result, sin ends for the moral rogue depicted in 3:3, who becomes a good neighbor capable of loving others as encouraged in 3:2. The two divine virtues Paul mentions in 3:4, "goodness" *(chrēstotēs)* and "kindness" *(philanthrōpia),* define the nature of a God who not only saves sinners but then restores their capacity to be good and kind toward others. That is, the believer's experiences of God's grace are first of God's love and then of one's new ability to love all people.

What follows in 3:5-7 is a richly textured confession of the grand evangelical affirmation that "God saved us." Its rhetorical design is framed by another contrast, expanding on the contrast just considered, between our failed attempts to earn God's salvation by "righteous works" (3:5a) and the triumph of God's mercy through Christ and in the Spirit (3:5b-7). Of course, this contrast is made famous by Paul's gospel, for which it is central. In this instance the conflict between human works and divine mercy is made even more emphatic in the Greek text by placing the main verbal idea, "God saved us," *after* the contrast is asserted (rather than before it, as in most translations). Often in Paul's letters the phrase "because of works" is attached to doing the law as an ineffective means of acquiring God's saving grace. Of course, in making this point Paul is responding to one of the great controversies during his law-free Gentile mission: sinners (= Gentiles) are initiated into their life with God by trusting the results of Jesus' messianic death alone, rather than by following those rites prescribed for Gentile proselytes by official Judaism. Here, however, the meaning of the phrase is much broader and intends to subvert *any* human activity, no matter how pleasing to God (= "righteousness"). God's saving grace breaks into our lives because of Jesus, not because of our good deeds. Clearly, Paul's point does not rule out good works from the believer's life, since he routinely calls for them (cf. 3:1-2); he simply rejects these same works as the condition for one to be initiated into life with God. The way into salvation has already been paved by the appearance of Christ alone, and we now experience salvation in the realm of his Spirit alone.

Confessions like this one are severely gapped statements. They provide a glossary of salvation words that is notoriously imprecise if read as a theological definition. (Some scholars suppose this passage, or something very similar to it, was used as part of a baptism liturgy in the earliest church when new converts were initiated into the congregation's life.) In Titus the primary purpose of this passage (along with 2:11-14) is rather more modest: to enlist those big ideas to help the reader recall Paul's powerful teaching about God's salvation. In particular, the passing reference to "in the Holy Spirit" (3:5) is linked to the believer's "washing, regeneration, renewal" — words that elsewhere in the Pauline writings refer to one's spiritual formation. Although finding logical relationships or fine distinctions between these properties of the Spirit's work in transforming the believer's life is difficult, the grammar seems to commend pairing the words "regeneration" and "renewal" as the sum effect of the Spirit's "washing" (= baptism). "Regeneration" refers to the Spirit's work in mediating God's salvation-creating grace, whereby the believer experiences life in brand-new ways. "Renewal" is similar in meaning, although in Pauline thought the idea seems to be associated with transforming the way we think (Rom. 12:2; Col. 3:10), not only to know God's will but then to embody what we come to know as the truth in public places — as "living sacrifices" to God (Rom. 12:1). In Acts, however, the Spirit's baptism (or "filling") is more "prophetic" and tied explicitly to the community's power to evangelize. The issue at stake for Paul is the believer's moral and spiritual transformation from a life of vice to one of virtue (cf. Gal. 5:16-26). In this regard, the meaning of "regeneration and renewal" seems to envisage, however vaguely, a maturing process (cf. 2:11-12) — some even think in two distinctive ("regeneration" and "renewal") stages — by which the new believer becomes a morally competent person.

Significantly, this Spirit is "poured out" upon the faith community "through Jesus Christ our Savior" (3:6). The idiom of the Lord pouring out the Spirit of prophecy recalls the Day of Pentecost when the third person of the Holy Trinity breaks into the history of God's people according to biblical prophecy (see Acts 2:17-18, 33). Paul extends the Spirit's work within the community beyond its initial Pentecostal filling to mediate God's transforming grace. The collaboration of God and Christ in the Spirit's work of moral transformation is indicated by reference to "Jesus Christ our Savior" (3:6), which repeats the earlier "God our Savior" (3:4). The preposition "through" commends the messianic mission of Jesus, and especially his death (3:7), as the trigger event of the Spirit's arrival at Pentecost. That is, there could be no Spirit baptism, with its effective results of regeneration and renewal, without the birth, life, death, and resurrection of the Messiah. What Paul instructs Titus to remind believers of in 3:1-2, and the reality of the believers' moral transformation that is implied by the contrasting vices of 3:3, would be utterly incomprehensible without Christmas!

Not only our present life with God in the Holy Spirit, but any idea of a future with God — any hope of becoming "heirs of eternal life" (3:7) — would be rendered moot without Christ. In fact, 3:7 states the ultimate purpose ("so that") of God's collaboration with Jesus Christ in our justification: sinners are justified by God's grace in order to live with God forever. Paul does not mean by eternal life "a slice of pie in the sky when we die." His hope of eternal life presumes a quality (not quantity) of real-life existence in a right relationship with God and each other that realizes the good the Creator originally observed when gazing upon human creation.

The Gospel lesson is centered by a Christmas carol, celebrated by the angelic host in praise of God that a Savior has arrived on earth with God's shalom (Luke 2:14). But the setting for this glorious confession is so unlikely as to be shocking. The first auditors are shepherds — outcasts, perhaps even outlaws, engaged in filthy and forsaken work. Rejected by other Jews but not by the God of Israel, they search for the Savior until they find a babe in a barnyard. The strange beginnings of our salvation on that first Christmas remind us that anyone in any place can "become heirs in hope of eternal life" because of what our loving God has done for us through Jesus Christ.

*Robert W. Wall*

# Sixteenth Sunday after Pentecost, Year C

First Lesson: Jeremiah 18:1-11
(Psalm 139:1-6, 13-18)
**Second Lesson: Philemon 1-21**
Gospel Lesson: Luke 14:25-33

It is important to paint in broad strokes the precedents for a critical view of slavery that Paul would have already derived from the Old Testament. On the whole, slave law in Israel was much milder and more enlightened than in the rest of the ancient Near East.

Although people from other nations could be enslaved by Jews for life, early law dictated that Hebrew slaves be released after six years of service and supplied with food and flock (Exod. 21:1-11; Deut. 15:12-18). Deuteronomic law even forbade the return of runaway slaves (23:15-16). Levitical law required that all Hebrews held as slaves be released every Jubilee (fiftieth) year; yet it also stipulated that Hebrews not be made to serve as slaves (i.e., treated with harshness), but rather as "hired laborers," and that kin had the right to buy back such "laborers" at any time (Lev. 25:39-55).

Both the Deuteronomic and Levitical law codes directly justified their aversion to enslaving fellow Hebrews on theological grounds: Yahweh had redeemed the Hebrews from enslavement in Egypt (Deut. 15:15; Lev. 25:42, 55; cf. Exod. 22:21; 23:9). Therefore, although slavery was practiced, Israel did not have a slave economy.

Also important to the general historical context are the differences between slavery in the Greco-Roman world and slavery in the antebellum American South. In the Greco-Roman world slavery was not based on race (Rome was an equal-opportunity oppressor). For most slaves (particularly urban or domestic slaves) slavery was not a permanent condition. For some people slavery was a means of climbing the social ladder or obtaining special jobs or rights (depending on the status of one's owner). Even if slavery did not bring any elevation in status, many undoubtedly considered it preferable to starvation (a not uncommon occurrence in the ancient economy). Slaves were also allowed to own property.

As for the particular historical context, Philemon appears to have been a host and patron for one of the house churches in or around Colossae (vv. 2, 4, 7, 22). Colossae was one of three textile centers in the Lycus River valley (Laodicea and Hierapolis are the other two) 110 to 120 miles east-southeast of Ephesus in western Asia Minor (modern-day Turkey). At the time of writing, Paul (who had not personally founded the church at Colossae; Col. 1:6-7; 2:1) was a prisoner *(desmios)* awaiting trial for his proclamation of the gospel (vv. 1, 9, 10, 13, 23). Ephesus or Rome is the most likely location of his imprisonment. If Ephesus, which is the more plausible of the two owing to proximity to Colossae and future travel plans (cf. Philem. 22 with Rom. 15:24), he is writing circa 55; if Rome, circa 60-64.

Onesimus, Philemon's slave (v. 16), had apparently "wronged" Philemon in some way or owed him something (v. 18; theft is a possibility). This slave, whose name meant "profitable, beneficial, useful" *(onēsimos),* had become "useless" *(achrēstos)* to Philemon (v. 11). Onesimus may have deliberately sought out Paul, not as a fugitive slave attempting to gain his freedom, but as one seeking a mediator who could effect improved relations with his master. (Several Roman jurists of the first and second century C.E. argued that an unauthorized departure of this sort did not turn a slave into a *fugitivus*.) Onesimus, however, got more than he bargained for: Paul converted him over to the Christian faith (v. 10), a feat that Philemon himself had not been able, or inclined, to accomplish. Onesimus then became "useful" *(euchrēstos)* to Paul, ministering to Paul's needs *(diakonē)* in and during *(en)* Paul's "imprisonment [lit. 'bonds, chains': *desmoi*] for the gospel" (vv. 11, 13). Paul was now sending Onesimus back to Philemon, in spite of Paul's desire to keep him with himself (v. 14).

In laying out the historical context, the preacher will want to make clear that Paul's conversion and recruitment of Onesimus for the work of the gospel had created an awkward new relational dynamic for Philemon. Previously Philemon related to Onesimus only as a master to a slave. Now, however, Onesimus had become Philemon's "beloved brother" in the faith (v. 16). Implicitly, too, both were now slaves to the same master or lord, Jesus (cf. 1 Cor. 7:22). Moreover, both Philemon and Onesimus now shared a similar relationship with Paul. Verse 19 ("you owe me in addition yourself") suggests that Paul had a hand in Philemon's conversion (perhaps at Ephesus; Acts 19:10). If so, then Paul had "begotten" Philemon; he was the spiritual father and patron of both Philemon and Onesimus (v. 10). Philemon, by virtue of his material and spiritual role in "refreshing the hearts of the saints" at Colossae (v. 7), was also a "coworker" *(synergos,* v. 1) and "partner" *(koinōnos,* v. 17) of Paul's in the propagation of the gospel. Paul implies the same status for Onesimus, at least on Philemon's "behalf" (v. 13). Philemon would have to figure out how to integrate two previously discrete realms of existence, two worlds now in collision, the one "in the flesh" and the one "in the Lord" (v. 16). Indeed, as Norman Petersen has argued in *Rediscovering Paul,* he might have to choose between being a master to Onesimus and being a brother to Onesimus — and choosing the former could have serious repercussions for his relationship to Paul as partner and coworker, his image to the church at Colossae as loving patron and leader, and even his relationship to God as a son.

The letter is carefully crafted for producing maximum effect with a minimum of words. Paul requests three things of Philemon, only one of which is explicit. He explicitly requests Philemon to welcome Onesimus back as if he were Paul himself (v. 17, meaning, minimally, not to punish Onesimus). He implicitly requests Philemon to manumit Onesimus ("have him back, no longer as a slave but more than a slave, a beloved brother, . . . both in the flesh and in the Lord," i.e., in the sphere of human society and not just the church; vv. 15-16) and to send Onesimus back to Paul so that Onesimus "might be of service to me on your behalf during my imprisonment for the gospel" (vv. 13-14).

That there are implicit requests in the letter is apparent from the wording of verse 21: "I know that you will do *even more* than what I am [explicitly] asking." Preachers should be aware that scholars disagree over whether Paul is implicitly requesting that Philemon free Onesimus. The dispute centers, in part, over whether the Pastoral Epistles and the letters to Colossians and Ephesians, all letters that seem to accept the institution of slavery for Christians, stem from Paul's own hand or from later disciples. Further confirmation for an implicit request to free Philemon can be found in 1 Corinthians 7:21, which views freedom from slavery as at least a penultimate good for Christians: "Were you called as a slave? Do not let it trouble you; but if indeed [or: even if] you can become free, use it [viz., your freedom] even more [or: rather]"; that is, use the freedom not as an opportunity to do whatever you want but rather to redouble your efforts to be a slave of Christ.

The differences between slavery in the Greco-Roman world and slavery in the pre–Civil War South can help explain why Paul did not simply command Philemon to give Onesimus his freedom. They lived in an empire where slavery was a normal part of human existence and sometimes the only alternative to starvation. Furthermore, Paul's authority to command Philemon to make the significant personal and financial sacrifice of releasing Onesimus was also limited (vv. 17-20). Paul desired Philemon to "do the right thing" voluntarily as a spur to the growth of his own faith and as an example to his house church (vv. 6, 8-9, 13-14, 22). Paul also trusted Philemon's good character and his capacity to do the right thing without command (vv. 4-7, 21).

In short, Paul could achieve his goal of Onesimus's release without destroying Philemon's credibility in the eyes of his own church. In the honor-shame culture of the time, Paul sought to free Philemon as well from bondage to worldly values, preserving his honor with a minimum of shaming, turning a defeat into a triumph for Philemon, the church at Colossae, and the cause of Christ.

Perhaps the most interesting aspect of the letter is the way Paul goes about convincing Philemon to "do the right thing" with respect to Onesimus. He points to his own acts of self-sacrifice such as his imprisonment for the gospel (vv. 1, 9, 10, 13, 23) and his return of Onesimus to Philemon (vv. 12-14). He also notes his abandonment of authoritarian ways toward Philemon (vv. 8-9, 19) as a model for Philemon to emulate in his dealings with Onesimus (vv. 1, 12-13). He turns Philemon's private matter into an event with public ramifications for his house church by addressing the letter not only to Philemon but also to "the church in your house" (v. 2) and alluding to a future visit (v. 22).

He appeals repeatedly to Philemon's goodwill and character (vv. 4-9), finding a way to lift up Philemon even as he seeks to correct his behavior. He then highlights the fact that Onesimus is an entirely new person in Christ (note the repeated relative clauses in vv. 10-13). Philemon *thinks* he knows who Onesimus is. In fact, to piggyback off a book title, he is "meeting Onesimus again for the first time." He points to Onesimus's previous departure as an act of divine providence that would ultimately benefit Philemon. Paul contends that Philemon is not losing a slave but gaining a Christian brother for fellowship, for the work of the gospel, and for assistance to Philemon's spiritual patron, Paul (vv. 15-16). Here one is reminded of Joseph's words to his brothers in Genesis 50:20: "Even though you intended to do harm to me, God intended it for good" (NRSV). We can let go of our self-centered desires when we see that God works for good in all things (Rom. 8:28).

Paul makes clear that whatever Philemon now did to his "client" Onesimus, he would also be doing to his spiritual "partner" Paul ("welcome him as me," v. 17), since Onesimus had become Paul's "heart" (*splanchna*, lit. "guts" [heart, spleen, liver, stomach, etc.]). The wordplay here is instructive, and the very sound of the word in Greek gives the congregation a light-hearted moment: Paul received encouragement in prison from the fact that "the *splanchna* of the saints has been refreshed through" Philemon (v. 7); Onesimus has now become "my [Paul's] *splanchna*" (v. 12); Paul urges Philemon to "refresh my *splanchna* in Christ" (v. 20). Obviously, the best way that Philemon can fulfill that last request is by refreshing the *splanchna* of Onesimus.

In his many-faceted appeal, Paul even offers to compensate Philemon for any loss he might have incurred from Onesimus's "wrong," despite the fact that Philemon himself owed Paul his very life (vv. 18-19). In making this offer, Paul models for Philemon the self-sacrifice that he is seeking.

The gospel, properly proclaimed, ought to have a liberating impact on oppressive social structures in the world, not just on individual self-understanding in relation to God. Christianity is not just an otherworldly, ethereal religion. Faith is concrete. Consistent with the cross, it calls all believers to die daily to worldly self-interest, especially in our interactions with other believers. The preacher will want to explore typical life experiences where believers fail to "do the right thing," not making the connection between the truth claims of the gospel and various segments of life, even when their hearts are otherwise basically in the right place.

Paul in this text shows us how to encourage fellow believers to do the right thing. Rather than tear down the offender, one should strive to make appeals to the good character, spiritual self-interest, and kingdom-oriented goals of believers. In short, effective exhortation honors the best in transgressors and helps them to see that acting rightly is consistent with who they have become in Christ and what they want to do for Christ; that obedience to God always results in a net gain even when such obedience feels like a loss (Phil. 3:7-11; Mark 8:34-38). Exhorters likewise are called on to model the self-sacrificial conduct they want to promote in others, just as Jesus provided such a model for us. Otherwise, exhortation appears arrogant and motivated by a desire to control others.

*Robert A. J. Gagnon*

## Nativity of the Lord (Christmas Day), Years A, B, C

First Lesson: Isaiah 52:7-10
(Psalm 98)
**Second Lesson: Hebrews 1:1-4, (5-12)**
Gospel Lesson: John 1:1-14

[This commentary is confined to 1:1-4; for 1:5-12 see the Twentieth Sunday after Pentecost, Year B.]

Hebrews begins with a ringing affirmation of the identity of Jesus Christ.

Initially the work of Christ is identified in terms of divine speaking. Divine speaking is an integral form of divine revelation; it is at the core of the Jewish understanding of how God is made known. God's speaking in Christ is set here in continuity with and in contrast to God's past speaking by the prophets. There is no suggestion of God's speaking through nature, although this is not excluded. Divine speaking, moreover, shows great versatility; it takes place in many and varied forms. Now there is a radically new form to God's speaking; God has spoken through the Son. This Son not only has superior status; he also has a role that transcends his earthly status, for he is heir of all things and the agent of God in creation. It is God who appoints the role assigned to Jesus. His arrival takes place in the last days, a term signifying the dawning of the world to come here and now.

The nature of Jesus is spelled out in terms of being and behavior, of ontology and action. He is the reflection of God's glory and the exact imprint of his being. These images capture both the distinction and identity between God and the Son. God and the Son are to be distinguished, yet the Son makes manifest the very glory and being of God. Moreover, the Son shares in the creative activity of God, for by his powerful word he sustains all things. God keeps the world in being through the agency of the Son's word. The imagery of creation through the word signals the ease by which the Son sustains the world.

The Son's historical mission in the world is described as that of having made purification for sin. The Son has given his life once for all as a sacrifice for sins. Consequent to this work he is exalted on high, taking a place of honor alongside God. He now shares the majesty of the divine. Hence he stands tall above the angels, inheriting a name as Son that is superior to theirs.

These four verses provide a sweeping and magnificent analysis of the person and work of Christ. They recast the narrative of the gospel in a way that knits the life of Jesus back through God's dealings with Israel into creation and forward through the present glory of God into the final destiny of the world. The ensuing network of scriptural texts drives this home by spelling out the way in which Christ surpassed the status and work of angels.

Today, Christmas Day, the glory of the Christian calendar in the Western Church, we are confronted anew by the marvel of the Christmas message and event. To come to terms with Jesus Christ is to cross a threshold in God's dealing with the world. Once we realize what has transpired, there can be no going back. We are introduced to the Son of God who has revealed the very mind of God, who has saved us from our sins, and who now reigns exalted forever before the throne of God. The crucial theme of divine revelation is worth pondering.

Revelation in the Christian tradition is progressive in nature. There is God's general revelation in nature, wherein God speaks in conscience and the natural order, making manifest his nature and power. Beyond that there is God's special revelation in Israel. The prophets of old are not important because they were especially learned, or because they had unique insights into the divine, or because they had special experiences of the divine. They were set apart by God to receive his Word of promise and judgment as God worked in the events of Israel's history. By speaking to them God made known his specific intentions and purposes. This special revelation is pre-

469

served and treasured in the Old Testament of the church. We may ignore this revelation, but it stands there in the Christian canon as secure as the Rock of Gibraltar against every effort to remove it.

Beyond this special revelation, there is extraspecial revelation. There is now a definitive and normative revelation given in the Son of God. There is a unique, irreplaceable, inimitable, unsurpassable Word from God in Jesus Christ. As Christians we await no further new revelation from God. The message of that revelation is so simple it can be printed on a postcard.

To be sure, there is personal revelation to us in our varied circumstances leading us in this or that vocation, calling us into the varied ministries of the church, sending us this way or that, and the like. This is a revelation given to the individual; it is not a public revelation given to the church. One test of the divine origin of such personal revelation is that it fits with the revelation given in Jesus Christ. Moreover, we await the final, awesome revelation of God at the consummation of the ages. This will indeed be a public revelation, but it will be a public revelation of the status and victory of the Son already achieved in human history.

In the meantime we live in the light of the revelation given in the Son. Ultimately we hear no other word, attend to no other voice, and accept no other message than that given here. To accept this revelation is to cease one's searching. In coming to terms with the manifestation of God through the Son, we now believe that we have knowledge of God. We no longer are weighing our options or hedging our bets; the times for sifting the options and sorting through the data have passed. We have left the world of human opinion and entered into the manifested knowledge of God. We have crossed the Rubicon of faith and taken up residence in the city of God. We now inhabit a new world, the glorious world of God made available to us in the Son.

Stretched to the limits of our intellects yet drawn by the wonder of what has happened, we now strain to see everything by the light of the Son. Creation itself is looked upon as the product of his creative handiwork. The origin and destiny of the world are enfolded in the creative activity of the Son of God, who was born among us.

There can therefore be no going back over the threshold into the old world, not even to the old and wonderful world of Israel. Whatever befalls us, we must stand firm in our faith and commitment. The temptation to draw back is of course real. It was so real for the recipients of the letter to the Hebrews that this epistle is a sustained argument insisting that there can be no return to Judaism as it was before the coming of Christ. The core of the argument is given here in a nutshell. Once we know who Christ is, we cannot go back over the threshold of faith. Not only do we have to treat the new revelation from God as genuine knowledge, that revelation requires commitment even to the point of death.

This remains in place for all time and calls for the same response today as it did of old. Many in our culture toy with divine revelation; they think it too good to be true and sit on the sidelines. Some dismiss it as a labor-saving device unworthy of the critical intellect. Others set it aside as arbitrary, or they interpret claims to special revelation as the last resort of those who are hell-bent on imposing their will upon others. Yet others decry the use of divine revelation to sanction violence and intolerance. The pressure to cave in and abandon the faith is subtler but no less real than it was in first-century Rome.

It is pivotal that Christians recover their intellectual nerve at this point. There is no substitute for robust theology in the recovery of faith in our generation. Sentimental feelings or diffuse forms of gratitude, welcome as they are, are not enough. Everything hinges on what we think of Jesus Christ. If all we have is a prophet, we are indeed blessed. If he is more than a prophet, and if he is in reality the Son of God, then the blessings pour out in abundance through all of creation from beginning to end, from first to last, from this glorious day to all the days of our lives. If he is what the faith says he is, then the debate is over; we have no alternative to flying the flag and sticking to our guns. Like Christ himself, we must live it through to the end, come what suffering there may be. There is no alternative once we see who he is, what he has done, and where he now reigns for evermore with the Father. To him be glory unto ages of ages!

*William J. Abraham*

## Twentieth Sunday after Pentecost, Year B

First Lesson: Job 1:1; 2:1-10
(Psalm 26)
**Second Lesson: Hebrews 1:1-4, 2:5-12**
Gospel Lesson: Mark 10:2-16

[This commentary is confined to 2:5-12; for commentary on 1:1-4, see the Nativity of the Lord (Christmas Day), Years A, B, C.]

The Jewish believers who received this letter clearly believed that angels had a crucial role in God's way of running the universe. Angels operated as agents of God, mediating, for example, the law of God to Moses. They had a high place in the divine economy. In the previous chapter the author insists that Christ had a superior status to angels. Here he resumes the theme by arguing that Christ's activity and destiny surpass that of angels. God did not subject the coming world to angels; rather, he subjected it to Christ, who gained his glory by suffering death for everyone. In doing so he fulfills God's plan for humanity; he achieves that plan not by setting aside human agents but by standing with them as an equal.

The style of argument used here is foreign to modern sensibilities, but it was not unusual in the ancient world. Thus vague allusions to texts ("someone has testified somewhere") are found in first-century authors, including Philo. The messianic reading of the Old Testament texts is common in Hebrews and was available hermeneutically as a reading strategy to Jewish Christians.

Here the meaning of Psalm 8:4-6 is deftly reworked to speak of the life of Christ. The psalm describes the lofty status given to human beings. While they are created lower than the angels, God has crowned them with glory and honor, subjecting all things under their feet. The gloss immediately following emphasizes the totality of human subjection; God left nothing outside of human control. However (and here we see the shift in meaning in motion), such subjection is not currently visible in creation, indicating that human beings have not yet fulfilled God's promise for them. This creates the opening for indicating how the promise is actually realized; that is, it is realized through Christ, who is now crowned with glory and honor. He is the human agent who led the way to the fulfillment of God's destiny for humanity. For a little while he was a little lower than the angels; he was truly human, living among us; he has now carried through God's intentions for human agents in the created order.

Christ's achievement in this regard did not happen accidentally. Christ received his status as a true human agent because he suffered death. By the grace of God he suffered death, so that he might taste death for everyone.

This way of fulfilling God's destiny for human beings, that is, bringing many children to their intended glory, was entirely fitting. It was right for God, through whom all things exist, to carry out his purposes this way, because it enables the one who sanctifies and those sanctified to have one Father. It makes possible a radical solidarity between the Savior and the saved; both can stand together in the congregation, praising God as children of the one God. Indeed, Jesus is not ashamed to call us brothers and sisters. There is, therefore, an extraordinary unity between believers and the one in whom they believe.

Teasing out the theological significance of this text is an enormous challenge. I suggest the following lines of thought.

We begin with the observation that, as it is, we do not see the world as it is meant to be. We do not see human beings crowned with glory and honor. On the contrary we see death, destruction, misery, sin, and disaster all around us. Rather than finding human beings fulfilling their God-given destiny, tending creation as God intended, we find human beings in bondage to themselves and to creation. Rather than seeing life lived in harmony with the divine order, we see the divine order disrupted by human nastiness and evil. Rather than experiencing life to the full, we experience life as a network of heavy burdens that threaten our security and well-being. We find things out of control; we see life riddled with anxiety; we experience disorientation and disruption.

Such observations do not, of course, always come easy. At times we prefer to look the other way or to drown ourselves in busyness and distractions. We switch off as best we can. We invent various illusions to hide the truth from ourselves. There are any number of feel-good schemes to enable us to whistle our way through the dark and keep our spirits alive. Indeed, life at times can be so brutal that we rightly welcome any help we can get to carry us through. It would be cruel in the extreme to cast aside any effort to make life bearable. Yet we can and should go deeper.

We can go deeper for this reason. We see Jesus, who for a little while was made lower than the angels but is now crowned with glory and honor. We have found one who has lived life on earth as God intended it to be lived. God has not abandoned his creation but has entered into it. On the scale of eternity and in the vastness of creation, this may appear to be a small thing.

We are told that it was for a little while that Jesus was made lower than the angels. But what a little while! What a momentous little while! What a critical little while! God has not abandoned his creation to sin and death; he has started anew from within human history in the person of Jesus. One life, one little while long ago, has become the turning point of human history. We see Jesus crowned with glory and honor.

Yet it is not the usual glory and honor; it is glory and honor on the other side of the world as it is, full of death and destruction. God has not achieved his purposes for the world in Jesus apart from life as we know it. Jesus has entered into every facet of human existence, drinking the dregs of suffering and death, tasting it on our behalf. God has broken the power of death and hell by entering into it, by taking the full force of sin and evil upon himself, by breaking through the brutality of disorder, and by coming through the other end unintimidated by sin and rebellion. It is precisely because we see this that we can look at the world and ourselves as they are; we can look the world in the eye and not be distracted or afraid. We do not need to run away, or be distracted, or be in denial. We can look at the world in hope, for we see human life as it ought to be, even in the midst of appalling evil. We see one of our own, flesh of our flesh and blood of our blood, crowned with glory and honor.

This Jesus is the pioneer of life, as it ought to be and now can be through his grace. God has planned things this way. Our natural response to the way things are is often one of shame and dismay. We are ashamed at what goes on around us; we are ashamed at what people do to one another; we are ashamed at the way we ourselves have behaved. But God is not intimidated by our shame. He has arranged a way beyond our shame, disgrace, and embarrassment by sending Jesus, who has gladly suffered and died for us. The Savior and the saved operate on the same playing field; the Healer and the healed share the same nature; the Liberator has become one of the oppressed; the one who sanctifies and those who are sanctified all have one Father. Jesus is not ashamed to call us brothers and sisters, leading us in praise in the midst of the congregation and pioneering the way of trust in God. He is bringing us to glory in God's inimitable and appropriate way.

Hence we recover our nerve as human beings. We no longer crave to fly away to the world of angels and give up on the human race; we seek no ethereal existence above us. Nor do we give up and descend into the life of the beasts; we seek no base existence below us. We are thrilled to be human! We are delighted to be what God made us to be! We do so because we see in Jesus what we are meant to be. Better still, we see that human life as it is meant to be can be lived out in history. We now face the future with ineradicable hope and faith. So let there be no more escapism, no more despair, no more false hopes and false starts. We look at ourselves as we are, and we remember what we are meant to be. We are neither angels nor beasts; we are children of God. We are brought to glory by a pioneer who has given his all for our salvation. Let us, with him, praise God in the midst of the congregation!

*William J. Abraham*

## First Sunday after Christmas, Year A

First Lesson: Isaiah 63:7-9
(Psalm 148)
**Second Lesson: Hebrews 2:10-18**
Gospel Lesson: Matthew 2:13-23

These verses are part of a tightly argued effort to establish that it was fitting for Jesus to suffer in providing salvation to those who believe. Where chapter 1 focused on the deity of Christ, chapter 2 insists on his humanity. Both features of his nature were crucial in the pastoral situation in view. The Jewish Christian readers were clearly facing pressure to abandon the faith. The antidote to such pressure was to get a clear grasp on the one they had come to believe. His deity makes it clear that he surpasses the status of the angels who mediated the Mosaic Law; his true humanity makes it clear that he truly understands and can minister to those undergoing persecution and suffering.

Christ reached his position of glory through suffering. It was fitting for this strategy to be adopted by God, for whom and through whom all things exist. Christ's role in salvation is that of a pioneer who brings many children to glory through his suffering. God has so arranged things that the one who sanctifies and those sanctified have one Father. Because of this strategy, rather than feeling awkward or embarrassed at having gone through suffering, Christ is not ashamed to call believers brothers and sisters. The Old Testament prophecies from Psalm 22 and Isaiah 8 show that the Messiah would indeed acknowledge them as such in the midst of the congregation;

in turn, such an acknowledgment would be the occasion for trust in God and praise of God. Hence this is not some accident of history but something long planned by God. God has intended all along that the pioneer of salvation be one with those he will save.

In other words, the children to be saved share flesh and blood, so their Savior should share their flesh and blood. By entering into human existence to the full, indeed to the very point of death, Christ has destroyed the devil, the one who has the power of death. And he has freed those who were held in slavery by the fear of death.

He came not to help angels but to minister to the descendants of Abraham. It was no accident that Christ became like his brothers and sisters in every respect. Knowing human existence from the inside, he was able to be a merciful and faithful high priest when he made atonement for the sins of the people. Moreover, because he was tested and suffered, he is now able to help those who are being tested by opposition, ridicule, persecution, suffering, and the like.

The likely pastoral situation addressed here is that of Jewish Christians who had come to Christ but were now having second thoughts about staying the course. Perhaps they had thought the whole nation would accept Christ as the Messiah, even though he had suffered, and that Christ would soon return and establish his kingdom. They are now moving into a second generation, and things have not quite worked out as anticipated. Perhaps they are facing pressure from friends and former teachers who challenge their allegiance to an impostor who was crucified. The writer confronts these challenges head-on by insisting that Jesus is fully divine and fully human. In his divinity he rises above all prior revelation and defeats the power of the devil; in his suffering humanity he comes alongside human beings in their sin and helps them in times of testing. The latter is the focus of the reading.

The temptation to abandon the Christian faith is a perennial one. It has been played out in the history of Western culture over the last three hundred years, reaching its climax in the last half of the twentieth century. For a host of reasons our culture has systematically set aside the Christian faith, becoming post-Christian in its media, its educational institutions, its legal arrangements, its political rhetoric, and its moral discourse. How should we respond to this crisis? This text supplies a number of clues.

First, we should do all we can to understand what has happened and why. Like the writer to the Hebrews, we should seek to get under the skin of those who have abandoned the faith or are in danger of giving up on it. This is not a time for scolding, or hand-wringing, or grandiose apocalyptic warning. We need to come to terms with the pressures that have led to a failure of nerve on the part of so many members of the church and enter sympatheti-cally into the thought world that produced the cognitive dissonance. Like the Savior who has come into our world as it is and not as we might like it to be, we should get alongside our unbelieving generation and feel the force of the intellectual, moral, and spiritual objections they explicitly and implic-itly have adopted. Yet we should do this with confidence, sure in our hearts of the faith we have received and certain that it speaks to the human condi-tion as it is.

Second, we can gain such confidence by returning to the bedrock basics of the Christian faith. In the end the faith is centered on Jesus Christ, fully divine and fully human. This is the bottom line; this is the end of the road; this is the heart of the matter. If this claim stands, then we can hold firm and not be intimidated or panicked by the loss of faith in our culture. If we enter a new Dark Ages, then this faith will sustain us. If we experience a Third Great Awakening, then this faith will be its foundation. To be sure, there is much more to the faith than this stark christological assertion. However, the Christian faith stands or falls with the status of Jesus. If in-deed he is fully divine and fully human, then we cannot cave in to the pres-sures of our culture. On the contrary, we have stumbled into the secret of salvation and healing for the world.

Third, the challenge is to bring this good news to life by persuading peo-ple that what God did in Jesus Christ is fitting. The standard of intellectual success is soft rather than hard; it is a matter of illumination rather than of proof. It is God who has come to us in Jesus. God has entered our world and defeated the powers of sin, death, and the demonic. We are not dealing here with an angel, a sage, a charismatic politician, a great philosopher, or the like. We welcome such folk and the treasures they bring; however, if we are to live as God planned and intended, we need to have God come among us and lead us. We need a divine agent, a divine presence, and a divine touch. Anything less is too weak and inadequate. Equally, we need one who is one of us, one of our own, one who has lived the life of flesh and blood that we ourselves live. We need a human agent, a human presence, and a human touch. Anything less is too distant and ethereal. This is precisely what we have in Jesus Christ. He is fully divine and fully human. His life and work represent a fitting and appropriate divine strategy to put things right for Jew and Gentile.

Fourth, in his humanity he has entered into the full contours and depths of human existence. He has taken on the demonic and defeated it. He has taken the fear out of death; we still have sorrow at the loss of loved ones and at the thought of our own deaths, but the terror has gone for good in the res-urrection of Jesus. He has become our faithful high priest, taking our needs directly into the presence of God. He has in mercy borne our sins in his sacrifice on the cross. Because he has suffered, he is now able to help us in our suffering both in our personal lives and in a culture that has lost hope in God.

Jesus Christ is not a paper Jesus. He is not someone hidden in the pages of a book or entombed in an ancient text. He came from God, lived among us as one fully divine and fully human, and did all that was needed to bring us to God and fulfill the destiny God has for us. He is now raised from the dead, ready and willing to lead us all to glory as his brothers and sisters. Exalted as he was and is, he knows us as we are. He has lived among us as bone of our bone and flesh of our flesh. He has done this for our sakes, so that he might share our sufferings and help us when we are tested. It was fitting that he should defeat the powers of evil and take us to glory in this manner. Because it is fitting, it is indeed true.

*William J. Abraham*

## Twenty-first Sunday after Pentecost, Year B

First Lesson: Job 23:1-9, 16-17
(Psalm 22:1-15)
**Second Lesson: Hebrews 4:12-16**
Gospel Lesson: Mark 10:17-31

This unit marks the end of a short sermon that declares that Jesus is superior to Moses and begins a new section that identifies Jesus as the superlative High Priest. In the wider narrative the author presses the case for remaining committed to Christ by showing the dire consequences of disobedience. While it would be natural to divide the material and relocate the two parts in their respective literary units, when read together they provide ample theological food for reflection. Throughout the text the author appeals to what God has said in the past as both a warrant for the claims advanced and a spur to persisting in the faith.

In 4:12-13 we have a brief comment on the nature and effectiveness of the divine Word working in the present. The Word of God is conceived not as a wooden word from the past, but as living and active in the present. The Word of God is compared in its sharpness to the best two-edged sword. Its ability to gain access to the inner recesses of the human mind is vividly captured in two metaphors. It can divide soul from spirit and slit joints from marrow. Humanly these are impossible feats; yet the Word of God can do it. Thus the Word is able to judge the thoughts and intentions of the heart. As a result, what is hidden is clearly visible to God. Hiding from God is impossible. All are naked and laid bare to God, who holds all responsible for their actions. God is a judge to whom all must render account.

These remarks drive home the impact of the preceding promises and warnings derived from Scripture. As the reader is drawn into agreement, they explain why he or she finds it so searching and evoke persistent, obedient trust. Should the reader disagree, they invite him or her to ponder the Word anew so that God may bring to light his or her true thoughts and intentions. Failure to understand cannot be attributed to failure in the effectiveness of the Word of God.

This is a sobering judgment. The encounter between God and his people is depicted in dramatic and even violent imagery. The reader is depicted as extremely vulnerable; the call to accountability is unmistakable. We are laid low, as if cowering before an inescapable and powerful foe who can strike us through the heart.

We are ready for the word of comfort and reassurance that follows immediately in verses 14-16. The switch to Jesus, the Son of God, as our great High Priest is welcome good news. God has wounded us to heal us and restore us. He has sent his Son, who acts as a great high priest on our behalf. We have a representative from God's side who has passed from earth to heaven. His heavenly presence guarantees help. Therefore we should hold fast to our confession. We are not left to flounder under pressure. Our High Priest knows what it is like; he is able to sympathize with our weaknesses; he has been tested and tempted in every respect, as we have. Yet he has never yielded to sin. We can now approach his throne, a symbol not of his distance from us but of his power to aid us, and we can do so with boldness. We will find there abundant grace and mercy to help in the current time of need.

What is the theological significance of this material?

First, we discern here the powerful dialectic between law and grace, between judgment and promise, between bad news and good news, and between diagnosis and prescription. The gospel of Jesus Christ can initially appear irrelevant, distant, and incredible. Cut loose from the wider story of what has gone wrong with the world, it floats in thin air. It can appear as high and dry as a handbook of medicine and medical remedies or as grim and boring as a catalogue of dry, dusty goods in an old warehouse. The handbook comes to life once we discover we are ill, and the catalogue is a treasure once we start looking in earnest for that precise piece of furniture that will fit in our new home. What God has done in Jesus Christ comes alive when we become aware of the ruin of the world and of our lives through sin and rebellion. Hence there comes a time when we have to ponder the ingenuity and depth of human evil if we are to grasp the wonder of God's salvation.

Very often this happens after we have begun the journey of faith rather than before it. It is relatively easy to be drawn to faith. The message may sound good initially; we like what Jesus stands for; the fellowship is warm and inviting; and religion is generally a good thing. It is only on the inside that we realize what we have gotten into. That is why some of the deepest experiences of God emerge well beyond the initial stages of commitment. Sometimes the experience can be so searching and humbling that we doubt our conversion and are liable to excoriate what looks like mediocre discipleship in others. When put to the test, the Word of God cuts to the core of our being and values; we discover pockets of rebellion and resistance that shake us to the foundations.

Second, such exposure and revelation is not of our own doing. We know the depth of our spiritual darkness only as we encounter the light of God. That light breaks forth from his Word as we ponder and internalize it for ourselves. We all know that our best insights take time to germinate. We readily give ourselves time to work through life-changing decisions that will have a long-lasting impact on others and ourselves. We talk to friends, sleep on the issues, ask for a second opinion, and the like. In our spiritual life, it is easy to forget this. We look for a big bang that will bring instant resolution and light. We set aside the patient reading of the Scriptures. We refuse to ponder them as they are, turning to outside sources for a handy remedy. God has appointed his own way of searching us and healing us. He has given us the Scriptures as a means of grace. Through the Scriptures God cuts through our confusion and self-deceit. His Word at times comes crashing in upon us, and we see ourselves as we are, naked, vulnerable, defenseless, caught in the act with nowhere to hide. This can be excruciatingly painful. It appears as if God is out to get us, to hunt us down and kill us. This is indeed God's doing. His grace comes over us in judgment and damnation.

Third, as we weather the storm and stay the course, we discover that grace indeed is at work. God has exposed the wound to heal it; he has shown us the problem so that we may reach for the solution; he has come near us in darkness that we may see the light; he has brought us to our senses to give us a way out. It is then that the tenderness and mercy of God become real to us. The gospel ceases to be high and dry; it draws us into the very life of God. We see the marvel of his coming among us in his Son, reaching down into the full depths of human existence and living within the historical conditions of our broken and rebellious world. The life and work of Jesus Christ take center stage; it is virtually impossible to grow weary of the good news he embodies for us. We awaken to the reality of God's love and mercy.

Yet there is not a hint of sentimental passivity. God's mercy and condescension are a spur to holding fast in the faith and storming the gates of heaven for fresh assistance. We cannot wallow in our vulnerable bondage to self-interest. Given all that Christ has done to bring our needs and requests into the throne room of God, we cannot cave in to the current pressures and walk away from him. He has become our High Priest, our advocate above in the courts of God. He is our hope for forgiveness and a fresh start. We rise up boldly in faith and bring our needs to him so that he may pour out his grace in abundance upon us. We are gripped anew in the marvel of God's generosity and given assurance of his enduring power.

The outcome of such active grace is the ending of sin in our lives. Our great High Priest has lived a fully human life, replete with temptation, frustration, suffering, and death. He has endured the full round of human misery. He has been exposed to the full blast of human envy, nastiness, jealousy, and evil. Joined to the lifeline he has thrown us, we too can live as he did.

*William J. Abraham*

## Twenty-second Sunday after Pentecost, Year B

First Lesson: Job 38:1-7, (34-41)
(Psalm 104:1-9, 24, 35c)
**Second Lesson: Hebrews 5:1-10**
Gospel Lesson: Mark 10:35-45

The image of a high priest is not one that resonates naturally with modern sensibilities. To Jewish readers it was a powerful notion that came naturally to them. The author exploits its significance to explore the superlative resources of Jesus Christ as the Son of God to provide eternal salvation for all who believe and obey.

The role of every high priest is to manage the intercourse between humanity and God. As such he is chosen from among mortals; he is to act on behalf of the people, offering gifts and sacrifices for sins. Being mortal himself and thus subject to weakness, he is able to operate gently with the ignorant and wayward. In the process of his duties, he must also provide sacrifices for his own sins. Following the example of Aaron, the priesthood is an honor given to him by God; it is nothing to claim or presume as a given.

Christ's work as a high priest was by divine appointment. He did not seek it as something to glorify himself. In appointing him God declared that he was his begotten Son and that he was granted a priesthood forever after the order of Melchizedek. Both designations bring out the superlative status of Christ's priesthood. The writer indicates in verse 11 that he is entering deep waters at this point.

While the status of the priesthood is clear (it is that of a Son and of an eternal order), the focus quickly shifts to the life actually lived by this high priest. The core of the material involves a clear echo of Christ's experience in Gethsemane. In the days of his flesh Jesus offered up prayers and supplications, with loud cries and tears, to the one who was able to save him from death. He submitted himself completely to the will of God; because of this submission, God heard him. As the Son of God, he might have expected to escape suffering. However, he was not spared suffering; on the contrary, through his suffering he learned obedience. Gaining perfection through suffering, he became the source of eternal salvation for all who obey him. It is precisely this one who is designated by God as a high priest according to the order of Melchizedek. God himself has appointed this manner of high priesthood, and God himself has prearranged the conditions essential to gaining salvation through him. It is through obeying Christ, and following him in suffering, that God has ordained us to receive eternal salvation.

In our current world we find two contrasting ways of handling the idea of priesthood. Within Protestantism, with its emphasis on the priesthood of all believers, there is little or no sense of the need for a priest. We feel perfectly capable of managing our relations with the divine in our way, at our own pace, and according to our own desires. The distance between God and ourselves is minimal, and we can bridge that distance on our own with relative ease. Within Catholic and Orthodox circles, there is a strong sense of distance and a concomitant sense of need for help; here we know that we need a priest. We need those who will go into the holy of holies and take care of business for us; their job is to do whatever mysterious thing needs to be done on our behalf. In the meantime we can carry on as usual, immersed in our secular interests and duties, leaving divine service to the spiritual officers in charge of the divine economy. One group ignores the distance between God and ourselves; the other conceives the distance in such a way that it can be managed by handing it over in an external manner to religious professionals.

It is important to recognize the real distance between God and ourselves. We think twice about sauntering into the presence of our heroes or of some great political or royal personage. We do not hesitate to find intermediaries who will pave the way and put in a good word for us. The Jewish tradition was deeply aware of the gap that needed to be bridged between God and us. We needed someone to deal with our sin and to bring our gifts to God. God himself had to appoint the appropriate way to do this; we were too self-serving to get it right on our own. In this way we could have some assurance that we had acknowledged the proper distance between the divine and the human, between the holy and the sinful. In following God's appointed priests, we could be sure that God would find our offerings acceptable. Having come to terms with our finitude and sin in this manner, we then capitulated to a different set of temptations. We turned the actions of priests into a system of works that sought to bring merit to our religious endeavors. We turned the distance between ourselves and God into an ingenious excuse to ignore God and get on with our lives as usual.

In the gospel Christ himself has become our high priest. On this analogy for the person and work of Christ, the need for priesthood is sustained. We really do stand at a distance from God, failing negatively by our sin and failing positively by refusing to bring the gifts that are his due. Now God has appointed a high priest, his Son, to bridge the gap and to cover the distance between us and God. This is no temporary procedure; it stands as God's eternal arrangement. God has come from his side of creation and furnished a high priest to stand alongside us.

This high priest shares our nature and thus understands our predicament. He is able to deal gently with the ignorant and the wayward. He understands our propensity to misread the nature of religion and invent our own ways of making it serve our interests. He knows how easily we become distracted and confused, how readily we turn things on their head, how spiritually stupid and obtuse we can be. In response he knows how to control and moderate his feelings toward us. He is unsparingly patient with us. He discharges the duty that befalls every high priest with consummate skill and tenderness, for he knows our weakness within his own very nature.

Indeed, he himself suffered at our hands. The high point of such suffer-

483

ing was in Gethsemane, when he wrestled with the final acts of brutality that were directed toward him. When he prayed, "All things are possible for thee, let this cup pass from me," he meant what he said. It was no theatrical display to heighten the effect when he said, "Thy will be done." He meant every word of it, crying with bitter tears and anguish. He offered up prayers and supplications, with loud cries and tears, to the one who was able to deliver him from death. Such was the depth of his voluntary commitment to come to us as we are, bearing in every fiber of his being the cost of exercising his priesthood on our behalf.

Precisely because of such submission to God's way of securing liberation from evil, he is now able to offer eternal salvation to those who obey him, to those who stay the course under pressure. He asks nothing that he has not himself endured. We can picture the stresses of some of the readers. They stand homeless, their furniture gone, their families split up and divided, haled off to prison, mocked and despised because they have come to faith. They break down in tears, their spirits exhausted and bludgeoned by suffering. They wonder if they had been wise in being baptized. They are drawn to returning to the priesthood and sacrifices they had known in Israel. Obedience has brought them to tears. Then they remember that first obedience brought Jesus to tears. There is nothing to be ashamed of if the cost of discipleship has broken them to the point where all they can do is weep before God.

They follow the rest of the plot. The Son of God submitted reverently to the Father; in his suffering he learned obedience; he was brought to perfection. He trusted God, and he proved that God is faithful to his word. He proved that God honors obedience and faith and brings it out triumphant in the end. So how can they draw back and cave in? How can they return to the old ways that have been superseded by God's new and superlative high priesthood in Jesus? They will continue in obedience and gain the eternal salvation now given by God through Jesus Christ. They will follow the way of suffering and submission that leads to perfection. They will lean on the One whom God has eternally appointed and designated to bring them to eternal glory.

*William J. Abraham*

## Fifth Sunday in Lent, Year B

First Lesson: Jeremiah 31:31-34
(Psalm 51:1-12)
**Second Lesson: Hebrews 5:5-10**
Gospel Lesson: John 12:20-33

This short passage, Hebrews 5:5-10, contains a wealth of imagery and numerous possibilities for a preacher. These verses, along with 4:14–5:5, introduce the enormously complex discussion in Hebrews of Jesus as the great high priest. The two notions of Jesus as Son (5:5) and as priest according to the order of Melchizedek (5:6, 10), which this passage highlights, are typically named as the two primary christological categories for the letter of Hebrews. Thus this passage opens upon the primary theological themes of the letter. Furthermore, images of obedience, prayer, suffering, perfection, and salvation are evoked in brief form in this passage. Each of these ideas plays a fundamental role in the overall theology of Hebrews. Thus this passage opens not only upon the primary themes of this letter but upon nearly every aspect of its theology. Finally, the curious and troubling notion of Jesus learning obedience (5:8) gives a puzzling edge to the passage.

The deep connectedness of this passage to the larger theological themes of Hebrews raises interesting issues for the preacher. It is not clear what an exegetical basis would be for choosing one of these themes over another. And if a theme is focused upon, it is not clear how much and how far to read in the rest of the letter. In some ways the introductory character of this passage means that it does not and perhaps even should not stand on its own. A case could be made that each of the key terms in this passage cannot be comprehended simply by a good reading of this single, isolated passage. Each term needs the longer and more complex accounts in the rest of the letter. We cannot, for instance, understand the import of Melchizedek in 5:6 without reading at least chapters 7 through 10.

Perhaps the best case can be made for the notion of Jesus as high priest being the governing theme of this passage. Both the internal rhetoric of the passage and the larger rhetoric of Hebrews point in that direction. The larger movement of the letter places this passage at the opening of the complex explorations of the new priesthood of Jesus, which runs in a general sense from 4:14 to 10:18. The section begins in 4:14 by combining the idea of priesthood with that of Sonship: "Since, then, we have a great high priest who has passed through the heavens, Jesus, the Son of God, let us hold fast to our confession." This claim initiates the first of many comparisons between the old priesthood and the new. Our passage in fact seems to constitute part of this comparative exercise. The internal rhetoric of the passage also points to this theme. The passage opens and closes with references to the character of Jesus' appointment as high priest.

Thus the priesthood of Jesus is the most natural entry into this passage. In this case it is difficult not to read this passage in light of 7:1–10:18, wherein the full implications of this priesthood are detailed. The complexity of the arguments of Hebrews about priesthood presents a challenge to any reader. It is particularly difficult to know how much of this complexity to read into this passage. At a minimum the conception of the superiority of the priesthood of Jesus seems applicable here, not only because this superiority is the guiding theme of 7:1–10:18 but also because this passage itself engages in a comparison between "every high priest" (5:1) and Jesus.

From 7:1 to 10:18 we learn of the superiority of Jesus in the character of Jesus as high priest, in the nature of the sacrifice, in the place of the sacrifice, in the temporal and cosmic range of the sacrifice, and finally in the effectiveness of the sacrifice for humans. The categories of the old Levitical priesthood are still intact in the new high priesthood of Jesus. But each of these categories becomes transformed because of the unique character of the Melchizedek priesthood.

At most, these many transformations are hinted at in our passage. We can hear echoes of superiority in the assertion that "Christ did not glorify himself . . . but was appointed by [God]" (5:5). The superiority of Jesus' appointment is further detailed in 7:15-22. There are further echoes in the quote from Psalm 110:4:

> You are a priest forever,
> according to the order of Melchizedek. (5:6)

The word "forever" will prove crucial to the character of this new priesthood (see, e.g., 7:24-25). Finally, the images of "having been made perfect," "eternal salvation," and the "all" who may obey in turn anticipate the superiority arguments which follow (e.g., 7:28; 10:1; 12:2; 9:12; 10:10).

Thus, initial linguistic space is put in place for Hebrews's exploration of the superiority of the Melchizedek priesthood of Jesus Christ to the old Levitical priesthood. There are no real hints in 5:5-10 of the ultimate failure of the Levitical priesthood. In chapters 7 through 10, Jesus' priesthood is initially declared to be "better" (see, e.g., 8:6-7). Eventually, however, the many weaknesses of the Levitical priesthood result in its abolishment (10:1-

10). The human character of the Levitical priesthood finally issues in its failure. No sacrifice done by human priests, with animals, in a temple of stone, can be ultimately effective. The human weaknesses of the priests will prove to produce fatal flaws in the whole system.

The assertions of 5:5-10 stand in wonderful tension with this outcome. Here the humanness, even the weakness, of a priest is seen as a good thing. The positive role of weakness, which is asserted in 4:15, sets the stage for our passage: "For we do not have a high priest who is unable to sympathize with our weaknesses, but we have one who in every respect has been tested as we are, yet without sin." This weakness of Jesus is then connected positively to the weakness of every high priest: "He [every high priest] is able to deal gently with the ignorant and wayward, since he himself is subject to weakness" (5:2). Not only is the humanness of Jesus affirmed here, but the weakness of Jesus. Only a high priest who knows weakness can properly intercede for humans who are fundamentally and persistently weak. Jesus has touched enough weakness to be a good priest. Yet this same Jesus must be without sin. Somehow Jesus is imagined as being both weak and without sin.

The nature of this combination of sinlessness and weakness is perhaps elucidated in 5:7-8. First of all, "In the days of his flesh, Jesus offered up prayers and supplications, with loud cries and tears, to the one who was able to save him from death, and he was heard because of his reverent submission" (5:7). These cries and tears must be understood as genuine. Jesus shed tears in anticipation of death. Yet these tears issued not in rebellion or flight but in prayers and submission. Weakness is not sin. Tears are not sin. Perhaps even terror before death is not sin. If this terror leads to prayer and gives way to obedience, then fear of death is not sin. In fact, this experience of "cries and tears" produces a necessary character in Jesus' priesthood. Without these weaknesses Jesus would fall short as high priest.

The precise logic of all this would be frustratingly unclear if not for the assertions of 5:8: "Although he was a Son, he learned obedience through what he suffered." The phrase "although he was a Son" probably signals an acknowledgment of the theological tensions in the superiority and weakness arguments of Hebrews. Nevertheless, the main point seems clear enough: Jesus learned obedience through suffering. While this idea does not solve all our problems and may in fact open up a whole other set of questions, this notion of learning obedience through suffering gives us a far better grasp of the positive role of weakness. Apart from the terrors of suffering, humans will never learn to submit to God. Suffering has the power to rip away human securities and to manifest even to ignorant (5:2) humans the true character of our weakness. The experience of suffering teaches humans about real weakness. Without a sense of weakness it is hard to have faith. Suffering is a necessary and even a positive force in the journey of faith (see the wonderful explorations of this in chaps. 11 and 12).

What is striking in all of this is the exemplary human character of Jesus. Jesus in Hebrews is not simply, as Son of God, the proper object of faith; Jesus is, as human, also the pioneer of faith (12:2). The humanity of Jesus means that Jesus can pave the way on this difficult journey of faith to which Hebrews calls us (see, e.g., the call to perfection in 6:1). The humanity of our high priest means that our priest has preceded us down the road of faith, with its sufferings, tears, and hopes. Jesus may be superior to the angels (1:5-14), but this same Jesus also must know weakness.

The opportunities for a preacher in this passage are numerous. This reading has focused on the wonderful combination of superiority and weakness in Hebrews's portrait of Jesus. But notions of "eternal salvation," "obedience," "perfection," and others also present intriguing possibilities.

*Lewis R. Donelson*

## Twenty-third Sunday after Pentecost, Year B

First Lesson: Job 42:1-6, 10-17
(Psalm 34:1-8, [19-22])
**Second Lesson: Hebrews 7:23-28**
Gospel Lesson: Mark 10:46-52

Three things are important for understanding the context of this passage. First, it constitutes the concluding two paragraphs of a section that probably began in 4:14: first is a hortatory section (4:14-16); then an exposition of what the office of every priest, including Christ, entailed (5:1-10); then an extensive second hortatory section (5:11–6:20); followed by this detailed description of Melchizedek and the fact that Christ's high priesthood was after the order of Melchizedek rather than in the Levitical order (7:1-28).

Second, Hebrews consistently affirms that God appointed the Son as high priest. This is specifically stated in 7:28: "The word of oath . . . appoints a Son who has been made perfect forever." This truth is also clearly affirmed in 5:5-6. God appoints Christ as high priest by using not one but two texts: Psalm 2:7 ("You are my Son, / today I have begotten you") and Psalm 110:4 ("You are a priest forever, / according to the order of Melchizedek"). Thus Christ is both Son and high priest.

Third, the Son as high priest in Melchizedek's order is part of what has been called the "parabola of salvation," which is so basic in Hebrews (used frequently and effectively by Thomas G. Long in other parts of Hebrews, *Hebrews*, Interpretation [Louisville: John Knox, 1997], pp. 22, 27, 43, 79, 104, 127). Already the opening paragraph, 1:1-4, exhibits such a parabola concerning the Son. It begins in heaven: the Son is the one through whom God made the worlds, who is also the reflection of God's glory and the exact imprint of God's being. Among other things, this Son left heaven, came to earth, and made purification for sin. After that he went back to heaven and sat down at the right hand of the Majesty on high, thus also being the one God appointed as the heir of all things.

In Hebrews 7 this "parabola of salvation" can also be used in elucidating Hebrews's typology concerning Melchizedek. 7:1-3 speaks of the Melchizedek of Genesis 14 as "resembling the Son of God" in that he has neither father, mother, genealogy, beginning of days or end of life, and thus "remains a priest forever." That is, Melchizedek was a "literary-historical" type of Christ. In that, in terms of what the biblical record both did and did not say about him, Melchizedek "resembled the Son of God" in heaven. But "on earth" Jesus was declared to be high priest after the order of Melchizedek. As such he went through genuine temptations and learned obedience from the things that he suffered (4:15; 5:7-9a). But since he also became priest by the power of an indestructible life (7:16), 7:28 can say that he was high priest as the Son who was made perfect forever. This "parabola of salvation" in typology might be pictured as follows.

| | |
|---|---|
| A. The Son of God is the heavenly pattern or archetype, 7:3; cf. 8:6 | D. The Son as high priest made perfect forever, 7:26-28; cf. 4:14 |
| Heaven | |
| --- | Heaven |
| Earth | |
| | Earth |
| B. Melchizedek as high priest is a type resembling the Son, 7:3, 8 | C. Jesus as high priest after Melchizedek's order, 7:15-17, 21; cf. 5:6 |

We turn now to the text itself. Hebrews 7:23-25 centers on one main idea, namely, that Christ is a *permanent* high priest. This is developed in verses 23-24 by the contrast between the "former" high priests and the one high priest, Jesus. The old covenant priests were "many in number"; according to Josephus's reckoning (*Antiquities* 20.227), there were eighty-three high priests from the time of Aaron to the cessation of temple worship in A.D. 70. Each died in turn; as our text states: "They were prevented by death from continuing in office." Such was not true of Christ, for he "holds his priesthood permanently." The Greek word here is *aparabaton,* which has the meanings "permanent," "unchangeable," "inviolable." The reason why his priesthood is permanent is "because he continues forever." In 7:16 it is affirmed that Jesus is high priest "through the power of an indestructible life," no doubt referring to his resurrection and especially his continued existence in heaven at God's right hand. Thus Jesus is not a continuing high priest in any symbolic way (as Melchizedek himself was; cf. 7:3) — he actually lives and is seated at the right hand of the Majesty on high.

Verse 25 gives the important consequence of this permanent priesthood of Jesus: "He is able for all time to save those who approach God through him." The phrase in Greek translated duratively as "for all time" may also be translated in the qualitative sense of "completely." Perhaps it contains both ideas at once and could be translated "absolutely." Remember that the book of Hebrews was written to encourage Christian people who were in danger of giving up. The author wanted them to know that there was absolutely no doubt about this Son High Priest and his saving ability. His salvation is "for all times" and "in every way."

The reason he can save absolutely is stated: "since he always lives to make intercession for them." Earlier (4:14-16) we were told that he sympathizes with people in their temptation and gives mercy and grace to help in time of need (cf. also 2:17). Here his work is summed up as "intercession." The work of intercession is attributed to the Suffering Servant in Isaiah 53:12:

> Yet he bore the sin of many,
>     and made intercession for the transgressors.

It is exemplified in the ministry of the earthly Jesus (cf. Luke 22:32 and John 17). But here it refers to Christ's heavenly intercession in our behalf. Saint Paul rarely speaks of Christ as high priest, but in the one passage that he clearly does so (Rom. 8:34: ". . . who is at the right hand of God, who indeed intercedes for us"), he is also referring to his heavenly intercession. Notably

Christ's heavenly intercession is not problematic, as if he were pleading our cause before a reluctant God. After all, he is the Son, God's Son, who is high priest, and his self-offering was utterly acceptable and efficacious. His heavenly intercession is never ending, and therefore his salvation is absolute.

It is sometimes said that 7:26-28 recaps what is said in 7:1-25. In a sense that is true, but it actually reaches back further to the beginning of this section (4:14–7:28), picking up ideas affirmed in 4:14-15 and 5:1-10. The idea of 4:14 ("we have a great high priest who has passed through the heavens, Jesus, the Son of God") is picked up here in the reference to Jesus as Son and as the one "exalted above the heavens." The idea of 4:15 ("one who . . . has been tested as we are, yet without sin") is picked up here in the description "holy, blameless, undefiled, separated from sinners." The idea expressed in 5:3 ("he must offer sacrifice for his own sins as well as for those of the people") is picked up in verse 27 with reference to "those" same old covenant high priests. And finally, the ideas of 5:5-10 (God appointing Jesus by using Pss. 2:7 and 110:4 and Jesus becoming high priest when or after he was made perfect) are picked up here in 7:28: "The oath . . . appoints a Son [as high priest] who has been made perfect forever."

There are two main ideas in this paragraph: Jesus is the *sinless* high priest, and he is the *perfected heavenly* high priest. In regard to his being sinless, the three words used can best be understood as referring to slightly different aspects of his sinless quality: "holy" refers to his religious qualification of being separated out to God's service; "blameless" refers to his cultic qualities — there is nothing that disqualifies him; and "undefiled" probably refers to his moral qualification — as high priest, he has done no evil. In verse 27 it is therefore said that he did not need to offer sacrifices for his own sins as did the old covenant high priests, and in verse 28 it is implied that the Son did not have "weakness" (Gk. *astheneia*) like the old covenant high priests. Indeed, as the author states in 7:26: "Such a high priest" meets our need!

Furthermore, he is our perfected heavenly high priest. His being "perfected" did not come easily. In 2:10 it was fitting that God should make "the pioneer of their salvation perfect through sufferings." Jesus did not need to become "morally perfect" (he was "without sin" — 4:15), but he did have to become qualified for the office of high priest by undergoing his own suffering. In fact, he shared our flesh and blood and therefore died to save us from fear of death (2:14). He himself was tested, tempted, tried (2:18; 4:15). He learned obedience from the things he suffered and then was made perfect (5:9, 10), Son though he was (5:8). Nevertheless, he did not shrink back but in faithfulness carried out God's plan for him. The note of encouragement is that he can help us through our testing, temptations, and trials.

And he is the heavenly high priest who has, as Son, God's approval: he is exalted with God in heaven. He is the true high priest for all times and for all situations. When we are discouraged, we can look up to him and find mercy and grace to help in time of need.

*Andrew Bandstra*

## Twenty-fourth Sunday after Pentecost, Year B

First Lesson: Ruth 1:1-18
(Psalm 146)
**Second Lesson: Hebrews 9:11-14**
Gospel Lesson: Mark 12:28-34

This passage belongs to a section that probably runs from 8:1 to 10:31. The thought in this section is developed in terms of two Old Testament texts: Jeremiah 31:31-34 and Psalm 40:6-8. The former is quoted and commented on in Hebrews 8:7-13 and 10:15-18. The Jeremiah passage speaks of God's intention to establish the more effective new covenant that is founded, as Hebrews says, on better promises. Psalm 40:6-8 is quoted and commented on in Hebrews 10:5-10. This passage is understood to refer to the better offering that Jesus gave in comparison to those of the old covenant in which God (no longer) delights. Thus the general theme of this section, 8:1–10:31, is that Jesus provides the better sacrifice under the new covenant that is more effective for providing sanctification, purification, and perfection than the old covenant sacrifices.

Chapter 9, in which our passage sits, functions as the bridge between the two main texts by developing the comparison between the sanctuaries (an idea introduced already in 8:1-6) of the old and new covenants with their respective rituals. 9:1-10 basically describes the sanctuary and rituals under the old covenant, especially the ritual reflected in the Day of Atonement. 9:11-28 involves a series of comparisons and contrasts between what was accomplished under the old covenant and under the new.

9:11-14 has two sentences: verses 11-12 and 13-14. The first has as its central premise that Christ as high priest, in gaining eternal redemption, entered once for all into the real Holy Place in heaven. The second sentence proclaims that while the blood sprinkled in the rituals of the old covenant had some efficacy — "sanctifying as far as fleshly cleansing is concerned" — the blood of Christ purifies our conscience from dead works so that we serve the living God. Thus the two main ideas of this text, very much worth preaching, are that the high-priestly work of Christ has gone both *higher* and *deeper* than the blood shed and sprinkled under the old covenant. It has gone *higher* because his work carried him in definitive fashion into the true sanctuary, the Holy Place in heaven, in gaining our eternal redemption. It has gone *deeper* because it penetrates to the very core of our being, to the cleansing of our conscience in order that we may serve the living God.

Hebrews 9:11-12. Two smaller points of interpretation need to be mentioned. First, there is a textual-critical item in verse 11: Is it "the good things that have come" or "the good things to come"? The former is to be followed, not only because it has good external support, but also because it fits much better in this context. In 9:10 the author had spoken of certain "fleshly regulations" that were in force "until the time of reformation," no doubt referring to the time of "these last days" with God speaking through his Son (1:2). Now that Christ has appeared, "the good things to come" are "the good things that have come." The second point is how to construct the phrase in verse 11 which in the Greek is introduced with *dia* with the genitive, which can be either "means/instrumental," "by means of the greater and more perfect tent" (thus referring somehow symbolically to Christ's body), or "local," "through the greater and more perfect tent" (thus referring to the first compartment of the heavenly temple). Some have argued that since in verse 12 *dia* is twice used in the "means/instrumental" sense, it should have the same meaning in verse 11. But this is not absolutely required, and the local sense certainly fits much better with the imagery of the Day of Atonement in which the high priest, under the old covenant, first went through the "first compartment" and then into "the Most Holy Place" (9:2, 8). Christ also went through the first compartment in heaven to arrive at the heavenly Holy Place directly in the presence of God.

Of greater import for understanding the main thrust of the text — and certainly much more seriously debated — is the exact force of the two *dia* phrases in verse 12 and the temporal nuance of the aorist participle at the end of that verse: *heuramenos*. All are agreed that the two *dia* phrases are to be understood as expressing "means/instrument," such as "by means of" or "by virtue of," but they differ on how much the work of Christ must be understood with reference to the Day of Atonement with which it is being compared. The temporal nuance of the participle raises the following options: Should it be understood as referring to an action antecedent to the main verb: "he entered . . . having obtained eternal redemption"? Or should it be understood as referring to an action coincident with or subsequent to the action of the main verb: "he entered . . . thus securing eternal redemption"?

In the main there are three views reflecting these decisions.

1. Emphasis is sometimes placed on the comparison of Jesus' work with what happened on the Day of Atonement when the high priest entered the Most Holy Place carrying or "with" the blood of animals. (The translation of the NRSV in 9:12 could be understood in that way — following 9:25, "with blood not his own.") It is therefore suggested that Christ's atonement was not completed on the cross but only when Christ entered the heavenly Most Holy Place and sprinkled the blood on the heavenly altar. Only then was atonement and eternal redemption secured. In this view the sacrifice on the cross is a necessary but preliminary work. This view does not appropriately translate the *dia* phrases (which can more correctly be translated "by virtue of . . .") and does not give sufficient recognition to other passages in Hebrews that speak of the cross as "the single sacrifice for sin" (10:12) and our being sanctified "through the offering of the body of Jesus Christ once for all" (10:10).

2. There are those, on the other hand, who emphasize that the parallel to the ritual on the Day of Atonement should not be pressed. The *dia* phrases indicate instrument or means, and even 9:25 (where *en* is used) may be understood in an instrumental sense. Besides, the participle at the end of verse 12 should be understood as giving antecedent action, and thus eternal redemption was secured on the cross, prior to Jesus entering into heaven. His entering into heaven is part of his priestly work but not an integral part of securing eternal redemption.

3. But, as many commentators have pointed out (cf., e.g., William Lane, *Hebrews 9–13*, Word Biblical Commentary [Dallas: Word, 1991], pp. 230, 239), the participle at the end of verse 12 seems to have a future look, since "securing redemption" is probably related to his work, stated in verse 14, of cleansing our consciences from dead works. In that case both stages of Christ's priestly work are necessary in securing our eternal redemption. The first stage is his offering of his body once for all as the one sacrifice for sins forever (10:10, 12); the second, his appearance before God as the one who has been slain (as in the case of the Lamb in Rev. 5:6). A choice between these last two views is difficult, but the third position seems best to represent all of the emphases in the book of Hebrews.

Hebrews 9:13-14. In contrast to the previous sentence, this second sen-

494

tence has only one difficult phrase to interpret — "through the eternal Spirit." It probably means that as the Suffering Servant, he accomplished every part of his ministry through the divine Spirit.

The construction is that of a first-class conditional sentence with a less-to-greater argument: if such and such is true, how much more is something else true. In first-class conditional sentences the protasis is assumed to be true and can often be translated as causal: "since the blood of goats and bulls. . . ." In verse 13 the author broadens his reference beyond the animals used on the Day of Atonement and includes other sacrificial animals, including the ashes of a heifer in cleansing defilement, as recorded in Numbers 19. The important thing to note is that such rituals did have a certain efficacy — they sanctified for the cleansing of the flesh. Thus they could do what was necessary for people under the old covenant to draw as near to God as was possible under that covenant. In terms of temple imagery, those sacrifices were efficacious for getting as close to God as the "court of Israel" and the "court of the women." But as the contrast of the two verses implies, the old covenant sacrifices did not touch the conscience of the worshiper (cf. 10:1-4).

The "how much more" argument has to do with the efficacy of the blood of Christ. The sacrifices of the old covenant could not "perfect the conscience of the worshiper" (9:9). But the blood of Christ can and does. It reaches down into the very center of the worshipers' being and cleanses the conscience from dead works. The word "conscience" is used here and in 9:9; 10:2, 22; and 13:18. It refers to the inward part of a person, and its cleansing means that there is no shame or guilt that would keep a worshiper from entering the very presence of God. Christ, who has "entered" into God's presence, takes his people with him — he is the pioneer of our salvation and he leads many sons and daughters into glory (2:10).

*Andrew Bandstra*

## Twenty-fifth Sunday after Pentecost, Year B

First Lesson: Ruth 3:1-5; 4:13-17
(Psalm 127)
**Second Lesson: Hebrews 9:24-28**
Gospel Lesson: Mark 12:38-44

According to Hebrews, the Melchizedek priesthood of Jesus changes nearly everything. Most of all, it changes the nature of priests, temples, and sacrifice. In fact, as this passage implies, the "once for all" character of Jesus' sacrifice puts an end to all other sacrifices, priests, and temples. If Jesus' temple is heaven itself, then the time of earthly temples has passed. Hebrews 9:24-28 explores the implications of Jesus, the high priest, entering not "a sanctuary made by humans hands," but "heaven itself" (9:24). The heavenly provenance of the sacrifice means that Jesus can indeed truly "save those who are eagerly waiting for him" (9:28).

At first glance this passage appears to summarize the contrast between the old priesthood and the new by way of an account of the radical superiority of the heavenly sanctuary to the earthly one. However, since chapter 10 continues and even intensifies this contrast, finally concluding with the abolishment of the first priesthood (10:9), we cannot read 9:24-28 as a conclusion. Instead, the passage is usually read as a gathering point in the series of contrasts between the old priesthood and the new which runs from 4:14 to 10:18. As a gathering, it mentions most of the fundamental ideas Hebrews makes about the new priesthood of Jesus, but it does not yet articulate the fatal conclusions of chapter 10. Instead, the emphasis of this passage is not on the failures of the old priesthood but on the excellence of the priesthood of Jesus. Thus the tone is not one of critique but of praise and celebration.

The initial challenge for any reader of this passage is its embeddedness in the larger arguments of Hebrews. Nearly all readers note that this passage effects some sort of conclusion to the arguments about the first tent (9:6) and the greater and perfect tent (9:12) which form the heart of chapter 9. But the passage also is a key moment in the whole sequence of comparisons about the old priesthood and the new. Thus in some ways it is not adequate to read this passage on its own, in isolation from the rest of Hebrews. In fact, the radical conclusions of 10:1-18 depend in explicit ways on the conclusions articulated in these verses. Only if there really is the kind of perfection suggested here can the first priesthood be fully and confidently left behind.

Although numerous themes are addressed in chapter 9, as the passage progresses the argument begins to focus on the power and necessity of blood. Blood is required for any entrance into the "second" tent (9:7). The high priest offers this blood for "himself and for the sins committed unintentionally by the people" (9:7). Blood effects covenants: "Not even the first covenant was inaugurated without blood" (9:18). The poignant conclusion is that "without the shedding of blood there is no forgiveness of sins" (9:22). This necessity of blood establishes the necessity of death. Thus the new covenant, the Jesus covenant, also requires both death and blood. At this point emerge the classic contrasts which structure 4:14–10:18. Jesus brings his own blood, a better and more potent blood. "For if the blood of goats . . . sanctifies . . . , how much more will the blood of Christ . . . purify our conscience" (9:13-14).

All of this sets up 9:23-28. First, there must be blood and death. Second, the blood and death of Jesus are more powerful than that of goats and bulls. Our passage explores the implications of this.

Our passage also adds a new piece. It takes into account the place of the sacrifice: "For Christ did not enter a sanctuary made by human hands, a mere copy of the true one, but he entered into heaven itself, now to appear in the presence of God on our behalf" (9:24). There seem to be echoes here of the well-documented Jewish distinction between the heavenly temple and the earthly one. The language of "a mere copy of the true one" seems to be drawn directly from this imagery. On the other hand, the language of Hebrews does not fit precisely within a dual-temple dichotomy. There seems to be no temple in heaven. Jesus enters "heaven itself." Unless there is simply a looseness in the imagery, this lack of temple in heaven must point to the eventual disappearance of all temples. When Jesus enters heaven instead of the temple with the ultimate sacrifice, this somehow marks the end of all temples.

Readers have raised many questions about the heavenly provenance of Jesus' sacrifice. When, for instance, did the efficacious death occur? Did Jesus die on a cross outside the walls of the earthly Jerusalem, or did Jesus die in heaven itself? Is the concept of place being undone here, so that Jesus in the moment of death is both on earth on a cross and in heaven with God? Hebrews does not work out either the geography of the moment of death or the precise sequence of it. Somehow the place of the death of Jesus is in heaven. Furthermore, the heavenly provenance of the sacrifice radically intensifies the power of the sacrifice.

The main intensification which our passage highlights is the once-and-for-all character of the death. Jesus dies only once. The onetime character of the death is connected somehow to the heavenly provenance of the death. Obviously, it is not manifestly clear why a sacrifice accomplished in heaven needs to be given only once, while sacrifices on earth need endless repetition. Hebrews will make several arguments.

First, the brief note about "blood that is not his own" in 9:25 recalls the arguments of 9:13-14 in which the power of Christ's sacrifice derives from the superiority of the blood that is spilled. The blood of Jesus is unique blood with unparalleled power. Second, if Jesus had to die more than once, "then he would have had to suffer again and again since the foundation of the world" (9:26). The logic of this argument is not obvious. Perhaps there is a hint here of the impossibility of a person dying over and over. Perhaps the horror of endlessly repeated suffering is also in play. And there may be new age assumptions in the background. With Jesus' death the new age has come. Jesus cannot go back into the old age and die again. Third, "it is appointed for mortals to die once" (9:27). Jesus, as a mortal, cannot die more than once. Thus his death must be once and for all. Fourth, most readers hear an implied argument about time and heaven in these verses. There may be a sense in these verses that in heaven sequences of time and endless repetitions do not have the same force they do on earth. In heaven, somehow time collapses in such a way that a deed or a sacrifice done once is eternal.

Whatever the probative force of these arguments, the conclusion is crucial. All of this means that Christ can "save those who are eagerly waiting for him" (9:28). For all the difficulties of the blood and heavenly sacrifice arguments of chapter 9, this conclusion has evident coinage for a preacher. We may have difficulty in the twenty-first century related to the blood and theology of temples. It is no mean task to try to articulate such on a Sunday morning in an American pulpit. We are so distant from the ancient world of temples. However, the question of the nature of the power of Jesus to save needs little translation. The question of the power of our sins to separate us from that salvation needs little translation. We understand, at least a little bit, the questions of sin, salvation, and Jesus.

"Without the shedding of blood there is no forgiveness of sins" (9:22). The negative leads to a positive: with the unique shedding of Jesus' unique blood at a unique place and time, the forgiveness of sins is possible. We are left with an ancient Christian formula: in Jesus' death our sins are forgiven.

In fairness to Hebrews, it is dangerous to end on that point. Hebrews always includes a warning. Hebrews will insist at the end of chapter 10 that for those who "willfully persist in sin after having received the knowledge of the truth, there no longer remains a sacrifice for sins" (10:26). Without taking up the endless discussion this warning, along with others (see esp. 6:1-

8), has occasioned in Christian theology, we must admit that Hebrews does not leave us with a simple and comforting mantra. We cannot simply say, "In Jesus' death, our sins our forgiven." Hebrews, I think, imagines that, in Jesus' death, not only are our sins forgiven, they are also taken away.

Because Jesus died, sins disappear from our lives. We cannot calmly assert, according to Hebrews, that whatever sins we might commit today or tomorrow are already forgiven in the blood of Christ. Hebrews imagines instead that because of the power of Jesus' death, we shall not commit whatever sins we might have committed today or tomorrow. This is a more unsettling theology.

*Lewis R. Donelson*

## Fourth Sunday of Advent, Year C

First Lesson: Micah 5:2-5a
(Psalm 80:1-7)
**Second Lesson: Hebrews 10:5-10**
Gospel Lesson: Luke 1:39-45, (46-55)

Two major Old Testament texts dominate this section (8:1–10:31) in which our passage is located. The first, Jeremiah 31:31-34, is quoted and commented on in Hebrews 8:7-13 and 10:15-18; it prophesies that God will establish a new covenant based on better promises (8:6). The second, Psalm 40:6-8, contained in our text, promises something better, more pleasing to God, than the sacrifices offered under the old covenant. That "covenant" and "sacrifice" belong together is not only implicit in the psalm, but the writer of Hebrews specifically interprets it in this way, namely: "he takes away the first in order to establish the second" (10:9).

A. *The introductory formula.* This is an appropriate Advent text, since the author of Hebrews places the words of the psalm on the lips of Jesus (10:5): "Consequently, when Christ came into the world, he said . . ." This is not the first time the author of Hebrews has understood Old Testament prophecies as being spoken by Jesus — see 2:11-13, where both Psalm 22:22 and Isaiah

8:17-18 are so used. As in those cases, also here it seems likely that the very personal confession of the psalm invites such attribution — "Then *I* said, 'See, God, *I* have come to do your will, O God.'"

In addition, certain things in the text, especially in the Septuagintal translation used here, invite attributing it to Jesus in his coming in the flesh into the world. (1) The second line of the quotation reads, "a body you have prepared for me." This, of course, suggests an incarnational context — more than the "you have given me an open ear" that translates the Hebrew of the Masoretic text. (2) The quotation, in both Hebrew and Greek, speaks of the mission of the one speaking, and in the translation given by the author of Hebrews the speaker specifically says, "I have come to do your will, O God." He accomplished this by dropping from the end of the quotation the word *eboulēthēn* (I have resolved), thus making the infinitive clause "to do" a purpose clause dependent on the main verb, "I have come." In both of these ways this portion of Psalm 40 appropriately reflects what is true of Jesus in his "coming into the world."

*B. The quotation itself.* (1) It seems likely that the four terms the psalmist uses for sacrifice are meant to cover all the main types of offering that were prescribed under the Levitical priesthood. And concerning these offerings it is said that God "did not desire" them or "take pleasure" in them (both the Hebrew and LXX versions have "did not require"). (2) In and by itself these statements already indicate that for the psalmist this order of things was, like the old covenant itself, "obsolete and growing old" and soon to "disappear" (8:13). The reason for this is indicated in part already by the reference to "but a body you have prepared for me." The Suffering Servant who has now appeared in the flesh has fulfilled all the spiritual principles that underlay these various types of sacrifice. His very incarnational existence is viewed as a voluntary submission of himself to God's will.

(3) Moreover, voluntary submission to God's will, says the psalmist, was the purpose of Christ's coming: "I have come to do your will, O God." This same truth is echoed by Jesus himself in John 6:38: "For I have come down from heaven, not to do my own will, but the will of him who sent me." For the author of Hebrews this purpose in coming not only covered all of the time known as "the days of his flesh" (Heb. 5:7-8), but also focused especially on "the offering of his body once for all" (10:10). (4) With reference to the phrase "in the scroll of the book it is written of me," the NRSV has a footnote that says "Meaning of Gk uncertain." That judgment is correct. Though a probable interpretation can be given, it seems wise not to make too much of it in a sermon, especially since it does not belong to the crucial part of the significance of the passage.

*C. The interpretation of the quotation.* There are two parts to the interpretation, coinciding with the two parts to the quotation. (1) The first, verses 8-9, makes explicit and direct what is implicit and indirect in the first part of the quotation. The author notes that the sacrifices and offerings referred to were those that were "offered according to the law." This interpretation is quite in accord with Hebrews's understanding of the "law," which has a different emphasis from that of Saint Paul. In Paul's writings the "law" refers primarily to the "demands" contained in the law of Moses, demands and prescriptions that must be kept or "done." In the book of Hebrews the "law" is primarily the instrument of God under the old covenant for regulating the cultic activities of priesthood and sacrifice (cf. 7:11; 9:19-22; 10:1-4).

As such, the law was not "bad," but rather something "obsolete" now that the "better" has come. And that is the point the author makes explicit when he says: "He abolishes the first in order to establish the second." In 8:13 the author interprets what God said in Jeremiah 31:31-34 about the "old covenant." When God said he would establish a "new covenant," he was thereby implying that the old covenant was "obsolete and growing old" and therefore "will soon disappear." In similar fashion, since God says he has no delight or pleasure in the offerings and sacrifices required under the first covenant, he clearly implies that they are to be set aside in order that something better can take their place. This has now happened, when in these last days God has spoken to us in his Son, who, after making purification for sins, sat down at the right hand of the Majesty on high (1:2-3; cf. 10:12). The whole epistle to the Hebrews has rightly been called "the epistle of the covenant." For even though the word "covenant" does not appear until 7:22, and is only made central in the discussion in 8:1–10:31, it had already been the basis of the comparison between the angels and the Son (1:5–2:18); the comparison of the faithfulness of Moses, the servant, and of Christ, the Son (3:1–4:13); and the comparison of the Levitical priesthood with that of Christ's after the order of Melchizedek (4:14–7:28).

(2) The second part of the interpretation, verse 10, is a grand statement of what is entailed in the will of God. Almost surprisingly, that will is our sanctification: "by which will we have been sanctified." It is noteworthy that our sanctification has been accomplished by means of "the offering of the body of Jesus Christ once for all." This, of course, is the body prepared for him at his incarnation, referred to in the psalm. And it was entailed in God's will, for he had come to do God's will. In 10:19, 29 our salvation is said to be "by the blood of Jesus" or "the blood of the covenant." This makes explicit that the "offering of his body" entails the offering of his body in death. Furthermore, his offering is said to be "once for all." Unlike the sacrifices under

the old covenant that are repeated year after year and could never make the consciences of the worshipers perfect (10:1-4), the offering of Christ under the new covenant was "once for all" because it accomplished our "sanctification" or "perfection."

The text says we "have been sanctified," using the perfect tense of the verb. Consistent with other parts of the New Testament, our author seems to hold to both "definitive sanctification" and "progressive sanctification." It would seem that the definitive aspect of our sanctification prevails when we see what has been accomplished by Christ in his definitive, once-for-all sacrifice. It seems that the "progressive" aspect of sanctification comes to the fore when we think of the experience of sanctification in our lives. Thus our author says in 10:14, "For by a single offering he has perfected [perfect tense] for all time those who are being sanctified [present tense]." In Hebrews our "sanctification" and "perfection" are two of the main words used to express the fact that we have been qualified through the work of Jesus to enter into the true sanctuary, into the very presence of God. When we look to the work of Jesus, it has been done once and for all; when we look at ourselves, we recognize that we are people in the process of sanctification. While "progressive" sanctification is a reality, in 10:10 he refers to our sanctification as being as unrepeatable as the sacrifice that brings it about. Thanks be to God for his great salvation.

*Andrew Bandstra*


## Twenty-sixth Sunday after Pentecost, Year B

First Lesson: 1 Samuel 1:4-20
(1 Samuel 2:1-10)
**Second Lesson: Hebrews 10:11-14, (15-18), 19-25**
Gospel Lesson: Mark 13:1-8


This passage has its setting in the fourth major section of Hebrews, which probably runs from 8:1 to 10:31. It is controlled by two major Old Testament texts: the first, Jeremiah 31:31-34, is quoted and commented on in Hebrews 8:7-13, and the second, Psalm 40:6-8, in Hebrews 10:5-10. The two themes, the "new covenant" of Jeremiah and the "effective sacrifice" of Psalm 40, are brought together in various ways throughout this section. Those themes also dominate the passage for today.

Hebrews 10:5 indicates that the author of Hebrews understands Psalm 40:6-8 as something appropriate to the incarnation of Christ and as fulfilled in his coming, in which coming the new covenant was also effected. Specifically, 10:10 sees the psalm fulfilled in Christ offering his body once for all, so that through it new covenant believers have been sanctified. Our section carries the idea of the effective sacrifice of the new covenant offered by Jesus at his incarnation into his session at God's right hand. It is the sacrifice of the presently enthroned high priest. Our passage has two main sections: 10:11-14 and 15-18.

A. *Hebrews 10:11-14*. This short paragraph begins with a contrast (indicated in Greek by the *men/de* construction) basically contained in verses 11-12. Verse 13 is an addition to the end of 12, a continuation of the allusion to Psalm 110:1. The effective ministry of Christ as expressed in verse 12 is further supported (indicated by the *gar* in the Greek) in verse 14.

1. Verse 11 affirms several things about "every priest" — that is, every priest under the old covenant. He "stands" to do his ministry as commanded by God (Deut. 18:5). He ministers "day by day," here, as in Hebrews 7:27, referring to the yearly cycle of daily sacrifices. In 10:1 the reference is to the sacrifice on the Day of Atonement and thus "year by year" (cf. 9:7). He offers the "same sacrifices again and again," and these "can never take away sin" (cf. "can never perfect the worshiper" in 10:1). Thus this verse expresses in sharp fashion the futility of the sacrifices offered under the old covenant.

2. Verse 12 contrasts the previous "every priest" with Christ (Gk. "this one"), whose incarnation and offering were described via Psalm 40:6-8 in Hebrews 10:5-10. In contrast to the sacrifices offered again and again, Christ offered a "single sacrifice for sin." In contrast to the Levitical "day by day" and "again and again," this one offered one sacrifice for sin "for all time." In 10:10 it is said that he offered his body "once for all," which is the same thought expressed here in terms of one sacrifice for all time. It is a matter of some dispute whether the phrase "for all time" goes with the previous phrase ("he offered") or the following ("he sat down"), but it more likely goes with the former since in Hebrews the phrase seems to follow the verb it modifies (cf. 10:14; 7:3).

The material in the preceding paragraph is given in verse 12 in a subordinate participial clause. The main affirmation (main verb) is given in the quotation or allusion to Psalm 110:1: after he had offered such a sacrifice, "he sat down at the right hand of God." In two ways this part of the psalm indicates the divinely accepted effectiveness of Christ's one sacrifice. First, it indicates that God has given his approval because Christ has sat down at God's right hand. Psalm 110:1 has been quoted or alluded to earlier — for example, 1:3, which has the two stages as here: "after he had made purification for sin, he sat down at the right hand of the Majesty on high." And 1:13 quotes Psalm 110:1 to indicate that the Son or Lord has a closer relationship to God than any of the angels; see also 8:1. The second indicator of his completed effective sacrifice is that he "sat down," in contrast to the "standing" of the old covenant priests. He sits because his sacrifice requires no repetition.

3. Some think that in Hebrews the last part of Psalm 110:1, quoted in verse 13, implies that Christ sits motionless (since Another places his enemies under his feet). Although it is true that Another (God) will put his enemies under his feet, Christ himself is engaged in a heavenly ministry of intercession in behalf of those who draw near to God through him (7:25) and assures them of their deliverance from Satan and the fear of death that comes from this enemy (2:14-15). The reason for quoting it here seems to be that it assures us of the heavenly stability of his position so that he can continue to perform his heavenly ministry.

4. Verse 14 supports (gar) and enlarges upon the affirmations of verse 12. The reference here is to the effect of that "one sacrifice." He suggests, first of all (using the perfect tense), that "he has perfected" forever those being sanctified. Christ himself, according to Hebrews, has been made perfect (2:10; 5:9); but the grace in his work is that by this same sacrifice he has accomplished our perfection — precisely what the old covenant sacrifices could not do (10:1). Since the verb tense is the same as in 10:10 ("we have been sanctified"), both verses probably refer to our definitive sanctification by which nothing keeps us from entering, through and with Christ, into the very presence of God himself (10:19-20).

But what is definitive in that sense is also a process. He has perfected forever "those who are being sanctified" (present passive participle). This idea of "definitive yet a process" fits with the "already but not yet" character of salvation throughout this epistle. For example, in 3:6 we "are [present tense] Christ's house," yet we need to hold on to that confidence. In 3:14 "we have become [perfect tense] partners of Christ," but we need to hold the beginning of our confidence firm to the end. In 12:22 "we have come [perfect tense] to Mount Zion," but we must see to it that we listen to the one speaking from heaven (12:25).

*B. Hebrews 10:15-18.* This paragraph has an introductory formula in verse 15, the quotation from Jeremiah 31 in verses 16-17, and in verse 18 the author's conclusion with references to these promises and Christ's sacrifice.

1. The author of Hebrews does not speak extensively about the Holy Spirit. He does connect him with the great salvation in 2:4 and closely links him to Christ's powerful sacrifice in 6:4; 9:8; and 10:29. But the author links the Holy Spirit to Scripture: whereas in 9:8 the Spirit is more generally the revealer, in 3:7 he "speaks" (present tense) through Scripture and here he "witnesses to us" (present tense) believers of the new covenant. By means of Jeremiah 31 the Spirit witnesses to the validity of the "perfection" that has come to us through the one effective sacrifice of our enthroned high priest. This affirmation makes this text especially appropriate for use in the season after Pentecost.

2. The phrase "after saying" in verse 15 implies something like "he also adds" in verse 17, though the latter is not in the Greek. In 8:6-13 Jeremiah 31:31-34 is quoted especially to remind us that the old covenant was aging and obsolete (cf. 8:13); here it is quoted to emphasize two of the "better promises" (8:6) of the new covenant delineated in Jeremiah 31.

The first promise important to the idea of our "perfection" is that God promised to put his laws in our hearts and to write them on our minds. God's laws are no longer out there on stone tablets but, under the new covenant, are written on our hearts (cf. 2 Cor. 3:3). Probably also implied, since it is the Holy Spirit who testifies this to us, this writing on our hearts and minds implies the power to carry the laws out.

The second promise important for the "perfection" of believers is that God promised to remember no more their sins and lawless deeds. What was impossible on the basis of the sacrifice of animals (10:4) has now been accomplished by God's forgiveness — the author identifies this nonremembrance with forgiveness in verse 18 — on the basis of the better sacrifice of Christ.

3. The term "forgiveness" implies the effective taking away of sin. The term goes back to 9:22, where one side of the axiom is stressed, namely, "without the shedding of blood there is no forgiveness of sins." Here the other side of the axiom is stressed, namely, where there is forgiveness of sins, there is no longer any need for an offering for sin. He thus ties the promises of God under the new covenant proclaimed in Jeremiah 31 with the sacrifice of Christ as portrayed in Psalm 40. Christ's sacrifice was the one sacrifice for sins forever, and there is no other sacrifice available (cf. Heb. 10:26). The only sacrifices appropriate to the Christian believer are the "sacrifice of praise" and the sacrifice of "doing good and sharing" (13:15-16). These sac-

rifices the believer does out of gratitude for the forgiveness and sanctification that come through the one sacrifice of Christ offered for us.

*Andrew Bandstra*

## Twelfth Sunday after Pentecost, Year C

First Lesson: Isaiah 1:1, 10-20
(Psalm 50:1-8, 22-23)
**Second Lesson: Hebrews 11:1-3, 8-16**
Gospel Lesson: Luke 12:32-40

Hebrews is a "word of exhortation" (13:22) to a community, possibly Jewish Christians in Rome under persecution (confiscation of property, imprisonment), not to shrink back to the synagogue and abandon their "better" salvation in Christ. The author (who is unknown to us but, in any case, certainly not Paul) employs a high Christology to combat a nostalgia for a past, pre-Christian life, depicting Christ as "better" than the angels (1:5–2:18), Moses (3:1-6), and primarily the Levitical priesthood (4:14–10:18).

Our text occurs in the last major section of Hebrews (viz., prior to the letter's conclusion in 13:20-25), 10:19–13:19, an exhortation to the audience to live a life of "fullness of faith" (10:22; cf. 10:38–12:2; 13:7) and "endurance" (10:36; 12:1; "endure" in 10:32; 12:2-3, 7) by directing their attention to the heavenly kingdom above and coming rather than to public persecution. This section, 10:19–13:19, can be broken down as follows. After an opening exhortation (10:19-25), warning (10:26-31), and recollection of the recipients' past faithful endurance of persecution (10:32-39), the author introduces in chapter 11 an encomium (a speech celebrating and praising the virtues of a person or persons as a basis for honor or remembrance), specifically an encomium on faith that lists exemplars of such faith in Israel's past (11:2; cf. 12:1: "a cloud/host of witnesses"). Based on this recitation of witnesses, the author exhorts his audience to endurance in 12:1-13 (alternatively, one could view 12:1-3 as the climax of chap. 11, with Jesus portrayed

506

as the ultimate exemplar of faith), then issues the fifth and final warning of the letter not to turn away from this salvation in 12:15-29. In 13:1-19 the author rounds off the section with parenesis (general moral advice), within which is inserted a brief peroration (conclusion) in 13:10-15.

Returning to the shape of chapter 11, an *inclusio,* or brackets, for this section can be found in the repetition of "faith" and "received attestation" in the introduction in 11:1-2 and the conclusion in 11:39-40. Within 11:3-38 two main sections are discernible: 11:3-31, the section where our lectionary text is found, which gives extended discussions of select heroes of faith from the preflood to Mosaic eras; 11:32-38, which provides a rapid summary of heroes of faith in the post-Mosaic era, both those who experienced triumph in this life (vv. 32-35a) and those who did not (vv. 35b-38). In 11:3-31 the author refers in verses 3-7 to preflood examples of faith (creation, Abel, Enoch, Noah); in verses 8-22 to examples from the period between the flood and Moses (Abraham in vv. 8-12, [13-16], 17-19; also Isaac, Jacob, Joseph in vv. 20-22); and in verses 23-31 to the era from Moses to the conquest of Canaan (Moses in vv. 24-28; also Moses' parents in v. 23; and in vv. 29-31 the people who passed through the Red Sea, the crumbling of the walls of Jericho, and Rahab). Within 11:3-31, summary interpretive comments by the author are inserted in verses 6, 10, and 13-16.

Verse 1 begins with the definition of faith, which is key for understanding the entire chapter, if not the entire letter: Now faith is a (or: the) *hypostasis* of what is hoped for, an (or: the) *elenchos* of things (or: matters) not seen. The meaning of the two transliterated words is subject to dispute. A range of meanings has been suggested for the first, *hypostasis* (lit. that which stands or lies under): (1) reality, substance (in contrast to what merely seems to be); (2) realization; (3) guarantee, title deed (recording ownership); (4) foundation, substructure; (5) assurance, confidence, being sure.

The last-named sense, though embraced by a number of standard translations (NRSV, NIV, NLT, CEV), is also the most difficult to document in texts of that period. The best-documented sense, and one that makes good sense here, is the first meaning: the underlying, transcendent, or objective reality of the believer's future hope.

Meanings that have been suggested for the second transliterated word, *elenchos,* include: (1) evidence, proof, proving, demonstration; (2) conviction, being certain. The objective character of hypostasis suggests the first sense; that is, *elenchos* refers not so much to the subjective feeling of certainty as to the objective certitude of things not seen. Moreover, when *elenchos* means "conviction," it is in the sense of a court's finding of guilt, not a firm belief.

Although the Greek literally translates as "faith is the reality . . . , the certitude [or proof] . . . ," it is doubtful that the author equates faith with that reality or certitude itself. Rather, in chapter 11 the author argues that faith is the belief that ultimate reality lies not in the here and now or in things visible to sight, but in things yet to come and things that cannot be seen. Faith believes that God "is" (i.e., exists, is real), even though God cannot be seen, and that God "rewards those who seek him," even when that reward is not forthcoming in this present age (11:6). Faith is the means, the eyes, by which the as-yet-unseen "heavenly country," the future inheritance of the faithful, can be seen "from a distance" (11:13, 16). Faith for the author does not make real something that has no intrinsic reality of its own. It merely recognizes that what God promises is more certain, better, greater, and more lasting than any boon that the "fleeting pleasures of sin" can offer (11:25). Consequently, the wording "faith is . . ." in 11:1 should probably be understood as an instance of metonymy, where the object of belief stands in for the belief itself: "faith is [a belief in] the reality of what is hoped for, [a belief in] the certitude of things not seen."

Verse 2 indicates that it is "by means of this" faith (lit. "in this") that Israel's "ancients" or "people of old" (*presbyteroi*, a generic masculine since women are included) "were attested" *(emartyrēthēsan)*; that is, they were recorded in the scrolls of Scripture as being people pleasing to God (see the use of the verb "were attested" in 11:4-5). Based on the examples cited in chapter 11, it is evident that the author means by faith a willingness to obey God in view of God's promise of future reward, even at the cost of enduring great personal sacrifice in this life. Two important corollaries follow. A faith/works contrast dissipates under such a definition of faith. Moreover, the author shows no reluctance to applaud a faith that is driven by the incentive of reward.

After speaking of the faith of the "ancients" in 11:2, the author takes what initially seems like a surprising turn by starting the list with an example of faith found by believers in the author's own day ("we"). Apparently the author wanted to connect faith with the dawn of creation to show faith's importance for the whole scope of salvation history. Since obviously no human being was around at the time of the creation of the world, the acceptance of the dogma that "the world was fashioned by the word of God" requires faith on the part of "us." While the author may be reacting in part against the perceived pagan notion that creation was accomplished by idols resembling created things (see the critique in Wis. 13:1-5), the "not" in the following result clause points primarily in a different direction.

The Greek for the result clause in 11:3 is a little ambiguous. One translation option reads: "so that from things not visible has what is seen come into being." The position of the negative particle in the Greek suggests a different reading: "so that not from visible things *(eis to mē ek phainomenōn)* has what is seen come into being." In either translation the sense is basically the same: God did not create the world from things that can be seen but by divine fiat, mere word. The notion that God brought the world into being by verbal fiat, without the aid of preexistent visible matter, appears elsewhere in Hellenistic Judaism (e.g., 2 Macc. 7:28; *2 Enoch* 24:2; *2 Bar.* 21:4; 48:8; cf. Rom. 4:17), so the author of Hebrews may have this in mind. Genesis 1 makes clear that God created by mere word, but it also suggests the preexistence of both cosmic "waters" and land beneath the waters, which God then separated by command (vv. 2, 6-10).

In the author's roll call of heroes of faith, Abraham receives the most attention. He is the center of the discussion in verses 8-22, with Isaac and Jacob mentioned marginally in 9b and 20-21, and Joseph in 22. The author's first summary in 13-16 refers to the experience of "all these" previously mentioned, but has Abraham primarily in view.

In verses 8-12 the author highlights three actions by Abraham that demonstrated his faith in God's unseen, future-oriented promises. First, *Abraham's call to leave Mesopotamia* (11:8). Abraham responded immediately and obediently to God's call (present participle: "as/while he was being called he obeyed") by starting out for a place that God had promised as an inheritance — even though Abraham did not know precisely "where he was going" (cf. Gen. 12:1: "Go . . . to the land that I will show you"). Abraham left his former settled and secure existence for an existence that, apart from faith, would appear to be unsettled and insecure.

Second, *Abraham's sojourn in Canaan* (11:9-10). When he arrived in Canaan, he, and later Isaac and Jacob, lived there as immigrants without citizenship status, dwelling not in a building with secure foundations but "in tents" (11:9). So not only did Abraham depart to the Promised Land without worldly title in hand, he also lived in the land as someone who had no ownership claim to it. Abraham "waited for the city that has foundations, whose architect and maker is God" (11:10).

Third, *Abraham's faith in God's promise of numerous descendants* (11:11-12). He dwelt in Canaan for almost twenty-five years without a child from his wife Sarah (Gen. 12:4 says Abraham was 75 years old when he departed Haran; Gen. 21:5 says he was 100 years old when Isaac was born). Yet he continued to have faith (Paul says "hoped against hope" in Rom. 4:18) that God would provide him with the offspring necessary to keep the family line going until the promise of a homeland could be fulfilled — despite the seemingly insurmountable obstacle of a barren wife and his own impotence ("as

509

good as dead" so far as procreation was concerned, 11:12; the same participle, *nenekrōmenos,* is used in Rom. 4:19).

Later, in 11:17-19, the author adds a fourth stage in Abraham's faith journey: surviving the test of offering up his son Isaac. (For a comparison with the image of Abraham in early Judaism, see my discussion of Rom. 4:13-25, Third Sunday after Pentecost, Year A, and Second Sunday in Lent, Year B.)

Verses 13-16 anticipate in a more detailed way the conclusion in verses 39-40. The main point of the summary is to confirm the opening definition of faith in verses 1-2: "all these" exemplars of faith believed in the transcendent reality of something as yet unseen and yet to come.

The key to any sermon on Hebrews 11 is to emphasize this profound understanding of faith; namely, the conviction that the truly real things of life, the transcendent reality for which all can and must be forsaken, lies in things that are for us both future and unseen. Developing "faith vision," the ability to believe from a distance and to accept as hard fact what the gospel promises, requires constant renewal of the mind (Rom. 12:2). Hebrews 11 attempts precisely such a renewal by citing a series of models from Israel's past. What God requires of believers today is nothing different from what God has asked of generations of witnesses gone by, including Jesus himself, the "chief leader and perfecter of faith" (12:2).

*Robert A. J. Gagnon*

## Thirteenth Sunday after Pentecost, Year C

First Lesson: Isaiah 5:1-7
(Psalm 80:1-2, 8-19)
**Second Lesson: Hebrews 11:29–12:2**
Gospel Lesson: Luke 12:49-56

The delimitation and structure of the last section of Hebrews (other than chap. 13) is much disputed. What makes the most sense to me is to see Hebrews 1–12 as comprising five sections — or better, five *homilies* (cf.

13:22) — each governed by one or two Old Testament texts that are quoted and commented on. The delimitation of the first four homilies with their respective Old Testament texts is relatively easy: Hebrews 1:5–2:18, based on Psalm 8:4-6; Hebrews 3:1–4:13, based on Psalm 95:7b-11; Hebrews 4:14–7:28, based on Psalms 2:7b and 110:4; and Hebrews 8:1–10:31, based on Jeremiah 31:31-34 and Psalm 40:6-8. In addition, one can make a good case for the hypothesis that the fifth homily runs from Hebrews 10:32 to 12:29. The key Old Testament text is Habakkuk 2:3-4 (LXX version), which is quoted and commented on in Hebrews 10:35-39. It is probable that this last homily has three main sections: the first, 10:32-39, providing the introduction based on Habakkuk 2:3-4; the second, running from 11:1 to 12:13, develops the meaning of "my righteous one will live by faith" as one who does not "shrink back." The third section, 12:14-29, develops various aspects of life in the end times, surrounding the word of prophecy which says: "The one who is coming will come and will not delay."

In terms of this suggested structure, our passage lies clearly in the second part of this last homily and deals with the meaning of "my righteous one will live by faith." Almost all of the well-known chapter 11 deals with what has been called "the heroes of faith." That includes the faith of the antediluvians (vv. 4-7), Abraham (vv. 8-22), and Moses (vv. 23-28).

There are four discrete sections in our passage. Hebrews 11:29-31 continues the recital of faith operative in the old covenant, but now includes the people of Israel and even Rahab. 11:32-38, while continuing to refer to the old covenant people, clearly changes the structure, as indicated by a rhetorical introduction and the more generalizing style. There is a further switch in 11:39-40 in that the preacher develops the relationship of the old covenant believers with the new covenant believers. 12:1-2 points especially to Jesus, the pioneer and finisher of our faith. As a homiletical strategy in handling this material, one might limit one's preaching text to 12:1-2 and cover the three segments of Hebrews 11 under the first clause of 12:1: "since we are surrounded by so great a cloud of witnesses."

*Hebrews 11:29-31.* In verse 29 it is affirmed that the people of Israel experienced the exodus "by faith." Although later in their wanderings they suffered much because of unbelief (cf. 3:7-19), at this point they acted out of faith. To be sure, on one level the exodus was an act of God (Exod. 14:14) and on another level it was caused by an east wind, but the people of Israel were there because of their faith, ready to see God's action on their behalf. A similar kind of faith motivated the Israelites, according to verse 30, when conquering Jericho. From a purely military point of view, what God asked them to do would have been considered foolish. But they trusted in God and obeyed him so that those walls came atumblin' down. Further, one can say many things about Rahab, her occupation, and her craftiness, but ultimately our preacher says in verse 31 that it was "by faith" that she was saved. (For helpful comments regarding the recognition of Rahab in the Christian tradition, cf. F. F. Bruce, *The Epistle to the Hebrews,* rev. ed., NICNT [Grand Rapids: Eerdmans, 1990], pp. 318-19.) In James 2:25 her actions in behalf of the spies are one of two arguments in support of the contention that faith without works is dead.

*Hebrews 11:32-38.* This section begins with a rhetorical introduction that is paralleled in other Greek literature: "And what more can I say? For time would fail me to tell. . . ." It points to a summary way of handling the material.

The references in this section can be seen as falling into two groups, delineated in verses 32-34 and 35-38. In connection with the first group, there are many questions concerning the order of the names listed in verse 32 and why Jephthah is listed among them. (For a competent discussion of these problems, cf. Harold W. Attridge, *Hebrews,* Hermeneia [Philadelphia: Fortress, 1988], pp. 347-48.) The first group expressed their faith in terms of military exploits and were involved in acts of deliverance. Through faith they, as the text says, "obtained promises" and "won strength out of weakness." Through faith they were victorious. The second group, verses 35-38, suffered terrible sufferings and apparent defeat. Yet through faith, under the most difficult circumstances, they persevered. They did not shrink back, but through faith received the salvation of their souls.

*Hebrews 11:39-40.* In 10:39 the author of Hebrews applies part of Habakkuk 2:3-4 to the congregation by saying: "But we are not among those who shrink back and so are lost, but among those who have faith and so are saved." Now in 11:39-40, after a long reminder about how faith functioned so vividly under the old covenant, he connects the experiences of the old covenant believers with the faith of new covenant believers.

Verse 39 reminds us that though these old covenant believers were commended for their faith or received attestation from God for their faith, they "did not receive what was promised." This sounds surprising since verse 33 speaks of those who "obtained promises." It may be helpful to remember that of Abraham (and those with him), it is said both that "he had received the promise" (11:17; cf. 6:15) and that these died in faith "without having received the promises" (11:13). It is therefore best to understand that when it refers in 11:33 to "obtaining promises," the reference is to the actual promise itself, and when it says in 11:39 that they did not receive the promise, it refers to the realization of that promise. Thus these believers, whose faith is attested by God, did not receive the realization of the promise that ultimately awaited the "something better" that God, through Jesus, had in store for us new covenant believers.

The ultimate goal was the unity of believers of both covenants, so that apart from us they should not be made perfect. Now that Jesus, the mediator of the new covenant, has offered himself in death so that the transgressions under the first covenant might be forgiven (9:15) and that the transgression of new covenant believers might be forgiven (10:11-14), we together have been made perfect. "For by a single offering he has perfected for all time those who are being sanctified" (10:14).

*Hebrews 12:1-2.* For preaching, an analysis of the grammatical structure of the Greek in this passage is important. It is one sentence, with one main verb which is a hortatory subjunctive: "let us run with perseverance the race that is set before us." This main clause is preceded by two participial clauses: the first, no doubt to be rendered as causal, "since we are surrounded . . . ," and the second, to be rendered as manner or means, "by laying aside every weight. . . ." The main clause is followed by another participial clause, to be rendered also as manner or means (i.e., the means or manner of running the race with patience), "by looking to Jesus. . . ." In this case the participial clause is extended by a compound relative clause further describing Jesus: "who . . . endured the cross . . . , and who has taken his seat. . . ." The whole sentence is connected to the preceding chapter by the particle *toigaroun*, indicating an inference, "therefore."

The main clause is expressed in an athletic metaphor of running a race. We are specifically to do that with "perseverance" or "patience," or "patient endurance"; the same word is used at the beginning of this section in 10:36: "for you have need of patient endurance. . . ." Obviously the race in which Christians are entered is not the 100-meter dash but the long cross-country (to the heavenly country) race. The first assurance is that we are surrounded by a great "cloud" or "host" of "witnesses." Because of the athletic metaphor, it is perhaps natural to think of them as "spectators." But given how the word is used in chapter 11 (that faith of old covenant believers is "witnessed" or "attested" using this same word group), it is better to think not of them looking at us but we looking to them — for encouragement.

One means for aiding us in running this race with patience is laying aside everything that hinders us in our running, that is, putting off every weight and the sin that clings so closely (or, as the footnote suggests, following a less-well-attested reading), the "sin that so easily distracts." The other supreme means by which we can run the race with patience is "looking to Jesus, the pioneer and perfecter of our faith." As the pioneer, he was made per-

513

fect through suffering in leading many sons and daughters to glory (2:10). As the perfecter of our faith, after he himself was perfected, he became the source of our eternal salvation (5:10). He knows about needing patient endurance, for he himself endured the cross, despising its shame, and is now seated at the right hand of the throne of God. So keep looking to Jesus as you run this race that God has laid out for us.

*Andrew Bandstra*

## Fourteenth Sunday after Pentecost, Year C

First Lesson: Jeremiah 1:4-10
(Psalm 71:1-6)
**Second Lesson: Hebrews 12:18-29**
Gospel Lesson: Luke 13:10-17

Our passage is the conclusion to what is probably the fifth homily in this "word of exhortation" (Heb. 13:22), running from 10:32 to 12:29. (For a fuller accounting of this view of the structure of Hebrews, see the introductory material for the Thirteenth Sunday after Pentecost, Year C, on 11:29–12:2.) The major Old Testament text for this fifth homily is Habakkuk 2:3-4 (LXX version), which is quoted and commented on in Hebrews 10:35-39. It is probable that this last homily has three sections. The first, 10:32-39, is the introduction that sets the stage for the quotation of Habakkuk 2:3-4. The second segment, running from 11:1 to 12:13, develops the meaning of the statement in the quotation that "my righteous one shall live by faith" as one who "does not shrink back." The third segment, 12:14-29, develops various aspects of life in the end times, surrounding the prophecy in Habakkuk 2:3, which says, "The one who is coming shall come and shall not delay." Chapter 13 of Hebrews is a kind of epistolary closing to the twelve chapters that are a series of five homilies on various Old Testament texts.

In terms of this suggested structure, our passage is part of that third segment about life in the end times — in fact, the concluding section. The author of Hebrews begins with a paragraph (12:14-17) encouraging the pursuit of peace and holiness and warning against finally not obtaining the grace of God. One must live seriously in the end times. In that connection, in 12:18-24 he reminds the Christian believers of the "better" gifts of the new covenant in comparison to the old. They have arrived at Mount Zion, but not at a mountain that could be touched and that burned with the fire of judgment. Rather, they had arrived at the heavenly Jerusalem. Serious but joyful living befits citizens of that great heavenly city. It is God's amazing gift of grace. But a warning is still appropriate (12:25-29): listen to the one who speaks from heaven. The appropriate response is the giving of thanks in acceptable worship.

*Hebrews 12:18-24.* A consistent pattern in the book of Hebrews is to declare the superiority of the revelation and great salvation given by the Son under the new covenant compared to what was given under the old. In this final segment the author does the same. In verses 18-21 he reminds Christian believers that they, in contrast to the people of the old covenant, have not arrived at a "mountain" that can be touched, etc. The word "mountain" is not in the better manuscripts but is implied, and refers to the Israelites' experience at Mount Sinai.

The account in Hebrews is based on the Old Testament, perhaps along with a Haggadic tradition that interpreted the account. Much of its account is found in Exodus 19:16-19; 20:18-21 and in Moses' recounting of it in Deuteronomy 4:9-14 and 5:23-27. Particularly reflected in Hebrews are the words of Exodus 19:18-19: "Now Mount Sinai was wrapped in smoke, because the LORD had descended upon it in fire; the smoke went up like the smoke of a kiln, while the whole mountain shook violently. As the blast of the trumpet grew louder and louder, Moses would speak and God would answer him in thunder." Also Exodus 20:18-19: "When all the people witnessed the thunder and lightning, the sound of the trumpet, and the mountain smoking, they were afraid and trembled and stood at a distance, and said to Moses, 'You speak to us, and we will listen; but do not let God speak to us, or we will die.'"

So holy was the mountain that even animals who touched it were to be put to death (see Exod. 19:12-13). It is a serious thing to offend the holiness of God. What may reflect a Haggadic tradition is that the writer says that even Moses was affected by the holiness of the spectacle and said, "I tremble with fear." This description of Moses' emotional state is not stated in the accounts of the Sinaitic theophany in Exodus and Deuteronomy. Perhaps the closest parallel is found in Deuteronomy 9:19, where Moses reminds the people of his supplication for them after the incident of the golden calf, and says: "For I was afraid that the anger that the LORD bore against you was so fierce that he would destroy you." Another parallel is in Stephen's speech in regard to Moses' encounter with God at the burning bush, where it is said (Acts 7:32): "Moses began to tremble and did not dare to look." Thus our author, perhaps from acquaintance with this Haggadic tradition, attributes fear and trembling to Moses at Sinai so that he could emphasize that element of fear associated with the old covenant and the giving of the law. Our author affirms that new covenant believers did not come to such a mountain.

On the contrary, as Hebrews 12:22-24 indicates: "You have come to Mount Zion and to the city of the living God." The word translated "you have come" (also used in v. 18) is the perfect tense of the Greek *proserchomai*. This verb is used throughout Hebrews to refer to the cultic and liturgical approach to God (cf. 4:16; 7:25; 10:1, 22; 11:6). The perfect tense of the verb gives expression to what might be called his "inaugurated" or "realized" eschatology, a reality that Christian believers "already" experience. In 3:6, 14 he affirmed that "we [already] are Christ's house" and "we have [already] become partners of Christ." In 6:4-6 he speaks of people who have already, among other things, "tasted of the heavenly gift" and "the powers of the age to come." There is also a "not yet" aspect to the believers' experience that calls for continuing listening to God, and the author will get to that shortly — in verses 25-29. But in this paragraph he wants to remind new covenant believers of their privileges, which are so much greater and more celebrative than under the old covenant.

Under the old covenant Mount Zion was the place for the tribes of Israel to gather in praise of Yahweh (cf. Ps. 122:3-4). But here it is the city of the living God, which is "the heavenly Jerusalem" (cf. Gal. 4:26-28). Christian believers, in coming to this heavenly Jerusalem, have also come to "myriads of angels in festal gathering" (cf. Rev. 5:11-12). The reference to "the assembly of the firstborn who are enrolled in heaven" suggests that we, though now on earth, are already enrolled with all God's people in that heavenly assembly of the firstborn, through union with Christ, who is truly the Firstborn. Here too we meet God, who is the judge of all, and "the spirits of the righteous made perfect," no doubt a reference to the believers of pre-Christian days referred to in Hebrews 11:39-40 as those who would not be made perfect apart from us. And, even above all, we have come to Jesus the mediator of a new covenant, whose blood is our admission ticket into God's presence (cf. 9:11-12). What amazing privileges we new covenant believers already possess!

*Hebrews 12:25-29.* Even though the author of Hebrews celebrates the great blessings that new covenant believers share, he does not cease to couple those blessings with a call for responsible behavior. Here he thus calls for his readers to see to it that they not refuse the one who is speaking. Hebrews began with a reminder that the God who spoke of old through the prophets has in these last days spoken to us in a Son (1:1-2). Here, as a kind of *inclusio,* he comes back at the end of his word of exhortation to call his readers and us to hear the one who is speaking. Much as he did in 2:1-4, he uses an *a fortiori* argument — they did not escape the one who warned them on earth (Mount Sinai), how much less will we escape if we reject the one who warns from heaven. He knows from the prophet Haggai (2:6, 21) that this final speech will be one that shakes not only the earth (as at Mount Sinai) but heaven as well. The author infers from the "yet once more" that this means the removal of what is (or can be) shaken. Further, the shaken things are those that belong to the created order and are under God's scrutiny and judgment. (Creation for the author of Hebrews does not belong to the eternal order of things [cf. also Heb. 1:11-12] — thus agreeing with the whole of the Bible against some of the Greek tradition.) This shaking has as its goal that only what cannot be shaken may remain.

The author then adds another exhortation based on this gift — we are receiving a kingdom that cannot be shaken. Such a gift of grace can lead to only one thing — a thankful heart. It is from such a thankful heart (cf. also Col. 3:16) that we offer to God acceptable worship with both reverence and fear. The final sentence underscores the responsibility that we new covenant believers have to continue to live responsibly before our gracious God, who is, at the same time, a consuming fire. The gifts of new covenant grace call for serious commitment to thankful living.

*Andrew Bandstra*

## Fifteenth Sunday after Pentecost, Year C

First Lesson: Jeremiah 2:4-13
(Psalm 81:1, 10-16)
**Second Lesson: Hebrews 13:1-8, 15-16**
Gospel Lesson: Luke 14:1, 7-14

This passage, especially without verses 11-14, reads as a gentle and wonderful exhortation to the classic Christian virtues. In fact, it would be hard to find a more representative account of Christian ethics in the New Testament. Readers are exhorted to love each other, to practice hospitality, to remember those in prison, to keep the marriage bed undefiled, and to keep free of love of money. These five admonitions occur in various forms throughout the New Testament and early Christian literature. Together they portray beautifully the peculiar Christian configuration of the ethical life.

The friendly tone of these verses is reinforced by evocative images in 13:15-16. There we offer sacrifices of praise, we do not neglect the good, and we share our possessions with one another. As configured in the lectionary and when read in isolation from the rest of Hebrews, these verses become an almost poetic call to simple Christian virtues. A preacher has much to build on here. There is proper warrant in these verses for congenial sermons of quiet entreaty. However, the larger context in Hebrews adds a more violent and bloody tone to these rather polite verses.

"For indeed our God is a consuming fire" (Heb. 12:29). When we read Hebrews 12 before we read Hebrews 13, then Hebrews 13 contains an aura of threat. We are called to the righteous life amidst warnings of the holiness of God. "You have not come to something that can be touched, a blazing fire, and darkness, and gloom, and a tempest . . ." (12:18). Hebrews 12:14-29 is a warning to Christians not to fall away. And, as Hebrews 13 indicates, falling away consists in failing to live the Christian virtues. Thus this call to Christian virtues is not a congenial "Would you mind, by the way, being nice to one another because God would kind of prefer that." The call to righteousness is carved out in the face of the unspeakable holiness of God. Without the gentle virtues enumerated here, we fall under the terrors of God's judgment. These virtues, overstating the case somewhat, save us.

Read this way, we find a startling contrast, an almost unbridgeable gap, between the absolute holiness of God and the vulnerabilities of the Christian life. But there is a problem with this reading. Simply put, it does not account for the formidable Christology of Hebrews. This Christology is per-

518

haps evoked in 13:8 — "Jesus Christ is the same yesterday and today and forever." The immediate context (13:9-10) suggests that the eternity of Christ counters the newness of heresies. But 13:11-14 connects the passage to the larger christological forces of Hebrews.

"Therefore Jesus also suffered outside the city gate in order to sanctify the people by his own blood" (13:12). This brief allusion evokes the powerful and complex sacrificial Christology of Hebrews. Without tracing the details of that here, we can note that the life of righteousness is not something we can accomplish on our own. God must act through the eternal priesthood and eternal sacrifice of Jesus. There is a permanent violence, an eternal sacrifice, which makes possible the ethical life. The sacrifice of Jesus makes us holy. This is, of course, the dominant theological image of Hebrews. It is evoked here, over the gentle virtues, as a reminder of the blood which makes love possible.

"Let us then go to him outside the camp and bear the abuse he endured" (13:13). In this call we hear a second crucial christological theme of Hebrews. Jesus is "the pioneer and perfecter of our faith" (12:2). Jesus models and prefigures the Christian life. Jesus shows the way. In this case he pioneers by leading us outside the tent to a place of abuse and death.

At this point we are reconnected to the moral imperatives in 13:1-5. We follow Jesus outside the gate, to the place of abuse, not by seeking abuse. We follow by obeying the moral exhortations which open the chapter. The larger context to 13:1-5 highlights the vulnerability, the risk, the danger which accompanies all acts of kindness. To love may be many things, but it always includes making oneself vulnerable. To love is to stand outside the safe camp; it is to open oneself to the violence of others. Even if Hebrews names love without either defining it or illustrating it, the text does give the sense of vulnerability which haunts love. To love is to let another person, an unreliable other person, inside your safe walls. This is so whether the one you love is your husband or your enemy. To love is to risk abuse.

Early Christians became famous in Roman literature for their hospitality. Christian hospitality is even on occasion ridiculed as the cheapest form of travel. Just announce yourself as a Christian and you can get free room and board for a few days. This ridicule intimates in a nonthreatening way the very real risk of hospitality. The command does not state "welcome your friends and loved ones into your homes"; it says, "Do not neglect to show hospitality to strangers" (13:2). To strangers! To let a stranger into your house is always a risk. These strangers might be "angels," but they might not. This call to hospitality is a call to ongoing vulnerability to the unknown other.

519

The mood shifts slightly in the call to "remember those who are in prison" (13:3). The imagery here is rather stunning. We are to remember "those who are being tortured as though you yourselves were in the body." We live in the very bodies of those in prison, of those being tortured. Here we partake of the violence and abuse done to others. Even if we ourselves survive a walk outside the camp, if anyone else does not and is abused, they become us. If anyone anywhere is in prison, we are in prison. If anyone anywhere is being tortured, we are being tortured.

As is typically the case in the Bible, there is scant consideration given the difficulty (impossibility?) of obeying these commandments. Hebrews displays beautifully the absolute character of most Christian imperatives. We are simply told to love, not love as best you can from time to time. The commands come as absolutes. Furthermore, the larger theology of Hebrews suggests that failure is not looked upon lightly. The warnings in 10:19-39 and 12:14-29 should be taken seriously. The commands expect obedience. And it is certainly true, as Christians have long admitted, that in this moment here, in front of this stranger or this prisoner, I can obey. Nothing prevents me.

The sense of belonging to others which is traced in the first two imperatives and absolutized in the third is again evoked in the reference to marriage. Husband and wife belong to each other. This belonging concerns everyone: the husband, the wife, and every potential adulterer. It is the task of the whole community to keep the marriage bed undefiled. It is hard not to hear in this the "one-body" imagery of Genesis 2:24. Just as prisoners are one body with us, husbands and wives are one body with each other.

The first four imperatives seem to focus upon a redefinition of the self. To be a self is to belong to others. To be a Christian self is to not belong to oneself. To be a self is to go outside the safe camp to dangerous places. To be a self is to let others take possession of you. To be a husband is to belong to your wife. To be a Christian is to have strangers rummaging through your stuff. To be a Christian is to "go to [Jesus] outside the camp and bear the abuse he endured" (13:13).

The final warning against money puts a different edge on Christian vulnerability. Early Christian nervousness about money is well known. The syntax in 13:5 is less threatening than many Christian admonitions against money, but even it incorporates the opposition between trusting money and trusting God. Money isolates. It isolates us from people by protecting us from dependence on them. And it isolates us from God, since it is money that gives us food and roofs and safety. To avoid money is to become vulnerable, both to people and God.

This final image of vulnerability leads to a wonderful call to trust God. If I am going to be so vulnerable, what or who will keep me safe? Hebrews adds a comforting promise by way of two scriptural allusions. The first is loosely drawn from Deuteronomy 31:6, 8 and/or Joshua 1:5. For God has said, "I will never leave you or forsake you" (13:5). The second is from the Septuagint version of Psalm 118:6.

> The Lord is my helper;
>   I will not be afraid.
> What can anyone do to me?  (13:6)

It is hard to imagine more fitting images of comfort for this passage than these.

Finally, we must note again the effective gathering of gentle images in the conclusion in 13:15-16. We have returned at this point to the quiet with which the passage began. "Let us continually offer a sacrifice of praise to God" (13:15). "Do not neglect to do good and to share what you have" (13:16). The loving and positive force of Christian virtue is herein echoed once again. These verses (and the opening ones) make the practice of Christian virtues sound like a pleasant and relatively easy task. And, I suppose, oftentimes it is.

The final phrase may shift the mood a bit: "for such sacrifices are pleasing to God." As we have seen, it is no idle thing to please or displease God.

The theological richness of this passage offers considerable opportunities and equal challenges to a preacher. There are so many possible images and texts from which a sermon might emerge. If there is a guiding image, I think it is that of risk. The Christian life is a life wherein we risk everything on God's promise not to leave us or forsake us.

*Lewis R. Donelson*

## Fifteenth Sunday after Pentecost, Year B

First Lesson: Song of Solomon 2:8-13
(Psalm 45:1-2, 6-9)
**Second Lesson: James 1:17-27**
Gospel Lesson: Mark 7:1-8, 14-15, 21-23

James is famous for his practical focus. His letter contains a higher percentage of imperatives than does any other New Testament book. And verses 22-27, where we find James's call to "do the word" and not just hear it, is the epitome of his concern for the actual living out of the Christian faith. Anyone preaching James faithfully must of course do justice to this intensely practical focus. But at the same time, it is important not to miss the underlying theology that informs James's specific exhortations. There is a real danger, in other words, that the preacher might treat James as a self-standing moral code and miss the theological underpinning of that morality.

For this reason it is particularly salutary that the lectionary includes verses 17-21 along with 22-27. For this earlier text enunciates the indicative of God's grace without which the imperative of human response is misunderstood and misapplied. Faithful preaching of this great text will take both emphases into account, seeking to help Christians understand how the gifts they have received from God are to be put into his service in specific and practical ways. Looked at from this perspective, these verses provide one of the fullest expositions in Scripture of the purpose and effects of God's word.

The verses for this lection actually span three separate paragraphs in James's letter. Verses 17-18 are the concluding part of a section in which James seeks to dispel any notion that God will tempt his people to sin. Verses 19-20 are a brief exhortation about anger and speech. And verses 21-27 are a long exposition about the proper way Christians are to treat God's word.

In verses 13-15 James warns us about ever thinking that God, who does "test" us (vv. 2, 12), would ever "tempt" us to sin. Such enticement to evil is simply not possible for God. After the transitional verse 16, James then turns to the flip side: rather than tempt to evil, God gives good gifts to his people. The Greek of verse 17 is semipoetic in form and might indicate that James here quotes a preexisting saying. The language reflects ancient speculation about the movement of the heavenly bodies. These bodies move and change, some regularly (the sun and moon) and others, apparently, irregularly (the planets; the name comes from a Greek word that means "wander"). But God, James reminds us, never changes but is ever constant in his grace and love for his people. The supreme evidence of this grace is the gift of the new birth (v. 18). God uses his word, the good news about Jesus, to regenerate people and so appoint them as "a kind of first fruits of his creatures." Christians, in other words, represent the first stage in God's kingdom work of reclaiming the world for himself.

James is not an easy letter to organize. It stubbornly defies our attempts to create neat, self-contained expositions and obvious transitions. To be sure, modern scholarship recognizes more unity and structure in the book than older scholars in the form-critical approach saw. But we force James into a mold to which the book does not belong if we insist on logical transitions and development of ideas. Verses 19-20 exemplify this point. They are not obviously tied to anything James is saying in this context. Integrating them into a sermon that seeks to deal with all the data of verses 17-27 is therefore something of a challenge. Perhaps, however, they are best aligned with verses 26-27, where James specifies some of the specific ways in which Christians are called to "do" the word of God. The connection between anger and speech that is hasty and harmful is widely recognized (see, e.g., Prov. 17:27). James makes clear that unjust anger and the violent speech that often results from anger do not meet God's approval (cf. "God's righteousness" in v. 20) and so violate the demands of his word.

Many Bibles and commentaries put a paragraph break between verses 21 and 22. But a more important break comes between 20 and 21. For 21 introduces the theme that will dominate the rest of chapter 1: the right response to God's word. The call to "welcome" or "receive" the word usually is a call to convert in the New Testament, but this is not James's intention here. He is writing to Christians, and his point is that we need to let God's word, already "implanted" in our hearts, have its full effect in our lives. Behind James's language lies the Old Testament prediction about the internalization of God's word that would come with the new covenant (Jer. 31:31-34; Ezek. 36:24-32). No longer would God's word be written on tablets of stone; it would henceforth be written on the human heart, making it possible for God's people to discern his will for them from within and to do that will because the heart of stone has been replaced by the heart of flesh. We emphasize, again, then, that James's call to "do" the word in verse 22 comes only after he has established the groundwork for that imperative in the regenerating and empowering activity of God's word in the hearts of his people.

But James is not content to let the matter rest with the rather vague "welcome the word" (v. 21). So he now spells out more particularly what welcoming the word involves: doing it. God's word brings blessing to his people, but it also brings demands. These demands cannot be ignored by anyone who has a genuine claim to know God. Those who think they can benefit from the word without obeying it are, James claims, "deceiving themselves." They are like people who see their image in a mirror but do nothing about it (vv. 23-24). Various attempts to find allegorical significance in this mirror have been made. But it is doubtful whether James intends anything but a simple illustration here. Looking in a mirror is to be followed by response. People look at their images to straighten their ties, adjust their makeup, comb their hair. It is natural, in other words, to make some response to the image one sees. So also, the purpose of looking into God's word is to respond to its teaching. We are not just to walk away mumbling "how interesting" or to use it as no more than a source for intellectual stimulation and academic debate. James indicates the aspect of the word of God that he is highlighting here by shifting from the term "word" to the term "law" (v. 25). And it is the one who studies and perseveres in doing the word who will be blessed (v. 25).

James concludes with some suggestions about specific ways we can put the word into practice. People who are truly "religious" will "bridle their tongues." (Here is where the preacher may want to integrate vv. 19-20 into the sermon.) Echoing a persistent Old Testament theme (Exod. 22:22; Deut. 14:29; Isa. 1:10-17; Ps. 68:5), he also calls for believers to care for "orphans and widows." In the society of that time, these were people who were helpless and needed assistance just to survive. We can contextualize the point by urging Christians today to reach to whoever in our society is helpless: the homeless, the mentally ill, the elderly without family help or support. But lest we think that doing the word is a matter of outward acts only, James ends with a reminder that faithfulness to the word is fundamentally a matter of one's worldview. "Keeping ourselves unstained by the world" means allowing God's word to reprogram our thinking so that our thought processes naturally emulate the values of Scripture rather than the values of the surrounding culture.

Lutheran theologians are famous for their focus on the "law/gospel" distinction. "Law," in this contrast, is whatever in Scripture makes demands of us; "gospel," on the other hand, is whatever God promises to do for us. James's teaching about the word in this passage follows this scheme fairly closely. He celebrates the fact that God in his word brings people into new life (v. 18) and that God graciously plants that word in our very hearts (v. 21). Here is the "gospel" side of God's word. But he also insists that believers respond to that word by obeying it — the "law" side. Broadly speaking, then, James helps us in this passage to understand what God's word is and how his people are to relate to it.

*Douglas Moo*

## Sixteenth Sunday after Pentecost, Year B

First Lesson: Proverbs 22:1-2, 8-9, 22-23
(Psalm 125)
**Second Lesson: James 2:1-10, (11-13), 14-17**
Gospel Lesson: Mark 7:24-37

One of the main challenges of Christian existence is to resist the temptation to pay lip service to one's faith (v. 16). James is concerned to remind his readers of this challenge in general (1:19-27), but also to explore some practical examples, such as the neglect of and even discrimination against the poor within a Christian context (2:1-17). In this latter passage he applies some principles established in the former, especially the following: (1) the need for Christian action; (2) the applicability of the perfect or royal law of liberty; (3) the value of compassion; (4) the need to avoid self-deception before God. To discriminate against the poor means to fall foul of all four principles. Having moved from the principles to the case in point (vv. 1-3), James demonstrates the sinister nature of such discrimination with three points: (1) God values the poor (vv. 4-5). (2) To honor the rich at the expense of the poor means tacitly to reinforce a regime of oppression (vv. 6-7). Such oppression presumably took the typical form of rich landowners exploiting day laborers and pushing aside those with small holdings, despicable actions in the opinion of prophets such as Isaiah, Zechariah, and Amos. (3) The law of liberty privileges mercy for the poor (vv. 8-13). But it is not just a case of not discriminating against the poor; Christian concern needs to be proactive; anything else would amount to lip service, not saving faith (vv. 14-17).

There is little doubt that James had in mind a specific scenario among his audience. This passage is not a theological treatise, it is borne out of con-

525

cern about an actual situation. But what is it? There are two plausible answers to this: either the discrimination happened as part of the normal Christian meetings, or it occurred in the context of a formal dispute among the local Christians such as that envisaged by Paul in 1 Corinthians 6. The reference to "judges" in verse 4 might support the latter (compare the similar use of such imagery in Lev. 19:15), the use of the word "synagogue" in verse 2 the former. But "synagogue" can have both meanings: "Jewish synagogue" or simply "meeting," such as a Christian meeting. In the New Testament it tends to mean the former. The latter tends to be expressed by the word *ecclesia,* a convenient way of distinguishing Christian meetings from synagogal ones. This would support the meaning "Jewish synagogue." But here James speaks of "your synagogue," as if to distinguish it from synagogal meetings. We know that he likes to refer to his readers in Jewish terms — this is clear from 1:1. After all, the renewed people of God stands in a covenantal continuity with the twelve tribes. However, we know from Luke 11:43 that privileged seating in synagogues was not unusual. Quite possibly James's Jewish Christians had carried such traditions over into their Christian meetings. As Luke 11 shows, Jesus found such practices reprehensible. Given James's frequent references in his letter back to Jesus' teachings, it seems likely that here too we have James reapplying his teacher's values. Such early Christian recontextualizations are tremendously useful as frameworks to guide our own efforts in reapplying biblical teaching for different contexts.

There is a subtlety in James's use of words here. By allocating the rich and the shabby their separate seating arrangements, the "evil judges" not only divide according to that which should not be the standard for any division, but in doing so they display the kind of "wavering" faith (a sense the word for "divide" in v. 4 has in 1:6) which James criticizes harshly in his introduction (1:6). A look forward to 4:11 and 12 confirms how strongly James feels about this issue. The basis for his strength of feeling is twofold: (1) The law of liberty promotes gracious reversal: the poor are elected to inherit riches. "Faith" which ignores this intended reversal is dead (vv. 5 and 15-17). (2) The only legitimate judge is God; the believer's responsibility is not to judge but to demonstrate proactive mercy (vv. 5, 11-12, and 15). All this sounds straightforward, but there are plenty of questions which require further clarification. Why the preference for the poor? What is the royal law? Why raise matters of adultery and murder at this point in the discussion? What is the link between works and faith?

If James had in mind a divine preference against the rich — and some have argued this by appealing to his "election" language in verse 5 — would he not thereby have replaced one type of discrimination by another? The answer depends on what we make of the word "poor." In the Old Testament it can refer not only to the materially poor, but also and specifically to the humble and meek who rely on God for their strength and salvation (Ps. 69; Isa. 29 and 62; Amos 2; and others). The Greek word used in the Septuagint translation of these OT passages is identical with that used by James here. This last sense is that intended in the beatitude "Blessed are the poor" (Luke 6:20), as a comparison with Matthew 5:3 shows. Here James is also using the word in the sense of "poor in spirit," that is, those who rely in their spirit on Israel's God. That is clear from the concluding comment in verse 5: "the poor in the eyes of the world" are those "who love him" — in short: God's people. Another (symbolic) way of referring to God's people is that found in the letter's opening verse: the twelve tribes in dispersion, that is, those addressed by the letter in the first place. James is reminding his recipients that he expects them as God's people (who are poor in their own way) to treat respectfully the poor who join the assembly. One might add that this sense of "the poor/humble" as God's people is entirely in keeping with such passages as Luke 1:51-53 where Mary expresses the hope and experience of her people. In fact, among the four Gospels it is especially Luke who is interested in the eschatological reversals motif which Jesus inaugurated (the first will be last, etc.). For a similar Pauline emphasis see 1 Corinthians 1:26ff.

What, then, is the royal law? Although most New Testament writers refrain from referring to Jesus' ethics as "law," in the case of James this would not be surprising. He is rather reliant on Jewish terminology elsewhere ("synagogue," "twelve tribes," etc.), presumably because of a combination of having a Jewish Christian audience and being thoroughly Jewish in upbringing and outlook himself. In terms of meaning, four points are worth making. (1) The proximity of the phrase to the "kingdom" reference in verse 5 suggests that we should translate "kingdom law." (2) The addition "royal" or "kingly" is meant to distinguish this law from the Jewish law, not dissimilarly to the way the addition "your" qualifies the "synagogue" in verse 2 as a Christian gathering. (3) The same applies to the addition "of liberty" in verse 12. (4) The matter is clinched by James's customary dependence on Jesus' own teaching, in this case from Matthew 22:37-40. Again we have a case of recontextualization here. Whereas Jesus expanded the OT teaching on neighborliness to include foreigners, James applies the same principle to a case of social discrimination in the context of the Christian gathering. This almost certainly happened not without some inspiration from Leviticus 19:15-18, where we find the topics of prohibiting partiality and neighborly love closely co-located. James's addressees would have appreciated the ethical continuity implied in this line stretching from the Old Testament law to Jesus and to their own sense of being God's people.

Why does James raise two examples from the Decalogue (v. 11)? It may be tempting to think there were those among the recipients who prided themselves on marital fidelity while at the same time committing "murder" (in the deeply symbolic sense used by Jesus — cf. Matt. 5:21-26) in the shape of discriminating against the poor. The second part of this suggestion is more secure than the first, though both are speculative. What is clear is the underlying logic: no matter how many laws there may be in detail, there is only one divine will behind each of them. Hence, to break just one law is to break that divine will, a view James shares with Paul in Galatians. It is not that the Old Testament law did not make provision for transgression; it obviously did, just as the new covenant makes gracious provision (v. 13). The point is that one cannot approach God's will with a "pick and mix" attitude and still expect to receive a gracious response. One's faith needs to be validated by the sort of action which emulates God's grace. Up to this point that action could be construed in passive or reactive terms. To avoid such misunderstanding, verses 15-17 unequivocally call for proactive action against poverty. This is a call to the corporate local church. How do we respond to it?

Finally, some comments about the expressed necessity to validate faith through works. Attempts to downplay this theme here by appealing to grammar are doomed. James is as clear as Paul that works matter (Eph. 2:10). Paul goes so far to say that "we must all appear before the judgment seat of Christ" (2 Cor. 5:10). So how do mercy and judgment relate to each other in verse 13? Most likely the mercy which triumphs over judgment is that of the believer, not God's. By exercising grace (for a negative example of this, see vv. 15-16), believers accumulate evidence of their intention to be judged by the gracious law of liberty (v. 12), not a law which has no place for mercy (v. 13a). In so doing they truly worship God (1:27). This is rather different from the retribution formulas so prevalent in antiquity. Grace, divine or human, was not generally associated with escaping divine retribution. The challenge today is to consider how to reflect such grace in a world that badly needs it. Again it is the local Christian fellowship(s) that needs to own up to this challenge in the first instance.

*Thorsten Moritz*

# Seventeenth Sunday after Pentecost, Year B

First Lesson: Proverbs 1:20-33
(Psalm 19)
**Second Lesson: James 3:1-12**
Gospel Lesson: Mark 8:27-38

One of the most common of all topics in wisdom literature is the righteous person's speech (see esp., e.g., Prov. 10:8, 11, 21; 11:9; 12:18, 25; 13:3; 16:27; 17:14; 18:7, 21; 26:22). James's epistle does not exactly fall into the category of a wisdom book. But he does manifest many of the same concerns that we find in the wisdom books of the Old Testament and Judaism. He briefly alludes to sins of speech in chapter 1 (vv. 19 and 26), and he will touch on them again in chapter 4 (vv. 11-12). But it is here, in chapter 3, that he develops the topic at some length. This paragraph is not obviously tied to anything in its context. But it does have some connection both backward and forward. James has just finished reminding believers that their works will be taken into account in God's final assessment of their spiritual status (2:14-26); and what we say belongs to the general category of our "works." More important perhaps is the way James's concern for our speech habits frames what seems to be an integral section of his letter, 3:1–4:12. This passage brings together themes that are often related to one another in both Greco-Roman and Jewish moral literature: "envy" (see 3:14, 16; 4:2), sins of violence (4:2), and sins of speech (3:1-12; 4:11-12). While therefore 3:1-12 can be preached as a self-standing paragraph, one should note how these connections provide a certain kind of context for the teaching. James is especially concerned about speech that manifests envy and selfishness and is harmful to fellow believers.

The passage unfolds without obvious breaks, but four successive emphases can at least be distinguished: (1) the special need for teachers to control the tongue (vv. 1-2); (2) the incredible power of the tongue (vv. 3-6); (3) the difficulty in controlling the tongue (vv. 7-8); and (4) the doubleness of the tongue (vv. 9-12).

Since James begins by referring to teachers, some conclude that the section is targeted to that group of people. But James does not address teachers, but any who might want to be a teacher. So the passage is directed quite generally to the Christian community. Especially against the background of first-century Judaism, the teacher, or the "rabbi," was a position of honor and prestige. Too many people in the early church may, then, have been an-

529

gling for such a public role in the early community. And we can find similar impulses among some believers in our own day. So James warns us by reminding us that the teacher is called to use regularly the most difficult of all "tools" to control: the tongue. Only a perfect person would be able consistently to keep the tongue under strict control (v. 2).

James is a favorite of preachers. One reason is his practical focus. But another is his rich use of a variety of evocative metaphors. James saves the preacher time by illustrating his own teaching. And nowhere do we find such a cluster of metaphors as in 3:3-6. James presses into service virtually universal illustrations: the bridling of the horse (v. 3), the steering of the ship (v. 4), and the violence of the forest fire (vv. 5-6). The first two metaphors are parallel, each showing how a small implement (the bit, the rudder) can direct the course of a much larger object (the horse, the ship). The tongue, James suggests, is like the bit and the rudder. While a comparatively small member of the human body, it has the ability to set the whole course of a person's life. Timely, well-chosen words can preserve friendships, bring reconciliation with others, and most important, please God, whereas hasty and ill-chosen words can wreak havoc in personal relationships, harm the people of God, and bring God's judgment. Consider, James says, what a great conflagration can be sparked by the wrong word at the wrong time (v. 5b). Verse 6 is difficult to translate, but the NRSV has it about right: "And the tongue is a fire. The tongue is placed among our members as a world of iniquity; it stains the whole body, sets on fire the cycle of nature, and is itself set on fire by hell." Two points in this verse are not immediately clear. First, in claiming that the tongue is "a world of iniquity" James probably means it is the conduit by which all the evil of the world comes to expression in us. Second, the phrase "cycle of nature," originally a technical philosophical description of the unending cyclical nature of existence, had percolated down into popular culture as a general way of denoting the course of life. James is simply saying that the tongue has power to bring disaster throughout our lives. How can the tongue have such power? James concludes this section by reminding us that evil spiritual forces ("hell") seek to gain power over our speech so as to disrupt our human relationships and sever us from God himself.

James returns (from v. 1) to the topic of the difficulty of controlling the tongue (vv. 7-8). Reflecting the Genesis creation account, James reminds us that human beings have been successful in taming all kinds of creatures. But the tongue, by contrast, "no one can tame." Augustine suggested that the Greek here implied the idea of "no one, apart from the power of God." With his help, however, the tongue could be tamed. This interpretation is probably oversubtle, however. James does not think human beings can reach perfection in this life, and that means that the tongue, the most difficult member of the body to perfect, will never be entirely and perfectly brought under our control. Does this mean that we should give up trying? Not at all! I may know that I will never be a perfect husband, but that knowledge should in no way keep me from striving to be the best husband I can be.

A key theme in James is the problem of "doubleness," or "dividedness." He coins a word, *dipsychos,* "double-souled," or "double-minded," to express this idea (1:8; 4:8). He wants Christians to overcome their tendency to serve both God and the world (cf. 4:4) and to give themselves wholeheartedly to their Lord. This being the case, it is not surprising that James concludes his warning about the danger of the tongue by citing its duality. We use the same tongue to bless God and to curse people made in his image. With the same mouth we sing hymns and gossip maliciously about our neighbors. We utter sincere prayers and berate our spouses and children. We teach the word and tell coarse jokes. This state of affairs is not natural, as James's illustrations in verses 11-12 reveal. The same spring does not gush forth both sweet and foul water, nor does a fig tree yield olives or a grapevine figs. What James is implying here is that the tongue of a sanctified person should be whole, single, and consistent in its speech. That this is not the case is "unnatural"; it goes against the new nature that God has created within his people. Yet it is our status as "already" regenerated (1:18) but "not yet" finally delivered from sin and temptation (cf. 5:7) that explains how the tongue could still remain untamed. As we preach these verses, therefore, we will want to steer a careful course between a naive optimism and a defeatist pessimism. We want to assure people who are genuinely struggling to control their speech that their struggle is part of what it means to be a Christian in this world, still looking forward to the final transformation into the image of Christ that comes at his return. But we want also to make clear that God expects his people to make progress in consistency in speech and not to excuse any lack of progress by appealing to the "not yet" dimension of God's work of salvation in our lives.

*Douglas Moo*

## Eighteenth Sunday after Pentecost, Year B

First Lesson: Proverbs 31:10-31
(Psalm 1)
**Second Lesson: James 3:13–4:3, 7-8a**
Gospel Lesson: Mark 9:30-37

Despite the break between chapters 3 and 4 suggested by some Bible translations, there are two reasons why the two paragraphs belong together. (1) Both are concerned with misguided envy, which leads to bitter quarrels in the community. (2) The two paragraphs develop this topic in a way reminiscent of other well-known (at the time of James) Hellenistic discussions of the same topical links: envy and jealousy lead to social ills in the community. The range of these ills typically includes slander and double-mindedness at one end and physical violence at the other. James's readers would have recognized the topical links. What would have surprised them is the call to achieve peace by demonstrating practical humility. This is a suggestion that did not typically figure in the texts referred to, for humility was not usually regarded highly in Greek thinking. For James practical humility is a sign of true wisdom. It appears that he has the whole community in mind — not just the leaders. Quite likely James is putting forward practical humility as the alternative to "presuming to be teachers" (compare v. 1).

The Greek in verse 13 is awkward, but ought to be rendered something like "Let them claim it [i.e., their wisdom and understanding] on the basis of their good conduct, their deeds done in wise humility." Such key ideas as the need for humility and good deeds are known to the reader from 1:21 and 2:14-26. Where did James get them? Good deeds were important in Roman life, and civic benefactors were usually accorded high honor. As for humility, we can confidently say that James would not have taken his inspiration from his contemporary environment. More likely is his dependence on the teaching of Jesus, the one who claimed to be meek and who blessed those who were humble (Matt. 5:5; 11:29; 21:5). Jesus in turn was in line with Old Testament thinking on the matter: wisdom begins with fear of the Lord (Prov. 1:7) and leads to good conduct (Prov. 2:20). The reason why all these sources, the Old Testament, Jesus, and James, stress the connection between wisdom and humility is that human strife demonstrates that claims to wisdom are often purely theoretical in nature, at best without any authentication — at worst contradicted by conduct. It is immediately evident that this type of argument powerfully subverts those forms of Christian faith which place such exclusive emphasis on confessional loyalty that practical conduct becomes almost immaterial.

There can be positive and negative ambition. Verse 14 makes it clear that James is here concerned with negative ambition. Was he thinking of particular situations where people boasted about an attitude that James regards as a false ambition? Not necessarily, for he seems once more to be inspired by the Old Testament, which insisted that no one should boast about such things as strength, wisdom, or riches. Instead let them boast about knowing Israel's God (Jer. 9:23-24). When James uses the phrase "deny the truth," he has in mind the opposite of "knowing the Lord," in Jeremiah's words. Put differently, by tacitly appealing to Old Testament wisdom, James is challenging his readers to assess whether their conduct is worthy of God's people. This is a phenomenon we also know from Paul. The new covenant people need to act in ways which are compatible with the best conduct expected of the people of God of old. After all, James addresses his readers as the dispersed twelve tribes (1:1), a clear affirmation of their continuity with Israel. It would be intolerable if God's renewed people (i.e., those committed to Jesus) were found to be less responsible in their conduct than those who preceded Jesus and his fulfillment of the Jewish covenants.

The language "from above" (or "heavenly") versus "from below" (or "earthly") is evidently not meant physically-spatially — space is a common metaphor here for "divine" versus "human"; or "in line with God's kingship" versus "in line with human ambition." Nor is it meant temporally, as if God only wanted his values to transpire in a future age. Again Proverbs could be appealed to in order to underline James's thinking (2:6): wisdom is a divine gift. In Judaism the main "gift from above" was thought to be the Mosaic Law. This gift was celebrated in a variety of cultic contexts. One thinks of the Jewish Pentecost festival, which originated as a harvest festival but was eventually changed in pre-Christian times to a Law commemoration event. Paul occasionally counters this by emphasizing the Christian Pentecost festival, which celebrates Christ as the ultimate gift, who in turn gives spiritual gifts to God's people (compare Eph. 4:8-10). James is not here interested in antithesis as much as Paul is. Rather, he highlights the fact — albeit tacitly by his use of traditions — that for God's people the question of separating between different types of "wisdom" has always been vital. The same applies to the criterion of "authentication by conduct." Continuity in these areas with the best values of the people of God of old is a reflection of the fact that "God is not a God of disorder, but of peace." This quotation, to be sure, comes from 1 Corinthians 14:33 (compare 2 Cor. 6:5 and 12:20), not James, but the perfect fit with the motifs discussed by James shows once more that the latter is here reverberating common early Christian beliefs. "Disorder" both in verse 16 (compare 1:8 and 3:8) and in 1 and 2 Corinthians is a reference to the schizophrenic situation in which Christians who are double-minded find themselves. They claim possession of wisdom from above on the one hand, while on the other hand they display the fruits of wisdom from below.

Verse 17 lists a number of fruits of the wisdom from above, but the greatest fruit is mentioned in verse 13. This verse also insists that humility itself needs to be "of wisdom," that is, "wise." Not all humility passes the exam of wisdom from above. Now we can make sense of a seeming non sequitur in verse 14. Why would anyone who harbors bitter envy want to boast? And what truth is being denied? Probably verse 14 offers the flip side of verse 13: there are those who, perversely, are proud of their "humility." The truth (which they deny) is that their false humility hides bitter envy and selfish ambition. Their false humility is exposed by their boasting. It is "unspiritual" (v. 15). Throughout the New Testament the word used here tends to denote those aspects of the inner human being ("the heart") which are in need of transformation. All three words used here by James ("earthly," "unspiritual," and "demonic") say the same thing, though with increasing degrees of directness. They all refer to envy and selfish ambition. This is clear from the repetition of those terms in verse 16. But what selfish ambition does James have in mind?

Clues are found in verse 13 (unsubstantiated wisdom claims) and in 4:1 (quarrels). This is reminiscent of the situation behind 1 Corinthians. So-called wise men (Sophists) claimed distinction in the art of argumentation and debate. This is a much-discussed topic in the ancient philosophical literature of the time. Eloquent language, such as that by the so-called Sophists, though seemingly humble, can easily be used in arrogant and boastful ways that lead to strife in the community. How does this fit with the astonishing claim in 4:2: "you kill and covet"? The best explanation is not the literal one, although some have suggested that literal killings were committed in early Christianity. This is an unnecessary assumption for a number of reasons. (1) Verse 18 shows that James is again dependent on Jesus' teaching. Jesus, however, spoke proverbially of killing each other (Matt. 5:22; cf. 1 John 2:15). In particular, he too argued that our use of language can amount to killing someone. (2) The phrase "and you covet" uses the same terminology by which the Jewish Zealots were known. James tacitly encourages some of his readers to think of themselves as equally fanatical as those Jewish terrorists. There the problem was nationalism; here it is selfish ambition. The solution to both situations would have been the "sowing of peace"

(3:18). If literal killings had taken place, James would undoubtedly have found much harsher words than he did.

Grammatically, verse 18 could be taken to promise a fruit of righteousness to those who make peace, or it could indicate the benefits to the community that arise from peacemaking. In any case, in line with its common Septuagintal use, the genitive should be translated "the fruit that is righteousness," thus defining the opposite of "denying the truth" (v. 14). "Righteousness" in turn is defined in 1:20 as that conduct which pleases God. Such conduct is not motivated by "desires within you." The terms used for this in 4:1 do not necessarily imply bodily desires, but more likely refer to thirst for honor (as in the "moral tradition" reflected in the Maccabean literature). There is undoubtedly a message here for those in Christian communities who, in their wrongful pursuit of leadership roles, leave a trail of pain and hurt.

Verses 7b and 8a clearly represent a common early Christian tradition. As in 1 Peter 5:5-9, Proverbs 3:34 is quoted (v. 6), followed by the command to "humble yourselves." James here reminds his readers of what they already know. In analogy to Old Testament language (Lev. 21:3, 21, 23, and others), the tradition he uses refers to the drawing near to God in worship. Where believers fail to resist the devil, they jeopardize the worship of the community.

*Thorsten Moritz*

## Third Sunday of Advent, Year A

First Lesson: Isaiah 35:1-10
(Psalm 146:5-10)
**Second Lesson: James 5:7-10**
Gospel Lesson: Matthew 11:2-11

Once again James alludes to traditions from the Old Testament as well as from Jesus. The image of the farmer who patiently waits for the rains comes from Deuteronomy 11:14, where it is an expression of God's faithfulness. Jesus uses it, according to Mark 4:26-29, as an illustration of the kingdom (compare 1 Cor. 9:7, 10 and 2 Tim. 2:6). Given James's frequent reliance on both these sources for his own theology, there is little doubt that here too they govern his intended meaning. The kingdom is currently growing (including the weeds, for which the enemy is responsible — Matt. 13:24-31). That growth will eventually be brought to a close which involves judgment as well as the gathering of the elect (again Matt. 13:30, 40-43 — cf. 1 Cor. 15; notice again the "gathering" motif in Deut. 11:14). It is that double event which James is looking forward to. In the meantime endurance is needed — this is one of the major themes with which James opened his letter (1:2-18). More immediately the paragraph explores the flip side to the condemnation of the unrighteous rich landowners who exploit the poor (5:1-6). The encouragement James offers his fellow believers is based on Psalm 37, a text well worth reading in connection with James 5:7-11.

James here combines two major biblical themes, one of which (God takes care of justice) has the function of backing up the other (believers should demonstrate patient endurance in the face of injustice). If the judge is already standing at the door (vv. 7-9), there is no need to do his job for him. Paul agrees (compare Rom. 12:19). Both are probably influenced by Jesus' teaching in Matthew 7:1. But the real question, of course, is whether or not James and the other early Christians who proclaimed the impending coming of the Lord were not themselves impatient. Was the judge really standing at the door? Is he still standing there?

Two thousand years later commentators can roughly be divided into two camps. There are those who argue that the early Christians' enthusiasm carried them away — they were simply wrong. Some would say the same of Jesus. The other main camp attempts to rescue both Jesus and the early Christians by suggesting that he never promised to return during their lifetime. To return in the "near" future was simply a way of saying that the end times had started and that the return would be sudden — it could happen at any point. In that sense his return would be "near" from anyone's perspective, even two thousand years later. One might have sympathies for aspects of both these views, yet ultimately both are unsatisfactory. The view that Jesus and/or the early Christians were wrong is difficult theologically. And in any case, what precisely did Jesus say would happen while some of his disciples were still alive (Mark 9:1 and 13:30)? What precisely is meant by the term "parousia," which is also used here in verse 7?

The alternative view is unsatisfactory because the relevant New Testament texts quite clearly imply a great deal more urgency than allowed by those who explain the issue away. The word "near" simply does not mean "sudden," however much we might wish it did. When Jesus explains that his miracles are a sign of the nearness of the kingdom (Luke 10:9-11), to give just one example, he is talking about temporal nearness, not suddenness. The "It is finished" on the cross amply testifies to this. So does John the Baptist when he refers to the impending appearance of the kingdom, an appearance which for Mark is so near, in fact, that he immediately tells the reader that Jesus was walking along the shore of the Sea of Galilee to find disciples who would group around him to represent the renewed people of God (Mark 1:15ff.). If, then, James, along with others, speaks of an imminent (not just sudden) parousia, what does he mean by that expression? And why hasn't it happened since, or has it?

The term "parousia" itself is not much help here, for the simple reason that (1) it is an innocent everyday word that means "presence" and (2) we cannot assume that in New Testament times it had acquired the exclusive technical sense of "bodily return of Jesus." Paul refers to his "parousia" when all he means is a visit to Corinth or Philippi (1 Cor. 16:7; also 2 Cor. 10:10 and Phil. 2:12). In other words, the word itself tells us precious little about what sort of presence is envisaged. To be sure, 1 Thessalonians 4:15, like James, applies the term to Jesus' future coming. John 5:24-30, on the other hand, with John's emphasis on the realized aspects of eschatology, speaks of the time when the dead will hear his voice and be raised as "having come now" (v. 25). To these brief examples that show that we must avoid simplistic conclusions one could add the fact that, in any case, the New Testament knows a variety of comings of Jesus. (1) We saw that John the Baptist refers to the coming of Jesus after him. (2) Jesus orchestrates his final arrival in Jerusalem in such a way as to evoke images of the returning God of Israel. This is equally plain from Jesus' "return" parables, which undoubtedly would have been interpreted by Jesus' contemporaries with reference to the return of Israel's God. (3) The so-called eschatological discourses in the synoptic Gospels interpret the coming of the Son of Man in judgment with reference to the impending destruction of Jerusalem. It is this (and probably only this!) that Mark 13:30 has in view when it speaks of an event that will come about within a generation of Jesus. Compare the parallel in Matthew 24:32, which is also about the destruction of Jerusalem and which — like James — combines the term "parousia" with the expectation that the parousia (of the judge) is right at the door. The Jewish War, of which the destruction of Jerusalem was the sad climax, happened within forty years of Jesus' prediction. (4) In John's Gospel Jesus himself predicts a future "return" or "presence" in the form of the Spirit who will take his place. The synoptics and Acts are agreed in insisting that the disciples must stay in Jerusalem until being endowed with this presence (Pentecost). Just as Jesus claimed by his words and actions to embody the coming (or returning) God of Israel, so the Holy Spirit embodies such a coming after the departure of Jesus. So where does this leave us with respect to James's reference to Jesus' future (from James's perspective) coming?

The number of close parallels between this text and various Gospel texts (something we are well used to from James) demands compatibility in interpretation between them. The parallel motifs include (1) standing firm patiently; (2) the impending coming of the Lord/Son of Man; (3) the farming imagery; (4) the judge at the door; (5) the need to be prepared for suffering; (6) the admonition not to judge each other as this is God's responsibility; (7) the reference to the prophets who spoke about this in the past; and finally (8) the blessing of those that persevere. On the assumption that we should avoid interpreting the eschatological "nearness" texts in the Gospels artificially as referring to the indefinite future (after all, they refer to these things happening within one generation!), they are most faithfully interpreted with reference to the impending Jewish War in A.D. 70. This would be the occasion when the Son of Man who was given power and glory according to Daniel 7 will exercise his role as judge in the shape of allowing the Romans to bring judgment upon the center of Judaism, namely, Jerusalem and the temple. Hence the various pieces of advice by Jesus to his disciples not to return to the city but to flee into the hills when this happens. Salvation is found in Jesus, not in Jerusalem and its (by now) corrupt temple. The bad surprise for Israel's much criticized leadership will then be that, rather than establishing his throne in the temple and exercising judgment upon Israel's enemies, the returning God of Israel will be seen to bring judgment upon his own people. As for those who put their trust in Jesus, they will escape judgment and participate in the eschatological restoration of God's people — they will *be* the renewed people of God.

It is likely that the "destruction of Jerusalem" scenario painted in Mark 13 and parallels, where the returning Lord establishes both justice and restoration among his people (note the same collocation of "bad news" and "good news" in James 5:9 and 11), is also envisaged here. Among commentators this is a minority opinion. But it has the decisive advantage of interpreting these texts more in line with first-century Jewish thinking, thus avoiding the need either to postulate error in the New Testament or to offer contrived and unlikely interpretations to keep face in light of the alleged delay. James's message for his original audience, in sum, was that they needed to stand firm and to await the bringing about of justice by God. There was no need to grumble against their Jewish brothers and sisters who denied their messianic claims. God himself would vindicate them.

*Thorsten Moritz*

## Nineteenth Sunday after Pentecost, Year B

First Lesson: Esther 7:1-6, 9-10; 9:20-22
(Psalm 124)
**Second Lesson: James 5:13-20**
Gospel Lesson: Mark 9:38-50

As he concludes his letter of practical exhortation and encouragement to Christians under trial, James touches on several themes. While the matter is not at all clear, this conclusion probably begins in verse 12, the phrase "above all" signaling the transition into the final statement of the letter. But verse 12 is a relatively independent exhortation, so the decision to focus on verses 13-20 does no harm to the natural divisions of the letter. Many New Testament letters conclude with exhortations to and requests for prayer. James is no exception. Verses 13-18 exhort us to pray in a variety of circumstances and encourages us to do so by reminding us of the great power of prayer. James follows the pattern of some other more literary letters (1 John; 2 Peter) by concluding not with personal matters or greetings but with a final exhortation — much like the conclusion to a sermon. Verses 19-20 provide a fitting climax to James's letter of exhortation by encouraging each of its readers to pursue any in the community who may be lagging in their obedience.

The preacher of this text must decide on his or her strategy in handling these verses. For, like many other texts, these verses contain one perplexing text that can easily dominate an entire sermon: the call for elders to anoint the sick with oil with the purpose of healing them (vv. 14-16a). The text is difficult, and the issue it treats one of the most emotional in pastoral ministry. The preacher will probably need to spend considerable time on the matter, as we will in this brief exposition. Nevertheless, the overall thrust of these verses is considerably wider than the matter of physical healing. A sermon on this *text* must ultimately respect its general emphasis even as attention is given to its most demanding section.

James begins with two general states that believers may find themselves in: "suffering" or "cheerful." In each case prayer is the appropriate response. It is natural that James should begin with suffering, since most of chapter 5 has been devoted to a situation of economic oppression in which the Christians to whom he writes find themselves. Those who suffer should ask God for help. On the other hand, those who are "good spirits" (a possible rendering of the Greek word here) should praise God for their good fortune.

In verse 14 James turns to a specific form of the suffering that he mentioned in verse 13: physical illness. To be sure, a few interpreters question whether James is really talking here about physical illness at all. They note that the Greek word rendered "sick" in the NRSV is actually the vague "weak" *(astheneō),* and that this word can denote spiritual weakness rather than physical weakness. They further argue that all the key terms in verses 14-16 — "save," "the weak," "raise up," "healed" — are regularly applied to spiritual conditions in the New Testament. They are right, to the extent that none of the words must have a physical reference. But what they miss is the way James's language in these verses (and this is true of his language throughout the epistle) echoes the language of the Gospels. And where we find this language in the Gospels, it is applied to Jesus' healing of sick people. So we are certainly justified in following the vast majority of interpreters, ancient and modern, and interpreting these verses in terms of a case of physical illness.

Just what the illness is, or how serious it is, is not of course said. But the fact that the elders must visit the person who is sick and pray "over" him or her suggests that the illness is a serious one. We should note that it is the elders, the spiritual leaders of the community, and not a specially gifted "healer," who are encouraged to pray for this sick person. Paul, of course, recognizes a special gift of healing (1 Cor. 12:28), and we have no justification for dismissing such a gift as no longer relevant to the life of the church. Nevertheless, in this, the key teaching passage on the matter, responsibility for healing is placed on the spiritual leaders in general.

That the elders should pray for the person who is sick is natural. But why does James call on them to anoint the sick person with oil? The Roman Catholic Church cites this text as support for the sacrament of extreme unction, or what, since Vatican II, has been called "the anointing of the sick." Other interpreters attribute sacramental significance to the anointing as well. But James makes clear in verse 15 that it is the prayer of the elders, not the anointing, that brings healing. So giving the anointing sacramental significance appears to go too far. At the opposite end of the spectrum are interpreters who think the anointing might have a medicinal purpose. The famous ancient physician Galen recommended anointing with oil for certain maladies, and we remember that the Good Samaritan ministered to the man beaten and robbed by pouring oil and wine on his wounds (Luke 10:34). However, we have no evidence that oil was considered a panacea; why would James recommend its use generally for those who are ill? The anointing here probably has, therefore, a symbolic function. Anointing with oil was common in the Old Testament. But especially significant for our purposes are those passages in which anointing symbolized the setting apart of a person or thing for God's special attention or use. Note, for instance, Exodus 28:41: "You shall put them on your brother Aaron, and on his sons with him, and shall anoint them and ordain them and consecrate them, so that they may serve me as priests." We suggest that James recommends anointing as a way of symbolically representing the way the sick person is being set apart, through the elders' prayers, for God's special attention.

What is the outcome of such prayer? "The prayer of faith will save the sick, and the Lord will raise them up" (v. 15a). Does James here promise an unconditional positive response to the prayer for the sick? Some Christians argue that this is the case, and fault either the sick person's faith or the elders' faith if healing does not occur. But such a conclusion misses some key biblical evidence. First, several texts make clear that it is not always God's will to heal his people from their diseases (see, e.g., 2 Cor. 12:7-10). Second, faith itself is ultimately in the hands of God. We cannot have the faith to pray for healing if God himself does not will that faith. The spiritual leaders are exhorted to pray for anyone who is sick and requests such prayer. We who exercise this ministry must prepare as sincerely and as fervently as we can. But we must ultimately recognize that our prayers will not be accompanied by the faith that will bring immediate healing unless God inspires that faith in us. Our preaching of this difficult text must be carefully balanced. We must, on the one hand, hold out the power to heal that God has invested in the prayers of the elders. We must encourage such prayer and hope fervently for it to accomplish the healing. But on the other hand, we must also acknowledge the limitations inherent in any prayer this side of glory, emphasizing that the result is ultimately in God's hands and that we cannot, by emotional exercises, generate the faith for healing apart from God's sovereign work to that end.

Physical sickness, James implies in the last part of verse 15, is sometimes the result of sin (see also 1 Cor. 11:29-30). And so it is appropriate also to

541

call on the sick person to repent of his or her sins as a means of bringing the healing about. And James concludes his discussion of prayer for healing by encouraging the community in general to engage in constant confession of sins and prayer for one another (v. 16a).

Verses 16b-18 conclude this section on prayer with a reminder of the power of prayer. "The righteous" of 16b is, it should be noted, not a "supersaint," but the ordinary member of God's people. And the example of Elijah's powerful prayer in verses 17-18 (alluding to 1 Kings 17–18) moves in the same direction. James cites him not as a great prophet of God, but as "a human being like us."

As a fitting conclusion to his letter, James calls on each of his readers to go after any among us who may be "wandering from the truth." If our intervention is successful, the sinner's soul is saved from the eternal condemnation ("death") that his or her course would have led to in the end. In promising, further, that such intervention will "cover a multitude of sins" (cf. Prov. 10:12; 1 Pet. 4:8), James leaves unexplained whose sins are covered. He may think that God rewards those who intervene by forgiving them their own sins. But the sequence makes it more likely that it is the person who has wandered whose sins are "covered" with the forgiveness of Christ.

*Douglas Moo*

## Second Sunday of Easter, Year A

First Lesson: Acts 2:14a, 22-32
(Psalm 16)
**Second Lesson: 1 Peter 1:3-9**
Gospel Lesson: John 20:19-31

First Peter addresses Gentile Christians, though it sometimes addresses them as if they were Jewish Christians. In one and the same letter they are regarded as the elect in the Diaspora, the royal priesthood, the holy people and elect (and therefore "Jews"), as well as previous aliens and strangers with an empty way of life (the latter being terms which were typically applied to Gentiles). Now they are believers, having become God's people, though not by virtue of their ancestral religion. Clearly, therefore, they are Gentile believers. But why, in that case, does the author regard them as "Israel," and what does he mean by that? The terminological constellation referred to above makes it abundantly clear that Peter buys into the widespread early Christian view that Gentile Christians have become incorporated into the renewed (namely, through Jesus) Israel. This is reflected not least in such details as the shift from the first- to the second-person plural in our text. Peter, the "renewed Jew" who relies on the blood of Christ (v. 2), identifies thoroughly with those Gentiles who have also become renewed in Christ. (Of course, we know from Paul in Galatians 2:11-21 that Peter was not always consistent in his own application of this principle!) In Christ ethnic distinctions are a matter of the past. In this respect our "Gentile Christian Diaspora" letter is entirely in keeping with texts such as Ephesians 2:11 and following. Importantly here as well as there, the authors have in mind what could be called displacement by renewal. God's people are now defined by christological renewal, not ethnic belonging. Because this displacement is based on renewal and missionary opening (a notion not in any way central to Judaism!), it brings with it both continuity and discontinuity. As far as continuity is concerned, God's re-creation through Jesus does not start from zero. We know from the Gospels that (1) it started with Jesus grouping Israel's remnant (i.e., the disciples who represent the twelve tribes) around himself and (2) that it continued with the decentralization of the gospel message (note Luke 9 and 10, where the remnant/disciples are sent into the villages, a movement reinforced by Jesus' Great Commission and reenacted in Paul's missionary journeys).

Our verses are part of what many call a liturgical piece. A close parallel — though a much more extensive one — is again found in Ephesians 1. Both texts major on praising God by giving thanks for the fact that in Jesus he is bringing history to a head. Both celebrate this as an act of grace. Both texts shift between first- and second-person plural pronouns for the sake of demonstrating continuity between those Jews who are in Jesus and those Gentiles of whom the same is true. Together they form God's true people, sometimes in the Bible referred to as the "remnant." To praise God by way of such a *berakah* (blessing) section is thoroughly Jewish. The fact that Peter expected his Gentile readers to relate to a Jewish way of expressing praise is explained simply by the observation that most Gentiles who became Christians in the first century did so because of their prior leanings as "God-fearers." They were people who were attracted by Jewish monotheism and who had therefore attended local synagogues. They would have been almost

543

as familiar with Jewish forms of worship as Jewish believers themselves. By employing the Jewish *berakah* genre, Peter uses his knowledge of their background to enforce their sense of continuity with the genuine people of God of old. This is not dissimilar to Paul's strategy in Romans 9–11. With this general background in mind, what are the major exegetical decisions and observations the interpreter has to make with reference to this text?

Verse 3 kicks off with a gloss of a major Old Testament *berakah* component. In the Septuagint one often encounters the phrase "praised be the Lord and God." Here the two titles are separated, so that "God" can still refer to the Father whereas "Lord" now applies to the Son (compare Eph. 1:17). God is now defined christologically. Christ lives as Lord, and it is he who embodies God. This is radical and markedly different from the more typical Jewish look back to the heroes of the past who tended to be celebrated as those who walked most closely with God. 1 Peter joins with the rest of New Testament Christianity in celebrating Christ as the fulfillment of the Jewish hope for the return of YHWH to his people: in Christ the Father has returned. Hence the splitting of the two titles "God" and "Lord." The primary point in this text is precisely not the subordination of the Son but his elevated status.

Verse 3 then offers the closest parallel in the New Testament to John 3:3-7 when it talks about our "rebirth" or "birth from above." Semantically both are possible, but there is no real difference in meaning. Rebirth happens as part of God's re-creative efforts for his people and is therefore, metaphorically, "from above." Christian rebirth terminology is new — what is not new in Judaism is the general hope for re-creation, nor the view that God's eschatological re-creation is an act of astonishing grace. Judaism had all along believed in a God of grace who was interested in renewing this creation. Paul agreed with this (Rom. 8:21-22). The Septuagint often relates God's mercy to his patience — 1 Peter 3:20, together with this text, concurs. The specifically Christian component here is the christological one, especially as it focuses on the resurrection. Titus 3:5 agrees that the divine mercy manifests itself in re-creation. 1 Peter extends such thinking by insisting that rebirth based on Jesus' resurrection leads to a living hope (v. 3) toward the inheritance (v. 4), which is salvation (v. 5). "Hope" can refer to the anticipation of good things in the future or to the content of that anticipation. The latter is more likely. In other words, hope, inheritance, and salvation all appear to describe the same thing. Such a piling on of nearly synonymous terms is characteristic of *berakah* texts — the example of Ephesians 1:3-14 makes that abundantly clear.

Underlying the author's talk of (re)birth, inheritance, and protection is the imagery of being God's children. The inheritance is indestructible, incorruptible, and unfading. All three terms have a negative prefix and have a poetic quality. We should not, therefore, press each word individually. The same applies to the "storage" of the inheritance in heaven. This is not about the locality of the inheritance, but about its quality. In the same vein Jesus advised against storing treasures on earth, thus discouraging attachment to earthly values (Matt. 6:19-20; compare Col. 1:5). Why is the inheritance stored? In other words, why is it not available now? The likely answer relates to the mention of Jesus' resurrection in verse 3. While Judaism expected physical resurrection to play a major role in the bringing about of the kingdom, no one expected this to be limited to one person. The big surprise was not that Jesus was raised as such, but that only one person should be raised in this way, at least initially. It is here that we find a major component of early Christian expectation: if Jesus only was raised, he must be the first fruit. His followers would follow in due course. Applied to our text, Peter seems to be saying that despite the current troubles and sufferings, there is a certain hope of future resurrection, and therefore salvation. Having said that, he is not content with pointing believers to the future only — in fact, our verses are devoid of future tense verbs. This raises the question of the meaning of the phrase "at the last stage" (end of v. 5).

What are we to make of this phrase? Some translate "on the last day," although *kairos* does not normally mean that. Terminologically it is not clear whether a definitive event which affects all believers or a time period such as the culmination of the suffering (v. 6) is in view. Some are quick to interpret the phrase as a synonym for "parousia," but that term too is ultimately indeterminate (meaning, quite generally, "presence"). Our best option is to make use of Mark 13 as the most likely background for this text. There as well as here we find the following elements: (1) suffering of the believers; (2) protection of those who follow Christ; (3) manifestation of Jesus for both salvation and judgment. In Mark 13 salvation refers in the first instance to being saved from the woes of the Jewish War in A.D. 66-70. Those who take Jesus' advice to escape seriously will be saved when the suffering culminates. Their loyalty to Jesus guarantees their salvation precisely because Jesus' (or, according to Mark 13, the Son of Man's) eschatological manifestation means that the end times or that last stage of salvation history has dawned. This scenario, which is expounded throughout the whole of Mark 13, makes equally good sense here in 1 Peter. Because the believers live in the last stage (compare vv. 11 and 20-21), loyalty to Jesus will ensure salvation for them. Salvation is here not just a metaphysical event, but a quality which works itself out in this life in the form of protection in the midst of affliction, opposition, and suffering. Its culmination, as we saw, is the believers' resurrection from the dead (though this is not made explicit in 1 Peter 1), but this should not cloud the fact that it is "ready to be manifested" now (v. 5) and that believers have reasons even now to rejoice (the verb in v. 6 is in the present tense), despite the troubles. One must insist that the term "salvation" in Judaism is not restricted to an eternal state of affairs, but often denotes the present enjoyment of God's grace. Those who insist — as some commentators do — that the writer has in mind two main periods, suffering now and rejoicing later, ignore not only the lack of future tense verbs here but equally the paradox of joy while suffering in 4:13. As in 1 Corinthians 2:9, the indescribable joy is not about future consummation of the kingdom, but about God's present redemptive aspirations in Christ. After all, if this is the decisive eschatological time of God's return to his people (in the form of Jesus), it is also the time when the eschatological joy mentioned in Isaiah 60:5 comes to fruition.

Two final remarks: (1) Verse 8 reminds the readers of a common early Christian conviction, namely, that faith outweighs sight when it comes to knowing God (compare John 20:29; 2 Cor. 4:18; 5:7; Heb. 11:1-3). This is somewhat reminiscent also of Jesus' farewell discourse where he promised his disciples to become visible to them after his departure, provided they continue in love for him and obedience (John 14:21-24). (2) Having insisted that this text should not be forced into a "now suffering, later joy" mold ("joy in suffering" would be more apt), we now ask what Peter means by the "salvation of souls" that is the "goal of your faith" (v. 9). "Souls" simply means "life" in its most wholesome sense: in the midst of suffering believers learn what true life is. This is what Jesus had already taught his disciples (Mark 8:35). The reason for the anarthrous term "souls" is that no physical salvation from death is promised here — what is promised is true life the other side of judgment (compare 3:20-21 and 2 Cor. 4:17-18).

*Thorsten Moritz*

## Third Sunday of Easter, Year A

First Lesson: Acts 2:14a, 36-41
(Psalm 116:1-4, 12-19)
**Second Lesson: 1 Peter 1:17-23**
Gospel Lesson: Luke 24:13-35

These verses are part of a section pervaded by the theme of hope. Hope is not just characterized as an optional feature of the Christian faith — at one point it is even demanded of the believer (v. 13). Hope looks forward to the resurrection of believers (an implication of Christ's resurrection — v. 3), but also to God's grace which manifests itself at the time of Christ's revelation (v. 13). It is supposed to determine Christian living, especially in terms of one's holy conduct, that is an approach to life that distinguishes itself by remaining free from the signs of uncertainty which characterized the believers' pre-Christian lives. These requirements are reinforced in verse 16 by a quotation from the well-known (even to the original audience! — they would have been familiar with this from their synagogal teaching) text in Leviticus 19:2. This is part of the Holiness Code in Leviticus 17–26 which was explicitly directed to Aaron and his sons, and to all the people of Israel. Peter is addressing his readers/hearers in distinctly priestly terminology here. This does not mean that he regards the church(es) as priestly-dominated societies. Rather, he reinforces the view that the Christian body operates within a framework of ethical continuity with God's expectations of this people of old. It is not that God had suddenly changed his ethical priorities for his people in the light of the Christ event. There is continuity — at least in this area — between God's people then and God's people now. It is instructive that the Levitical Holiness Code (which the Pharisees at the time of Jesus strove so hard to apply to all people) was indeed addressed to all Israelites. There was precisely no distinction in God's ethical expectations placed on the priests and the people. To that extent the Pharisaic endeavor was a legitimate one. It was their legalistic, purity-based interpretation of what holiness meant that was rejected by Jesus. He preferred a paradigm of mercy because that reflects more closely God's own holiness. That such thinking determined not least Peter's own is clear from verse 22 (see below).

So much for the context of these verses — it is a context of hope and purity in the midst of adversity. The adversity suffered by the readers is represented by their own past which is threatening to catch up with them once more, but also by the surrounding environment in which they live as "strangers" (2:11). Peter has specific ethical advice for them, but not until a little later (2:11ff.). For now he seeks to reinforce their sense of community by reminding them of their confessional status in Christ. They "appeal to the Father" (v. 17), and in doing so demonstrate that they are the ones for whose benefit the prophets offered revelations (vv. 10-12). The sheer privilege of being in this position tended to be celebrated in early Christianity (cf. Luke 1:70). Even as the readers are positioned at the time of the climax of God's people's history (v. 20), they represent continuity with God's people of old, both confessionally and in terms of irreproachable conduct as a witness to outsiders (2:12ff.).

Why then is God's fatherhood introduced at this point (v. 17)? The reason is that it is this fatherhood that enabled the possibility of the "not a people" to become "a people" (2:10) together with those among the people of old who accept the cornerstone (2:6). This illustrates that God does not show favoritism (v. 17). Every person's works will be judged by him who is not just Christ's father (1:3), but that of the addressees too (1:2). This emphasis on God the Father is somewhat unusual in Judaism. It echoes Jesus' innovative reference to God the Father in places such as the beginning of the Lord's Prayer. But there are two other subtleties. (1) Given the importance of the Levitical Holiness Code for this text, we note the command in Leviticus 19:3 to revere one's father. Peter is hinting that Christian purity requires not just reverence of one's biological father, but especially of God the Father. Hence the reference in verse 17 to living "in fear." This is Jewish stock terminology for reverence; it does not imply "terror." (2) Fatherhood is a particularly important notion for those in the dispersion (v. 17). Peter links the two not only here but also at the beginning of the letter (1:1-2). He understands their sense of alienation and therefore their need to relate to God as a father. This sets them apart from those contemporaries who have other cultic allegiances (many of which also employed fatherhood terminology).

Something else that sets them apart is the fact that their "work" is already under the Father's scrutiny. Peter does not have in mind individual "works" — the word is deliberately in the singular — but the life of each believer. Eventually each person will have to account for himself or herself at the day of reckoning (4:5), but that is not what is in mind here. Peter is here concerned with holy living. But what does it mean to live "in fear"? In 3:6 and 14 fear of human enemies is explicitly discouraged. But 2:17 demands fear of God. We know that the society in which Peter's recipients lived was dominated by a kind of *Weltangst*, that existential fear of all sorts of real and imagined evil powers. Hence the perceived need to possess and use amulets and so forth very likely played, as far as we know, a major part of their daily lives. Here Peter advises to take a strikingly different route: if Christians live in fear of God, based on an awareness of the price paid for their redemption (v. 18), they will have no need to resort to all sorts of means of placating human and supernatural enemies. This message may be more explicit in epistles like Ephesians, but the many parallels between these two letters underpin the view that Peter is here thinking along the same lines. There is an interesting contrast between the price paid for redemption (the blood of Christ) and the perishable things that dominated the believers' previous lives. Quite likely the implied reference here is to the means which were "handed down by the fathers" (v. 18) and were used to placate human and spiritual opponents. The message is: If you were redeemed at the price of Christ's blood, why would you need to worry about the powers at work in your preconversion life?

Peter's interest in the ransom paid reflects the interpretation of Jesus' death along the lines of Isaiah 52 and 53 in Mark 10:45. Isaiah 53 is also in the background of 2:21-25. In Isaiah the servant represents Israel. By assuming the role of the servant, Jesus not only becomes the perfect lamb for Israel, he effectively takes Israel's fate upon himself — he truly is the Christ. This, verse 20 argues, has now been revealed. Some (including some translations!) wish to play down the emphasis on Christ having already been revealed by pointing to 1:13. But there the experience of grace in the form of the revelation of Christ is a present one, much as in 5:12. The idea is clearly that believers live in the eschatological age. In his description of the lamb, Peter also draws on Jewish sacrificial language, in this case Passover language, from Exodus 12:5. However, in this case the perfection of the lamb was not a function of it being properly chosen by those bringing the sacrifice, but an expression of God's eternal ordination (v. 20). As usual in the New Testament, God's foreordination is in the first instance about the mode of salvation (namely, in Christ), not about who will be saved or who will not (cf. Eph. 1:3-8).

So far the faith of the letter's recipients has been affirmed, but now Peter looks at the nature of this faith (v. 21). They are believers "in God"; this is an important addition as they would have been "believers" (presumably in other deities) before their Christian conversion. Jesus too encourages his disciples to "believe in God" (John 14:1), but only to specify that the only way to achieve this leads through him (14:6). Our text tells us why: because he is the one who was raised and exalted (v. 21). The question of the salvific exclusiveness of Jesus is closely tied up with that of his uniqueness. So far only he was raised and exalted. From a Jewish perspective that was a surprise

— would not all believers be raised in the eschaton? Peter delays his answer to this implied question, but he offers a different one straightaway: what matters in the near term is rebirth, which in turn implies the hope in resurrection, hence the talk of "imperishable seed" in verse 23.

By quoting from the Greek version of Jeremiah 6:16 in verse 22 ("purify your lives"), Peter is not suggesting here that the Christians he addresses needed to purify their lives — they have already done so by showing their commitment to the fellowship (or "brotherhood"). It is interesting and inspiring to find that Peter here relates issues of purity and holiness not to the life of the individual (as one might in the West), but to the sense of belonging to and depending on the local fellowship. As in the Johannine epistles, here too mutual love is a nonnegotiable sign of rebirth. This is something akin to the Qumran fellowship. The latter, however, relates such love to ritual initiation, not rebirth. Moreover, at Qumran the initiates are encouraged to hate the sons of darkness. Here the emphasis is more on winning them over by living by example (2:12). The Christian faith is not about initiation rituals (at least it should not be!) — it is about the kind of faith that leads not just to the transformation of the self, but to the subversion of a surrounding world of darkness. It is outgoing, in other words. And that is not something that could be said, for instance, of the Qumran fellowship.

*Thorsten Moritz*

## Fifth Sunday of Easter, Year A

First Lesson: Acts 7:55-60
(Psalm 31:1-5, 15-16)
**Second Lesson: 1 Peter 2:2-10**
Gospel Lesson: John 14:1-14

This passage contains two of the most famous theological images in 1 Peter: "spiritual milk" and "spiritual house." Readers have long noted that both are deeply embedded in the overall theology of the epistle. 1 Peter connects the image of milk to notions of new birth and to the nourishing power of the word. It connects the image of a spiritual house to christological notions of election, rejection, and holiness, and to ecclesiastical notions of a holy people and the priesthood of believers.

This means that this passage is a rich one for preaching, since it connects to so much of the theology of 1 Peter. But this also means that this passage resists any quick and simple reading, since it drags so much of 1 Peter with it. In particular, 2:2-10 builds upon and continues the theological arguments of chapter 1. And it lays a foundation for the exhortations for good conduct which follow. In fact, many readers have insisted that it is incumbent upon any reader of this passage to maintain the interconnectedness of it to the larger arguments of 1 Peter. Especially the constant effort in 1 Peter to connect holiness and good deeds, Christology and ethics, should be recalled in our reading of these verses. In some ways this passage gives only passing nods to ethics. But the larger theology of 1 Peter suggests that these nods are crucial to the logic of this passage. For instance, God's milk does not just nourish us for our own sake; this milk enables the ethical life.

This image of "pure spiritual milk" (2:2) builds upon the idea of new birth in 1:23. Thus this milk is probably to be understood as a metaphor for the "word." In fact, most readers understand this entire passage as an exploration of the nature of Jesus as word. The word, we learn in 1:23, is that which creates new birth. In 2:2-3 the word is "spiritual milk." In 2:4-10 this word is a "living stone," which founds other living stones. Thus the word is the force which inaugurates, undergirds, and nourishes the new life.

This image of spiritual milk highlights the sense of newness which characterizes the Christian life. What makes us like milk is that we are like babies. We are just beginning this new life. And like babies (the Greek actually refers to "nursing babies"), we depend for our very life on our mother's milk. Jesus, the word, is our mother's milk. Without it we die. Thus we should "long for the pure spiritual milk," just as babies long for their mothers' milk. Thus the passage names for us the source of our life and calls us to want this source. There is an exhortation here for us to increase our longing for the word. Want the word with the same absolute focus that a baby wants her mother's milk.

This milk, this word, enables us to "grow up to salvation." There is no apparent sense here that we shall ever outgrow a need for this milk. All Christians are always babies needing milk. There is never another source. Always, Jesus is the word which nourishes. Furthermore, even if this milk reaches within us so that it in some way becomes us, it always comes to us from outside. Thus there is in this image of milk a sense of the exterior origin of the word. God is not simply inside us in the sense that something in us is God.

551

God's word comes from the outside even if it resides in us. To be a Christian is to be fed from the outside; it is not just becoming more of who we already are. And, in a nice touch, this opening section (2:2-3) ends with a reminder (or a confession) that we have "tasted" this milk and it tastes like "kindness."

How we drink this milk or where we find it or what it looks like is not explained here. However, in some ways the entire focus of 1 Peter is to explore the shape and force of Jesus in our lives. Jesus is word; Jesus is milk; and then, in 2:4-10, Jesus is a living stone. In this image of stone we encounter some of 1 Peter's sense of how we drink this milk.

The familiar metaphor of "living stone" opens upon a whole range of connected images — temple, priesthood, sacrifice, holiness, and a spiritual house. As commentators have long noted, this phrase has a quite common and literal meaning. A stone is "living" if it is uncut and still in its natural place. Thus an uncut stone is the worst of all possible stones to serve as a cornerstone. The whole point of a cornerstone is to have a "perfect" reference for the rest of the building. A cornerstone needs to be accurately cut and accurately laid. A "living stone" is neither. Of course, in 1 Peter this stone is "living" also because it has a unique connection to life. This stone is not simply uncut; it is alive. Jesus is himself alive and is the source of life for us.

This alive Jesus is also a cornerstone in the sense that we, who are his "spiritual house," depend on him for both support and orientation. As a stone, Jesus belongs to the ancient sacred house of Israel. There has been some attempt on the basis of an ambiguity over the word "royal" in 2:9 (it can be read as a noun and translated "royal house") to read "spiritual house" as not necessarily invoking the temple. However, it is very difficult for any reader not to think of the temple when confronted with the series of temple-related images in these verses. "Priesthood," "sacrifice," "Zion," and the whole notion of "holiness" all connote temple. Jesus as stone is the source not just of life but of holy life.

We should put in play here the quote from Leviticus 11:44 in 1 Peter 1:16: "You shall be holy, for I am holy." In fact, "holiness" may be as close as we can get to a governing image for these verses. The stone quality of Jesus connects him to the temple and to the whole complex of holiness traditions therein. When we in turn become living stones, we become holy because our cornerstone is holy. This is the origin of our status as "holy nation" and "royal priesthood" in 2:9.

But we should not at this point forget the larger context of this passage. The reference to "spiritual sacrifices" (2:5) points to the larger ethical arguments of 1 Peter. Holiness is obedience in 1 Peter, as it is in most of the Old Testament. The spiritual house which we become is a house made of holy deeds, love, and even the submission patterns of the household (2:13–3:7). This holiness is also configured by a powerful no toward our former lives and their passions. In fact, beginning the passage at 2:2 instead of 2:1 is a bit misleading. The milk and stone support and nourish us in the context of our "putting away" our former vices.

Key to the whole force of this argument is the series of scriptural quotes and/or allusions in 2:6, 7, 8, 9, 10. The quote in 2:6 comes from Isaiah 28:16; 2:7 is from Psalm 118:22; 2:8 is from Isaiah 8:14; 2:10 is from Hosea 1:9 and 2:23; and the four images which begin 2:9 are pulled from Exodus 19:6 and Isaiah 43:20-21. These quotes serve first of all to focus upon the determinative status of Jesus. Jesus is the stone laid in Zion. For those who believe, this stone is "precious" (2:7). Those who do not believe "stumble because they disobey the word" (2:8). The truth of Jesus as "living stone" can be found in the attributes of various stones in Scripture. This is classic early Christian exegesis. If Jesus is the stone in this text, other texts about stones may also be about Jesus.

The force of these texts may also illustrate how the "word of God" might nourish us. Jesus is the word. These texts may also be the word. The word of God nourishes us through the words of the ancient texts and through the real living stone of Jesus.

The passage concludes in 2:9-10 by returning to the sense of new life with which it began. As 2:10 insists, quoting loosely from Hosea 1:9,

> Once you were not a people,
>   but now you are God's people.

These are the people who depend on the word and enjoy the gifts of Jesus the living stone. The four descriptive phrases of these new people — "a chosen race, a royal priesthood, a holy nation, God's own people" — invoke classic images of Israel. Now that Jesus is the special stone, he takes on these classic names of Israel for himself and those who believe. A stone has been placed in Zion. This stone is the center of everything blessed about Israel. Those who are attached to that stone enjoy the ancient blessing. Those who do not believe "stumble" and "fall."

Finally, this passage ends with an emphasis on the communal nature of this new life. I am not a new person. We are a new people. This new life is plural, not singular. Holiness is not any individual's own possession; it exists when someone loves another. The kind of holiness that comes from the "living stone" exists only in community.

*Lewis R. Donelson*

## Fourth Sunday of Easter, Year A

First Lesson: Acts 2:42-47
(Psalm 23)
**Second Lesson: 1 Peter 2:19-25**
Gospel Lesson: John 10:1-10

In this section we discover one of Peter's typical rhetorical strategies. He starts briefly with a specific situation – in this case that of suffering slaves – and then quickly moves to draw out some general lessons for Christian life. He does so partly because he believes that life cannot or must not be divided into niches, which have their own, at times incompatible, principles. It is not that he leaves the specific situation of the slaves behind after verse 18, but he ensures that their situation becomes an example for Christian existence in general (*nota bene:* "someone" in v. 19).

Peter's strategy here is also reminiscent of other so-called household codes in the New Testament (Col. 3:22–4:1 and Eph. 6:5-9). Despite the order of Peter's argument (slaves first, then Christians in general), the underlying logic of such passages is not that we can draw general moral lessons from specific situations, although there might be examples of this elsewhere, but rather that the general principles inform the specific situation. Where possible, the household codes base such general principles in Christ's example and sacrificial death. In the present text the move from slaves (v. 18), via general Christian principle (vv. 19-20), to Christ's example (vv. 21-23) and a theological interpretation thereof (v. 24a-d), eventually leads to a reminder that the reality of faith in Christ must be reflected in their behavior (vv. 24c-25). The principle that true grace is embodied in the willingness to respond to injustice with perseverance is an obvious interpretation of Jesus' own teaching in Luke 6:27-35 (cf. 1 Pet. 2:20). "Grace" here is shorthand for the "credibility of faith." Where in a situation of crisis or persecution Christians act in nondistinctive ways, their faith credibility is undermined. Jesus talked of rewards, Peter of its flip side, which is punishment. The principle at stake is precisely the same.

Interestingly the account of Jesus' way to the cross (cf. 1 Pet. 2:21-25) is couched in language indebted to one of the Servant passages in Isaiah, here chapter 53. This is significant because of the role of that text in pre-Christian Judaism and early Christianity. In modern times (and, in fact, well before that) Christian believers have often pointed to Isaiah 53 as a clear reference to Christ in the Old Testament. This is not wrong, but the conclusion sometimes drawn that Jesus' Jewish contemporaries had no excuse for not recognizing Jesus as the Savior is precipitate. In the various Isaianic servant songs the "Servant" is often code for Israel's remnant. In light of this it would have been reasonable, indeed expected, to interpret Isaiah 53 in the same vein. This means that the application of the Servant imagery and texts to Jesus in the Gospels had a particular theological implication: Jesus assumed the role of the righteous remnant, and so did those who grouped themselves around him, starting with the Twelve. Israel's future therefore lies in the renewed Christ-centered remnant. Some have suggested that Peter follows in verses 21-25 not the text of Isaiah 53, but an early Christian hymn based upon it. That may be so, but it changes little in terms of the implied theology. If anything, it would add to the evidence that early Christianity had indeed understood the point about Christ's relationship to the righteous remnant of the Old Testament: the raison d'être of the remnant depends on Christ's willingness to suffer on its behalf. What is the practical relevance of this Christ/remnant theology? For Peter it is evident: if Christians are serious about belonging to the righteous remnant, their lives must be distinguishable, just as Jesus' attitude on the way to the cross was decidedly different from what most expected (including his own disciples! — cf. Mark 8-10) from a messianic pretender. The implied remnant theology therefore explains why Christ should function as an example to be followed (1 Pet. 2:21). It is worth emphasizing that this kind of theological reasoning is prevalent throughout early Christianity. Because it usually works by intertextuality with the Old Testament rather than being made explicit, it is not always obvious to modern readers. It is worth remembering, however, that to read epistles like those by Peter is like listening to one part of a phone conversation while guessing what is being said and assumed at the other end. Fortunately the frequent use of Old Testament quotations and allusions provides us with significant pointers in the right direction. With this general background in mind, a few more specific features of the text call for attention.

The reference to "masters" in verse 18 is carefully distinguished in the Greek from references to the "Lord" *(kyrios)*. The other household codes achieve that by qualifying the word "Lord" or "Lords" with a phrase like "according to the flesh." Peter achieves much the same thing by simply using a different word for the masters *(despotēs)*. Importantly, Peter is not suggesting (as might be thought from the word order) that Christian slaves should "fear" their masters. Instead they should submit to these masters as a reflection of their fear of God. Submission under human masters yes; fear no. Reverent fear *(phobos)* is due only to God (2:17). In this regard Peter's household section is no different from those in Colossians and Ephesians. Where it does differ is here: the latter consistently deal with pairs of relationships (such as masters and slaves), but Peter does not address masters. Given the normally fixed form of household codes, this appears to be deliberate and ought to be explained on the basis of his assumptions that there were no Christian slaves among his recipients. Whether or not he thought there should not be Christian slave masters by definition is unclear. Possibly he left any Christian masters out because his spotlight was firmly on the Christian call to be ready to suffer, something that would have been difficult to illustrate by addressing Christian masters.

The term "grace" does not here (v. 19) refer to that free gift from God (as elsewhere — 1:10, 13; 3:7; 4:10; 5:5, 10, 12), although that is not totally out of the picture. Peter has in mind the lifestyle or attitude which is the appropriate response to that grace. Put differently, he encourages the sort of radical behavior (vv. 19-20!) which serves to authenticate any claims to having received God's grace. The question must be asked how radical the behavior demanded by Peter really is. By modern Western standards it seems almost unacceptably subservient and out of touch with reality. In ancient Greco-Roman times the contrast between demand and reality would have been somewhat softer because that culture demanded that people live in line with their inherited status. To want to be "upwardly mobile" was viewed with suspicion, because it indicated an arrogance of betrayal toward others in the community who shared the same inherited status. Even within Judaism it was proper to live according to one's inherited position in the community, though this did not apply nationally. It was not seen to be a good for God's people to have to be subservient to overlords such as the Romans, but within the community acceptance of one's inherited standing was seen as the proper attitude to adopt. Needless to say, in today's Western world such thinking tends to be met with derision. But Peter is actually asking for more than the ancient Jewish ideal of living within one's inherited status: he demands subservience even where the master's behavior is unjust. From a modern perspective his requirement is astonishingly radical, but importantly it is backed up by Jesus' own behavior. The radical nature of this call to emulate Jesus must not be watered down. The clash of cultures needs to be acknowledged, and the question must be raised what kind of Christian behavior would achieve in today's world what Peter expected from his readers at the time, namely, to demonstrate what is possible in terms of relationships where a person is at ease with his or her true Lord (v. 24).

There is some discussion among scholars about the best translation of the word *syneidēsis* (conscience) in verse 19. Is Peter thinking of a gift or of

God-pleasing behavior? There is much to be said for the translation "for God's sake." The action to be taken as a result of this attitude is not resistance, but passive endurance. Christ's example consists of his willingness to suffer. It is that which is meant to be emulated, not his death as such. And even then the enduring suffering only makes theological sense in the context of "doing good" (cf. Eph. 2:10). This must refer to what is good in God's eyes (in contrast to what the human masters want); why else would the masters wish to punish their Christian slaves? In other words, Peter has in mind situations where a conflict arises between the wishes of one's earthly masters and one's divine Lord — in such cases the latter takes priority! This puts a new complexion on the earlier advice in verses 13-17, which appeared to be based on a naively optimistic view of human rulers. Now it is clear — even if only by implication — that there are limits to one's obedience toward human masters. The underlying principle of Peter's advice is this: in principle submission under one's human masters is godly, fear of them and blind obedience to them is certainly not. Peter resolves the seeming tension by implying that submissive endurance of human punishment, which results from acting in godly ways, achieves a threefold aim: (1) It shows that God's will is privileged over that of human masters — it is God who deserves reverent fear, not the human masters. (2) At the same time it demonstrates something of God's grace in the lives of those who are prepared to submit to human masters in the sense of enduring unjust suffering. (3) Most importantly it serves as a pointer to Christ's radical self-giving, an act which, in a paradoxical fashion, itself combines (1) and (2). Like wives who seek to win over their husbands for Christ (3:1), a slave might turn his master to the true Shepherd. Not surprisingly, that last point is again made with the help of a well-known text from Isaiah (cf. the Greek translation of Isa. 6:10). True healing occurs where people turn to Christ. One's human masters are no exception. Where slaves (or Christians in general for that matter) are discouraged by the paradox of serving God and submitting under one's human masters, Peter responds by reminding them that that was the very paradox endured by Jesus himself!

*Thorsten Moritz*

## Sixth Sunday of Easter, Year A

First Lesson: Acts 17:22-31
(Psalm 66:8-20)
**Second Lesson: 1 Peter 3:13-22**
Gospel Lesson: John 14:15-21

This section is about vindication in the face of evil and suffering. It falls naturally into two parts. The first (vv. 13-17) effectively offers an application of the quotation from Psalm 34 in verses 10-12. The second part extends the discussion by looking at Christ's role. It actually does so by once more moving back to an Old Testament text which throws light on Christ. This pattern, from Old Testament text to Christ's example and back to the Old Testament, is typical of Peter's approach (cf. 2:21 and v. 22 for two such "hinges"), and indeed of early Christianity. There was a pervading desire among the theologians of the earliest Christians to demonstrate that the Christian fulfillment of Judaism did not entail a fundamental discontinuity, certainly not on the level of behavior and attitudes. Peter's use of texts and traditions affords us an insight into how Scripture and knowledge of Christ can combine to inform Christian behavior and understanding. Even at the microlevel (clauses and phrases, rather than paragraphs and sentences), Old Testament allusions and Gospel traditions are allowed to intrude in Peter's own argument. For instance, the admonitions in verses 14-16 are dependent on the Greek translation of Isaiah 8:12-13. The exhortation not to "fear them" recalls Jesus' reported teaching in Matthew 10:26-33 and Luke 12:2-9 (compare also Luke 15:1ff.), texts which are also about facing injustice and suffering. Peter's very own application comes in verse 16: by allowing the teaching of the Old Testament and the experience of Christ to inform their behavior, believers should be able to keep a clear conscience. It's an argument that Peter conveys by means of the rhetoric and genre of wisdom. Clear indicators of this are the beatitude of verse 14 and the "it is better" saying of verse 17. Because of this particular genre, interpreters must be careful not to press any literal meanings of those phrases that are not intended.

The sentiments that if God is on one's side what harm could possibly come to those who do good (v. 13), are widespread in the biblical literature (Pss. 56:4; 91:7-10; 118:6; Matt. 10:28-31; Luke 12:4-7; 21:18; Rom. 8:31). Here the striking expression "zealots for what is good" adds further emphasis. While not certain, it is at least possible that Peter is here thinking of an alternative way of being a "zealot," namely, not that of rebelling against the overlords, but of enduring their oppression in a way which testifies to one's following of the suffering Jesus. Such suffering involves the kind of blessing (v. 14) Jesus promised in his beatitudes (Matt. 5:10). Does this admission of suffering not contradict the thrust of verse 13? No, because suffering and blessing function on different levels. This is reminiscent of the "panoply" passage in Ephesians 6:10 and following, where on the one hand the believers suffer the threat of death in the arena, but on the other they are safe spiritually. Importantly, that spiritual dimension transcends that of "blood and flesh" (Eph. 6:12).

Some have argued that the optative in verses 15 and 17 shows that Peter is not thinking of actual present suffering, but rather of the possibility of future suffering. In the light of 1:6-7; 2:18; 4:12-19; and 5:8-10, this is an unlikely inference. The optative indicates not that suffering is not a present reality, but that not everyone is affected by it. What did it involve for those who encountered it? Sometimes in 1 Peter it refers to death, sometimes not. Translations of verses 14 and 17 would do best not to read "death" into the term "suffer." Whether it is implied or not is unclear. More importantly, however, we have here a promise which rates among the most prevalent in the entire Bible: do not be afraid of your opponents and do not be troubled! Biblical references of this type are endless. In this particular case (v. 14) Peter draws on the Greek translation of Isaiah 8:12, although he turns the singular "of him" into a plural ("of them"). Verse 15 continues to reflect his dependence on Isaiah 8, this time verse 13, though he again makes a small adaptation: for Peter it is specifically Christ who is set apart, for he embodies the Lord that Isaiah 8 has in mind. This is one of those important New Testament texts that celebrate the fact that Christ fulfills the expectations Israel had attached to their "Lord." This explains why Christ is due the same reverence or even worship as Israel's God. It also explains why the writer thinks that acknowledgment of Christ as Lord "in one's heart" is the key to overcoming fear of enemies.

The injunction to be ready to account for one's hope to anyone who demands it employs the language of the courtroom. But here it is not used formally. It is not even clear that Peter primarily has in mind a verbal account of one's hope. What matters most for him is not the mode of one's accounting, but the frame of mind or worldview conveyed by it, namely, "humility and reverence" (v. 15). The envisaged reverence is almost certainly directed to God (cf. the continuation of Isa. 8:12-13, which Peter does not quote but which is likely to have influenced his choice of words here — also see Acts 5:29). The resulting "good conscience" has both moral and spiritual qualities, insofar as it reflects one's keen awareness of a God who allowed himself to be humiliated in suffering for the sake of replacing people's innate *Weltangst* with a "fear of the Lord." In that sense verse 17 — which is an extension of 2:20 — is far more than a tautologous insistence that good is better than evil. Moreover, it prepares the way quite deliberately for what follows.

The second half of our section, then, offers a christological basis for the foregoing. Christ did exactly what verse 17 demands of believers, and he did so with a view to bringing people to God. The big question is, what does that have to do with Noah and the "spirits in prison"? It is probably best to start with some fairly incontrovertible features and claims of this text. (1) A major emphasis is on Jesus' resurrection — see the *inclusio* of verses 18 and 21. (2) At the center of the *inclusio* lies the water analogy between baptism and Noah's flood. (3) The Noah analogy is likely inspired by Jesus' use of a similar analogy in Matthew 24:38-39 and Luke 17:27. At the same time, it is extended to include Christian baptism. (4) Despite the history of effect of this text, it speaks neither of a "descent" nor of "hell." (5) Verses 18-19 and 22 insist that Christ's journey from resurrection to the right hand of God led to the submission of authorities and powers. This pairing of the resurrection motif and the submission motif draws on the typically early Christian combination of Psalms 110:1 and 8:7 (cf. Eph. 1:22; 1 Cor. 15:27-28 — also Heb. 1). (6) There is a contrast between the disobedient spirits and those who get saved. (7) Despite the phrase "this water . . . saves you as well," baptism is not here seen as a means of salvation, as the immediately following sentence (v. 21b) makes clear. The "good conscience," as demonstrated by the use of the same phrase in verse 16, is evidence of good conduct in Christ, thus forming the basis of baptism, not its result. (8) The proclamation of verse 19 follows rather than precedes the resurrection. (9) The phrase "made alive in the Spirit" is much more likely to say something about the means of achieving the resurrection ("by the Spirit" — cf. John 6:36 and especially Rom. 8:11) than about the resurrected Jesus being just spirit, not body. (10) There is a deliberate contrast between Christ's exaltation and the powers' submission.

The following points are less clear: (1) Are the disobedient spirits (v. 19) and the submitted authorities (v. 22) identical? (2) Should we translate "spirits in refuge" or "spirits in prison"? Semantically both confinement and protection seem possible (for the latter, cf. Rev. 18:2 and Mark 5:10-12). (3) What should we make of the seeming temporal tension between Christ's postresurrection proclamation and the recipients of that proclamation who were around at the time of Noah? And what was the nature of the proclamation? (4) Is there an intended analogy between the building of the ark, which provided refuge from judgment, and the building of the spiritual house (1 Pet. 2:5), which will also provide refuge at times of judgment, albeit in the future (4:17)?

To take the last question first, some such analogy between ark and church may well be intended, not least in light of 4:17-18, which picks up the same contrast between salvation of the righteous and judgment of the disobedient as does our present text. It also sits well next to the implied analogy between the new start of humanity after the flood and now after the resurrection. Presumably, then, Peter does not press the analogy because it could be misconstrued as implying that the church saves people. The truth, on the contrary, is that the church is the result of people having been saved. If the analogy is indeed present in the text, it probably follows that the authorities and powers (v. 22) are at least analogous to the disobedient spirits at the time of Noah. The analogy itself is a slight development of that employed by Jesus in Luke 17:20-37. Some have argued that the term "spirits" would be an unusual reference to people, either at the time of Noah or that of Jesus or Peter. But this argument loses weight when it is seen that the term "spirits" was chosen as a counterpoint to the "Spirit" that was responsible for Jesus' resurrection (v. 18). Jesus used the Noah analogy with regard to his generation. Why should Peter not have intended the same? We must remember that it was prudent for Peter to refer to the enemies of his readers in covert fashion. Not to have done so would have created unnecessary additional problems for the Christians addressed.

What was the nature and timing of the proclamation? The set of interpretations that does the best justice to all the variegated factors mentioned is that the proclamation happened as the result of, that is, after, the resurrection. It took the shape of the victorious vindication of the Spirit evidenced by Christ's resurrection and the submission of the "powers." As it was in the days of Noah (though without the vindication achieved by the resurrection), it is directed at the powers/spirits as manifested in the behavior of people who were and are disobedient. The difference is that at the time of Noah God simply "waited patiently," whereas now Christ, by virtue of having been raised and exalted, proclaims God's victory over the powers. They are now in submission, at least in principle, and await judgment (cf. 4:5).

Finally, what about the "prison" or "refuge" of the "spirits"? Traditionally the former term tends to be used. However, it now seems better to opt for "refuge." As is the case in Revelation 18:2, the spirits reside in the people and structures of this world, confidently expecting to be safe in it. That was the case at the time of Noah, indeed at the time of the building of the tower of Babel. It was also the case with those who — contrary to Jesus' advice to his followers! — sought refuge in Jerusalem in the face of the on-slaught by the Romans (Jewish War — Mark 13 and parallels). It is still true in Peter's day. The "spirits of the day" need to be and now are being chal-lenged, not least to make them understand that their "refuge" is in fact any-thing but that. Christians participate in this challenge by their Christlike behavior — and they now do so on the strength of his resurrection. The ba-sic principle hasn't changed between Noah and the advent of Christianity. But the postresurrection challenge has considerably more force than that in the days of old.

*Thorsten Moritz*

## First Sunday in Lent, Year B

First Lesson: Genesis 9:8-17
(Psalm 25:1-10)
**Second Lesson: 1 Peter 3:18-22**
Gospel Lesson: Mark 1:9-15

1 Peter 3:18-22 was the center of controversy in nineteenth-century missiological debates. Its message returned in the twentieth century as a response to the challenge of religious pluralism. (On both, see John Sanders, ed., *What about Those Who Have Never Heard?* [Downers Grove, Ill.: InterVarsity Press, 1995], pp. 71-106). New Testament scholar Benjamin Robinson calls the passage "the most difficult in the New Testament." Given its history and challenge, humility is in order for every exegesis ventured.

We begin an exploration of these four verses in the context of the letter as a whole. The writer addressed the epistle to Christians in exile, driven there by early persecutions. The message to them is: Christ suffered and rose again. Now you are reliving the same drama. Expect to pay a great price for your witness. But closure will come to your pain and grief. Indeed, that end is a future life in glory with your risen Lord. Therefore, do not grow weary in well-doing. Show your antagonists how a Christian lives and dies.

With its theme of suffering and hope, 1 Peter is a disquisition on theodicy, its refrain a variation on Job's final cry in the face of his own quandary, one memorialized in Handel's *Messiah*:

I know that my Redeemer lives,
and that at the last he will stand upon the earth.    (Job 19:25)

Thus eschatology speaks to the question, "Why do the 'good' suffer if God is all-powerful and all-loving?" Biblical theodicy treats all three assertions as nonnegotiables. It rejects the standard solutions that eliminate one or the other, either by declaring evil unreal, or God limited, or God unloving. The canon's answer, itself shrouded in final mystery, addresses the enigma by challenging the conventional wisdom about divine power. No, it is not despotic, instant, and omnipresent control. God's omnipotence is a patient, vulnerable, cruciform love, suffering the world's assaults, yet one vindicated at Easter and victorious at the eschaton. Thus the word of 1 Peter to those in agony: "By his great mercy he has given us a new birth into a living hope through the resurrection of Jesus Christ from the dead, and into an inheritance that is imperishable, undefiled, and unfading, kept in heaven for you, who are being protected by the power of God through faith for a salvation ready to be revealed in the last time" (1:3-5).

Note, contrary to the Marxist critique of an eschatological theodicy — it's just "pie in the sky by and by" that undercuts action in the here and now — that the letter does not counsel Christians to lie down and play dead. Rather, they are urged to "resist the powers" in the revolutionary role of a priesthood of all believers (2:4-5) called to sacrifice for its faith. True, however, that the expectation of an imminent eschaton did forestall the more radical critique of the status quo that later developed, making for the household codes given to the letter's immediate audience, ones that did not challenge there and then the cultural practices of slavery (2:18) and male hierarchy (3:1). Here a hermeneutic is needed that can separate Scripture's "why" and "wherefore" basics from culture-relative "when" and "where" conventions. The why-and-wherefore theodicy of 1 Peter — through suffering to victory — is the context for probing our passage, one that deals with a related issue and its corresponding penultimate quandary and ultimate hope.

Exegetes ancient and modern have linked the allusion to "proclamation to the spirits in prison" (3:19) with the assertion in the next chapter that "the gospel was proclaimed even to the dead" (4:6), reading them as variations on the eschatological refrain of the epistle. The problematic is about

563

the destiny of those who never hear the gospel. This time the postmortem hope has to do not with the persecuted but with the unreached. Our exegesis stands in that stream of interpretation.

The passage begins with the letter's refrain: you are suffering, so did Jesus. But he suffered not only *from* the sins of his persecutors, but also *for* their sins. "Christ also suffered for sins once for all, the righteous for the unrighteous, in order to bring you to God" (3:18). The basis of this encompassing work of salvation was his crucifixion and resurrection: "He was put to death in the flesh, but made alive in the spirit" (3:18). The groundwork is thus again laid for eschatological hope, but this time for those of the unrighteous "all" who are "the spirits in prison" (3:19). They too have to be brought "to God."

Many are the theories as to who these "spirits" are. The verse that follows speaks of them as those "who in former times did not obey, when God waited patiently in the days of Noah" (3:20). Could the author be speaking of those in the Noachic covenant yet to be reached by an ark of salvation? (See the exegesis of Acts 4:12 in the commentary for the Fourth Sunday of Easter, Year B.) It appears so, for they are contrasted with the ark-rescued "eight persons . . . saved through water" (3:20). The counterparts to the latter now are the *few* saved by baptism (3:21). And the former, both then and now, are the *many* "spirits in prison," devoid of the saving Word, to whom proclamation will be made by the same divine patience in the person of Jesus Christ, "who has gone into heaven and is at the right hand of God, with angels, authorities, and powers made subject to him" (3:22).

What is the question on the mind of the author of these sentences in this late letter who is facing an uncompleted mission to preach the gospel to the ends of the earth and anticipating a soon-coming finale? It appears to be: Is there hope for those who have gone to their deaths without hearing the good news? Are they locked into the universal disobedience, prisoners of a fall who are denied knowledge of the cruciform word of forgiveness? And the answer: not so, "For this is the reason the gospel was proclaimed even to the dead, so that, though they had been judged in the flesh as everyone is judged, they might live in the spirit as God does" (4:6).

So understood, the eschatology of 1 Peter speaks to the enigma of the unreached as well as the sufferer. For both there is a length as well as a wideness in God's mercy. For the former, a Hound of Heaven will pursue the last and the least down the corridors of eternity itself. The good news is preached to the unreached by the risen Christ, who, "alive in the spirit . . . went and made a proclamation to the spirits in prison" (3:18-19). All imprisoned in sin, here or hereafter, have the choice to make: stay where you are or walk free through the door now opened by grace. There is no "universalism" here in the eschatological proclamation, any more than in the earthly one. But the mercy and justice of God are vindicated by the work of the risen Lord.

1 Peter, as a whole, is a joyful word to that time and ours. The lection echoes the whole letter's triumphant faith in the victory of Christ over suffering and death. Victims of first-century persecutions take heart. Fling your faith boldly in the air, and live toward your death in the confidence that all the saber-rattling political and social powers and principalities are already dust and ashes after Christ's resurrection victory. So too Christians today who look about and see the powers of this time and place strut and swagger, know that they have already met their match. Jesus Christ alone is our future. "He's got the whole world in his hands!" Therefore, "He calls us into his church to proclaim the gospel to all the world and resist the powers of evil" (a contemporary church statement of faith).

This eschatological-cum-action message is not limited to the church suffering but is for all, for those who have been saved by grace through faith and for those who never heard this good news. The knowledge of the pursuing love of Christ for every sinner, his indefatigable sharing of the gospel with the last and the least, spurs us to action in kind. As the trust in Christ's final victory over all evil evokes not complacency and withdrawal but active struggle against evil, so that same confidence in an ultimate offer of mercy to all does not cut the nerve of evangelism but evokes a zeal to share the Word. Those who have found a pearl of great price want to beckon all to come over and see it.

The paradox of ultimate confidence and penultimate action regarding the unreached has been present in the periods of the church's most vigorous mission outreach. Scholars of the early centuries tell us that by A.D. 150 Christians believed firmly in an eschatological Hound of Heaven, as in the Apostles' Creed's declaration of Christ's descent to the dead, conjoining it to the determined spread of the gospel. And in the midst of the movements of overseas outreach of the nineteenth century, trust in the divine perseverance beyond the gates of death was common in European and American missionaries who held to the teaching of "second probation" regarding the unreached, even as they passionately shared the faith around the world.

Theodicy poses agonizing questions about the purposes of God. 1 Peter replies with the confidence that Christ shall have the last Word. There is no better answer for preaching and teaching today.

*Gabriel Fackre*

## Seventh Sunday of Easter, Year A

First Lesson: Acts 1:6-14
(Psalm 68:1-10, 32-35)
**Second Lesson: 1 Peter 4:12-14; 5:6-11**
Gospel Lesson: John 17:1-11

Once again Peter launches into his "favorite" topic, if that's not a misnomer given the seriousness of persecution. The first part of the passage (4:12-14) is very reminiscent of that earlier text, 3:13-22. The same cluster of motifs is present: suffering is a function of sharing in Christ; therefore it comes not as a negative surprise but, paradoxically, gives cause for gladness; hence the exhortation not to be troubled. Importantly the sharing in Christ happens neither by sacramental rite nor by mystical union but by suffering. However, Peter does not just repeat what he had said earlier. He adds some other elements, such as the fiery ordeal, a stock Jewish metaphor for eschatological judgment (in the case of God's enemies) or testing (in the case of believers). There is also the expectation of the revelation of Jesus' glory and the assurance that the Spirit rests on those who suffer for Christ's name's sake. And yet, despite these assurances, from one's detached perspective as a reader of this epistle two thousand years later, one wonders how realistic it is for Peter to expect his readers to rejoice in the midst of persecution. Why not simply commend endurance?

The relatively straightforward answer is twofold: Peter's thinking is governed by an overarching meta-narrative which involves the notion of God's care and control over the fate of his people. Secondly, it is particularly Jesus' experience and teaching that sets the agenda for Peter. The rejoinder to be glad almost certainly derives from the tradition behind Matthew 5:12, or even Matthew 5:12 itself. Throughout his letter Peter displays a persistent dependence on parts of Matthew 5:11-12 and, in this case, Luke 6:22. This dependence on Jesus traditions also accounts for the Spirit promise (Matt. 10:20; Luke 12:12; Mark 13:11). Jesus' sufferings took place in the context of his trust in the Father. He was rewarded with the endowment of the Spirit who made him alive. The same is now being promised to his followers. Jesus brings his disciples "to God" (cf. 1 Pet. 3:18), both by virtue of being a trailblazer and by modeling their present and future experience. It is here that we find the foundation for the "rejoicing."

Given Peter's infatuation with the Old Testament, it is not surprising to find him quoting from it once more in 5:5, this time from the Greek translation of Proverbs 3:34. Verses 6-11 provide an exposition of this verse. Others in early Christianity used this Old Testament verse. James, in 4:6-10, quotes it and offers his own exposition. Like Peter, he is interested in the lesson that believers should humble themselves in order then to be lifted up by God (both in this life and into the next). Perhaps it is coincidental that Peter and James seize on the same verse and come to the same conclusion. More likely, however, is the assumption that such a use of this verse was fairly conspicuous in early Christianity. This is backed up by the observation that Peter's exposition has further points of contact with New Testament material. The "panoply" passage of Ephesians 6:10-17 comes to mind. There too is talk of "resisting," "God's might," "evil," and the need for "faith." There too the context is one of suffering in a hostile first-century environment of religious oppression. (Such oppression is not the norm in the Roman Empire of the first century, but Ephesians and 1 Peter certainly assume this type of local context. We are well aware that local cults in the relevant areas tended to be powerful enough to exert this kind of pressure.)

Another example of a New Testament writer addressing this type of "spiritual warfare" situation is found in 1 Thessalonians 5:6-8. Although today's worldview issues are somewhat different — especially as they relate to postmodernism — there are significant similarities too. When confronted with the claims of the Christian meta-narrative for this world (one Creator God, election of a people, the need to address the problem of sin, etc.), even postmodernism tends to lapse "religiously" into a mode of intolerance. In view of this, our text seems as relevant now as it was when it was written. But how so? A close reading should yield some clues.

The phrase "being humbled under someone's hands" is a metaphor for being overthrown by enemies (Ps. 106:42). Here it is used positively of submission under God. That "God gives grace to the humble" is clear from Proverbs 3:34. Peter's thinking here is also reminiscent of the reversal motifs in the synoptic Gospels (Matt. 18:4; 23:12; Luke 14:11; 18:14), especially when combined with the promise of divine exaltation. The phrase "mighty hand" recalls Israel's deliverance from Egypt. There are about a dozen references to this effect in the Pentateuch. This invites the conclusion that here Peter has another exodus ("in due course") in view, presumably from the oppression suffered. Typically Peter seeks to provide encouragement by relating the story of his readers to that of the people of God of old. In times of hardship believers need to be reassured of the consistency of God's dealings with his people. The continuity between Israel and Peter's Gentile audience rests on Christ's achievement, which served to bring the Jewish story to its climax while in the process opening it up to non-Jews. It is no surprise that

Peter feels free to underpin his encouragement with another piece of advice in verse 7 ("All your anxieties throw upon him, for he cares for you") which, once more, is as suggestive of Jesus' teaching (Matt. 6:25-34 and Luke 12:22-32) as of the teaching of the Old Testament (Ps. 55:22-23).

Verses 6 and 7 gave the theory. Verses 8 and 9 offer a hint of application. Compared to Ephesians — which shares so much of the thinking of our letter — 1 Peter is relatively thin on application. This may simply be because Peter does not know enough about the readers' precise situation. In any case, his advice to be "self-controlled and alert" has a close parallel in 1 Thessalonians 5:6, the context being the coming of the Lord. Perhaps the verb combination was code for the expectation of Christ's return. Some such denouement must have been in mind, otherwise the advice of verse 9 to resist the devil and to keep standing firm in the faith appears insufficient. How long can one resist if no help is on the horizon? And for what purpose? Peter's advice is predicated on the conviction that divine help is indeed coming. This he spells out in some detail in the next two verses, but not before making two further revealing comments.

The first concerns the archenemy of God, the devil and accuser (Job 2:2 and Zech. 3:1-2). It is because he is seen as the embodiment of all evil that he is referred to in the singular. All other references to opponents in 1 Peter are in the plural. Interestingly he is portrayed as "prowling around" (again see Job 2:1) and "roaring like a lion." A comparison with the Passion Psalm 22:13 turns out the same phrase. That psalm was interpreted messianically by some (4 Ezra 12:31-32). On the other hand, the term "lion" could also refer to Satan, or generally to God's people's enemies. It appears that our text plays on the ambiguity, thus reminding its readers tacitly that they are engaged in a battle between Jesus and Satan. The second comment relates to the scope of the battle. It is worldwide (v. 9). The reason for that is simply that the Christian fellowship has worldwide proportions, thus extending the battleground, certainly from the devil's point of view. One might object that, at the time of writing, this was geographically not the case. However, in the first century any philosophy that had reached Rome was regarded as having impacted the whole world, simply on the grounds that Rome was regarded by many as the center of world dominion. Like Peter, Paul is familiar with this thinking, as is clear from some of his comments about the geographical impact of the gospel in Colossians 1:6, 23.

Resisting the devil is not the same as attacking the devil, as both 1 Peter and Ephesians 6 state. The former is a wise approach for believers, the latter is not — it falls into the domain of Jesus or God (cf. 4:19 and 5:6). This puts a strong question mark against some contemporary Christian attempts to promulgate a view of evil as something to be attacked. The advice of the New Testament is not to attack but to resist. The point is reiterated in verse 10 and is made the basis for the doxology in verse 11. Peter is not suggesting a triumphalistic note when it comes to engaging the "powers." Triumph should properly be rooted in Christ's achievement and hoped-for return, not in one's own attempts to attack the "powers." Having said that, this letter is about the threat posed by evil, not about the question of how Christians should react to injustices in the world. Put differently, Peter's advice to resist rather than to attack should not be misunderstood as a carte blanche endorsement of religious quietism in the face of injustice.

So what is the relevance of this text in a postmodern world? The crucial area is that of meta-narrative. 1 Peter clearly assumes that the story of the world is one where God is in control, but also one where a battle rages between God and his opponent. The existence of evil is acknowledged and interpreted in terms of a divine power struggle. The battle manifests itself in the area of interaction between God's people and the society in which they live. This yields a perspective on evil which is significantly more focused and demanding than that found in most Western societies. Believers are expected to engage the threatening powers not by self-preservatory action, but by trusting in God's final victory. The aim of believers must be to subvert culture, not to overpower it in bursts of hostility. This admonition alone serves to demonstrate the demanding character of the call to authentic faith as trust. It will not do for Christians to retreat from the world and to leave it to its own devices. On the face of this text, that conclusion might be drawn, but it is hardly what Peter has in mind (cf. 2:12, 15; 3:15).

The faith envisaged by Peter derives its raison d'être from a biblical understanding of the story of God, his people, and the world. It is precisely this understanding of history as a relationship story that postmodern worldviews tend to challenge as too restricting. Christians will not want to give way in this ideological debate, but they need to participate in the debate as such (and do so with gentleness and respect for others — cf. 3:15!) if they hope to continue making a meaningful impact on this world.

*Thorsten Moritz*

## Last Sunday after the Epiphany (Transfiguration), Year A

First Lesson: Exodus 24:12-18
(Psalm 2)
**Second Lesson: 2 Peter 1:16-21**
Gospel Lesson: Matthew 17:1-9

These six verses contain two of the most difficult passages in 2 Peter. The difficulty does not lie in the meaning of the individual words or in the structure of the sentences themselves. The difficulty with both passages lies in our uncertainty over the force and direction of the argument. It is not clear what is being argued for or against in either passage.

1:16-18 consists largely of an account of the transfiguration. The version here reads much like a condensed form of the version in Matthew 17:1-8. Embedded in the account in 2 Peter are several indications that some sort of polemic is being engaged in these verses. For instance, the passage opens with a denial that suggests some sort of accusation has been made. "For we did not follow cleverly devised myths when we made known to you the power and coming of our Lord Jesus Christ" (1:16). Although we cannot be very precise about the content of "cleverly devised myths," the real question is who is accusing whom of following cleverly devised myths. Is the author of 2 Peter implying that unlike his opponents, whom he is accusing of following myths, he himself does not do so? Or has the author been accused of following such myths and is here denying it? Readers are divided about which scenario makes more sense.

If the author is accusing his opponents of doing this, then he is simply reminding readers of the well-known unique status he enjoys as eyewitness. If he is himself being accused of following myths, then he is pointing to the well-known quality of the transfiguration to which he was witness.

In either case it is a bit puzzling as to who is authenticating whom. Is the unique revelatory character of this event bestowing authority on its witnesses? That is to say, is Jesus authenticating Peter? Or should we say, the author of 2 Peter? When the passage is read this way, it opens up all the questions of authorship and the role of apostolic authority in the early church. Many readers suggest that an unknown author, who is certainly not the apostle Peter, is trying to accrue apostolic authority for this letter. He is announcing that he, unlike most other people, was an "eyewitness of his majesty." Thus the edge in 1:18 is that "we ourselves," unlike you or anyone else you know, heard God speak on the mountain. We should then underline the "we" in "we were with him on the holy mountain" (1:18). In this case the primary purpose of this passage is simply to add apostolic weight to the rest of 2 Peter.

Or is the acknowledged apostle Peter reminding his readers of some theological truth contained in the story of the transfiguration? Some readers suggest that this passage is elaboration of the rather unusual theological notion found in 2 Peter 1:4, where it is asserted that, by way of the virtues of the Christian life, Christians "may become participants of the divine nature." This notion has been attacked as "myth" by the "false prophets" who are denounced in chapter 2. Thus Peter is reminding his readers of the details of the transfiguration wherein Jesus partook of the divine nature. The edge of this passage becomes the terms "majesty," "honor," and "glory," all of which belong to the character of a God who is named here as "the Majestic Glory." Jesus partook of God's own glory. Jesus gives us this same glory.

Most readers favor this latter scenario. Read this way, this passage becomes a reinforcement of the possibility of the ethical life. It is possible to escape from our ancient "lust" (1:4); it is possible to have "goodness," "knowledge," "self-control," "endurance," "godliness," "mutual affection," and "love." These things are possible because it is possible to partake of the divine nature from which these powers come. We know this is possible because Jesus himself received divine glory on the mountain. Peter was there. He heard God and what God said. He saw what happened to Jesus.

The argumentative force of the passage is exhortation. You can live the righteous life. Perhaps you underestimate yourself. Perhaps your many failed attempts to become a loving person have convinced you that love is beyond your reach. But Jesus gives you the power to partake of the divine nature. Your faith will lead to real love.

The second passage (1:19-21) has occasioned as much debate as the first. These verses open with a conclusion derived from the preceding account of the transfiguration: "So we have the prophetic message more fully confirmed" (1:19). It is not at all clear at first glance how this account of the transfiguration might confirm the prophetic message. Furthermore, it is not clear what this passage might mean by either "prophetic message" in 1:19 or "prophecy of scripture" in 1:20. Although numerous options have been suggested, most readers see either a reference to a specific prophecy that is somehow confirmed in the events of the transfiguration or to prophecy in general. Given that readers have been unable to agree on a specific prophecy which might fit here, most readers think the passage is asserting that the account of the transfiguration confirms the general validity of all scriptural prophecy or perhaps even all of Scripture. The phrase "prophecy of scripture" in 1:20 leads most readers to exclude ongoing Christian prophecy from the possible range of "prophetic message" in 1:19.

We are still left with a puzzle. How does the transfiguration confirm prophecy? Puzzlement over the logic of this assertion has led many readers to point out that the meaning of the Greek is extremely unclear. This passage might be translated as "We hold prophecy even more firmly" than the transfiguration, or "We hold very firmly to prophecy" also. The first option creates its own problems — why would prophecy be more potent than the transfiguration? The second solves the problem of confirmation and has prophecy be a second force for authentication of the apostolic voice. This is nice and clean, but most readers regard this reading as undoing the whole force of the passage wherein "prophecy" and the voice of God at the transfiguration somehow belong to one another.

In fact, one of the key theological points of 2 Peter may be the inseparability and even the overlap of the apostolic memories of Jesus, the apostolic summaries of the gospel, and the words of Scripture. In particular, many readers point to attacks on opponents in 2 Peter 2:1-22 wherein scriptural allusions and apostolic teachings interpenetrate one another. In these verses it becomes almost impossible to tell where Scripture ends and apostolic teaching begins. And this may be the point. Scripture and apostolic teaching are one. If this is so, then any attempt to draw a precise map of how the transfiguration or God's words at the transfiguration might confirm or reinforce Scripture is misguided. They always reinforce and implicate one another. The point may simply be: gospel stories and Scripture cohere, in this case as in all cases.

After this confirmation of the prophetic message, the passage moves naturally to a series of famous images about prophecy and inspiration. The passage points the readers to the "prophetic message" with three images of light: a lamp shining in darkness, the dawning of day, and the rising of the morning star in "your hearts." All three denote the power of Scripture to "enlighten." These images have inspired many a sermon.

This power of Scripture to enlighten leads to two statements about inspiration, both of which have occasioned controversy. We read first that "no prophecy of scripture is a matter of one's own interpretation." This sounds like a defense of apostolic authority. Peter was an eyewitness. Peter heard God on the mountain. Peter saw the honor and glory of Jesus. The apostolic tradition that comes from Peter is reliable and is able to "interpret" Scripture. Thus individual or idiosyncratic readings of the text that do not conform with apostolic teachings are not reliable. Scripture tells us how to understand the apostolic tradition. And the apostolic tradition tells us how to understand Scripture.

However, the clarification in 1:21 complicates such a reading. There we read that "no prophecy ever came by human will." Rather, people "moved by the Holy Spirit" spoke. Prophecy does not come from the mind of humans but from the mediated voice of God. This suggests that prophets do not always understand their own prophecies. The basic point is clear enough. Prophecy neither begins nor ends in human thought. It emerges from the divine and settles in the divine. It is spirit speaking to spirit. There is, thus, no prophetic voice unless God authors both its speaking and hearing.

We are touching at this point the whole issue of the inspiration and reading of Scripture. On the one hand, 2 Peter, in its attempt to place the real force of Scripture with God, seems to open the voice and authority of Scripture to many possible readings. As long as the spirit is present, then spirit is speaking to spirit and proper reading is occurring. On the other hand, there may be an initial attempt to confine proper readings of Scripture to those readings which cohere with tradition.

It is clear, in any case, that in these verses 2 Peter is addressing both the power and danger of biblical texts. Modern Christians know both well. Biblical texts often speak to us with all the wonder and clarity of the morning star rising in our hearts. These same texts divide us from one another. As we well know, we often choose who will be in or out of a community by how they read or do not read certain texts. 2 Peter witnesses to both. It includes as aggressive an attack on Christian opponents as we have in the New Testament. And it includes a series of wonderful and gentle images of the Christian life. The Bible is a powerful and dangerous text.

*Lewis R. Donelson*

## Second Sunday of Advent, Year B

First Lesson: Isaiah 40:1-11
(Psalm 85:1-2, 8-13)
**Second Lesson: 2 Peter 3:8-15a**
Gospel Lesson: Mark 1:1-8

In the popular imagination a "last will and testament" is thought of as a rather arid legal document through which a now-dead person parcels out possessions to his or her heirs and assigns. Every once in a while, however, we witness — either in a movie or, for some of us perhaps, in real life — a will which is also a "testament" in the sense of communicating the deceased person's final thoughts. Sometimes the words chide family members for past sins. Other times the testament expresses unfulfilled yearnings for reconciliation. At still other times the words are fond remembrances of the past as well as the deceased's loving hopes for the future.

Each person could ponder what he or she would write if composing his or her final communication to loved ones. The apostle Peter thought about this, too, when penning the words of his second epistle. Many scholars believe this letter serves as a kind of last will and testament from Peter as he saw his own time on this earth drawing to a close (cf. 1:13-15). Peter sensed he might not get another chance to address his friends, and so he needed to make every word count. Among the items on Peter's agenda in writing this letter was an attempt to deal with the painfully obvious fact that Jesus had not yet come back even though Christians, and now the apostles as well, were dying.

Given these circumstances, it is not surprising to find Peter concluding with apocalyptic thoughts. As an Advent lection, this passage properly inclines also our thoughts toward the second coming of Christ Jesus. Although no one wishes to reduce Christian eschatology to the personal, subjective encounter each person has with death, there is an inevitable sense in which death is the individual's penultimate encounter with "the last things." Hence, Peter's own imminent death (and the ongoing deaths of many other believers) led him to point forward to the new heavens and the new earth — to that realm which is each believer's ultimate hope beyond the grave.

But as an Advent text, 2 Peter 3 has still more to recommend itself. After all, Peter wrote to people who were highly concerned about the fact that Jesus had *still* not returned after a whopping thirty or so years. Thus Peter needed to remind them that our time is not God's time: "With the Lord a day is like a thousand years, and a thousand years are like a day" (v. 8). But if the passage of time was of concern to the people in Peter's day, how much more pressing it is now! Peter no doubt intended his "a thousand years" analogy as simple hyperbole for people who thought three or four decades were a long time to wait. But for contemporary Christians, thinking in terms of thousands of years is neither metaphor nor hyperbole — it is reality. It *has* been a long time now!

Peter reminded the people of his era that no matter how much time passed, the Day of the Lord was still coming. After two whole millennia, this reminder has become even more vital for believers today. After all, considering the chasm of years that now yawns open between Jesus' lifetime and now, the ongoing annual celebration of Advent (with its twin horizons of Bethlehem and "The End" of history) is either the height of folly or an indication of just how powerful a force faith truly is.

For Peter, John, Paul, and the other writers of the New Testament, however, the sustaining of imminent eschatological expectations had little to do with the passage of time and everything to do with the presence of Christ through the Spirit. The reason the church has managed to stay on its collective tiptoe for two thousand years is not by repressing how much time has passed but by basking in the *ongoing* presence of Jesus in the church — a presence so real and so warm and so loving to those with faith that time's passage cannot blunt the knowledge that Jesus is already here and so can, at any moment now, fully reveal himself in the second coming.

That's why Peter can encourage his readers by saying that although we look forward to a great and glorious future day, for now the ongoing reality of Christ is what leads to "spotless, blameless" lives which are at peace with God. We don't need to focus on what will happen when God salts this earth with fire in a renewal of all things. We have enough to focus on right now as we already live in God's salvation. Part of such living means that we make good use of the parousia's delay by declaring salvation to as many as possible.

As much as any time in the church year, Advent reminds believers of their in-between status: we dwell between the distant past of Bethlehem and the indeterminate future of Jesus' return. But this in-between time is not empty time but very full. Believers are not simply suspended between Bethlehem and the parousia with nothing to do. Faith is not a kind of fly-caught-in-the-amber stasis which freezes one in a blind clinging to ancient histories and distant futures. Instead time bursts with opportunities for us to live "holy and godly lives" (v. 11) — lives redolent of shalom and transparent to the salvation in whose midst we live every day.

For this same reason Peter's return to the original creation in the verses just prior to this lection, and then his segue from that to the new creation, may be instructive. Of all the things Advent and Christmas may mean to the average person, themes related to the physical creation are almost surely not among them. The angels' message of "Peace on earth" may mean many things to many people, but peace *for* the physical earth is not often one of them. Yet in this Advent passage Peter's thoughts bend back to the word of God which created all things and which will, after a cleansing fire, remake them too. Although it is easy to read Peter's apocalyptic words as pointing only to the destruction of all that we know, it is clear that when the smoke clears and the fire goes out, what will be left will not be some vapory realm of clouds and ether but "a new heaven *and a new earth.*" This new creation will be "the home of righteousness" or, in Eugene Peterson's delightful paraphrase, a place "landscaped with righteousness" (*The Message: The New Testament in Contemporary English* [Colorado Springs: NavPress, 1993], p. 499). Since this is the home to which we "look forward," it makes sense that a part of our holy and godly living in this present world will be a celebration of, and a protection of, the creation of our God. Christians draw strength from the creation. The power of God displayed in this cosmos affirms that this same power can and will re-create it all one day as well.

So this is a passage of utter realism. In some ways Advent could be so easily caricatured as a flight from reality. Angels who dance in the night sky, virgins who deliver babies in feed troughs, stars melting — none of these things is a part of ordinary experience. Likewise in December many neighborhoods briefly transform themselves into little fantasy kingdoms of twinkling white lights. But such things are temporary. Real life isn't about fantasy kingdoms, and soon enough our neighborhoods go "back to normal" as dried Christmas trees litter the curbs and the pretty lights get unplugged and tossed back into their boxes. Then the only lights to be seen are security floodlights to keep lurking thieves at bay in the dead of night. *That* is reality.

But Peter reminds his readers that Advent is a time of realism. It's a time to think of the Word of God who created all things, who continues to hold all things, who dwells in our hearts every day, and who one day will return to make all things new. This is reality. And so it needs to be our reality every day as we lead holy, godly lives. Instead of hermetically sealing Advent off from the rest of our lives, we are reminded that what the birth of Christ portends is nothing short of the renewal of everything, starting with everything in our lives today.

One day, as Peter wrote, every last thing in the cosmos will be affected by God's deluge. For now, the life of each believer is supposed to be a minipreview of that as each component of also our lives bears the stamp of God's presence. Advent is not so much a season as a window — a portal through which to glimpse the landscape of righteousness as it already exists now in our hearts and as it will one day exist to the ends of the universe.

*Scott Hoezee*

## Second Sunday of Easter, Year B

First Lesson: Acts 4:32-35
(Psalm 133)
**Second Lesson: 1 John 1:1–2:2**
Gospel Lesson: John 20:19-31

The lectionary division makes sense, as 2:3 begins a new unit focused on obedience, ethics, and commandments and uses a different structure than 1:6–2:2. 2:1b-2, furthermore, contains the response to the disapproved conditional sentence of 1:10 (see below) and finishes off the discussion on the forgiveness of sins (1:7, 9). Even so, the larger unit of 1:1–2:2 could certainly be subdivided (as below) since there is quite a bit of material here — certainly enough for several sermons!

1. *1:1-4 (The Prologue).* Most translations are misleading, as the Greek does not begin with a verb at all but simply with "What was from the beginning. . . ." This may be awkward English, but this opening clearly evokes the opening of the Gospel of John (1:1-18). Indeed, 1 John does not begin as most New Testament letters do, and this has led many scholars to argue that it is not a letter but rather a sort of commentary or homily on the Gospel of John proper.

Be that as it may, the "commentary" begins not with a *verb* of proclamation (contra NRSV) — indeed, no such verb is found until 1:2 — but with the *subject* of proclamation. To be sure, *the fact that* someone proclaims is important (see Rom. 10:14), but here it is of secondary importance compared to the *content* of that proclamation. (This is an insight that ought to humble many a preacher!) And if that content is so important, then it is imperative that one get it straight. (This is an insight that ought to motivate many a preacher!) In this case the content concerns the "word of life." This is probably a reference to Jesus, who in the Gospel of John is called both "the Word" (John 1:1) and "life" (John 14:6). Here, then, the two are combined, perhaps implying that this word *brings* life (D. Moody Smith, *First, Second, and Third John,* Interpretation [Louisville: John Knox, 1991], p. 36, thinks "word of life" may also be an allusion to early Christian preaching. If so, the text would be a text *about* preaching as much as one *for* preaching [Smith, p. 41]).

That Jesus is "the word of life" is confirmed by the language used in this opening unit. "What was from the beginning" clearly echoes John 1:1, "In the beginning was the Word," where the Word is clearly Jesus Christ (see John 1:14-18). The verbs used also point to Jesus. What the author proclaims has been *seen, looked at, touched, heard,* and so forth — indeed, by many (the "we" is probably the author and his community or perhaps the author and the community addressed, traditionally thought to be Ephesus). These verbs have to do with sense perception, signaling that the prologue is concerned with Jesus' "revelation" — a term that is repeated twice in 1:2. And this isn't the only instance of repetition: "heard" occurs twice (1:1, 3), "seen" three times (1:1, 2, 3), and "proclaim" twice (1:2, 3). Other terms, closely related though not repeated, are also used: "looked at" (1:1), "touched" (1:1), "testify" (1:2). All this repetition — both verbal and semantic — not to mention the specific content, indicates that the prologue is dealing with the issue of Jesus' very real, very tangible, very human revelation. Indeed, in this light perhaps the prologue is an "elaboration" of John 1:14 (Smith, pp. 38-39).

This insight is underscored not only by the verbs used, but also by their *tenses.* Some (e.g., "heard" and "seen") are in the perfect tense, indicating that the action took place in the past and yet its results are still operative. Other verbs, such as "revealed," "looked at," "touched," are in the aorist tense, describing action limited to the past. The author is stressing two points: Jesus was revealed once, back then, historically, at which point he could be looked at, even touched (aorist). Yet the effect of that revelation lives on: Jesus is still heard, is still "seen" — even today (perfect)!

The emphasis, both contextually and grammatically, is clearly on the first point. The author is emphasizing the reality of Jesus' historical revelation. Why? Probably because the epistle was written, at least in part, to combat false teachers — called "antichrists" — who denied that Jesus had come in the flesh (see 1 John 4:1-3; 2 John 7-8). This false doctrine was evidently a type of Docetism, which rejects that Jesus was really, truly, fully human. Instead, he only appeared or seemed (Gk. *dokeō*) to be so. But the author of 1 John will have none of this. Jesus really was human, was truly revealed —

"we" heard him, saw him, looked at him, even touched him with our own hands (see Luke 24:39)!

The problem of Docetism continues to haunt many contemporary Christian communities, especially of the "conservative" variety, which tend toward "Superman" Christologies. In such contexts the reality and totality of Jesus' incarnation (*fully* human) must be stressed, as the efficacy of the atonement hangs on it. But 1 John fights on two fronts: it is not only bothered by a Christology that is too high, it is also concerned with a Christology that is too low (see 2:18-22; the use of the full title "Jesus *Christ*"; the emphasis on Jesus' divine Sonship [e.g., 5:13]; and especially 5:20). This latter problem also plagues many contemporary Christian communities, especially of the "liberal" variety, which tend toward "Really Nice Guy" Christologies. For these contexts, it will be the reality and totality of Jesus' divinity (*fully* God) that will need to be stressed, as the efficacy of the atonement hangs equally on that. That is, with either error, orthodox Christology is threatened (see Athanasius's *On the Incarnation of the Word*).

But if 1 John is about theology and Christology, it is equally about ethics and community. Indeed, these are deeply connected. Proclaiming these truths about the very real, very tangible revelation of Christ enables very real, very tangible fellowship with one another, not to mention fellowship with God and Christ (1:3). Such real, tangible, divine-and-human fellowship makes our joy complete (1:4).

*2. 1:5 (The Message).* 1:5 begins the next unit, and what follows in 1:6–2:2 is a kind of meditation on it (Stephen S. Smalley, *1, 2, 3 John,* WBC 51 [Waco, Tex.: Word, 1984], p. 26; hence, one might say that if 1:5 is the text, 1:6–2:2 is the sermon). Even so, 1:5 is also closely tied to the prologue. It contains, after all, the message *(angelia)* that "we have heard" (same verb and tense used in 1:1, 3) "from him." This "him" is probably Jesus given the emphases of the prologue and because Jesus was the last person mentioned by name (1:3). This message is nothing new, therefore (cf. 2:7-8; 2 John 5), and this may be the reason the author uses a slightly different verb for "proclaim" in 1:5 (*anangellō* vs. *apangellō* in 1:2, 3). While this might be stylistic variation, the verb in 1:5 may indicate that the author is reminding (proclaiming *again*) the community of the message originally presented to them. If so, the author highlights a consistency between what was *once* taught and what is *now* being taught (again), even if version 2.0 will contain further clarifications (see 1:6–2:2). This reminder may contain a subtle criticism: they have had the right message the whole time, but in light of the community's problems (e.g., 2:19) that message evidently bears repeating!

The content of this message — whether new or repeated — is "God is light." Virtually everyone in antiquity would have agreed with this. But the author continues, using a double negative that might be translated woodenly: "in him there is no darkness, not one bit." This clarifies the light considerably and testifies to, among other things, God's absolute goodness as well as God's consistency, integrity, and unity (the latter may be at work in Deut. 6:4). Yet this theological statement also has profound ethical ramifications. If God is pure light and we want to be involved with this God, then we better lose our darkness quickly! If we don't and continue to claim we are part of God's community, we are nothing more than liars (see 1:6–2:2!). This confession ("God is light") has further ramifications. For starters, it means that it is only in God — and only in this God — that we can find such light. It simply will not do — despite our many valiant (?) and tragicomic attempts — to search for light anywhere else.

One final question might be leveled at 1:5. Exactly where and when did the author hear this message about God from Jesus? Is this one of the many statements made by Jesus that simply weren't preserved in the four Gospels? Perhaps. But the incarnational emphasis in the prologue may imply that the author thinks this is what shows that God is light. Could it be that it is in the historical revelation and person of Jesus Christ, a Palestinian Jew who came from Lower Galilee, who lived and taught, who was crucified outside the walls of Jerusalem by Roman soldiers sometime around A.D. 33, and who was raised from the dead by God on the third day, that we learn the truth that "God is light and in him there is no darkness, not even one bit"? What an astonishing sermon from an equally astonishing text!

*3. 1:6–2:2 (Explication of the Message).* The final subunit unpacks the abstract assertion that "God is light." This section comprises three pairs of conditional statements. Each pair begins with a statement that is rejected (1:6, 8, 10); a positive conditional statement follows (1:7, 9; 2:1b). The former have to do with *boasting, claiming,* or *saying,* and the latter with *walking, confessing,* or *having.* A contrast is being drawn, therefore, between what one *says* and what one actually *does.*

Most scholars agree that the disapproved conditions are quotations of the false teachers (see esp. Raymond E. Brown, *The Epistles of John: A New Translation with Introduction and Commentary,* Anchor Bible 30 [New York: Doubleday, 1982]; also Smalley, *1, 2, 3 John*). This has great bearing on how these statements are employed in the contemporary context. Nowhere is this more critical than in 1:8-9, a text often used liturgically in the call to confession. In short, such a usage may be problematic, especially if there are no Christians in the particular church body claiming such doctrines in the same manner as the false teachers! Even so, it should be noted that the author uses "we" language throughout this section — perhaps as a rhetorical device. Despite the fact that these false teachers "went out" (2:19), they evidently are still having an impact and posing a threat to the community. 1 John's "we" challenges the community to decide whether or not their sentiments are really "our" position after all.

a. 1:6-7. 1:6 highlights the deceit at work in those who would claim fellowship with the God of light while walking around in darkness. Such a scenario is simply impossible. Alternatively, the author holds out the very real possibility that we *can* walk in the light *just* as God is in the light! This right walking again enables true fellowship *with one another,* something highlighted in 1:3 but noticeably missing from the opponents' boast in 1:6. Walking in the light also enables complete forgiveness — cleansing from *all* sin. Why would any choose to continue in darkness?

b. 1:8-9. Here the false teachers claim to have no sin. In Johannine literature the verb "to have" often connotes a state of being (Brown, p. 205). The false teachers may thus be saying that they are (now and continuously; note the present tense) free from the state or guilt of sin. Alternatively, the claim might reflect a heretical type of libertarianism or perfectionism (for the latter, see John Bogart, *Orthodox and Heretical Perfectionism in the Johannine Community as Evident in the First Epistle of John* [Missoula: Scholars Press, 1977]; there is, as Bogart's title implies — not to mention texts like 2:1a; 3:4-10; 5:18 [see below] — an orthodox type of perfectionism in 1 John). Whatever the case, the opponents evidently claimed that sin, in some way, had no relevance for them. But the author also calls this a lie and states that the truth (a christological allusion?; cf. John 14:6) is not in any who make such a claim. Sin is not dealt with by *denial* but by *confession.* Such confession was probably meant to be public (see 2:23; 4:2-3, 14; 2 John 7; John 1:20; 9:22; 12:42). Why? Perhaps because, as Bonhoeffer noted, "He who is alone with his sin is utterly alone" (*Life Together* [San Francisco: Harper San Francisco, 1954], p. 110). A confessing sinner, on the other hand, has company to help on the journey home! Such confession is certainly not painless but leads, again, to complete forgiveness: he (probably God) is faithful and righteous *(dikaios) with the exact purpose* to forgive our sins and cleanse us from *everything* that is not like God ("unrighteousness"; *adikias*). Truly such a God is good — light — with no darkness at all (1:5; cf. James 1:17).

c. 1:10–2:2. In the final claim (1:10), the opponents evidently deny that they have ever sinned and that they still don't (another perfect tense verb). The author's reply is strong: such a claim makes him (probably God) a liar, and his word (another christological allusion?) is not in such a claimant. Note the development: It is bad enough to be a liar and live in darkness

(1:6). It is worse to say that our wrong ethic creates no guilt because that is self-deception (1:8). Worst of all is to deny that our wrong actions are really wrong, that they are really sin (1:10). That is to pervert the order of things; it makes light into darkness, falsehood into truth, and God into the devil, who is a liar (John 8:44) (Brown, p. 236).

The author interjects in 2:1a. He can't continue this semipolite diatribe with the opponents any longer. He must be clear about his motives: he is writing these things (the letter?; cf. 1:4) to his beloved "little children" (cf. John 13:33) *so that they may not sin.* Idealistic? Perhaps, but the author is also realistic: he is not writing so that they *will not* sin. That would be beyond his ability. Rather, he is writing an exhortation that they *should not* or *might not* sin (subjunctive). Still, 2:1a is further evidence of 1 John's belief that it is possible for one to *really* walk in the light as God is in the light (1:7), to *really* live without sin (see also 3:4-10; 5:16-18). The latter point is also additional proof that 1:8 is not the author's last word on sin or its place and status in believers (on the use of 1:8-9 as a call to confession, see above; on the contradictions between 1:8, 10 and 2:1; 3:4-10; 5:16-18, see Bogart, *Orthodox and Heretical Perfectionism*). While acknowledging the serious and real nature of sin, 1 John will simply not permit us to believe that it is unconquerable (note Smith, p. 45: "No New Testament writing manifests the tension between the reality of sin — even in believers — and the demand of Christ for perfection more dramatically than 1 John"). Its rule can (and must!) be stopped (cf. Rom. 6:12-14).

Yet the possibility of future sin must be reckoned with. If 2:1 doesn't work out, there is still hope: we have an Advocate (Paraclete) "with the Father" (see 1:2; cf. John 1:1) — Jesus Christ. This advocate is a good one; he is described as "righteous," just like God (1 John 1:9). His sacrifice (cf. 1:7) is also completely efficacious — indeed, more than we might expect. It covers our sins, and not only ours but also the sins of the whole world *(kosmos)!* This is no small statement, especially from a text that usually speaks of the "world" in negative terms (see 2:15-17; 3:1, 13; 4:1, 3-5; 5:4-5, 19; cf. 2 John 7). But it is exactly that world that Jesus entered and ministered in (4:9, 14; John 1:9-13), and where we must do the same (4:17). Negative or not, then, Jesus' death is effective for the entirety of this world as well.

*Brent A. Strawn*

## Third Sunday of Easter, Year B

First Lesson: Acts 3:12-19
(Psalm 4)
**Second Lesson: 1 John 3:1-7**
Gospel Lesson: Luke 24:36b-48

The author of 1 John has heard or watched as teaching about Jesus Christ has been distorted and reshaped into something other than the truth. Liars deny that Jesus is the Messiah (2:22). The anti-Christ denies the Father and the Son (2:23). Deceivers (2:26) or others claim we have no sin (1:8). Deceivers claim that our righteousness is not connected to our fellowship with God (3:4-10). They seem to be saying that we can know God without knowing Jesus Christ, that the incarnation (Son) is not necessary and that our conduct doesn't matter because it does not interrupt our fellowship with God.

Into this distortion of what has been taught the author of 1 John writes a pastoral letter, out of love for both his people and the gospel. His aim is twofold throughout this letter and in this particular passage: to encourage believers to hold on to what they've been taught about the truth of Jesus Christ, and to clarify the gospel in unambiguous terms. While the letter is a clear denial of false beliefs, its purpose is to affirm the gospel and encourage its readers to hold on to what they already know. (The phrases of encouragement "you know" or "we know" or "this you know" or other variations appear over twenty-three times in this letter.)

The truth of the gospel, in contrast to the false teachings of the day, is articulated throughout in clear terms: Jesus Christ is God incarnate in the flesh, we live or abide in him as we obey his commandments, and our love of God is and must be lived out in our love of neighbor (2:9-11).

The intent of the letter is summed up near the end: "I write this to you who believe in the name of the Son of God, that you may know that you have eternal life" (5:13). Preaching should thus reflect its tone. The passage invites exploration of the attraction of false believing (you can be spiritual without having to worry about your behavior, for example) and is clear about its ultimate falsehood. But its tone and intent is encouragement, not so much to condemn and tear down false teachings, but in love to reveal their emptiness so that the life-giving truth of God's love in Jesus can be grasped more firmly by those who believe.

This letter and this particular passage, 3:1-7, hold a mirror to our current times. Our responsibility in love to our congregations is both to encourage them and to clarify the differences between the Christian gospel and lesser spiritualities. It leads us to ask some pertinent and difficult questions of our day: What will motivate people to hold on to the truth of the gospel? How do we encourage people to see the preciousness of a received tradition? And in a culture of multiple perspectives and religious beliefs, is Christian language about the "truth" of the gospel dead or alive?

In this passage the message of assurance and encouragement to believers is made with the introduction of the language of love and hope — the only place hope is mentioned in 1 John. The passage breaks itself into two separate teachings: 3:1-3 assures us of what we've been given, and 3:4-7 refutes false teaching regarding sinfulness. While it is easier and tempting to preach on only one of the two halves (most likely the first), throughout this letter the author states that the two cannot be severed — as false teachers claim. To preach on God claiming us as his children without calling the congregation to right behavior, or preaching right behavior without the certainty of our adoption as children — and thus falling into a futile debate over faith and works — is to rend the connection between abiding in Christ and faithful living. It is no small challenge to preach on both halves.

The author states that we are claimed by God as his children and expresses his amazement over such steadfast love. He affirms three things about our status as God's children. First, our relationship to God in Christ is certain: "See what love the Father has given us, that we should be called children of God; *and that is what we are*" (3:1). Second, we are God's children even if the world does not recognize us as such (3:2). Third, we are God's children *now,* even when it is not apparent, even before it has been fully revealed to the world (3:2b).

In a world where we so often see ourselves as the creators of our lives and their meaning, where belief is no deeper than our feelings, this threefold proclamation of our unshakable identity as God's children invites preaching on its meaning. The conviction that what's important is not only *who* we are but *whose* we are is grounded in this passage. What is our primary identity? To whom do we belong? For teens searching for a way to navigate all the claims on them (of parents, peers, school, a culture of violence and sex, their own ambitions or fears), the unshakable certainty of God claiming us as his children can be both a firm foundation and a compass. In a world filled with false spiritualities and cafeteria-style approaches to God, Christ, and Scripture, where do we receive the unshakable assurance that God has sent Jesus Christ in the flesh? We can preach with boldness to all ages that God in Christ is claiming us as his children.

Hope in this passage rests on the assurance that our future is in Christ's hands. Even though we do not know precisely what to expect when Christ comes again, we can be confident that we will see him as he is, and in seeing him *be like him* (3:2). This is an invitation to preach clearly on the meaning of the Christian life: we are not called to become successful or fulfilled but to become like Jesus Christ. We can hope for that with confidence; it will happen! What do we do with this confidence about our futures, given to us as a free gift of God's love? Believing it is true, we become like him. We purify ourselves as Jesus is pure. For all ages — searching teens, ambitious career-oriented parishioners, those nearing death — this articulation of our destiny can serve as a compass and comfort.

The third verse is the bridge between the first and second part of the passage. It invites listeners to make the connection in their lives between God's certain claim on us as beloved children and how we live out that hopeful certainty in our lives. Jesus is not simply our friend, our comforter, our savior. He is our *future* because we are to become like him: "And all who have this hope in him purify themselves, just as he is pure" (3:3).

In 3:4 the author then answers a claim made by false teachers that some people were above sinning. Everyone sins, he says in 3:4, and to sin is to commit lawlessness, that is, to ignore God's commandments. He then again makes the connection between the life we have in Jesus and our behavior. It's all a matter of where we "abide." Those who abide in Christ have no sin; those who abide in sin have not yet seen or known Christ (v. 6). Again the author is answering claims made in the community that first received this letter. Unless listeners today can overhear those claims and counterclaims, grasping the good news in this passage will remain difficult. All of us sin, even the most faithful, even those who abide most deeply in Jesus Christ, who "was revealed to take away sins" (3:5).

The preacher must find a way for this language to come alive. Otherwise the congregation will leave it at the door when they exit the church. It needs careful reinterpretation. This is no small challenge. For many the language of sin is dead (or at least on life support), and to have such a claim made does nothing to resuscitate it for most ears. The reminder in 3:7 comes to our assistance: we live in a world that proudly holds on to our right to set the terms for our existence and lifestyle. But as Christians we are called to challenge that assumption, knowing with confidence that we are God's children, not children of this world. To hear the language in 3:4-7 in light of the broader assumptions and values that permeate our culture is one possible way to revive language about sin and righteousness.

Preaching from this passage provides an opportunity to loosen the claims of the world on those who listen and fill them with the confidence that they know who they are and whose they are, this day and forever. The passage challenges the false teachings of today and reveals the love of God for us in Jesus Christ and the glorious call and certainty of becoming like Jesus, which no false teaching, no lesser spirituality, no self-made sense of sin and righteousness can touch in its depth of love and hope.

*Annette G. Brownlee*

## Fourth Sunday of Easter, Year B

First Lesson: Acts 4:5-12
(Psalm 23)
**Second Lesson: 1 John 3:16-24**
Gospel Lesson: John 10:11-18

1 John is a beautiful set of meditations on love. The letter makes its point not so much by developing a logical argument, but by intertwining key themes and phrases about confessing Christ, obeying his commandments, and abiding in God. Scholars believe the author is writing around A.D. 100, perhaps from Ephesus, in response to a group that left the church and rejected its beliefs. These early opponents of the church were probably Docetic. They emphasized Christ's divinity at the expense of his humanity. They failed to see that God in Christ had fully entered the human situation. 1 John insists that such a position undermines the ethical implications of the gospel. Its adherents are unable to grasp the depth of God's love for the world and hence are unable to live in true communion with God and their brothers and sisters in the faith.

Our passage — verses 16-24 — focuses on the character of Christian love. Of particular significance for the church today is the author's effort to describe the shape of the love that God demonstrates and to which God calls us. Contemporary American society tends to romanticize love. We are told that true love springs forth from within. It is spontaneous and free. It gives us a feeling of ecstasy — of transcending ordinary life, of being connected to powers larger than ourselves. 1 John, by contrast, insists that God's love is self-giving. It is not a spiritual high that lifts us above the problems of everyday life or takes us out of the world. On the contrary, God's love sends us into the very world for which Christ lived and died. It directs us to life in true community, here and now. It calls us to bring all of life into the light of the gospel.

Our passage reminds us that we come to know what God's love is all about when we look at the cross. "He laid down his life for us — and we ought to lay down our lives for one another" (v. 16). This emphasis on the cross should not be understood as diminishing the significance of the incarnation or the resurrection. The Son of God who emptied himself to become human is the Christ who gives himself for us on the cross (cp. Paul's great Christ hymn in Phil. 2:6-11). Similarly, the Christ who has been crucified is the Savior who has been raised from the dead and draws us to himself today. Incarnation, crucifixion, and resurrection are of one piece. They tell the one story of God's love — a love that turns us away from self-interest and self-centeredness to the needs of others.

Throughout history Christians have struggled to understand just how God's self-giving love comes to expression in the cross. Our passage seems to emphasize Christ as moral example. Because Christ laid down his life for us, we should lay down our lives for each other. Because Christ has given himself to us, we should give ourselves to each other — particularly by caring for those in need (v. 17). The cross is a summons to action, not speculation (v. 18). But in fuller context, 1 John clearly relates a moral understanding of the atonement to a theological understanding of God's saving work on our behalf. Christ "is the atoning sacrifice for our sins" (2:2). The "Son of God was revealed . . . to destroy the works of the devil" (3:8).

Here again we have an indication that 1 John is not so much a logically argued theological treatise as an extended doxology. Any of our explanations of the cross fall short. Theories of the atonement (as penal satisfaction, moral example, or cosmic victory) merely point, more or less faithfully, to the wonder of God's love — a love that is more than "word or speech," having proved itself in Christ in "truth and action" (see v. 18).

What God has done in Christ, expressed most deeply in the cross, calls us to worship. We need not — we cannot — reduce the gospel to one formulation of belief or one program of action. But alternatively we cannot worship without attempting to find words and deeds that express our adoration and gratitude.

In 1 John key elements of our worship come to expression in Christian community. Our passage reminds us that life in Christian community is more than a matter of friendly words and similar interests. We are called to share our lives with each other in concrete and particular ways. Verse 17 focuses on the brother or sister in economic need. It is striking how often the New Testament takes up this theme. In Acts "all who believed were together and had all things in common; they would sell their possessions and goods and distribute the proceeds to all, as any had need" (2:44-45). James reminds us to supply the bodily needs of a brother or sister who "is naked and lacks daily food" (2:15). These passages do not commend a particular economic system. They are speaking of our worship! They tell us that we respond in adoration to the God who has loved us in Christ only as we also bear each other's burdens and are stewards of our gifts and goods for the sake of our brothers and sisters.

If the cross is one central element in defining and shaping Christian love, a second is obedience. It is not enough to have Christ's example; we also need his commandment. Love is not simply a spontaneous response to God's mighty acts in the life, death, resurrection of Jesus; it also comes to us as a demand. The freedom that Christ has won for us and the obedience that he requires of us are two sides of the same coin. Discipleship is already/ not yet. We already adore God, yet we still need to grow into the image of Christ more fully. We already experience the reality of God's love, yet we still need to practice that love more faithfully. The command to love directs us to all of God's commandments, as fulfilled in Christ.

Our passage closely connects the command that we "love one another" with the command "that we should believe in the name of his Son Jesus Christ" (v. 23). We again see 1 John's insistence that God in Christ really walked among us. God came into the world as one of us. God became fully present to us in flesh and blood. We can know the love to which God has called us only as we know the love that God has shown us in the life, death, and resurrection of Jesus. Belief and practice are inextricably interconnected. We must obediently hear and believe the story of God's mighty acts in Christ — and we must obediently embody that story in our way of life in Christian community.

A third element in defining and shaping Christian love is the notion of "abiding" (v. 24). Christ's death on the cross and Christ's commandments open us to life in God. Christian love is self-giving; Christian love is disciplined; and Christian love is relational. It draws us into the very presence of the living God, and the God with whom we share intimate, abiding relationship calls us into relationship with each other.

This life in God is stronger than sin. We may fall short in our worship. We may falter in our obedience. But "whenever our hearts condemn us . . .

God is greater than our hearts" (v. 20). God's love gives us the assurance (v. 19) and confidence ("boldness") (v. 21) that we know God and belong to God.

The rich poetry of 1 John does not easily lend itself to homiletical exposition. It is the language of devotion and meditation. Nonetheless, our passage is replete with insight for the church today. It reminds us that when we say, "God is love," we also have to say more. First, Christian love is christological. Its only source is the life, death, and resurrection of Christ. No matter how noble our own definitions of love, we must set them aside to hear the story of God's work in Jesus — the One who really lived among us, the One whom people saw, heard, and touched (see 1:1).

Second, Christian love is deepened through lifelong disciplines of belief and practice. It is not a state that we achieve once and for all, nor is it a feeling that ebbs and flows. It is not simply a set of tips for better living or a series of suggestions that we can choose to ignore or modify. Rather, Christian love is defined and shaped by the way of life to which God has called us. To love in the way of Christ is to learn obedience to his will.

Third, Christian love springs out of communion with God and seeks community with others. 1 John focuses on the household of faith — community with brothers and sisters in the faith. But its author knows that Christ came not only for an elect few but for the whole world (see 2:2). Christians are called to a way of life together that embodies Christ's self-giving love. They are called to care for each other in time of need. This self-giving love surely seeks to draw others into its orbit, that the whole world might know God rightly and abide in him.

*John P. Burgess*

## Fifth Sunday of Easter, Year B

First Lesson: Acts 8:26-40
(Psalm 22:25-31)
**Second Lesson: 1 John 4:7-21**
Gospel Lesson: John 15:1-8

All the great themes of 1 John — believing in Christ, obeying his commandments, and abiding in him — echo in this passage and are woven together into a hymn of praise to the God of love. John does not cite "love" in order to develop a detailed ethic. We do not know what his position would be on issues of war, abortion, or sexuality if he were living today. Rather than clarifying the specifics of a Christian response to difficult moral issues, he is concerned to lay down spiritual foundations of the Christian life that will be lasting and unchanging.

Our passage speaks to the basic orientation points of Christian existence. It describes the context of faith that should guide and direct all our thinking and doing. It reminds us: Wherever we turn, we face God. Whatever we do, we stand before God. Love is not adequately defined by human conceptions of what provides for a good order. It is more than a celebration of human diversity. Love is, first of all, a divine reality. It is nothing less than the abiding presence of God.

At the heart of John's hymn of praise is "God is love" (v. 16). Love begins in God; love is from God (v. 7). Our efforts to treat each other with respect, to value the diversity of human backgrounds and interests, and to provide for the flourishing of every human life can be noble and important, but we do not truly know God if we make God nothing more than a projection of our values. 1 John suggests that we will know how to treat each other respectfully and how to value each other's unique possibilities only if we have first been drawn into the life of God. Love is best understood not as an abstract concept that can be easily expressed in general philosophical or experiential terms, or as just another of the many attributes of God, such as righteousness and holiness. To speak of the love of God is to speak of what God has done, is doing. Whatever love is, it is defined by the character of the active God who has moved and is moving in our midst.

God's activity in the world has a trinitarian shape. At the time of the writing of 1 John (probably around A.D. 100), the church had not developed a theory of the Trinity. Yet it is striking that Christians already did not know how to talk about God except in terms of Father, Son, and Spirit. They had experienced the love of God in a threefold manner.

According to our passage, we know God's active presence in the world first in the Son, who is "the atoning sacrifice for our sins" (v. 10). Christ truly walked among us, bearing our sins, "that we might live through him" (v. 9). He is "Savior of the world" (v. 14).

This Son was more than a good human being. He did not simply discover an inner human capacity to heal people and call them into a new way of life. Rather, he was "sent" (vv. 9, 14). He has a "Father." God's activity in Christ thus belongs in the larger context of God's intentions for the world. The story of God's love reaches back beyond the birth of Christ — and forward beyond his death — to God's sovereign purposes as the source of all that is.

1 John also refers to the Spirit, who assures us "that we abide in [God] and he in us" (v. 13). Like the Son, the Spirit has been given to us. The Spirit is not an inner feeling ("I've got the Spirit") or a sacralized institution ("the Spirit belongs to the church"). The Spirit does not simply spring up from within us or magnify powers that we already possess. Rather, the Spirit comes from beyond us and (as John notes in the passage that immediately precedes ours) confesses that "Jesus Christ has come in the flesh . . . from God" (v. 2). The Spirit thus convicts us and comforts us by confronting us with the story of God's love in Christ. Through the Spirit, what God has done for us in Christ is no longer an abstract, intellectual proposition that we could thoughtfully consider (and accept or reject) but becomes the truth by which we live and die.

Our passage not only refers to the three "persons" of the Trinity, but also explores their interrelationships in the economy of salvation. Father, Son, and Holy Spirit belong together. They are not three independent entities but the one love of God, expressed in God's own being and in God's coming to us. The significance of the trinitarian shape of our passage is, above all, doxological. The point is not to figure out an abstract puzzle about three-in-one, but to worship the living God whom we know as Father, Son, and Spirit. The trinitarian shape of our passage also protects John's key insight about love: "We love because he first loved us" (v. 19) and "In this is love, not that we loved God but that he loved us" (v. 10). The Trinity points to the story of God's love that precedes us, holds us, and goes before us. The Trinity is a way of telling us of a God who is love in his very being.

It follows from the character of God's love for us that our lives before God should also be defined by love. Our passage can go so far as to say that "everyone who loves is born of God" (v. 7). Father, Son, and Spirit invite us,

591

stir us, into a new way of life. There are two dimensions to this love, and they are intimately interconnected: love of God and love of our brothers and sisters. 1 John rejects the notion that we could love God without loving our brother or sister: "Those who do not love a brother or sister whom they have seen, cannot love God whom they have not seen" (v. 20). But it is equally clear that love of brother and sister cannot replace love of God, for it is love of God that leads us to our brother or sister: "Those who love God must love their brothers and sisters also" (v. 21). Thus Christian faith cannot be reduced to platitudes about the way we should treat each other. We will know how to love each other only as we come to know God's love for us and abide in God as he abides in us.

Here our passage injects an eschatological note. The God of love is also the God of judgment. Our love must be perfect if we are to stand confidently (in "boldness") before God (v. 17). "Perfect love casts out fear; for fear has to do with punishment" (v. 18). This emphasis on perfection (also, see vv. 12, 17, 18) reminds us of Jesus' admonition to his disciples in the Sermon on the Mount: "Be perfect, therefore, as your heavenly Father is perfect" (Matt. 5:48). At times John affirms that this perfection is already ours; at other times he suggests that sin still infects the Christian life (see 1:8). Augustine, one of the tradition's great commentators on 1 John, argued that our love is in training. We must learn day by day to love in the way of Christ until we love perfectly in eternity.

The theme of love is basic to many a sermon, and we are often tempted to focus on examples of costly human love in order to move and inspire our listeners (and to win their approbation?). John asks us to discipline these homiletical possibilities. First, we must be careful not to play "the two loves" off against each other. Love of God cannot be the basis for ignoring the cries of our brothers and sisters in need. Neither can love for others be the basis for ignoring what God has done for us in Christ. We cannot know God apart from the neighbor, yet the neighbor is not God. Adoration of God and service to the world go hand in hand, and neither can take the place of the other.

Second, we must carefully reflect on "love perfected." Some Christian traditions have emphasized the possibility of achieving holiness; others have argued that even our most noble works of love remain tainted by self-interest. This debate must not obscure the obvious: whatever progress we make in the way of Christian love is fed by God's gracious presence and in Christ. The love that casts out fear is not our achievement but an eschatological reality — a possibility that hinges on God's in-breaking into the world.

Third, Christian ethical action has no foundation outside of the trinitarian story of God's love for us. Christian ethics is not simply a question of "right decisions." It involves more than implementing one human project or another. Christian ethics is an exercise in fear and trembling before the living God. Christian ethics describes the story of God's love to which we have been joined by the work of Christ and the power of the Holy Spirit. We will know ourselves only as we know God — and as we know that he abides in us and calls us to abide in him.

*John P. Burgess*

## Sixth Sunday of Easter, Year B

First Lesson: Acts 10:44-48
(Psalm 98)
**Second Lesson: 1 John 5:1-6**
Gospel Lesson: John 15:9-17

The rich themes of the witness of the Beloved Disciple converge and interweave intricately in the First Letter of John. In this pericope a few short verses give us a typical, especially abbreviated bundle of Johannine themes. Among them are faith, loving God the Father by loving the Son, obedience to the commandments, love of the children of God, prevailing over the world, the incarnation, the sacramental presence and reality of Jesus Christ, and the testimony of the Spirit.

John is not systematic or tidy, yet the rich themes of his witness support one another like the stones of an arch. The witness cannot be laid out or proclaimed in several easy steps. It is not possible to start out at one spot and progress to an obvious conclusion. For instance, though this pericope ends with an emphasis on the truth that is the Holy Spirit, it might easily have begun there. For only through the Spirit can we "believe that Jesus is the Christ" and that faith is necessary to be "born of God." Only in the Spirit can we keep the commandments and conquer the world. A similar exercise could be conducted with each of the other themes I have listed.

593

Such a witness is offensive to the modern mind. It does not lend itself well to PowerPoint presentations — or to three points and a poem. An outline will not help much; the text is so spare as to be an outline already. The text is not like a catechism. It is not like a philosophical argument. Yet it is stunningly clear.

There is a good reason why it is so unmodern and unlinear yet so clear. Revelation is more like life than a syllogism, more like the story of God in Christ reconciling the world to himself than like a proof. The beginnings of the Gospel and the First Letter of John remind us that the Word of God has become flesh, that is, a person, Jesus of Nazareth. God's Word and revelation will not take the form of a neat outline. It will be like a life, the life of Jesus and then the life of his church. So in this text the riches just fall before us, bearing their witness and inviting the church and the preacher to use and proclaim them.

The scholarly consensus on 1 John is pretty firm. It is generally placed at a somewhat later date than the Fourth Gospel and is something of a commentary on it. It reaffirms the themes of the Gospel of John and rules out the gnosticizing interpretation that has plagued the Fourth Gospel from that day to this. Plainly, part of the community has abandoned the church and the gospel for some sort of proto-Gnostic new age religion. The apostolic witness is brought to bear on those who remain, to confirm them in their faith and in their resistance to sin and schism and to the bizarre claim that the Word did not come in the flesh.

Because this pericope is so tightly packed, it is useful to take a brief look at each verse separately.

Verse 1 reaffirms the central claim of the Johannine literature. The Word became flesh, and the Father is known and loved in the Son and vice versa. It reaffirms the divine origin of Jesus and also his true humanity, for to deny that the man Jesus is the child of God is to repudiate the Father — "everyone who loves the parent loves the child." Denial of Jesus' identity alienates a person from the Father.

Verse 2 applies the same argument to brothers and sisters. To love the parent is to love the child; therefore, to love God means to love all his children. This implies not just sentimental affection, but also preserving the unity of the church by obeying God's commandments and avoiding the schism effected by anti-Christ and false prophets, those who deny the incarnation.

The next verse continues to fill out the meaning of the love of God. It too is not just a matter of sentimental affection. To love God is not to feel good about God but to obey his commandments. It is probably best to interpret "the commandments" not as the Decalogue, though that is certainly not ruled out, but as the fundamental commandment of love, the new commandment laid out in John 13 and reiterated as 1 John addresses the crisis of schism in the community. Surely the commandments of Moses are not abrogated, and they are consistent with the love enjoined upon the Christians, but in this context — emphasizing the love of God and the love of the children of God — it is the new commandment that is under discussion.

Verse 3 ends with the reminder that the commandments are not burdensome, and verse 4 reminds us that faith, born of God, conquers the world. Note the multiple layers of meaning involved in the image "born of God." The children of God are those born of God; the Son is the child of God; and faith is born of God. And according to verse 4 and then verse 5, the one who believes Jesus is the Son of God (the critical central theme of the epistle) conquers the world.

In verse 6 we are reminded that Jesus, who came in the flesh and in whom we are to believe, is not distant or inaccessible. He came by water and blood. Verse 6 may be terribly obvious, but here the obvious should be stated.

The allusion is to the piercing of Jesus' side on Calvary and to the blood and water that poured forth. The image in the Gospel and here in the epistle is powerfully incarnational and sacramental. The water is baptism; the blood is the Eucharist. (In the letter, as in the Gospel, it is still necessary to distinguish Jesus from John the Baptist, who came "with the water only.")

The reassurance to the community is very aggressive. He came with the water and the blood in the sense that he was truly human. Only the spirit of anti-Christ would deny it. He comes also to his people in the water and blood of their sacramental life. He is real; he is present. He does indeed live in them and they in him. And the real Spirit testifies to this. The real Spirit not only testifies to the truth but is the truth. The Spirit is also the Spirit of the church's sacramental life. There is here, it should be noted, an apparent reference to John 3:5, "No one can enter the kingdom of God without being born of water and Spirit." The truth that is the Word-made-flesh is the truth (and, we may say, the Spirit) of the church's sacramental life.

It all holds together, although, as I said at the beginning, the pieces of the argument can be rearranged with kaleidoscopic variety. Still, the picture is clear, and the opportunities for application to Christian life in the early twenty-first century are as real as the incarnation.

To the false and ephemeral "spirituality" oriented primarily to helping middle-class people accept and cope with things as they are, the First Epistle of John holds out the realism of the incarnation, the sacraments, the church, and the truth. It tells us that hope lies there, not in psychic exercises. To the deep individualism of such religious notions, the gospel offers instead the community of brothers and sisters and the hope of real joy in loving God and his people.

To postmodernist relativism this text proclaims that the "Spirit is the truth." It is a striking phrase, but its reminder that the deepest truth and hope are with God warrants the epistle's striking usage. Truth is not something we invent in our own subjectivity; it is the gift of God. 1 John tells us, as we all know, that "God is love." But it also tells us that God is truth.

Finally, it tells us that freedom and wisdom are not freedom from commandments, freedom from neighbor, or freedom from God. Our problem is not that some heteronomous authority is controlling us and depriving us of the opportunity to be all that we can be. Our problem is that our faith, our love, and our obedience are lodged in the wrong place. The lack of freedom that we experience comes from failure to have and trust the right God, and only this pericope's emphases on love, faith, community, sacraments, the reality of Christ, and the truth of the Spirit can offer people what they truly seek.

The reading, indeed the whole epistle, opens up a magnificent opportunity to bring the water of life to satisfy the spiritual thirst that exists inside and outside the church.

*Leonard R. Klein*

# Seventh Sunday of Easter, Year B

First Lesson: Acts 1:15-17, 21-26
(Psalm 1)
**Second Lesson: 1 John 5:9-13**
Gospel Lesson: John 17:6-19

Many of the false teachings to which this letter was in part responding were about Jesus Christ. The letter counters claims that Jesus was not the Messiah (2:22; 5:1), that he did not come in the flesh as the Son of God

(4:2, 3), and that we can know God without knowing Jesus Christ (5:20). If these claims were true, then Jesus Christ is optional in our life with God and one another.

Such false teachings still flourish today. In a large bookstore on spirituality there recently were books about Jesus Christ among others on angels, channeling, aromatherapy, Eastern chants, candles, calming music, and so on. In other words, the culture is presenting Jesus today as one of many options, each equally valid, depending on our preferences and lifestyles.

This passage near the end of the First Letter of John claims that such an attitude or teaching is not only false but also cuts us off from the very source of life (5:11-13). In addition, by resting on God's testimony to Jesus Christ, it shows us a better way than the popular idea of choosing for ourselves what we believe. Thus to be faithful to this text, the preacher, as a messenger of the gospel of Jesus Christ, is compelled to proclaim to his or her listeners the absolute necessity of belief in Jesus Christ in the flesh and the purpose and primacy of the received tradition as given by God and passed down through the generations. However that faith may be interpreted and applied in specific pastoral contexts, it cannot be avoided. Jesus and God's testimony to Jesus are not one of many options, but rather, as the author says in this passage, eternal life itself.

This is the goal of this passage — and the entire letter in fact — "I write this to you who believe in the name of the Son of God, that you may know that you have eternal life" (5:13). It is written to believers, encouraging them in love to hold on to what they already know. Its tone and intent is encouragement, not so much to condemn and tear down false teachings, but in love to reveal their emptiness so the life-giving truth of God's love in Jesus can be grasped more firmly by those who believe.

The passage invites clear articulation of what we have been given in Jesus Christ that can be found in no other place — not in ourselves or any lesser spirituality — and what the death and resurrection of Jesus does for us that we cannot do for ourselves. While it might seem that we are preaching apologetics to those who are already Christians, the text invites us to encourage our sisters and brothers to recognize, remember, and hold fast in hope to what they know, that they may know that they "have eternal life." Preaching should reflect the tone of the letter: encouragement in light of the false teachings about Jesus Christ or false spiritualities.

This passage can be summed up as follows: God, and not just humans, has testified and given witness to his Son, Jesus Christ. God's testimony is far greater than any human testimony; thus we are to receive it and assent to it as we would no other. If we believe that Jesus Christ is God's Son in the flesh, we have taken him into ourselves and into our way of life. To deny the truth of Jesus Christ in the flesh is to deny God's truthful testimony and thus make God, the author of truth, into a liar. The testimony God gives us about Jesus Christ is that through him God has given us eternal life, and that this gift comes from God through the cross of Jesus Christ. Finally, the author writes this so that we may hold fast to this teaching about Jesus Christ that we have already known, and thus hold fast to the gift of eternal life given through him.

This passage invites numerous approaches to making its message come alive to its listeners. But all themes in this passage converge in the unveiling of God's love. Love is the reason for the testimony, for the gift of Jesus, and for the gift of eternal life.

The first theme is the superiority of God's testimony to human testimony (5:9). We have a God who speaks out of love, not a God who is silent. This is the biblical record. God's word gives life to the world, and the Word made flesh redeems it. Though there are differences in interpreting the content of God's testimony to Jesus Christ in this portion of 1 John, what demands our attention is the fact that God has communicated to us the nature and purpose of his Son through his life, death, resurrection, the Holy Spirit, and the whole of Scripture. At a time when received authority is no longer given assent, the preacher has the opportunity to explore what we miss for the living of our lives when we either do not pay attention or too easily write off God's testimony to his Son. We do not have a mute God or a mute faith. The text says that when we ignore God's testimony to Jesus — or deny it — we do not silence God but rather, in effect, treat God as a liar. The ignoring of God's testimony invites us to imagine what the world would be like if we had a God who remained silent, who did not speak (5:10b, 11). Such strong language can serve as a wake-up call to us who can too easily dismiss God's testimony to Jesus.

A second theme to explore is the promise that "those who believe in the Son of God have the testimony in their hearts" (5:10a). This is not superficial assent to Jesus Christ, a confession without conversion, agreement without integrating faith with life. What, then, does it mean to take the testimony — the truth of Jesus Christ — into our hearts? To take him into our worries, our families, our work, our money, our health, our priorities, our hopes and fears? The certainty of the testimony that eternal life is in the Son (5:11) is life- and world-shaping.

The third theme — and the point of the letter — is the promise of eternal life in the Son. Eternal life in Jesus — the gift of God's love — stirs us to distinguish the love God commands from the hatred of brother or sister (2:9-

11) and from the love of "the world" (2:15-17). Here is an opportunity to clearly make the distinction between "love [for] world or the things in this world" and loving the world as God loves the world. Receiving eternal life in Christ is the source of the love God commands.

Jesus Christ cannot be optional because it is only Jesus who on the cross bore in his flesh all the things that separate us from God — our hate, our misguided love of the world. Out of love and God's unwillingness to let go of his creation, Christ bore all this in his own body, to free us to live and love and to rise with him into eternal life.

*Annette G. Brownlee*

## Christ the King, Year B

First Lesson: 2 Samuel 23:1-7
(Psalm 132:1-12, [13-18])
**Second Lesson: Revelation 1:4b-8**
Gospel Lesson: John 18:33-37

## Second Sunday of Easter, Year C

First Lesson: Acts 5:27-32
(Psalm 118:14-29)
**Second Lesson: Revelation 1:4-8**
Gospel Lesson: John 20:19-31

This passage focuses the reader's attention on the divine origin of the book of Revelation. The identity of the God who brings believers "grace . . . and peace" (cf. Paul's salutations; e.g., Rom. 1:7) is no less than "him who is and who was and who is to come." This tripartite divine name ascribes authority from on high to the book of Revelation — as high as it gets. The divine name here echoes the Tetragrammaton, the holiest name for the God of Israel. Framed in its current setting, the implication is clear:

no one less than YHWH is about to speak — albeit through various intermediaries, including John, angels, and the Spirit (or spirits). All Jews, and especially Greek-speaking Jews, would readily identify the deity in verse 4 with
the most sacred name for God. The Lord's designation as Alpha and Omega
(v. 8) is another form of the divine name since it also attributes eternality or
timeless being to God. The mention again of the tripartite name in verse 8b
places emphasis upon the Lord who rules all time: past, present, and future.
The divine name thus envelops our particular passage and gives us a hint of
what is to come in this apocalypse (lit. "unveiling") that we call today the
book of Revelation (cf. 4:8).

We might observe that the entire book of Revelation is little more than
an unfolding of the third leg of the tripartite divine name: "is to come." The
chronology of the Bible's last book tilts forward. Even though much of the
imagery is borrowed from Israel's past, the signs, portents, and vindication
of God and God's people, at least from the perspective of the author and his
early readers, will take place in the future.

It is not too soon to draw out an important point for sermonizing
from this book. No small percentage of preachers have misgivings and ap-
prehensions about tackling passages from the book of Revelation. We are
in good company: Luther and Augustine, among others, steered mostly
clear of the book (to their theological harm, in my view). On the other
hand, purveyors of dispensational literature have been much less shy about
espousing their explanations of Revelation. While dispensational interpretations will either prove true or be susceptible to ridicule and rejection with
the passing of time, it is good for us to be reminded by their piquant interest that the last book of the Bible *is* canon. There is an important reason
why Revelation remains in our Bibles. If we went with Augustine and Luther and only highlighted, for example, Saint Paul's thirteenth chapter of
Romans (vv. 1-7), we could soon forget an important part of our calling as
the church. While Christ's followers are called to be good citizens of this
world and its various governments (Rom. 13:1), it is equally important to
remember that our Christian witness may sometimes swim against the
stream of the surrounding culture (cf. Rom. 12:1-2). We are also called at
times to rub against the grain of this world's *rulers* (for this we find no sequel in Paul). The book of Revelation serves as a vivid reminder of the
church's potential for conflict with corrupt rulers of the present wicked
age. Here in Revelation is presented an enormous challenge not to be overly
conformed to this world, especially not to be cowed by temporal authorities when they turn to the dark side.

Comfort too comes in surprising places in Revelation; for example, when we look closely at 1:5-6, the theme of the entire book begins to unfold. It is this: God reigns in the future just as much as in the past and present. This is affirmed by nothing less than the divine name. YHWH, God's sacred covenant name (see Exod. 3:14), has always held an element of timelessness in its form and content; the Great I AM is also the one who WAS and WILL BE. John builds on the past, present, and future tenses implied in the divine name, YHWH, and expands it. His lengthy greeting identifies the eternal God as the source of grace and peace. And this comes not only as we look on the past and live in the present, but also as we trust God with our future. The future belongs to the Lord. "Is to Come" is another name for God.

Here an awesome homiletical opportunity arises. Many of us can trust God when we look at the past and remember the ways grace and peace have been supplied even in the most difficult of circumstances. The present is busy, at least for moderns in the West, and if forced, many of us might admit how seldom we pause in order to see God's hand at work sustaining our world and guiding our lives. Yet, uncertainty about the future is where many draw up short of breath and break into a cold sweat. The future with its daunting possibilities and enormous uncertainties contains a frightening number of unknowns. Both things under our control and things out of our control can frighten us when it comes to the future. The burden of responsibility or the fear of having no responsibility at all can both be magnified from the present and projected into a terrifying future. Our own mortality and hopes for immortality lie in the future. For too long the church has shrunk away from the future as if God held only the present and the past in his hands. This passage points us toward the future so that we can face it, not only realistically, but also with hope.

In verse 5 John affirms that Yahweh self-reveals as Jesus Christ. Several interesting titles are used for Christ in this passage. The "faithful witness" (*martys*, from which we derive "martyr") alludes to Jesus' martyrdom on earth, recounting that his life was voluntarily laid down (cf. Rev. 2:13; 11:3; 17:6; and 1 Tim. 6:13; Titus 2:14; Matt. 27:11-14; John 18:33-38). Of course, the historical Jesus who went to the cross is also the risen Christ of faith, who in his exalted condition authenticates this revelation (cf. Rev. 22:20).

The designation of Christ as "firstborn" alludes to his resurrection and implies that many others will follow. Beyond death the faithful have the promise of resurrection.

The first two verses of our passage then declare much about the christological motif of the book of Revelation. YHWH, the great "I AM," has spoken definitively in Jesus Christ, who (v. 5):

601

a. *as* a faithful witness during his life on earth, thus leading to his crucifixion,
b. *is* the firstborn from the dead — referring both to his royalty and triumph over death by resurrection, and finally
c. *will be* ruler of kings on earth. (cf. Rev. 11:15)

Having explained the divine authority of this revelation, John then describes in a doxological poem what God has done for us in Christ. Here once again is divine love which frees us from sin through his blood; that is to say, Christ's death is the chief expression of God's love (v. 5b; cf. Mark 10:45; Eph. 5:25). The love of Christ calls us into a kingdom that at present remains a spiritual kingdom with many diverse expressions, some tangible and others intangible. Yet the kingdom also awaits a glorious future consummation. The same Messiah who died in bloody humiliation on the cross will return in glory and dominion for everyone to see (v. 7; cf. Dan. 7:13). Even those who pierced him will look upon him and wail either with regret or awe (cf. Zech. 12:10b; Luke 21:27).

The repetition of the divine name in verse 8 concludes our passage and completes the thought begun in verse 4. One more divine predicate is added; it is the last word in our text: "the Almighty" *(pantokratōr)*. This refers to God's supremacy over all creation. A final point worth preaching from this text is the certainty with which the author proclaims God's sovereignty over all things. At the time John received this revelation there was little evidence in the Roman world for the universal appeal of Christ, let alone his reign over all the earth and its rulers. The worldwide spread of the church might be taken as a sign of Christ's proleptic reign; but even with the proliferation of the numbers of Christian faithful worldwide, it requires faith to adhere to the proclamation that Christ is not only the one who *was* and *is,* but also the almighty ruler of all things who is *to come.*

The eschatological comfort and challenge of this passage are captured wonderfully by Katharina von Schlegel, whose words are often put to the familiar tune "Finlandia":

Be still my soul,
thy God doth undertake
to guide the future
as he has the past.

*Daniel J. Price*

## Third Sunday of Easter, Year C

First Lesson: Acts 9:1-6, (7-20)
(Psalm 30)
**Second Lesson: Revelation 5:11-14**
Gospel Lesson: John 21:1-19

In this passage John is recording what he sees: "then I saw" ("then I looked," NRSV) is a phrase that connects the sequences of John's apocalyptic vision in chapters 4-21 of the book of Revelation. The paragraphs preceding our passage provide important background for our text. For example, what John saw in 5:1 created a sense of nervous expectation because portents of doom were about to break loose. A heavenly scroll sealed with seven seals was held in hand by the one on the throne (cf. Ezek. 2:9-10). Its contents are never spelled out specifically, but it promises to contain cataclysmic historical events: perhaps the "lamentation, mourning and woe" predicted by Ezekiel. Yet no one had been found worthy to open it until the Lamb came forth.

The symbolism of the seven seals on the scroll is possibly taken from first-century Roman laws relating to a person's will. A last will and testament would often be sealed with seven seals. At the end of the person's life, a sealed scroll could be opened delineating the conditions of the will. This is John's way to indicate what events will unfold, not at the end of an individual life, but at the end of history. Some scholars refer to this chapter as a "book of destiny" containing God's predetermined plan for the world in its final hours.

In spite of the ominous sense of judgment hanging over the opening of the scroll, John weeps because no one is able to open it. This would indicate that there is not only judgment but an element of hope attached to the opening. After a long lament over not finding anyone worthy to open the scroll, John finally hears from the elders that the Lion of the tribe of Judah can open the scroll and its seals. Here at last is found one worthy to break the seals.

In a single verse John shifts messianic metaphors from the Lion to the Lamb: in 5:5 Christ was the conquering Lion of the tribe of Judah, the Root of David; in 5:6 and following Christ becomes the Lamb who was slain. This is one and the same Messiah. The simultaneous identity of the Messiah as both Lion and Lamb provides much food for sermonic thought.

The Lamb takes the scroll and is about to break the seals when we witness a dramatic interlude. Just as there is calm before the storm, there is worship before the terrible apocalyptic judgment breaks loose. Our passage thus begins with a worship scene that interrupts the judgment narrative begun in chapter 4. This passage might be described as an elaborate heavenly liturgy. Let us first ask who these heavenly worshipers might be, then why they worship, and finally what implications their heavenly worship might have for us on earth today.

Who are these worshipers? First, many angels surround the throne of God. These impressive heavenly messengers rejoice and lift their voices as they proclaim the worthiness of the Lamb to open the scroll. In addition to angels, "living creatures and the elders" and a vast throng break into song. John does not bother to explain the identity of all these worshipers. What seems of greater importance is their vast number and the focus of their attention: they glorify the Lamb.

To the voices of the angels and elders are added those of "every creature in heaven and on earth and under the earth and in the sea." The myriads are singing (v. 13); in other words, to the angelic choirs are added the voices of the entire congregation breaking into a doxology of praise directed at the one on the throne and the Lamb. The unsparing use of adjectives like "many" (polloi), "myriads" (a transliteration from the Gk. myriades), and other numerical terms like "thousands of thousands" recalls the final judgment vision of Daniel (7:10; cf. Jude 14-16; 1 Enoch 14:22). Our exegesis thus brings to light another important homiletical point, namely, the cosmic authority of the Lamb. John could not affirm more strongly that this Lamb is no local deity. The Lamb worshiped here is adulated in tandem with the Ancient of Days, the great I Am, the one seated on the throne. Even though this is not the place for a theological discussion of Christ's deity, this much is plain from the text: the Lamb is to be venerated as God. The investiture of the Lamb with status worthy of worship receives the approval not only of the myriads who surround the throne, but also of the one seated on the throne (cf. Matt. 11:27; 28:18; even though the one on the throne is surprisingly quiet in this scene).

Why do they worship the Lamb? There is a certain irony in John's depiction of countless multitudes worshiping the Lamb. The irony is that the Lion of the tribe of Judah, who is deemed worthy to open the scroll of judgment, is transformed into the Lamb that was slain. A lion is a creature of great ferocity and strength, the so-called king of beasts. A lamb is weak and virtually helpless. Yet it is not the Lion who is praised; rather, the Lamb receives songs of praise from the heavenly host. The multitudes worship the Lamb because, by implication, this Lamb was slain and therefore accomplished something remarkable by his death (cf. Rev. 5:9). In spite of the weakness of being slaughtered, this Lamb is now deemed worthy to receive the highest accolades available in the Greek language: "power and wealth and wisdom and might / and honor and glory and blessing!" (v. 12). John's vision thus inspires us to see Jesus as a person worthy of veneration. He is worthy of the heavenly accolades not only because of his divine power and office, but because of his character. He has endured the test of suffering and proved faithful.

John's vision of heavenly creatures worshiping this Lamb is intended to be didactic: we are to honor on earth as they honor in heaven. More to the point, we are to honor on earth *whom* they honor in heaven. Thus Christ is proclaimed as worthy of our adoration and praise alongside God (v. 12; cf. v. 9). As the Lamb of God, Christ is worthy to receive power and wealth, etc., because he has entered into our humanity and suffered alongside us. Divesting himself of all power and glory and might and wealth, he became weak; yet all things of which he has been divested are now reinvested by divine fiat. This is the God Christians worship. The God who sends his Son, little and powerless, now paradoxically deems the Son worthy to judge the nations and consummate history.

Irony transforms into paradox in our passage as we discover it is the Lamb who sits on the throne — not the Lion (v. 13). The Lion of the tribe of Judah was expected to be a conquering king like David. The Lamb, on the other hand, is the suffering servant, hinted at in passages like Isaiah 53. The Lion is a military conqueror, the Lamb is a quiescent vicarious sufferer. The Lion and the Lamb are one and the same Messiah, and Christians through the ages believe that the Lamb of God, who suffered under Pontius Pilate, will return as the conquering Lion of the tribe of Judah. This passage therefore highlights a central theme of the book of Revelation. The Lion is the Lamb. The powerful Messiah is weak, and in his righteous weakness is power. These seemingly opposing symbols for Christ, the Lion and the Lamb, hold in tension the paradox on which Christian worship must balance.

Fyodor Dostoyevsky, one of the great novelists of all time, wrote in his masterpiece, *The Brothers Karamazov,* "So long as man remains free he strives for nothing so incessantly and so painfully as to find someone to worship."

Even in an increasingly secularized Western world, the impulse to worship remains strong. Cultural signs are easily discovered that reveal our desperate impulse to find someone to venerate, worship, praise, and adore. If we do not worship God, we will invest our energy for worship elsewhere, shifting the object of worship from God to others. Whether it be a sports hero, a political leader, a wealthy individual, or wealth itself, today no less than in biblical times or Dostoyevsky's time, we strive incessantly to find someone or something to worship.

As followers of Jesus Christ, we are called to worship in faith the God who became weak. And we are reminded by God's identification as the Lamb that the worship of raw power is misplaced. Our God is revealed most clearly in the weakness of Bethlehem and Calvary. The Lion of God who will sit on the throne and judge nations is none other than the Lamb that was slain.

*Daniel J. Price*

## Fourth Sunday of Easter, Year C

First Lesson: Acts 9:36-43
(Psalm 23)
**Second Lesson: Revelation 7:9-17**
Gospel Lesson: John 10:22-30

This passage begins with the simple statement ". . . I saw" (*eidon:* "I looked," NRSV), a phrase that frequently links John's vision narratives in the book of Revelation. More importantly, "I saw" discloses something about the mode of revelation itself. Seeing is a receptive sense, and John therefore distinguishes himself as the chronicler, not the innovator, of these visions.

What John sees here is most impressive. A multitude beyond counting is standing before the throne and the Lamb. John employs several Greek superlatives to emphasize the vast size and number of creatures worshiping in the heavenly court, thereby signifying a fulfillment of God's promise to Abraham (Gen. 13:16; 15:5). Some equate this multitude with the 144,000 mentioned in the earlier part of the chapter (7:1-8), but these arguments are unconvincing. Even in the ancient world the author would have known enough math to distinguish between 144,000 persons and an innumerable host. If the 144,000 were intended to be symbolic of all the faithful, it is difficult to explain their enumeration by each of the twelve tribes of Israel. The contradistinction between the 144,000 and this current multitude grows when we note that John mentions not only the impressive size, but also the amazing diversity of this huge assembly: gathered from every ethnic group *(ethnous)*, tribe *(phylōn)*, people *(laōn)*, and tongue *(glōssōn)*. This motley crowd from many nations will in the end of time become the one people of God. How will this come to pass?

Today we in the West are learning to celebrate ethnic diversity; thus our text has a certain contemporary appeal. The inclusive nature of this celestial crowd, however, is due *not*, as in our own age, to the laws of jurisprudence prohibiting discrimination, nor to an enlightened point of view, but to the compelling character of the one worshiped. This polychrome multitude is united by its worship of the Lamb. Here will be fulfilled the other part of the promise originally made to Abraham and his offspring (Gen. 12:3; 17:4ff.), which reverses the divisive confusion of the tongues at the tower of Babel (Gen. 11:1-9).

The rich diversity of the people of God is something that the church has sometimes overlooked. Sadly, Sunday morning has been and continues to be one of the most segregated hours of the week. If rightly preached, this heavenly worship scene should inspire cross-cultural fellowship.

The scene continues as the loud cries from this multitude commence worship (v. 10). They ascribe salvation to God and the Lamb. The christo-centric worship at the end of time continues as it opens out into ever widening circles of worshipers. To the multitude worshiping with loud voices are added an angelic host, elders, and "the four living creatures," who all break into singing. The four living creatures are most likely cherubim, winged intercessors who guard the tree of life (Gen. 3:24), the gilded images of which stand over the ark of the covenant (Exod. 25:18ff.).

Here, as in many parts of the Bible, a victory celebration marks an occasion for worship. Interestingly, it is the *Lamb* who unites the saints from every corner of the earth, not the *Lion* of the tribe of Judah (v. 14; cf. 5:5).

The white robes signify that these worshipers are martyrs (v. 14) — or have at least suffered persecution. They are now vindicated because they have washed their robes in the blood of the Lamb. The whiteness of their robes also symbolizes purity; in conjunction with the palm branches, their attire most likely indicates victory. The palm branches may serve as a reminder of Palm Sunday. Here, however, Christ's followers celebrate the ultimate victory that the Lamb has won. Ascending first to the cross, then to receive his crown, he has won the victory through obedience — not power. The multitude in white robes have followed the Lamb through their own sufferings (*thlipseōs*, v. 14b; cf. Matt. 24:21; Dan. 12:1), and are therefore encouraged to expect vindication (vv. 15-17). This is John's way of reminding his readers that the communion of saints is a communion of sufferers who will ultimately conquer, not conquerors who happen to suffer.

The reward for the fidelity of the martyrs will be the opportunity to worship "day and night within his temple" (v. 15). By contrast, the Jerusalem temple doors closed each evening after sacrifice and remained closed until morning (Ezek. 46:1-2). The one who is worshiped by the multitudes day and night will "shelter them" (v. 15b). This passage alludes to the prophet Ezekiel (37:27) and envisions the prophetic fulfillment of the promise "I will be their God, and they shall be my people." The Greek verb used here to describe God's presence *(skēnōsei)* is literally translated "to encamp with," denoting the direct presence of God with his people. The image of God's tabernacle comes readily to mind, as do the booths required for the Feast of Tabernacles; whether the author accents the former or latter meaning is a matter of exegetical debate. Regardless, the important emphasis here is that God's Shekinah presence, accompanied always with awesome cloud and fire, is with his people (cf. Lev. 23:42-43). The images of both protection and divine immanence are communicated in this verse. The God who is seated on the throne is no longer seated on a distant throne. The God of cloud and fire will no longer be so transcendent as to be potentially lethal to those who have direct contact. Rather, the awesome fire and cloud will be a signature of divine protection over the people of God.

Not only is God's divine protection with the faithful, there is also an abundance of provision. Verse 16 is a reference to Isaiah 49:10, where the promised escape from hunger, thirst, and scorching heat is a sign of divine deliverance. The promise that they will "hunger no more, and thirst no more; / the sun will not strike them, / nor any scorching heat" stands in striking contrast to the fate of those who are later afflicted by the fourth bowl (16:8-9), where the sun was allowed to burn people with fire.

The author spins a mixed metaphor in order to inform the reader that the "Lamb at the center of the throne" is at the same time the "shepherd" who guides the faithful to "springs of the water of life" (v. 17). The latter employs an ancient pastoral metaphor in which the king is described as a shepherd who leads the flock. The implication of the conflated metaphor is that the shepherd-king is also the Lamb. While this shepherd has the power to comfort the people and lead them to the verdant pastures and still waters, the suffering this king has endured is not forgotten. This Davidic Messiah (David's shepherding days could hardly be discarded or overlooked in this context) is also the Suffering Servant. Of course, the Lamb who is the shepherd is identified as Jesus (cf. Matt. 15:24; 25:32; John 10:2, 11, 12, 14; Heb. 13:20; etc.).

The affirmation of Jesus Christ as both the Lamb and the Good Shepherd is intended to be of comfort to those who were suffering hardships for their faith. How do we preach this passage to some whose greatest suffering for their faith might be enduring a long sermon or teaching a testy group of children on Sunday mornings? On the other hand, many in the congregation know far more about suffering than the person in the pulpit.

There exists a fine line between challenge and scolding when we preach the need for suffering on behalf of Christ. Yet there is a compelling need for all who follow Christ to be informed about his suffering. In light of Christ's suffering, our own sufferings make sense, and the people of faith begin to realize that suffering creates opportunity to grow in faith rather than signaling God's abandonment. Sharing honestly our own suffering is a legitimate usage of the pulpit. But the dangers of manipulation, obsession, or exaggeration should be kept in check. The ultimate comfort of all believers who endure times of suffering is to be yoked to one another in the fellowship of *his* sufferings. The purpose of the preacher is thus to point to *the Lamb at the center of the throne who will shepherd the people.*

Finally, the colorful description of the worshiping heavenly host can inspire us on earth. It is the pull of Christ's love more than the push of duty that ultimately unites worshipers. Messages that free Christian worshipers from the legalistic baggage they often bring to worship can hardly be proclaimed too strongly. These celestial worshipers are pulled by the magnet of Christ's love; let the sermon attempt to do likewise by helping the congregation to capture a glimpse of the immense joy of all creatures who worship their Creator.

*Daniel J. Price*

## Fifth Sunday of Easter, Year C

First Lesson: Acts 11:1-18
(Psalm 148)
**Second Lesson: Revelation 21:1-6**
Gospel Lesson: John 13:31-35

This climactic passage is familiar on its own terms and also because it re-capitulates many of the eschatological portraits painted in the Old Testament and intertestamental literature. It is a fitting penultima to Revelation, framed by angelic visions in chapters 17–20 and 21:9–22:9. In it John transitions us to the end of time where the new Jerusalem comes to earth from heaven with the following results: God dwells with mortals and wipes all tears away, death is banished along with mourning, all things are made new as the former things pass away. In verse 5 God speaks for the first time since 1:8 and proclaims his work "done." There could hardly be a more colorful conclusion to John's apocalypse. Let us take a closer look at this striking text.

The literary form of the first five verses of this passage is interesting in that it is a chiasm. Simply put, a chiastic structure is one where the first phrase and the last phrase are parallel expressions (e.g., v. 1a and v. 5a), then the second and second-to-last phrase likewise, and so on; in other words, sequence *a, b, c, d* is followed by *d', c', b', a'*. This may not provide any preachable information, but it can help the preacher better understand the text, its structure, and therefore its ultimate meaning. In this passage this structure is important because it places emphasis on the God who comes to dwell with his own people. More will be said about this below.

Also of interest with regard to our text is the fact that some scholars believe 21:1-4 was originally connected to 22:3-5 without the intervening verses. This would mean that 21:5–22:2 is an insert. However much the plausibility of an insert might make sense poetically and source-critically, there are still good reasons to preach from the text as it is. The final form of our passage here is anything but arbitrary even if it does break the poetic flow, for it emphatically places God in the midst of the dialogue. It is God who makes all things new, God who was Alpha in the beginning and climaxes history at its omega point, God who offers to the thirsty a gift of living water. The theocentric insert therefore serves as a fitting summary of the entire book of Revelation: it is the same God who commissions John to write "for these words are trustworthy and true" who comes to dwell on the earth with his people.

There is good news in this passage even though a *prima facie* glance may indicate otherwise. In the first verse of chapter 21 John obliquely mentions nothing less than the passing of heaven and earth. The disappearance of heaven and earth had already been announced (20:11), and there are countless antecedents predicting this event in ancient literature, among them Isaiah 65:17ff., 66:22, *1 Enoch* 45, Paul (Rom. 8:21), and even the Gospels (e.g., Matt. 19:28). Whether the first heaven and earth are utterly destroyed and replaced with the "new heaven and new earth" *ex nihilo*, or simply renovated on a grand scale, is not clear. Whatever the case may be, the old order is replaced by the new.

While the literary style and structure of this text is complex, the content is simple. This is a text about God coming to earth at the end of time and dwelling with mortals. It is of interest to see how John communicates this basic theme in several ways.

First, the preexistence of Jerusalem had been written about by various prophets for many centuries. Also, a new Jerusalem was often hoped for, especially during times when the old Jerusalem was either destroyed or occupied by foreign powers (or both). Few things would indicate God's presence more than a renewed Jerusalem (cf. Heb. 11:10; Gal. 4:25-26).

Second, the home or tabernacle *(skēnē)* of God is now pitched among mortals who live in the new Jerusalem. The connection of this text with the holy tabernacle and the ark of the covenant actualizing God's presence with his people would be familiar to any Jewish person familiar with the Old Testament. "He will dwell with them; they will be his peoples" (plural reading preferred here). This too had been predicted by the prophets (cf. Ezek. 37:27): a time would come when God would be neither distant nor terrible, but fully present for his people. Emphasis on the divine presence comes at the end of verse 3: "God himself will be with them."

An important preaching point is occasioned by the message of the first three verses. Regardless of what the preacher or the congregation believes about the eschatology of Revelation and its many possible interpretations, the theology of this passage preaches to any group of Christians. It contains a clear affirmation of God's desire for communion with human beings, and thus provides a fitting conclusion to the whole book. God with us! The promise of incarnation will be consummated at the end of time. This central tenet of our faith has often slipped through the cracks of the church. God-with-us is the *sine qua non* of the church, the primary and only real reason for her existence. The church that is not seeking communion with God is not a church, but a secular institution with religious trappings. The church that strays from the Lord that seeks her is not the bride of Christ,

611

but more like the harlot described in chapter 17. This is the immensely preachable theological message of this passage and the book of Revelation: the God of staggering power, glory, and holiness deems it good to dwell with mortals like us. The God who has acted in history through Israel and Jesus Christ reveals to us that history will be consummated with sweet communion between God and the faithful. Eschatology may sell books and pique people's interest, but the theology of this text is far more relational than eschatological. God will ultimately win the faith of the faithful; consequently, they will find God encamped in their midst.

The compassion of God is shown to the faithful by the statement: "He will wipe every tear from their eyes" (v. 4; cf. 7:17); this statement, along with the banishment of death, is a reaffirmation of Isaiah 25:8. The ultimate annihilation of death is an apocalyptic theme in many pre–New Testament books (e.g., 4 Ezra 8:53), and in other parts of the New Testament itself (cf. 1 Cor. 15:54-55). The subject of death deserves some careful reflection. Our culture has become very adept at skirting issues that surround death. Of course, there is the hospice movement, but this is merely the exception that proves the rule. We are generally so insulated from death that we have to create an institution to get people through the final chapter of life. The topic of death could of course provide food for discussion for countless days. The comfort of this verse is that mortality will be swallowed up by immortality; at the end of time we will be cloaked not in mortality, but in immortality. The great I AM who sits on the throne will one day make all things new, including our own bodies. This is a comforting passage for the people of God and should be preached as such.

Verse 5b likely refers to not only this passage but the entire preceding passages in the book. In other words, this is a truthful revelation and not a false one.

The final verse of the passage alludes once again to the prophet Isaiah (55:1) and reminds us of one very important point. The thirsty shall have their thirst quenched by nothing less than the living water from the God who is the fount of all blessings. There is of course a certain amount of responsibility implied in the metaphor of being thirsty; those with no thirst will not imbibe the divine elixir. Yet the thirst-quenching water is a gift, and therefore flows not from human thirst but from divine grace. A preacher could hardly do better than to invite his/her hearers to freely drink of the living waters Christ offers (John 4:7-15). It is, after all, the only satisfaction offered without price.

*Daniel J. Price*

## Sixth Sunday of Easter, Year C

First Lesson: Acts 16:9-15
(Psalm 67)
**Second Lesson: Revelation 21:10; 21:22–22:5**
Gospel Lesson: John 14:23-29


It is worth noting that the beginning phrase of 21:9 is a verbatim repeat of 17:1. Hence the judgment of the great whore in chapter 17 and the reward of the bride in chapter 21 contrast starkly.

In 21:10 John's majestic transport recalls a vision of the prophet Ezekiel, who pictured the messianic kingdom as a city perceivable from the mountaintop (40:2). In this passage, however, the holy city is not yet fully constructed but is in the process of descending from heaven. Hence John's portrait of the holy city is painted with an eschatological brush. The heavenly descent of John's Jerusalem asserts that this will be the city of cities: a "new" (21:2) Jerusalem that will never perish because it has not been built with human hands (cf. 4 Ezra 13:35-36).

The place of mountains as a site of divine revelation is common in ancient literature (cf. Deut. 34:1-4). Because John describes the mode of his vision as "in the spirit," we should not take his journey to a "great, high mountain" too literally. To any modern-day lover of mountains, it is tempting to postulate that John had visions of snow-capped peaks and azure rivers running through glaciers. John's metaphor, however, is likely based on the apocalyptic idea that the closer one's proximity to the heavens, the more likely one is to gain a divine perspective. Just as standing on a pinnacle enhances one's physical range of vision, so standing on this summit in the spirit provides a vantage point for spiritual truths and revelations otherwise obscured (cf. Matt. 4:8; 24:3). John is thus transported to a place where he can see what few of us are privileged to perceive. An apocalypse is literally an "unveiling," and John's apocalypse ultimately unveils more than a series of portentous judgments; it reveals a divine perspective. It is truth revealed. It is God revealed.

The idea of a heavenly Jerusalem is rooted in Jewish and New Testament literature. For example, the pseudepigraphal authors spoke of a preexistent Jerusalem which God showed to Adam, Abraham, and Moses (e.g., *2 Bar.* 4:2-7). The New Testament speaks of the heavenly Jerusalem as the place where God dwells (Heb. 11:10). It should not be overlooked that the new Jerusalem is also the place God and the saints cohabit. The vivid image of the Lamb seeking the love and companionship of his bride is yet another reminder that the purpose of the church is to bring the faithful into fellowship with the living God (see Heb. 12:22; also Gal. 4:26, where Paul contrasts the "present Jerusalem" with the "Jerusalem above," the latter referring to the new Jerusalem).

The heavenly Jerusalem is described in detail in the verses following 21:10. For the important theological interpretation of this vision, however, we skip down to verse 22, because here the theological importance of this grand vision is developed. The preachability of the text thus comes alive.

In verses 22 and following John makes some observations about this new Jerusalem that would surprise many Jews and Jewish Christians. The phraseology in the Greek suggests that it startled even John. (Given the impressive nature of these successive visions, what could possibly startle John?) There is no temple in this celestial city.

Why would the most sacred building in all Judaism be missing from the heavenly Jerusalem? Because "the Lord God the Almighty and the Lamb" *are* its temple. Historically this surprising absence might be explained by looking at other so-called antitemple literature. A good deal of antitemple sentiment can be found in both Jewish and Christian literature. For example, the sectarian group at Qumran was so disillusioned with the temple practices of the first century that they rejected the established temple and its priesthood. Instead they developed the idea of the community of God's true believers as the new temple (naturally, they thought themselves the most likely example of this divinely inspired community). Christians too were accused of proclaiming an antitemple theology. Jesus' cleansing of the temple foreshadowed its destruction (Mark 11:15-19; Matt. 21:12; Luke 19:45), and Stephen's martyrdom resulted largely from his perceived threat to the temple and its priests (Acts 6:13-15).

Theologically, something important is being affirmed here; first in the negative because of the startling absence of the holy temple, then positively in the following verses. There is no temple because God is present in a direct and unmediated manner with the people of God. The Lord God the Almighty and the Lamb *are* the temple.

Here we bite into something substantial for the preacher and parishioner alike to chew on. The awesome experience of entering the first-century Jerusalem temple rebuilt by King Herod is something we can only scarcely imagine, being so far removed by time and space. Pictures of prayers planted in the Wailing Wall scarcely capture the holiness and sacredness of this ancient edifice. The temple became the central focus for Israel's religion — and remains so today for many Jewish people — despite its absence. Perhaps the last few scenes from the movie *Jesus of Nazareth* provide the best reminder of the immense reverence ancient Judaism held for the temple. The audacity of the Essenes and the Christians in supplanting this holy place with their own communities now comes into clearer focus.

In light of our discussion we may propose that the end result of the preaching of the Word and the fellowship of the people of God should be nothing less than a "temple experience." All the sacredness, mystery, and holy transcendence of God should be found in our worship of God and fellowship with one another. Nothing less will do. The role of the preacher is thus clarified and made all the more daunting: as tempting as it is to impress the listener with our own presence and sermon preparation, the building, choir, youth programs, or social advocacy, we must refrain and rather preach the presence of God. The church is called to be a sign of the age to come when God will dwell with his people in direct and unmediated communion.

The glory of God and the Lamb supplant not only the temple but also the solar bodies. There is no need for sun or moon because of the glory of God and the Lamb (cf. Isa. 60:19). The divine presence provides more than physical light, for the same light enables kings and nations to walk by its illumination. This divine light thus imparts both life and the wisdom to direct life toward godly purposes. The final verse of our passage even sees this divine light as the source of eternal life (22:5).

Two important themes are developed in verses 24-27. First, the universality of this new Jerusalem is affirmed. While it seems very much to be a specific place, it will be visited by the nations and kings of the earth. This, then, is no local deity ruling over a provincial and narrow-minded group of followers. No one less than God is worshiped in this place, and while there are certain boundaries, no national, ethnic, or social lines are drawn that would keep away anyone who desires to enter. Secondly, the fact that the gates will not need to be shut indicates the utter safety and security of this heavenly city. The messianic prophecies that express the longing for safety and prosperity have been fulfilled. All persons thus have immediate and full access to God. There is no exclusion based in prejudice; only those who by their false practice and attitudes distance themselves from God will not be allowed to enter (21:27).

With the final verses of our passage we arrive at the Bible's last chapter, and with it are introduced to the "river of the water of life, bright as crystal, flowing from the throne of God and of the Lamb." Once again a natural metaphor is used to impart a spiritual truth. The river and its waters provide a symbolic means of conveying God's life-giving presence in the new Jerusalem. Commentator George Ladd puts it well: "The presence of the river of life in the new Jerusalem is a picturesque way of saying that death with all its baleful accompaniments has been abolished and life reigns supreme." This river of life flows through the center of the new Jerusalem. While it is unwise to take the symbolism too literally, it is also difficult to imagine that such a beautiful fount of life is nothing more than a symbol. For we now arrive in a place where symbols and reality merge, and the river which spawns trees with their life-giving fruit, the throne of God, and the light of God's glory all fuse to present a picture of what it will be like to be in the direct presence of God. The challenge of preaching from this text is to allow it to speak in such a way that many will thirst for the waters of the new Jerusalem.

*Daniel J. Price*


## Seventh Sunday of Easter, Year C

First Lesson: Acts 16:16-34
(Psalm 97)
**Second Lesson: Revelation 22:12-14, 16-17, 20-21**
Gospel Lesson: John 17:20-26


With this passage we reach the conclusion both of John's revelation and the New Testament. This text belongs to a complex and sometimes choppy epilogue (22:6-21). Some commentators refer to the Bible's last chapter as the "scattered limbs of the poet." Others, however, see this as a single composition, comprising liturgical formulae for worship that lead up to an early church participation in the Lord's Supper. It very well could be both.

Regardless of how one reconstructs this text (admittedly, a complex task), the fact that this is a judgment text should be kept in mind. The words of this exalted Christ picture him as the end-time judge. The role of Christ as eschatological judge may not be a popular theme for preaching today (especially in the mainline denominations), but it is not uncommon in many parts of the New Testament (cf. John 5:22; Acts 10:42; Rom. 2:16; cf.

Rev. 2:23). Western theology learned early in the twentieth century that any theology which excludes ethical exhortation is truncated and runs the risk of making grace a cheap commodity. Dietrich Bonhoeffer powerfully illustrated this by his life and writings, as did many others of the so-called neoorthodox school. Since then, however, the developments of liberation theology, feminist theology, or even postmodern pluralism may seem to have pushed aside the palatability of judgment — especially from the pulpit. Secular trends in the West, especially in America, provide few footholds for prophetic proclamation. Nevertheless, preachers in the twenty-first century need not flinch at preaching the judgment texts — even if we may preach them differently than someone like Jonathan Edwards.

If this passage and many others like it compel us to preach on divine judgment, the counterbalancing truth should also be kept in mind, that the judgment of God transcends a preacher's pet peeves or emotional storms. It comes from outside our emotional condition and in many cases is quite independent of one's emotional stability or instability. Most importantly, let the preacher keep in mind that judgment, faithfully preached, prepares the heart for grace.

John inserts the statement of Jesus, "See, I am coming soon," three times in this chapter. It is noteworthy that in verses 7, 12, and 20 it is Christ himself announcing his return, no longer an angel who mediates Christ's message. What does "soon" mean? In other words, when will Jesus end the human narrative as we know it? Church history is littered with the false claims of charlatans and well-intended but misguided zealots who claimed particular insight into how soon "soon" would be. We therefore are well advised to carefully consider its meaning.

The Greek word (*tachy*) can be translated into English as either "quickly" (KJV, Phillips) or "soon" (RSV, NRSV, English Bible). If translated with the latter meaning, "soon," it would mean before long in time. If we therefore interpret "soon" to mean within a few years of the time of writing, then John's prediction of Christ's imminent return has been terribly disappointing. If, however, we interpret the chronology of "soon" more loosely, we may take it to mean a span of time considerably longer than a few years. This could be warranted if we remember that God does not measure time as we do (Ps. 90:4). Today even astronomers and cosmologists talk about billions of years as if it were no great stretch of the imagination. Thus "soon" could be anytime in the next few thousand years or centuries, or millennia. Honesty compels us to admit, however, that this looser interpretation would surprise the early church members, most of whom expected Christ's return before the death of the first generation of believers.

617

Another possible translation of *tachy,* "quickly," could mean that when Jesus comes, it will be with surprising suddenness. Accent would then be on the swiftness of his coming and not a specific point in history. This latter meaning softens the tendency to construct charts and fix dates for the second coming; in fact, it very much discredits such practices because the swiftness of the coming will surprise everyone — to a lesser degree even the saints (cf. Matt. 24:36-44). Since the Lord has chosen not to return after nearly two thousand years, the latter meaning gains credence.

Nevertheless, it is important to keep the expectation that God *could* invade history soon. Both contemporary dispensationalists and last century's neoorthodox theologians have made it their task to remind us that whenever the church loses sight of the eschatological dimension of the gospel, it runs the risk of becoming a slumbering and inert institution. Belief in the importance of both the First and Second Advent is usually linked; therefore, those who eschew the latter tend to impugn the former. Thus verses 12 and 20 contain an important theological affirmation that should not be overlooked in preaching; namely, the church is summoned to live the Christian life as though Christ is coming soon.

"My reward is with me, to repay according to everyone's work." With this verse comes the question for someone of the Protestant tradition: How do I reconcile this statement with Paul's emphasis on salvation by grace through faith? If grace saves us, then how can Christ's return focus on reward and payment for "everyone's work"?

The seeming violation of grace in verse 12 is mitigated by some of the following verses. For example, in verse 14 we can arguably allow the textual evidence to lead to the translation "Blessed are those who wash their robes" rather than "Blessed are those who do his commandments." We then point to the probable interpretation of washed garments as a sign of baptism and sanctification. The image of washing one's robe harkens back to 7:14, where this is a requirement for gaining entry into the heavenly kingdom. These references to saints washing their robes are deeply rooted in the sanctification rituals of the Old Testament, both for the people of God in general (Exod. 19:10, 14; Num. 8:7, 21) and for the priests in particular (Lev. 11:25, 28, 40; 13:6; etc.). In the Bible physical washing often symbolizes moral and spiritual renewal. The need to produce good works subsequent to being saved by grace has never been questioned, either by Paul (cf. Rom. 6:1-23; Gal. 5:16-24) or the Gospels (e.g., Matt. 7; 16:27) or even reformers like Calvin. The washing of one's robe *in the blood of the Lamb* therefore is a complex metaphor that alludes to the efficacy of Christ's death on the cross and at the same time illustrates the need for humans to respond to grace by washing in Christ. In other words, through being baptized and earnestly continuing the process of sanctification, the believer gains the right to eat from the tree of life (v. 14) and enter the holy city by the gates. Christian discipleship is therefore a wholehearted and unconditional response to the unconditional grace offered in Christ, and any faith that fails to produce good works would not be considered genuine.

Having washed their robes, the saints have regained access to the tree of life (v. 14b), thus reversing the expulsion of Adam and Eve from the Garden of Eden. An echo of the Adam-Christ typology (cf. 1 Cor. 15; Rom. 5:14-19) can be heard in this passage. A powerful means of expressing this theologically is found in patristic authors like Irenaeus, who proposed that what was lost in Adam is regained in Christ (cf. Eph. 1:10). Where Adam's disobedience brought banishment, Christ's obedience gives his followers free access to the tree of life and the city of life (presumably the new Jerusalem). This new condition of spiritual relationship to God is freely offered by God through his Son, and must be freely chosen by any who would follow. Again, choosing to follow Christ could be the "work" Christ will reward upon his return.

In verses 16-17 Jesus invites everyone to participate in his cleansing sacrifice. First he serves his credentials as a descendant of David, thus substantiating his messianic claim, then he offers to quench the spiritual thirst of anyone who comes to him. Here the metaphor of water is sustained but altered slightly: water is no longer the source of cleansing, but is pictured as the means of quenching one's spiritual thirst.

It is clear that the offer of Christ is to everyone:

Let *everyone* who hears say, "Come."
And let everyone who is thirsty come.

On the other hand, it is also clear that not every sort of practice is to be allowed in the eschatological kingdom (v. 15); nor will those who tamper with John's message be admitted (v. 19).

In verse 20 John has the Lord repeat for the third time in chapter 22 that he is coming "soon." This highlights the tension between the dramatic fall of the curtain and the certainty of the need for daily grace. Interestingly, John concludes with "The grace of the Lord Jesus be with all the saints. Amen."

It is most fitting that the last verse of the Bible would be a benediction of grace.

*Daniel J. Price*

# Preaching from the Letters

## COLIN GUNTON

"Everything is what it is and not another thing," famously wrote Bishop Butler many years ago. He could have been writing about the New Testament epistles, whose particularity is the first, as well as last, thing with which we must engage. Much has been written in recent years about the details of their social setting, though it must be questioned how much of this is speculative, as one suspects is the case with much of the theorizing about "Johannine communities." Although we scarcely need to go beyond the internal evidence to realize the unique setting, problems, and aims of the different books, we cannot evade the problems this presents to the modern expositor. What, to us, are the particular tendencies of the Corinthian Christians and Paul's instancing of his unmarried state? Much, in every way, we shall see, and for the most important reason of all: that the gospel itself is universal only through its particularity.

The first general point to be made about preaching from the epistles is that one cannot — as one can with the Gospels, though only by trying very hard — avoid direct engagement with the doctrinal content of the Christian faith. What is interesting about Paul is that the explicitly doctrinal content often takes the form of brief confessions of faith, fragments of what Dodd called the apostolic preaching, which were later to be ordered into the early "rule of faith" and finally the creeds. The fact that they are often incidental to the main argument and introduced to support a pastoral or moral point reinforces the point about the epistles' particularity. The confession of

Christ the Creator in 1 Corinthians 8:6 — "for us there is one God, the Father, from whom are all things and for whom we exist, and one Lord, Jesus Christ, through whom are all things and through whom we exist" — is here instructive. If we think that is mere doctrinal abstraction, a glance at its place in the argument will disabuse us. It is truly practical, deeply concerned with the life and worship of the church. Paul's opponents appear to believe that, because the idols do not exist, it is a matter of indifference whether or not they eat the food at the pagan temples. Abstractly speaking, that may well be the case. But Christians are not abstract monotheists. Their monotheism — and Paul quotes the confession of Deuteronomy 6:4 that "the Lord our God, the Lord is one" — is now defined through Jesus Christ.

To cut a long story short, Paul's argument is to the effect that because this is the God from whom, in whom, and for whom is everything, the church's life and conduct should be shaped by love rather than by "mere" theology. Or rather, the point is that there is no "mere" theology, because the God we worship makes all the difference to the way our life in community is formed. Here, however, as in all preaching, we must beware of abstraction: of making too easy an application of the lesson of love taught in this epistle apart from an engagement with the particular question with which it deals. The point always is to enable the text to shape our "application" of it. How often we can approach a text expecting that it is just the one to point a message we think we must convey, only to find that it compels us — or will, if we let it — to say something quite different. That is one aspect of what we call Scripture's inspiration, and it leads us into a consideration of the work of the Spirit. We begin with Christology.

Scripture's God is one who achieves his universal purpose — to reconcile all things to himself in Jesus Christ (Eph. 1:10) — by particular means. Central among these means are Israel and Jesus, the particular Israelite in whom the fullness of the deity lives embodied (Col. 2:9). Here the trinitarian matrix of all Christian theology makes the crucial difference. The incarnate Lord is the presence of God on earth, and so the mediator of all the Father's creating, providential, and saving work. He is the center and soul of all the epistles, from Paul's insistence in 1 Corinthians that he and he only should be proclaimed — and not the rival theories of those who preach him — through to Revelation's celebration of him, the lamb bearing the marks of slaughter, as the one who from his throne rules all the nations, even the demonically mighty Roman Empire. That is the first particularity which we have to bear in mind, the brute historical particularity that in the crucified and risen and ascended Jesus we have the concrete and universal expression of God's eternal love for man and woman alike and together.

Conventional scholarship, and that which so easily dominates our approach to these matters, is that Jesus is a figure moored in the past, recoverable, if at all, by historical reconstruction and the votes of the priest-scholars who mediate truth in the modern academy. That, however, is not the assumption of our writers, whose understanding of time is not that of the modern rationalist who still lives in Newton's mechanistic world. Rationalists typically displace God the Holy Spirit with the power of unaided human intellectuality, and so completely misconstrue the situation. But we must beware of oversimplification on the other side also. It is not that Jesus belongs in the past and the Spirit miraculously brings him into the present, although that may be part of it. It is rather that he is a figure who indeed lived, taught, died, and was raised in the past, but whose living reality encompasses our present and what we call the future as well. Let us now explore something of how these things might at once be held together and contribute something to our understanding of the task of preaching from the Letters.

We must begin with a broader conception of the work of the Spirit than simply making to happen what is otherwise difficult or impossible. Our pneumatology must be resolutely christological. We have seen that Jesus is the particular action of God by whose life his universal purposes are achieved. The Spirit is also the mediator of God's particular action, yet in a way related to, although also distinct from, this. In this instance the Spirit is the one who realizes Jesus' saving action, making it to be the kind of action that it is. The key is to be found in the Letter to the Hebrews, a wonderful preaching resource despite the apparent bookishness of the writer and the antiquity of the things he uses in illustrating his argument. "How much more, then, will the blood of Christ, who *through the eternal Spirit offered himself* unblemished to God, cleanse our consciences from acts that lead to death, so that we may serve the living God" (Heb. 9:14). Here we meet our past tense, not, however, with reference to some supposedly reconstructed event, but with a focus on the whole story of Jesus as the one created being who was enabled by the Spirit to realize his true being and action. And at what cost! Like us in all things, sin apart, as this writer insists perhaps above all his colleagues, Jesus went through it all, for us and indeed with us, for our sakes, as the second part of the verse makes clear. That is why the past act has a bearing on the present: at stake in this historical figure is all the difference between life and death.

Why? The reason is that this is not only a past figure. With Paul, this author reaffirms at the beginning of his treatise the apparently universal early Christian confession of Christ as the mediator of creation who, having triumphantly shared our lot, has now taken his seat at the right hand of the

Father. Forget the difficulty moderns are alleged to have with such imagery in order to see the point made by the symbolism. *This* human life is perfected, through the Spirit, so that ours also might be made perfect through the offering and the sacrifice, and by that same Spirit. It is not, then, merely that the past bears upon the present. It is that the one who realizes the perfect sacrifice that is Jesus' obedience to the Father becomes the means, through that same Christ — the author and pioneer of our faith — of all human obedience, wherever and whenever.

The action of the Spirit in perfecting Jesus' self-offering enables us to perceive how the Spirit perfects all things, including the work of the preacher. The Spirit is the one who enables particular things to be and become what they are created to be by bringing them to God the Father through Jesus Christ. For our purposes there are two foci of his work with which we must engage. First, the epistles are in this light more than, while remaining, pieces of particular writing mainly engaged with particular pastoral problems. Just as the Spirit is the one who enables Jesus of Nazareth, the incarnate Lord, to remain true, through temptation, suffering, and death, to the one who sent him, so it is with the authors whose writings are authorized to bring to human speech the gospel of God's love and judgment in Jesus Christ. To say that these writings are inspired means at least this: that they, in all their particularity, are the unique gift of God to church and world so that the one may be built up and be sent, as was Jesus himself, to the other.

Second, so far as the preacher is concerned, the peril and the promise are this: that it is only through the sheer differences of the conditions of those to whom the epistles were addressed that we shall discover their point for today. That is an essential focus for our attempt to pinpoint the work of the perfecting Spirit, and we shall once again seek illustration from the first letter to Corinth. There is, to be sure, much to be said for the likenesses between then and now, as well as for the differences. Socially they are clear. If we are tempted either to idealize the first days of the church as Acts presents them or to despair because we are no longer like that, then the Corinthian correspondence will remind us how alike we are, beset by problems on every side. It will also suggest that those unique social conditions, a church set about by paganism, are not so unique after all. For in its worship of the material world, modern culture is not so different from the proto-gnosticism which appears to be the fruit of the Corinthian church's denial of the resurrection of the body. Neither knows how to live redemptively in the created world which God has given us to inhabit, because neither acknowledges the sovereignty and authority of the Creator, so that much of the argument of that letter concerning the clash of ultimate loyalties which acceptance of the gospel involves speaks as directly now as then. Yet the differences also remain crucial, and it is the very strangeness of some of the considerations Paul advances that enables the preacher to make manifest today the demands of the gospel. We may not be troubled by the eating of meat offered to nonexistent gods, but are we not tempted all the time to submit to the "gods many and lords many" that characterize our particular times? And is not Paul right that it is in our sexual relations that the challenge to the ultimacy of Christ often comes in our day also, and is that not a point far too often forgotten in the modern church? By attending to Paul's struggle to articulate the gospel for and with his church, we gain a perspective on today's similar struggle.

The reason for the astonishing concreteness of this letter is that beyond the particularities of the Corinthians lie the universals. At the center is the polarity of cross and resurrection, which still presents the preacher with a framework for all proclamation. Paul will preach nothing but Christ and him crucified; and yet that gospel falls unless the resurrection is equally proclaimed. And not far below the surface are other factors which are equally intrinsic to the theology of any era, factors which are again based on the particularities of God's universal action. Among them are reconciliation, holiness, and law. Paul is insistent that something has happened to change the status of those to whom he is writing: they have been redeemed. His understanding of this new standing is deeply shaped by his engagement with what we call Old Testament Scripture, but which for him was simply Scripture. All New Testament Scripture is but an interpretation of the Old, and Paul's engagement with this can be seen throughout his letters. From there he shows that holiness and law are interrelated, so that those who have been redeemed must seek the direction of their sanctification from the Torah, which is repeated in summary in chapter 6.

I have used the first letter to Corinth as the primary example because of its unique combination of sometimes apparently alien particularities and universal theological moment. Similar points could be made of the other epistles. For example, the so-called "new perspective on Paul" has, by attending to previously neglected particularities, enabled us to correct an imbalance in the way his theology, and particularly that of Romans, has been treated. That does not, however, alter one salient fact: that we are justified through faith in God, and not by any achievement of our own. This remains an article by which the church stands or falls, because unless our strength and our salvation come from God alone, we are lost. The same can be said of Galatians, the letter most frequently linked with Romans in that respect.

That must not allow us to forget the new insights, so relevant to our times because Christian relations with the Jewish people remain as central to our concerns now as then, but must continue to remind us that our particular acts of proclamation are undergirded by the one eternal gospel.

Preaching from the epistles is, accordingly, a matter of bringing the particularities of the literature into conversation with the particularities of our own times, but always within the common framework of the universal gospel as it bears variously on the human condition. The acts of God in creation, covenant, the incarnation, life, death, resurrection, and ascension of Jesus Christ and their implications — reconciliation, justification, sanctification — together provide the foundations which underpin both the particular teaching of the writers and the particular preaching of today. Preaching is proclamation of the present act of God, but its shape is given by the great themes of the gospel as they are embodied in the details of the letters. And the Spirit is the one who, through the living and ascended Christ, grants the connections between teaching and proclamation, then and now, which is the point of the exercise.

Just as the Letter to the Hebrews enables us to make the link between the Spirit and Jesus, the Spirit and the text, and the Spirit and the preacher, so also it enables us to be both realistic and positive about the preacher's task. Far from making Jesus immune to toil and suffering, the Spirit rather took him through them to "the joy that was set before him." "During the days of Jesus' life on earth, he offered up prayers and petitions with loud cries and tears to the one who could save him from death" (Heb. 5:7). Engaging with these ancient and difficult texts is hard work, involving "prayers and petitions," and sometimes perhaps "cries and tears," especially if we are to begin to come to terms with the wisdom of both the tradition and contemporary scholarship. There is no guarantee that we shall get it right. Two qualifications of that point have, however, to be made. The first is that unless we engage with the text of Scripture, there *is* a guarantee that we shall get it wrong. The second is that, guarantee there may not be, but promise there is that the text will be enabled to speak, not always in ways that can be predicted, but nonetheless really and effectively.

# Contributors

William J. Abraham
Perkins School of Theology
Dallas, Texas

Elizabeth Achtemeier
Union Theological Seminary
Richmond, Virginia

Ronald J. Allen
Christian Theological Seminary
Indianapolis, Indiana

Dale C. Allison
Pittsburgh Theological Seminary
Pittsburgh, Pennsylvania

Gary A. Anderson
Harvard Divinity School
Cambridge, Massachusetts

Martyn D. Atkins
Cliff College
North Sheffield, England

Raymond Bailey, Pastor
Seventh and James Baptist Church
Waco, Texas

Andrew Bandstra
Calvin Theological Seminary
Grand Rapids, Michigan

Andrew H. Bartelt
Concordia Seminary
St. Louis, Missouri

Charles L. Bartow
Princeton Theological Seminary
Princeton, New Jersey

Richard Bauckham
University of St. Andrews
St. Andrews, Scotland

C. Clifton Black
Princeton Theological Seminary
Princeton, New Jersey

Robert L. Brawley
McCormick Theological Seminary
Chicago, Illinois

Annette G. Brownlee
Ascension Episcopal Church
Pueblo, Colorado

## CONTRIBUTORS

John P. Burgess
Pittsburgh Theological Seminary
Pittsburgh, Pennsylvania

Richard A. Burridge, Dean
King's College
London, England

Charles L. Campbell
Columbia Theological Seminary
Decatur, Georgia

Lewis R. Donelson
Austin Presbyterian Theological Seminary
Austin, Texas

Patricia Dutcher-Walls
Knox College
Toronto, Ontario

Craig A. Evans
Trinity Western University
Langley, British Columbia

Gabriel Fackre
Andover Newton Theological School
Boston, Massachusetts

Lawrence W. Farris, Pastor
Presbyterian Church (USA)
Three Rivers, Michigan

Stephen Farris
Knox College
Toronto, Ontario

Robert A. J. Gagnon
Pittsburgh Theological Seminary
Pittsburgh, Pennsylvania

Thomas W. Gillespie, President
Princeton Theological Seminary
Princeton, New Jersey

John Goldingay
Fuller Theological Seminary
Pasadena, California

Colin J. D. Greene
British and Foreign Bible Society
Swindon, England

Sidney Greidanus
Calvin Theological Seminary
Grand Rapids, Michigan

Colin E. Gunton
King's College
London, England

Sarah Henrich
Luther Seminary
St. Paul, Minnesota

Scott Hoezee, Pastor
Calvin Christian Reformed Church
Grand Rapids, Michigan

John C. Holbert
Perkins School of Theology
Dallas, Texas

David E. Holwerda
Calvin Theological Seminary
Grand Rapids, Michigan

Leslie J. Hoppe
Catholic Theological Union
Chicago, Illinois

Arland J. Hultgren
Luther Seminary
St. Paul, Minnesota

George Hunsinger
Princeton Theological Seminary
Princeton, New Jersey

Robert W. Jenson
Center of Theological Inquiry
Princeton, New Jersey

Robert Jewett
Garrett-Evangelical Theological Seminary
Evanston, Illinois

Karen Jobes
Westmont College
Santa Barbara, California

Scott Black Johnston
Austin Presbyterian Theological Seminary
Austin, Texas

Donald Juel
Princeton Theological Seminary
Princeton, New Jersey

James F. Kay
Princeton Theological Seminary
Princeton, New Jersey

Craig S. Keener
Eastern Seminary
St. David's, Pennsylvania

Leonard R. Klein, Pastor
Christ Lutheran Church
York, Pennsylvania

Joel E. Kok, Pastor
Trinity Christian Reformed Church
Broomall, Pennsylvania

James Limburg
Luther Seminary
St. Paul, Minnesota

Tremper Longman III
Westmont College
Santa Barbara, California

F. Dean Lueking, Pastor
Grace Lutheran Church
River Forest, Illinois

Lois Malcolm
Luther Seminary
St. Paul, Minnesota

Martin E. Marty
The Fairfax M. Cone Distinguished
  Service Professor
The University of Chicago
Chicago, Illinois

Peter W. Marty, Pastor
St. Paul Lutheran Church
Davenport, Iowa

J. Clinton McCann, Jr.
Eden Theological Seminary
St. Louis, Missouri

Douglas Moo
Wheaton Graduate School
Wheaton, Illinois

Thorsten Moritz
Cheltenham and Gloucester College
  of Higher Education
Cheltenham, England

Roland E. Murphy, O. Carm.
George Washington University
Washington, D.C.

Hughes Oliphant Old
Research Theologian
Trenton, New Jersey

Dennis T. Olson
Princeton Theological Seminary
Princeton, New Jersey

Earl F. Palmer, Pastor
University Presbyterian Church
Seattle, Washington

Steven D. Paulson
Luther Seminary
St. Paul, Minnesota

Mary Margaret Pazdan, O.P.
Aquinas Institute of Theology
St. Louis, Missouri

## CONTRIBUTORS

Christine E. Pilkington
Christ Church University College
Canterbury, England

Daniel J. Price, Pastor
First Presbyterian Church
Eureka, California

Paul R. Raabe
Concordia Seminary
St. Louis, Missouri

Ephraim Radner, Rector
Ascension Episcopal Church
Pueblo, Colorado

Stephen W. Ramp, Pastor
First Trinity Presbyterian Church
Laurel, Mississippi

Barbara E. Reid
Catholic Theological Union
Chicago, Illinois

Stephen Breck Reid
Austin Presbyterian Theological Seminary
Austin, Texas

André Resner, Jr., Pastor
Lamington Presbyterian Church
Bedminster, New Jersey

Michael Rogness
Luther Seminary
St. Paul, Minnesota

John M. Rottman
Emmanuel College
Toronto, Ontario

The Reverend Fleming Rutledge
Priest of the Episcopal Church
Diocese of New York

Timothy E. Saleska
Concordia Seminary
St. Louis, Missouri

Marguerite Shuster
Fuller Theological Seminary
Pasadena, California

Graydon F. Snyder
Chicago Theological Seminary
Chicago, Illinois

Frank Anthony Spina
Seattle Pacific University
Seattle, Washington

Brent A. Strawn
Candler School of Theology
Atlanta, Georgia

Roger E. Van Harn, Pastor
Christian Reformed Church
Grand Rapids, Michigan

Robert W. Wall
Seattle Pacific University
Seattle, Washington

William H. Willimon, Dean of the Chapel
Duke University
Durham, North Carolina

Paul Scott Wilson
Emmanuel College
Toronto, Ontario

Stephen I. Wright, Director
College of Preachers
London, England

# Index of Authors

631

# Index of Readings for Years A, B, and C

## YEAR A

### First Sunday of Advent
Isaiah 2:1-5   I:295
(Psalm 122)
Romans 13:11-14   II:128
Matthew 24:36-44   III:140

### Second Sunday of Advent
Isaiah 11:1-10   I:320
(Psalm 72:1-7, 18-19)
Romans 15:4-13   II:137
Matthew 3:1-12   III:12

### Third Sunday of Advent
Isaiah 35:1-10   I:324
(Psalm 146:5-10 or Luke 1:47-55)
James 5:7-10   II:535
Matthew 11:2-11   III:64

### Fourth Sunday of Advent
Isaiah 7:10-16   I:310
(Psalm 80:1-7, 17-19)
Romans 1:1-7   II:10
Matthew 1:18-25   III:1

### Nativity of the Lord (Christmas Day)
Isaiah 9:2-7   I:316
(Psalm 96)
Titus 2:11-14   III:456
Luke 2:1-14 (15-20)   III:294

*OR*

Isaiah 62:6-12   I:388
(Psalm 97)
Titus 3:4-7   II:460
Luke 2:(1-7), 8-20   III:297

*OR*

Isaiah 52:7-10   I:360
(Psalm 98)
Hebrews 1:1-4, (5-12)   II:468
John 1:1-14   III:476

### First Sunday after Christmas Day
Isaiah 63:7-9   I:392
(Psalm 148)
Hebrews 2:10-18   II:475
Matthew 2:13-23   III:8

634

# YEAR B

# YEAR C

646